Contemporary
Republic of China

THE TAIWAN EXPERIENCE 1950-1980

Edited by

JAMES C. HSIUNG

and others

PRAEGER

PRAEGER SPECIAL STUDIES • PRAEGER SCIENTIFIC

Library of Congress Cataloging in Publication Data

Main entry under title:

Contemporary Republic of China.

     Bibliography: p.
     1. Taiwan—History—1945-   —Addresses, essays,
lectures.   I. Hsiung, James Chieh, 1935-
DS799.8.C66   951'.24905   81-11993
ISBN 0-03-060298-X   AACR2

Published in 1981 by Praeger Publishers
CBS Educational and Professional Publishing
A Division of CBS, Inc.
521 Fifth Avenue, New York, New York 10175 U.S.A.

© 1981 by James C. Hsiung

123456789 145 987654321

Printed in the United States of America

BOARD OF ADVISERS

Published under the auspices of

The American Association for Chinese Studies

with a grant from

The Pacific Cultural Foundation
Taipei, Taiwan
Republic of China

ACKNOWLEDGEMENTS

Grateful acknowledgements are made to the following for permission to reprint:

Asian Affairs for "Education in Taiwan" by William J. F. Lew (May-June, 1978); and for "Taiwan's Options" by John F. Copper (May-June, 1979).

Asian Survey for "A Comparison of Political Attitudes of Taiwanese Children and Mainlander Children on Taiwan" by Richard W. Wilson, copyright 1968 by The Regents of the University of California; for "Modernization Process in Taiwan: An Allocative Analysis" by Yung Wei, copyright 1976 by The Regents of the University of California; for "Taiwan's Foreign Policy in the 1970's" by Thomas J. Bellows, copyright 1976 by The Regents of the University of California; for "Taiwan's Recent Elections" by John F. Copper, copyright 1981 by The Regents of the University of California; and for "The Social and Political Impact of Education in Taiwan" by Sheldon Appleton, copyright 1976 by The Regents of the University of California.

Barrie & Jenkins for *The Republic of China under Chiang Kai-shek* by F. A. Lumley, copyright 1976.

China Quarterly for "The Socialization of Children in China and on Taiwan" by Roberta Martin, copyright 1975 by China Quarterly.

Chinese Materials and Research Aids Service Center for *Moral and Social Values of the Chinese: Collected Essays* by Wolfram Eberhard, copyright 1971.

Columbia University Press for *The Committee of One Million* by Stanley D. Bachrack, copyright 1976.

Cornell University Press for "Foreign Trade" by Maurice Scott in *Economic Growth and Structural Change in Taiwan,* edited by Walter Galenson, copyright 1979 by Cornell University and for "Agricultural Development" by Erik Thorbecke in *Economic Growth and Structural Change in Taiwan,* edited by Walter Galenson, copyright 1979 by Cornell University.

Economic Development and Cultural Change for "Urbanization and Migration in Taiwan" by Alden Speare, Jr., copyright 1974 by University of Chicago Press.

Harvard University for *Island China* by Ralph N. Clough, copyright 1978 by Harvard University Press.

Institute of International Studies for *The Taiwan Relation Act and the Defense of the Republic of China* by Edwin K. Snyder *et. al.,* copyright 1980 by Institute of International Studies, University of California, Berkeley.

Journal of Asian Studies for "Social Class and Rural-Urban Patterning of Socialization in Taiwan" by Nancy J. Olsen, copyright 1975 by University of Michigan Press.

MIT Press for *Learning To Be Chinese* by Richard W. Wilson, copyright 1970 by MIT Press, Cambridge, Massachusetts.

M. E. Sharpe for *The Future of Taiwan* by Victor Li, copyright 1980 by M. E. Sharpe, Inc.

Table of Contents—An Overview

Table of Contents

Section 1
Cultural Values and Cultural Continuity
Cho-yun Hsu

Contents

Section 2
The Educational System
Theodore H. E. Chen

Contents

Section 3
The Taiwan Experience in Economic Development
Yuan-li Wu and Jan S. Prybyla

Contents

Section 4
Social Conditions and Social Change
Yu-ming Shaw

Contents

Section 5
Law and Justice
Hungdah Chiu and Jyh-pin Fa

Contents

Section 6
Domestic Politics
John F. Copper

Contents

Section 7
Foreign Relations
Winberg Chai

Contents

Section 8
Security and Defense Capabilities
Michael Y. M. Kau

Contents

Foreword

by James C. Hsiung

General Editor

This is a book about Taiwan, a society whose $2,280 per capita income (1980) brings it to the threshold of the industrially developed world, while the gaps in distribution have also been significantly narrowed. These achievements, made in the span of the past thirty years, have often been described as "phenomenal" or "miraculous." Taiwan, however, is also a subject that may evoke different responses and comments, depending on one's political opinions and extent of understanding. The Republic of China (ROC) on Taiwan has its share of detractors and well-wishers alike in America. While the latter are generally impressed with the island's economic advance and political stability, the detractors may hold negative views for a number of reasons.

There are, first, those who harbor resentments about Taiwan because it was for some time a "stumbling block" in America's attempts to normalize relations with Peking. That stigma dies hard even after President Carter derecognized the ROC in his decision to switch recognition to the People's Republic of China (PRC) as from January 1, 1979. The same group now are afraid that continuing a good relationship with the ROC even at the present "unofficial" level—especially if it entails arms sales which would court Peking's ire—could jeopardize America's "China connection." The value of the China card to this group lies in its potential (or alleged) usefulness in Washington's fight with the Soviet Union, and in this brute power game Taiwan is dwarfed by the colossus that is mainland China. If the PRC claims Taiwan as part of its own, the United States, in this reasoning, should not offend Peking by holding on to its close ties with the ROC.

These China card-players are joined by at least two other groups with their own axes to grind. One group consists of those who for a variety of reasons are politically disposed to Peking and therefore negative toward its rival, Taiwan. The other is a loose coalition of those Taiwanese Chinese and their sympathizers in America who advocate the "independence" of the island, totally cut out from that abstract China of which Taiwan is considered by all other Chinese to be a part. To this group, an "independent" Taiwan would not only be detached from all claims by mainland China, but would have a government to be established only by its own members, to replace the current ROC authorities. Their favorite target against the latter has been the ROC's human-rights record, which received the most vociferous attack during the four years of the Carter Administration. On this score, they were at times joined by certain human-rights purists who otherwise would have little or nothing in common with the group.

These three groups—the China card-players, the pro-Pekingers, and the Taiwan independentists—do not, however, share the same vision for Taiwan. The China card-players entertain the ultimate possibility of "returning" the island to mainland China, in order to make Peking a more willing pawn to be played against the Soviet Union, which is after all their foremost concern. But they are in no hurry to see this happen, for once the candy is given out there will be no way to control the child, as it were, as before. The pro-Pekingers, on their part, want a speedy amalgamation of Taiwan with mainland China, in the name of "national reunification." The independentists, however, want nothing less than a separate Taiwan state under their own aegis and control. The disparate goals and motives held by the three groups are sufficient to discount a conspiracy against Taiwan on their part, although occasionally some of them do find common cause for joint action (such as in the attacks on Taiwan's human-rights record thus far). The fact remains, nevertheless, that each of the groups has its own reasons for not wanting Taiwan being presented to the American public other than in the manner that it thinks will best serve its own purposes.

The Purpose of This Book

In making this point, we are less interested in condemning any of them as in noting a problem and a justification for this book. The problem is that while the subject of our book will attract the more immediate attention of these three groups than many others among the American public, the way we present the Taiwan record will most certainly grieve them, as it will fail to serve their special interests and purposes just noted. But, here also lies the justification for the book. Most if not all discussions of Taiwan thus far have been linked to one or another of the party lines of these three groups: Taiwan is discussed either (a) as a potentially dispensable chip in the U.S.'s China card-playing, or (b) in the context of Peking's claims to the island, or (c) in terms of the independentists' attempts to justify why Taiwan must be freed from anyone else's control only to be placed under their own.

We propose to discuss Taiwan quite differently, because we have a different concern and interest. Our concern is that the truth be known to the American public in the way truth ought to be told. Our interest is in the reasons behind the success story of Taiwan's economic strides, about which there is almost no dispute. Even leaders in Peking from Mr. Deng Xiaoping on down have stated that they can and should learn from the "Taiwan model." However, the reasons why Taiwan has been successful, we believe, have yet to be fully explored and presented in a more coherent fashion, which is the *raison d'etre* for the present volume.

Let me, however, make a few disclaimers or clarifications:
• This is a collaborate volume involving many scholars of diverse backgrounds and political opinions, and it makes use of diverse published sources already available in the English language, not all of which agree on the same issues. The key word, parenthetically, is *diversity*. None of the

members of the editorial board, or among the advisors, either has an axe to grind or has any personal stakes or professional reasons for being partial about the subject of our study. It is not a book written with any partisan designs in view.

• This book covers only the thirty years after the relocation of the ROC government in Taiwan, from 1950 to 1980, and does not go back to the mainland years unless there is a compelling reason for doing so (such as the inseparable continuities in the legal system and reforms extending from the pre-1949 period to the present, as noted in the "Law and Justice" section). We do not claim to cover the entire history of the Republic of China, which in 1981 is celebrating its 70th anniversary since the success of Dr. Sun Yat-sen's revolution of October 10, 1911. The thirty-year Taiwan phase is long enough and its substance is challenging enough for an entire volume such as ours to be devoted to it. Even within the period under its coverage, the book has had to leave out much that is not directly relevant to its major thesis (see below) or offers only a tangential interest.

• In its selections, concededly, certain harsher critical works have been left out, because we do not believe their inclusion would enhance our understanding of the Taiwan experience, which has been complicated already by the partisan problems noted above. The book does not purport to represent all points of view, but endeavors to stay in the middle, steering clear of both the left and the right extremes. But it contains enough diversity and constructive criticisms to justify, we believe, its claim to being a balanced representation.

The major thesis of the book is that successful economic development must be supported by salutary political and social conditions, as is borne out by the Taiwan experience. Although there is awareness of the socio-political "overhead" of economic development in much of the developmental literature (beginning with, for example, Holt and Turner, *The Political Basis of Economic Development*),[1] there is little evidence that the links between Taiwan's economic success and its political and social foundations are taken to heart by many development theorists, much less by the American public. Usually, Taiwan is not studied by development theorists in the same light as the other Third-World developmental cases, and its success therefore has not been similarly examined with a view to discovering its multiple but related underlying causes. The possible intellectual pay-off from a systematic study of Taiwan as a relevant model for Third-World development may in itself be a rationale for this book.

A Classic Example of Macro-Development
The negativism held and advanced by the detractors mentioned before may also have been responsible for the fact that Taiwan has been relatively under-studied as a classic example of macro-development in which economic growth is one component. If Taiwan is only a passing phase, as the China card-players and the pro-Pekingers would have us believe, why should one bother to study it in the first place? If, as the independentists

charge, Taiwan's human-rights record is so bleak, then what is there to speak of in terms of the socio-political "overhead" which might make Taiwan's economic success meaningful? Obviously, we disagree with all this in our assessments, as will be made plain throughout the book.

Development may be defined in various ways, but in the context of the thirty years of the Taiwan phase of the ROC's existence, it is conterminous with modernization. We are dealing with an all-out modernization involving societal mobilization orchestrated from the top in a structure which, as Chalmers Johnson notes in the Introduction, must be understood in terms of a non-socialist but close public-private cooperative framework. Where modernization generates psychic, physical, and social mobility, Taiwan's political stability and social cohesion have cushioned the shocks and dislocations that usually accompany rapid modernization. Where the modernizing process entails the increasing use of inanimate power, scientific and technological knowledge, and massive organization, Taiwan's political and social self-discipline has provided the necessary conditions (including a healthy cultural and educational environment) for achieving all these without incurring drastic effects. There is enough planning and orchestration at the top to provide purpose, but not so much as to stifle private initiative. Taiwan is a successful example of development-by-design,[2] although not many successful cases of this brand of development can be cited outside East Asia.

The ultimate function of political authority in the Taiwan system is not merely "government," but "governing," to borrow a term from Richard Rose,[3] in that it has to steer the statecraft through untold storms and tidal waves (especially on international waters) toward pre-set directions. From its loss of the China mainland (1949) to its expulsion from the United Nations (1971) and U.S. derecognition (1979), the Republic of China has weathered many an international storm. Thus, its impressive economic performance to date is a testament as well as result of the island's political and social attributes, however imperfect they may appear at times.

As a case of development under great adversities, Taiwan is probably matched only by Israel in terms of the overwhelming scope of its surrounding odds and foes. However, unlike Israel, there have been no comparable efforts at making the Taiwan story better known to the outside. We believe that it is a story that deserves to be more widely told.

The layout of the book bespeaks its major thesis. The eight sections, each edited by a specialist or team of specialists, cover various aspects of Taiwan's thirty years of developmental experience. As suggested, development has to be supported by the right cultural and social milieu, an education system that turns out a new generation of citizenry equipped for the ever-changing needs, a legal or normative order that provides the minimal protection and stability in basic human relationships, and above all political stability and vision to guide and sustain systematic economic transformation. Thus, the book begins with a section on "cultural values and cultural continuity" (Section #1), followed by separate sections on the "education system" (Section #2), "social conditions and social change" (Section #4), "law and justice" (Section #5), and "domestic politics" (Section #6), alongside a hefty two-part section on "economic development" (Section #3). Since Taiwan's development has taken place in the face of external adversities, an understanding of its "foreign relations" and "security and defense capabilities" will be instrumental, as is provided in two additional sections (#7 and # 8, respectively).

Each section begins with an introductory commentary by the editor or co-editors for the section, followed by selections from published sources in excerpts. The commentary for each section sets out the frame of reference, identifies the subtopics, points out the significance of the issues under discussion, and outlines the context in which the excerpted materials are being presented. The editors have made conscious efforts to choose a cross-section of materials that reflect different views as well as cover various aspects of each topic under discussion. They have also endeavored to preserve the meaning and integrity of the original sources from which the excerpts were drawn. Where there are gaps or areas not covered in the reproduced selections, the commentary also attempts to supply the missing links within its allocated space.

If we did not call this volume a "reader," it is because it is more than that, if a "reader" is essentially a collection of selections, either in full or in excerpts. The commentaries for the eight sections can be read independently of the supporting documentary materials, and when read together by themselves they provide enough about Taiwan as any book could. The excerpted selections, for their part, serve to flesh out or document the ideas or points made in the commentaries. Hence, to us the book is not just a "reader."

The co-editors could have written an original book without resorting to reproductions from published sources. But we have decided to combine original writing (i.e., the commentaries) with reproduced materials, in order to achieve two purposes. First, we hope to be able to demonstrate that the views expressed here are not limited to the co-editors alone but are shared by a larger community of scholars and observers. Secondly, the reproduced sources, we hope, can be better strung together when placed in a more meaningful context such as the commentaries can provide. As our reader will notice, the footnotes for many of the reproduced materials are omitted, on the theory that our readers can always go back and find the footnotes in the original sources, should there be such an interest. All the sources are properly identified for that purpose. The omission of the footnotes, in these cases, is mainly to save space in order to make the volume less unwieldy than it would be otherwise.

Although we make no pretensions about having put together a most definitive book about Taiwan, we hope that it will prove to be a handy volume comprising most vital issues and that it will have helped to generate a renewed dialogue on a fascinating topic.

Acknowledgements

This book was written under the aegis of the American Association for Chinese Studies, with a grant from the Pacific Cultural Foundation, Taipei, which I gratefully acknowledge. Besides those members of the Board of Advisors who have simultaneously served as the section editors, everyone has helped—either in bibliographical suggestions or in offering ideas or topics for inclusion, or in other ways—to make this book possible. The section editors have made special efforts to meet an almost impossible deadline, in order that the book can be out in time to coincide with the 70th anniversary of the Republic of China alluded to earlier.

During the initial stage of the project, an extensive bibliographic search was undertaken to survey the existing literature, for which I had the good fortune of being aided by my able assistant, Peter K. H. Yu, while a number of other people also helped, including Barbara Solomon and two of my children, Susette, 18, and Eric, 17. Another team headed by Dr. Si-kuen Lee, of *Academia Sinica,* also joined in the search by locating published materials available in Taiwan. The select bibliography appended to this volume is a partial result of that search. Peter Yu, who had helped me on two previous book projects, also assisted me in many other ways, including corresponding with publishers for copyright permissions for the reproduced materials and a variety of other clerical and editorial chores. Ramon Myers, a member of the Board of Advisors, even went out of his way to assign "weights" to all the items included in our composite bibliographical lists on Taiwan after having checked up on all of them. These "weights" followed the same criteria as were used in an earlier set of evaluative "scales" worked out by Peter Yu, who had also gone over all the items listed in the composite bibliography. On the basis of these two sets of evaluative scales, which gauged the quality and reliability of each of the items on Taiwan, the editors were able to select the finalists for inclusion in the sections.

Some of the advisors, including Ramon Myers, C. Martin Wilbur, and Robert A. Scalapino, made suggestions or raised questions regarding the proposed format for the book. I alone, or course, remain responsible for the final format and design adopted for the book. My editors, on whose specialized expertise I have had to rely heavily, will share the responsibility with me for the quality and substance in each of the eight sections of the book.

As General Editor, I have carefully read and edited everything that was sent to me by the section editors, to make the final manuscript read and look like one whole piece in terms of its organization, style, and frame of reference. I would, however, be the first to admit that there are still some weaknesses, such as overlaps between sections, though not to the point of redundancy. In these cases of overlaps, I have allowed them to stand because of the importance of the subject matter involved and also because each section has a different context. There are also gaps not filled, mainly because the book has to focus on its main thesis, as was explained in the disclaimers before.

I had a wonderful team and it was a wonderful experience. The team's professional competence, congeniality, and shared eagerness to see the work completed in time—all have made my job much easier than it otherwise would have been. Chalmers Johnson graciously agreed to write the Introduction under enormous time pressure but, amazingly, managed to complete it a considerable time before the deadline. I am indebted to all of them.

NOTES

1. Robert T. Holt and John E. Turner, *The Political Basis of Economic Development* (Princeton, N.J.: Van Nostrand, 1966).

2. I am borrowing the concept from Chandler Morse, (ed.), *Modernization by Design* (Ithaca, N.Y.: Cornell University Press, 1969).

3. Richard Rose, *Politics of England* (Boston: Little, Brown, 1974), p. 32.

Introduction–The Taiwan Model

by Chalmers Johnson

The high-growth capitalist developmental states of East Asia—Japan, Taiwan, Korea, Singapore, and Hong Kong—are not well understood by either their allies or adversaries. The Anglo-American countries tend to believe that the high-performance Asian economies are merely variants of their own essentially regulatory states, refusing to acknowledge that there are other ways to organize capitalism than on the North American model, or they tend to ignore the special institutional arrangements of these states in favor of an explanation that stresses cultural differences, a lingering Confucian ethos, or the primacy of the group over the individual. The Communists have come only belatedly to concede that these states have actually delivered to their peoples what Communism claims to deliver but everywhere has failed to do. During the Thermidor that followed the death of Mao in mainland China, some of the contributors to Peking's short-lived "democracy wall" noted ruefully that Taiwan and the other capitalist developmental states had decisively broken through the $1,100 per capita income level (1970 prices), while thirty years of Communist experimentation still left the mainland Chinese only dreaming about such prosperity. [1]

The five main cases—Japan, Taiwan, Korea, Singapore, and Hong Kong—are not identical, nor have they pursued identical development strategies. But there are similarities among them in terms of their priorities, their reliance on the price mechanism rather than direct governmental control, and some of their key institutional arrangements and social supports for high-speed growth. They also resemble each other in that for the twenty-year period lasting from approximately 1955 to 1975 they experienced exceptionally high growth rates—from 7.8 percent to 9.5 percent in real output and above 5 percent in real per capita income. This performance distinguishes them from both the Anglo-American regulatory capitalist states and from the Soviet-type command economies. In the pages that follow, I shall attempt to sketch in the main political and institutional features of these high-growth systems and then detail some of the special characteristics of Taiwan, which is perhaps the purest example of the type and the most successful of them all.

Public-Private Cooperation Essential

The operative mechanism of the high-growth economies has been public-private cooperation in a non-socialist environment in order to shift the

Chalmers Johnson is Professor and former chairman, Department of Political Science, University of California, Berkeley. He has written extensively on the politics of modern China and Japan, including *MITI and the Japanese Miracle* (Stanford University Press).

effort. The international trade of the Communist countries since the time of Stalin has been concentrated in raw materials rather than finished products because of the inability of their enterprises to compete in quality and design, since they are cut off from international standards of taste and marketing information.

Second, the high-growth system seems to require certain specific political arrangements. The most important of these is a marked, if never openly acknowledged, separation between reigning and ruling; the politicians reign and the state bureaucrats rule. The functions of the politicians are to maintain political stability by holding off the demands of pressure groups or political claimants that would contradict or divert the main developmental effort and by providing space for an elite, highly educated bureaucracy to operate. At the same time, the politicians perform "safety valve" functions, forcing the bureaucrats to respond to the needs of groups upon which the stability of the system rests (above all, the farmers) or forcing the bureaucrats to alter course slightly when they have gone too far (as, for example, in their insensitivity to levels of environmental pollution that constitute threats to health).

Although there are marked differences in the political systems of the high-growth nations, they are all characterized by a virtual monopoly of political power in a single party or institution for a long period of time and by a "soft authoritarianism" when it comes to maintaining the interests of economic development vis-à-vis other interests or claims. The twenty-five year uninterrupted reign of Japan's Liberal Democratic Party has provided the space for the elite bureaucracy to carry out its economic development plans and to foster a government-business relationship that has made Japan a businessman's paradise. Although not directly elected and therefore resting on less secure consensual bases, the Kuomintang in the Republic of China, the late president Park Chung Hee in the Republic of Korea, Prime Minister Lee Kuan Yew in Singapore (an elected official but one who has held office since 1959), and the British colonial government in Hong Kong have all performed essentially the same reigning and safety-valve functions.

Democracy of the Anglo-American variety does not prevail fully in any of these societies, but the trade-offs of these political systems have been tolerated and accepted by their populations because of the situational imperatives of all the nations involved. These imperatives include Japan's large population and utter dependence on international trade, Taiwan's and Korea's similar dependencies plus acute security threats, Hong Kong's position as an enclave of free enterprise on the Chinese mainland, and Singapore's status as a Chinese community in a Malay world. Opposition parties are tolerated in all these systems, and they often come to power and are effective at the local government level. It is when political issues or communal fissures threaten to break the stability on which the economic development effort rests that either the people rally around their reigning politicians or the soft authoritarianism is put into effect to suppress the conflict.

The actual rulers in these systems are the state bureaucrats—the ministerial officials in Tokyo, the Executive Yuan in Taipei, the economic bureaucrats in Seoul, and similar elites in Singapore and Hong Kong. They are, however, less "rulers" than "managers," which leads to the third component of our model: the commitment in all of these systems to market-conforming methods of intervention. In order to promote economic development, these officials (who normally occupy the highest social statuses in the society and constitute an intrinsic elite based on demonstrated merit) do not need to resort to the direct mobilization of resources, as for example occurred during the Great Leap Forward in mainland China. They have learned that the price mechanism is a less painful, more effective, and not necessarily less speedy means of mobilizing resources than direct governmental control. All of these systems depend to a high degree on public-private cooperation between the managers of the state and the managers of private enterprise. This cooperation is achieved through innumerable, continuously operating forums for coordinating views and investment plans, sharing international commercial intelligence, making adjustments to conform to the business cycle or other changes in the economic environment, deciding on the new industries needed in order to maintain international competitive ability, and spreading both the wealth and the burdens equitably. Examples of such forums include the Industrial Structure Council in Tokyo and the Council for International Cooperation and Development in Taipei.

One consequence of this public-private cooperation is that non-strategic sectors of the systems will on occasion vent their grievances at lack of access through public demonstrations. These grievances may arise because interests have developed that are not but should be tended to by the bureaucrats and political leaders or simply because of the frustrations of relatively limited political participation. Examples of such demonstrations include the Security Treaty riots in Japan during 1960, the Kaohsiung demonstrations in Taiwan during December 1979, the unstable conditions in Korea following the assassination of Park Chung Hee, and the Mongkok riots in Hong Kong during 1966. Such outbursts are important. The political leaders must anticipate and effectively ameliorate them, sometimes suppressing them and sometimes altering policies in order to reduce their causes. But it should not be thought that they indicate fatal flaws in the systems or that fully open political processes would necessarily end them (demonstrations and riots are far from unknown in the Anglo-American democracies). They arise from the inevitable strains of high-speed growth, from the rigidities of single-party reigning and bureaucratic ruling, from the effects of mass media of communications, and from the intense work discipline these societies impose. The costs of high-speed economic growth are not negligible, but they are insignificant in comparison to the costs of the forcible demobilization of the non-strategic sectors as practiced in Communist command economies.

The fourth and final element of our model is the existence of a "pilot agency,'' or a planning and guiding organization. I am referring to such organs of state as Japan's Ministry of International Trade and Industry, the ROC's Ministry of Economic Affairs, Korea's Economic Planning Board, and Singapore's Economic Development Board and Jurong Town Corporation. (In Hong Kong the functions of the pilot agencies are performed by the banking community and by cartel-like organizations of private entrepreneurs.) These organizations perform "think tank" functions for their economies, chart the route for economic development, obtain a consensus for their plans from the private sector, act as "gatekeeper" for contacts with foreign markets and investors, and provide positive governmental supports for private economic initiative. They are invariably staffed by the best non-political administrative talent in the respective societies; it is testimony to the political inventiveness of the high-growth nations that they have seen the need for such agencies, have staffed them properly, and have given them the scope, under political supervision, to operate. These agencies have no precise equivalents in the Anglo-American democracies or the Soviet-type command economies. Although they certainly do not have unblemished records of accomplishment and are often engaged in bitter controversy with rival bureaucratic organizations, their role of coordinating the capitalist developmental state is indispensable.

Taiwan a Successful Capitalist Developmental System

This four-fold model of the high-growth system—education, separation between reigning and ruling, reliance on the market and price mechanisms, and government-business cooperation guided by a pilot agency—is merely a sketch. To give it full contours would take us well beyond this introduction to a collection of papers and essays on Taiwan. Taiwan today is certainly one of the world's most prominent and successful capitalist developmental systems. It is properly compared with Japan and the other developmental states of East Asia, not with the Anglo-American democracies, the Communist countries, or the maldeveloped systems of Africa and Latin America. On the eve of the June 22, 1980, general election in Japan and fearing that the Liberal Democratic Party was about to lose its majority (it actually won handsomely), the *Economist* of London wrote editorially: "During the LDP's third of a century in power the party and the mandarinate have provided Japan with 15-fold economic growth, a 20-year increase in life expectancy, a sharp reduction in violent crime and a maintained social cohesion, all for taxes which have taken only just over 20 percent of gross national product. This can plausibly be called the most successful government in any big unwarlike country during all the history of the world."

Leaving aside the hyperbole of the last sentence, we might add that the achievements of Taiwan under Chiang Ching-kuo are no less impressive, particularly given the base from which Taiwan started and its inauspicious security situation. It is one of the greater ironies of our time that a nation that raised its per capita income from about $244 in 1967 to about $1,000 a decade later is not a member of the Economic and Social Council of the United Nations; that a nation that achieved 99.64 percent elementary-school attendance in 1978, with 94.70 percent of the graduates continuing on to secondary school, is not a member of UNESCO; and that a nation that has virtually eradicated disease from what was under the Japanese imperialists a quite unhealthy island has been expelled from the World Health Organization.

An Example for the Third World

Taiwan is not a small country. With a population of about 18 million, it has approximately the same number of people as Australia (14.4 million) and New Zealand (3.2 million) combined. (One cannot help but wonder whether the American people would have agreed to Jimmy Carter's unilaterally cancelling the American defense treaties with Australia and New Zealand in order to change the name of the U.S. mission in Peking from "liaison office" to "embassy"). Taiwan's economic development strategy is one of the soundest ever created and is (or should be) a model for the underdeveloped nations.

The program began with land reform. In 1949 the government reduced all rents to 37.5 percent of the estimated annual yield of the tenant farmers' main crop. In 1951 public lands were sold to incumbent tenants. Then, in 1953, individual ownership of land was limited to 7.4 acres. Any land owned over this amount had to be sold to the government and was resold to tenants. From 1952 to 1965 agricultural products, especially sugar, were Taiwan's most important foreign exchange earners. Since 1950 crop production has doubled, livestock production has gone up four times, and fishery yields have increased eight times. Simultaneously with this agricultural transformation the government launched an industrialization program, oriented at first toward manufacturing substitutes for imported goods. This industrialization campaign absorbed surplus agricultural labor, decreasing the farming population from 76 percent in 1950 to 37 percent in 1976.

Around 1960, the government began shifting the strategy of industrialization from import substitution to the production and promotion of export goods. After about 1970 it changed the strategy again, to emphasize captial-intensive heavy industrialization and enlargement of the industrial infrastructure. Most recently, the strategy is aimed at building "knowledge-intensive" high-technology industries. Simultaneously with these developments, the government made major investments in health and education. By 1979, Taiwan was turning out about 25,000 new engineering graduates per year, thereby fulfilling the most important prerequisite for knowledge-intensive industrialization. In the twenty-five years from 1952 to 1977 Taiwan raised industry's share of the net domestic product by 21 percent, an achievement that is virtually without precedent in the history of economic development. According to the current Ten-Year Economic Development Plan, the Taiwan authorities expect by 1990 to achieve a per capita income of US$6,200, a total GNP of US$110 billion ($32.3 billion in 1979), and a level of foreign trade approximately equal to GNP (in excess of $100 billion). Given Taiwan's sustained economic development for the past thirty years, these estimates are realistic, certainly more realistic than mainland China's "four modernizations"[3]

Every observer agrees that Taiwan's economic development has been phenomenal, but not everyone agrees on why it has occurred. There is a persistent myth that Taiwan is exceptional or has enjoyed a "free ride" because of its former alliance with the United States (it seems that some of mainland China's post-Mao reformers hold this view of all the high-growth economies and expect similar miracles from their new relations with the United States, a view that could prove to be tragically misinformed). It is sometimes supposed that Taiwan was left singularly well-endowed by Japanese imperialism or that U.S. economic aid was the key to its rapid economic growth.

The fifty years of Japanese rule in Taiwan (1895-1945) did see the introduction of widespread education, for example, into Taiwan, but it is often forgotten that this was almost entirely a Japanese education. From junior high school on, classes were conducted entirely in Japanese; and most of the teachers and students *were* Japanese. In 1944, when the highest number of secondary-school students was recorded, Japanese students numbered 16,179 and Chinese 12,826. During 1950 the number of students in each thousand of population was 139.6, a figure that by 1978 had raised to 262.3. Moreover, the amount and quality of higher education increased enormously over what it had been during the Japanese era. By the late 1970's Taiwan had about a hundred colleges and universities, more than the total number of institutions of higher learning on the mainland.

U.S. economic aid has similarly been overstated. Total U.S. economic assistance to Taiwan since 1949, including grants, loans, and food, has amounted to only about $1.7 billion, or roughly one-third of the value of the goods the United States imported from Taiwan during the year 1978. The U.S. Agency for International Development (AID) mission in Taiwan was closed in 1965. This U.S. aid to Taiwan was not unimportant at the time it was given, but it was not out of line with the U.S. Marshall Plan aid to Europe or the offshore procurement orders placed in Japan from the time of the Korean War throughout the 1950's. It was certainly not sufficient to have fueled the industrialization drive of the 1960's and 1970's.

Foreign investment in Taiwan has been much more important. But this was not a "free ride"; it was an integral part of Taiwan's economic development strategy. Differing from the Japanese and more like the Singaporeans and the Koreans in this respect, Taiwan's economic managers have not been afraid of foreign capital. They learned how to make the multinational corporations work for their own developmental, export, and employment goals and encouraged foreign investment. Their policies included the construction of some 42 industrial districts for plant sitings and the development of export processing zones in Taipei, Keelung, and Taoyuan, together with extensive financial inducements to promote their use. The result is that such major American companies as Ford, IBM, Goodyear, RCA, Zenith, and Texas Instruments have long been established in Taiwan.

Again, however, total private foreign investment in Taiwan, which has averaged roughly $100 million per year during high-speed growth, has always stood at around 2 percent of Taiwan's annual rate of capital formation. Even if all foreign investment in Taiwan were suddenly cut off, the impact on Taiwan's economic growth would not be very great. Some 250 American firms have certainly been among the largest groups of investors in Taiwan (representing about 30 percent of all private foreign investment, as compared to Western Europe with 21 percent, Japan with 17 percent, and the overseas Chinese with 32 percent), but this has been as much to their advantage as to Taiwan's. The funds for Taiwan's high rates of investment have come primarily from the high rates of domestic savings, for which the government offers strong incentives, and from the overseas Chinese.

The most distinctive problem of Taiwan's development has been the management of the fissure between the majority group of native Taiwanese—or descendents of earlier mainland immigrants—who comprise about 85 percent of the population, and the mainland Chinese who moved to the island in 1949. The native Taiwanese not unnaturally resented the monopolization of political power by the mainlanders (needless to say, they are not the least interested today in replacing their present mainlanders with a new group who are also Communists), but the mainlanders contributed enormously to the island's economy by bringing with them managerial skills and in some cases actual factories that were hitherto unknown in Taiwan.

The tensions that do exist between mainlanders and native Taiwanese are complicated by disputed claims in the Chinese civil war and by differing strategies of international recognition. However, the situation is not as unusual as is sometimes supposed. Polyethnic nations, such as Malaysia, or nations with radically different rates of economic and institutional development between center and periphery, such as Thailand, the Philippines, or Indonesia, are not dissimilar. And although historical reflection may suggest alternative solutions to the problem as it existed on Taiwan, the one chosen has been neither unsuccessful nor inhumane.

In essence, the political leaders of Taiwan have opted to let time resolve their problem, while compensating those who oppose it with high levels of material prosperity and cultural freedom. Today, a new group composed of born-in-Taiwan mainlanders and urbanized, educated Taiwanese is coming to the fore and replacing the old guards of the Kuomintang and the Taiwan independence movement. Under Chiang Ching-kuo, Taiwanese representation in local government has expanded rapidly, and the inequalities that existed between the two groups at the outset have been ameliorated. The population of Taiwan has not yet totally escaped from the dangers this issue poses, and a program of political development must be on the agenda for the future, as is true of all the societies of East Asia, the high-growth ones, the low-growth ones, and the Communist ones. But given the intractable nature of all ethnic or cultural divisions in a society, Taiwan's solution to its own share of such problems compares favorably with most others (e.g., Israel and the Palestinians, mainland Chinese and the Tibetans, not to mention England and the Irish, or America and its own polyethnic problems). One thing is certain about the Taiwan solution: time will make all the inhabitants into Taiwanese, and economic prosperity will make all Taiwanese into some of the richest people on earth.

NOTES

1. On the significance of the $1,100 per capita income barrier, see Edward K. Y. Chen, *Hypergrowth in Asian Economies: A Comparative Study of Hong Kong, Japan, Korea, Singapore and Taiwan* (London: Macmillan, 1979), pp. 179-80.

2. Ministry of Economic Affairs, Republic of China, *Economic Development in the Republic of China* (Taipei, May 1980), p. 6.

3. On the prospects for continued growth in Taiwan, see the testimony of Jan S. Prybyla in U. S. Senate, Committee on Foreign Relations, 96th Congress, 2nd Session, *Taiwan: One Year After United States-China Normalization* (Washington, D.C.: U.S. Government Printing Office, 1980), p. 82.

Section 1

Cultural Values and Cultural Continuity

Edited by Cho-yun Hsu

Section 1

Cultural Values and Cultural Continuity

by Cho-yun Hsu

The term culture can be defined in many ways. It may be regarded in a narrow sense to mean ideology; it may also imply the expression of ideology, which includes literature, creative arts, and performing arts, the cultural forms that are called "high cultures." Thus, cultural creations and activities can serve as indicators of the basic orientation of a given culture. In this section, however, the term culture is defined as the way of living and the manner in which people organize themselves to carry on this livelihood. In other words, the definition is an anthropological one. The selection of excerpts in this section is mostly from the anthropological monographs. Religious faith is one of the most common means by which people share their cultural values. Literature, as well as the arts, serve to express the values of a given group. Therefore, observations on religous practices and literary styles are also useful in identifying the mood and characters by means of which people share their culture.[1]

In this section, the main theme is the continuity of, and change in, Chinese cultural values during recent decades in Taiwan. For centuries, Chinese cultural values were derived from a long tradition of rural surroundings that emphasized coherent human relationships in small communities and which can be described as a particularism. Kinship ties were especially strong and buttressed communal ties. Since the mid-nineteenth century, China underwent changes in response to the intrusion in China by Western civilization. Industrialization and foreign trade turned coastal cities into a Westernized China, while the massive population in inland villages, who still retained much of the rural cultural tradition, felt that their brethren in the cities no longer shared the same value system. Even the vocabulary used by the city people was very different from that in the countryside. Such cultural alienation, compounded by many other factors, finally led to a showdown in the 1946-49 civil war, in which urban China was defeated by rural China, a national tragedy which has yet to reach its conclusion.

This section is an investigation of cultural development in Taiwan. A brief summary of the historical background of this small island society should be helpful in order to appreciate its patterns of development, which somehow evolved into a distinct lifestyle. First, Taiwan was a frontier island to which migrants brought their cultural heritages, especially folk cultures with little elite influence. The demands of the frontier situation

Cho-yun Hsu, the editor of this section, is Professor of History, University of Pittsburgh (Pittsburgh, Pa.). He notes that the advice of Professor Yih-yuan Li was most helpful in editing this section.

created an emphasis on some cultural values, such as communal cooperation, while deemphasizing others, such as formalism. Second, because it
had been a colony of Japan for 50 years, Taiwan had experienced the early
phase of modernization along a course different from that in Mainland
China. Third, the rapid pace of economic growth in recent decades pushed
Taiwan into thorough industrialization and urbanization. The result was an
integration of the old Chinese cultural values and the new pattern of life of
the modern industrial world.

Behavior and Values

The selections in the following pages fall into two categories, one on behavior and one on values. Human behavior reflects cultural values, as seen
in the interaction of individuals within the framework of the community
and of kinship organization. In Wang's paper, Chinese family structure is
viewed as a channel facilitating movement toward developing enterprises
rather than as a barrier to change. Taking this step further, Pasternak's
presentation demonstrates the value of communal solidarity in the process
of adopting technological improvements such as modern irrigation. The
excerpts from papers on migration from villages to cities by the Gallins
reveal how the migrants adjust to the urban environment by huddling together around old communal ties. Deglopper's narration on the behavior of
small town merchants discloses the blended effects of personal intimate
relationships of the old *Gemeinschaft* combined with the contractual relationships of impersonal modern business dealings. From these selections,
we see that the transition from a rural to an urban society was achieved in
Taiwan without serious alienation between the two. Many of the old behavior patterns, such as the maintenance of intimate personal ties, served positive functions. Close family relations, for example, served to bridge spatial
and social distances among members of the same family. There were new
factors as well, of course. The development of irrigation, the use of bank
checks, the absence of migrants from their home villages, and their city
jobs—all were new elements imposed on old institutions or old situations.
Particularism in human relationships somehow seemed to adapt with
changing environments. New elements were incorporated into traditional
values in a positive manner. The polarization of an urban-rural schism and
the consequent cultural alienation such as that suffered by the Chinese in
the 1930's and 1940's simply did not appear in Taiwan.

Some of the essential elements of Chinese cultural tradition, such as
kinship relationship and communal ties, are surprisingly adaptable to new
socioeconomic conditions. It has often been said that interindividual relationships, as a trademark of Confucianism, could have caused retardation
of the modernization of China. In the case of Taiwan's development, such
a simplistic statement seems to face serious challenge. Many of the traditional values and notions, with proper revisions, actually served as lubri-
cants to facilitate the transformation ushered in by industrialization and
urbanization. Much of Confucian ethics, after all, can be conducive to the

modernization of an economy and society. Taiwan is not the only place the successful transformation of a Chinese society has been achieved. Hong Kong and Singapore, both Chinese societies, testify to similar success. In the case of Taiwan, because it is a more pure Chinese nation, the testimony seems loud and clear.

The second group of articles deals with values. In Eberhard's analysis of notions on love and marriage, the continued emphasis on traditional attitudes toward marriage as an institution to form a family indicates concern with its social implications rather than with unions based on sexual attraction. Western customs are adopted, including relatively free courtship. Western individualism, which might have weakened the concept of social responsibility and therefore the bond between husband and wife, however, does not appear to have prevailed. Feuchtwang observes that religious faith as reflected in characteristics of Taiwanese temples underwent some profound changes during recent decades. Especially noticeable is the movement away from folk beliefs toward national elite religions. It should be pointed out, nevertheless, that Taiwanese religious faiths are essentially the same ones which the early settlers brought from southern Chinese coastal provinces. The transformation which Feuchtwang records is a consequence of the impact of high religions which were brought by new refugees after 1949. There is no distinct separation between high religions and folk beliefs. The two forms represent the two ends of a continuum, with many gradual steps between them. In the selections on literature, the Taiwanese products are clearly recognized as continuations and extensions for the mainland tradition. A setback was suffered during the early 1950's due to the fact that major figures in Chinese literature did not come to Taiwan. The themes and styles, however, originated from the legacy dominating mainland literature since the May Fourth Movement (1919).

The selections on cultural values reflect the fact that the Chinese in Taiwan generally retained values very similar to those which prevailed in mainland China before 1949, although they probably leaned more toward urban than rural patterns. After all, urbanization in Taiwan transformed the whole island to an urban environment with an urban-oriented population. Both the excerpts on behavior and those concerning values appear to confirm one another, since in both a preservation of traditional values is shown to be balanced by some degree of revision to accommodate present-day life in Taiwan.

Uniformity of Rural and Urban Values

The phenomenon of relative uniformity of values in the city and in the countryside should be attributed to the widening of communication channels that took place in Taiwan. Education, of course, is extremely significant in making information accessible to an entire population. The expansion of education is the subject matter of another section, so there is no need to discuss this topic here. Channels of communication are also broadened as a result of the proliferation of public media. The attached charts (Charts 1 and 2) clearly show that radio was the most popular medium until television assumed dominance. The number of television receivers per 1,000 persons leapt, in the late 1970s, while radios, especially electronic ones, have become such a commonplace that no statistics have been taken since 1977. The statistics on the production of books demonstrate a similar trend. By the late 1960s, the publication boom took off drastically. Excluding books of general interest, the combined number of titles in the humanities and social sciences exceeded the number in pure and applied sciences by about a three-to-one ratio. This trend demonstrates titles related to cultural concerns are readily available and that in Taiwan people are seriously concerned with cultural issues. Uniformity of attitudes on culture can easily be accomplished by means of the penetration of the public media. Charts 3 and 4 show the growth of the daily circulation of *China Times,* one of the leading newspapers in Taiwan. The year 1965 is a watershed line after which the growth rate was spectacular. The case of *China Times* is cited here for illustration. The other newspapers fared equally well. Together the big four, the *China Times, United Daily, Central Daily,* and *Taiwan Times,* are approaching a total circulation of three million. A score of local and evening papers brings the total circulation to between four and five million daily. For every four persons, adult and child, there is one copy of a newspaper. The impact of the public media indeed can be tremendous.

The fact that the late 1960's was a turning point is related to the economic growth spurt which took place at that time. Due to the expansion of

Chart 1.   Radio and television receivers and number of receivers per 1000 inhabitants

End of year	Radio receivers		Television receivers	
	Number[1]	Per 1000 population	Number[1]	Per 1000 population
1964	1 212 756	98.95	36 026	2.94
1965	1 306 778	103.48	62 434	4.94
1966	1 362 366	104.86	108 415	8.34
1967	1 402 073	105.45	163 918	12.33
1968	1 421 307	104.12	243 735	17.86
1969	1 429 456	99.72	338 816	23.64
1970	1 443 858	98.38	510 228	34.77
1971	1 451 297	96.79	672 721	44.86
1972	1 464 423	95.78	835 279	54.63
1973	1 470 783	94.49	900 646	57.86
1974	1 480 123	93.37	908 872	57.33
1975	1 486 376	92.04	912 942	56.53
1976	1 493 057	90.44	913 910	55.36
1977	...	...	1 309 059	77.86
1978	...	...	2 505 360	146.21

Note: [1]Regulation for registration to radio and television had been abolished since Feb. 1977, hence data for sets of radio are not available from that time. Sets of television, however, could be obtained by subtracting the exports of each of month from the sum or production of Jan. 1977 and each month.

Source: *Statistical Year Book of Republic of China, 1979* (Teipei: Directoraᵤe General of Budget, Accounting and Statistics), p. 550.

the public media, the impact of the economic prosperity resulting from industrialization and foreign trade expansion spread all over the island instead of being felt only in the cities. In mainland China the gaps between the cities and inland areas became wider as modernization took place because the impact of outreach and economic growth was limited to the urban areas. In Taiwan, the pattern has been one of reduced distance between urban culture and its rural counterparts.

In the last four or five years, there has been a growing interest in reviving traditional arts, dances, drama, etc., including both folk and elite culture. The younger generation has been primarily responsible for this movement. For instance, Mr. Lin Huai-min experiments in dance by incorporating traditional Chinese opera motions into modern Western-style performances. In another case, Miss Kuo Hsiao-chuang revises traditional opera with new modes of expression. The popularity of folk songs has been growing on college campuses, and artists have been attempting to revive the skill of Chinese brush painting. All of these efforts represents a trend which, as shown in one of the selections here, is shared by the creative writers who look for guidance and inspiration to classical Chinese litera-

Chart 2. Production of books and translations by subject

Year	Total	Generalities	Philosophy	Religion	Social science	Philology	Pure science	Applied science	Arts	Literature	History & geography
1954	1 380	...	...	...	...	...	...	...	...	...	...
1955	958	...	...	...	...	...	...	...	...	...	...
1956	2 763	...	...	...	...	...	...	...	...	...	...
1957	1 549	42	40	53	280	127	90	124	127	409	257
1958	1 283	38	62	17	266	481	68	102	43	—	206
1959	1 472	71	62	43	472	371	69	89	36	—	259
1960	1 496	...	...	...	...	...	...	...	...	...	...
1961	761	34	16	20	173	239	36	86	37	—	120
1962	2 404	134	61	49	337	70	60	132	44	1 135	382
1963	2 601	57	93	47	550	125	117	211	133	881	387
1964	3 095	73	103	56	587	1 082	137	229	142	128	558
1965	1 104	31	51	27	239	67	83	55	111	224	216
1966	2 199	34	93	67	524	306	160	196	180	238	401
1967	2 252	140	72	73	338	132	310	236	120	580	351
1968	3 950	313	186	114	385	269	269	384	144	782	1 104
1969[1]	22 556	9 115	861	567	2 461	1 011	1 835	2 256	624	2 615	1 211
1970	8 714	350	252	225	1 901	82	334	1 129	66	2 401	1 974
1971	8 504	295	231	195	1 894	201	367	1 167	72	2 219	1 863
1972	8 216	208	241	180	1 794	235	375	1 171	79	2 180	1 753
1973	8 547	295	236	189	1 897	212	389	1 153	86	2 214	1 876
1974	8 799	924	263	245	1 506	276	548	1 247	376	2 118	1 296
1975	8 921	942	268	254	1 516	284	567	1 264	382	2 138	1 306
1976	9 109	844	314	271	1 554	304	618	1 294	336	2 195	1 379
1977	9 304	859	324	281	1 574	314	638	1 334	346	2 235	1 399
1978	9 416	870	335	292	1 585	325	649	1 345	357	2 246	1 412

Note: [1]In 1969, many Chinese classical works were reprinted by different publishing companies in Taiwan. Thus, the production of books was greatly increased. Ye-Wen Publishing Company, for an example, printed more than one hundred collections of Chinese classical works comprising altogether 8,832 volumes. These volumes and many others were all counted as newly produced books by the National Central Library.

Source: *Ibid.*, p. 551.

Chart 3.   The China Times Circulation Growth

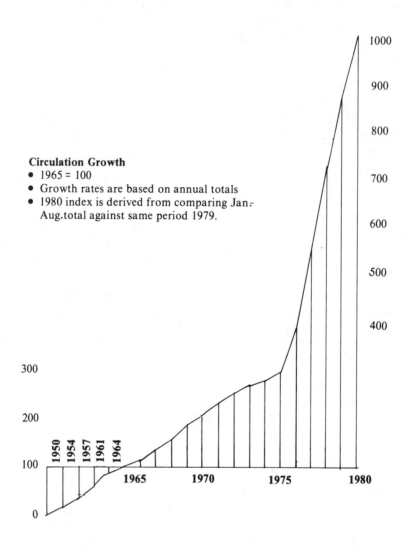

Circulation Growth
- 1965 = 100
- Growth rates are based on annual totals
- 1980 index is derived from comparing Jan.-
  Aug.total against same period 1979.

ture. It appears the rapid pace of development of a uniform culture tending toward Westernization has aroused a counter-action among the younger generation, which is reflected by their swaying toward Chinese tradition and creating a new synthesis.

A Dark Cloud on the Horizon

On the one hand, the cultural transformation taking place in Taiwan is a success. On the other hand, there is a dark cloud on the horizon. The rapid transformation is gathering momentum. Taiwan has been increasingly drawn into the orbit of Western, especially American, culture due to the growing contact with the West through trade and other interaction. The

Chart 4. The China Times Readership Composition

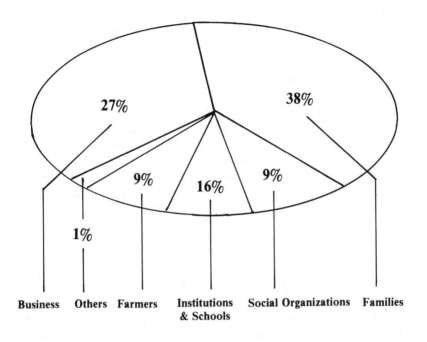

expansion of the influence of the public media is also accelerating. There-fore, much of the Chinese population in Taiwan finds itself captured by Western culture, and drawn toward conformity with it. The tremendous momentum of this movement may eventually become so formidable that the Chinese will be completely assimilated into the American civilization, historically a product of industrialization and urbanization. In Chinese there is a proverb which tells of a young man who tried to imitate the style of walking in a foreign country and who eventually forgot his natural way of walking and had to crawl home on four limbs. If Taiwan indeed becomes another occidental nation located in the Orient, as Japan is often described, the consequence will be two-fold. First, there will be no possibility of sharing a cultural heritage with mainland China compatriots, because the continuity will have been lost and the similarity erased. Second, there is a more imminent danger. The ills that American culture suffers today, for instance, the disintegration of community and the alienation of individuals from one another, will appear in Taiwan. The Chinese cultural legacy in-cludes a built-in antidote to these problems of modern life. It would be a pity for the Chinese in Taiwan to give up these valuable preventatives. Culturally, Taiwan is now standing at the fork in the road. The resurgence of interest in tradition on the campus and among the young artists and writers very likely reflects their awareness of the dangers of the change in cultural values. Their influence, however, is far too little to overcome the formidable weight of the public media and the entire Western world. More serious and organized efforts are urgently needed to mobilize available resources in order to accomplish the noble task of continuing progress without loss of the individual.

This task will not be an easy one. An awareness of loss of identity seems to have been growing. Large public buildings in Taiwan, hotels, museums, and memorials, are often decorated with traditional designs and motifs. Below the glittering tiles, within the vermilion columns, and behind the shining ceiling paintings, modern steel and concrete support the structure. Traditional Peking opera stages performances every evening, sponsored by public funds. It seems that both the government and the general public are concerned with the preservation of symbols of the old cultural heritage, symbolically at least. The illusion of old architecture, however, can provide only temporary relief for nostalgia for the past. The Peking opera is filled by an audience of middle age or older. The government-sponsored cultural renaissance movement never became more than an ornamental effort. As long as the small three-room apartment continues to displace the old-style compound, the family ties which somehow survived the first stage of the transformation toward a modern urbanized society will become weaker and weaker. As long as there is continuing rapid turnover of neighbors in the condominiums, communal relationships will also rapidly disappear. While the rate of transformation continues as it is now, the old cultural values, which appear to be surviving at the present time, most probably will disappear. If this is allowed to occur, it would be a quixotic dream to speak of checking the growth of alienation in an urbanized and industrialized society. The lonely crowd could never fight back against an impersonalized brave new world. If there is any hope of preserving the ideological assets of Chinese culture to somehow redeem the problems of modern industrial and urban cultures, the effort to conserve them must be much more than an ornamental paint job. The public needs to be educated, the media needs to be educated, the government also needs to be educated, so that the cultural values that helped the Chinese to survive a thousand years and that proved conducive and adaptive to the modern transformation of today, still can be serviceable to the Chinese society in Taiwan and shape an alternative to the Western model of post-industrial culture, an option the whole world will gratefully appreciate.

1. Family Structure in Rapid Modernization

Sung-hsing Wang

This paper will touch mainly upon the study of the Chinese family system in this age of rapid modernization. Generally speaking, studies regarding this subject are divided into two categories: the first one is concerned with pinpointing the effects of economic change on the family system and the second one deals with the opposite—knowing the effects of the family system on economic development.

Taking the first category—how economic change affects the family system—we can consider changes such as the atomization of the family when society enters a market economy system, the changing role of parents, the changing relationship among family members, and the problems of youth delinquency as parts of this discussion.

As for the second one, the consideration is whether the family system has a positive or negative effect on economic development or whether family system assists or hinders economic development. In discussing this point, it is rather difficult to arrive at a definite criteria of what constitutes a positive or a negative effect. Very often, we get into contradicting conclusions regarding one particular system. In other words, one system can at the same time be beneficial and detrimental to economic development, depending on the viewpoint we take in making the examination.

Let us take Chinese familism as an example. A number of scholars in Japanese and Chinese modernization conclude that the Chinese family system is the culprit in the slow modernization of China. However, bringing the same family system to Southeast Asian countries, we can also say that Chinese extended family and web of kinship relations is a positive catalyst in the development of a captalist entrepreneurial system in most of these countries . . .

It is a general observation that because of the practice of dividing family property equally among sons, no affluent family can stay affluent for three or four generations. Another observation is that in traditional agricultural societies, it is a common practice for a poorer brother to become a dependent of the wealthier brother. Under such circumstances, development of a system of capital accumulation appears to be quite an impossible task . . .

We all know that the Chinese family is built upon patrilineal descent. It is from this that Chinese derive the concepts of succession and inheritance. To the great mass of people without special social position, succession does not have any meaning at all and attention is placed on the question of inheritance. For the Chinese, succession is secondary to inheritance and both are expressed by the same term: *Ch' eng chi.*

However, if we take the Japanese family system for comparison, then we realize its distinctiveness. Inheritance, for the Japanese, bears no importance whatsoever. In contrast to the Chinese, succession plays a central role in Japanese society. Inheriting the property of a family is the result of succeeding to family and both are designated by the same term: *Sozoku.*

A short time after the Japanese occupation of Taiwan, scholars studying the family institutions in Taiwan made this conclusion in comparing Chinese *Ch' eng-chi* with Japanese *Sozoku:* "The object of *Ch' eng-chi* is property but the object of *Sozoku* is the authority to which the property is attached." In other words, the Chinese are inheritance-oriented while the Japanese are succession-oriented.

In a family under an inheritance-oriented society, the continuity of a family line depends not only on having generation follow generation, but also upon the uninterrupted transmission of the family's common property. In a report on *Social Change in a Suburban Village of Taipei* Huang Hsun-erh points out that the inhabitants of the place possess strong attachment to the land and property left by their ancestors. They will not easily put such land bequeathed by their ancestors for sale, because such an action means an interruption of the family line. Records of land selling from 1950 to 1971 gives this evidence:

From Sung-hsing Wang, "Family Structure and Economic Development," *Bulletin of the Institute of Ethnology, Academia Sinica* (Taipei), No. 44 (1977), pp. 1-11.

Table 1

	Total	Land acquired by land reform	Ancestral land
Area	38.9104 ha	30.5006 ha	8.4098 ha
%	100.0%	78.4%	21.6%
Cases	170	159	11
%	100.0%	93.5%	6.5%

Table 2

	Land acquired by land reform	Ancestral land	Total
Sold	30.5006 (56%)	8.4098 (45%)	38.9104 (53%)
Unsold	24.4344 (44%)	10.0249 (55%)	34.4593 (47%)
Total	54.9350 (100%)	18.4347 (100%)	73.3697 (100%)

The opening statement of the "Contract of Family Division" best described the situation mentioned above. It said, "The division of a main branch into smaller branches is a natural occurrence." This exemplifies that the division of a family is inevitable. In an inheritance-oriented society, the emphasis in cases of family division is essentially property division. Take a contract, for instance: It states that "the ancestral land, house and all farming elements acquired by myself will be divided into three parts . . ." Generally, each son has one part, a concubine's son one-half, a step-son one-fourth. In this process of family partition, we find that the son's share in the family property takes the form of a stock-share. Furthermore, the property of a family, a basis of the Chinese family system, can be regarded as a joint-stock. The joint-stock is formed by the number of sons a family has. For instance, if a family has three sons, it is accepted that family property is formed by three shares; if another son is born much later, it follows that property will be composed of four shares. This concept is in great contrast with the Japanese norm of family property which is treated like a 'fund' and cannot be divided.

Because family property has the characteristic of a joint-stock, we easily find the mechanisms of pooling and sharing built within the family system. The economic activities based on such a family can be defined as an 'inclusive economy.' In contrast, we have the 'exclusive economy' of the Japanese which has *ie* as its basis.

Let us talk about the inclusive economy of the Chinese family. Lin Yueh-hwa in his *The Golden Wing* described how Dunglin and his sister's husband jointly opened a store in the city. Dunglin's share of the store, together with the land in the village, became the property of Dunglin's family. Dunglin stays in the city managing the store, his wife stays in the village together with Dunglin's mother, his brother and sister-in-law, and their children. The capital and income of the store, as well as the revenues from the village farm, are shared by the brothers. The two of them are much concerned with each other's work and both strive hard for the welfare of their family.

Let us take a more complicated example. Myron Cohen in 1965 made a study of Meinung, with Lin Shang-yung as the head of family. There are forty-two people in all. The estates of this family are scattered into four areas, each area forming a household. These are:

1) The buildings and fields in the original village

2) A rice mill in an adjoining village

3) A merchandise store in the neighboring village dealing with fertilizers and animal feeds

4) Another farm and house twenty-five miles to the south

This example is often seen in families which are not yet partitioned.

Cohen went further to point out that the diversification of economy, such as the example given above, induces the formation of joint family.

Now, let us go to the exclusive economy of the Japanese family system. In Japan, only the eldest son can succeed the family head, and all family properties come under his name.

From the second son below, all must leave their natal family and seek their own fortune, usually even before they are married. In most occasions, they go to the city to seek their fortune and make a fresh start. Their only connection with their village family is that it usually arranges for their jobs or positions in the city, and then later arranges for their marriages. After marriage, the young couple establishes its own home and then terminates its relationship and communication with the village home. Vogel, in his work on kinship structure and Japanese modernization, believes that this kind of family system has rendered impetus to the industrialization of Japan and the emergence of a system of capital accumulation. Since the Meiji reformation, it seems that the number of rural households has not increased. At the same time, the young people who leave their hometown village for the industrial cities usually bring their *ie* or family loyalties into the new entrepreneurial group. I will add here that they brought this family loyalty even to the military group during World War II.

To recapitulate, scholars of Japanese modernization and industrialization all agree that the family system mentioned above is a valuable asset to an exclusive economy such as that existing in Japan. I agree with this statement too. However, I find it unfair and too simplified to use this criteria to judge the problem of Chinese modernization. Many have argued that the Chinese family system forms a stumbling block to economic change. I am not a confirmed nationalist but I do think that scholars should avoid jumping into conclusions without first giving the Chinese family system a broader and more open analysis. Let me discuss this pitfall further by going back to the original topic of the distinctive features of the Chinese family structure.

Based on the above discussions, we can name three distinctive features of the Chinese family system:

1) It has an in-built mechanism of pooling and sharing
2) It is an inclusive economy
3) It has a natural tendency for diversification

The economic environment allowing, once these three features are given maximum expression, there is no doubt that the Chinese family system has a salutary effect on economic development. Its functions are incongruent with the characteristics of the Japanese family system. Naturally, in an agricultural economy, capital is limited and diversification is hardly possible. One brother becoming a burden on the other is also a natural phenomenon. However, since industrialization in Taiwan has taken off after the Japanese occupation, we cannot see and nobody has talked about the family system hindering economic development. To ascertain what role the Chinese family system actually plays in the path of Taiwan's economic development, we can bring up the following points:

1) *Increased Job Mobility* — In the example of Lin Shang-yung mentioned above, his family is founded on agriculture but he established two other enterprises besides his farm. Eberhard made a survey of businesses in Ching-mei, a suburban district of Taipei City. In 106 business families in this area, 43.4% or 46 households are first-generation business-men. This mobility, of course, also applies to those who have gone to the cities as laborers. Like the Japanese family system, we can see the influence of the Chinese family system in pushing people out of the farm into the city-industries. But there is a divergent point from that of the Japanese. Those who have left their hometown villages, unlike the Japanese, do not disregard their origins and they retain their attachment to their home villages. O. Lang made a survey in the nineteen thirties with these findings: In Peking, the working class and the lower middle class are the tradition-bound group. They persist in the practice of sending financial aid home to feed their parents and family in rural areas. In Shanghai, a study reveals that 28 out of 44 labourers in textile factories and 13 out of 43 in civil service still possess landed property back in their hometowns. However, this property exists only in form because they receive no benefit from the produce of the land. The land is left to their brothers to be cultivated and they do not share in the revenues from the farm. These lands are but symbols of security, something to go back to in case they lose their jobs in the cities.

This case is similar to our study on Rice Farming in Taiwan in 1971. Remittances from the city consist of 29% of the income in rural families. From this we can draw one conclusion. Because of this particular family system, relationship between the rural folk and the urban industrialized city folk are not terminated abruptly. A balance between these two groups is maintained by this particular system. The unproductiveness of agriculture in Taiwan, reaching its peak in 1971, did not create the destruction of the agrarian economy. Likewise, the ill-effects of the energy crisis in industry starting a few years ago did not create the same deterioration and damage as in other countries. Of course we also can mention the timeliness and effectiveness of state policy in warding off economic disaster, but the family system definitely can be credited for its salutary influence in maintaining economic balance. The demarcation between industrial and agricultural sectors is not very clear in Taiwan. But within the given family system, there is great flexibility between the two sectors.

2) *Leverage on Capital Flow* — My colleague at the Institute of Ethnology, Mr. Chuang Ying-chang, discussed this based on field work done in a village in Central Taiwan. He maintains that people both in the village and town still consider themselves as part of the family even after it has been divided. Mr. Chuang has coined a new term for such a family unit: the "federal family," which he defines as "a family unit in which the members do not share the same residence but maintain close social contacts, do not share common property but maintain a high degree of economic cooperation." He goes further to point out that this new family system is a product of modernization in Taiwan. This is an advantage to capital formation in a closer analysis. William Parish in 1970 gave us some figures to exemplify this point.

	adult offsprings receiving financial aid from parents	among sibilings
Tainan City	63%	47%
Kaoshiung	71%	43%
Detroit	30%	15%
Cleveland	47%	6%

Information of this kind cannot be found in the Japanese society. Perhaps, this kind of capital flow, especially among siblings, does not even exist in an exclusive economy.

From here we see that the Chinese family system is important to intersectoral capital flow, and this is another point worthy of our attention. We often see some people from the cities returning to their village hometowns and initiating some innovations in their farm activities like setting up fish ponds, farming and others. We can also see here examples of an agrarian economy turning into the industrial sector.

T. H. Lee in his *Intersectoral Capital Flow in the Economic Development of Taiwan, 1895-1960* (1971), has discussed in detail the capital flow in two sectors. He confined his information mainly to the public sector. But capital flow in the private sector still needs further investigation, especially after the rise of small-scale enterprises in the 1950's.

3) *Management of Industrial Enterprise*—Most of the industrial enterprises in Taiwan have been formed since the late 1950's. At this early stage of industrialization, people have already taken advantage of the diversification potentialities of the family system in expanding their enterprises. Such activities may be considered as a kind of multiformity and multilateral expansion. In such cases, a mother-enterprise is usually augmented to form several smaller related enterprises. The main rationale behind this can be traced to the lack of supporting or auxiliary industries to a certain enterprise, the desire of families to spread risks, and from the desire of individuals to pursue ventures of their own interest. In such related enterprises, capital is drawn from the family itself, with individual proprietors investing in each other's businesses. To minimize conflict, management of each particular enterprise is usually left to the interested party.

The three points discussed above substantiate the contention that instead of having a baneful influence, the family system can serve the ends of economic development. Furthermore, we wish to emphasize the point brought up at the beginning—that in determining the interrelation between the family system and economic development, we cannot confine ourselves merely to the influence of the family system on economic development and vice-versa. A more positive approach to this question is to look for the distinctive characteristics of a certain family structure and how these features can be utilized under specific economic set-ups to achieve the desired results.

2. Communal Solidarity in Technological Advance

Burton Pasternak

In any densely populated rice-growing community, frequent conflicts over water would certainly not be surprising, if indeed they were not taken for granted. What might be surprising on first thought, however, is the precise and almost paradoxical relationship between such conflict and the means developed to manage it. For the very existence of feuding seems to stimulate the emergence of both cooperative networks and managerial structures to preclude or at least restrain overt expressions of hostility. And the greater the danger of such hostile outbreaks, the more extensive and powerful the networks and structures seem to be. Exactly what they will be like in a particular case will be influenced by the character of the factors that generate them—that is, by the nature of the specific irrigation system involved. Changes in the system will, of course, cause changes in the kind and intensity of conflict prevalent in the community and, consequently, in the means of dealing with it.

With this in mind, let us consider a specific irrigation system and a specific community, the Chia-nan Irrigation System and the village of Chung-she on the Chia-nan Plain of southwestern Taiwan. The plain, which includes the *hsien* of Tainan, Chiayi, and Yunlin and the city of Tainan, has a total area of approximately 4,884 sq km, or virtually one-seventh that of the island. Rainfall on the plain is unevenly distributed throughout the year (roughly 80 percent of the mean annual precipitation of 3,000 mm falls between May and September), and underground water is not abundant, but the region is otherwise well suited to agriculture. About two-thirds of it is flat and fertile, and the temperature does not normally fall below 17°C. except in January. The area is often referred to as "the granary of Taiwan."

Chung-she Village lies in the southeastern portion of the plain. According to my census in 1968, 174 of its 194 households cultivated land, 104 of them as full owners (161 households owned at least part of the land they farmed). Its total cultivated area was 249 hectares in 1968. The principal crop has always been rice.

Before the Chia-nan Irrigation System was built, a small part of Chung-she's farmland drew water from public or private ponds scattered about the landscape. The farmers dependent on each pond functioned as a group to obtain "common water," and to manage disputes arising over it. The larger ponds had radiating canals. When the water in such a pond was sufficient, the canals drew water in a scheduled sequence, with farmers at the shallow end operating foot-treadles or opening gates before those at the deep end. The drawing period for each farmer was determined by the area of his fields, and measured by burning incense sticks. When water in the pond was low, however, each canal might draw water without regard to schedule. The only rule was that water would be taken only by foot-

From Burton Pasternak, "The Sociology of Irrigation: Two Taiwanese Villages," in W. E. Willmott, (ed.), *Economic Organization in Chinese Society* (Stanford, Ca.: Stanford University Press, 1972), pp. 193-213. Reprinted with permission of the publishers, Stanford University Press. Copyright 1972 by the Board of Trustees of the Leland Stanford Junior University. Footnotes omitted.

treadle. Farmers located at the deep end of a pond sometimes broke this rule. While pretending to pedal, they would covertly open a gate, forcing farmers to the shallow end to pedal furiously, and causing conflict. Farmers who were caught at this trick were denied access to the water in the canal. The smaller ponds were usually capable of supplying water only to the fields immediately surrounding them. So few farmers were involved that there was no need for schedules; each field-owner and his family simply treadled at will. Cooperation was not necessary.

Most of the fields cultivated by Chung-she villagers during this period depended exclusively on rainfall, and were referred to as *k'an-t'ien t'ien*, or "fields that depend on the heavens." Generally speaking, then, either all farmers had water, or no farmers had water. Before 1920, cooperation and conflict in irrigation were minimal and involved only individuals. Households needed to cooperate for only a few purposes, such as providing drainage for each other's fields, or equalizing the supply of water by passing it from one field to another. Theft of water was rare, and usually involved farmers cultivating fields irrigated by ponds. There was a saying that "a good field is made by a good field-neighbor; a good house is made by a good house-neighbor" . . .

The water supplied by the Chia-nan System is not sufficient to allow the cultivation of rice every year throughout the entire region. For this reason, a three-year rotation schedule has been established for about 75 percent of the system (122,167 hectares), including the area cultivated by Chung-she Village. The rotation area is divided into *hsiaoch'ü*, or "small areas," of about 150 hectares each, which are in turn divided into three roughly equal sections. In any one year only one section is to be planted to rice, while the second is to be planted to sugarcane, and the third to a crop that requires even less water, perhaps none at all from the system. The intent of this plan is to give every farmer equal access to the available water.

Putting the plan into effect is a complex matter, as the operation of the Wu-shan-tou portion of the system (serving Chung-she) may illustrate. Water is furnished to the main canal every day from June 1 to October 10. All the water in the canals during this period is intended for the rice-growing areas. During December, all gates are opened for a period of approximately twelve days. Water supplied during this period is intended for the irrigation of dry crops. For fifteen days in February or March, the canals are again filled to supply water for the cultivation of sugarcane. When newly released irrigation water has reached the terminal points of the main canal, and when water levels have been determined to be correct, all gates exiting from them are simultaneously opened. Two or three times a day while these gates are open, the water level is checked at various points along the canal and adjustments are made to keep it constant. As water is led into each lateral canal, gates exiting from it are partially opened, starting from the top gate and working down to the last one, as water passes each gate. When the water has reached the end of the line, the level of water at various points along the lateral canal is checked and adjusted accordingly. Thus, all gates in the system are actually kept open at the same time, and their apertures are adjusted as necessary.

The preceding description illustrates the integrated nature of the irrigation operation and the high degree of coordination that is required. The coordinating body is the Chia-nan Irrigation Association. Below the system level, however, cooperation prevails. The local irrigation station hires one or two villagers each year and assigns them to manage water distribution in a "small area." In fact, however, these men do little more than make ritualistic patrols. The actual channelling and distribution of water is handled by the farmers themselves.

In fact, it would probably be fair to say that cooperation in the handling of water resources is more prevalent in Chung-she today than it was before the irrigation system was built. Most village households own from two to four fields located in different places. When fields were watered by rainfall, as already noted, households needed to cooperate in only a few ways, such as providing drainage or equalizing the supply of water by passing it from one field to another. Theft of water was rare, and usually involved farmers cultivating fields irrigated by ponds. For the most part, either all farmers had water or no farmers had water. Since completion of the Chia-nan System, water is supplied to fields on a schedule and from a localizable source. Since each field has to be filled and drained several times during the growing season, and since not all fields border on canals, it is clear that a farmer must articulate his activities with those of other farmers. Not only must he cooperate with the owners of adjacent fields, but he must also arrive at understandings with farmers farther up the line on the canal, who receive water first.

In addition to cooperating in the day-to-day operation of the irrigation system, many farmers cooperate to steal water. They even establish complicated rotation schedules among themselves. Actual plantings of rice during much of the period since 1930 have far exceeded official estimates (the forty-five hectares scheduled to grow rice plus those areas given special permission to grow rice out of turn). This excess area could have been watered only with water illegally diverted from the irrigation system. It should be noted that the mean hectarage cultivated by individual households in this area has steadily decreased since 1935, and that the smaller a farmer's holding, the more likely he is to feel compelled to plant rice every year rather than sugarcane, in order to be sure of feeding his family.

The potential for conflict in Chung-she has obviously increased greatly since the Chia-nan System was built. Yet conflict over water in the village has not increased in the proportions that might have been expected—except possibly for disputes arising from thefts of water. . .

The Chia-nan Irrigation Association has taken several steps specifically designed to reduce conflict over water. The various farm ditches served by a single small-supply canal initially drew water simultaneously. But the water flowed so slowly that much of it seeped away, and it took a long time to irrigate the area supplied by each ditch. Farmers with fields located at terminal points had to wait a particularly long time. Besides, farmers whose ditches were higher on small-supply canals were in a position to draw water faster at all times and to draw more water in times of shortage. Water passed their ditch entries first, and the openings could be widened to let in a greater quantity of water. Conflicts therefore arose between the owners of ditches fed by a single small-supply canal.

A year or two after the Chia-nan project was completed, however, a plan was devised whereby each ditch received water by rotation. The time allotted for each ditch depended on the type of soil and the total area to be watered, and was measured by burning incense sticks. All the water in the small-supply canal could now legally pass into the entitled ditch. The water flowed faster, and less of it seeped away.

When conflicts arose because certain farmers sheltered their incense sticks to make them burn more slowly, alarm clocks were introduced to standardize timing. The first farmer on a ditch would open it and draw water. Because conflicts over timing arose between farmers along a single ditch, the irrigation station devised rotation schedules for each ditch. When the last farmer on the schedule has drawn his share, he passed the clock to the first farmer on the next lower ditch, who opened its entry and closed that of the upper ditch. If anyone claimed that the clock was running slow, it would be checked against the one in the local train station.

In a further attempt to reduce conflict over water, the irrigation station created the water patrol a few years after the Chian-nan System was completed. Steam-powered tillers used in the planting of sugarcane worked very deep, causing the soil to absorb great quantities of water during a short period. Simultaneous drawing of water from a small-supply canal, such as was still being practiced in rice areas, was no longer possible. Rotation among ditches in the sugarcane areas was therefore established early, and the patrol was set up to supervise it and to watch for flooding in the canals. It was later extended in modified form to rice areas as well.

In summary, then, the extension and integration of irrigation that occurred when the Chia-nan Irrigation System was built required a parallel expansion of the cooperative and managerial networks previously developed by the farmers of the Plain. Bernard Gallin has described the same sort of expansion in Hsin-hsing, another Taiwanese village. In that village, as in Chung-she, the extension of canal irrigation during the Japanese period made water available to a greater number of farmers, extended the area of interdependence, and broadened cooperative networks. . . .

The experience of Chug-she and Hsin-hsing contrasts sharply with that of Ta-tieh Village on the Ping-tung Plain farther to the south. Before 1956, the 220 hectares of farmland cultivated by Ta-tieh farmers were tied into an integrated irrigation system. Conflict over water in this area, already sharp because of population pressures and ethnic rivalry, was intensified early in the twentieth century when subsurface dams and new canals built upstream for the benefit of a new sugar factory deprived the system of much of its water.

Beginning in 1956, pumps designed to tap underground water were installed at various points along the canals in Ta-tieh and the rest of the Ping-tung system. These pumps were intended to counterbalance the drying up of older sources and to ensure more equitable and timely distribution of water for irrigation. An unintentional effect of introducing the pumps has been to split the system into more or less independent units, each drawing most of its irrigation water from a single pump, and there have been noticeable sociocultural adaptations to this change. Conflict over water has significantly diminished, and cooperative networks have contracted. The irrigation association still functions, and a small-group chief is still elected every three years to collect irrigation fees, to disseminate information passed down from the irrigation association, and, theoretically, to help arbitrate water disputes arising within each large-canal system. But the real authority lies in the hands of natural groups consisting of the twenty to twenty-five farmers who draw water from a single pump. It is within and between these groups that rotation and other forms of cooperation mainly occur.

Each pumping station is assigned a watchman by the irrigation association, but the selection usually follows the recommendation of pump-group members. The watchman is responsible to the members of the group he serves for the day-and-night security of his pumping station. During the dry season, especially during periods of severe drought, a pump group may also employ one or two field watchmen to ensure an equitable distribution of water day and night. Such watchmen are paid directly by the owners of the fields they guard. Once a rotation schedule has been agreed upon, usually by drawing lots at a group meeting, these watchmen must see that it is followed. They cannot change it without unanimous prior authorization from the group. During periods of really severe drought, farmers stay in their fields all night to double-check the watchmen.

Where local groups of farmers request it, the irrigation association may investigate the feasibility of and arrange loans for the construction of special pumping devices. The association then assumes responsibility for the maintenance of these facilities, passing both construction and maintenance costs on to the farmers. the irrigation association also assumes responsibility for major water projects such as dikes along the river, but its presence is rarely felt in the areas of water distribution and conflict resolution at the local level. These activities are normally regulated and managed on a face-to-face basis within and between pump groups. Major decisions are enforced by public opinion.

Labor Supply and Demand

Before the Chia-nan Irrigation System was built, the labor supply in Chung-she consisted of the farmers and their grown sons. Only a few wealthy families had permanent laborers attached to their households or living elsewhere in the village. The demand for labor was characterized by brief but intense peaks followed by relative lulls. Rainfall, unevenly distributed throughout the year and lasting only barely long enough at certain critical points in the rice cycle, had to be taken advantage of when it came. Every farmer was reportedly ready to begin preparing his rice fields (about 2.5 hectares in the second cropping season) as soon as the rains began. During the few days when the fields were actually wet enough to allow proper preparation, he and his sons and their buffalo would work as hard and fast as they could. But work as they might, they would sometimes not finish in time and would have to plant a faster-growing but lower-yielding strain of the native *tsai-lai* rice.

When rice seedlings reach the proper stage of development, they must be transplanted within a certain period of time, or they will be lost. Even if rainfall was adequate, the farmer and his sons had to work steadily to finish the job in time. Obviously under these circumstances there was no labor available for exchange or for hire within the village. Nor was there labor that could be brought in at these crucial times from villages just to the north, south, or west. As in Chung-she, farmers in these areas were under pressure to prepare their fields and plant their crops and with the rains. Labor could not even be imported from areas farther away where the planting and harvesting times were different, because transportation was so expensive. In 1920 a round-trip train ticket from the city of Tainan to Chung-she, for instance, cost the equivalent of 50 catties of rice. The average yield per hectare at that time was only 1,000 catties. The only hired labor in the village of Chung-she consisted of a few work teams from the western coastal areas brought in to help with the second-season harvest of rice.

The Chia-nan Irrigation System has changed all this. More land is irrigated and can therefore be more intensively cultivated. Yields per hectare are higher. Fields are no longer perpetually flooded, and each rice crop must be weeded at least three times, instead of once as before. The total demand for labor has accordingly increased. However, the prolonged availability of water has spread this demand over a longer period of time. Farmers do not all have to carry out the same operation at the same time, and the peaks in demand are considerably less sharp.

Exactly the opposite happened in Ta-tieh. In a system where farmers once received water in sequence, water was suddenly available to most villagers at about the same time of year, so that households were in a position to prepare, transplant, and harvest their fields almost simultaneously with everyone else. Peak periods of demand for labor (when rice is transplanted or harvested and when beans are planted) were therefore contracted.

Interestingly enough, these opposite patterns of demand for labor have not produced opposite patterns of labor supply: both villages began to hire far more labor than before. An increase in the hiring of labor would be predictable in Ta-tieh, where peak periods of demand were suddenly created. In Chung-she, however, where these peak periods were considerably eased, it might be thought that the villagers would begin to exchange labor. On the contrary, they began to hire workers for transplanting, for routine care of plants, and for harvesting. Brokers even appeared in some villages in the area to accommodate the new damand for hired labor. Perhaps the best explanation for this similarity is that in both villages the irrigational changes I have been describing brought substantial increases in annual income for most residents.

3. Integration of Rural and Urban Patterns

Bernard Gallin and Rita Gallin

To what extent have Hsin-hsing migrants continued to rely on kin- and village-based networks to satisfy their needs in the city? We have seen that upon arrival in Taipei, almost all of the migrants depended upon village-derived connections to take care of their immediate needs for employment and housing. As a result, the majority have jobs in the Central Market, which has natural centripetal consequences. The vegetable merchants have daily contacts with their fellow migrants. The cart drivers work and relax together every day; the gossip in which they engage tends to foster a community of interest and makes the Central Market the communication node of the Hsin-hsing community and, to a lesser extent, of the migrant community of Chang-hua county as a whole.

Within the market many of these people have organized themselves into groups somewhat akin to guilds and *pang*, which the government allows to function as "monopolies" in the interest of orderly market operation. The first such group organized was the Vegetable Merchants' Association. In order to maximize their profits, merchants needed two kinds of predictable labor services: delivery of wholesale produce to their stands in the market, and delivery of large loads of produce to major buyers outside the market. The association's first efforts, therefore, were directed toward organizing workers into two stable labor groups to perform these services. Migrants from Chang-hua county and particularly from Hsin-hsing dominate these groups. Over half of the members of one group, which has a contractual arrangement with the Vegetable Merchants' Association, are from Hsin-hsing and most of these men are from one patrilineage. The other group has the tacit recognition of but not a contract with the Association. It was organized by a Hsin-hsing villager and more than half of its members are from the village.

The preponderance of Hsin-Hsing migrants in the two labor groups is not surprising; men from Hsin-hsing were among the earliest arrivals in the market, formed the largest village grouping there—compared with any other single identifiable place—and were most familiar with the vegetable merchants. In addition, at the time the two labor groups were formed, many of the migrants' relationships still were based on kinship or village identity or both. It was reasonable, then, that when organization occurred such criteria defined the membership.

One might have expected, however, given these conditions, to find a much higher proportion of Hsin-Hsing migrants in these groups. Since their arrival in the city though, all of the migrants have developed new and intense reciprocal relationships with people not from Hsin-hsing—usually also migrants — on the basis of such shared experiences as being employed in the same market or living in the same area. (We will return to this point below.) Over time, many of these bonds have come to be considered more effective bases for developing the trust and cooperation necessary for the effectiveness of the groups than the ones brought from the village. As a result, when positions became available in the groups over the years, they began to be offered to city-based friends rather than to kinsmen or fellow villagers.

Despite the admission of "outsiders" to the groups, however, Hsin-hsing workers continue to exhibit a sense of unity among themselves within the market. Along with non-group villagers—later arrivals who were not able to find places in the more favored groups and who deliver small loads of produce on hand carts—Hsin-hsing laborers form an informal coalition that tries to protect its members against police harassment for alleged violations of regulations, demands for protection money from police and *liu-mang* (hoodlums), and competition from other groups. The coalition's success in this endeavor depends not only on sheer numbers, but also on support from influential merchants who sometimes help when they feel orderly market operation might be affected by problems among the laborers.

From Bernard Gallin and Rita Gallin, "The Integration of Village Migrants in Taipei," in Mark Elvin and G. William Skinner, (eds.), *The Chinese City Between Two Worlds* (Stanford, Ca.: Stanford University Press, 1974), pp. 331-358. Reprinted with the permission of the publishers, Stanford University Press. Copyright 1974 by the Board of Trustees of the Leland Stanford Junior University. Footnotes omitted.

The coalition's performance has varied over the years, but Hsin-hsing laborers view membership in the coalition as a means of obtaining a degree of security within the market and so it remains an active grouping.

Outside the market however, the Hsin-hsing laborers have failed to organize themselves into a cohesive mutual-aid group. Nor have they joined with other migrants from the Lukang or P'u-yen township areas to form a formal regional organization. This is partly because they have only a small population of natives in Taipei and only a few potential members from these places commanding resources, and partly because they do not feel much threatened as a group.

Nevertheless, laborers do report that they are "looked down upon" by Taipei natives because they are "outsiders" *(ch'u-wai jen)*—a term apparently applied to anyone from outside the immediate area of Taipei. And they believe that this attitude, along with their limited personal relationships with influential people, are responsible for their failure to secure government welfare benefits and services such as credit, legal aid, and protection. Thus, despite the limited threats directed against the migrants as people from a particular place, their belief that they are discriminated against and do miss opportunities came to provide a founding principle for a county-based association in Taipei. The group was organized in the early 1960's by several politically ambitious men from Chang-hua county who, in order to develop a clientele and following, used these beliefs and "t'ungism" to recruit members from among the large number of Chang-hua migrants in the city. Suggesting that ties based on a common county of origin were meaningful links that implied acts of reciprocity, these men promised prospective members patronage in exchange for political support.

Almost all the Hsin-hsing migrants responded to these recruitment "pledges" and joined the Chang-hua County (Regional) Association. Few, however, report having derived benefits from their membership. The association leaders' regular promises of aid appear to be met in part only around election time, when the association acts as a viable grouping representing the community of migrants. At all other times it serves primarily as an arena in which its more successful members organize alliances they can translate into social, economic, and political advantages. However, since the Hsin-hsing laborers usually manage to organize relationships through their associational activity only with people whose resources are as limited as their own, their membership fails to provide them with any beneficial ties to patrons or power brokers.

As a result, the only groupings to which the laborers belong that enable them to counter threats directed against them are their occupational groupings. But these groupings are exclusively economic in interest and proletarian in membership and provide them limited opportunities ouside the Central Market. Thus the laborers believe that their most promising avenue to success to the city is close and effective relationships with the Hsin-hsing merchants, who they hope will call upon their ties with people of higher standing on the laborers' behalf when necessary.

The merchants, for their part, are integrating themselves into Taipei by means of their increasing participation in sociopolitical associations. They take care, however, to preserve their village-based relationships. Such relationships enable them to make a contribution to the leaders of their new groupings and help ensure that they will remain welcome among them. Many of these associations serve primarily as a vehicle for the ambitious, and the merchants are recruited into them so that they can exert their influence on the lower-class migrants to promote the leaders' political interests. Thus the continuing ties maintained between the Hsin-hsing laborers and the Hsin-hsing merchants are mutually useful. On the one hand they bolster and secure the merchants' positions among their new associates and on the other hand they provide the laborers with an indirect access to power. The two groups of migrants therefore continue to depend, at least partially, on each other in the city.

In addition, village-based relationships continue to have significance within the two distinct groups of migrants. For example, laborers frequently lend each other small amounts of money without any interest or join each other's moneylending or credit clubs. At the time of a wedding or other festive occasion when many people must be entertained, they will offer their services as hosts. And often they will send *hung-pao* (a gift of money wrapped in red paper) on the occasion of a wedding, even when they are not planning to attend the dinner for which such a gift is obligatory.

The explanation they give for this practice is "that it is done to make *jen-ch'ing*," a term meaning the expression of good will or feeling. The gesture, however, is more than merely expressive, since laborers anticipate that the gift will be reciprocated when they celebrate a similar occasion. A migrant, in fact, when he uses the compound *jen-ch'ing* in speaking of its occurrence in his relationship with another, always uses it with the word *ch'ien*, meaning to owe. Thus, the practice is used as a means of creating personal-obligation ties with others.

The main reason laborers seem to take this care in maintaining their relationships with each other is that in the city an uncertainty exists about such relationships. The migrants no longer live in a small community in which residential concentration, socioreligious and political activities, and formal organizations draw them together, foster reciprocal relations, and exert pressure on individuals to conform to expected norms of behavior. (Their joint participation in occupational groupings has tended to reinforce their pre-existing kin and village ties but does not commit them to become involved with one another in other contexts.) As a result, although kinsmen and fellow villagers represent a source of help and security that most likely can be tapped in times of need, these relationships are considered voluntary, not obligatory, and laborers believe they must be nurtured.

In addition, the laborers believe it is necessary to seek out people other than kinsmen and fellow villagers with whom they can ally themselves and on whom they can depend. Most frequently they establish friendships with workmates or neighbors, also usually migrants. At the outset, these relationships are casual and primarily involve occasional get-togethers to eat and drink. Over time, many increase in intensity and evolve into close and cooperative ones involving exchanges of goods and services in both ritual and nonritual contexts. On festive occasions friends are entertained and at the time of a wedding or death, friends help out with gifts of money or with actual physical assistance. In addition, friends frequently visit each other's homes informally and, in time of financial need, furnish short-term loans without interest.

These relationships, however, like village-based ones, involve only voluntary actions of individuals or families. Friends, therefore, in order to be more certain of each other's potentiality as sources of aid, will sometimes organize themselves into a sworn-brotherhood group. Migrants believe that such groupings "unite people" by encouraging subscription to a common set of norms and by introducing a degree of obligation into relationships. Thus, they tend to guarantee that aid will be forthcoming when needed, since the sanctions of the group can be mobilized to oblige individual sworn brothers to fulfill their obligations.

Despite the utilitarian quality of these groups, however, the emotional ties of friendship define and characterize the relations among and between its members. Not all sworn-brotherhood groups, however, are organized as an outgrowth of warm and close friendships. Sometimes such groups are formed solely to maximize the socioeconomic and political opportunities of their participants; friendship may be used as a vehicle to enroll members and solidify their loyalties, but participants are recruited selectively with consideration given to the potential contribution of each individual to the group.

All five of the Hsin-hsing Central Market merchants belong to one such group, which includes among its 28 members a Taipei city council-woman whose father is a National Assemblyman; the neighborhood chief *(lin-chang)* of Ch'eng-chung district; a member of the board of the Ch'eng-chung Cooperative Bank; the head of the Chang-hua Regional Association; and the vice-chief of the Provincial Water Bureau. During the proceedings that culminated in the formation of the group, the anticipated contributions of the different members were articulated: the merchants were to develop a following for the politically ambitious "brothers" in exchange for economic and sociopolitical favors. Notwithstanding this frank statement of expected advantage, the group does attempt to foster camaraderie by holding dinner parties at members' homes every third month, and members participate in the life-cycle rituals of each other's families in their role as fictive brothers.

Joint participation in the sworn-brotherhood group and overlapping membership in other groupings have reinforced pre-existing ties between the merchants and encouraged closer relations among them. Since they compete for both customers and farmers' agents (from whom they buy their produce), they had previously maintained only rather formal relationships with each other. Their close and intense relationships usually were not with their fellow merchants, but with others whom they had met since their arrival in the city. As they have become more involved in associational activities, however, they have had the opportunity to meet and relate with each other in an arena other than the one in which they normally compete. As a result, they have developed closer and more cooperative relationships with each other, and village and kinship ties continue to have meaning for them.

Summary and Conclusions

Earlier we saw marked differences between the people who move from villages to nearby urban towns and cities and those who move to the larger and more distant cities. Unlike Speare, we found that these migrants to large cities did not have above-average educations and were not better off financially; on the contrary, they had below-average educations and usually were the more economically depressed residents of the areas from which they migrated.

The variance between these two findings may be due in part to differences between large cities such as Taichung (the focus of Speare's work) and urban-industrial centers such as Taipei, the historical fact of the influx of mainlanders into these latter cities, and a host of other factors. Taiwan's fine systems of communication and transportation make the most distant city easily accessible. A chain of relationships with earlier migrants—like the one that drew Chinese from southeast China to southeast Asian countries over the past several hundred years—attracted the Hsin-hsing area migrants to large distant cities. Most of these migrants therefore were not part of the stepwise migration stream in which rural migrants first move to urban towns—perhaps taking the jobs of townspeople who have migrated to cities—and later move to cities. Instead, the great majority of migrants from Hsin-hsing and the three other villages we considered emigrated directly to the distant industrial centers where well-paying employment is available for people with limited resources.

Within the city, the migrants from one village, Hsin-hsing, do not form a cohesive urban community, but they are bound by certain formal and informal ties. Most work in related occupations within the Central Market. When occupational organization occurred there, particularistic criteria determined the core membership of the favored labor groups, and Hsin-hsing villagers dominate the groups. Membership in these groups, however, is not based solely on ascribed bonds of common origin; many men were recruited into the groups in later years on the basis of common experience. Nevertheless, as the largest single village grouping within the market, Hsin-hsing laborers have organized an informal coalition there that actively protects and promotes their economic interests.

Outside the market however, the Hsin-hsing migrants have neither a large enough population nor enough wealthy or influential people to organize an active "t'ungist" group. In fact, the only regional level with a large enough population to support a *t'ung-hsiang* group in Taipei was the county from which the migrants emigrated. The county-based association that was organized, however, is seen as essentially irrelevant by most laborers since it neither helps them to counter the discrimination directed against them, nor helps them to articulate with and operate within the institutions of the city and the wider society. The association is, however, seen as an active and viable grouping by its more successful migrant members, who use it to create advantage for themselves outside the group.

The sociopolitical integration of migrants into city life depends, then, to a large degree upon class. The Hsin-hsing laborers for the most part lack meaningful relationships with people of higher standing within the city, and many of the problems they face are not easily solved. The Hsin-hsing merchants have extended their relationship upward in the city's social and political structure and have increased their ability to maneuver socially, politically, and economically.

The two groups of migrants, however, continue to maintain relationships with each other in order to satisfy their needs and to promote their interests. These relationships, not surprisingly, tend to resemble patron-client models, rather than alliances of equals. The merchants offer to exercise indirect influence on these with power to help the laborers meet certain economic or personal threats. In exchange, the laborers offer a clientele and political following, thus providing the means by which the merchants can secure cooperation from those with power.

Thus, kinship and village-based relationships continue to be significant for most Hsin-hsing migrants, even though institutional supports that help ensure unity and cooperation in the village—such as ritual, politics, kinship organization, and concentrated residential patterns—cannot and do not function in the city. These relationships, however, are less structured in the city and are not oriented around the total group as a group. Instead they operate mainly on the individual family level and on a selective and voluntary basis. Nevertheless, the ties of mutual identification that are reinforced by overlapping social networks and modes of social participation—especially those stemming from related occupational activities—function to hold the majority of this migrant group together as a quasi-community within the city of Taipei.*

---

*At the same time, the relationships between the members of this quasi-community in the city are reinforced by continuing relations with their home village of Hsin-hsing. These relations are maintained through money remittances, necessary activities connected with village landholdings, occasional visits organized around kinship functions, and a few elaborate Hsin-hsing village festivals that draw both laborers and merchants—along with their money—back to the village for one or two days at a time.

4. Rural to Urban Migration

Bernard Gallin

The new environment of the city with its different residence and work patterns and the ensuing lessening of social pressure precipitates most of the change that occurs in the social structure in which the migrants participate and in the cultural behavior they exhibit; these alterations, at least initially, are not made by cultural transmission through contact with the urban population, nor are they a result of the rejection of traditional values.

In the city, villagers are allowed their first opportunity to limit their contact and relations with fellow Hsin-hsing people, relatives, and even brothers (both in the village and in Taipei). Migrants can select their own residential locations and economic forms of endeavor and are free to determine the degree to which they wish to participate in religious or other ritual activity. In the rural area, traditional social institutions and pressures prevent such free action and enforce virtually complete participation in all village and kinship oriented activities.

A few migrants have taken advantage of the possibility for anonymity and lack of community or lineage social control and have forged a new and freer life for themselves in the city. Most of the Hsin-hsing migrants, however, apparently still feel a need for the identification and security they derive from village fellows and especially lineage relatives in the home community. These migrants, then, have structured their lives, as much as the dissimilar city environment will allow, on the bases of these traditional and supportive relationships. The choice of these relationships as the most significant bases of their lives in voluntary. So, too, is the choice migrants make to maintain close ties with the home village. Direct linkages with the village, in and of themselves, foster and encourage relationships with fellow villagers and kinsmen who live in Taipei and influence the activities and behavior of the migrants.

From Bernard Gallin, "Rural to Urban Migration in Taiwan: Its Impact on Chinese Family and Kinship," in David C. Buxbaum, (ed.), *Chinese Family Law and Social Change in Historical and Comparative Perspective* (Seattle, Wash.: University of Washington Press, 1978), pp. 261-282. Footnotes omitted.

The village migrants live and work in fairly heavy residential and occupational concentrations. There are outsiders—usually also migrants to Taipei and some few Taipei people—involved in the work or business activities with the Hsin-hsing migrants. Nevertheless, most migrants maintain their closest and most basic relationships and groupings with their fellow villagers.

Fellow villagers and kinsmen join together socially, when possible, for festive occasions such as weddings. The new environment of the city, however, places several limitations on the amount of socializing possible among migrants. Time and money often are limited. And, in addition, migrants say that they "are in the city to make money for their families, not to play." As a result, migrants in Taipei do not exhibit as much social cohesiveness as they did in the home community.

The migrants also do not exhibit any great sense of "larger-group" cohesiveness. Despite the great many Hsin-hsing villagers living in Taipei, nearly half the number actually living in Hsin-hsing itself, the migrants have not formed a village association. Nor have the small kinship groups, which have many members in Taipei as do some active lineage organizations in the rural area, formed any kinship associations. The most obvious explanation for this lack is the basic difference between the village and urban environments and the socioeconomic consequences of each.

In the village, for instance, but not in the city, an organization of villagers based on community identification or relatively formal organizations based on lineage are feasible. These organizations can exist and manage in the village because ritual and localized socioeconomic and political activities continue, for the most part, to regularly function as unifying forces for them. In the city, however, patrilineal or lineage relatives, and villagers generally, have more diversified interests and relationships—at least when compared with those they have in the village—and are unable to unify all the members and organize any operative socioeconomic and political manipulative force. (A group such as that of the cart drivers, while significant, includes neither all the Hsin-hsing villagers nor whole groups of fellow kinsmen, and its membership is not limited to people only from Hsin-hsing.)

As a result, although kinship and village based relationships continue to have significance for most villagers living in Taipei, they are limited to exchanges between individual kin-related and village-related families. They are not significant as the basis of membership in formal or informal kin or village organizations.

Formal associations that focus on kinship do exist in Taipei, however. But these broader based surname or clan associations are not necessarily based on strict or real kin relationships and generally serve as sources of identification, solidarity, and security only for people who have been socially and economically successful or, perhaps, have lived for a long time in the city. Large area associations also exist in the city, but they, too, operate only for the benefit of the more prosperous.

The concepts of kinship or localism as foci for orienting relations are not defunct in urban Taiwan. A particular form of kinship organization, that is, lineage, is defunct there; it simply does not suit the broad based, heterogeneous, large-scale society of the urban center. The new environment of the city influences and results in the modification not only of many cultural forms of behavior, but also of the rural form of the traditional lineage organization. Chinese urban life—even that of the emerging urban-industrial type as in Taipei—is not at all antithetical to kinship as a focus for socioeconomic and political organization and behavior. Rather, it is antithetical only to particular, non-functional forms but apparently not to clan associations in Taipei, as Fried has recently pointed out. (It must be remembered, however, that a gradual functional decline in the lineage form of kinship organization is currently taking place even in rural Taiwan as it feels the impact of and becomes more involved in national life.)

Nevertheless, kin and village based relationships continue to be significant for migrants, even though in the city these relationships function only on an individual rather than a group level. They still provide some of the socioeconomic, political, and psychic security so often needed by the migrant in the city.

This desired and needed psychic security is also offered by the symbolic tie the migrant maintains with his natal home. Frequently, however, the perpetuation of this tie involves a loss of some economic security, for it may be maintained through financial privation; that is, when a migrant continues to keep land or a house which he does not use, but on which he must pay taxes. Nevertheless, for many of the migrants, to break the symbolic tie would leave them virtually isolated.

Finally, most of the rural-to-urban migrants from Hsin-hsing village cannot yet be considered urbanized. In fact, many of them are probably not even very far along in the process of being urbanized.

Although Taipei is a city that is rapidly industrializing, the majority of her migrants share in limited aspects of the new urban industrial complex in which they find themselves. Most of them work in unskilled and service type jobs and live in residential concentrations, just as they might if they were to live and work in a pre-industrial city. Other than taking advantage of the opportunity to enroll children in the public education system (as they do in the village area), and increasingly seeking the services of Western-style medical practitioners, most migrants do not and in some cases cannot take advantage of the other services available in the urban center; for example, they make no use of credit facilities, wide organizational networks, or legal facilities.

Nevertheless, the new environmental arrangements of the city provide the migrant with alternatives that enable him to bring a new voluntarism into his behavior and his relationships. The new conditions of the urban setting both necessitate and make possible the modification and adaptation of many rural institutions such as family and kinship relationships; they do not necessitate rejection or replacement of rural institutions with urban-industrial type institutions. In Taiwan, then, the urban condition does not necessarily carry with it newly introduced cultural forms and values.

5. Personal Bonds and Business Ties

Donald R. Deglopper

If the people of Lukang stress the distinctions between themselves and everyone else, they minimize distinctions among themselves. They recognize certain obvious differences—some are rich, some poor; some live in one neighborhood, others in another; some have one surname, others another; some earn their living in one way, some in another. But each distinction cuts a different way. There are no highly visible or corporate subgroups within the population of the city. Lukang consists of a number of named neighborhoods, each with its own temple. But every neighborhood contains rich and poor, people of various surnames, and men who earn their living in many different ways. One can speak of the people of a neighborhood as a unit, a group, only when they are contrasted with the people of another neighborhood, as they may be on certain ritual occasions. Lukang's population bears three major surnames and a host of less common ones. But those of one surname have little in common besides that name. A man's surname is important if he is worshiping his ancestors or considering a marriage, but in other situations its significance is less certain. In short, within the general category of "Lukang men," every individual is a potential member of many subgroups, each defined by different criteria and important in certain specific contexts. There are no bounded corporate groups between the town itself and individual households.

From Donald R. Deglopper, "Doing Business in Lukang," in W. E. Willmott, (ed.), *Economic Organization in Chinese Society* (Stanford, Ca.: Stanford University Press, 1972), pp. 297-326. Reprinted with permission of the publishers, Stanford University Press. Copyright 1972 by the Board of Trustees of the Leland Stanford Junior University. Footnotes omitted.

Businessmen I talked with were unaminous in asserting that such categories as surname or neighborhood, in and of themselves, were of no importance in doing business. Membership in such categories was acknowledged as important for some purposes, but not for business. The field of potential partners to a business relation extended to all natives of Lukang, and was not limited to fellow members of a defined segment of the town's populace. The autonomy and the freedom of the individual businessman were stressed, and I was assured that one was free to establish business relations with anyone one wanted to.

This does not mean, however, that business relations within Lukang are established at random, or that they consist only of relations of exchange, based on pure economic rationality in a free market. There are certain constraints on business relations, and pure economic rationality is not the sole determinant of the structure of economic relations. It is simply that some of the factors that influence business relations in overseas Chinese communities or in large urban centers do not operate in Lukang. After all, if all of one's potential partners in a business relation are one's *t'ung-hsiang*, and every third one bears the same surname, one cannot use such criteria to narrow down the field of possible partners, as one could perhaps in a large city or an overseas community. Other criteria will be used.

The very first thing to say about the structure of business relations in Lukang is that one does not do business with people one does not know. No one deals with strangers. Business relations are always, to some degree, personal relations. They need not be very close, but both participants in a business relation should be acquainted, familiar, "siek-sai" as the Taiwanese say (cf. Mandarin *shu-ssu.*).

In every case the most important concept, the term most often used in discussing business and its problems, in *hsin-yung*. This is a fairly complex concept, and can be translated in several ways, depending on its context. The dictionary definition is "credit," and it is used in this way in the term for a credit cooperative. Colloquially it means "to credit, to have confidence in; to be worthy of confidence and credit." One speaks of a man's *hsin-yung*, meaning his trustworthiness, his willingness and ability to meet his business and financial obligations. A man who can't pay his debts who for whatever reason fails to meet his obligations, immediately losses his *hsin-yung*. Business relations of mutual confidence are described as having *hsin-yung*. The word also refers to the quality and reliability of goods. One may ask of a piece of cloth of a radio, "How's its *hsin-yung?*" Is it sturdy, does it work well, will it fall apart in a month?

Hsin-yung refers to an individual's or a firm's reputation, reliability, credit rating. It is the most important thing in business, a firm's most valuable asset. People say that to start a business one needs capital, but capital isn't enough. On must have *hsin-yung*, and to have *hsin-yung* one must know people, have a good reputation with some set of people, such as the other members of one's trade. Similarly, when a business fails, as often happens, the failure is described as the result of a loss of *hsin-yung:* "If someone, for whatever reason, can't pay his bills when they are due, he immediately loses his *hsin-yung*. No one will advance him any more money or goods, and his creditors start demanding immediate repayment. That's the end—he goes bust."

Hsin-yung is predicated on performance in business. It is not given or ascribed. Nobody has good *hsin-yung* just because his surname is Lin or Chen. It has no direct relation to an individual's moral character or general popularity. An unpleasant man who pays all his bills on time will have better *hsin-yung* than a good fellow who can't meet his obligations. In at least one sense *hsin-yung*, like a credit rating, is a scalar quantity, of which one can have more or less. And one can gain or lose it by increments, or, in the case of losing it at least, all at once.

Hsin-yung in the restricted sense of credit and *hsin-yung* in the more general sense of reputation and trustworthiness meet in the nearly universal practice of doing business with postdated checks. Retail transactions are usually in cash, but those between businesses almost always involve payment with a check dated anywhere from ten days to a year later. Thirty days seems to be the most common period, followed by ten and then by ninety days. The use of postdated checks is explained as being the "custom" of businessmen, "the way you do business. If you are a serious businessman, then you use checks." It is claimed that even marginal retailers and petty traders will open an account with the credit bureau of the farmers' association or the credit cooperative, simply so that they can write checks and thus be proper businessmen.

At one point the Ministry of Finance ruled that postdated checks are illegal and may be cashed immediately. Since anyone who refuses to accept postdated checks will have great difficulty doing business at all, the ruling has had little effect. Certainly no one I talked with in Lukang seemed aware that postdated checks were illegal, for everyone said that one great advantage of checks was that they were legal documents, admissible in court. If someone failed to pay his check when it was due, he could be taken to court. Even if he formally declared bankruptcy, one could at least get a settlement of 30 percent of what he owed. In fact very few people actually resort to the courts, but it is claimed that since everone knows what would happen if they did, they simply settle for 30 percent of the debt.

People say that in the past, before 1945, there were no checks, or that they were used only by big businessmen. Business then was said to be based solely on verbal agreements, which made *hsin-yung* and mutual confidence far more important than they are now. The stress on *hsin-yung* and verbal agreements is said to have restricted the number of people one could deal with, since they had to be very well known to be trusted. The present system of checks is said to be better because it permits greater flexibility, and allows dealing between businessmen in the absence of very close personal ties.

The businessmen of Lukang recognize a category of relations called "business relations." With the exception of retail sales, business relations can be described as those in which postdated checks are exchanged. In such relations *hsin-yung* and some degree of intimacy are important. But all the businessmen I talked with insisted quite firmly that business relations can be established with anyone at all, and that they are not influenced or constrained by such things as kinship, co-residence, sworn brotherhood, or relations that could be said to involve an element of sentiment, of *kan-ch'ing*. *Hsin-yung* is said to be determined entirely by a man's performance as a businessman, and to have nothing to do with the solidarities of common surname, schooling, or worship. Business relations are described as explicitly predicated on economic rationality and mutual self-interest. They are narrowly defined, functionally specific ties, based on the satisfactory performance of contractual obligations and sanctioned ultimately by the legal system. As one man said after I had been asking about the relation of such things as affinal kinship, co-residence, and common schooling to *hsin-yung*, "Look, *hsin-yung* is just a matter of whether or not someone pays his checks when they come due. That's all there is to it."

The owner of a furniture shop carefully explained that although he could be said to be "intimate" with the owners of the sawmills from which he bought his timber, and that he might occasionally go to a feast or wedding at their homes or invite them to his, such social relations were not necessary for the conduct of business and did not influence his decision to buy from one sawmill rather than another. "There are many kinds of wood, and the quality of each kind varies. I need several kinds of wood to make furniture, depending on just what I'm making. If this week I should need some cedar or *wu-t'ung* wood, I go out and see which sawmill has it and how good it is. I buy it from the place that best suits my particular needs. And the quality of the timber is very important. A lot of the quality is determined by the skill of the workers in the sawmill. I bought a lot of wood last week from Mr. Chen's mill, because his craftsmen are so skillful. The man who runs the planer is careful, so the planks are smooth and of uniform thickness. My workmen don't have to waste time planing them down by hand, and I don't have to pay for expensive wood like cedar that gets wasted as shavings and scrap. In this business it's the quality of the materials and the skill of the workmen that counts. That's the most important thing. It's not a matter of intimacy or sentiment *(kan-ch'ing)* at all."

The same man employs some twenty-five skilled cabinetmakers and apprentices. None of them are his kinsmen. When he wants more craftsmen he tells his workers, who recommend their "friends" or *nei-hang jen,* who are not their kinsmen either. He decides to hire or fire workers, and determines their wages, on the basis of their skill, on how well they perform their jobs as craftsmen. He sells his furniture to customers who walk in from the street. They come from all over central Taiwan, for Lukang furniture has a high reputation. He estimates that perhaps 30 percent of his customers come because other satisfied customers have recommended the shop to them. But, like all the owners of furniture firms with whom I talked, he insists that customers always visit a number of shops to compare quality and prices, and that recommendations do not determine where a customer will buy.

People in Lukang tend to deny that other sorts of social relationships or solidarities have any relation to business. One restaurant owner responded to my questions about the utility of sworn brotherhood in business by replying, "No, no, you don't understand. Business is an affair of money. Sworn brotherhood has nothing to do with money. It's fust an affair of sentiment, of *kan-ch'ing*." People from the same neighborhood are described as "intimate" because they all know each other, and they form a group defined by their relation to their neighborhood temple and its annual festival. But this sort of relation or intimacy is said to be one of pure sociability, with no instrumental purpose.

In ideal terms, people in Lukang describe the sum of their social relations with a set of discrete categories. There are business relations; there are kinship relations; there are neighborly relations; and there are what are usually called "social" relations. Each of these has its own principles and purposes, its own satisfactions and problems. One expects different things from, and owes different things to, the people in each category. If one defines business relations narrowly as relations of buying and selling, then other sorts of relations can be seem to have little to do with business. Here, it is important to keep in mind the extensive structural differentiation and the degree of integration with the national economy that characterize Lukang's economy. It is unlikely that the owner of a factory that makes scissors, some of which are exported to Ghana, will have very many kinsmen or neighbors who are even potential participants in his business relations. Nor will a retailer who deals with a fairly large number of wholesalers, many of them residents of other communities, be able to call on presumed solidarities of common residence or schooling.

But business involves more than just buying and selling, and in practice the different categories of social relations tend to overlap somewhat. Simple economic rationality and functional specificity suffice to explain much of the pattern of economic relations in Lukang, but they are not the only forces at work. If one looks at other aspects of business life, one finds that, in certain situations, what may be loosely described as particularistic and functionally diffuse personal relations are of considerable significance. Their importance is most easily seen if one looks at problems of credit, of access to restricted or limited supplies or markets, and of partnership.

Most business operate partially on credit extended by suppliers through postdated checks, on the basis of some degree of "intimacy" and mutual confidence. But since a few satisfactory cash transactions must take place before a check will be accepted, it is impossible to start a business on credit. Nor is it assumed that a business will regularly yield such smooth profits that all checks can be paid when they come due. Difficulties and slack periods are to be expected. Yet if checks are not paid on time, *hsin-yung* is lost. Often it is necessary to borrow or somehow raise funds to pay a check and preserve one's reputation, or simply to meet operating expenses during slack periods. Neither the bank nor the credit cooperative is a practical source of credit for most small businessmen. Given the norm of extreme reticence about financial affairs, the common practice of keeping two or more sets of books, and the absence of certifed public accountants and of any reliable public system of credit ratings, the banks are in no position to make rational economic decisions about which businesses are good risks. They perforce fall back on making loans only with substantial collateral, a practice not very different from pawnbroking. Small businessmen in Lukang often remark that the only people who can get loans from banks are those who don't need them. To start a business and to meet unexpected difficulties, businssmen must rely on credit obtained through informal, private channels.

The term used to describe such informal relations of credit and mutual assistance is *min-ch'ing*. Rotating credit societies, sworn brotherhoods and unsecured personal loans provide examples of *min-ch'ing*. People say that *min-ch'ing* depends on verbal agreements; nothing is written down. Obligations predicated on *min-ch'ing* are thus not legally enforceable, since there is no properly witnessed and sealed piece of paper to introduce as evidence in court. Such arrangements are sanctioned by reciprocity and appeal to community opinion. There is some risk in all such relations, and people are reluctant to participate unless they know and trust the others involved. It is assumed that people one has grown up with, who are committed to life in Lukang and bound up in its complex nexus of local social relations, are most worthy of trust than are strangers. People who have a family in Lukang, who have a general reputation for probity and have demonstrated a concern for community opinion are good candidates for an association of relation based on *min-ch'ing*.

Min-ch'ing is described as quite distinct from "business relations," and indeed it is. But *min-ch'ing* relations have an important, if somewhat indirect, effect on business. Relations with others in temple or festival committees, in rotating credit societies, in sworn brotherhoods, or in the informal groups that habitually sit in shops and exchange gossip are not described as "society," as "knowing people," or as affairs of generalized sociability, sentiment, or *kan-ch'ing*. By particpating in such activities, by contributing time and money to temples, and by occasional acts of charity, a man defines himself as a responsible member of the community, a moral person concerned with the affairs of others and with their opinion of him. Such a person is likely to receive aid, including financial aid, when he needs it. It is possible to abstain from such activities and suffer no immediate injury to one's business. As long as checks are paid on time and the goods one purveys are of competitive price and quality, there is not loss of *hsin-yung*. But should troubles arise, the unsociable merchant is on his own; no one will go out of his way to help him.

In an emergency it is possible to borrow money from close kinsmen, or from such people as sworn brothers, if one has any. But such aid, even from borthers, may be given grudgingly, and it may be made clear that it represents a favor. The favor as well as the money will have to be returned. People dislike being under a special obligation to anyone else, even their own brothers. It is also possible to get a personal loan from one of several wealthy men in the city who act as moneylenders. This is to be avoided if at all possible. Not only is the interest high, but one is obligated to the wealthy man and perhaps to the person who acted as go-between in arranging the loan. The men who make such loans are in many cases local political figures who use moneylending as one way to extend their influence. Once indebted to such a man, in any way, a small businessman loses some of his autonomy, and his freedom to do business with whomever he pleases is curtailed. He may find himself under pressure to deal with associates of the moneylender, or to extend favors or support to them.

To become rich one should be of course be willing to work hard, but that is not the essential quality. What one needs is brains, cleverness. It is recognized that some people have a talent for doing business and making money, and others do not. Anyone can work hard and get by, or run a small shop, but only a few are clever enough to become wealthy. A Lukang proverb says: "It's difficult to raise a child who can do business." Another points out: "Without cleverness on will never become a merchant."

Cleverness is important, but success in business is not usually ascribed to sharp practice or low cunning alone. Success takes more than that. The essential quality of a good businessman could be summarized as the ability to look at a situation, interpret it in terms of business success, and adapt one's own behavior to the situation. The world is complex, and it is difficult to perceive just what a given situation holds in the way of business advantage, or how it is likely to change. The man who can best do this, and thinks of a way to turn a situation to his advantage, is the one who succeeds, who becomes rich.

A cloth retailer explained that in the cloth business one has to be smart and use one's head. "When a customer comes in you should be able to size him up, to know just what he wants and how much he's willing to pay for it. Cloth is very complex now; there are all sorts, colors, patterns, and degrees of quality." The retailer has to match up the customer's specific wants, which the customer himself may not be very well aware of or able to articulate, with one of the several hundred possible sorts or combinations of cloth. To sell cloth successfully one has to be able to think fast, to empathize with each unique customer and respond to him in the appropriate way. "You have to research, to know all kinds of people and what is in people's hearts."

Rather than discussing competition with other businessmen in the same line, the merchants and craftsmen of Lukang prefer to speak more vaguely of an impersonal market or "conditions." To succeed, one must be able to meet the demands of the market. Business failures are usually described as the result of insufficient capitalization, getting too far in debt, and inability to satisfy the market, rather than as the result of the competition of other businessmen. Rather than recognizing an antagonistic relation between those in the same line, the *nei-hang jen,* people speak of an abstract "market" or "conditions," which everyone in a given sort of business must try to satisfy. Retailers stress the contest with the customer rather than that with the *nei-hang jen.* Cloth sellers ascribe success to their ability to size up customers and manipulate them, and celebrate the virtues of the salesman. "People say that a really skillful Lukang cloth seller can go up to a dead person and start talking with him, cajoling him, and gradually the dead person will rise up, bit by bit. In this business a clever tongue is what really counts." Craftsmen such as furniture makes or wood-carvers stress their skill and the quality of their products, the *hsin-yung* of these products as well-made objects. They say that one has to satisfy customers, give them what they want, but that customers can recognize quality, and will choose to buy from one firm rather than another because of the quality of the goods offered.

The emphasis is on fitting, matching up with what seem to be impersonal, given conditions. One merchant said that each person has his own way of looking at things, his own orientation to conditions and the market. Some ways of approaching things are better than others, for they accord with the demands of the market, and the man who is able to fit in with the conditions of the trade will prosper. A good cabinet-maker has to select the right kind of wood and decide the best use for each unique piece. A retailer must treat each customer differently, cater to him. He must know which customers like to look at a lot of things and bargain hard before they buy, and which prefer a simple transaction and will walk out if the merchant quotes his initial bargaining price instead of the one he is willing to sell for. Circumstances are constantly changing and one must keep up with them. Behavior that is appropriate in some circumstances will be inappropriate in others.

The qualities of a good businessman are summed up in the success story of Mr. Kin, a Lukang man who made a fortune in Taipei. As a young man Mr. Lin was very poor and could find no work in Lukang, so he went to Taipei to seek his fortune. There he worked at seal carving, a genteel but low-paying street trade. Somehow he managed to save or get his hands on a little money. With it he bought a small piece of land. The land was the least desirable in the city, the waste land where trash was dumped and burned. It was therefore quite cheap, and Mr. Lin gradually bought more and more until he owned two whole trash dumps. Taipei grew and the price of the land rose tremendously. Mr Lin's two trash dumps, close to the center of the city, became very valuable and he sold them at an immense profit. He invested the money in an import-export business and so became very wealthy.

Like the protagonist of a Taoist parable, Mr. Lin succeeded because he was able to see the value of the useless and the unwanted. He saw an advantage that others did not, and was able to adapt his behavior to the demands of the situation, the market. And he succeeded because he was free to invest in trash dumps; he did not have to explain what he was up to, or get the approval of anyone else. He was clever and he maintained his autonomy. Many of the small businessmen in Lukang could be said to be trying, each in his own way, to emulate the legendary Mr. Lin. By insisting on their freedom to do business with whomever they choose, by maintaining strict secrecy about the details of their financial affairs and their intentions, and by spreading their debts and obligations as widely as they safely can, they are maximizing their autonomy and their ability to take advantage of any opportunity that comes their way.

6. The Ideal Marital Partner

Wolfram Eberhard

Our data have several traits: they represent the voices of men as well as of women on topics of common interest. They present mainly the voices of the younger generation, the more urban, the better educated sector of the population. On the other hand, the different sources which we have used tap different spheres of the personality and the results, therefore, of the our analyses do not agree completely with one another. If a person is asked to describe an "ideal" partner, he is bound to be more detached, more "idealistic" than the person who wants to find an actual partner. And a person who writes to the "Mail Box" is usually a person who has already experienced problems of married or social life.

Since the beginning of modern times, not too many changes seem to have occurred in the interpersonal relations in the family. We know that the economic situation and the technical household equipment have changed greatly in recent years, and that the actual role of the family in society in general is no longer the same. But the feelings about the family and its function seem largely unchanged. There is a trend—as in other countries—to regard cooperation, equality, and mutuality in marriage as desirable and important. Characteristically, these "new" traits are mentioned by female writers more often than by male writers, since inequality in the traditional family meant that the wife had fewer rights and privileges than her husband. Therefore, modern women, stimulated by Western influences, stress equality more than men. But it is significant that all writers, male and female, are moderate in their statements and avoid extremes. Our writers still seem to value role differentiation between men and women, husbands and wives, and we agree with them that role differentiation and even authoritarian attitudes of men do not at the same time mean a lack of real warmth and love. If each person's role in the family is clearly defined, many differences and quarrels can be avoided; the feeling of mutual obligation and duties is stimulated; the individual partner knows that in a marriage he cannot expect to get a complete fulfillment of all his personal needs, to get perfect satisfaction for himself, but that sacrifices and consideration for the personal needs of the other are a necessary correlate of his own happiness. The case can very well be made—and many thinkers in the Far East and in Europe have expressed this opinion—that marriages based upon complete equality and without clarification of the roles of each partner, at first lead to a lack of security, as families of this type tend to be nuclear families, limited to the couple and, for a few years, their children; relations to the other relatives are so superficial that no feeling of security can be gained from such relations. But if the roles of married partners are not defined so that the duties and obligations as well as the rights and privileges have to be redefined in each instance, and if each partner expects a maximum of satisfaction for himself or herself, any change which occurs, such as waning of sexual attraction, shift of interests, physical changes by age or disease, endangers the security of one or of both partners. It seems to be a necessary correlate to the nuclear, modern family that both partners have a maximum involvement in non-family organizations, so that only one of the partners can participate in a given organization, while the other participates in other organizations. In spite of the ideal of "romantic love" and "complete understanding," this type of family seems to have lead to alienation and loneliness once the original sexual attraction, mistaken for "love," has worn out. The ideal of marriage which our writers seem to have in mind would like to avoid extremes in role differentiation, especially extremes in patriarchialism, but at the same time preserve basic differences in the life spheres of men and of women, to preserve the security and the feeling of "belonging," to find love as a tie between partners who understand one another and who can be assured to the unchanging devotion of the one to the other partner.

The Lonely Heart columns are much briefer than the full-size essays which the *Hsin-sheng-pao* survey published. The writers, too, are definitely strongly influenced by modern trends as they obviously have taken a stand against the traditional "go-between" arranged-marriage. The writers in this column, furthermore, do not write in the abstract, about some

From Wolfram Eberhard, *Moral and Social Values of the Chinese: Collected Essays* (San Francisco and Taipei: Chinese Materials & Research Aids Service Center, 1971), pp. 260-267.

vague ideal they may have, but they are interested in finding a partner—a real living being; and they know that no human being can possibly be perfect. Yet, in many ways, the column reveals attitudes and values similar to those in the essays: women are most afraid of husbands who have "bad habits;" men are most interested in a warm, understanding wife. Physical traits are for both partners in both surveys of relatively little importance; except some mention of health and sometimes height.

In one field, the Lonely Heart writers show more modernism than the letters about the ideal partner. On the one hand, a number of men are not against marrying into the family of their wife; on the other hand, there are seven men who state that they would consider marrying a widow, and two of these would take even a widow with daughters. Furthermore, one man was willing to marry a divorcee as well as a widow, while a second man would do so only if there were no children. These nine men have overcome the traditional prejudice aginst marrying widows and the still stronger prejudice against divorcees. Only two men mention that the woman should be able to conduct a good household, none mentions cooking or sewing or other feminine occupations as highly desirable.

The "Mail Box" leads directly into problems of life, pre-marital as well as marital. The discussions give guite a different impression than the descriptions of "ideal" partners or of persons which one imagines he would like to marry. In the real-life problems which are described in the letters, people are much more modernized than one would have thought. Several points stand out as important. In general, girls and boys seem to enjoy modern, free relations with each other in school and in the office. Girls seem to have no difficulty in getting to know boys, though they often cannot easily get enough information about the boy. In a number of cases, the relation between the sexes seems to go quite far, especially when marriage plans have been discussed. Parents, as everywhere, are not always enthusiastic about the behavior of their children and often try to intervene if they object against a specific boy or against the kind of relationship which is about to develop. Often the relations between boys and girls seem to last over many years without leading to marriage. In such cases, the relations may consist of an exchange of letters or also of telephone calls only, and a gradation of terms of intimacy seems to have developed beginning with "pen pal" over "friend" to "brother/sister" to "boyfriend" or "girlfriend." These conditions remind us more of the situation in Europe some 40 or 50 years ago and of the situation in contemporary Japan than of the United States today, but all of this behavior is in direct contrast to the relations as they werc supposed to be and most probably in general were in traditional China. Of course, we should not forget that the writers of letters are, by definition, already modernized boys and girls; conservative persons would not discuss such problems in public, even if they had the same problems. Occasionally we find indications in the letters that there still are quite conservative girls in the country: girls or boys who do not know how to find partners, who do not date or engage in premarital contacts. The coeducational schools, however, seem to promote that new behavior. Boys and girls meet during classes and recess; they go on trips together and walk home together.

Yet, in spite of all modern conditions, some old attitudes continue: the influence of parents is still quite strong. We still find women who were forced by their parents to marry unloved men; girls who were forced by their parents to stop seeing boys whom they liked. In general, one gets the impression that boys and girls normally followed the rules set up by their parents, and the newspaper editor regularly supports the parents' point of view. Virginity is still quite important for a girl who wants to marry and wants to be happy in marriage. Extramarital relations, even if they consist of nothing but occasional letters to a former boy-friend, present serious problems to a marriage, as do such socially discredited jobs as bar-maid or beautician. On the other hand, when husbands err, the wife is usually asked to be tolerant and to try to win the husband back, although many wives already think of divorce in spite of the legal discrimination under which they suffer.

In general, the "Mail Box" section seems to be a good source for the study of behavior towards the other sex in and before marriage, but mainly among the urban and more modernized, more articulate sector and especially among youth. Taken together with the other material which exhibited the ideals of the same sector of the population, one gets a fairly complete picture of the complexities of the present-day situation in urban Taiwan, of the gap between ideals and values and actual behavior.

7. Blending of Mainland Religious Influence in Taipei

Stephan Feuchtwang

The Japanese destroyed all the temples in the official walled city, but few temples outside it. The effect of this upon the local gentry and merchants was to remove the orthodox examples of their religious and cultural institutions, leaving their own institutions intact and releasing them from the ideological control of officials. The Japanese did build Shinto and Buddhist shrines and pursue a policy of slow conversion to Japanese culture, but theirs was an alien and colonial regime that, in the fifty years it lasted, never acquired the cultural legitimacy of the former Chinese rulers.

The Japanese resorted far more than the Ch'ing to direct, legal, and supervisory means of controlling temples. They were interested more in the orginization than in the culture of the temples, though the latter was of course indirectly affected. The Republican regime also lacked, at least initially, the ideological controls of the former Chinese imperial government, and also resorted to legal and direct controls. In this respect the two post-Ch'ing regimes can be considered together. In general, the controls imposed on temples are part of the extension, originally undertaken by the Japanese but continued under the Republicans, of central-government power in Taiwan below the county level, reducing the local political autonomy of gentry and merchants. Two other long-term effects of Japanese policies should be noted for their impact on local temples. One was the halting of migration and trade with the mainland; the other was the replacement of guilds with secular trade associations defined on a commodity basis. Their effect was to undermine the compatriot parochialism that had so strongly marked the settlement of the Taipei basin and the organization of its overseas trade. Taiwan's economy was "rationalized" to make the island produce as much surplus as possible for the Japanese homeland. As a result of these policies, compatriot temples, and especially guild temples, lost their former social significance.

Only the Amoy Guild continued, being revived at the time of a rebuilding of the Tz'u-sheng kung in 1908. But this exception was itself an example of Japanese methods of controlling temples. We have seen that a temple's renewal could occasion a change in the leadership of its management. The Japanese and Nationalist governments caused almost all the main Taipei local temples to need renewal, simply by billeting troops in them. The Pao-an kung and Lung-shan ssu housed troops just after the Japanese take-over. When Taiwan was returned to China, they and the Ch'ing-shui-kung miao, the Ch'ing-shan-wang miao, and the Tz'u-sheng kung were used first to house troops and then, for many years, to house retired soldiers. A Japanese city-planning and road-widening scheme had necessitated the demolition and rebuilding at another site of the Tz'u-sheng kung in 1908. The local government of Taipei contributed funds for the rebuilding and at the same time revived the incense-burner association of the Amoy Guild as a model religious organization for the island of Taiwan. This body, the Shen-ming Hui, had a separate building in the forecourt of the temple, but all twelve members of the temple's management committee belonged to it. In the temple forecourt were also the offices of a branch of the quasi-governmental Buddhist Youth Association, and a school for the study of Confucian scriptures. From none of these did the temple receive rent.

This method of control, by infiltration of management committees, was and is made possible by the requirement that a temple (or any other association) must be registered with the competent local authority. This means having a formally constituted management committee which is responsible to the government for taxes, where previously there had been an informally defined and unfixed management. Membership in the registered committee was held permanently, there usually being no provisions for elections, and was inherited, a practice that has continued even into the present period.

Under the present regime, elections for the replacement of retiring members should be

From Stephan Feuchtwang, "City Temples in Taipei under Three Regimes," in Mark Elvin and G. William Skinner, (eds.), *The Chinese City Between Two Worlds* (Stanford, Ca.: Stanford University Press, 1974), pp 263-301. Reprinted with permission of the publishers, Stanford University Press. Copyright 1972 by the Board of Trustees of the Leland Stanford Junior University. Footnotes omitted.

supervised by a representative of the government. In fact when a membership has lapsed or been resigned (for instance, when none of the sons of a member want to take their father's place), in many cases it has been phased out, no replacement being elected. Official records, such as those of the Taiwan Historical Commission, give numbers of "the followers" *(hsin-t'u)* of the temple, as if they constituted a congregation. In fact there is always a number of worshippers who attend the temple more regularly than others, and when elections have been held it is they, according to the temple keepers and managers interviewed, who are the electors.

One effect of this government interference in temple organizaton has been to consolidate any existing tendency toward exclusiveness in the management committees. Another effect has been that temples once open to a local community, with a very vague religious definition created by the repute of the god, have tended to become more like membership organizations, no longer focused on the community at large, but specifically as religious institutions.

Some temples have changed their registration from "association" *(hui)* to "nonprofit corporation" *(tsai-t'uan fa-jen)*. The advantages of taking this step are, as one of the managers of the Ch'ing-shan-wang miao said, that tax need no longer be paid and official sanction for the temple's activities is more easily obtained. However, nonprofit status means that the authorities not only supervise elections, but also inspect the temple's books. The Ch'ing-shan-wang miao has not yet taken this step. Those temples that have seem to conform to a certain standard organization, one of the features of which is running a charity. Some temples that have not formally become charitable organizations have also nevertheless started small charities. These involve the annual collection and redistribution of money, rice, and clothing to those in the temple's locality who are listed in government records as being below a certain socioeconomic standard. The local Kuomintang party branch or the local government office supervises or even takes over the distribution side of the charity—indeed the Kuomintang has its own winter charity. But collection is best left to the temple, since temples are acknowledge to have a more powerful moral pull than party or government.

Two other measures taken by the Republican regime may be thought to have had an effect on temples: land reform and local elections. Land reform has reduced the amount of land that can be held by an association or corporation. Regrettably, I could find out very little about Taipei temples' landholdings, knowing only that they had their forecourts and some real estate in the immediate neighborhood as sources of rent. When the reform has in fact succeeded in reducing temple landholdings, and there are numerous ways of circumventing it, the effect must have been to turn the interest of management committees toward maintaining their temples' large daily offerings of cash and meeting the expenses of their annual festivals.

Elections for local government office make the local politician's position, between a partly alien and dictatorial central government and his local constituency, ambivalent. The temple, in its capacity as the focus for local community, is used as an instrument to legitimate local power and as a proper medium for the publicization of a name. In other cities of Taiwan, T'ai-nan and Lu-kang for instance, local temples are used as symbols for competing local factions, but to my knowledge no politician has ever been able to use a temple or network of temples as a power base in the way that Farmers' Associations have been used. Nevertheless, appearing, at least in name, on the management of its temple, charity, or festival is a virtual necessity for winning support in a locality. The brothers Wu of the Ch'ing-shan-wang miao and the Lung-shan ssu achieved their local government offices by election. All of the managers of the Ch'ing-shan-wang miao and of the Pao-an kung are heads of wards (*li-chang;* also elected offices).

Even so traditional a form as sworn brotherhood still plays an important part in the weaving of a local network. One kind of local power is wielded through the groups of young men called *liu-mang,* their loyalty often sealed by sworn brotherhood, who run a kind of righteous protection racket. They are, of course, secret; but local groups of young men in general manifest themselves publicly in festival processions, in bands of musicians, as lion dancers, or in military arts troupes. Groups of men who act as volunteer fire brigades also frequently join festival processions as lion- or dragon-dancing contingents. During a festival lion contingents compete with each other for prowess, measured by the number of times they are asked to perform privately for individual households or firms. Above all, they are sponsored by the festival managers. In short, a festival procession is one occasion on which the holders of local informal power show themselves.

The translation of informal power into official authority, or its association with official authority, is difficult. The Kuomintang's former reliance on the power of secret societies notwithstanding, such societies and the sworn brotherhoods that form their nuclei are generally if not rigidly proscribed. The Ch'ing government also occasionally prohibited sworn brotherhoods. The Japanese government's thorough efforts to register every religious organization in police records was part of a more successful campaign against them. On this firm basis, with an even larger police force, the present government maintains a keen watch against religious organizations that might become fronts for political activity. At the same time, local police and government officials are expected to reduce the number of festivals in their areas, ostensibly, as in the Ch'ing period, because of the economic waste, the extravagance of the feasting, the frivolity of the theatrical performances—in short, because of the unproductive spending of time and money. As has already been remarked, however, it is precisely the feasting, the processions, and the theater that express and reaffirm local solidarity.

Sworn brotherhood and feasting have not been stopped; indeed they are still important means of sealing alliances and forming networks. Yet they are officially deplored and have to some extent been curtailed. How is a local politician to use them and at the same time remain a member in good standing of the Kuomintang or its government? The resolution of this problem in the context of temple organization has implied, and also in effect been made possible by, the contrast between festival and corporate management. The festival manager and his assistants continue to be selected anew at every festival, whereas the management of the temple itself has, as we have seen, become a long-term and exclusive group. The festival is an open and demonstrative local community occasion, whereas the kind of management molded by the government turns the temple into a self-contained institution. Festivals are not intrinsically—or, in the initial development of an incense-burner association, in practice—attached to a temple. The two look easily separable. But as long as festivals are still sponsored by temples, the two forms of management, that of the festivals and that of the temple, the two forms of managment, that of the festivals and that of the temple, provide separate but linked loci for the legitimization of the two kinds of power, unofficial and official, related to the same local base.

Possibly as a result of the government's ideological influence, there has been an increased orientation toward lay Buddhist practices in all but one (the Fa-chu-kung kung) of the eight local temples discussed previously. The period of increasing prosperity from the mid-fifties onward, when there has been more surplus to spend on ritual activities, has seen either the introduction of Buddhist liturgy chanters or an increase in their numbers. These are groups, mainly of women, led by or having been instructed by a Buddhist priest or monk, who chant sutras and abstain from meat on certain days in the month. Even the Hsia-hai ch'eng-huang miao, which does not house any god with a Buddhist name or legend, has a small group of devout women who chant sutras in the temple nine times a month and run a small charity. The exchange of resident groups to chant in each other's temples, and of congratulatory wreaths of flowers and baskets of fruit at festival time, are the ways in which the temple managements express their links with each other. The same period has seen in Taipei, but nowhere outside the city, a decrease in the number of *chiao*. In fact, apart from one in a suburb in 1963, there has been only one *chiao* in Taipei since the war. Presumably this reflects the greater effectiveness of government influence in its capital. . . .

If there is anything like a center it would be the Chüeh-hsiu kung, because it was there that the new religious style first developed. This temple supplied ritual experts to the Hsing-t'ien kung before the Hsing-t'ien kung started training its own practitioners, and still supplies them to the Sheng ch'eng-huang miao. The Chüeh-hsiu kung began in the 1910's (as the Hsing-t'ien kung began later) as a spirit-writing and reformist association. But it was also a curing cult and a center of Han medicine. The Chüeh-hsiu kung has continued to promote proper ceremonial, training practitioners of a new religious style that shuns the ritualistic and magical arts of Taoists yet professes Taoism, and bases itself largely on the civil ceremonial of the state cults. The curing side of its activities seems to have lapsed, but spirit-writing sessions are still held wherein personal problems can be put before the gods as well as new texts composed for its litany. Since the Republican period, the Chüeh-hsiu kung has become a nonprofit corporation organized into three departments, one for instruction, one for charity, and one for publishing. Several of its texts have been printed and distributed free, particularly through the modern temples discussed in this section. It is considered to be an act of merit to sponsor the publication of morally edifying books. The chairman of the Taipei municipal assembly has sponsored many of them and is honorary publisher of the Chüeh-hsiu kung's monthly journal *Cheng-yen* (Correct words). He is also on the managing committee of the Pao-an kung. Officials who are in the national government, and thus of even higher standing, have contributed congratulatory calligraphy and articles for the journal.

Another link between the temples may be found in the person of Huang Tsan-chün, who seems to have waged a one-man campaign for Chinese cultural renaissance until his death in 1952. Not only did he manage the Pao-an kung and contribute to the establishment of the K'ung-tzu miao, he also contributed to the building of the Chih-nan kung and published a number of magazines on culture and ethics. Later, he participated in the activities of a number of cultural and good-works organizations that had moved to Taiwan from the mainland. One of these was the Universal Ethical Society *(Wan-kuo tao-te hui),* which at one time established branches in the Tz'u-sheng kung and the Sheng ch'eng-huang miao.

Receiving texts and guidance can and does turn into receiving advice on personal and practical affairs of the same kind as that for which Taoist practitioners are consulted in the Hsia-hai ch'eng-huang miao and the Pao-an kung, a development that dissolves all sense of moral reform and rearmament against "superstition." In fact it is for beneficence in this practical sense, in the hope that a god will respond with practical benefits, that the mass of worshippers attends the Hsing-t'ien kung and the Chih-nan kung. In these temples they are saved the costs of traditional religious practitioners and of expensive offerings. The exponents of the new religious style receive no fees. They are trained for self-cultivation and the propagation of propriety in the five relationships *(wu-lun).* They must be clean, and in the temple ceremonies wear long blue gowns that entirely cover their worldly Western-style clothing. The emphasis is on simple and direct communication between individual and deity, without the mediation of priests, elaborate offerings, or spirit money—just incense, flowers, and fruit. Self-manipulated divination by lot is the most mediation allowed in the Hsing-t'ien kung. People who come for solutions to personal and practical problems take the texts thus selected (they are in classical, poetic form) to post-office-like kiosks for interpretation by the blue-gowned helpers. Their monetary contributions to the temple are collected, now that the new buildings have been completed, for charitable work. Loudspeakers harangue them with moral teaching from the roof beams.

But apart from this mass of worshippers, the trained practitioners and regular attenders of the Hsing-t'ien kung and the Chüeh-hsiu kung are much closer to a congregation than are the regular attenders of the local temples. The Chüeh-hsiu kung has an association of followers *(hsin-t'u hui),* membership in which cost (in 1968) ten new Taiwanese dollars a month. The "congregation" of the Hsing-t'ien kung must be much larger. In addition, both have something more like a Christian church's weekly assembly, held in a congregation hall with pictures of the President at one end and of the National Father Sun Yat-sen at the other, like all civic halls in Taiwan, and starting (as do all civic meetings) with the national anthem and bows to these two pictures. Unlike the local temples, these two temples and the Chih-nan kung and K'ung-tzu miao have no processions, no theater, no bands, and no professional ritual practitioners. The K'ung-tzu miao and the Sheng ch'eng-huang miao have a territorially defined community, within Taiwan, by virtue of their much closer identification with the old Ch'ing state religion. Otherwise they are autonomous institutions to which the mass of worshippers has no diffuse bonds of loyalty, just specific ritual needs. People come to the Hsing-t'ien kung and the Chih-nan kung from all over the island, without distinction of place.

Among the twentieth-century temples here considered, the Sheng ch'eng-huang miao is the only exception in this regard. It is local, has theater and a procession containing generals Fan and Hsieh that tours its borough on Retrocession Day which (in contrast to the practice of the Fa-chu-kung kung) is reckoned by the solar calendar and so always falls on October 25. But its locality is that of all the central government offices and some of its residences, and of the offices of Taiwan's main financial and commercial enterprises. The management of its procession is taken in turns by the heads of the administrative wards *(li)* of the borough. It was built after Retrocession at the instigation of the head of the borough, in order, so one of its present managers said, to restore patriotism. Thus it is not surprising, given its location and its origins, that it is linked to the networks of the more eminent and universalistic Chüeh-hsiu kung, Hsing-t'ien kung, and K'ung-tzu miao.

Conclusion

It looks as if these twentieth-century temples are developing a Republican version of the imperial state religion. Certainly their religious style is sufficiently distinct from that of the local temples so that quite eminent government officials can openly associate themselves with it. Among the local temples, the old guild temples and maybe the Pao an kung have been sufficiently transformed in the direction of the new religious style of the five to be on the verge of adoption into it. The degree of government control over the management of the old guild temples has to some extent forced this development.

The new religious style departs most radically from the imperial state religion in having a mass following of worshippers. Only the K'ung-tzu miao is not open every day to all worshippers who wish to make offerings and seek guidance and response, although in all of them regular active participation in their ceremonial is reserved for a defined and trained group of members.

Taipei has become a large city in a very short time, submerging or dissolving the former local communities by means of cheap modern transport. The texts of the new temples appeal to a mass readership. Transportation across the whole island having become faster and cheaper, Taipei's industry has attracted a great number of immigrants from elsewhere in the island, as well as from the mainland. The gods of the new temples have no local significance, nor are they branches of older local cults. They stand for power on a national scale. The morality preached in their name, and the stress of their religious style, is on the individual as a universal atom, receptacle of and responsible to "society" and "Chinese culture," and duty-bound to perform good works.

This amounts to what many social scientists would call the natural process of "modernization" or, more significantly, Westernization. But perhaps the sponsorship of temples that can attract a mass following, and whose deities and ceremonials at the same time transcend local loyalties, was and is a matter of conscious political decisions made by a government of Nationalist mainland exiles on Taiwan for the sake of enhancing its own legitimacy.

It is perhaps surprising that local, territorial temples continue to flourish at all. But when one looks at all the temples considered in this paper, one sees a sharp division between the festivals of the territorial temples in the poorer and older parts of Taipei and the autonomy of the universalistic temples in the newer and wealthier parts of the city, their ceremonials closely identified with the central government.

8. Old and New in Literature

Chi Pang-yuan, et al.

Poetry in Taiwan

When Chi Hsien and Ch'in Tzu-hao began anew in Taiwan, they were over forty but not yet established literary figures. On the other hand, they were already looked upon as forerunners because they had brought the latest influences of the mainland days to bear upon the new poetic scene and because, at that early stage, the budding poets on the island were mostly young men in their twenties. After a few years of simmering, modern Chinese poetry was ready for a contemporary taste. Suddenly, around 1954, all was astir. Three groups came into being almost simultaneously.

First of the three was the Modernist School, established under the leadership of Chi Hsien, whose basic program included an emphasis on intellectualism as a remedy for sentimentalism, a replacement of conventional poetic diction with plain prose, and a transplantation of recent Western poetry since Baudelaire. Though he advocated intellectualism as a theorist, Chi Hsien the poet was extremely emotional, almost exactly the opposite of what he tried to inculcate in his followers. It was in Fang Ssu, instead, that we find a serene poet and solid scholar, who of all the members best fulfilled Chi Hsien's requirements for intellectualism. By no means a prolific writer, Fang Ssu offered his fellow practitioners the example of his small output wherein the neat style, restrained tone and spare imagery proved the point that to go modern does not mean to go sloppy. As a poet, Chi Hsien has been for less consistent, but it was his magnetic personality and undaunted spirit rather than Fang Ssu's quiet merit that attracted a wide following for the movement. Among other notable members of this group whose poetry has survived the general iconoclasm of those years, mention must be made of Yang Huan, for the bitter-sweetness of his nostalgia, and of Cheng Ch'ou-yü and Lin Ling, for their melody and grace.

Close on the heels of the Modernists emerged the Blue Star Poetry Society, founded by Ch'in Tzu-hao, Chung Ting-wen. Hsia Ch'ing and Yü Kwang-chung. More a friendly union than a programmed movement, the Blue Stars were quietly creative and sought to maintain some critical balance. Influenced as they were by Western literature, they thought it unwise to disown native Chinese tradition and were strongly opposed to Chi Hsien's proposal for radical Westernization. In creative practice, they preferred spontaneous lyricism to contrived intellectualism. As for the use of prose in place of verse, the response of the Blue Stars was divided: while some showed a leaning towards free verse, others wanted to keep some of the virtues of rhymed verse. Chi Hsien's advocacy of simple, unadorned prose to replace ornate poetic language did clear a way for some to greater freedom and freshness of expression, but it was also abused by many others as an excuse for their unshapely "prosiness" of style. Other members of this group included Wu Wang-yao, Jung Tzu, Lo Men, Chou Meng-tieh, Hsiang Ming, Huang Yung, Chang Chien, and Hsiung Hung. Ch'in Tzu-hao played a leading role, both as an editor and a prolific writer, in the early years (1954-63) of the Society's history, but it was Yü Kwang-chung whose influence as a poet and a critic came to be strongly felt in and outside the Society. His insistence on the vital importance of national identity maintained a balance between selective and indiscriminate Westernization.

The third group, the Epoch Poetry Society, drew its principal members from the Chinese armed forces. While the Modernists were either Chi Hsien's friends or students, and the Blue Stars formed a motley group of people from the office, the camp, and the campus, the Epoch poets were a flotilla of naval officers stationed at their base in southern Taiwan. At first its leaders, Ya Hsien, Lo Fu and Chang Mo, aimed at setting a "model for national poetry," which did not materialize. After a few years, they suddenly switched to the other extreme and advocated avant-garde writing; including a form of French Surrealism. To

From Chi Pang-yuan, and others, (eds.), *An Anthology of Contemporary Chinese Literature: Taiwan, 1949-1974* (Taipei: National Institute for Compilation and Translation, 1975), Vol. I, pp. 3-7 and Vol. II, pp. 1-5.

carry out this program, they later enlisted Yip Wai-lim's help because of his greater ac-
quaintance with Western poetry. Thus, they plunged head-long into the inner world of the
unconscious and tried to present their private experiences, unprocessed by the "distortion"
of reason, in the so-called automatic writing. Theoretically, they sought to free the unconscious from such cultural and social inhibitions as morality, logic, grammar and rhetoric,
and to cut all links of textual association. Such a willful doctrine, if seriously pursued,
would have resulted in total anarchy, though in practice it proved virtually impossible to
follow such teachings all the way. However, the Epoch's promotion of surrealist experiments did lead to a state of nihilism and obscurity in the sixties which brought upon modern
Chinese poetry bitter criticism from both outsiders and fellow groups. Ya Hsien began in a
lyric vein and with a fresh ballad flavor, but gradually drifted to the edge of obscurity,
though he never let himself fall in. Lo Fu did, in his controversial collection, *Death in the
Stone Cell*, but eventually pulled himself out to explore a less dubious current of experience. While the surrealist adventure did accelerate the maturing process of the leading
members of the Epoch Society, their less gifted imitators suffered greatly from meaningless
obscurity and stylistic mannerism. In retrospect, it seems the main contribution of this
movement in Taiwan was its startling use of imagery, whose shock effects were gained at
the expense of other poetic virtues. Among other members, attention should be paid to
Shang Ch'in, Kuan Kuan, Hsin Yü, Ch'u Ke, Ta Huang, Mei Hsin and P'u T'i. Yang Mu is
an independent figure who is equally associated with the Epoch and the Blue Stars.

The furor of modern poetry has since provoked two major controversies, first between
the alienated public and the practicing poets, and then among the poets themselves. The
former raged most vehemently in 1959-60, when detractors of modern poetry complained
of its clumsiness of style, obscurity of language and irrelevance to society. In retort, its
defenders accused the critics of being unsympathetic, unimaginative and unreceptive to
anything original. In addition, the chagrined poets cited instances of raggedness and difficulty in such masters of classical poetry as Li Ho, Li Shang-yin and Huang T'ing-chien for
self-justification. The quarrel between the poets themselves centered on the problem of
modernization. They were unanimous that Westernization was a necessary step in modernizing Chinese poetry, but then they became divided as to whether, in the modernizing
process, native tradition was only an obstacle or properly inherited, a great help. The anti-
traditionalists would rather have thrown the native heritage overboard. On the other hand,
the neo-traditionalists argued that anything so uprooted from its native soil could not thrive,
however invigorating the alien weather. The debate went on until the end of the sixties,
when the anti-traditionalists realized the importance of their national heritage more and
more.

At the threshold of the seventies, the established poets were beginning to command
respect when they were suddenly challenged by aspiring poets of a younger generation. The
newcomers, who had learned their trade from the work and theory of the older poets,
became disillusioned with the heavy style typical of poetry of the early and middle sixties.
Above all they were fed up with the thick, clogged images and involved syntax of their
predecessors. They tried to mold a new poetry that was quiet, unaffected, lucid in language,
relaxed in tone, spare in imagery, and committed to social awareness. Yet, reactions to
prevalent absurdities can easily be carried by their own momentum to opposite ones. Unfortunately, there have been instances already where the new experiments turned out unin-
spired pieces that just look plain, loose, sparse, and dogmatic.

The Li Poetry Society was founded in 1964 by a handful of native Taiwanese including
Lin Heng-t'ai and Pai Ch'iu, former members of the then disintegrating Modernist School.
Li, meaning "bamboo hat" in Chinese, clearly indicates their quiet but confident affinity to
the rural, the earthy, and the broad experiences of Chinese life. Among their guiding principles are: exploration of life intself instead of cultural abstractions, use of daily speech as the
legitimate medium of poetry, and rejection of pretension and egotism. Unlike the three
societies founded a decade ago, Li owed something to modern Japanese poetry in addition
to Western influences. Important members of the group include Pai Ch'iu, Huan Fu, Lin
Heng-t'ai, Chao Tien-i, Fu Min and Tu Kuo-ch'ing. It is felt that the contribution of Li to
contemporary verse has been more critical than creative.

In 1971, a few members left Li and joined some outsiders to launch the Dragons Poetry Society. As the name suggests, the Dragons take pride in the tradition of Chinese culture, but intend to rejuvenate it into something lively and contemporary. With the single exception of Lin Huan-chang all members were then under thirty. They share practically the same critical beliefs as the Li poets, but as a body seem to surpass the latter in creative writing. Other groups include Ta Ti (Great Earth) and Chu Liu (Mainstream). Lin Huan-chang, one of the most mature of these young poets, marks a departure from the Existentialist-Surrealist mood of the early and middle sixties. Another young poet, Lo Ch'ing, keeps independent of societies and schools; his poems breathe a sobering freshness into the contemporary scene with their solid structure, simple language, thematic coherence and technical resourcefulness, the best answer to the call of intellectualism.

Of the older generation, Yang Huan and Ch'in Tzu-hao died long ago. Poets of stature such as Fang Ssu, Ya Hsien, Chou Meng-tieh, Hsia Ch'ing, Cheng Ch'ou-yü, Fang Hsin, and Shang Ch'in have, for many years, either produced little or ceased to be creative altogether. We are happy that, in addition to the young talents that are rising, older poets like Pai Ch'iu, Yang Mu, Lo Fu, Lo Men, and Yü Kwang-chung still remain active in their changing styles and keep adding new dimensions to our contemporary experience.

Somehow, modern Chinese poetry in Taiwan has gone full circle in its wild pursuit of the Western Muse and its lover's quarrel with tradition, and has just come to the point where the odyssey ends at a new beginning. Now is the time for the prodigal poets to review critically what they have done and plan sagaciously what they will do. It is true that in their rush toward the West, they have learned much about the technique of literary mining, but genuine gold still lies unexplored in the mines at home, in the reality and tradition that are China. Westernization is only a means, but not the end, of the modernization of Chinese culture. For us, Taiwan is the place where the creative Chinese mind is able to pursue its own course; it is our best chance for a cultural renaissance.

Fiction:

The fiction that has come into existence in Taiwan over the last twenty-five years has been produced among difficulties and challenges that are unusual if not unique in the literary history of China.

The number of writers coming across the Straits to Taiwan around 1949 was small. Even these few, pressed by the necessity of earning a living, took up teaching or some other occupations. Their productivity was low and literary activity long remained stagnant.

Realizing that a more vigorous cultivation of literature might have blunted the Communist propaganda offensive, the government sponsored a Chinese Literature and Art Award in 1950. These awards encouraged writers to produce a positive literature in the defense of humanity and freedom against totalitarianism and Communism. About forty writers were aided by these awards.

Most of their works were naturally reminiscent of the struggle against the Communists or reflected nostalgia for the families they had left behind. The majority were servicemen, who depended more on their own indefatigable efforts than on formal training for their cultural background. Because they were writing in circumstances that encouraged sentimentality or exaggeration, their stories tended to lack conviction, though realistic and sometimes moving enough.

Their oft-repeated fighting experiences gradually became banal and monotonous; worse still, these stories degenerated into stock formulas or pure propaganda. Then, in the early 50's, certain writers with a keener consciousness of literary technique rose above this scene, trying to incorporate into their works the contemporary approaches taken by the stage, movies, and Western fiction. Although they by-passed some traditional methods, the basic approaches to plot and tone were kept. Still, this beginning stage was largely experimental and not every experiment was an unqualified success. However, we still harvested a good bit of grain from our first crop of writers such as Lin Hai-yin, P'an Jen-mu and Meng Yao. The title of Pan's *Little World of Joys and Sorrows* is symbolic as well as realistic. Lin Hai-yin, whose command of the Chinese language brought literary writing to a new level of excellence, adds dignity to nostalgia when she shares her eloquent recollections of a child-hood spent in Peiping. An Meng Yao, whose interest in the here and now is effectively embodied in her novels, opened readers' eyes to the many contented people living about us, who confidently look forward to bettering their lives with their own diligence.

In the ten years after 1950, the scene was actually dominated by more mature writers who, now settled and looking upon the past more calmly, began to produce novels of enduring value. Among the best were Wang Lan's *The Blue and the Black,* Chiang Kuei's *The Whirlwind,* Ch'en Chi-ying's *Fools in the Reeds* and *Eight Years in the Houses of Hua and Hsia.*

Also worth mentioning was the sudden upsurge in sheer quantity of writing. There were at least fifty authors writing for literary magazines and newspaper supplements. Among them were quite a few women writers. But these offerings tended to be a tireless repetition of certain themes: nostalgic reminiscences of the past, recollections of friends, anecdotes of the war or fabricated love stories. However, these publications kept the fire of creativity burning, and nurtured many promising young writers whose permanent worth was to emerge clearly in the sixties.

In 1956, a serious magazine, *Literary Journal,* came into being, which contributed greatly to the development and modernization of literary writing in Taiwan. Its editor-in-chief, the late Professor Hsia Tsi-an, advocated an honest realism. In the inaugural issue, he says, ''We should not try to escape stark reality. Our belief is that an earnest writer makes it his duty to reflect the reality of his age, tries to present the spirit of his age through his work.''

This announcement was spurred, of course, by his impatience with the trend toward pessimistic nostalgia then prevalent among writers. According to Hsia, these authors seemed to have totally disregarded life as it was actually lived in Taiwan, while other professions were making remarkable progress in a heroic effort to establish on the island an even better home away from home. The *Literary Journal* encouraged and fostered a healthy climate of criticism conducive to the maturation of many promising writers (very much like the *Atlantic Monthly* and its contribution to American realism). Among the rising young writers were Pai Hsien-yung, Wang Wen-hsing, and Ou-yang Tzu. At this time, they were still college students whose experience with the kaleidoscopic human society around them was rather limited. Furthermore, their contact with the works of post-May Fourth Move-ment writers was not very extensive. Naturally, they turned first to Western writers, and Henry James, James Joyce, D. H. Lawrence. Hemingway, Camus, Sartre, and Kafka served as their models. Still, in Wang Wen-hsing's words, they "describe Chinese charac-ters, move in a Chinese setting, develop Chinese themes. No man is named John, no woman Mary. They eat rice with chopsticks.'' (Preface to *Modern Short Stories,* 1962).

In 1960, this group of young writers founder *Modern Literature,* a bimonthly that has contributed greatly, in its turn, to the rise of a still younger generation of writers. There is no denying that they have freely adapted the Western expression of such techniques as stream of consciousness, point of view, symbolism, etc. Freud has also had his influence on their analysis of human behavior. Thus, sex and sexual repression tend to dominate their world. Of this young group, Pai Hsien-yung is closer to the Chinese tradition and his achievement is also greater. Because of his own family background, he witnessed as an insider how declining aristocrats reacted to their changed circumstances. With the fresh and cool eyes of a young critic, he could examine objectively, almost clinically, the decay of a once proud generation, as in his *One Winter Evening* and *Jung's by the Blossom Bridge.* His ironical attitude is somewhat ruthless yet sympathetic. As a gifted writer, he doesn't depend on clever employment of language. His use of the Chinese language is natural, his characteri-zation is truthful and broader in scope than is indicated by the title he has given to his best-known collection of stories—*The People of Taipei.*

Wang Wen-hsing, however, followed a quite different path. He is more interested in the middle and lower classes, and succeeds in probing into the world of children and youth. He is much more obsessed with the imaginative use of language, and often creates new expres-sions. To achieve the desired tone of his style, he frequently takes long-accepted idioms and twists them into new meanings or new ambiguities, as manifested in his recent controver-sial novel, *The Runaway.*

Ou-yang Tzu is also very important in this group. She has been deeply influenced by Henry James, and successfully combines an objective observer's point of view with subtle irony. Her characters are mostly women, young college graduates who are mainly preoccupied with love, or merely sex. In a country where traditional morality is still powerful, she has to tread very carefully lest her art encounter social disapprobation.

There came a yet younger generation, mainly composed of native Taiwanese writers, products of a successful educational system conducted in Mandarin which involves about 98% of school-age children. By the 1960's they had become college graduates. Some had gone abroad for advanced studies and adopted new life styles. These young writers had naturally developed a deeply ingrained consciousness of commitment to an independent future that was uncompromisingly Chinese and distinctly their own.

Their characters, quite different from the aristocrats, generals, scholars, and intellectuals, are people of humble origins, reduced to a humiliating status by the circumstances of a marginal existence—as the character Hu K'un-shu in Huang Ch'un-ming's *His Son's Big Doll;* or the old timers eking out an existence from their meagre shed in Shih Shu-ch'ing's *The Old-timer;* or the old folks at home, living a leisurely life amid familiar scenes in Lin Huai-min's *Homecoming.* As these writers contemplate such aspects of their ancestral heritage which are rapidly vanishing from this island in the face of our recent material affluence, it is evident that their attitude is both critical and affectionate.

Section 2
The Educational System
Edited by Theodore Hsi-en Chen

Section 2

The Educational System

by Theodore Hsi-en Chen

The experience of the Republic of China in Taiwan has been described as a remarkable success story. It is no overstatement to say that educational growth is a major aspect of this experience and story. Education not only reflects the economic development and the social and political progress of the last three decades, but it must also be recognized as a potent force laying a firm foundation for continuing Taiwan's growth and advance from a developing country to the threshold of an industrialized and modernized society.

The sources cited in this section fall under two categories: those in Part One describing the contemporary school system, and those in Part Two reporting research studies and indicating some of the problems of education.[1] The first three selections present a general view of the school system, while the fourth and fifth discuss the educational aspect of the land reform and thus direct attention to education in the rural areas. Selections 6 to 10 inclusive, are samples of research studies on specific phases of the educational program. We regret that we have not been able to locate sources reporting more up-to-date research studies. Furthermore, the sources here cited tend to reflect the approach of political scientists interested primarily in the problem of political socialization; valuable as they are, we wish that we could include some studies by scholars in other disciplines, for example, students of education, who would use a different approach and methodology. Nevertheless, the studies here reported should stimulate fruitful thinking and the methodology. Nevertheless, the studies here reported should stimulate fruitful thinking and the methodology they suggest may be useful in future studies based on up-to-date data.

The Schools: The current system is a product of seven decades of evolution. The first system of modern schools in China was introduced in 1902 and was fashioned after the Japanese model. After the revolution of 1911, the Japanese model was considered inadequate for the young Republic and a new system was promulgated in 1912. World War I and the rise of democratic aspirations opened the way for escalating American influence, and the adoption of the 6-3-3-4 system of schools in 1922 reflected the American practice of two levels of secondary education, with three years of junior high school leading to the three-year senior high school. The basic structure of 6-3-3-4 remains today, but the aims and methods of education

Theodore Hsi-en Chen is Professor Emeritus of Education, University of Southern California (Los Angeles, Ca.).

and the content of the curriculum have undergone much change since 1912.

In the decade prior to the Sino-Japanese War, which began in 1937, the Nationalist government was attracted by the educational experience of European countries, especially the highly centralized administration of French education. European educators were invited to visit China to make recommendations for curriculum development, teaching methods, and centralized educational planning. European influence overshadowed the American influence of earlier years. In recent years in Taiwan, closer contacts with the United States have again led to an increase of American influence on education. We see today a blend of European and American influences guided by an over all aim to make use of the experience of foreign countries to design an educational program that would meet the conditions and the needs of the changing society of Taiwan.

The vast expansion of this program is evident in the excerpts from the first three documents. The nmber of schools jumped from 1,504 in 1950 to 4,950 in 1979, and the student population soared from 1,055,000 to 4,570,000. Six-year compulsory education is well enforced: 99.68 per cent of school-age children are reported to be attending schools. Since 1968, the junior middle school has been added to the elementary school to form a period of nine-year free education without the barrier of entrance examinations from the elementary school to the junior middle school. Entrance examinations are required for admission to the senior middle school, but there is talk today of gradually permitting graduates of the nine-year school to advance without entrance examinations to different types of vocational schools that parallel the senior middle school; if so, free education will have been extended to 12 years, from age 6 to 18. In view of the popular demand for education and the economic prosperity of the island, it is not impossible to realize this hope in the foreseeable future.

Rural education: The growth of education is not limited to the cities. The land reform in Taiwan has been hailed, at home and abroad, as a most significant movement that has transformed the social and economic life of the rural population. An important phase of the land reform was to institute free, compulsory education for the young and training classes and farmers' organizations to teach the adults in the villages. We have cited at length (in Selections IV and V) the studies made by Martin M. C. Yang, Mark C. Thelin, and others showing how education played a key role in social-economic reform during and after the land reform. Rural children studied in the schools that had produced a literate young generation in the cities, young people joined the 4-H Club, the Home Economic Teaching Program reached into the homes, and the farmers learned to go beyond individual effort to work together in farmers' associations and to adopt farm innovations to increase their productivity. Community participation not only showed a new way of getting things done, but also engendered a new spirit of community-mindedness that brought a new life to the villages.

The years since the above mentioned studies have witnessed an acceleration of progress in rural education. An investigation in the same villages today would undoubtedly reveal different conditions, some continued progress, and some new problems. For example, the language situation has improved. The teaching of *Kuo Yu* (Mandarin, or the National Tongue) in schools has produced good results and helped bring about a common tongue and a convenient medium of communication among all people in Taiwan. At the same time, many girls from the villages have gone to the cities to work in factories and earn independent wages, thus creating new problems of adjustment in the rural communities.

Broadening the scope of education: There is approximately 7 per cent illiteracy in the population at large. Most of the illiterate are adults beyond school age and those unable to attend schools on account of disability or handicaps. To remedy this situation, the school system has been extended to provide special education for such people. As shown in the chart in Selection 1, alongside the regular schools are special schools and supplementary schools at elementary and secondary levels. Special schools serve the needs of the blind, the deaf, the physically handicapped, and the mentally retarded, while supplementary schools provide education for adults who missed schooling in their childhood, and for drop-outs and young people in employment. Statistics published by the Ministry of Education in 1978 showed nine special schools enrolling 2,855 students, among whom were 1,332 deaf students enrolled in schools for the deaf. There were 192,704 students enrolled in 324 supplementary schools, among which were vocational schools in agriculture, industry, and technical fields rising to meet the needs of the fast-growing economy.[2]

Recognizing that education is more than schooling, many forms of education outside the school are promoted in what is generally known as social education. In addition to the radio and television, there are libraries, museums, science exhibits, art displays, zoological gardens, an observatory, and other forms of informal education. There are 134 radio stations and three television networks offering programs ranging from Mandarin lessons and English lessons to entertainment and sports. News and commentaries on domestic and foreign news, available throughout the day, reach millions of people and inform them of daily happenings on the island and important international events. Big events are carried live by way of the Pacific satellite. In addition to general programs, "School on TV" and "School on the Air" actually bring the classroom into the home. Most of the radio stations and all the TV stations are under private management and ownership. Television has become a major medium of public information and entertainment. The China Yearbook (ROC) 1979 reports 3,360,000 television sets in use in 1978, which means that most of the population of more than 17 millon are within reach of television. Most of the TV programs are broadcast in color.

The newspapers are also a potent force. Among the 31 daily newspapers, the two biggest papers, *United Daily News (Lien Ho Pao)* and *China Times (Chung Kuo Shih Pao),* both privately owned, have a daily circulation of around 1,000,000 copies. According to the 1979 Yearbook, the 31 newspapers have a daily circulation of 2,300,000 copies. Bearing in mind that subscriptions by individuals and offices are shared by family members and fellow workers, and many people read newspapers regularly in libraries and other public places, one may get some idea of the influence of the newspapers.

Prosperity Creates More Leisure

Economic prosperity and a higher standard of living make possible more leisure and lead to a proliferation of activities in the enjoyment of leisure. This situation could create new social problems, some of which seem to be endemic to highly developed societies, but it also opens up new opportunities for social education. The National Palace Museum in Taipei, which houses and displays objects of art representing the cultural heritage of 4,000 years and is a major attraction to foreign visitors, has been an effective vehicle of education for students, scholars, and the public in general. The continuous stream of visitors to this museum and other museum, notably the National Museum of History, consists of individuals and groups from all parts of the island. In like manner, the libraries play an active role in stimulating interest and study. Besides the well-supplied National Central Library, there are libraries established by city and county governments and private libraries which are also open to the public. Together, these agencies of informal education have encouraged young and old to spend some of their leisure hours in educating and acquainting themselves with China's cultural heritage.

In connection with the use of leisure time, it its appropriate to mention in passing the growth of popular interest in sports, in music, in travel making extensive use of the train as well as the highways, in mountain climbing, distance hiking, and other recreational activities. There is much interest in Western music, classical as well as modern; symphony orchestra concerts draw capacity audiences. Young and old, people on the island have the chance to live a much richer life on a broader scale than their predecessors in Taiwan and in mainland China.

To summarize, education in Taiwan is assured of stability and continued growth, thanks to the dependable financial support from the budgets of the central government and the provincial and local governments. The educational ladder consists of well-articulated levels of schools, with tracks provided for the benefit of the disabled and the handicapped, and adults who missed regular schooling in their early years. Moreover, the educational program extends beyond the schools and incorporates a wide variety of out-of-school educational activities usually known as informal education. The actual school attendance of 99.68 per cent of school-age children is second only to that of Japan, and adult literacy is taken for granted in most parts of the island.

This is not to say that there are no shortcomings or serious problems. It is not a simple task to fashion an educational program including and coordinating various types of schools and out-of-school educational agencies. The task is complicated by the need to preserve the essence of an old and highly prized cultural heritage, while recognizing at the same time that modern life and modern society create pressing demands for knowledge, skills, attitudes, etc. that were not a part of the education of past centuries or even past decades. It behooves the planners to make a critical study of the past heritage as well as present needs and to examine the experience of other countries in order to benefit from their successes as well as failures.

To carry on this complicated task, it is necessary to explore the wisdom of people who know China's past and present, of statesmen who have the vision of a regenerated and invigorated China in a changing world, of sociologists, economists and political scientists as well as of educators and educationalists, of scholars in the humanities as well as the sciences, and of outstanding thinkers from other countries who understand Chinese society and have a broad view of the trends and problems of education in their own countries.

Not all the problems of education can be solved by scientific methods of inquiry. The "science" of education has made significant contributions by methods of treating objective data and research studies using concepts and hypotheses that facilitate evaluation and comparison. It is not without its limitations, but its objective methods can be of valuable help in identifying and defining problems. In striving for objectivity, researchers find it advisable to focus attention on specific problems or phases of a problem instead of dealing with too big field at one time. Their studies should be understood and appreciated with such limitations in mind.

We cite in Part Two of the excerpts a number of studies which may stimulate thinking on specific phases of education on Taiwan. Selections 6 and 7 are writings of a political scientist who has made outstanding studies of what is generally known as political culture or the process of politcal socialization. Richard W. Wilson's studies of political socialization of children in mainland China and Taiwan were followed by others using more of less the same methods of research. It would not be inaccurate to say that the authors of Selections 8 and 9 reflect the influence of Wilson and other political scientists who set forth basic concepts of political socialization and the framework for research in this area. They focus their attention on the molding of political attitudes. Moreover, following the basic concepts set forth by the pioneers in this field of study, they are concerned especially with such maifestations of political behavior as conformity, dissent, deviance, reactions to authority, attitudes toward government, etc.

Critics may question the value of picking out a narrow phase of the educative process and emphasizing it at the risk of losing perspective in regard to the educational progam as a whole. The answer is that any phase of education deserves careful study, and the investigation of behavior changes beyond the conventional school subjects serves to reinforce the broadened concept of education to include family life, the influence of peers and "peer groups," and other factors that affect the formation of beliefs, attitudes, and behavior patterns. It may be noted that in the study of students attitudes some American researchers may have been influenced by the rise of student activism in American colleges and universities in the 1960's. Their interest in student activism may have turned their attention to a phase of political behavior that may not appear to be such an important topic for research today. In an article with the title "Silent Students and the Future of Taiwan," Sheldon Appleton stated his concern clearly in the beginning sentences, as follows:[3]

> In the United States, France, Germany, Canada, Czechoslovakia, and Spain, in Latin America and Africa, in Japan, Indonesia, the Philippines, and even Mainland China, students in the 1960's have been on the march in the name of multitude of causes, ideas, and concerns. But somehow, the Republic of China on Taiwan has managed to escape all this; throughout the sixties, when a new generation, educated on Taiwan, has come to maturity, Taiwan's campuses have been silent.

The above quotation may help one to understand the emphasis in Selection 8 on student dissent. Roberta Martin's study (Selection 9) of the socialization of children in Taiwan (as compared with the process of mainland China) also reflects this general point of view. In her analysis of elementary-school textbooks, she found that the teaching materials stressed such virtues as filial piety, patriotism, duty, diligent study, academic achievement, and the acceptance of authority, all of which meant an over-all goal of developing "a Confucian society." Her article was severely critized by a Chinese writer in Taiwan, who pointed out that Martin had examined selected textbooks from two different editions and left out lessons which could not support her conclusions.[4] He also cited from textbooks in the same editions to show that they contained materials designed to develop a balanced personality rather than narrow concentration on filial piety, loyality, diligent study, and other Confucian virtues. Nevertheless, Martin's studies could well be brought up-to-date and her methods may well be improved upon in order to avoid the limitations of her study.[5]

Taiwanese and Mainlanders

Another topic that has engaged the interest of political scientists is the relationship between the Taiwanese and the immigrants from mainland China after World War II. It is pertinent to not that researchers using the same methods and the same objective data may draw different conclusions. In this case, Wilson (Selection 7) concluded from his study that "the general overall similarity between Mainlander and Taiwanese children, with regard to both politically relevent and specific political attitudes, is quite marked and of sufficient strength to suggest that Mainlander and Taiwanese groups both have continued to adhere closely to political cultural norms despite their separation during the first half of this century." Though he did not dispute Wilson's findings, Sheldon Appleton (Selection 8) seemed to put more emphasis on "a very substantial degree of social division between Mainlanders and Taiwanese."

Provincial sentiments do not disappear quickly. But if the same investigations should be repeated today, they will probably reveal that the "social division" observed earlier has appreciably diminished. Several factors have contributed to a reduction of this division. One of them is language. The school has done such a good job in teaching the *Kuo Yu* that many young people from Taiwanese families now speak the national tongue more fluently than the Taiwanese dialect. The radio and television have also helped to popularize the common spoken language. Besides, the schools on all levels have proved to be a great unifier. By the time students enter college or university, many of them are not conscious of social differences or barriers. Intermarriage between individuals from Taiwanese and Mainlander families is becoming more common. Among Chinese students in the United States who came from Taiwan, this kind of "mixed" marriage hardly arouses any comment or attention. Additionally, another potent cohesive force is the general contentment of the population at large, thanks to the improvement of the quality of life that economic prosperity has brought. The housewives, the storekeepers, the farmers, the workers have at their disposal more things to enjoy and cherish than ever before, and they tend to be unenthusiastic about any big change of the status quo. The school population, naturally, is predominantly Taiwanese; young people from Taiwanese families have a much better opportunity of upward mobility than ever before.

This is not to say that there is no tension at all related to provincial origin. While capable Taiwanese do wield economic and financial power as captains of industry and finance, the politically-minded look to politics and governmental power for new opportunities for advancement and leadership. Taiwanese leaders have in recent years taken over the control of provincial (for the administration of Taiwan as a province) and local governments, but there is agitation for a larger share of top-level policy-making in the central (national) government. The incumbent Vice President, the Vice Premier, five Ministers, the Governor of the Province of Taiwan and mayors of cities, are native Taiwanese, but there is a demand for a larger share of top-echelon leadership and power by Taiwanese. This is not an unreasonable demand and it can be met with sympathetic understanding and high vision. The policy initiated by President Chiang Ching-kuo of the Republic of China to recruit more Taiwanese into government service has produced good results. It will undoubtedly be continued and broadened. An increasing number of capable people of Taiwanese descent have emerged from the education they received in recent years and the good life they have enjoyed, and the government can be greatly strengthened by the participation of such new talents in public service at high levels.

Recent years have witnessed a growth of interest in the study of Chinese language and culture in many countries of the world, and foreign students have gone to Taiwan as a part of a program of educational and cultural exchange. It was reported that among the 3,170 students from 52 countries who went to Taiwan in 1979, there was 882 from Japan, 828 from the U.S.A., 154 from France, 88 from West Germany, 46 from United Kingdom, and fairly large numbers from other Asian countries. As may be expected, most of the foreign students were enrolled in the humanities and the social sciences, but engineering, medicine, fine arts, agriculture, and education have attracted quite a few, also. The medical schools have received more applications from foreign students than they can accommodate. As a matter of fact, so great is the domestic need for physicians that a decision was made some three years ago to suspend the acceptance of foreign students in medical schools in Taiwan.

The "Brain Drain"

The excerpts in Selection 10 serve to call attention to a problem in regard to Chinese students abroad. The problem of "brain drain" is, of course, not peculiar to Taiwan; other countries also have been disturbed by the tendency of their well-educated and highly trained personnel to be attracted by opportunities in the United States, which induce them to establish permanent residence in America instead of returning to their homeland. As far as Chinese students in America are concerned, those who went in early years generally planned and expected to return to their homeland after the completion of their study. There was no question of a prolonged stay abroad partly because there was little meaningful employment available, but largely because the homeland offered good career opportunities. The situation began to change with the outbreak of the Sino-Japanese War in 1937, and a new trend appeared. On account of the difficulty of travel and unsettled conditions in China, many Chinese students were stranded abroad. The U.S. government and other agencies offered scholarships to help these stranded students. Those who had completed their study found their way into the faculties of American colleges, universities, and research organizations. After World War II, a change in American immigration policy made it possible for established scholars to apply for permanent residence. The opportunity of continued study and research in the midst of favorable conditions such as up-to-date research facilities and good salaries induced many to think of settling down. Brain drain became a live issue.

There are indications that the trend is now being reversed, or at least arrested. Industrialization and development have created new needs for highly trained personnel in Taiwan and the government has offered salary inducements and other benefits to attract scholars to return from abroad. A report in the *United Daily News*[6] stated that among more than 50,000 students who went abroad from Taiwan in the years preceding 1978, only 6,000 had returned to Taiwan. This percentage figure is higher than indicated in Selection 10. The Ministry of Education reported that while the annual return of students from foreign study did not exceed 63 before 1963, several hundred returned each year after 1970. A report of the National Youth Commission in Taiwan stated that 4,262 young scholars had returned to Taiwan for employment in the period from July 1971 to the end of 1978.[7] All the returnees had had graduate study in universities abroad, 1,091 had obtained doctoral degrees, and 2,561 Master's degrees. Some 45.75 per cent were employed by colleges and universities, and the rest were hired by government agencies, industrial and business organizations, hospitals, and other agencies. The decline of employment opportunities abroad (for various reasons) and the emergence of new opportunities in Taiwan have combined to accelerate the new trend.

The government has tried to attract highly trained Chinese scholars residing abroad. Enthusiastic over the progress and prosperity in Taiwan, and pleased with the prospect of making significant contributions to a promising program of modernization and development, more and more young scholars are now more inclined to respond to the call for patriotic service to the homeland. Meanwhile, in addition to the assurance of adequate salary and acceptable living conditions, the government is making an effort to provide an environment which will enable talented scholars to continue their research and keep abreast of developments abroad in their fields of specialization. The Academia Sinica, the National Science Council, the Atomic Energy Council, and the research departments of universities provide encouragement and facilities for scholars in the humanities and the social sciences, as well as in the natural and biological sciences. Outstanding foreign scholars have been invited to Taiwan to give lectures and to participate in seminars to share their research activities with Chinese counterparts. The plan of inviting visiting scholars from abroad is likely to be pursued actively and intensively. Meanwhile, support is given to scholars with notable achievement to enable them to attend and participate in international conferences in order to maintain contacts with foreign scholars in their fields. The National Science Council is reported to have included funds in its current budget to enable 200 scholars to go abroad for international conferences in 1981.[8] These arrangements may help allay the fear of some scholars that return to the homeland will result in isolation from the world community of scholars.

An international conference on sinology was held in Taipei in August 1980. Many participants came from European countries as well as the United States. Another link with intellectuals abroad is the development of sister-institution relationship between a number of colleges and universities in Taiwan and American colleges and universities. An active program of educational and cultural exchange will help engender a stimulating intellectual atmosphere which will be attractive to Chinese scholars at home and abroad. Related to this topic of discussion is the expansion of facilities for post-graduate study and research in Taiwan. Eight more universities were authorized in 1969 to establish post-graduate departments awarding master's and doctoral degrees. Among them are departments of veterinary medicine, oceanography, pathology, pharmacology, electronics, law, architectural engineering, urban planning, industrial management, and Chinese literature. A total of 5,443 students were enrolled in the graduate schools in 1979.[9] Expanded provision for graduate study and research will not only encourage some students to seek advanced study at home instead of going abroad, but will also give an added impetus to the fostering of an intellectual atmosphere in Taiwan.

Private Education in Taiwan

Private education plays a significant role in Taiwan. The Constitution of the Republic of China stipulates that the State "shall encourage or subsidize . . . private educational enterprises." Of the total educational expenditures of NT$36,690,330,000 in 1977-78, NT$6,818,877,000 came from private sources for the support of private education.[10] The list of colleges and universities in Taiwan in the 1980 Chinese Yearbook contains 33 public institutions and 68 private institutions. To this is added the newly established National Sun Yat-Sen University, a public institution in Kàohsiung). The larger figure for private institutions is due to the fact that most of the colleges and junior colleges in specialized fields of technology, business, commerce, nursing, journalism, medical technology, pharmacy, etc. are private institutions. At the secondary-school level, private education has played a big role in the establishment of vocational schools, special schools, and supplementary schools: out of 184 senior vocational schools, 10 are private schools, two of the nine special schools in operation are private institutions, and 157 of the 332 supplementary schools are private.[11]

A report by the Ministry of Education states that "most of the newly founded 5-year junior colleges are private ones" and that "educational expenditures from private sources have increased about four times in the last ten years."[12] Private schools have had a tradition in China for many centuries. Evidently, there is no lack of individuals or groups of individuals who are ready to give money for educational purposes. Private education is not permitted to enter the field of teacher training; all teachers' colleges are public institutions. Since the inauguration of nine-year free and compulsory education, there is a tendency to have the public schools take over the full responsibility for basic citizenship education, and the role of private schools at the elementary and junior high levels is consequently minimized. At the same time, in recognition of the fact that the academic-type senior middle school could not meet the needs and ambitions of all who desired further education beyond the 9-year basic education, there arose the need for a variety of vocational schools at the level of the senior middle school. The 5-year junior college, which actually is an extension of the senior vocational school to include the 2-year junior college, was introduced as an additional alternative to the senior middle school. The fact that such a high proportion of senior vocational schools and the new 5-year junior colleges are private institutions shows that private education plays an important role in Taiwan's educational system. It has proved its vitality and sensitivity to changing educational needs and its ability to fill a gap as soon as it appears in the educational system.

The place of private education in a national system of education is an important question no matter whether the control or supervision of education is centralized or decentralized. Under the centralized administration established by the Nationalist government in the 1920's and 1930's, which is still in effect today, the proper role of private education is something that requires careful thought. Is private education needed only when there are needs unmet by public education? Should private schools and public schools be governed by exactly the same standards in regard to curriculum and administrative procedures? Should private schools be allowed any leeway for trying out new methods and new programs as long as they do not violate the general regulations or broad educational policies of the government? Would there be any need for private education if the government should at some future time have enough financial resources to provide public school programs to meet all the needs of the country and the population? In other words, will private education outlive its usefulness in the future? Educators in the private sector have now and then raised such questions. They are concerned about the future of private education, its justification and its opportunities. A thought-out and clearly stated policy would help in planning for the future.

In the first decade of the Republic of China (1912-1922), public education was poorly financed and badly administered. Private education played a dominant role and private schools and colleges, with few exceptions such as the prestigious Peking University, were the best and most highly respected educational institutions in the country. At the same time, there were private schools which existed merely as commercial or business enterprises or schools which were diploma mills, at best. To bring order out of chaos and to prevent the abuse of educational privileges, it was necessary to place all private education under strict government control. One purpose of control and supervision was to make sure that all private and public schools followed the same regulations. To rectify the chaos and abuses, the regulations tended to emphasize restrictions and demand uniformity and there was little evidence of serious consideration of the positive role of private education in the long-range program of national education.

The situation has changed today. The chaos of the early years is no longer found in Taiwan today. A firmly established and well-supported system of public education is in place. To be sure, the possibility of reckless entrepreneurs who would exploit children and youth under the guise of education is not entirely non-existent, and it is necessary for the government to watch out for abuses. But there are many people in private education who are dedicated educational workers for whom restrictions are not as necessary. Private enterprise plays a big role in Taiwan, not only in the economic growth and industrial development, but also in various types of formal and informal education. There are signs that the government is moving toward an evolution of policy that will recognize the positive and permanent role of private education. Only recently, the government made an important move which gave much encouragement to the teachers, staff, and managers of private schools. Since 1958 an Insurance System for Public Functionaries has been in effect which provides medical care, hospitalization, and disability benefits; teachers and staff of public schools have been protected as public functionaries. Now, the coverage has been extended to include the teachers and staff of private schools. This is a move in the right direction and we hope it will lead to other specific measures to encourage those who work in private schools. Such developments may indicate a turn to a positive policy of education beyond the prevention of abuses and mismanagement, a policy that expresses a philosophy of education that will enable private education to maximize its contributions to national education.

Students from Taiwan have made an impressive record in American universities. They are recognized as outstanding students and researchers. The success of academic education in Taiwan, however, has brought perplexing problems. Competetion is keen on all levels of the school system, and the pressure for success is great. The excerpts in Selections 2 and 3 have called attention to "the congestion in academic high schools," the oppressive effects of competitive examinations, and the "rigidity" of curriculum and teaching methods aiming above all things to enable students to pass examinations. Out of this situation has risen a prevalent practice of intensive study which is actually no more than feverishly cramming for examinations. Bearing the euphemistic name of "review lessons" or "supplementary study," the process of cramming starts with elementary school pupils (even in the villages, as reported in Selection 5) and has become a major activity throughout the schooling years. Parents worry about the health effects of such after-school cramming sessions day in and day out. The limitation of allotted space permits only a passing mention of these problems. Suffice it to say that newpapers, forums of teachers, parents, and educators, and articles in journals have joined in a chorus of demand for reforms. There are many other problems of education that cry out for urgent reform. Some of them grew out of the very success achieved in the last three decades. Many suggestions have been made for changes and adjustments in the light of the new social-economic-political conditions. It is encouraging to note that the public is aroused and much concerned about education, and that the complaints and proposals for reform are openly aired in forums and in current literature. Such open discussion provides hope that solutions may be forthcoming and appropriate action may ensue.

NOTES

1. The author wishes to express his thanks to Dr. Vera Young, Assistant Professor Education, University of Southern California, for her valuable assistance in the selection of excerpts from various sources.

2. ROC Ministry of Education, *Educational Statistics of the Republic of China*, pp. 102, 104, Taipei, 1978.

3. *Pacific Affairs*, Summer 1970.

4. *Chinese Communist Affairs Monthly* (a Chinese language publication in Taipei), March, 1977.

5. Related to the point of view of the researchers here cited is a statement of the function of the Government of Taiwan as "the custodian of Chinese culture" by Richard L. Walker, in Paul K. T. Sih, *Taiwan in Modern Times* (New York: St. John's University Press, 1973), p. 381: "While much of the curriculum in the *Kuo-min Hsueh-hsiao*, national schools, could be criticized for its failure to provide relevant instruction for vocational goals, the subjects stressed throughout the system related to the Chinese tradition, Chinese history, and traditional morality."

6. *United Daily News* (Taipei), May 3, 1980.

7. *Free China Weekly* (Taipei), December 17, 1978.

8. *United Daily News,* January 1, 1981.

9. ROC Ministry of Education, *Educational Statistics of the Republic of China* (Taipei, 1979), p. 93.

10. *Ibid.,* p. 46.

11. *Ibid.,* pp. 74-76.

12. ROC Ministry of Education, *Education in the Republic of China* (Taipei, 1980), p. 24.

Part I
The Education System, Growth & Curriculum

1. THE CURRENT SCHOOL SYSTEM
1979

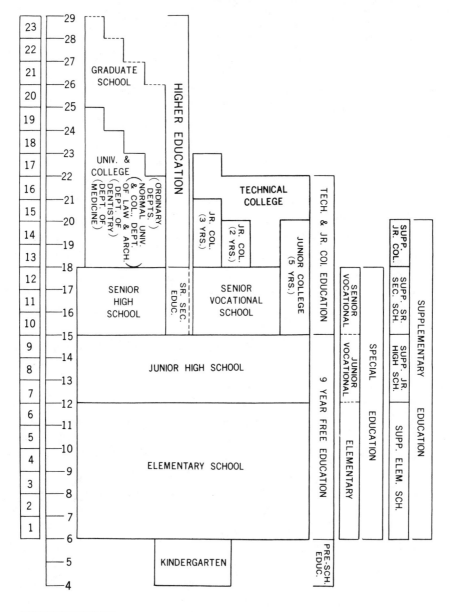

From Ministry of Education, ROC, *Education in the Republic of China* (Taipei, 1979), pp. 11, 40, 35-36.

Educational Growth, 1950-1979

Comparison of number of
students and population

Percentage of school-age children attending schools
and percentage of graduates pursuing advanced study

School Year	Population (1,000)	Number of Students (1,000)	‰		School Year	School-Age Children Attending Schools(%)	Graduates Admitted to Next Level of Education (%)		
							Elementary School	Jr. High School	Sr. High School
1950	7,554	1,055	139.64		1950	79.98	31.99	61.38	72.57
1951	7,869	1,135	144.19		1951	81.49	36.55	59.21	67.93
1952	8,128	1,188	146.14		1952	84.00	33.76	62.89	46.21
1953	8,438	1,276	151.22		1953	87.75	35.56	66.97	70.11
1954	8,749	1,383	158.08		1954	90.83	38.73	72.19	75.17
1955	9,078	1,535	169.15		1955	92.33	43.03	75.82	78.42
1956	9,447	1,679	177.71		1956	93.82	46.69	72.95	76.17
1957	9,748	1,848	189.57		1957	94.61	48.52	74.43	67.03
1958	10,092	2,037	201.85		1958	94.84	50.30	74.34	66.22
1959	10,485	2,213	211.03		1959	95.44	50.71	78.36	65.94
1960	10,851	2,375	218.91		1960	95.59	51.24	79.56	76.37
1961	11,210	2,541	226.64		1961	96.00	52.51	81.85	76.75
1962	11,575	2,703	233.50		1962	96.52	54.36	80.04	72.74
1963	11,949	2,824	236.30		1963	96.71	53.49	77.34	78.14
1964	12,325	2,964	240.51		1964	96.83	55.14	79.31	77.51
1965	12,699	3,117	245.49		1965	97.15	57.40	85.36	67.78
1966	13,065	3,253	249.03		1966	97.16	58.95	79.77	68.11
1967	13,371	3,406	254.75		1967	97.52	62.29	79.13	71.77
1968	13,726	3,615	263.35		1968	97.67	74.66	89.36	71.19
1969	14,412	3,810	264.35		1969	97.62	76.01	86.72	72.46
1970	14,754	3,992	270.54		1970	98.01	79.81	90.13	71.93
1971	15,073	4,131	274.04		1971	98.02	81.39	71.35	75.17
1972	15,367	4,269	277.81		1972	98.13	83.86	70.55	83.43
1973	15,642	4,334	277.90		1973	98.09	84.26	65.43	74.84
1974	15,927	4,395	275.94		1974	98.46	88.62	64.61	73.41
1975	16,223	4,449	274.24		1975	99.29	90.06	67.06	78.76
1976	16,580	4,479	270.15		1976	99.42	91.01	60.02	77.05
1977	16,882	4,522	267.86		1977	99.57	94.21	60.00	77.20
1978	17,202	4,530	263.31		1978	99.64	94.70	60.15	74.27
1979	17,543	4,576	260.51		1979	99.68	96.20	62.44	79.57

Curriculum

TEACHING SUBJECTS AND WEEKLY TEACHING HOURS IN ELEMENTARY AND JUNIOR HIGH SCHOOLS
(Weekly Minutes for Elementary Schools)

Grade	Elementary School 1-2	Elementary School 3-4	Elementary School 5-6	Junior High 1	Junior High 2	Junior High 3
Civics & Ethics	120	120 200	200	2	2	2
Health Education				2		
Mandarin	400	400	400			
Chinese						
English				6	6	6
Mathematics	120	160 200	240	2-3	2-3	
Social Studies	80	120	120	3-4	3-4	3-4
History				2	2	1
Geography				2	2	1
Natural Science	120	160	160	3	4	4
Singing & Playing	160					
Physical Education		120	120	2	2	2
Music		80	80	1	1	1
Fine Arts				1	1	1
Craft work	} 80	120	120			
Industrial Arts (Home Economics for girls)				2	2	2
Selective Subjects: Plantation of Agricultural Products						
Drawing					2	
Abacus						
Agriculture						
Industry						
Commerce						
Home Economics						
Marine Products						
English						6-9
Mathematics						
Music						
Fine Arts						
Boy Scout Training				1	1	1
Group Activities	80	80	80			
Guidance Activities				1	1	1
TOTAL	1160	1360 1480	1520	30-32	31-33	31-35

Notes:
1. The teaching hours of foreign language (English) and mathematics at junior high school are flexible in order to meet actual local requirements.
2. In the second year of junior high school, plantation of agricultural products, drawing and abacus are electives. The student may elect any one of the three courses for two hours weekly.
3. In the third year of junior high school, electives are divided into two categories, namely, professional electives and other electives. The former is again divided into agriculture (including agricultural plantation, agricultural processing, poultry and animal raising courses), industry (including drawing, metal works, and electronic works courses), commerce (including abacus, bookkeeping, and statistical drawing courses), home economics (including meal management, dress-making and home electrical appliances courses). The latter is subdivided into natural science, English, music and art courses. Industrial courses have 4-6 hours weekly, while other courses are two hours each week. The student must elect two courses out of the two-hour weekly courses with at least one professional course, or three courses with at least two professional courses. But only one elective from industrial courses is required.
4. One hour each week for weekly-meeting, and extracurricular activities in junior high school are not included in this list.

Teaching Subjects and Weekly Teaching Hours
In Senior High Schools

	(A) Major in Natural Sciences						(B) Major in Social Sciences					
Grade	1		2		3		1		2		3	
(Semester)	I	II	I	II	I	II	I	II	I	II	I	II
Chinese	6	6	5	5	5	5	6	6	7	7	7	7
English	6	6	5	5	5	5	6	6	7	7	7	7
Civics	2	2	2	2			2	2	2	2		
Three Principles of the People					2	2					2	2
History	2	2	2	2			2	2	2	2		
History of Chinese Culture											2	2
Geography	2	2	2	2			2	2	2	2	2	2
Mathematics	4	4	6	6	6	6	4	4	4	4	4	4
Physics					6	6					3	3
Chemistry			6	6					3	3		
Biology	3	3					3	3				
Earth Science					2	2						
Physical Education	2	2	2	2	2	2	2	2	2	2	2	2
Music	1	1	1	1			1	1	1	1		
Fine Arts	1	1	1	1			1	1	1	1		
Industrial Arts (Home Economics for girls)	2	2	2	2			2	2				
Military Training (military Training & Nursing for girls)	2	2	2	2	2	2	2	2	2	2	2	2
Selective Subjects					2 ≀ 6 ≀ 32	2 ≀ 6 ≀ 32					2 ≀ 5 ≀ 33	2 ≀ 5 ≀ 33
TOTAL	33	33	36	36	36	36	33	33	35	35	36	36

2. The Educational Ladder

William J. F. Lew

The educational ladder starts at the kindergarten level, and ends with graduate school, either at home or abroad. Now there are more Taiwanese than mainlanders at every rung of the ladder. Elementary education is compulsory. Since 1968, free education has been extended to nine years, encompassing the six-year elementary school and the three year junior high school. To popularize education still further, tuition at the upper levels is standardized at an extremely low rate. For the academic year 1975-76, for example, tuition per semester at a public university was $60, and $170 at a private university.

Contrary to the Chinese tradition favoring large families, Taiwan reluctantly, but successfully launched a family planning program in the early 1960's. The birth rate has now declined from a high of five percent in 1951 to 1.8 percent in 1974, a figure lower than for most other Asian countries . . .

The Ministry of Education has recently completed a census of mentally retarded and physically handicapped children, who are said to total 42,560. Of these, 25,566 are already in school; and when special education programs are fully implemented, 100 percent attendance of school-age children in elementary schools may be expected.

To popularize education, and eliminate the detrimental effects of competitive entrance examinations on mental and physical health, the government in 1968 extended free basic education from six to nine years. Although not compulsory, every child who graduates from elementary school is entitled to go on to public junior high school in the district where he resides. In consequence, the percentage of elementary school graduates entering junior high school has been increasing. The greater percentage of boys over girls entering junior high schools may reflect traditional sex discrimination by some parents (usually among the lower socioeconomic class). The gradual narrowing of the difference between sexes from 22 percent in 1967-68 to ten percent in 1975-76 therefore signifies an important social development.

The junior high school provides both general and vocational education. Since 1950, an average of 75 percent of junior high school graduates have gone on to senior secondary schools of various types. Those who do not seek further schooling are quickly absorbed by the labor market. Female factory workers are in even greater demand than males. Indeed, special arrangements were made for girls of the 1976 graduating class to leave school one or two months early in order to meet the urgent demands of industry. To improve their marketable skills, the government is planning to provide compulsory vocational training on a part-time basis for junior high school students who do not continue formal education.

There are two major types of senior secondary or high schools: academic and vocational. To meet the growing need for medium-level manpower in business and industry, efforts have been made to open new vocational high schools as well as to expand existing ones. Since 1971, students in vocational schools have outnumbered those in academic schools. While enrollments in vocational schools have grown steadily in the past quarter of a century, the number of students in academic schools began to decline in 1973. This is an exceptional development. In other Asian countries, such as Japan, senior secondary schools are predominantly academic in nature.

In a further effort to promote vocational education at the secondary level and to alleviate the congestion in academic high schools, five-year junior colleges—for the most part privately operated—were inaugurated in the early 1960's. In such colleges, general education at the senior high school level is offered during the first three years, and vocational training at what is actually the junior college level is provided during the last two years. It has been estimated that of all junior high school graduates seeking further education in 1975, 45 percent were admitted to vocational high schools, 35 percent to academic high schools, and 15 percent to the five-year junior colleges. The remaining five percent entered the nine five-

From William J. F. Lew, "Education in Taiwan: Trends and Problems," *Asian Affairs*, Vol. 3, No. 5 (May-June, 1978), pp. 317-322. Footnotes omitted.

year junior normal colleges for elementary school teachers, the four three-year military academy preparatory schools, and numerous private preparatory schools which offer short-term courses preparing students for entrance examinations to senior high schools and colleges.

Despite the face that congestion in the academic high schools has been somwhat alleviated in recent years, competition to get into the "good" schools (usually government-supported) via the entrance examination remains keen. To some extent, this competition distorts education in the junior high school, which is primarily involved in mass preparation for the academic high school. A substantial number of candidates choose public vocational or private academic schools after they have failed to gain admission to the public academic schools.

The competition is even more severe when it comes to the joint entrance examination held each Summer to select applicants to the nine universities and 15 senior colleges. Graduates from vocational high schools, though at a disadvantage when competing with those from academic schools, are also eligible to take the examination if they wish to do so. While most of the 76 junior colleges offer five-year programs, there are several two-year and three-year junior colleges or technical institutes that also select their students from among senior secondary school graduates. Since 1950, an average of 72 percent of academic high school graduates have been admitted to colleges and universities, while only ten percent of vocational high school graduates were admitted.

Since many private schools and colleges are either profit-making or inadequately funded, government-supported schools generally enjoy higher prestige. Of the nine universities, six are operated by the national government and three by churches (one Catholic and two Protestant). Only one of them—National Taiwan University with 12,852 students—had an enrollment over 10,000 in 1974-75. In addition, three private senior colleges were also at this level—Tanchiang College of Arts and Sciences (14,546), the College of Chinese Culture (13,905), and Fengchia College of Commerce and Technology (11,302).

It must not be inferred, however, from the relatively small enrollments at colleges and universities that the number of applicants is limited. It is the policy of the more prestigious institutions (as well as the government) deliberately to restrict enrollment in order to maintain the quality of higher education and, more importantly, to prevent unemployment and underemployment of college and university graduates.

During the past decade, the number of applicants taking the joint entrance examination increased from 49,141 in 1966 to 98,073 in 1973. The percentage of those admitted to institutions of higher learning decreased from 39 percent in 1966 to 30 percent in 1973. In a recent three-year period, the number of applicants stabilized at 93,205 in 1974, 97,859 in 1975, and 94,807 in 1976. The percentage admitted to the universities and colleges has also hovered around 30 percent. This stabilization is certainly an encouraging development. Counting those admitted to the evening divisions of some institutions and to the military academies (which assume the status of senior colleges), an estimated 60 percent of all applicants have been admitted to institutions of higher education in recent years— about 75 percent of academic high school graduates and 20 percent of vocational high school graduates.

The issue of whether higher education should be selective or universal has been much debated. The government has been severely criticized for failing to meet the demand for more colleges and universities, and for more places in existing ones, but continues to adhere to a restrictive policy. Presumably this stems from a perception that the expansion of formal education is not always to be equated with national development. As unemployment or underemployment spreads among degree holders (including Ph.D.s) not only in Asian countries such as India and the Philippines, but also in advanced Western countries, the situation must be kept under control in order that economic growth and social development will not be impeded.

Another way to prevent unemployment among college and university graduates is to allow them to go abroad for further education, and to remain abroad if they so desire. Although local universities have graduate schools offering Master's and doctoral programs, most of those who aspire to advanced degrees prefer to go to some developed country if they are academically and financially capable of doing so. Nearly 90 percent of those studying abroad have gone to the United States. Students from Taiwan constitute one of the largest foreign student populations in this country. Of the 219,721 foreign students in America during the academic year 1974-75, 10,250 were from Taiwan. In contrast with most other countries, the great majority of students from Taiwan were attending graduate school, since normally only students who have already graduated from colleges and universities in Taiwan are allowed to study abroad . . .

As has been implied by the foregoing, education in Taiwan has been effectively geared to economic development. The political situation has remained stable; and coupled with this political stability, education under a centralized system has contributed significantly to the ROC's widely reported economic growth.

Education is not only a chief determinant of economic growth, but also a key factor in political development. It goes without saying that economic growth and political development are closely interrelated. It has been Taiwan's governing philosophy since 1949 that no national development is possible without social and political stability; hence the slogan, "progress with stability." Today, Taiwan enjoys as much political stability as any country in Asia, and a major reason for this has been the success of political socialization through education and mass communications. While support for the regime is not uniform across the society, and dissenting voices may still be heard at home and abroad, few people on the island would like to see Taiwan become part of the People's Republic of China. It is also something of a miracle in international politics that although the ROC lost its seat in the United Nations in 1971 and is now recognized by only 27 countries, Taiwan seems to be growing stronger in both political and economic terms.

But in spite of its accomplishments, Taiwan's educational system is not without problems. It may be worthwhile to examine some of them briefly.

Entrance Examinations. The most serious problem seems to be the entrance examination, first to senior high school and then to colleges and universities. While it is carefully administered, the examination has at least three disadvantages: (1) In order to allow efficient grading by computer, tests must be constructed for objective, rather than creative, reponses. (2) Examination results are the sole yardstick for the selection of students, ignoring entirely the cumulative record in schools at a lower level. (3) The Entrance examination is held only once a year; anyone who fails must wait for a whole year in order to try again.

The most obvious shortcoming of the entrance examination is that it is generally a test of factual knowledge, with insufficient stress on synthesis and creativity. This tends to shape the pattern of instruction in the educational levels below. Thus in elementary and secondary schools alike, teaching is formal and rigid, with much emphasis on drill and homework; pupils are frequently tested, usually weekly and sometimes daily. Class size ranges from 45 to 55. Although academic standards are high in comparison with Western schools, overreliance on memorization in teaching and testing, plus the traditional Chinese emphasis upon conformity, discourages creative and critical thinking in the learning process, and thereby hinders intellectual development.

Development of the Young. A related problem is the overemphasis on academic achievement in elementary and secondary schools to the neglect of social, emotional, and physical development. As a result, extracurricular activities are given only superficial attention. Students are overburdened with constant tests and daily homework without sufficient time for rest and recreation. This, plus a rigid lecture method of instruction, authoritarian teachers, and parental pressures in the form of high expectations, has made the average Chinese student in Taiwan more hardworking, submissive, and reserved, and less creative and flexible than his Western counterpart . . .

3. The Educational Reform

F. A. Lumley

For the first 15 years after 1945 the educational expansion proved a great success, but by the sixties the demand for knowledge was creating its own problems, closely allied to the population explosion. The faults of traditional methods became apparent; vocational and technical education remained subordinate to the academic; while the six-year period of free schooling was insufficient for the children of poor families. In 1968 the period was extended to nine years. Demand for places has meant that entrance examinations have become increasingly stringent, and the number of drop-outs has caused some anxiety. The Ministry has been forced to bring to bear a new concept of more functional training, introducing vocational and technical courses from the 10th grade, with programmes ranging from three to five years.

The results are beginning to be felt. In 1963 over 60 per cent of students were at high school and only 40 per cent at technical and vocational colleges. Figures have now been reversed to 45 per cent and 55 per cent respectively, while in the next few years the figure of 40 per cent at high school and 60 per cent at technical and vocational colleges should become stabilized. In the school year 1975 there were 4,450 schools at all levels. Full-time teachers numbered 143,968 for 4,448,587 students. The schools may be divided into kindergarten, mostly private, public ones accounting for less than 10 per cent, usually affiliated with public elementary schools. Elementary schools are mainly public (only 1 per cent private) and junior high schools are also mainly run by the government (only 10 per cent in private hands). In the category of the senior secondary school, only 20 per cent are private. Vocational schools, since the introduction of the nine-year free education program, are now at senior level.

In recent years the government has been encouraging, at the junior college level, the opening of private schools, now twice as numerous as public ones. In the cases of universities and colleges, numbers of schools and students are about equal in both public and private, though the public ones have more full-time staff; similarly, the graduate schools of research centers are all affiliated with public and private universities and independent colleges. The numbers of private research institutes and students are fewer than the public ones.

There is no religious teaching. Another feature is the relationship between the private and the public school facilities. At the primary level only 5 per cent of children go to private schools. At the secondary level 25 per cent go to private schools, while in the higher education field 50 per cent of enrollments are in private colleges, high schools and universities. Around 70 per cent of those who sit the university entrance examinations pass; those who fail may sit again later. Though the majority of universities in cities are not residential, a growing number of campuses are organized on American lines. In 1972 there were 9 universities, 14 colleges, 76 junior colleges and 129 graduate institutes in the field of higher education, with over 1 quarter of a million students—36 times the number of students in higher education in 1950.

The most controversial aspect of university and college courses in Taiwan is the arbitrary way prospective students state their order of preference for both faculties and places. Theoretically such a freedom of choice might be thought to ensure that a student follows the course he or she wants, but in practice it can lead to an unsatisfactory compromise. Each student states his priorities for university (or college) and subject; selection is also based on the score achieved in the entrance exam. Many students, however, prefer to stay with their parents instead of going to a residential campus. In cities like Taipei the demand for entrance at, for example, the National Taiwan University is much higher than for a campus situated in an isolated part of the island. A student who had intended to study law, therefore, in order to stay in Taipei may prefer to follow a course in another faculty, should the law one

From F. A. Lumley, *The Republic of China Under Chiang Kai-shek — Taiwan Today* (London: Barrie and Jenkins, 1976), pp. 79-83.

no longer be available, rather than read law elsewhere. Meanwhile the Ministry of Education has to make serious long-term decisions; even over whether Taiwan is not in certain fields educating too many students. Is it possible to make long-term plans in education at all, without closely considering the needs of the economic plans, and forecasts? The very existence of a quota system in education has been questioned; should a government decide how many lawyers, engineers, doctors or scientists there should be? Or on the other hand can the expense of unlimited education in fields where there is little likelihood of subsequent employment be justified?

In Taiwan back in 1955 the Nationalist government decided to promote nuclear research and established the Institute of Nuclear Science Research as part of the graduate school of Tsing Hua, which was re-opened, with the aim of creating in Taiwan an equivalent of the Massachussets Institute of Technology. This was to be the first Nuclear Institute in Asia, before the founding of the Japan Atomic Energy research Institute.

The Tsing Hua University grew from a graduate institute with 20 students in 1957, with the addition of the Institute of Mathematics in 1963, the Institute of Physics in 1966, the Institute of Chemistry in 1968, and in 1970 the Institutes of Nuclear Engineering, Applied Chemistry and Applied Mathematics, Applied Physics, and Materials Science and Engineering. In 1972 the Institutes of Power Mechanical Engineering and Industrial Chemistry were added. The undergraduate departments now include Chemistry, Industrial Chemistry, Materials Science and Engineering, Mathematics, Nuclear Engineering, Physics, and Power Mechanical Engineering. There are at present 1,300 students (of whom 100 are women) 300 of them post-graduate researchers. The teaching staff consists of 140 permanent faculty members and 50 visiting professors from overseas.

Research includes the carrying out of co-operative projects with, among others, the U.S. Argonne National Laboratory and the Japan Atomic Energy Research Institute. The objectives of the university include the promotion of the peaceful applications of nuclear energy and the training of young scientists.

The development of nuclear science and technology in particular has been made possible because of the research nuclear reactor (Tsing Hua open pool reactor—THOR) and the Van de Graaf accelerator. The nuclear reactor section has answered requests from all over the island to utilize the THOR for irradiation purposes, and several requests have come from overseas areas such as the Philippines—mainly from medical and agricultural circles.

The question must remain unanswered whether through her advanced nuclear research Taiwan plans to follow the Indian example and become a member of the nuclear club, with nuclear weapons as the main support of her defense if and when the American nuclear umbrella is removed. The task would not be difficult, for to date Taiwan has five nuclear research reactors, four of which are fueled with 20 per cent enriched uranium sold to Taiwan by the United States, which keeps close watch on the fuel and the by-products, such as plutonium, that it generates. The fifth reactor, of Canadian origin, being built for the Institute of Nuclear Energy Research is understood to be capable of producing about 22 pounds of plutonium a year—more than enough plutonium to fashion a nuclear weapon. It is the first reactor to be fueled with natural uranium, which can be purchased on the open market, whereas enriched uranium is sold only by the United States and the Soviet Union under agreement.

In one generation educational reforms have transformed Taiwan, enabling her to cope with whatever technological demands arise, with knowledge and know-how on par with many industrial giants.

Part II
Social and Economic Implications in Education
4. Effects of the Land Reform on Education

Martin M. C. Yang

Formal education gave to farm people, who had been largely illiterate and, therefore, looked down upon, some social status and a feeling that "I am as good as others." Such status and feeling can be of significant help in getting a farmer to join to some sort of social life or group activity. But it is not invariably so for every person. Farmer Wang may be a graduate of the township's First Primary School, but may yet feel that he is nobody and so refuse to participate in the parents' association on behalf of his children.

In rural Taiwan today there are numerous organizations and activities which give farm people both practical education and some social experience. They are learning to produce, whether in farming or related businesses, more efficiently and more profitably. But since this teaching is always conducted through doing, and the doing always involves group cooperation and, therefore, new personal interrelationships, the whole process of this kind of education is actually a new social life. This aspect of rural life can be much better evaluated today through the functions of the educational organizations than through the traditional social or civic collections. Since the most active organizations among farm people are created by, or related to, the agricultural-extension service, it is necessary to understand this function of education in Taiwan.

Farm organizations sponsored by farmers' associations. Agricultural-extension services conducted by the farmers' associations exist in three main branches: The Farm Advising Program, the Home Economics Teaching Program, and the rural youth or 4-H Club Program. The chief task of the Advising Program is to acquaint the farmers with new and better crops, farm planning and management, techniques and implements, agricultural economics, and marketing. The Home Economics Program teaches farm women new and better ideas, methods, and materials in homemaking and how to build a satisfactory home life. The 4-H Club's work is to inspire young boys and girls to become good citizens through learning skills and discipline, and by providing them with information which will lead to good citizenship. Principal methods and mechanisms used in these programs are personal contact, group projects, and community organization. It is the down-to-earthness which makes this type of education more effective than others in turning a timid, group-shy farmer into a community-participation man.

The extension services undertaken by the other agencies have been primarily limited to farm advising. But the Taiwan Sugar Corporation has recently broadened the scope of its service, and its programs now cover virtually all the subject matter and interests described in the foregoing and employ the same methods and mechanisms.

Extension education fairly well blanketed rural Taiwan ten years after land reform: In 1964 85 per cent of the township-level farmers' associations were conducting extension programs. Each township had one farmers' association, so this meant that 85 per cent of Taiwan had agricultural-extension services. In 95 per cent of the townships, farm-advising service directly, or indirectly, reached all farm people. There were 544 township-level farm advisors and 35 county-level farm supervisors in 1966. About 50 per cent of all farm villages had agricultural demonstration projects. To emphasize the principle of working through group organizations, a number of extension supervisory committees were established. In 1960 these committees involved 316 persons on the county level, 2,772 persons at the township level, and 14,129 persons at the village level. Members of the township and village committees were, with but a few exceptions, farm people. There were also 2,668 village supervisory committees, and each committee averaged 5 or 6 members.

From Martin M. C. Yang, *Socio-Economic Results of Land Reform in Taiwan* (Honolulu, HI.: East-West Center Press, 1970), pp. 389-414. Reprinted by permission of the University Press of Hawaii, copyright 1970 by the East-West Center Press. Footnotes omitted.

The most important extension unit at the village level is the farm-study class. A total of 4,416 such classes with 78,700 members were recorded in 1966. Members of these classes were adult farmers. At a farm-study class the farmers, the extension agent, and, on some occasions, a farm specialist gathered together to discuss some particular problem existing in the locality and to exchange knowledge and experience. On some occasions, civic affairs, current problems, and social events were discussed along with farm innovations.

The demonstration-farm-household was another technique through which better methods were shown and the farm people socialized. A demonstration-household was a more advanced or enlightened farm household which was selected to plant a certain proved but not yet extensively adopted crop, using certified cultivation methods. If the result was good, the farm then became a model to demonstrate the new crop and its good points to other Farmers, with the anticipation that they might adopt the new crop and method of cultivation. The chief objectives of such a project were (1) to install the demonstrating farmers as local farm leaders with a considerable amount of socialization and (2) to establish the teaching (demonstrating and showing) and learning (observing) relationship among the farmers themselves. Behind such projects there was the belief that farmers will accept and adopt what they have personally seen to succeed, and that one farm family gains confidence in its own capability after witnessing the success of another farm family. In 1966 there were 4,035 demonstration-farm-households. In 1960 there were 5,051 demonstration fields. To these demonstration fields, 1,744 observation tours were conducted for 120,036 farmers.

The township and village, agricultural-extension, supervisory committees and the village, farm-study classes could also call special meetings to discuss any emergency in farm affairs. Up to the end of 1960, the township supervisory committees had met 355 times for this purpose and 4,147 farmers had participated. The village committees had had 1,685 such meetings involving 17,121 persons. The village, farm-study classes called 14,838 emergency sessions and the farmers attending number 244,544.

There was also short-term job training for local farm leaders. In 1960, 7,958 persons participated in 135 such training meetings at the county level. At the township level 1,604 training meetings were held and 68,106 local leaders attended.

The recently created, and rapidly developing, joint-cultivation system is another effective way of instituting intimate and in-depth community participation. By joint cultivation it is meant that farmers of the same village who have adjacent fields enter into agreement to plant, cultivate, and harvest their crops cooperatively. They work together and pool farm implements.

There is no need to emphasize that by joining in these joint-cultivation projects, the farmers and their families enjoyed a much fuller social life. The chief group activities in such projects are discussion study and talks centered on the dissemination of agricultural information, the exchange of experience, and the exploration of new crops, improved cultivation methods, better farm tools, etc. Recreation and civic discussion were secondary, but they served to make the meetings interesting and offered a change in the farm people's tiring routine. Participation was largely voluntary, but sometimes persuasion was necessary. Meetings were held in seasons when they would least interfere with the operation of the farm. And, importantly, there was almost no political talk or partisan indoctrination.

The home economics branch of agricultural-extension education had programs designed to get farm women and girls into group activities. In 1966 they were staffed by 235, township-level home economics demonstration agents employed by the farmers' associations and 4,488 volunteer local leaders. There were 2,244 home improvement study classes with a membership of 40,452 women. In addition, 1,201 irregular or emergency meetings, held to discuss special homemaking problems or topics, were attended by 38,301 women. Children's centers were operated in busy farm seasons. These centers had 1,522 classes in 1966 and enrolled 70,840 children. Large numbers of farm women were directly or indirectly involved in these projects, and they were effective in putting farm wives in touch with each other. Out of such interrelationships, community cooperation is born and strengthened. In addition to regular business meetings, the home-improvement classes sponsored home-industry training: weaving, knitting and sewing. There were, in 1966, a total of 558 such classes attended by 26,781 rural women.

Farm women's community participation can also be seen in the implementation of the various home-life improvement programs where women of different households, and different communities, work together. Thus, each woman's mind and world were widened. In 1966, there were 68,067 home-life improvement projects carried out in rural homes.

To bring knowledge and socializing to the farm boys and girls under the age of 25, there were 4-H clubs with their work, civic, and recreational projects. The chief function of 4-H clubs is to plan and carry through various group activities among rural youth related to farm production, home improvement, health buildings, recreation, civic exercise, and trade-skill training. At the end of 1964 there were 351 4-H club advisors or organizers, 4,756 local volunteer leaders, of whom about three-fifths were men and two-fifths were women. These clubs had a membership of 64,825, of whom 42,767 were male and 22,058 were female. These members undertook 4,867 work projects with an average participation of 13 boys and/or girls.

In addition to the regular work projects and work discussion meetings, 4-H club members organized recreational activities such as movies and stage plays. In 1964 they put on 1,610 shows and involved 449,589 farm people. In 1966 the 4-H club members banded themselves into groups or teams and went into such community work projects as planting and caring for trees along public highways, construction or repair of village roads, helping farmers in rice transplanting and in the sterilization of rice nurseries, eradicating rats and insect eggs in the rice fields, building or repairing irrigation canals, weeding rice fields, cleaning ditches and drains, and repairing dams. Altogether, 102,179 young people participated in these activities which had both economic and social values.

4-H clubs also conducted method demonstrations for their own members and for other farm young people. In 1959, 3,743 method demonstrations were attended by 13,956 young people who learned new ways of doing things and also enjoyed the experience of group life. The numbers of members who participated in such programs as *kuo-yü* (Mandarin Chinese) speech contests, demonstration talks, achievement-judging contests, educational tours, and physical check-ups were 2,264, 4,408, 13,668, 27,618, and 12,417, respectively.

These statistics show that in the seven years between 1959 and 1966, the farmers' association-sponsored, agricultural-extension service alone had been able to get about two million farm people, including men, women, and youth, into active community participation.

Farm organizations sponsored by the Taiwan Sugar Corporation. Each year there are, on the average, about 150,000 private sugarcane growers. These are the objects of the services of Taiwan Sugar's agricultural-extension branch. The corporation regularly employs an extension staff of 1,700.

Formerly, the Taiwan Sugar Corporation did its extension work mostly through individual contacts. Its extension men went to grower households one by one, to encourage the farmers to plant more hectares in sugarcane and to teach them the best know-how for growing the crop. In recent years, however, extension personnel of the corporation have been deeply impressed by the conspicuous success of the extension work done through the various farmers' organizations. Because of this, the extension branch of the corporation also began to encourage and assist the sugarcane growers to organize themselves into study groups. At the end of 1966, more than 600 such classes were functioning. Each class averaged 20 to 30 active members. . . .

Today the membership of these classes must be around fifteen thousand. According to the corporation's personnel who were in charge, they plan to establish 5,100 classes within a period of ten years. When this goal has been reached, there will be more than 150,000 sugarcane-growing households participating in these classes. Assuming that each household averages three adult persons, there will be 450,000 farm people in direct or indirect community participation through this program.

The sugarcane growers' class is, in principle, a village-level organization. The growers of each village organized into one, two, or more study groups. Each group was to have from 25 to 30 members. Under ordinary conditions, one village will have from 25 to 60 households growing sugarcane. If they number more than 40 but less than 60, there should be two classes. All sugarcane growers whose ages were between 20 and 45 could join the classes, or were persuaded to join. But they must be literate, or have had a least one primary-school education. Each class elected its president, vice president, and secretary. All affairs of the class were democratically managed by the officers and members themselves, but the class was supervised and assisted by the local township government, the township farmers' association, and the corporation's branch office or plant located in the vicinity.

The reason for describing the activities of the farmers' associations at such length is the need to show that farmers in Taiwan have already been deeply involved in, and affected by, the farmers' associations. In this involvement, the associations help make farming progressive and farm life prosperous, and, in return, the farmers give life and power to the associations. This is community participation in its full and democratic meaning.

Land Reform and Community Participation

More than 62 per cent of the former tenants said it was land reform that aroused community spirit in them, and it was land reform that caused them to foresee the benefits of being members of community organizations. More then 44 per cent claimed that their becoming community-minded was chiefly due to the improvement of their living conditions following land reform. If the improvement of living conditions in these households was, for the most part, attributable to land reform, then the rise of community spirit in these households can also be considered a result of land reform, although an indirect result.

In general, whether people have or do not have a lasting interest in any kind of community organization or group activity depends to a great extent on whether they have a role, and particularly an important role, to play in the organization or activity. About 36 per cent of the former tenants admitted that their satisfying experience in the various organizations was due largely to the fact that they had specific roles and that these roles were, in most cases, more important than those they had had occasionally before. The reason for their having been assigned more important roles was that they had become farm owners. In community organizations owner-farmers' positions are usually higher than those held by tenants. •

According to information presented elsewhere in this study, those farmers who were still tenants at the time of the research conducted themselves much the same as did the former-tenant-now-owners, in respect to community constructions and social-welfare programs. Their households had not acquired owner status, but they had been beneficially affected by land reform. The rent limitation program not only released tenants from the heavy burden of high rental, and so increased their annual income, it also rid them of the feelings of fear, humiliation, and inferiority they had had in relations with their landlords. Since land reform, tenants and landlords have really been standing in equal positions. If this has not as yet been entirely realized in their material possessions, it has been clarified in social and psychological relations. With improved income and bettered social position, and with awareness of a new freedom from fear and humiliation, today's tenant-farmers have morale and ambition equal to the owner-farmers. If the former-tenant-now-owner's newly aroused or increased interest in community participation was a product of the land-to-the-tiller program, the current tenant's new interest must have been due to the rent limitation program. . . .

In the countryside, even today, one's education or lack of it has, in many cases, great bearing on one's feeling at ease and respected in a community organization. It is true that some people will be shy and timid in group relations whatever their education; nevertheless, it is commonly acknowledged that educated people have the greatest potentiality for important roles, feeling assured, finding enjoyment, and contributing much toward the fulfillment of joint purposes in group activities. At any rate, it is safe to say that education is a prerequisite for spontaneous and satisfying community participation. The influence of education is not limited in the sense that the farmers themselves must be educated; just having their children in school could have about the same effect. There is no question but that many small or tenant-farmers have risen in social status since land reform because of their children's education. It could be very possible that it was this very fact that has made them no longer the grass-seed, ignored, poor-peasant type of farmers.

5. Education in Taiwan Villages

A. Elementary school in *Hsinchuang*

Hsi Ju-chi

There are four villages situated on the ridge of Tatu Hill: Hsinchuang, Nanliao, Juiching, and Chepu. The two former villages are in Lungching Hsiang, i.e., Township, and the latter two villages are in Tatu Hsiang. Administratively, both Lungching Hsiang and Tatu Hsiang are in Taichung Hsien, i.e., County. Geographically, these frontier-like villages are situated in a mountainous area which is unique. There is a primary school in Hsinchuang which is attended by children from all four villages. It is this school which is the subject of our report.

About forty years ago Hsinchuang built its first one-room schoolhouse. Today, the Lungfeng Elementary School is crowded with more than a thousand schoolchildren. The main purposes of this report are to trace the historical development of the school and to describe its current situation and its activities in the rural area it serves. A brief biography of a local teacher is also given to show the role and status of the teacher in the community. The data of this report were obtained through field observations and intensive interviews by the present writer and some senior students of the Department of Sociology at Tunghai University.

Before the time when the one-room schoolhouse was built in Hsinchuang, the number of children in the four villages who attended school was quite small. Some attended the elementary school in Lung ch'üan, situated on the western slope of Tatu Hill. The distance from their homes to the school was considerable. It took about one hour and forty minutes for them to walk up and down the hillside paths to get there. Most of these schoolchildren were boys, who were more energetic than girls in making such a long trip every day. Even now, since the families of cane farmers need several helpers either in the household or in the fields, daughters frequently are not sent to school. Most farmers think that formal schooling for boys is more important than for girls. This is a vestige of the situation which existed forty years ago. Then, public opinion held that it was not worthwhile to educate girls.

In 1920 a one-room school was built in Hsinchuang. Later on the school building was enlarged and the number of pupils increased. Up to the time of the restoration of Taiwan to China in 1945, there was a total of eleven classes in six grades at the school. In the spring of 1946 all the Japanese teachers were repatriated, and the school was reorganized as the Lungfeng Elementary School. In December of 1960 there were 18 classes, from the first grade through the sixth grade, totaling 988 pupils. Of these 549 were boys and 439 were girls. The average class had 60 pupils. Since there were only 14 classrooms at the school then, the pupils in the first through the third grades were (and still are) attending only half-day sessions, either in the morning or in the afternoon. As elsewhere on Taiwan, this is called "the Dual System."

There are 21 staff and teachers in the school now: the principal, the superintendent of teaching affairs, and 19 teachers, one for each class, including the kindergarten, which offers a two-year, preschool source. Most of the staff are Taiwanese (13 of 21 teachers and staff), six are from Shantung, and two are from Kiangsu and Hopei. Only three of the twenty-one teachers are female, and they all teach the lower grades. As the school is in a frontier-like mountain area, most of the teachers are not likely to stay permanently in the village offering their services to people who need to be educated, except for some native-born teachers whose homes are in Hsinchuang or in the villages nearby. Because school-

From Mark C. Thelin, ed., *Two Taiwanese Villages* (New York: United Board for Christian Higher Education in Asia, [1976]), pp. 48-54. Footnotes omitted.

teachers are appointed by the Department of Education in the Hsien (County) Office, some Mainlanders have earnestly applied for transfer to the urban area, but only a few have succeeded. Seven teachers are living in houses owned by the school in the village. Four commute from Ch'ingshui and Shalu. The others are staying with their families in their homes in Hsinchang or in the nearby villages. . . .

As elementary education is compulsory in Taiwan, there are no tuition fees from the first through the sixth grades, and all the textbooks are supplied and distributed by the government. But, as reported by our informants, each pupil contributes about NT$50 per semester as contributions for the PTA, the fund for the encouragement of military personnel, fees for the pupils' clubs, the fund for teachers as an expression of esteem, and the usual charges for notebooks, paper, etc. Most parents in the village have no such amount of cash in hand for their children to pay it all at once to the school. The solution to this difficulty is to make collections separately, even if the amount is only one or two dollars at one time. This is a convenient and satisfactory way as far as both sides are concerned. The regular administrative expenses of the entire school are limited to NT$500 per month. For other expenditures the limit is NT$85 for each class per semester. All these funds are supplied by the Educational Affairs Section of the County Government Office. In 1961 the regular administrative expenses at the Lungfeng Elementary School amounted to slightly less than NT$10,000. The deficiency between this figure and the amount furnished by the County Office was made up from other sources such as the County Governments contingency account, or from the PTA. As Mr. Wang Pai-nien said, "All the parents of our pupils are legally members of the PTA, so each must contribute NT$5.00 per semester to a fund which can be used to defray the school expenses." . . .

In regard to the attendance rate of school-age children in this rural area, there are different figures from different sources. According to the principal of this elementary school, attendance ranges from 95% to 97% of the nearly 1,000 students enrolled.

The content of the subjects taught is regulated by the Ministry of Education. The textbooks used by the children are printed by the Provincial Government and are distributed free to each child in each class. The subjects of study in the fifth and sixth grades include Chinese, arithmetic, "social science" (which covers civics, history, and geography), and natural science. Besides these there are "the technical subjects" which include fine arts, physical education, music, and labor education (periodic sweeping and cleaning of classrooms and classroom equipment). Children in the lower grades (Grades 1 through 4) study three subjects, Chinese, arithmetic, and "general knowledge."

The official language of instruction is Mandarin Chinese, but most of the pupils and teachers are Taiwanese who speak the Amoy dialect, except for those who have come from Mainland China since 1945. At the beginning of the first grade, the children learn the *Chu Yin Fu Hao*, the national phonetic symbols. Several weeks later, they begin to read textbooks in which the *Chu Yin Fu Hao* symbols appear alongside the Chinese characters. It is in this way that the children learn to speak and to read Mandarin as quickly as possible. In Hsinchuang, however, the teaching of Mandarin is not as successful as at other places in Taiwan. The situation is very much like that of teaching English in Chinese schools. Most people in Hsinchuang speak the Amoy dialect, so there is no fundamental need for them to use Mandarin to communicate with each other in their daily activities and, thus, there is little opportunity for effectively practicing it.

The daily schedule is very busy for all the pupils and teachers. At 7:50 in the morning, there is an assembly of all teachers and pupils on the playground for the flag-raising ceremony. After that four class periods occupy the time until noon. When the lunch hour is over, there are another three class periods, each lasting from thirty to forty-five minutes, according to the importance of the subjects scheduled.

The main defects in the system of rural education are in terms of the content of the subjects which are being taught at the elementary level. The important things the pupils want to know are the ways through which they may improve their living standards, but what they learn in school is not directly related to this interest. It would help if the children could be taught how to plant sugarcane, how to use improved implements to increase crop production, or how to use the fertilizer needed to enrich the fields. They are only being taught how to pass the competitive examinations for entrance into junior middle (high) school, as are children of the urban areas.

The situation has an additional complication: the classrooms are very crowded, averaging more than 60 children per class. The children can neither effectively nor even satisfactorily carry out the primary purpose of preparing adequately for the highly competitive middle school examinations. Even an energetic teacher cannot take care of a large group of children in one class.

With regard to the harmful "reviewing courses and supplementary classes," the case of the Lungfeng Elementary School is just like that of other schools in Taiwan. When we visited the school in 1960, we noticed that several classrooms were full of children "behind closed doors," and a teacher walked to and fro on tiptoe to supervise them. Whenever a child enters the fifth grade, he is asked whether he wishes to take part in the junior middle school entrance examinations during the following year. If he answer is yes, he is then assigned to a special class to prepare for the coming tests. He must pay extra money to the teachers each month—a fee which ranges from NT$10 to NT$50. The total amount of these extra fees is allocated by the principal to the other senior teachers as "extra payments." If, for one reason or another, a child does not choose to prepare for the entrance examinations, he will be classified as a pupil in another class called "the class preparing for employment," or vocational class. The children in these classes do voluntary services on the campus such as cleanup work and other labor programs in addition to their regular class meetings. . . .

The population of Taiwan has been increasing rapidly, but the number of classrooms has not been increased at the same rate. Other educational facilities have lagged behind, too. All the primary schools are crowded with children, as are the middle schools in Taiwan today. All parents want their children to be educated in the modern school curriculum. They do not care what they learn, only that their children will successfully pass all the competitive examinations from the junior middle school admissions test up through the test for university graduates who wish to study abroad. Both the students and their parents make a great effort to achieve this goal. The means to succeed is to study harder than usual in the supplementary courses, either in their own schools or in the private night classes in supplementary courses offered outside of the school. Some say that the supplementary courses are a necessary evil, even though they are harmful to the health of the children. Some parents in Hsinchuang have the same attitudes as the parents in urban areas. Some villagers do not think it is necessary to send their children to middle school.

B. Education in the Villages: Some Survey Findings

Mark C. Thelin

In each community roughly one-fourth of the males in our sample households six years of age and over have had no formal schooling whatever, while half the females in the same age bracket are similarly classified. As expected, the modal class in both communities is the elementary or grade school level, though it is unusual that more than twice as many males in the Shuichueht'ou as in the Hsinchuang sample have gone no further than Grade 6. The same is true of the females in both communities. We have commented above that Shuichueht'ou is the more "modern" community, yet its women and girls are less well educated than those of Hsinchuang. As for the men and boys, the data show that more have gone further up the ladder of formal education in Shuichueht'ou (including four individuals with at least some college education) than their Hsinchuang counterparts, provided we exclude the junior middle school level (Grades 7 through 9). It seems very unusual, indeed, that such a great disparity exists between communities in the elementary and junior middle school grades. Perhaps a comparatively small group within the sample (shopkeepers or merchants in the "Business" occupational class and civil servants) disproportionately contributes to the upper levels of formal education. Perhaps, also, the age-structure of school-age children in these families may be lacking at the seventh-through-ninth-grade levels. This might account for the "inflated" number of children in Grades 1 through 6 as "compensation" for the dearth of children at the next higher level. It is obvious that a more definitive treatment of this anomalous datum must await further research.

This interpretation would, presumably, hold for formal education among females in our samples as well as males. It seems very unusual that only two female individuals in the Shuichueht'ou sample had received any formal education beyond the sixth grade, especially when 65 females among our Hsinchuang informants had done, or were doing, so. Our hypothesis of disproportionate representation of business and civil servant families might still explain the difference, provided, of course, that the data obtained are reliable.

The data on whether the local school could assist in improving living conditions within the community are revealing. Between one-third and two-fifths of the respondents in Hsinchuang as Schuichueht'ou replied in the negative to the question. It must be kept in mind, of course, that the local school in each case was an elementary school. The negative and "Don't know" opinions may reflect the view that a school would at least have to be a middle (high) school before it might have any significant positive impact on the local community.

Another interpretation could be that formal education is essentially "a consumption commodity" which has little relevance to the main occupation of both communities, i.e., farming. To be sure, our informants quite likely recognize the value of well-learned reading, writing, and arithmetic—particularly in an age when agriculture on Taiwan is becoming increasingly commercial. Courses in hygiene and in the national language (Mandarin Chinese) may be perceived as having utilitarian value, but the content of the curriculum has no direct relevance to farming.

To the contrary, numerous informants may feel that "educating their children out of the village" is a good thing—recognizing that many occupations may be preferable to farming as a way of life. In other words, formal education may increasingly be recognized as the primary ladder of upward social mobility.

6. Political Socialization of the Children

Richard W. Wilson

Years ago Sun Yat-sen, pondering the problems of China's modernization, wrote: "If we are to recover our lost nationalism, we must have some kind of group unity, large group unity." It is, I think, by no means accidental that Sun should have conceived of China's problems in group terms, for the sense of belonging to a group is one of the oldest and most enduring observations that Western analysts have made of the Chinese.

And yet, as Sun's remarks hint, there is also the sense of a lack of group unity, of a need for something that did not exist, for Sun speaks of large group unity and in traditional China it was not the society but the family which absorbed the most intense loyalties. Indeed, of the five ideal Confucian loyalties (subject to ruler, son to father, younger brother to elder brother, wife to husband, and friend to friend) four are on a primary group level of interaction, and three are in the family. The first, subject to ruler, while theoretically perhaps the most powerful bond, was in normal practice so vague and distant as to be almost meaningless in the daily context of mutual rights and obligations. On the other hand, family terms were widely used to describe many relationships and family loyalties seen as the model for all others. This family, of course, was not simply the natural family but often included members of one's extended family and clan as well. These people worked together, lived in the same village, and had a sense of mutual responsibility and identity reinforced by government policies which held all group members mutually responsible for the conduct of each other.

It is the very fact that no individual can escape being a member of some group that makes an investigation of the qualities and aspects of group life essential to an understanding of any society. The types of responsibilities group members owe each other, the strength of internal group cohesion, the attitudes held by members toward other groups, and the ways in which conformity to group norms is enforced are only some of the pertinent questions. In China training for group life is so intensive and begins so early that no study should never be undertaken without a thorough knowledge and grounding in the social framework in which Chinese live.

Yet modern Taiwan is not traditional China, for the focus of group loyalties is enlarging, and while the presence of older loyalties is still easily discernible, one can also detect a new intensity of group loyalty in areas less dominant traditionally. What is happening, in fact, is something very new, the birth of that large group awareness that Sun Yet-sen perceived would be necessary for the creation of a modern society.

Children in Taiwan, even at a very young age, have a developed sense of their membership in society as a whole. Furthermore, at least ideally, they conceive of themselves as having a primary duty and loyalty to society. In giving reasons for why a person should do this or that, why a person has succeeded, or why some person is famous, they will frequently invoke the name of society and do so with evident feelings of conviction. This is more clearly discernible among children than adults but even with the latter there is a recognition of the growing preeminence of society. One friend, discussing face with me, gave as his opinion that face embraces much the same circle of people now as before—friends, classmates, the company one works for, the family, etc.—but at the same time, he said, it is also less strong, particularly in the family. He implicitly recognized that wider loyalties now command attention.

The emotions concerned with face and the loyalties to a group were, in traditional China, involved to a great extent with such primary groups as family or close friends. This focus, however, was always a source of societal disunity and a catalyst to political breakdown. The attempt today is to transform the particularistic relationships that characterized small groups into broader, more universal ones, yet the emotional content of the older particularistic relationship is not so readily changed.

From Richard W. Wilson, *Learning To Be Chinese: The Political Socialization of Children in Taiwan*. (Cambridge, Mass.: The MIT Press, 1970), pp. 43-79. Reprinted by the permission of the MIT Press, Cambridge, Massachusetts.

In Taiwan there is a conscious attempt on the part of the educational authorities to maintain an emotional congruence between already established primary group relationships and the new patterns which are being formed; there is a process of identifying the primary group with the state. To some extent this is similar to traditional Confucian concepts. The difference is that the society's needs and claims are now always and unequivocably given precedence. In a book on elementary school social science teaching methods in Taiwan, the author says: "Social science ought to emphasize the development in children of moral concepts, group consciousness, partriotic thoughts, habits of cooperation, the attitude of service, and the spirit of sacrifice, etc., making children's group sense achieve adequate development." Individual achievement becomes group achievement and the highest emphasis is placed on the society's achievement as a whole. This conception is widespread in education and finds expression in Chiang's statement that "All virtues are based on 'loyalty' and 'filial piety.' To fulfill the principle of complete loyalty to the state [government] and of filial piety toward the nation [people]; to be altruistic and not seek personal advantage; to place the interests of the state ahead of those of the family; such is the highest standard of loyalty and filial piety."

Education may not only develop in the child a sense of awareness of society as a group to which he belongs but also make him aware of, and subject to, the values of that society. The learning process whereby actions are committed in terms of such values is a complicated one. Principles of behavior theory would suggest that a reinforcement in educational materials of certain stimulus and response patterns of primary groups may create similar patterns of behavior with regard to the society.

I was visiting a class in the men's teachers' college in Taipei when the question came up of what was a proper topic of conversation for a speech class in elementary school. After discussion it was agreed that to bring up a topic such as the differences between boys and girls would be wrong. Also inappropriate would be citizenship topics, better left to the citizenship class itself. Fitting topics for discussion would be such items as "My Home" or "How We Should Respect Our Parents." Throughout the elementary school years there is emphasis on home life, linked at the same time with development of general group spirit.

The purposeful development in school of a general group spirit, which must be distinguished from nonpurposeful but equally important aspects of group training, is not without an ultimate goal. Educational authorities seek to create a powerful loyalty to Chinese society and, specifically, to the state as exemplified by the government of the Republic of China (the Kuomintang government). Political training and the rudiments of group discipline begin in kindergarten with flag-raising ceremonies quite formally carried out. There are also, during the term, simple references by the teacher to the Republic of China and the President. In elementary school the flag is introduced into the textbooks and is on the cover of the readers the children use from first through fourth grade, waving over a group of playing children. Such insertions of national symbols are by no means accidental or merely decorative; educational authorities told me that these insertions were made with the definite intention of familiarizing children with an appropriate symbol for the country. The society itself is the object of considerable glorification. In kindergarten children begin to hear "We are Chinese and we all love China. Our China's national territory is the largest, the population the greatest, and our products the most abundant." In fourth grade there is a poem that children chant, each of the three stanzas starting with "China, China, lovable China, there is no other country in all the world greater than you." In the fifth-grade history reader there is a series of lessons on Chinese civilization. One of them makes the statement: "The Republic of China has also the world's most exceptional race. The facts of the following historical examples can prove this . . . Three thousand years ago, while other races of the world were still leading a primitive life, our country had already developed a writing system and simple writing implements . . ." In a sixth-grade history class the children were told about the age of exploration. The topic under discussion was Magellan and his feat of sailing across the Pacific. No mention was made of Magellan's being the first to circumnavigate the globe; the important point was that China could now be reached from the East as well as from the West. Ethnocentrism begins early.

At the same time that children are taught to admire and respect their society, they are also introduced to a conception of priorities with regard to the groups in which they concurrently live. At first educational emphasis is on the fact that aspects of already learned behavior in primary groups are acceptable as a standard in other areas. Thus, in third grade, children will be expected to answer True to a statement in a true-false quiz which says: "In the school we are good students; in society we ought to be good citizens." By fifth grade, in the citizenship reader, children are enjoined to love their relatives, and just as they love them, to love friends, the people, and the country. Start now in school, they are told. There are two stories together in the fifth-grade reading primer of a mother writing to her son. Work for the country, she tells him in the first story, for sons must be brave and mothers must be brave too. Love of country must come before love of family. The moral is repeated in the next lesson when she exhorts him to kill the enemy and be brave, for the country and the people are more important than the family or an individual.

By sixth grade the priorities are expected to be well established. There is a multiple-choice question in a review section on citizenship training where the children are asked: "The responsibility of young people is to (1) read books conscientiously, (2) exercise the body, (3) build society, (4) establish the family." Here all the answers are desirable goals, but, as the principal of the city public school told me, only (3) can be the right answer. The nation as a focus for one's loyalty and effort receives reinforcement outside the school as well. A sign in the T'ao Yuan local government office, for instance, requests the local people to speak Mandarin, for "To speak Mandarin expresses love for one's country." Just as cooperation is stressed as the ideal of group life in general, so patriotism, loyalty and bravery are the specific ideals of the good citizen.

Today in Taiwan the moral influence of the leader is augmented by, and identified with, the state's power and dignity. One educator has stated: "In the modern era the leaders of states not only represent the people's determination and power but at the same time symbolize the state's honor and dignity. Citizens, therefore, ought to express respect toward their leaders." The same writer, talking about the desirability of encouraging children to participate in group activities of service outside the school, had this to say: "In the group, no matter what one's responsibility or work is, one ought to obey the guidance of the leader; if oneself is the leader than even more one must know how to guide others."

The children were asked whether, when they were playing a game with their schoolmates, they were the ones who usually decided what to play. About one third of the children responded that they were the decision makers, a half said they were not, and one sixth admitted that they didn't know. When asked whether they *wanted* to be the one who decided 59.2 percent responded Yes, 27.2 percent responded No or Don't Care, and 13.7 percent said they didn't know. There were no significant differences between Mainlander and Taiwanese children, but there was a significant difference between boys and girls, the boys being slightly higher than the girls in their desire to take command. There was also a significant difference between grades, with the number of Yeses (indicating a desire to be the one who decides) declining (except for a high fifth-grade figure) from 61 percent in first grade to 52.7 percent in sixth grade.

While many children indicate a desire to be a decision maker, the number who so desire decreases with age, presumably as realization of female roles develop. Another important factor could well be an increasing awareness of the necessity for conformity and a hesitancy to be the one to establish a course of action which might possibly challenge an established leader or prove unacceptable to the group, for as children grow older, they show marked increases in their feelings that a leader is necessary for group action. When asked whether a basketball team (basketball is widely played in Taiwan) should have a leader or not, 82.5 percent of the children who were asked said Yes, with a slightly significant increase with age and slightly significant difference between Mainlanders and Taiwanese, the Mainlanders being more emphatic in their desire for a leader. There was no significant difference between boys and girls. When asked to explain why there should be a leader, children almost never responded with such replies as "Because the leader plays the best basketball" or "Because he is the best liked." Rather they saw the leader in groups terms similar to a twelve-year-old sixth-grade mainland boy at the city private school who said that if "there is a team captain, then there will be order, and when they begin to play, no one will be reckless."

If the extent and nature of actual political training in the home is difficult to assess, the emphasis by parents on education as a goal is not. No other topic in Taiwan is of such consuming interest, and children early learn that education is a goal of paramount importance. The emphasis is undoubtedly greater in some homes than in others, the rich versus the poor and the urban versus the rural, for instance, but despite such differences it is a topic generally emphasized throughout the society.

The Schools

In the schools there is a hierarchy of strictly defined roles. At the apex is the principal. Next in rank come the department heads, teachers who spend part, or all, of their time giving overall direction to maintenance, health, curriculum, teachers affairs (absences, changing schools, poor teaching, etc.), and discipline (lining up, regulations, safety outside the school, etc.). Last are the teachers themselves.

Boys seem to be picked more frequently than girls for such jobs as starting games, and this tendency seems to carry over into the selection of class leaders. In the city private school I analyzed the sex of the class leader and assistant class leader for all grades for the spring term of 1965. In all, girls held these posts 19 times versus 17 times for boys. When examined in detail, however, it can be seen that by the upper grades girls are not frequently elected to the top position.

The status of students leaders is quite high, possibly because, according to one teacher, leaders are selected not simply on the basis of intellect but also on the basis of leadership factors. Elections are carried out in class meetings, the procedures for which are precisely set forth. Nominations are made from the floor, and the names are written on the blackboard. In some classes the children then stand up and, with remarkable candor, praise and criticize the candidates for their strong and weak points. The children then write their choice on a piece of paper, fold it, and give it to the row leader, who takes the collected slips to the class leader. After another student has been delegated to observe that the class leader reads the results fairly, the ballots are opened and checks put against the name of each candidate as he receives a vote. There is often much cheering as the result of each ballot is read off. In one case a teacher made comments after the election, saying that the opinion of the class shared by her as this child was very diligent, not naughty, and constantly improving. In this case, at least, the elected child's status is a model for emulation was heavily reinforced by the teacher's praise.

Such respect and concomitant high status are also afforded the teachers and principals themselves. One fourth-grade mainland girl at the city private school described her principal in these glowing terms, "Very nice. When we do somthing wrong, she tenderly talks to us." This recogition of a principal as compassionate and good was shared by a second-grade mainland boy at the same school. He wrote of the meeting scene as one between the parents and the principal after a traffic accident when some children were taken to the hospital. (A tragic bus accident in which many children were killed had taken place shortly before, just outside Taipei.) He makes the principal say: "I feel that your children are my children, so that what has happened to you is just as if it has happened to me. I feel so sorry for you."

There is a conscious attempt in education to utilize the feelings children have toward the teacher and principal. In the second term of fourth grade, for instance, there are three lessons together that clearly reveal this attempt. The primer begins with a story about how studious Sun Yat-sen was. This is followed by a lesson on Lincoln and his love of reading. In the third lesson a teacher praises an industrious student to the class. Political figures are used as models, yet it is the teacher who serves as the one who praises this activity and who sanctions it for the class by his approval.

In the fifth grade there is a story in the primer that categorizes the teacher as loving and nurturing. The children are precious, the teacher says, because they are like a family. Then we get a repetition of the loyalty theme, for the teacher makes his affection conditional upon the absolute acceptance of his authority position. The children are like a family; more than this, the teacher wants the class to be just like a family—responsible and obedient.

At a very early age children develop an awareness of certain national symbols. The generally favorable identification with such symbols is probably due to their association, quite early in the child's experience, with models, such as the principal, who are accepted as leaders in the child's own immediate environment. It seems that a response developed during something like morning exercises, where political symbols and school authority figures are often paired, many generalize to individuals other than some known to the child who is also associated with such symbols. I would posit that the association with the principal and teacher is far more important with respect to learning about specific political symbols than are parents, for school authorities are most closely associated with these symbols. Both parents and teachers provide generalized training in authority situations, but it is in school, under the influence of the school authorities, that organized political learning really begins.

James C. Davis has found that children, by seven years of age, have a warm and positive attachment to their schools, to the beauty of the country, and to the goodness of the people. Attachment to the flag becomes almost religious, with this attitude reaching a plateau by the time children are nine or ten years old. This is certainly true in Taiwan. In the first grade of the city public school, when told to draw pictures of the out-of-doors, 23 of 69 students included the national flag as some part of the picture. In Taiwan, however, the most intense feelings surround not the flag but the political leaders, and there is a conscious effort throughout all the school years to foster and encourage this feeling. This is not to posit, however, that the two symbols are not frequently used to reinforce each other, because they are. Thus, for instance, in the first part of second grade, there is an exercise sentence about every house hanging out the flag and every classroom having a picture of Sun Yat-sen.

7. Political Attitudes of Taiwanese and Mainlander Children: A Comparison

Richard W. Wilson

One of the basic problems bedeviling all current research on modern China is how to test the accuracy and reliability of our assumptions about that society. With no foreseeable hope of doing field studies on the Chinese Mainland and with only a relatively scant flow of refugees coming each year to places like Hong Kong, a complex challenge presents itself. For to lack knowledge of a quarter of the world's people not only is frustrating from an academic point of view but also impoverishes our general national understanding of a society critically important for American foreign policy.

Scholars are facing this challenge by employing a variety of techniques, many of which have led to remarkably insightful and productive results. Careful interviewing, monitoring of broadcasts, and constant and tiring perusal of the written word have all been successfully utilized. Some scholars have gone to other societies in Asia, hopeful that their work there with Chinese minority groups may have broader implications for Chinese society as a whole. Of all such societies it is probably Taiwan which today receives most attention from American scholars. Yet the problem remains that assumptions concerning Chinese society as a whole when tested with regard to a sample on Taiwan may have no real relevance for mainland China. Where relevance is predicated it is done so on the assumption that there are certain basic Chinese values, common to all Chinese people, which derive from a largely similar traditional life experience and are still held by most Chinese despite the recent intrusion into their daily lives of different political systems.

The object of this paper is twofold: first to investigate the differences and similarities in political attitudes between Mainlander and Taiwanese children, the types of political attitudes held and the ways in which they are acquired, and second to make an assessment on the basis of these differences and similarities of the persistence and strength of political culture values in Chinese society as a whole.

The Taiwanese children were born to parents who grew to adulthood in the latter part of Japan's fifty-year domination of the island and who were largely subjected to Japanese political education and other forms of Japanese influence. The Mainlander children, on the other hand, were born into families which fled from the Mainland at the time of the Communist victory. These children have grown up in families which, while influenced by the historical process of Western penetration into China, were on the whole much less subject than the Taiwanese to the systematic efforts of a foreign government to change patterns of allegiance. Clearly, however, while certain life experiences over the last fifty years have been different for Mainlanders and Taiwanese, to the extent that aspects of a similar basic cultural tradition continued to be commonly held by both groups during the period of Japan's domination we would not expect to observe at the present time large differences between Mainlander and Taiwanese children.

Specific Political Learning

Following a test form outlined by Easton and Dennis, a 10-picture symbolic association quiz was given to both Mainlander and Taiwanese school children in order to test their responses toward authority in the context of their national group life (it should be noted that by sixth grade both groups of children on Taiwan had developed strong loyalties to the state as a whole, a not unexpected finding in view of the emphasis in school on group loyalty and loyalty to the state in particular). The pictures, in order, were of a policeman, Sun Yat-sen, Double Ten Day (equivalent to the American Fourth of July), voting, a law court, the Presidential Palace, the Legislative Yuan, the flag, the "Three Principles of the People"

From Richard W. Wilson, "A Comparison of Political Attitudes of Taiwanese Children and Mainlander Children on Taiwan," *Asian Survey* Vol. VIII, No. 12 (December, 1968), pp. 992-998. Copyright 1968 by The Regents of the University of California. Reprinted by permission of The Regents.

(the political ideology of the Kuomintang Party), President Chiang Kai-shek, and a final space for "I Don't Know." From these ten pictures the children were asked to pick two in response to a question asking which two first came to mind when they thought of government. Using the same scoring techniques as Easton and Dennis, where any picture which exceeded 20% or more of the responses was considered significant, it was found that for Chinese children on Taiwan cognitive images of national government centered around four symbolic associations. There were: Sun Yat-sen (55.13%), the flag (26.27%), the "Three Principles of the People" (22.39%), and Chiang Kai-shek (44.59%), from a total from all schools of 540 responses. Mainlander and Taiwanese children from the two public schools both tended to choose the same pictures with slight differences.

On a second question in the symbolic association quiz, scored in the same way, the children were asked: Who makes the laws? (Because there is no tense in Chinese, this question could be read: Who made the laws?) In the responses, four pictures again predominated—Sun Yat-sen, the law court, the Legislative Yuan, and Chiang Kai-shek, with the choice of the Legislative Yuan and Sun Yat-sen tending to increase with age, the law court first increasing and then decreasing, and Chiang decreasing steadily. (The "Three Principles of the People" also tended to be selected by the older children, but it is not included here because on an overall basis it did not achieve the 20% level.) Again, both groups of children responded in the same way and in the same direction with little difference between them.

It is apparent from the evidence presented so far that there is little difference between Mainlander and Taiwanese children with regard to the significant national political symbolic association they hold and to their awareness of who makes the laws. Yet despite the fact that at the national level cognitive associations and awareness of who makes the laws are reasonably similar for both groups of children, there is some evidence that the local political process as such is less salient for Taiwanese children than for Mainlanders, a point made forcefully clear from the responses of the children to questions dealing with political knowledge below the national level. The children were asked if they knew who the head of the city government of Taipei was and how they felt about that person. In terms of gross results, being able or not to name some government role or person, there was no significant difference between the two groups, with only 54.3% of the children being able to identify this as a government function. However, when these responses were analyzed for differences between Mainlanders and Taiwanese, it was observed that in terms of being able to name the actual role, that of mayor, the Mainlander children who named a government role were far more competent in selecting the exact role than were the Taiwanese. Although this ability improves with age it is still far below that of American children who, despite a general lack of specific political training in grade school, have been found by fourth grade to be generally aware of both the president and the mayor. These findings are borne out by further data. In order to find out if they could identify a local government function, the children were asked who in Taipei City ought to decide whether a new park should be built. Mainlander children showed a significantly higher propensity to name some government figure or role as the locus of responsibility for this decision. Regardless of the small differences between the two groups of children a general lack of affective attachment to local political leaders is characteristic of both Mainlanders and Taiwanese and further indicative of the lack of meaningfulness which politics at the local level has for these children. . . .

Authority orientations are acquired quite early in the life of a child, the earliest orientations generally tending to correspond to those most important in the behavior of adults known to the child. Much of this learning is quite casual in nature, taking place within the family in the daily interaction of children with adults. Even in school most politically relevant attitudes, as against specific political education, are acquired as a by-product of the more general educational process. In any case, by the time a child has reached the age of six to ten years we can speak of the "authority inception period" as having ended. By the middle of the primary school years most children should have acquired a knowledge of the "ranges of acceptable behavior for almost all situations of action" and a knowledge of what constitutes conformity or deviance, what is legitimate and what is not.

There is a sign directly outside a fifth grade classroom in Taiwan which announces to all who enter and leave: "To Obtain the Victory of the Group Is Each Individual's Victory." The solidarity of the group and the submersion of the individual's identity into a larger more important identity is perhaps the most constant and enduring theme of childhood education for both Mainlanders and Taiwanese. Signs in classrooms proclaim such slogans as "Happy Group" and such group-associated themes as "Cooperation."

The content of educational materials is consciously designed to stress group values. An analysis of the reading primers which all grade school children use reveals that fully 25% of the stories directly stress in some way the value of the group. In the first term of third grade the children read the following story which is typical in its group-oriented content: Some geese were flying in a flock when one small goose broke formation and flew on his own. The other geese said to him, "This kind of wild flying is wrong. When we are in a group we should keep order (discipline) and not just leave as we wish." The small goose returned but then flew off again and was warned again. He still failed to mind, however, and a hawk, spying him, swept down and caught him. When his compatriots thought to go and help him it was too late. As the chairman of the committee in charge of compiling elementary text-books in the Ministry of Education told me, the formation geese fly in is roughly similar to the Chinese character for man and therefore the teacher can use this device to bring the point of this story into the context of a human group.

Beyond such conscious manipulation of the group theme is a whole area of human interaction which stresses the same point often in a wholly implicit way. Norms of conformity and deviance are among the most heavily sanctioned in the society. Whatever one's inner feelings, loyalty to the group—to one's family, school, friends, and above all, political loyalty to the state—is the *sine qua non* of adequate conformity. From early childhood on, expressions of disloyalty or deviance, of whatever nature, call into question one's membership status in the group and subject one to punishment, usually ostracism and shaming. There is no concept of a loyal opposition.

A question dealing with group orientations was posed to the children as follows: If on a walk to a park all the group decides to go one way, but one person knows of a much shorter path, should that one person say so? Why? The two groups of children showed no significant differences in answering the first part, over 80% of them believing a person has an obligation to speak up and tell the others. The second and more important part of this question was analyzed to see if the responses to the first part contained some positive reference to the group as a reason for such behavior. Here there was a significant difference: The Taiwanese gave group responses 42.3% of the time, Don't Know responses 51.9%, and Other 5.9%, while the Mainlanders were more articulate in their espousal of group responses, responding in this way 58.7% of the time, with 37.8% Don't Know, and 3.6% Other.

The less positive formulation of norms in group terms evidenced by Taiwanese was confirmed on another question where the children were asked if they felt a basketball team should have a captain and why. Mainlanders showed a slightly (.05 level) greater desire for defined leadership (84.6% vs. 74.3%) and also placed more emphasis on the leader serving group needs. Mainlander children gave group content responses 60.0% of the time, Don't Know 36.8%, and Other 3.2%, while Taiwanese children responded with group content responses 45.3% of the time, Don't Know 53.0%, and Other 1.8%.

Although these differences between the two groups of children indicate some dissimilarity in acculturation patterns, there is, I believe, a reasonable congruence for Mainlanders and Taiwanese in the desire for clear-cut leadership and belief in the necessity for group conformism. Moreover, the children begin to learn quite early which group level and which leaders are most important. Emphasis on the societal level begins in kindergarten where one lesson reads: "We are Chinese and we all love China. Our China's national territory is the largest, the population the greatest, and our products the most abundant." School achievement is consistently related to the theme of working for society. In fifth grade, when the priorities are expected to have been well learned, the children read a story in their textbook of a mother writing to her son. Work for the country, she says, for sons must be brave and mothers must be brave too. Love of country must come before love of family.

In general, authority figures are always supposed to exhibit correct group-approved behavior. This is very explicit in traditional Confucian moral injunctions, and despite the decline of direct references based on this ethical system there remains in child training on Taiwan highly articulated values and norms regarding the roles and statuses of leaders and followers within the group. A father is ideally the head of the family, and the excellence of the family as a whole and of each member depends greatly on the father's deportment. The same is true for the teacher and the principal. The most important point, however, is that whatever the group, members are expected and encouraged to model their behavior on that of the group leader, for the leader presents the cues for correct conformist behavior. There is, in addition, a corresponding emphasis by group members on enjoining the model to perform his role properly. Only by "proper" behavior, which is the ideally correct authority behavior as conceived by a majority of the people in the group, is the model entitled to his status. When behavior is proper the follower is expected both to defer to and to accept loyally the leader as the correct model on pain of punishment.

The children were tested with regard to who is the major authority figure in the home and with regard to status differences defined on the basis of sex and age. In no cases were there any significant differences between Mainlander and Taiwanese children, both emphasizing the father with regard to authority in the home but deemphasizing the special privileges of male and elders as such.

With regard to the general veracity of authority figures there was also no significant difference between the two groups of children. Two questions were asked: (1) Do you think your mother and father are always right? (2) Do you think your teacher is always right? The children came down overwhelmingly on the side of belief in these authority figures, over two-thirds of the responses being positive for both questions and only 12% being negative.

While it is questionable whether we can assume any direct causal link between attitudes toward primary group authority figures and those toward secondary group authority figures, observation of the elementary education on Taiwan reveals a constant and consciously stressed interaction between the feelings, attitudes, and patterns of behavior with regard to such authority figures as parents, teachers, and principals and those toward the major political leaders, the emphasis on modeling shifting over time from the former to the latter and occurring largely simultaneously with the development of national group consciousness. Very early, Chiang Kai-shek and Sun Yat-sen, the national leaders, become the major political symbols in the society and the paramount models for correct behavior, but for the role of citizen and even, as the children are constantly told, for how a child should behave in primary groups. Filiality, respect for teachers, loyalty, courage, love of country, etc., are introduced to the children through countless stories based on the real or apocryphal lives of Chiang and Sun. No other personages or roles in the society approach the emphasis on these two men. Moreover, reinforcement between formal learning and informal training in respect for leadership generally supports the importance of these two universally known figures. They become the legitimation of and models for the acts of others lower in the authority hierarchy. Indeed, adherence to and knowledge of these national leaders and their works become the basic proof of good citizenship.

Conclusion

Although the data presented has been far from exhaustive, the general overall similarity between Mainlander and Taiwanese children, with regard to both politically relevant and specific political attitudes, is quite marked and of sufficient strength to suggest that Mainlander and Taiwanese groups both have continued to adhere closely to similar political cultural norms despite their separation during the first half of this century.

With regard to politically relevant attitudes, observations revealed a strong similarity in training practices while the questionnaire date indicated a high level of congruence in response patterns challenged only with regard to the strength of group orientations. Even here the data do not suggest a radical difference between the two groups of children, since a similar tendency in the responses is quite marked for both Mainlanders and Taiwanese.

Mainlander children show a greater propensity to emphasize group cohesion and to want clear-cut group leadership, factors which may possibly reflect real differences between the two groups but which more probably suggest a sense at both conscious and subconscious levels of the Mainlander minority refugee status. Interestingly, a political ideology—the "Three Principles of the People"—is a stronger association for Taiwanese than for Mainlanders, suggesting that while the specific political attachments of Taiwanese children may be less by identification with a specific national leader they may still associate with the leader's political program. While differences in politically relevant orientations and specific political knowledge exist between Mainlander and Taiwanese children, these differences are not significant when compared to the overall congruence. The results therefore support some confidence in the belief that basic Chinese cultural patterns of a politically relevant nature are persistent.

8. The Social and Political Impact of Education
Sheldon Appleton

Studies of the educational process in Taiwan, and of students' reactions to it, have been conducted at every educational level from elementary school through college. The schools have been characterized as group- and authority-centered and paternalistic in their methods of operation. There is an apparent effort, according to Wilson, to shift the children's loyalty somewhat from the family to the nation and its leaders, and to have them internalize a universalistic rather than a particularistic set of moral values. These efforts seem to be relatively successful through the elementary grades. Beginning with junior high school, however, and proceeding through the college years, disillusionment seems to set in— perhaps as the behavior of adult models is seen to deviate from approved norms. In junior high school, the students become preoccupied—often to the point of suffering considerable emotional anxiety—with school grades and the need to pass competitive entrance examinations for senior high school and college. By the college years, at least in the late 1960s, political interest was low, and cynicism and conservatism relatively high. A process of withdrawal toward particularistic values and relationships seemed to take place, culminating in some cases in emigration for study abroad, and in many more in an "inner migration" toward personal rather than social and political concerns.

Mainlanders and Taiwanese
The differences in attitudes and values reported in these studies between students from Taiwanese and Mainlander families were relatively small. Yet in the population at large, there are substantial demographic differences between people in these two groupings. Mainlanders are better educated and concentrated in the cities. Taiwanese predominate in the countryside and in rural towns. The extent to which these differences will continue to characterize future generations of Mainlanders and Taiwanese is of great potential importance for the island's social and political development.

Statistics issued by the Taiwan provincial government during the late 1960s—the last time they were available—show that Mainlanders have maintained a sizable lead in educational enrollments. At that time, when Mainlanders constituted about 14% of the total population and probably and somewhat lower proportion of school-aged youth, almost a quarter of the island's non-vocational high school students, 30% of its college students, and almost 40% of those enrolled in the top-ranking national universities, were Mainlanders. If

From Sheldon Appleton, "The Social and Political Impact of Education in Taiwan," *Asian Survey*, Vol. XVI, No. 8 (August 1976), pp. 704-716. Copyright 1976 by The Regents of the University of California. Reprinted by permission of The Regents.

this pattern continues, the educational superiority of Mainlanders in the next generation will be lower than in the present one, but will remain quite substantial.

It should be emphasized that none of this appears to be the result of deliberate government policy. There is every reason to believe that the competitive examinations for senior high school and college entry are fairly administered and scored; but Mainlanders come from more educated and urban families to begin with, and some may benefit also from the fact that a northern dialect *(kuo yu)*, rather than Taiwanese, is the language of instruction in the schools. Similarly, there is no indication of systematic job discrimination that disadvantages Taiwanese. Grichting's data show, on the contrary, that Taiwanese with comparable levels of education are rated as slightly better off by interviewers than their Mainlander counterparts. Once again, it is the latter's continuing educational superiority that seems to be the critical variable. This superiority, in turn, may be due more to social class than to the educational system itself. But, as many American liberals have learned in recent years, class and ethnic factors are often difficult to separate. If education in Taiwan has not created the occupational and income differences referred to, it appears to have contributed relatively little to their elimination. In the absence of any "affirmative action" policies, or special advantages in admissions such as those provided in the People's Republic of China for the offspring of workers and peasants, we can apparently expect a good part of the educational advantage held by Mainlanders today to continue for at least another generation.

Responses to Grichting's survey reveal also a very substantial degree of social division between Mainlanders and Taiwanese. Over 97% of the three best friends reported by Taiwanese repondents were also Taiwanese, while 87% of the three best friends reported by Mainlanders were Mainlanders. There was little difference by educational groupings. Ninety-three percent of college-educated Taiwanese and 88% of college-educated Mainlanders, for instance, said their best friend was from their own grouping. The slightly greater tendency for college-educated Taiwanese to have Mainlanders as their best friends is most likely due to the relatively larger percentage of college-educated Mainlanders rather than to any effect of education per se. Younger Mainlanders (under 35) were, however, somewhat more likely than their elders to have Taiwanese friends.

Paradoxically, respondents to this survey were more likely to choose spouses than friends from outside of their own groupings. Just over a third of the married Mainlanders, and 7% of the Taiwanese had chosen a spouse from the other group. Three quarters of these "exogamous" marriages, however, involve Taiwanese women under 35 and middle-aged (35-54) Mainlander males. It seems likely that this is due in large part to the unbalanced sex ratio among (especially older) Mainlanders, many of whom migrated as soldiers or military officers. A good number of Mainlander-Taiwanese marriages therefore probably represent unions between eligible young Taiwanese women and older, comparatively better established Mainlander men. Ninety-nine percent of the Taiwanese men in the sample and 94% of the Mainlander women married within their own grouping, and there is little variation by age in these figures. Thus the rate of inter-marriage appears to be increasing only very slightly. The effect of intermarriage on friendship patterns, moreover, seems to be minimal both at the individual and at the group level. In this context, the impact of these marriages on Taiwanese-Mainlander relations in general is uncertain.

Additional evidence on the extent of social division between Taiwanese and Mainlanders comes from surveys of high school and college students. These students were asked some questions about the person who accompanied them to the movies the last time they attended one. Most had gone with school classmates, and close to 90% were able to recall the provincial origin of this movie companion. Over 70% of the Mainlanders in each group of students said their companion had also been a Mainlander, While 85-91% in each group of Taiwanese said theirs had been Taiwanese. The pattern of responses did not change after a three-year interval.

Value Changes

Taiwan's generation of educational expansion has failed to eliminate the bulk of either the social division between Taiwanese and Mainlanders, or the educational, economic and occupational advantages presently held by the Mainlander minority. But education does seem to have affected the values and even the personalities of Taiwan's populace.

Studies of the effects of economic development on values have been carried out in a number of countries. Data collected by Inglehart for a number of Western European states shows successive generations raised in increasing material comfort assigning greater priority than their predecessors to "post-bourgeois" values ("protecting freedom of speech"; "giving the people more say in political decisions") and lower priority to "acquisitive" values ("maintaining order in the nation"; "fighting rising prices") Ike's analysis of successive generations in Japan yielded different conclusions:

> I am inclined to believe that in Japan there is less a shift from acquisitive to post-bourgeois values than a long-term change from collectivity orientation to individualism . . . It is my contention that in Western culture, which has long stressed individualism, youth may seek a sense of belonging, whereas in Japanese culture, which has emphasized the group, youth may yearn for individualism and privatization.

Grichting's data reveal virtually no significant differences in the value rankings of successive age cohorts among the Taiwan respondents. But the value rankings assigned by both student and adult respondents at different educational levels strongly suggest the kind of movement toward individualism and privatization found by Ike among Japanese youth. Among the students, the value assigned to "a meaningful life" rises sharply with increasing education, and the valuation of "wisdom," "true friendship" and "freedom" also rises somewhat, at the expense of such social values as "national security," "equality," "a world at peace," and "respect for others." For the adult sample, similarly, "inner harmony" and "friendship" are valued more, and "a comfortable life" and "family security" less, by the most highly educated. (The relationship between level of education and the ranking assigned to each of these values is statistically significant.)

There are other indications of this shift in values as well. The college educated in Grichting's sample were the least likely to say that ability to earn money was the most important thing to be gotten out of college, and to cite personality formation or ability to get along with others instead. Similarly, while the least educated respondents defined personal success largely in terms of education, money and career, the college educated cited education, development of talents, good citizenship and good character most often. The grade school educated believed that obedience and cooperation were the values most to be stressed in child rearing, while the high school and college educated said independence should be emphasized most. In questioning stratified samples of the mothers of Taiwanese school children in parts of Taipei and Changhua county, Olsen found that less educated mothers did in fact emphasize obedience, conformity and physical punishment in their child-rearing practices, while the well educated tended to employ affection and "love-oriented" discipline and to stress self-reliance.

This shift in values seems to be reflected in the personalities of young people in Taiwan. Abbott administered the California Personality Inventory and other psychological tests to a random sample of 13-17 year-old boys and to their parents in the Kuting district of Taipei. The personality profiles of the better educated fathers of these boys were closer to American norms than were the personality profiles of the less educated Taipei fathers; and the personality profiles of the Chinese and American youths were closer together than their parents' profiles had been. Abbott concluded that:

> Generational differences as well as the median position of the Japanese group suggest a general movement toward the position now held by Americans. . . . Chinese psycho-social functioning, responding to the values and socialization practices of an increasingly technological and industrial society in which it functions, *is changing by adaptation and adjustment* to be more overtly aggressive, individualistic and direct.

Education and Discontent

These value shifts provide a clue to the further finding that, despite the material benefits they have reaped from Taiwan's generation of economic growth, the best-educated residents of Taiwan seem by and large to be the most discontented with political and social developments on the island. Grichting's island-wide sample was asked whether each of nine specified familial and social relationships had changed for the better or for the worse over the preceding ten years. They were also asked whether they expected each of these relationships to change for the better or for the worse over the next ten years, and whether the state of each of these relationships in Taiwan at present was better, worse, or about the same as in the United States.

In every case, without exception, a plurality of those with a grade school education or less believed these changes had more often been — and would continue to be — for the better, while a plurality of the college educated believed they more often had been — and would continue to be — for the worse. In every case but one, moreover, the high school and college educated were more likely than the less educated groupings to rate Taiwan higher than the U.S. on these dimensions. In each instance the most positive responses came from those with grade school education rather than from those with no formal education at all. We might speculate that those in the grade school grouping have been most likely to feel some of the benefits involved in some loosening of the rigidities of traditionalism without yet experiencing the impact of the alienation and disruption of social networks that comes with urbanization and further social change. This relationship between level of education and discontent with social change is strengthened, rather than weakened, when age is controlled. Though differences by age level are relatively small, it is the youngest age groups, despite their higher levels of education, who are most positive about past and future changes in these relationships.

The college educated were also the most likely to be dissatisfied with their present place of residence (i.e., country vs. city), and to say it was more difficult to raise children these days than a generation ago. Thirty percent of the college educated grouping said that the reason it was harder to raise children these days was that society as a whole had gotten worse. Only 6% of those with a grade school education or less gave this response.

Mitchell's survey of attitudes and social conditions in five Southeast Asian cities also reflects the discontent felt by Taiwan's better-educated residents. Taipei has the highest education level in Taiwan, and also the highest of any of the five cities included in Mitchell's study. Its residents were the most likely to say they were dissatisfied with what they had achieved in life, and were second only to Hong Kong residents in expressing dissatisfaction with their present living situation, and in feeling unable to control the course of their own lives. Some of this dissatisfaction seemed to be due to their feeling that their jobs held lower prestige than they desired. Within the Taipei sample, the best educated were the most likely to complain about the erosion of traditional codes of behavior.

The data we have reviewed suggest that one factor underlying this discontent may be the increasing difficulty experienced by successive cohorts of college graduates in finding careers and status rewards commensurate with their aspirations and efforts. Analysis of the elementary school textbooks used on Taiwan shows that, unlike those used on the mainland, they place little emphasis on farming or on any hard manual labor. Instead, the models held up for students to emulate are generally famous scholars, officials and soldiers, who have often received material rewards and social recognition for their outstanding achievements. Education and academic achievement are portrayed as ends in themselves. It is no surprise, then, that a study of the attitudes of Taipei junior high school students found that they "showed a tendency to have broad, but indefinite goals. . . . They all aimed at high but unrealistic goals; everyone wanted to become 'a great man' with little interest in being an ordinary person.

A second source of discontent may be the apparently deep ambivalence felt by many educated residents toward the Westernization that seems to be accompanying Taiwan's rapid urbanization and economic growth willy-nilly. For familial, friendship and human relations in general the traditional pattern is most preferred and what respondents perceive to be the Western pattern is most disliked. For relationships involving economic or management skills, or technology, the Western model is most admired. In the legal and political areas, there is substantial division among the respondents. Among the student samples there seems also to be a preference for Western models in relationships between individuals and groups not joined by bonds of kinship or friendship. . . .

The picture that emerges from this data is that of a generation strongly oriented toward a conception of modernization close to that espoused by 19th-century Chinese reformers — "Western learning for practical use, Chinese values for essentials." Whether this kind of modernization is any more achievable in contemporary Taiwan than it was a century ago may be at the core of a number of the problems Taiwan's government will have to deal with over the next generation or more.

Evidence of the impact of education on political attitudes is of course more difficult to come by. But the little that is available is consistent with the pattern of social attitudes we have described. Voting turnout—but not interest in politics—seems to fall as levels of education rise, possibly due to a growth in political cynicism. One set of surveys shows lower levels of political interest and pride in governmental and political institutions on the part of college students than on the part of vocational high school students. The college-educated respondents in Grichting's island-wide household sample were more likely than the less well educated to listen to radio and television news broadcasts, which suggests a greater interest in public affairs. But they were less likely to discuss a political matter—the election of a mayor—with their neighbors or spouses, and no more likely to discuss it with friends, than the grade school educated. A study of voting behavior among Taipei residents also found a negative association between level of education and voting turnout in local elections, despite a positive relationship between educational level and political interest.

9. Socialization of the Children

Roberta Martin

The predominant feature of the texts used in Taiwan is their emphasis on filial piety. . . . Model individuals in the texts are defined by their fulfilment of duty to their parents. Patriotism and diligent study are also heavily emphasized, but they are presented as manifestations of filial piety, the ultimate virtue.

Old Lai-tzu, the famous Chinese model character, is described to children in the third grade reader as the epitome of filial respect and duty. Although Lai-tzu himself has reached the age of 70 with white hair and the troubles of old age, he still must play the role of respectful son to his even older parents. Everyday he serves them devotedly, choosing their favourite food for each meal and dressing to please them. His parents are often low in spirits because of their age. To cheer them, Lai-tzu dresses as clown and, using a small drum, sings and dances in front of them like a child—refusing to stop until they have laughed. "Although old Lai-tzu was very old," the story concludes, "he continued to show his filial respect in this manner and thus he was most respected by everyone."

Shortly thereafter, in the same grade text, the story of Yüeh Fei is presented. Here the relationship between filial piety and patriotism is underlined. While duty to family remains the primary concern, the story stresses that the sanctity of the family relies on the strength and unity of the nation. Yüeh Fei lived during the Sung Dynasty when China was attacked from the south by the Chin tribe. The emperor was kidnapped. Yüeh Fei wished to join the army and fight to protect the country, but his mother was very old and he felt that it was his filial duty to stay with her. His mother, however, realizing that he was remaining at home for her, urged him to go. "If the country falls, where will the family be?" she asked him. "When one must choose between the virtues of loyalty to the country and filial piety," she instructed Yüeh Fei, "one must decide which is the more essential, which the less. Go quickly and defend the country!" Yüeh Fei went and fought bravely, and the Chin soldiers were defeated.

From Roberta Martin. "The Socialization of Children in China and in Taiwan: An Analysis of Elementary School Textbooks." *China Quarterly,* No. 62 (June 1975), pp. 242-262. The findings here were based solely on analysis of elementary-school language textbooks that teach children to read in grades one through five.

Diligent study is the third major behavioral pattern emphasized. The "good student" who "gets up early and goes off to school" every day is introduced several times in the first grade reader. In the second and third grade readers the "good student" is presented as a child who, having lost his father at a very young age, studies hard under the guidance of his mother to become a great scholar. He succeeds despite poverty and hardship, thus bringing honor to his mother and fulfilling his filial duty. Ou-yang Hsiu, presented in the third grade reader, is the model for such behaviour. Ou-yang Hsiu was a famous scholar of the Sung dynasty. His father died when he was young, leaving his mother to raise and educate him. Everyday she would teach him reading and writing, but since they were very poor and did not have enough money to buy paper and brushes, Ou-Yang Hsiu learned by writing characters in the sand with branches.

Ou-yang Hsiu's mother often told him about his father, a man who was "exceptional in his display of filial piety." She told him how his father used to weep after his grandmother died, remembering how his poverty prevented him from providing her with enough to eat in her lifetime. Ou-yang Hsiu took these stories to heart. He modelled himself on his father and "not only showed his mother great respect, but . . . read books incessantly and became a great and very famous scholar."

The family in the texts is presented as a unit of activity, moral and social example, warmth, security and happiness. A family is shown going to visit grandmother; parents take children on pleasure trips and on trips to the park introducing them to natural phenomena and to historical spots on Taiwan; when father is away the children write him letters, or, with mother, telegraph him when there is a very bad storm, to assure him of their safety. Children are also shown performing outstanding feats of filial piety. The traditional stories of the little boy who, in winter, jumps into a cold bed to warm it for his father and, in summer, fans his father to sleep, and of Old Lai-tzu, who at the age of 70 puts on comic plays for his still older parents, as related before, are examples. . . .

Patterns of Interpersonal Relations. Patterns of personal interaction in the Taiwanese texts appear to be hierarchical in nature, resting on traditional, ascriptive authority relations. . . . The types of individuals who assume authoritative positions in the texts are limited and closely linked to the child's immediate world of home and school. They are teachers, school principals, parents and President Chiang. Their positions of authority are demarcated in a variety of ways: teachers are bowed to as a sign of respect in the stories; the school principal gives a speech urging respect for elders, adult birds are analogously shown to be more intelligent than baby birds; and New Year cards addressed to teachers and elders are shown to carry more formal, deferential wording than those addressed to peers and brothers. . . .

Manual Labour. Working with one's mind rather than with one's hands was the ideal in traditional China. The Taiwanese texts, which put much emphasis on diligent, academic study and book learning but very little emphasis on hard, manual labour, appear not to foster any deviance from the traditional ideal. The Taiwanese readers on one level express a positive attitude towards manual labour, proclaiming that the labour of farmers should be appreciated because they "toil bitterly but do not fear it," and revealing that even President Chiang "from the time he was little, did not fear labor. Every day he wished to draw water, sweep the floor, and help his mother plant in the garden." The Taiwanese texts offer very few examples, however, of people engaged in manual work and there is no attempt to present model workers to children in the stories.

The Taiwanese texts devote very little attention to farm life and no attention to agricultural skills. They do, nonetheless, attempt to present farm life as "acceptable" as, for example, in "My Father is a Farmer." This story describes how very hard the father toils during the day before coming home to his family at night. Many other urban occupations are held up to the child as desirable, however, such as those of teacher, soldier, administrator, fireman and engineer. . . . Stories in the Taiwanese readers describe a mother waking her child up early to see the newly opened flowers in the garden, a brother and sister listening to the noise of a cicada bug and attempting to discover how the bug makes sounds, and sunrise at sea. They emphasize an appreciation of an affinity with nature.

Education. The emphasis of the Taiwanese texts on diligent study and academic achievement tends to encourage education as an end in itself. Many stories focus on the school, describing either activities within the classroom or the school institution itself. Individuals from history, who did not have today's advantageous conditions for study, but who nonetheless attained an education, are held up as models. One child is described as having been so poor he was unable to buy any books to read. He therefore went to work in the homes of wealthier people and rather than accept payment for his labour, he asked only to have the privilege of access to his employers' libraries. His employers were only too willing to allow him this privilege, as "they respected him very much." The boy cut a small hole in the wall of his room to gain light from the living room and would sit up until the family went to bed reading from the tiny hole of light. Eventually he became a great scholar. His knowledge, it is stressed, came from hard and bitter study.

Conclusion

The political symbols which appear in the Taiwanese stories can be classified in three categories: those relating to the war with Japan and the Japanese occupation of Taiwan (four instances), those relating to the Communist occupation of the mainland (11 instances), and simple national symbols (seven instances)—the flag, National Day, Confucius, democracy, Sun Yat-sen's birthplace, the military and the establishment of the Republic of China.

The Taiwanese Government is promoting a revitalization of the traditional Confucian system of social behavior and personal mores. Filial piety, patriotism, academic achievement, an aesthetic appreciation of nature and a sense of propriety in interpersonal relations are to be the attributes of a model citizen in Taiwan. The individual's focus is to be the family unit, and he is encouraged to have little political awareness or involvement. Although contemporary roles are not clearly suggested in the Taiwanese texts, such citizen-individuals are apparently meant to step into roles in the quickly developing capitalist economy of contemporary Taiwan and become "model citizens" engaged in building a modern China.

The question which remains, of course, is to what extent the picture presented in the textbooks corresponds to reality in Taiwan. As the texts constitute only a minor agent in a child's socialization experience, it is impossible to know what "message" the child is receiving from other socializing agents, such as his family, his friends, or the larger society in which he is living. Is it possible for the Taiwan regime to achieve its goal of developing a Confucian society in the context of a modernizing socio-economic system?

10. Taiwan's Brain Drain

Charles H. C. Kao

The only source for compiling information about the returned students from abroad is the Guidance Committee for Students Educated Abroad. Established in 1955, its major function is to help the returned individuals locate suitable jobs. It also takes care of other details such as arrangement of free transportation to return home, obtaining an entry permit to Taiwan, etc.

The total number of American-educated returned students reported by the Guidance Committee is somewhat underrecorded due to the fact that some returned students from abroad simply did not report to the Committee. To cite an example, eight of my personal acquaintances; with American Ph.D.s in social sciences returned to Taiwan during 1964-68, but none of their names was included in the list of 298 cited above. Through their own arrangement or because of their committment prior to studying abroad, these Ph.D. holders found no need to contact the Committee upon their return from the U.S. They had already arranged a job or returned to previous positions. A hypothesis may be advanced: For a returned specialist, the higher the academic degree, the less likely he needs the Committee's assistance, and thus the more likely that his name will be left out. Accepting the hypothesis tentatively, one has to conclude that the reported return of 31 Ph.D.s during 1964-68 was a gross underrecording. The author's speculation suggests that at least 30 percent of the returned specialists were not included. If so, the total number of returned specialists might be close to 390 during 1964-68, or an annual inflow of about 80.

During 1960-67, the National Council for Sciences also sent 297 individuals abroad for advanced studies. Of these 134 went to the U.S. As of the summer of 1969, 102 had completed their programs and returned to Taiwan. Other organizations such as the Taiwan Provincial Government, the Kuomintang Party, and many others have their own training programs for sending their employees abroad. In view of these programs and other complications mentioned above, the reported figure of 298 returned specialists during 1964-1968 should not be considered as the total figure of Taiwan's brain retention.

Given the data on the outflow of college graduates and returned students in the 1960's, the rate of the Chinese brain drain into the U.S. and its brain retention can now be calculated and further analyzed. An attempt is made to estimate the maximum rate of brain drain, crude rate of brain retention, and weighted rate of brain retention.

The crude rate of brain retention over the period 1960-1968 is only 4.5 percent. However, it is significant to note that for every 100 college graduates going to the U.S. for advanced studies in a given year, on the average only about five American-educated Chinese returned home. By any standard, such a rate must be considered extremely low. One government official in Taiwan made a terse comment: "We cannot perhaps place all the American-educated Chinese students into good positions if they all decide to come home at once, but we certainly can afford to have many more."

In recent years, prominent Chinese scholars and scientists have been invited by the Chinese government in Taiwan for short-term assignments. In the academic year 1967-1968 alone, at least 14 Chinese American-educated Ph.D.s were serving as visiting professors in the field of mathematics, botany, civil, mechanical, and electrical engineering, agronomy and social sciences at National Taiwan University. All of them received their undergraduate training in Taiwan. Fifteen more also served as visiting professors at National Tsing Hua University, and National Chaiotung University, not to mention many other scholars who went back to Taiwan for short-term teaching or research in other universities. To cite two more examples, in the field of economics, three prominent Chinese economists in the U.S., Dr. T. C. Liu of Cornell University, Dr. S. C. Tsiang of the University of Rochester, and Dr. Anthony Y. C. Koo of Michigan State University, all members of the

From Charles H. C. Kao, *Brain Drain: A Case Study of China* (Taipei: Mei Ya Publications, 1971), Chapters 3, 8, and 9.

Academia Sinica, return to Taiwan periodically either serving as government consultants or visiting scholars. In science, Dr. T. Y. Wu, a noted physicist, of the University of Buffalo, travels back and forth between Taiwan and the U.S. Dr. Wu, serving as the Director of the most prestigious National Council for Sciences, formulates the long range policy of scientific development in Taiwan. Many examples can be found in other fields. It would be wrong to suggest that Chinese scholars and scientists in the U.S., all lulled by the handsome salary and material comforts and preoccupied with their own research, have made no contribution to their homeland.

We have studied the reasons for Chinese scholars' decision to stay in the U.S., and also the reasons for scholars' decision to return to Taiwan. There remains one important question: What reasons account for the Chinese college graduates' initial decision to leave Taiwan for the U.S.? One popular and seemingly convincing answer was given by Dr. George Baldwin in 1970. He argues that the professional migration from developing nations appears to be not a drain, but an overflow. Taiwan, along with South Korea, the Philippines and other developing countries, are cited to substantiate his thesis. He states, "The less developed countries (LDCs) are not being stripped of manpower they badly need; more often than not they are being relieved of manpower they cannot use."

Is his "overflow thesis" applicable to Taiwan? It will be argued below that its application to Taiwan's situation is largely invalid. Taiwan's brain drain is more related to factors other than "overflow" or the lack of effective demand for university graduates and employment opportunities.

Taiwan's job market in the 1960's for university graduates in humanities, and to some extent also in social sciences and agriculture, was indeed tight, but the demand for engineering, science and medical students has been strong. One recent labor employment survey shows that for 315,000 people with college education, only 2,000 were unemployed. Their unemployment rate is less than one percent.

The shortage of high-level manpower becomes more acute in view of Taiwan's attempt to implement a highly ambitious 12-year science development program. It was estimated that Taiwan has to recruit an additional 2,296 scholars and scientists with advanced degrees or training from aboard in the period 1968-72, an additional 1,542 in 1972-76, and 1,422 in 1976-1980.

In short, Taiwan's manpower problem is the shortage of highly trained scholars and scientists as well as the undersupply of university graduates in sciences, engineering, education and medicine.

Based on my research findings and judgment, the key factors which account for the initial outflow of Taiwan's university graduates include: pursuit of knowledge, lack of promotion, search for new opportunity, availability of financial assistance in American universities, social and family pressure, lack of research facilities, intellectual atmosphere and adequate pay at home. Granted, some of these factors could be partly the result of the oversupply of university graduates in certain fields, but it is grossly misleading to say that overflow is the major explanation for Taiwan's brain drain.

In a more realistic view, the relevant question to ask those well-established Chinese scholars in the U.S. today is: Would they be interested in going back to Taiwan for a short-term assignment—a year or less? If so, under what conditions?

To explore this possibility, they were asked in the survey: "Would you be interested in teaching or working in Taiwan, say, in the next three years?" Fifty-six percent, or 208 of the sample scholars, expressed an interest, but forty-two percent did not. As expected, more scholars (61 percent) from Taiwan said "yes" than scholars (48 percent) from mainland China—although the former were more critical of Taiwan than the latter group.

Since most of them have decided to stay in the U.S., what are the reasons for their willingness to return for short periods? "Making contribution to Taiwan" and sharing experience and knowledge" were the two most important reasons given. The next two important reasons were to "acquaint their children with Chinese language and culture" and "family reunion."

Their interest in returning may be partly related to the fact that 97 of the scholars had visited Taiwan in the past five years. Only 13 individuals found their trip discouraging. The other 44 were encouraged to return and 40 were neutral.

It would appear that they can indeed make contributions to Taiwan in view of their answers to the question regarding the relevance of their major field to Taiwan's needs. Seventy four percent of the sample scholars indicate their specialization had "much" or "some" relevance to the need of Taiwan. Their answers here seem inconsistent with their worry over the lack of the demand for their specialization in Taiwan discussed earlier.

A bleak view of the brain drain from developing to developed nations has been dominant in academic circles since the early 1960's. That pessimism, however, is now being partly disspelled by the fact that increasing numbers of foreign scientists and students are leaving the U.S. for their home countries, and Taiwan may prove to be an encouraging case in point.

According to statistics released by the Ministry of Education in Taiwan, 399 foreign-educated Chinese students returned home in 1970. Of these, 233 returned from the United States. This number may still appear to be small when it stands alone, but it is certainly gigantic when compared with the number of returned students in previous years. Two hundred thirty three is close to the total number of returned American-educated students in the immediately past four years, 1965-69. Equally important to note is that the annual total of U.S.-bound students from Taiwan has significantly dropped from between 2,500-3,000 in 1968 and 1969 to 1,800 in 1970. From the brain retention viewpoint, both of these sets of figures are encouraging: not only are more highly trained individuals returning to Taiwan, but also fewer college graduates are leaving for the U.S.

An analysis of 399 returned students indicates that slightly more than half earned master's degrees, and slightly over one third earned doctoral degrees; two fifths specialized in engineering and sciences, and one third in social sciences and humanities; slightly over half were employed in academic institutions, and one tenth in government. One must conclude from these facts that these returned students were highly trained, and devoted themselves to academic work. Their specialities are greatly needed in Taiwan today.

A single year's figure, of course, cannot be viewed as a trend. But all the indications seem to suggest that Taiwan's brain drain is slowing down and its brain retention is now improving. My own prediction is that Taiwan's college graduates will continue to enter into the U.S. for advanced studies, but the annual outflow from Taiwan will probably be in the neighborhood of 2,000 instead of 3,000 as in the recent past. On the other hand, the number of students returning annually from the United States will increase from 50-60 in the late 1960's to over 200 or even 300 in the future. If the ratio of the outflow and returning students can be maintained at less than eight to one, I would venture to suggest that the term "brain drain" should be replaced by a new term—"brain exchange."

Factors such as research facilities and funds and job promotion, once unfavorable in Taiwan, have been gradually improving. The Chinese government has indeed made more efforts in this direction in recent years. Among them, improvement of research institutes and graduate programs, availability of more research funds and government programs to select people to study abroad, are the major ones. In addition to such academic improvement, the government's relaxation of exits from and entrance into Taiwan, better communication with students and scholars abroad about job information, more liberal promotion policies, all make Taiwan more attractive than before. But I suspect that students' returns are more due to the lack of jobs in the U.S. than improvement on the island. In other words, in my judgement, the deterioration of "pull" factors is more influential in the decision-making process than the improvement of the "push" factors.

Now we turn to the second question: Why are decreasing numbers of college graduates going to the U.S.? In a broad sense, the domestic conditions in Taiwan are steadily improving as briefly described above. People now tend to believe that one can be successful, and more importantly, happy in Taiwan without necessarily going through the phase of "studying aboard." In this connection, a sense of national self-confidence has been somewhat restored. Besides, a prosperous economy provides enough challenge and opportunity to many college graduates and the rising living standard also means a more comfortable life in Taiwan today. Recent novels and stories in the media about some Chinese students' painful struggles and failures in the United States also make college graduates themselves more apprehensive about coming to the United States and their parents less persistent and eager to push their children to leave Taiwan. Furthermore, social attitudes toward studying abroad have been changing from the once unconditionally admiring to today's cautious endorsement.

Despite the importance of all these favorable factors, perhaps the most immediate reasons for the decreasing number of college graduates leaving for the United States are twofold: first, the tightening admission standards and financial assistance in the American universities, and second, the periodical raise of the TOEFL scores moderated by the American Embassy in Taipei and the more difficult Study-abroad Examination given by the Chinese Ministry of Education.

Undoubtedly, at the present time, this two-way flow benefits both countries. A crucial question to ask is: Will this new development just be temporary and return to one-way movement. When the job market in the United States becomes loose again? There is always such a possibility, but I doubt very much that it will happen in the next five years or so. First, unless unexpected events take place in the United States, "academic depression" and saturation of qualified scientists and other high-level manpower will not be over perhaps until the end of this decade. Secondly, the Taiwan economy can utilize many more returned students at its present stage of development. A recent survey conducted by the National Youth Commission shows that there are 819 positions available this year to those with doctoral and master's degrees. If 400 would return this year, half of the positions would still remain unfilled. The one-way flow witnessed in the 1960's, in my view, is unlikely to happen again with the strong demand for high-level manpower and the better conditions in Taiwan, and oversupply of Ph.D.s and greater uncertainty of job market in the United States. From Taiwan's point of view, yesterday's brain drain finally becomes today's brain gain.

Specific Policy Measures

We have shown that China's brain drain into the U.S. is multi-faceted—a combined result of the "pull" and "push" factors. By comparing these factors, the Chinese scholars have found that research and teaching facilities, income, academic freedom, fair competition, political climate, intellectual atmosphere and acknowledgement are far better in the U.S. than in Taiwan. They were also more satisfied with the American way of life than the Chinese way of life.

To avoid sowing seeds of dissatisfaction and emigration, a nation's educational system must produce the "right" kind of products and the "right" quantities of each. The Chinese government should push forward its manpower planning and forecasting program so that the surplus of college graduates in some fields and shortage of others can be prevented. Moreover, a comprehensive review of the numbers and kinds of specialists needed to achieve national development objectives should be a part of the educational planning. Such review should be carried out on a continuous basis. If the shortage of high-level manpower is discovered, as the case will be, a logical step is to recruit some of the Chinese scholars and scientists to return home. The Manpower Development Committee of CIECD has made various useful manpower studies and projections. With further improvement of these studies, the government would be better equipped to review its manpower policies with special reference to the need to stimulating the return flow.

A drastic increase of salary at least initially offered to those highly-educated individuals returned from abroad is an essential step for recruitment. Such action may cause local resentment, but is justified on the grounds that this is what they are "worth" abroad. Ideally speaking, not only has salary to be raised drastically for these highly trained individuals, but also the increase has to be made more flexible. A uniform salary schedule for the people holding the same ranks, though it appears to be fair, destroys the incentive. Incentive is the key for Taiwan's development and should be encouraged even if it has to be carried out at the expense of the so-called "fair principle".

But as our statistical analysis has shown, improvement of salary alone cannot assure their returning. Other non-monetary factors, e.g., research facilities, political climate, career advancement, fair competition, intellectual atmosphere, have to be improved concurrently with, if not prior to, salary improvement. As a matter of fact, these factors are much more difficult to improve. They take more money, time and effort to change. For example, to establish a modern library or research laboratory cannot be done in a short period of time. To improve the political climate is much more easily said than done. The lack of fair competition, poses another hindrance. The pressure exerted upon the government for more improvement might be one of the few desirable effects of the brain drain.

Section 3

Economic Development

Edited by Yuan-li Wu
and Jan S. Prybyla

Section 3

The Taiwan Experience in Economic Development*

Overall Commentary by Yuan-li Wu

Since the latter part of the 1970's, the economic success of the ROC on Taiwan has become progressively better known in the world. Numerous statistical indicators of success can be readily cited.[1] For instance, Taiwan's mid-1978 population was 17.1 million, or 1.8 percent of that of the PRC (People's Republic of China); yet Taiwan's per capita GNP in that year was, according to the World Bank, six times that of its much larger "neighbor" on the Chinese mainland. At 1976 prices, Taiwan's per capita GNP rose from NT$10,521 in 1952 to NT$19,523 in 1965 (an 85.9 percent increase), and NT$54,359 in 1979 (an increase of 416 percent).[2] Labor productivity, measured in terms of GDP (gross domestic product) per person employed, rose from NT$68,467 in 1965 to NT$145,850 in 1979 (an increase of 113 percent), both at 1976 prices. Total foreign trade turnover (exports plus imports) increased from the paltry figure of US$303 million (current dollars) in 1952 to US$1,006 million in 1965 (an increase of 232 percent) and then to US$39,484 million (an increase of 12,910 percent) in 1980. Taiwan's foreign trade was 1.0 percent of the IMF's world trade in 1979 and 14.6 percent of the foreign trade of Japan, although in 1978 Taiwan had only 0.4 percent of the population of the world's 125 nations listed in the World Bank's *World Development Report* (1980). These figures and others are more than enough to secure a place for Taiwan in the world economy. They highlight the rapid economic growth of Taiwan in less than thirty years (1952-1980) and especially during the decade and a half (1966-1980) after the termination of U.S. economic aid in 1965.

Economic Development: A Prudent Strategy

However, the developmental experience of Taiwan should not be understood purely in a recitation of production and trade figures. For it is above all a story of the ROC's successful strategy of development, which has meaning for other countries. This is a strategy that has in three decades done what is politically necessary and prudent, while never pausing for

---

*There are two subsections in this section on Taiwan's Economic Development, one on internal and the other on external aspects, for each of which there is a separate editor and separate commentary. Here is an over-all commentary by Dr. Yuan-li Wu for the entire economic section. — *General Editor.*

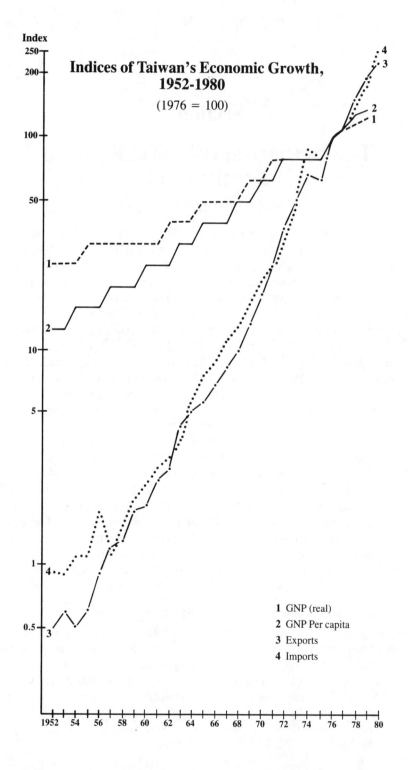

Indices of Taiwan's Economic Growth, 1952-1980

(1976 = 100)

1 GNP (real)
2 GNP Per capita
3 Exports
4 Imports

long to move the economy in a forward direction. The story of Taiwan is one of sustained rather than sporadic economic advancement. Furthermore, it is a story of economic *development*, rather than of economic *growth*, in quantitative terms alone. In fact, but for its simultaneous emphasis on stability, equity, and growth, Taiwan may not have succeeded in enjoying the safe passage it did, politically no less than economically, through the stormy decade of the 1970's. Because of its prudent, pragmatic, yet energetic approach, Taiwan now offers an example of continuous development of a country from a poor LDC (less developed country) with meagre natural resources to an industrializing, trade-oriented open country for which further betterment of the economic well-being of its citizens no longer seems a problem. Not that Taiwan's economic problems have all been solved; nor are the principal issues on the agenda today any less challenging than before. Yet the constantly pressing new issues have become somewhat less forbidding, they have become "old hat," as it were. There is a growing confidence on the part of the ROC authorities and the business community in Taiwan in their economy and in their own ability to meet new challenges which, they are convinced, will never cease to occur.

The manner in which Taiwan's prudent strategy of development has unfolded over the years is demonstrated by the country's embarkation, time and again, on new phases of development that are pre-conditioned by steps taken in earlier stages. Thus, in the very beginning, U.S. aid, primarily technical, was prudently used, both by the donor and by the recipient, through the JCRR (the Joint Commission on Rural Reconstruction) in order to help restore the political credibility of the newly transplanted government and to create a sense of accomplishment which had been wanting for so long. This is why a program of land rent reduction was followed by the establishment of an owner-cultivator program of agrarian reform and why these first institutional changes were followed by continuous efforts to increase farm production in which experienced Chinese technicians, many recent arrivals from the mainland, provided effective help to an intelligent and responsive agricultural labor force.

In the economy as a whole, restoration of price stability was regarded by all concerned as the prerequisite for any sustainable development program, as was the restoration of the economic infrastructure—power, transportation, communications, and irrigation—which had been devastated by the effects of World War II and post-war inflation. Once these preliminary objectives had been attained, Taiwan then opted (especially in 1958-60) for a lessening of foreign-exchange and trade controls and an expansion of the private—relative to the public—sector of the economy. Import substitution gave way to export promotion, finally leading to a process of import liberalization that has not yet seen its end. The expanding emphasis on foreign trade as the leading sector of economic growth is of course natural and logically necessary for an island economy. Yet export expansion would have been very difficult if marketing overseas had not been undertaken by enterprises run by foreign investors both inside and outside the export processing zones (EPZS). Foreign investors would not, however, have come to Taiwan if the investment climate, including the island's then large, unskilled, but well disciplined labor force, had not presented high prospects of profitability and stability. Nor would greater import liberalization have been economically, as well as politically, feasible without the prior success of export promotion.

Breaking through the Savings and Payment Constraints

Opting for labor-intensive manufacturing for export with a quick capital turnover was decidedly the key to Taiwan's initial rapid entry into the ranks of the fast-advancing LDCs that are not exporters of vital natural resources. Once this course had been set, rising income succeeded in speeding domestic savings, capital formation, and further development. From the point of view of most LDCs, the rate of capital formation and the availability of foreign exchange earnings to pay for imports are among the foremost strategic growth variables. In this connection, Taiwan's gross capital formation was already close to 20 percent of GDP (19.3 percent in 1964) on the eve of the termination of U.S. economic aid in 1965. This rate rose steadily thereafter, hovering around 30 percent (33 percent in 1979) in the 1970's. The foreign trade (goods and services) balance rose from a deficit of $66.8 million in 1965 to a sizable surplus in the 1970's, the principal exceptions being 1974 and 1975, when OPEC's large oil price hikes made their initial impact. In terms of the current account balance, which used to register a small deficit around the time of U.S. aid termination ($89.1 million in 1964), there was a surplus balance throughout the 1970's with the sole exception again of 1974-1975. Thus Taiwan was able to overcome the vexing investment and foreign payment gaps confronting many another LDC during a period when the world economy reeled under the repeated blows of OPEC's oil price onslaughts, not to mention the cessation of U.S. aid in 1965 and the diplomatic setbacks Taiwan suffered in 1971-73 (withdrawal from the U.N.) and again in 1979-80 (U.S. derecognition).

Two-way Foreign Investments

The inflow of foreign investment, even if not absolutely necessary for reasons of financing, can nevertheless play an indispensable role as a means of technological transfer and export marketing. In 1965, when direct foreign investment during the year amounted to only $10 million, the figure of $100 million a year was noted in Dean Jacoby's assessment for the U.S. Agency for International Development (AID) as a landmark to which to look forward. In 1979, direct foreign investment, albeit in current dollars, stood at a net balance of $121 million ($143 million into Taiwan from abroad, $22 million from Taiwan), not to mention other inflows of long-term private capital (more than 300 million dollars in 1979). Approved foreign investment applications, including reinvestment of earnings in Taiwan, according to the American Institute in Taiwan (A.I.T., the "unofficial" representative of the U.S. government since diplomatic dere-cognition), totalled $350 million in the first ten months of 1980 and were expected to reach $480 million for the year. Some 40 percent of the $480 million came from the United States.

These figures are especially remarkable in view of the high sensitivity of foreign investment to the international political situation. The inward flow of foreign capital dipped following the initial impact of the 1971 announce-ment of President Nixon's visit to Peking. It fell again during the 1974-75 period of world-wide readjustment to the first oil shock. Each time, how-ever, the flow was able to resume after a pause and even to expand, as it has done after the "Carter shock" of Christmas 1978.

Why have confidence and profit expectations from investment in Taiwan managed to bounce back? For an explanation of this resilience one must again look into Taiwan's domestic policies and developments.

Co-emphasis on Equity and Stability

The open initiation of U.S.-PRC rapproachment in 1971 was met by a political and, therefore, economic response in Taiwan greatly at variance with that of South Korea, which was then anticipating a similar U.S. re-trenchment and strategic retreat elsewhere in the Western Pacific that could lead to the withdrawal of U.S. forces from the Korean peninsula. While the South Korean authorities opted for stepped-up economic expansion fi-nanced through increasing foreign indebtedness, their ROC counterpart in Taiwan characteristically chose a path of steadier if slower growth with co-emphasis on equity and stability.

Both equity and stability are goals which Taiwan has long stressed in its economic policy. In 1964, the top 20 percent of Taiwan's households on the family income ladder accounted for 41.1 percent of all family incomes. This ratio declined further to 38.7 percent in 1970 and 37.5 percent in 1975. In contrast, households constituting the lowest 20 percent on the income ladder registered 7.7 percent of total family income in 1964, 8.4 percent in 1970, and 8.6 percent in 1979. Farm family income in relation to non-farm income stood at 96.6 percent of the latter in 1964. After falling to 67.1 percent in 1970, the ratio climbed back steadily during the next de-cade, reaching 79.7 percent in 1979. Unemployment, which registered at 4.3 percent of the labor force in 1964, fell to 1.7 percent in 1970 and 1.3 percent in 1979. Even during the worst post-oil shock year of 1975, it was no more than 2.4 percent. The same can be said of the relative stability of the annual rate of GNP (gross national product) growth in real terms (ad-justed for changes in the terms of trade). While its fluctuations rose sharply during 1973-76 as a result of the first shock wave of oil price increases, the real growth rate returned in 1977-79 to the same degree of steadiness as in the 1961-66 period.[3]

Price inflation which arose once more in the last several years of the 1970s presents one of the most serious economic challenges today. Much of it, however, is imported inflation, sustained by credit expansion. Leaving it aside for the moment, one can clearly point to the far greater social and political stability that has accompanied Taiwan's economic growth in the 1970s in comparison with that of South Korea, another rapidly developing country in the Western Pacific. (The "city states" of Singapore and Hong Kong are not appropriate comparisons.) This record of steady growth in spite of major external economic and political shocks has finally moved Taiwan to a new point of departure in economic development in the 1980s. Further growth in the coming decade is bound to assume some distinctly new characteristics.

An Economic Agenda in 1965

It will be instructive at this point to note what Jacoby thought in 1965 should be on Taiwan's development agenda.

> Development raises new problems as it resolves old ones. As Schumpeter observed long ago, a free economy grows by a process of 'creative destruction.' Taiwan's promising future could only be realized by timely solution of the social and economic problems that confronted this transitional society in 1965.
>
> Some basic social needs of Taiwan have already been described. Excessive growth of population on a crowded island needed to be curbed by national measures for family planning. Unemployment had to be reduced by policies to expand employment, and by raising the period of compulsory public schooling over six years. The educational system needed reorientation to the requirements of an industrializing society. A radical upward adjustment of civil service salaries was essential to keep able men and women in government service. Growing inequalities in income called for a greater reliance upon progressive income taxation. The population needed sanitary sewerage facilities and potable water. Removal and rebuilding of the industrial slums in the cities were urgent, as well as transportation and traffic controls. Adequate safety and social security laws were needed to protect the industrial worker and his family against the hazards of life. All such measures to modernize the apparatus of social welfare would contribute to the rise in productivity of the work force and, thus, fortify economic growth.
>
> Taiwan also had developed gaps in the economic institutions and policies required for its rapid future progress. It had reached a stage in which effective investment banking and capital market institutions were needed to channel public savings into industrial investment. It lacked adequate home mortgage and consumer credit financing facilities. The size, independence, and prestige of its public accounting and management-consulting professions were gravely deficient. Local insurance, banking, and foreign trading firms needed the energizing effect of more competition from new Chinese enterprises as well as from branches of foreign firms.

We have already noted the improvement in income distribution and unemployment in Taiwan. As is noted in the Education Section of the present volume, free public education has already been extended from six to nine years since 1968. A further extension to 12 years will be introduced on a trial basis in 1983 in the vocational schools. A series of pay raises during 1979-80 has significantly improved the comparative standing of the pay scales of both civilian and military personnel in government service, in relation to remuneration in the private sector. An on-going large investment program in paved roads, street lighting, drinking water and sewage systems, market places for stall keepers, public meeting places, mobile medical teams, and the social infrastructure is aimed at a substantial amelioration of the quality of life in both urban and rural areas. By the same token, sharply increased urban public housing construction and arrangements for installment purchase have made Taiwan a progressively more developed society over and above economic growth in purely quantitative terms.

Agenda for the Eighties

Even as many of Jacoby's 1965 agenda items were or are being taken care of, others remain and new ones continue to arise. Notable among the unfinished tasks are the development of capital and money markets for mobilizing domestic savings, dispersing ownership of private industry among larger segments of the population, and more effective monetary policy. Still other institutions are now needed to facilitate investment overseas from Taiwan, to develop multinational financial and other links with neighbors in Southeast Asia and beyond, and to effect technological transfers in both directions. These needs were not as urgent in 1965, when Taiwan was still at a lower stage of economic development.

Other economic issues now confronting Taiwan have arisen from radically changed international circumstances. The U.S.-ROC diplomatic break in December 1978 and the greatly altered American military stance in the Western Pacific have increased Taiwan's perceived need for greater military build-up of its own defenses and the necessarily accompanying adjustment in economic policy. Moreover, continuously rising oil prices pose an external payments and terms-of-trade problem which requires a sharply increased "value-added" of Taiwan's exports by changing their composition and the supporting indstrial structure.

The 1960s and most of the 1970s saw rising real income and imports in U.S. and world markets. This condition which made Taiwan's rapid export growth possible can no longer be assumed without question today. Competition from other developing countries has increased, as has the drive in developed countries, including Taiwan's major markets, to keep out more imports. Continuous expansion of the same categories of exports requires spreading out the exports among more countries and diversifying into more new markets. The small supplier in a large market is likely to attract less hostility as a competitive supplier. There is also the accompanying call for more bilateral settlement of accounts or, at least, buying more from where one sells, not to mention other reasons for import diversification by source. In short, among Taiwan's new challenges is the need to continue its trade-pulled economic growth in a world growing less hospitable to interdependence and multilateral trade expansion.

Attempts to deal with some of these emerging needs are already being made. For instance, new rules were incorporated in December, 1980, in the revised Statute for Encouragement of Investment, which entered into force on January 1, 1981, to urge Taiwan investors to "explore, exploit or process natural resources outside the country." A concerted effort is being made to speed up technology transfer and to expand the industrial application of R&D (research and development). The Hsin-chu Industrial Park, designed for this purpose, was officially opened in December, 1980.

Finally, an immediate issue that must be dealt with is inflation. From an annual rate of increase of 5.6 percent between the last quarter of 1975 and that of 1978, the rise of the consumer price index of Taiwan accelerated to an annual 17.2 percent rate of increase between the first quarter of 1979 and the third quarter of 1980. While the record still compares favorably with the performances of Thailand, the Philippines, South Korea, and Indonesia in the Western Pacific, it is not as good as the records of Japan, Singapore, and Hong Kong. Unless the rate of inflation can be first arrested and then sharply reduced, both internal stability and external competitiveness will suffer.

In this connection, it may be well to recall the manner in which inflation was brought under control in Taiwan before. The following words, taken from an address[4] by Shirley W. Y. Kuo to an international audience are instructive:

> Immediately after the war the most urgently needed policy was price stabilization, because during the period 1946-1948 prices rose at an annual rate of about five-fold and then accelerated to about 30-fold in the first half of 1949. Stabilization policies were implemented through various measures, among which monetary reform was essential.
>
> **(1) Monetary Reform**
> The New Taiwan Dollar Reform was put into effect on June 15, 1949, amidst the situation of hyper-inflation. The old currency was devalued at a rate of forty thousand to one, the most conservative full reserve system was adopted, and the limitation on issuance was strictly regulated. Speculation in gold was strictly prohibited, and the government sold gold periodically. This mechanism stabilized the price of gold on the one hand, and absorbed money supply on the other.
>
> Right after the monetary reform the inflation rate slowed down and increased only three-fold in 1950. Compared with the 30-fold increase experienced in the first half in 1949, this was a great success. The inflation was more controlled after 1951, and the annual increase in prices was 8.8 percent during 1952 to 1960, before it became 3 percent in 1961 and afterwards. Although it took twelve years to accomplish this, the contribution of the monetary reform to the stabilization and to the economic development was great.
>
> **(2) Interest Rate Policy**
> Another very important measure promoting stabilization was the introduction of "preferential interest savings deposits" in March, 1950. Due to the then prevailing hyper-inflation, the duration of the deposits was set very short, only one month at the outset. Longer-term deposits were gradually added

later as price stability was gradually achieved and the amount of deposits gradually increased.

The principal characteristic of the preferential interest savings deposit was its high interest rate. At that time, the yearly interest rate for one-year time deposits was 20 percent. The interest rate for these new deposits was 7 percent per month, which, if compounded, would amount to 125 percent per year. Although the interest rate was actually still below the inflation rate in 1950, a setting of such a high interest rate required the government's intelligence and determination.

The preferential interest saving deposit was very effective. At the beginning of 1950, time deposits in all banks amounted to only NT$2 million. After the inauguration of the preferential interest deposits, the amount increased to NT$35 million in eight months, making up about 7 percent of money supply. The interest rate was once lowered from 7 percent per month to 3.5 percent and 3 percent in 1950. However, a decrease in deposits was observed, and the interest rate was raised to 4.2 percent again. The interest rate was gradually reduced to 2 percent in November 1952. At that time preferential interest saving deposits accounted for 44 percent of the money supply.

After 1953 the government gradually provided preferential interest saving deposits at longer terms. The deposits on these longer-terms gradually increased.

On March 5, 1956, the authorities started a new kind of time deposit which matured in six months and one year and could not be mortgaged, bearing monthly interest rates of 1.5 percent and 1.8 percent, respectively. These rates were higher than those for the deposits that could be accepted as security for loans, the interest of the latter having been reduced to 0.85 percent and 1 percent respectively for deposits in one-month and three-month accounts. Because of the reduction in the interest rates for shorter-term deposits, all deposits tended to be of longer maturity. At the end of 1956, deposits of one-year accounts comprised 27 percent of the total deposits.

On July 16, 1957, the Bank of Taiwan began to accept time deposits maturing in two years and, in the meantime, abolished the one-month deposits. The interest rate for deposits of three-months duration was further lowered to 0.85 percent, and that for deposits of two-years duration was fixed at 1.9 percent. Within the year 1958, the total amount of one-year deposits more than doubled; from the middle of 1957 to the end of 1958, the amount of six-month deposits was nearly doubled.

At the end of 1958, the authorities suspended the preferential interest savings deposits. The total outstanding deposits at that time amounted to NT$1,500 million, or 29 percent of money supply. In a period of about nine years, from March 1950 to the end of 1958, the financial authorities had relied on these savings deposits as the means to call in a tremendous amount of idle capital from the market, thus contributing greatly to the stability of the economy on the island during these years.

On the other hand, the Bank of Taiwan, then functioning as the central bank, succeeded in bringing credit expansion of the commercial banks under its effective control. Extension of loans to business are carefully coordinated with the overall policies.

The present threat of inflation, far less serious than in the late 1940s and early 1950s, is nevertheless taken seriously by the authorities. Taiwan can congratulate itself on having proponents of sound monetary and credit policies to advise its leaders.

Thus, one needs only to contemplate the array of problems we have enumerated in order to appreciate the many economic issues on Taiwan's agenda for the 1980s. In order to tackle these economic issues and to avoid the political consequences of failing to find adequate and timely solutions. Taiwan must strive not only to sustain the original conditions of economic growth and stability but to add to them. The original work ethic needs to be reinforced by greater productivity based on more investment in equipment, skill and technology. Thrift must not give way to conspicuous comsumption, while heavy investment in equipment has to be made with one eye on the potential fickleness of external demand and another on the availability of real savings. The island must above all keep its adaptability. Its economic nimbleness must not be replaced by ossification through the emergence of strangling vested interests, whether they originate from capital or labor or excessive government control. Finally, a consensus based on public understanding must be reached on potential conflicts between the requirements of economic growth and the protection of environmental and social values. One could continue in this vein almost *ad infinitum*.

The conditions for long-term steady development are many, and none can, offer unconditional assurances of success. Yet past experience suggests that Taiwan's policy makers and the island economy's working population are not likely to be overawed by the challenges they will have to face. One can, however, be optimistic, just as the A.I.T. has been optimistic. The following paragraphs, taken from the Institute's report on "Taiwan: Economic Relations in 1980," provide some fitting comments:

If 1979 was the year in which Taiwan's economy withstood and overrode the shocks of 'normalization' and surging oil prices, 1980 was the year in which Taiwan demonstrated an ability to broaden and deepen trade and financial partnerships and other nongovernmental linkages dramatically, not only with major traditional trading partners—the United States and Japan—but increasingly in Europe, East as well as West.

The real gross national product expanded in the range of 6-7 percent over 1979, down slightly from the planned target of 8 percent but still, at US$40 billion in current prices, among the highest growth rates in the world. Economic developments in Taiwan, long primarily a function of events in the U.S. and Japan—particularly the levels of interest and exchange rates and of retail demand—are increasingly responding to demand and financial flows in Europe. There is also a triangular dimension: the strength or weakness of the U.S. dollar, to which the Taiwan dollar is pegged at about 36:1. The strength of the dollar heavily influenced Taiwan exports to Japan (down) and to Europe (up) in 1980, with the result that the European Economic Community countries in 1980 surpassed Japan as Taiwan's second largest export market, and Taiwan emerged as 16th on the global list of major exporters. Two-way trade totalled about $39.5 billion in 1980; it totalled $31 billion in 1979. However, because the oil import bill of $4.1 billion was more than double the cost of crude oil imports in 1978 and 1979 combined, the merchandise trade surplus was only about $50 million in 1980; in 1979 it was about $1.33 billion. In 1980 Taiwan was the United States' eighth largest trading partner worldwide, and second only to Japan in Asia. It is evident that the loss of diplomatic relations with the U.S. has not adversely influenced the economy, nor has there been any sign of interference with commercial relations.

Taiwan has overcome the chronic problems which afflict many developing societies; illiteracy, poverty, hunger, social and political instability, insufficient supply of or access to raw materials, uncontrolled population growth, and shortages of capital and technology.* On the contrary, Taiwan's main economic problem as an export-oriented industrial society is price inflation fueled by: (1) vibrant domestic demand, and (2) rapid and artificial increases—in effect an externally-imposed tax—of crude oil prices. In truth, however, planners in Taiwan are concerned less about the absolute increase in the price of crude oil than they are about: (1) asssured oil supplies; (2) the total oil bill as a percentage of GNP and; (3) the influence of high oil prices on export competitiveness. At year-end the cost of oil was 10-12 percent of GNP and the concern is that the ratio may increase in 1981. The planners fear that if oil cost as a percentage of GNP increases faster in Taiwan than in Japan, Hong Kong, South Korea, and Singapore, then domestic price inflation will increase at a correspondingly higher rate, with a concommitant loss in the competitive export position.

Taiwan's imperative—as it is elsewhere in the industrial world—is to export goods and services to world markets at rapidly increasing and profitable rates in order to pay for its oil which is imported at ever increasing prices only partially responsive to market mechanisms, and to restrain the upward ratchet effect of oil prices on domestic wage and price levels. In the absence of abundant natural resources, great resourcefulness will have to be displayed—as it has to date—to meet such objectives.

---

*Taiwan lacks minerals and other resources and is over-populated, but as a result of the adoption of sound policies and effective management of the economy, these shortcomings do not pose social and economic burdens.

NOTES

1. The statistics below are mainly taken from *Taiwan Statistical Data Book, 1975 and 1980,* compiled by the Council for Economic Planning and Development, Executive Yuan, Republic of China, and *Social Welfare Indicators,* Republic of China, 1980, published by the Manpower Planning Committee of the same Council.

2. In 1952 the new Taiwan dollar (NT$) was quoted at NT$15.55 (buying) to NT$15.65 (selling) per U.S. dollar for exchange settlement by government agencies. Between 1960 and 1972 the exchange rate was pegged at NT$40.00—NT$40.10 to one U.S. dollar. The NT dollar was revalued on February 16, 1973 to NT$37.90—NT$38.10 per U.S. dollar—and again on December 10, 1974 to NT$37.95—NT$38.05. The exchange rate since 1978 has stayed at NT$35.98—NT$36.88 per U.S. dollar.

3. The rate of fluctuations (f_t) used here is the ratio of (1) the square-root of the three-year average of the variances of the real GNP growth rate to (2) the 3-year average growth rate of the previous year. That is:

$$f_t = \frac{\sum_{i=t-1}^{t+1} (x_i - \bar{x})^2}{3} \qquad \bar{x}_{t-1} \qquad \text{where } \bar{x}_t = \frac{1}{3} \sum_{i=t-1}^{t+1} x_i$$

x being the rate of real GNP growth, adjusted for changes in the terms of trade. According to the *Social Welfare Indicators, Republic of China, 1980,* the values of f_t in 1973-79 were: 1973–55.7; 1974–73.1; 1975–168.5; 1976–80.3; 1977–25.2; 1978–14.4; 1979–21.2: f_t varied between 15.4 (1966) and 29.0 (1962) in 1961-1966 and between 6.9 (1972) and 9.2 (1967) in 1967-1972.

4. Professor Kuo, who is also Deputy Governor of the Central Bank of China, spoke on "Effects of Trade on Growth, Employment, and Income Distribution in Taiwan, the Republic of China, 1952-1979" at a conference on U.S.-Asia Economic Relations at Rutgers University on April 18, 1981.

Part 1

Domestic Economic Construction

by Jan S. Prybyla

Despite what in the early 1950s were formidable odds, Taiwan's economy in the last thirty years has shown enormous vigor, resilience, and flexibility. By every available yardstick the economy has done very well in comparison with others placed in similar or more propitious circumstances. Although much of the Taiwan experience (including some of the developmental policies pursued by the government in partnership with the private sector) is specific to Taiwan and not readily transferable elsewhere, the study of that experience provides many useful lessons for developing and industrialized countries alike. Among those who could vastly benefit from such study are the authorities on the mainland of China.

The selections which follow deal primarily with the domestic aspects of Taiwan's economic development. They are divided into three major parts. Part I provides a general survey of the island and of its economy, and outlines some of the key problems which the Republic of China had to face in its early years on Taiwan. Part II addresses itself to the economy's quantifiable performance. The record is examined in two perspectives: growth (of gross national product, agriculture, and industry), and stability (of prices and employment). In the course of this examination, attention is given to the contribution of the land reform movement to both stability and industrial growth, the rapid urbanization of the country, and the future direction of agricultural development. The record of industrial growth and its prospects are noted in two essays, the relative brevity of which in no way subtracts from the awesome record of industrial achievement. The history of industrial progress in the Republic of China on Taiwan should be read in conjunction with the discussion of Taiwan's external economic relations. Industrialization was and remains closely geared to foreign trade and relies significantly on international technology transfers. Finally, in Part III, the distribution of the fruits of economic growth is analyzed and compared with the record of a number of other developing countries. A special aspect of distribution, particularly important in the economic history of the Republic of China on Taiwan, namely the distribution of educational opportunity, is the subject of the last essay in this section.

Prof. Prybyla, editor of this subsection, is Professor of Economics, Pennsylvania State University (College Park, Penn.).

I.   The Taiwan Economy: General Background

Taiwan: A Survey

Henry Y. Wan, Jr.

Tawian is an island of 13,885 square miles, slightly smaller than either Switzerland or the Netherlands, or the combined area of Connecticut, Massachusetts, and Rhode Island. Less than one third of this is arable. Irrigation and much chemical fertilizer are required for good crops. The rest of the area is mountainous, covered by forests of indifferent commercial value. Coal, limestone, and natural gas are present in quantities insufficient for local needs. The same holds for hydroelectric energy. For "The Beautiful Island," nature has not been bountiful.

Under Japanese rule, 1894-1945, Taiwan supplied tropical produce and rice to fulfill the import-substituting goal of the Japanese Empire. Japan left three legacies: (1) good roads and port facilities, (2) some food processing industries, and (3) a peasantry conducive to technical change. The naval blockade and aerial bombing in World War II reduced (1) and (2) to pale shadows of their old selves.

The postwar years, 1946-1952, were a time of turmoil and trial. During the first three years, the government of the Republic of China at Nanking was locked in desperate civil strife. The best administrators and technicians went to Manchuria; all resources were mobilized for war. Nothing could be spared for Taiwanese reconstruction. War damage was noticeable in Taipei until 1949. Railroad shipping reached its prewar peak only by 1951. The recovery has not been rapid. From 1952 to 1956, both Japan and mainland China were no longer sheltered markets. About 1.2 million evacuees had to be absorbed in an economy of less than 7 million. Military preparedness assumed top priority to stop any invasion forces across the strait of Pescadores. Inflation raged: 3400 percent in 1949, 306 percent in 1950, 66 percent in 1951, and 23 percent in 1952. The currency reform in 1949 failed to stem the tide, and the government deficit was financed by money issue. As a last resort, a multitude of controls were clamped down on trade and foreign exchange to preserve the remaining foreign assets. By late 1950, much needed U.S. aid came on the heels of the Korean War. Yet the repeated reversals suffered by the UN Command in the first year of the war did not inspire investors anywhere off the Asian mainland.

The decade 1953-62 was one of consolidation and stabilization. With U.S. aid, both the double-digit inflation and exchange rate devaluation came to an end by 1960. Import substitution policies were adopted to secure supplies of chemical fertilizer, textiles, and cement. Under the 1953 land-to-the-tiller program, shares of state enterprises were distributed to landlords to secure their titles. Titles were given to tenant farmers against their installment payments in grain over a decade. A series of trade and foreign exchange liberalization measures were adopted between 1958 and 1963. Per capita real income grew at the average annual rate of 3 percent, a creditable but average record for other LDCs. Some structural change of the economy also occurred. The percentage of rice and sugar—traditional staples exported from Taiwan—in total exports fell steadily, reaching 50 percent in 1960. The changing structure of the economy is depicted by the following figures:

Henry Y. Wan, Jr., "Manpower, Industrialization and Export-led Growth—The Taiwan Experience," in Yuan-li Wu and Kung-chia Yeh (eds.), *Growth, Distribution, and Social Change: Essays on the Economy of the Republic of China, Occasional Papers/Reprints Series on Contemporary Asian Studies*, (University of Maryland, School of Law), No. 3–1978 (15), pp. 138-141. Footnotes are omitted.

Percent of Employment		Percent of GDP		Percent of Export	
Agriculture	Industry	Agriculture	Industry	Agricultural Good and Products	Industrial Products
(1953) 61	9	38	18	93	7
(1962) 55	12	29	26	49	51

The years 1963-73 represented a period of sustained growth. Various fiscal schemes— e.g., tax holidays and tariff rebates on imported material processed for exports—were adopted to encourage foreign investment and export. Export cartels for farm products, export processing zones for manufactured exports, industrial parks designed for land purchases and setting up infrastructure were all adopted. The government recognized that close international economic contacts may promote both economic prosperity and international support to forestall or offset diplomatic reversals. In this period, population growth slowed down from 3.2 percent to under 2 percent. Per capita real GDP grew at an average rate of 7 percent per year. The changing structure of employment, GDP, and exports has continued. The data on employment and GDP will be shown later. The structural change of exports continued, the percentage of agricultural goods and products fell from 43 percent to 17 percent and the percentage of industrial products went from 55 percent to 83 percent. Within the "industrial exports," 90 percent were manufacturing products. Structural changes also took place.

The fastest growth between 1966 and 1971 belonged to the electronics industry. This industry attracts most of the foreign investment and exports most of its output. Its subsectors, telecommunication and generators/motors, grew at annual rates of 80 percent and 54 percent. In 1971, 60 percent of textile products were exported. The subsectors of knitted products and processed apparel also grew at 65 percent and 41 percent per year between 1966 and 1971. Another industry that attracted foreign investment and exported much of the output is rubber, chemical, and petroleum products. Its output growth in 1963-72 kept pace with the industrial sector as a whole—i.e., its output rose by five times. Finally, food, beverages, and tobacco industries increased their output by a factor of 2.5 in that decade. Consequently, their weight among all manufacturing outputs fell over time. During this period of rapid growth, the average increase of wholesale prices was 3.5 percent. The official exchange rate to the U.S. dollar remained at 40:1 throughout, and there was scarcely any difference between the official and black market rates. Unemployment was insignificant, but the real wage was rising. The ratio of exports to GDP rose to about 50 percent.

This years 1974-76 were a period of external disturbances and internal adjustment. Near the end of 1973, the rise of world prices over Taiwan prices caused an explosive export boom. Stock-in-trade was quickly depleted and export revenue was instantly transformed into domestic money supply. The shortage of soy beans was followed by the oil crisis. The government briefly subsidized imported farm produce at an untenable fiscal cost. When this measure was finally abandoned, it was coupled with a sharp increase of public utility rates. In early 1974, prices rose by more than 50 percent in one year. By then the recession in the developed world deepened. Export markets for a while disintegrated and factories started laying off workers. Per capita GDP fell but prices stabilized under a tight monetary policy. As recovery in Japan and the United States finally came, the Taiwan economy also started to recover. The surprising resilience of the economy shows that even during an acute international recession Taiwan could weather the storm without resorting to quotas and controls.

II. Growth and Stability
1. Gross National Products

An Overview on Taiwan's GNP

Kung-chia Yeh

Taiwan emerged from the Second World War a backward, war-torn economy. In six years, it more or less restored its prewar productive capacity. During the following two decades, it has become one of the fastest growing economies in the world, and its living standard has risen far above levels prevalent in most Asian countries.

Figure 1. Indexes of Real GNP, Population, and GNP per Capita

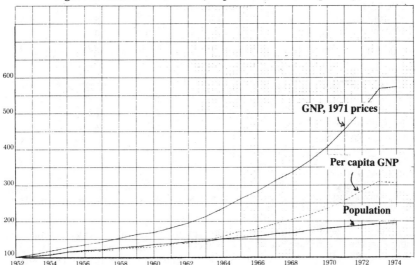

Data underlying this chart refer to GDP in constant 1971 prices and are taken from *Statistical Yearbook 1975*, pp. 194-195; and *Monthly Bulletin*, November 1976, p. 18. In general, there are two conceptually different measures of total product: gross national product (GNP) and gross domestic product (GDP). GNP refers to total output attributable to the factors of production supplied by the nationals of Taiwan; GDP refers to total payments from abroad. GNP is the appropriate measure of its productive capacity.

The most common yardstick for evaluating economic performances is the growth of real gross national product. Figure 1 shows changes in Taiwan's GNP, population, and per capita product in 1952-72. The tremendous growth of total output since 1952 is unmistakable. By 1972, GNP rose to more than five times its initial level, and per capita GNP was 186 percent higher than in 1952. Growth was continuous throughout the period and has actually accelerated since the early 1960s. The oil crisis in 1973 and its disruption of the world economy also brought a halt to Taiwan's growth in 1974, but since 1975 the economy has been turning upward again.

Kung-chia Yeh, "Economic Growth: An Overview," in Yuan-li Wu and Kung-chia Yeh (Eds.), *Growth, Distribution, and Social Change: Essays on the Economy of the Republic of China, Occasional Papers/Reprints Series in Contemporary Asian Studies* (University of Maryland, School of Law), No. 3–1978 (15), pp 11-23. Most footnotes are omitted.

Table 1. Rates of Growth of Population and
GNP, 1952-1972†

	1952-72	1952-60	1960-65	1965-72
GNP per captia				
Republic of China	5.6	3.6	6.4	7.3
Japan	8.5	7.2	8.8	9.5
South Korea	4.8	2.7	3.6	8.4
Philippines	2.7	3.1	1.6	2.9
Communist China	3.3	3.6	2.9	3.3
India	1.3	1.8	0	1.8
GNP††				
Republic of China	8.8	7.2	9.6	10.1
Japan	9.6	8.3	9.8	10.8
South Korea	7.2	4.9	6.4	10.3
Philippines	4.7	6.2	5.0	5.6
Communist China	5.6	6.0	4.7	5.7
India	3.5	3.8	2.6	3.9
Population				
Republic of China	3.2	3.6	3.2	2.8
Japan	1.1	1.1	1.0	1.3
South Korea	2.4	2.2	2.8	1.9
Philippines	3.0	3.1	3.4	2.7
Communist China	2.2	2.3	1.8	2.3
India	2.2	2.0	2.6	2.1

†The initial year for South Korea is 1953.

††For Republic of China, the growth rates are based on gross national product in constant market prices of 1966; for Japan, South Korea, and Communist China, gross national product in constant prices; for the Philippines and India, net domestic product at constant factor cost. Source omitted.

To show how fast the Taiwan economy has been growing compared with other countries, Table 1 presents the average rates of growth of GNP, population, and per capita product for Taiwan and five selected Asian countries in 1952-72 and three subperiods.* The year 1952 has been selected as a base point for appraisal mainly because by then the economies had fairly well recovered from the war and were entering a new phase of economic growth. In Taiwan, the land reform program initiated in 1951 was just about completed. Agricultural output had regained its prewar peak. The focus of U.S aid, which began flowing in soon after the Korean War, now shifted from rehabilitation to expanding social infrastructure and agriculture. For Communist China and India, the year 1952 marked the period immediately before they both launched their first five year plans. In Korea, the war had by then stabilized, and rehabilitation and growth got underway soon afterward. The choice of 1972 as the terminal point is not a compelling one; indeed, a more recent year might have been preferred. However, it was the last year before the worldwide economic disruptions caused by the oil crisis in 1973 and thus provides a convenient vantage point from which to take stock of developments in the last two decades.

The striking feature suggested by Table 1 is the rather high growth rate of Taiwan's per

*The measures of total product for the six countries are not uniform. Some represent gross domestic product, others refer to gross national product. Some are net, others are gross of capital consumption. Some are based on constant market prices of a certain year, others are based on constant factor cost of another year. Even if uniform measures were available, international comparisons of rates of GNP growth would still be beset with numerous conceptual and statistical difficulties. For a brief discussion of thoses complexities, see Simon Kuznets, *Economic Growth of Nations*, (Cambridge, Mass.: Belknap Press), 1971, pp. 3-10.

capita income of 5.6 percent per year since 1952, which exceeded those in all other countries except Japan. In particular, Taiwan's growth rate is much higher than those of the Philippines, mainland China, and India. The rapid growth of Taiwan's per capita income is all the more remarkable if one notices that Taiwan's population increased very rapidly during this period. In fact, all the five developing countries in Table 1 had quite high rates of population growth of more than 2 percent per year. But Taiwan's population increased the fastest, at an average rate of 3.2 percent per year during the last two decades. Yet, despite such a high rate of population growth, per captia income expanded at a phenomenal pace, faster than in the other developing countries. This implies, of course, that Taiwan's aggregate income expanded even more rapidly than those of other countries. In the two decades since 1952, Taiwan's real GNP rose at an average rate of 8.8 percent per year, second only to Japan's 9.6 percent, and higher than those of others, which range from India's 3.5 percent to Korea's 7.2 percent.

Table 1 also shows the growth rates in three subperiods: 1952-60, 1960-65, and 1965-72. The main reasons for taking 1960 and 1965 as intermediate time points are that there had been a major shift in Taiwan's developing policy around 1960 and that economic assistance from the U.S. terminated in 1965. It is of interest to examine how the economy performed after these crucial events took place. For other countries such a periodization might seem arbitrary, but it apparently introduces no serious distortion except perhaps in the cast of India, which had a poor year in 1965.

During these three subperiods, growth of Taiwan's per capita income has been accelerating. The growth rate in the 1960s was distinctly higher than in the 1950s. The higher growth rate since 1965 is of particular interest, for it signifies unmistakably a sustained growth without external economic aid. Among the countries listed in Table 1, only Japan and South Korea experienced a similar pattern of accelerating growth. For the others (the Philippines, Communist China, and India) no acceleration occurred. In the latter case, the average growth rates in the second subperiod (1960-65) declined rather sharply and they hardly recovered to their initial levels in the third subperiod (1965-72).

In contrast to total GNP, Taiwan's population growth has been declining, from 3.6 percent in the 1950s to about 3 percent in the 1960s, quite possibly as a result of the population control program. Again, no comparable downward trend can be found in the other countries during the same period. However, up to the early 1970s, Taiwan's population growth rate remained the highest, more than twice as high as Japan's. If population growth should continue to slow down as is likely, per capita income could increase even faster.

As a result of rapid growth in the last two decades, Taiwan now ranks high among the Asian countries in terms of per capita income. It is substantially higher than that of neighboring Korea, not to mention the average for the world developing countries. But equally clear, it still has a long way to catch up when compared with the developed countries.

Economic Stability

Economic stability refers here to stability in the domestic price level and in the growth of total output with reference to a long-term trend. Clearly, economic stability is a highly desirable development goal. Fluctuations in prices and output not only disrupt economic growth, they generally result in underutilization of the economic capacity and more inequitable distribution of income. In an important sense, economic stability is also an essential element in political and social stability. Has the Taiwan economy been able to maintain relative stability in the process of rapid growth? We focus first on fluctuations in its total economic activity.

Table 2 compares the year-to-year fluctuations in GNP for Taiwan and five other Asian economies in the last two decades. For reference, we also include the averages for 18 free market economies and eight planned economies in 1950-60.* The measure of the degree of

---

*The 18 free market economies are: Austria, Belgium, Canada, Denmark, France, Germany (F.R.), Greece, Iceland, Ireland, Italy, Luxemburg, the Netherlands, Norway, Portugal, Sweden, Turkey, the United Kingdom, and the United States. The 8 planned economies include: Bulgaria, Czechoslovakia, East Germany, Hungary, Poland, Rumania, the Soviet Union, and Yugoslavia.

Table 2.   Fluctuations in GNP, Selected Countries

Country	Period	Degree of instability
Taiwan	1952-72	2.0
Philippines	1950-70	2.0
Japan	1952-72	3.0
India	1950-72	3.1
South Korea	1953-72	3.3
Communist China	1952-72	9.5
Eighteen free market economies	1950-60	5.7
Eight planned economies	1950-60	2.7

Source omitted.

instability is the antilog of the square root of logarithmic variance of the series $Yt/Yt1$, with unity subtracted from the antilog. The value ranges from zero to infinity. If there were no fluctuation at all, the value would be zero. The higher the value, the less stable the path of growth. As Table 2 shows, economic growth in Taiwan has been much smoother than in almost any of the other five countries and the averages for planned and free market economies in the 1950s. Of particular interest is the exceptionally high degree of instability in Communist China. While the European Communist economies were subject to wider fluctuations than those of the free market economies, Communist China had even greater instability in growth than the other planned economies.

The Chinese Communists claim that fluctuations result in higher rates of growth. The implication is that the pace of development and smoothness of the growth path are trade-offs. A rough test of this proposition is made in a scatter diagram relating the rates of growth to the measure of instability in Figure 3. If the Communist claim were empirically true, the data should show a positive correlation between the growth rate and the degree of instability. But the scatter diagram for the six countries indicates no such relationship. It is not clear whether a larger sample would yield results that corroborate the proposition. In any event, data for all the countries except Communist China suggest that both high and low rates of growth could be achieved with fairly low degrees of instability. Among these six countries,

Table 3.   Average Annual Rates of Increase in Wholesale
and Consumer Prices, Selected Countries, 1952-73
(Percent per year)

	1952-60	1960-73	1952-73
Wholesale prices			
Taiwan	8.8	3.4	5.4
Japan	0.3	2.0	1.3
S. Korea	—	11.8	—
Philippines	0.9	8.3	5.4
India	2.6	6.9	5.2
	Consumer prices		
Taiwan	9.7	4.0	6.1
Japan	2.4	6.2	4.7
S. Korea	18.9	12.2	14.7
Philippines	0.2	3.6	2.3
India	2.2	6.9	5.1

Source omitted.

Figure 2.   Scatter Diagram: Growth Rate and Instability

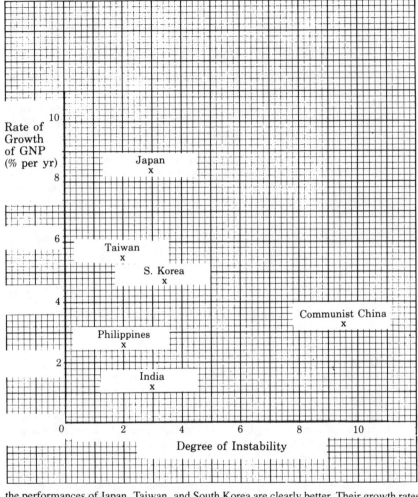

the performances of Japan, Taiwan, and South Korea are clearly better. Their growth rates are higher and their paths of growth have been quite smooth. That of Communist China is perhaps the worst. Its growth rate is considerably lower than the three best countries, and its economy exhibited a much higher degree of instability.

Taiwan was also successful in maintaining price stability. To be sure, there were considerable inflationary pressures immediately after the war and following the massive evacuation from the mainland. However, since 1952, the implicit GDP deflator rose at a moderate rate of 6.8 percent per year. This is well within the limit of 10 percent considered by some economists as the maximum justifiable price of rapid development. The path to price stability has not been a smooth one. During the earlier period 1952-60, the inflationary rate was about 10 percent per year. It was not until the 1960s that it fell to about 5 percent. In 1974-75, prices rose sharply by 34 percent, but the rate of increase has since declined.

Table 3 compares the rates of increase of the wholesale and consumer price indexes in Taiwan and four other countries in 1952-73. The comparison shows that, for the period as a whole, Taiwan's wholesale price and consumer price indexes rose at a rate faster than those of all others except Korea. Taiwan's higher rate of inflation than Japan's should not be surprising. The finanical system in a developed country like Japan is apparently more efficient in mobilizing and economizing the use of money in the face of inflation, and the degree of mobility of resources is likely to be higher so that the response of output to price changes might well be faster and more flexible. The higher inflationary rates in Taiwan than in other developing countries seem to suggest that Taiwan had been less successful than others in controlling inflation. This is clearly true of the period 1952-60. Wholsale and consumer prices in Taiwan rose at a rate many times those of others, except Korea, which was still feeling the effects of the war. However, the picture was very much different in the 1960s. Although the inflation rates in Japan, the Philippines, and India were higher than in the 1950s, those in Taiwan declined markedly. It may be recalled that Taiwan's economic growth during this period (1960-72) was much faster than 1952-60. The experience of Taiwan suggests that inflation need not be a concomitant of rapidly rising per capita income, either as an instrument of development policy or an inevitable outcome of structural change.

The comparison in Table 3 leaves out the case of the Chinese mainland, mainly because data on price changes are lacking. Official sources claim that prices have been stable (in the past). However, almost all prices are administratively set. Changes in demand and supply conditions generally are reflected in quantity changes rather than in price variations. Price stability under these conditions thus has a different meaning and cannot be easily interpreted.

GNP Growth and Stability: The Record To-Date

Jan S. Prybyla

Gross National Product (GNP)

It is well known that Taiwan's growth record since the early 1950s has been remarkable. Together with West Germany and Japan, Taiwan's performance should be included in the post World War II catalogue of economic "miracles." Dissimilar as are the details and points of departure, in all three instances the mircale is basically attributable to three domestic factors: an able, motivated, healthy, educated, disciplined labor force; a dynamic private enterprise sector; and enlightened governmental economic leadership. The combination of these provided fertile soil for initial American aid.

In real terms (constant prices of 1971) Taiwan's GNP increased 700 percent between 1952 and 1978, at an average annual rate of 8.4 percent, and a per captia annual rate of more than 5 percent (possibly higher if the bugs were taken out of the price deflator). Of the 700 percent 1952-78 GNP increases, 117 percentage points are attributable to increased employment; the remainder to increased labor productivity. Except for the imported OPEC-sponsored recession of 1974-75, Taiwan's real GNP growth has been smooth. Both as regards the pace and path of growth, Taiwan's record is superior to that of a number of Asian developing countries, including the People's Republic of China (Table 1). At the time of derecognition (end 1978) per capita GNP (1976 prices) was U.S.$1,337. (Per capita national income in 1976 prices was U.S.$1,218 an increase of 9.8 percent over 1977.) Around the time of derecognition Taiwan was listed by the Organization for Economic Cooperation and Development (OECD) as one of ten newly industrializing countries that were rapidly rising from low income levels to comparative affluence.

Jan S. Prybyla, "Some Reflections on Derecognition and the Economy of Taiwan," in *Taiwan: One Year After United States-China Normalizaton*, A workshop sponsored by the Committee on Foreign Relations, United States Senate, and Congressional Research Service, Library of Congress, (Washington, D.C.: U.S. Government Printing Service, 1980), pp. 72, 78-79, 82.

Table 1—Growth of Gross National Product
[Increase rate percent, at 1976 constant prices]

	Increase rate
Year:	(percent)
1970	11.27
1971	12.90
1972	13.31
1973	12.82
1974	1.12
1975	4.24
1976	13.48
1977	9.86
1978	13.85
1979 (preliminary)	8.10
1980 (expected)	6.5-8.0

Sources omitted.

Price Stability

Taiwan's phenomental growth had been accompanied in the past by remarkable price stability. In the 10 years preceding the OPEC price increases (1963-72) the annual increase in Taiwan's wholesale price index was 1.8 percent with a GNP growth rate of about 10 percent a year. The escalating price of imported oil and raw materials destabilized the domestic price level in 1973-74; wholesale prices shot up 41 percent in 1974. After 1974 and until 1979 wholesale price increases were kept down to about 3 percent a year. In 1978 the wholesale price index rose by 3.5 percent and the index of consumer prices by 5.8 percent. (In 1980 the inflation rate was in excess of 20 percent.)

Employment

Since 1968 the annual unemployment rate has been below 2 percent: 1.7 percent in 1978. An emerging problem consists in the conjunction of labor scarcity (hence strong, if unorganized, pressures on the wage level) and employer reluctance to raise wages due to the fear of losing an already slim competitive price edge in the world market. In recent years manufacturers' response to the problem has increasingly taken the form of importation of labor-saving machinery. One side effect of labor scarcity has been the expansion of fringe benefits provided to workers by the larger employers, including subsidized meals in factory canteens, free dormitories, payment of tuition fees for workers attending schools, free movies, and improved working conditions.

Prospects

As in the developmental experience of Japan, Taiwan's domestic market is becoming gradually a significant contributor to growth. If all goes well, by the end of the present decade per capita income is scheduled (by the 10-Year Economic Development Plan, at least), to reach U.S.$6,200 in current prices with a total GNP of U.S.$110 billion (U.S.$24 billion in 1978).

The immediate as well as longer term concern is with the twin problem of growth and inflation. Continued foreign investor confidence in Taiwan and the expanding domestic market are counted on to sustain the first; determined monetary and fiscal policies taken by the central bank and the government are relied on to keep down the second. The upgrading of the technological content of industry, accelerated writing-off of obsolete equipment, and merger of small manufacturing firms are intended to bring about dramatic increases in productivity and relieve pressures on the labor market. This combination, plus the addition of 200,000 recruits to the labor force, will hopefully keep wage increase rates well below the rate of labor (and more generally factor) productivity increases.

2.   Agriculture and Rural-Urban Migration

The 1949-53 Land Reform

Ching-yuan Lin

On April 14, 1949, within three months after he was appointed governor of Taiwan, General Chen Cheng put into effect a rent-reduction program for farmlands in Taiwan. This was well before its formal enactment by the legislative body. Together with the land-to-the-tiller program that followed in 1953, the determinedness shown by the general in the pursuit of land reform can be fully comprehended only by reference to the circumstances under which he became governor. In his own words:

> At that juncture the general situation on the mainland was deteriorating fast, the morale of people in Taiwan was low, economic confusion and social unrest were rampant, and it looked as if anything might happen. To safeguard the island as a base of operations for national recovery, we required social stability, and the first prerequisite had to be satisfactory solution of the problem of the people's livelihood.

In his capacity as a wartime provincial governor on the mainland, Chen had had success with experimentations in rent reduction in Hupeh in 1940. Seeing that the rise of the Communist regime on the mainland was rural-based, the general naturally believed that "social stability, improved people's livelihood and economic development could take place only through land reform." Thus the land-reform measures instituted in Taiwan at the turn of the 1950s can be understood more accurately as a political preventive act taken in order to prevent repetition of the widespread social unrest that had occurred on the mainland. The fact that these measures were taken does not necessarily mean that the tenant-landlord relationship in Taiwan was at the boiling point at that time.* For, although "social and economic conditions of Taiwan still rested on an agricultural basis and farmers constituted more than three fifths of the population and the numbers of tenants was more than two thirds of the farm families." the tenant-landlord relationship was basically no longer feudal in nature after the first land reform instituted by the Japanese governor-general a half-century earlier. Furthermore, although land rents were high (owing to the worsening man-land ratio), perhaps the more urgent problem confronting the rather price-responsive rural economy of Taiwan at that time was the depressing effects of the loss of preferential markets in Japan and mainland China for many farm products, plus runaway inflation, which raised the cost of living on the one hand and which forced the authorities to adopt a low rice price policy on the other. As the rent-reduction program was instituted in 1949, well before the imposition of foreign-exchange controls in 1951, it would be misleading to claim that the land-reform program was originally intended to be part of the measures designed to facilitate Taiwan's inward-oriented development in the 1950s. Nevertheless, by replacing a great number of landowners and keeping food prices low, land reform and related measures did contribute to the rise of urban-centered industrial development; it did this by giving a "push" effect to the outflow of rural resources, in combination with the "pull" effect exerted by foreign-exchange and import controls.

As a matter of fact the 1948 fixing of tenanted-land rent at 37.5 percent of the volume of the main crop harvested, together with the stringent conditions under which landlords could recall their lands for their own use or for selling to a third party, deprived the landlords of any incentive to reinvest in farmlands, for they were no longer able to share in the fruits of

---

Ching-yuan Lin, *Industrialization in Taiwan, 1946-72: Trade and Import-Substitution Policies for Developing Countries* (New York: Praeger Publishers, 1973), pp. 50, 52-58. Some footnotes omitted. Copyright 1973 by Praeger, used with the permission of the publisher.

*In this connection it must be pointed out that the social upheaval in Taiwan in February-March 1947 was urban—not rural—in character.

any increase in land productivity on tenanted land.* Therefore the market value of farmland immediately dropped, amid the upsurge in the prices of industrial goods. By 1952, the year before implementation of the land-to-the-tiller program, a piece of tenanted land fared only around one-third of its price in 1948 (Table 1). Many landowners, therefore, were compelled to relinquish their lands at only a fraction of the real worth, even before the government started compulsory purchases at the lowered prices in 1953 for resale to the tenants. In these transactons both the government and the tenants benefited from the lowered land prices. And as a result of the voluntary and compulsory redistribution of private lands, plus the sales in 1948, 1952, and 1958 of public lands formerly belonging to Japanese landlords (including the sugar corporations), the number of owner-farmers increased and the number of tenant-farmers declined in both absolute and relative terms. The pattern of landholdings became more equitable, albeit fractured. In 1955 a total of 583,000 families held 35 percent of all farmland in individual holdings of one hectare or less, compared with 1952, when a total of 432,000 families held 25 percent of all farmland in such smallholdings. According to the Food Bureau's own estimate, farm families tilling 0.8 hectare of less of farmland had little marketable surplus of rice after paying in kind for land taxes, fertilizer barter, and debts in installments on land acquired through the government. One consequence of transforming former tenant farmers into owners of small-farms, coupled with the low rice price policy taken as a part of anti-inflationary policy, was therefore to raise the propensity of the farmers as a group to consume goods, particularly rice.

Immediately after taking over the island's administration, the Chinese authorities imposed government control on inventory speculation and export of rice by the private sector; they did this in order to stabilize food prices under the inflationary condition. A provincial food bureau was created in January 1946, and it was charged with the task of procuring rice from the farmers for distribution to the great number of servicemen and civil servants, and of controlling its market price. To secure an adequate supply of rice, the Food Bureau was authorized to collect in rice (1) taxes and surtaxes on farmland, (2) rents on public lands, (3) repayments for fertilizer, cotton fabrics, soybean cake, and other farm inputs distributed, as well as agricultural loans made, to the farmers, and (4) repayments for the land distributed or sold to the farmers after the inception of the land-to-the-tiller program and sales of public lands. The volume of rice thus collected did not exceed more than 30 percent of annual rice output; based on estimates by the Food Bureau of the pattern of rice consumption and disposal by average farm households, however, the volume of rice may have amounted to as much as 70 percent of rice not consumed in the farm sector (Table 2). Aside from exporting some rice to Japan in exchange for ammonium sulfate, the Food Bureau used its rice stocks to intervene in the market whenever necessary and managed to keep the rice price low in relation to general price levels during the 1950s—except in 1953 and 1959-60, when abnormal conditions prevailed.

In addition to the unfavorable price of rice, farm incomes from most other major export crops (bananas, canned pineapple, and tea) must have been depressed in the early 1950s, judging from the greatly reduced export volumes of these products as compared to the normal prewar years. The only exception was the temporary prosperity enjoyed by the recovery of sugar exports in the immediate postwar years. Owing to the deemphasis on sugar production in Taiwan by the expanded Japanese empire and the need to boost rice production in the last war years, the area planted to sugarcane declined to only 33,700 hectares in 1946-47—roughly one-fifth of its peak (1938-39). With the mainland supply meeting only about one-fourth of China's estmated demand of 120 metric tons, the Chinese authorities took to resotre sugar-refining capacity and to restimulate cane planting in Taiwan. In June 1946 the Taiwanese farmers were given a direct share in sugar production instead of supplying canes to the sugar corporations at a price linked to changes in rice

---

*The actual ratio of rent to output for tenanted land declined over the years following the increase in land productivity. By 1960-61 it was down to 22-23 percent of the volume of actual harvest. See T. Sasamoto and S. Kawano, *A Comprehensive Study of the Taiwan Economy* (in Japanese) (Tokyo, Institute of Asian Economic Affairs: 1968), Vol. 1, p. 168.

Table 1
Decline in Value of Paddy Fields After the
37.5-Percent Rent Reduction
(1948 = 100)

Year	7th Grade	10th Grade	16th Grade	22nd Grade
1948	100	100	100	100
1949	65	71	67	65
1950	67	63	57	41
1951	56	48	42	38
1952	38	43	35	27

Note: Paddy fields in Taiwan are graded, from 1 to 26, for taxation purposes. The lower the number, the better the land. Source omitted.

changes in rice prices, as had been the practice during the Japanese period.* With the farmers receiving a share in rising sugar prices, Taiwan's cane-planting area rapidly recovered; this however, worked only to intensify the depression of domestic sugar prices in 1949, when the mainland market was lost. In the middle of that year the price ratio between sugar ad rice turned to 3:1 in favor of rice, and thus caused the farmers to delay the planting of sugarcane. At this the authorities hastened to restore the sugar-cane-rice linkage by offering to cane farmers a one-to-one price guarantee for sugar relative to rice. Nevertheless the planting area for the 1950-51 season was low, and the Chinese government therefore largely missed the windfall gain from the Korean War price boom. The boom in world sugar prices, however, was short-lived; during 1952-53 the Taiwan Sugar Corporation was placed in an impossible situation of having to pay the cane farmers a tremendous price subsidy owing to the coincidence of a low sugar export price and a high rice export price. This had prompted the government to permanently sever the direct link between the prices of sugar and rice. Instead a minimum price calculated on the basis of net earnings from potential competing crops was offered as of the 1953-54 season. With the world sugar price staying low for the rest of the 1950s, the planting of sugarcane thus retreated from the paddy fields, particularly in the northern part of the island.

While the prices of major farm produce were thus depressed, the prices of farm inputs and daily essentials, including chemical fertilizers, bicycles, cotton fabrics, and salted fish, were made relatively high, owing either to fiscal consideratons or to the imposition of import controls. In addition to the payment of taxes and nontaxes in rice at prices 30 percent or more below the market prices, the farmers were required to barter rice for fertilizers at a one-to-one ratio-fertilizers that the government imported at only one-half or even one-third of the export price of rice. Such deterioration in the farmers' relative income positon, and the increase in their tax burden would not have been possible without bringing the tenant farmers' sufferings to a dangerous point under the tenancy conditons that existed before 1949. In retrospect, therefore, the land-reform program, which redistributed farm income in favor of the tenants or former tenant farmers, made it possible for the agricultural sector to meet its increased fiscal burden and to support the urban-centered industrial development.

For the 143,000 "chias" of farmlands they gave up, 106,000 landowning families received compensation at 2.5 times the value of the annual yield of the land, with 70 percent in land bonds payable in kind (in rice or sweet potatoes, depending on whether the piece of land given up was paddy or dryland) in installments in 10 years, and 30 percent in shares of four industrial corporations owned by the government. In the process the landowners suf-

*The farmers share, originally set at 48 percent, was raised to 50 percent in 1947, and to 55 percent in 1961.

Table 2
Estimated Output and Disposal of Rice Grain
per Hectare, for Average Owner-Farmer of Average
Size Land-holding, 1960

Category	Amount per Hectare (kilograms)	Percent of Total yield (percent)	Percent of Surplus (percent)
Yield of grain [a]	3,151	100	
Farm Consumption and seed use [b]	1,853	58	
Surplus for nonfarm use	1,298		100
Payments or repayments in kind to government [c]	942	30	73
Marketable surplus [d]	356	12	27

[a] Based on the following computation: 38 percent of the yield was derived from two-crop paddy, 23 percent from one-crop paddy, and 39 percent from dryland fields, with all growing areas being in the tenth-grade category.

[b] Based on consumption of 252 kilograms per person for a family of seven members, plus 30 kilograms for farmhands.

[c] Based on the rates prevailing of land taxes, etc. in 1960.

[d] The average small farmer had a deficit rather than a marketable surplus. The average holding of 0.8 hectares per household had a deficit of 68 kilograms; one of 0.5 hectares per household had a deficit of 704 kgs.

Source omitted.

fered substantial capital loss, because of the undervaluation of the land they gave up on the one hand, and because of the overvaluation of the industrial shares they received on the other. The land they gave up used to command a price not just 2.5 times, but as much as 4 times greater than its annual yield during the prewar period.* In contrast the value of the industrial shares they received was substantially watered in the process of revaluation before the transfer of ownership, as may be surmised from the steep decline in the market value of three of the four corporations after the transfer. Except for the shares of the cement corporation, whose product enjoyed strong domestic demand, the market values of the corporations stayed at one-half or even one-third of their face value for several years amid the rise in general price level. Although the landowners were given compensation, it thus appears that such compensation was by no means fair and equitable, and that the litte resistance the Chinese government had had in the whole process of land reform in Taiwan, as in the previous case of land reform under the Japanese, can be explained better by the fact that in both cases the ruling authorities enforcing the reform program were outsiders who did not have anything to lose in the process. (This point must be borne in mind when considering the applicability of Taiwan's land-reform measures to other countries).

In the process of Taiwan's land reform a great number of small landowners had no doubt suffered tremendously, but over time the attention of the great masses of people was redirected from the traditional rural activity to the new urban-centered activity. Although some former landlords succeeded in getting a footing in the nonindustrial sector, that sector came to be dominated by owners of family factories and former merchants who took advantage of the government's new policy emphasis by moving into manufacturing activity from the conventional import-export businesses.

*According to an expert estimate the yield of rice per hectare and the value of paddy per hectare in terms of paddy rice averaged 5,241 kilograms and 22,387 kilograms respectively for 1936-40. See Teng-Hui Lee, "Intersectoral Capital Flows in the Economic Development of Taiwan, 1895-1960" (unpublished Ph.D. dissertation, Cornell University, Ithaca, N.Y., 1968), p. 151, Table 5.4

Land Reform and Land Ownership

Yung Wei

It has often been asserted that one of the major reasons for the Nationalist defeat on the Mainland was their failure to carry out land reform as envisaged by Dr. Sun Yat-sen. After the Chinese Nationalists retreated to Taiwan, a successful and peaceful land reform has been realized on the island. Through a series of policy measures such as the reduction of land rent, sale of public land, and ownership of the land for the former tenants, the government of Taiwan has by and large achieved its goal of equalization of land ownership.

The effectiveness of the land reform can be measured by the ratio of tenant farmers, partially self-tilling farmers, and self-tilling farmers. In 1949, the ratio was 39 percent tenant farmers, 25 percent partially self-tilling farmers, and 36 percent self-tilling farmers. After the land reform, the respective figures were 10, 12, and 78 percent in 1971. The effect of the redistribution of land can be further illustrated by using a widely used measurement of inequality—The Gini index. As data in Table 1 indicate, the Gini index was diminished to 0.457, which indicates a much lower level of inequality in land distribution. In comparison to Colombia, India, Mexico, Philippines, and U.A.R., Taiwan has a higher equity in the distribution of land ownership (see Table 1).

Table 1
Gini Index of Land Concentration in Selected Countries

Country	Year	Gini Index[a] (C)	Year	Gini Index (E)	Decline in Gini Index, in Percentage $\frac{(C) - (E)}{(C)} \times 100$
Colombia	1960	0.864	1969	0.818	5.32
India	1953-1954	0.628	1960-1961	0.589	6.14
Mexico	1930	0.959	1960	0.694	27.64
Philippines	1948	0.576	1960	0.534	7.26
Taiwan	1952	0.618	1960	0.457	26.08
U.A.R.	1952	0.810	1964	0.674	16.74

Source omitted.

According to statistics released by the Taiwan government (GRC), land reform has clearly led to higher per acreage production by the self-tilling farmer, which in turn led to an increase of income. Martin M. C. Yang notes that land reform in Taiwan has brought about a significant socio-economic change in rural Taiwan including increasing interest in participation in community affairs, inclination to adopt innovative farming methods, and rising expectation in the educational level of children of farmers. In contrast to the former tenant farmers the former landlords (who had been compensated by the GRC for their land by government bonds and stocks) have diverted their interest increasingly to economic pursuits in urban centers, and have gradually lost interest in politics in the rural community. Their previously dominant role in local politics was gradually assumed by the self-tilling farmers. Thus a redistribution of land ownership in rural Taiwan has also led to a redistribution of political power in the countryside and in small towns on the island.

Yung Wei, "Modernization Process in Taiwan: An Allocative Analysis," *Asian Survey,* Vol. XVI, No. 3 (March, 1976), pp. 257-258. Copyright 1976 by The Regents of the University of California. Reprinted by permission of The Regents.

Agricultural Output

by Chi-ming Hou

The increase of agricultural production in Taiwan since 1945 has been very impressive (see Table 1), with a growth rate averaging 6.2 percent a year for 1947-1975. During the recovery and rehabilitation stage after World War II—that is, from 1947 to 1952—the average annual growth rate was nearly 14 percent (Table 2). By 1952, the previous peak level reached in 1939 was restored. (During the years from 1939 to 1945, agricultural production declined sharply at 12.3 percent a year. In 1945, the level of production was the same as in 1910.)

Table 1. Index of Agricultural Output in Taiwan
(1971 = 100)

Year	Total	Farm Crops[a]	Forestry Products	Livestock Products	Fishery Products
1946	20.3	26.8	10.6	10.3	7.7
1947	25.4	33.5	16.8	12.1	9.3
1948	32.8	38.2	28.1	14.7	13.0
1949	33.5	44.6	20.7	15.0	12.4
1950	37.4	48.7	25.9	20.0	13.2
1951	39.0	48.7	28.5	26.2	15.9
1952	42.3	52.3	35.3	27.3	18.5
1953	46.3	56.7	36.0	33.8	19.0
1954	47.3	57.1	38.0	34.4	22.7
1955	47.6	56.3	40.0	35.7	26.2
1956	51.2	61.1	37.8	38.1	28.1
1957	54.9	64.6	43.8	42.6	31.0
1958	58.6	68.2	50.1	47.8	31.8
1959	59.6	68.0	64.2	47.4	33.9
1960	60.4	69.1	66.6	45.8	35.3
1961	65.7	74.2	76.0	50.7	40.6
1962	67.4	75.2	77.9	55.0	42.2
1963	67.5	74.2	77.6	56.4	45.4
1964	75.6	83.5	95.9	59.9	49.4
1965	80.5	90.2	97.9	61.6	51.4
1966	83.1	91.6	90.3	68.3	59.0
1967	88.3	95.4	91.9	78.0	66.7
1968	93.5	95.3	91.4	89.5	91.2
1970	98.7	99.9	95.7	98.3	95.3
1971	100.0	100.0	100.0	100.0	100.0
1972	102.6	101.1	93.7	107.9	107.1
1973	108.0	102.1	88.5	127.2	119.6
1974	108.5	107.6	81.8	117.5	114.0
1975	106.3	104.7	74.7	109.8	125.0

[a]Includes food products and other crops such as fibers, tobacco, tea, and coffee. Source omitted.

Chi-ming Hou, "Institutional Innovations, Technological Change and Agricultural Growth in Taiwan," in Yuan-li Wu and Kung-chia Yeh (eds.), *Growth, Distribution, and Social Change: Essays on the Economy of the Republic of China, Occasional Papers / Reprints Series in Contemporary Asian Studies* (University of Maryland, School of Law), No. 3-1978 (15), pp. 113-119. Footnotes omitted.

Table 2. Annual Growth Rates of Agricultural
Output in Taiwan

Year	Total	Farm Crops	Forestry Products	Livestock Products	Fishery Products
1947	25.1	25.0	58.5	17.5	20.8
1948	29.1	14.0	67.3	21.5	39.8
1949	2.1	16.8	−26.3	2.0	−4.6
1950	11.6	9.2	25.1	33.3	6.5
1951	4.3	0.0	10.0	31.0	20.5
1952	8.5	7.4	23.9	4.2	16.4
1953	9.5	8.4	2.0	23.8	2.7
1954	2.2	0.7	5.6	1.8	19.5
1955	0.6	−1.4	5.3	3.8	15.4
1956	7.6	8.5	−5.5	6.7	7.3
1957	7.2	5.7	15.9	11.8	10.3
1958	6.7	5.6	14.4	12.2	2.6
1959	1.7	−0.3	28.1	−0.8	6.6
1960	1.3	1.6	3.7	−3.4	4.1
1961	8.8	7.4	14.1	10.7	15.0
1962	2.6	1.3	2.5	8.5	3.9
1963	0.1	−1.3	−0.4	2.5	7.6
1964	12.0	12.5	23.6	6.2	8.8
1965	6.5	8.1	2.1	2.8	4.0
1966	3.1	1.4	−7.8	10.9	14.8
1967	6.3	4.1	1.8	14.2	13.1
1968	6.7	4.1	5.4	7.1	9.2
1969	−0.7	4.0	−5.7	7.2	9.2
1970	5.6	4.8	4.7	9.8	4.5
1971	1.3	0.1	4.5	1.7	4.9
1972	2.6	1.1	−6.3	7.9	7.1
1973	5.3	1.0	−5.5	17.9	11.7
1974	0.5	5.4	−7.6	−7.6	−4.7
1975	−2.0	−2.7	−8.7	−6.5	9.6
Average					
1947–52	13.5	12.1	26.4	18.3	16.6
1954–60	4.6	3.6	8.7	7.0	8.6
1961–65	6.0	5.6	8.4	6.1	7.9
1966–70	4.2	2.1	0.3	9.8	13.4
1971–75	1.5	1.0	−4.7	2.7	5.7
1947–75	6.2	5.0	8.4	9.3	10.8
1953–75	4.3	3.2	3.7	6.9	9.4

Source: Table 1.

After 1952, total agricultural production continued to grow, but at a lower rate. It increased at an annual rate of 4.6 percent from 1953 to 1960 and at 5.1 percent in the 1960s. The acceleration was particularly noticeable for livestock and fishery products. For farm crops, the annual rate of increase was 3.6 percent for 1953-1960 and 3.8 percent for 1961-70.

But starting in 1971, the rate of growth has declined substantially for all groups of products. For total agricultural production, the average growth rate was 1.5 percent from 1971 to 1975; for farm crops, 1.0 percent; and for livestock products, 2.7 percent. Forestry products declined at nearly 5 percent a year from 1971 to 1975. Only fishery products managed to grow at nearly 6 percent a year during this period.

If the averge of a five-year period is used, the growth rate started to decline rather sharply for farm crops and forestry products since 1961-65. Farm crops grew at 5.6 percent a year in 1961-65, and then only 2.1 percent in 1966-70. Forestry products hardly increased at all in 1966-70, after an annual increase of 8.4 percent in 1961-65. But livestock and fishery products continued to increase at an accelerated rate until 1970.

For the 23 years from 1953 to 1975, the average growth rate of total agricultural production was 4.3 percent, considerably higher than the growth rate of population, which averaged about 3 percent for the same period.

Among the categories of agricultural production, the growth rates varied substantially. For farm crops and forestry products, the average growth rates were 3.2 percent and 3.7 percent, respectively, for 1953-75. But for livestock and fishery products, they were 6.9 percent and 9.4 percent, respectively.

Table 3. Annual Growth Rates of Production of Farm Crops in Taiwan (Percent)

Years	Total	Rice	Other Dry Land Food Crops	Special Crops	Fruits	Vegetables	Mushrooms
1947–52	9.9	10.0	10.3	27.8	17.0	11.4	—
1953–60	3.2	2.6	5.4	5.0	7.5	3.9	—
1961–65	3.9	4.2	4.3	6.1	20.6	7.1	142.1
1966–70	1.0	1.1	0.2	− 3.3	9.1	14.2	− 5.1
1971–74	3.8	3.8	4.3	8.1	12.7	4.4	16.7
1947–74	3.8	3.8	4.3	8.1	12.7	8.0	—
1953–74	2.2	22.2	2.6	2.7	11.6	7.1	—

Source omitted.

Divergent growth rates also occurred among various farm crops. For major food grains, the growth rate was substantially lower than that of fruits, vegetables, and mushrooms, as Table 3 shows. The explanation probably lies at least in part in Engel's Law and the expansion of external markets.

For the population in Taiwan, Engel's coefficient (food expenditures as a proportion of total private consumption expenditure) declined continuously in the past two decades. It was 56 percent in 1951, 51 percent in 1961, and 41 percent in 1971. The income elasticities of demand for major farm products are, in general, low, though with great variance. They have been estimated as follows:

Rice	− 0.0219	(1961-69)
Fish	0.3069	(1952-69)
Pineapples	0.5921	(1952-69)
Pork	0.5958	(1953-69)
Sugar	0.6637	(1962-69)
Duck	0.8032	(1963-69)
Vegetable	1.0129	(1952-69)
Chicken	1.0139	(1963-69)
Citrus fruits	1.6934	(1952-69)

For products for which income elasticity of demand was high, growth rates were also high, namely, fruits, vegetables, livestock, and fishery products. For food grains, the income elasticity of demand was low; so was their growth rate.

For certain farm products, foreign markets have helped their expansion. This is particularly true for fruits and vegetables. The increase of exports of mushrooms and bamboo shoots, for example, has been phenomenal. The degree to which a product is dependent on exports may be measured by the ratio of domestic production to domestic consumption, which may be called the self-sufficiency rate. A coefficient of less than one indicates imports, and a coefficient of more than one indicates exports. The coefficients of self-sufficiency of various farm products are given in Table 4. It can be seen that, up until the end of the 1960s, Taiwan was about self-sufficient in rice and meat, had a great deal to export for fruits, vegetables, and sugar, and was dependent on imports for wheat, corn, soybeans, and milk. For food crops as a whole, Taiwan was about self-sufficient.

Table 4. Self-Sufficiency Rates of Major Food Items in Taiwan
(Percent)

	1952-56	1957-61	1962-66	1967-71	1952-71
Rice	111.9	106.5	108.4	103.8	107.6
Wheat	10.1	13.4	7.9	3.4	8.7
Corn	95.0	61.7	69.4	17.1	60.8
Soybeans	19.4	31.2	27.9	13.6	23.0
Fruits	126.3	131.5	197.7	179.7	158.8
Vegetables	99.9	99.8	139.4	156.4	123.9
Sugar	834.3	823.1	687.5	461.7	701.7
Meat	100.0	100.7	100.5	100.9	100.5
Milk	7.5	6.2	14.3	14.5	10.6
Sea Products	91.6	99.2	101.1	117.6	102.4
Total Food	103.2	100.0	03.5	95.7	100.6

Source omitted.

But, from 1971 to 1975, farm crops increased at only 1 percent a year, whereas population increased nearly 2 percent, so the self-sufficiency rate must have declined. According to one estimate, the self-sufficiency rate of food grains has actually dropped from 100 percent in 1968 to 88 percent in 1974.

Urbanization and Migration

Alden Speare, Jr.

Thoughout most of this century, Taiwan has experienced a rapid rate of urban growth due to the combined effect of a high rate of natural increase and a continual flow of people from the rural areas to the cities. Taiwan is not unusual in this respect as most other underdeveloped nations have experienced similarly high rates of urban growth. However, the study of urbanization in Taiwan is of particular interest for three reasons. First, among underdeveloped nations, Taiwan is one of the very few to have experienced rapid economic growth.

Second, industrial growth has been accompanied by increased agricultural productivity and land reform. These changes have resulted in a reduction of some of the rural population pressure which might have resulted had the rapid population growth occurred without increases in yield and with the disparities in land ownership which existed prior to the 1953 Land-to-the-Tiller Act. The combined effects of rapid industrial growth and improved rural conditions may have been to give the rural resident more of a choice between staying in the rural areas and moving to the city than is afforded in most developing countries.

Third, Taiwan is one of the few nations to possess a household registration system which is sufficiently accurate and complete to permit a detailed study of the urbanization process from official records. The Taiwan houshold registration system provides both a continual record of the population and a record of all reported moves made by the population.

*   *   *

Since World War II, the cities of Taiwan have grown at an average rate of close to 5 percent per year. Although a small part of this growth was due to the influx of migrants from the mainland of China around 1949, the effect of this migration on city growth was small compared with the migration of Taiwanese from the countryside. In fact, the postwar growth of cities was shown to be only slightly greater than the growth earlier in this century.

The rate of net out-migration was found to be the highest in areas where a high percentage of the males were employed in agriculture. With the exception of a relativley small movement to the east coast of Taiwan where some new land has been put to cultivation, recent net migration in Taiwan can be explained as almost entirely a move from agricultural areas to cities and large urban towns (over 50,000). While it is easy to point to the fact that virtually all available land in Taiwan has been intensely cultivated for some time and that the rural population has been growing rapidly during this period, these facts do not necessarily imply that the rural urban movement has been primarily due to a rural "push."

While the rural population has been growing, the population growth has been more than offset by increases in agricultural yield resulting from the introduction of new seed, fertilizer, and improved irrigation. Land reform, by dividing the land more equitably, may have made farming more attractive for many who otherwise would have left the rural areas. Furthermore, some of the industrialization in Taiwan has permeated the countryside, and there has been increased opportunity for nonagricultural employment both within rural areas and within commuting range of these areas.

With a few exceptions, rural-to-urban migration in Taiwan can be viewed as a rational response to changing economic conditions. The growing rural population has adjusted to the pressure of population on limited resources by sending to the major cities those members of the rural population who are best qualified for urban employment. The migrants have been drawn disproportionately from the young adults, from the more highly educated, from those working most recently in nonagricultural employment, and from the larger farms.

Alden Speare, Jr., "Urbanization and Migration in Taiwan." *Economic Development and Cultural Change*. Vol. 22, No. 2 (January 1974), pp. 302-306, 318-319. Footnotes omitted.
Only the barest essentials from the Spear article are reproduced here, as more excerpts from the same article are reproduced in the section on Social Change in the present volume—General Editor.

Other members of the rural community have responded in other ways. Those with less education or from smaller farms have tended to seek other employment nearby either through seasonal employment as an agricultural laborer or in local nonagricultural employment or by daily commuting to nonagricultural employment in a smaller urban place.

Although the major net flow of migration was from rural areas to the major cities, this net flow was only a small part of the total internal migration in Taiwan. On the average, for every four migrants who entered the major cities there were three migrants who left these cities, most of them probably returning to their original places of residence. The finding that these "return migrants" were approximately equal to the primary-stream migrants in education could not be completely explained.

Prospects for Agricultural Development

Erik Thorbecke

The role of agriculture in Taiwan's economic development appers to be switching from that of a supporting sector providing important resources to the rest of the economy to that of a dependent and protected sector. A strong case can be made that if land and labor constraints are binding, the increased application of capital inputs, including both current intermediate inputs and farm machinery, yields diminishing returns—at least in an institutional setting of extremely small farms. Because of the setting and the difficulties involved in implementing schemes such as joint operations and managment, which would amount to de facto land consolidation, mechanization appears to have been relatively unsuccessful in replacing human labor as a major source of energy, as judged by the deceleration in the growth rate of agricultural output since 1968.

Indeed, in addition to the organizational and administrative problems of bringing fifteen to twenty farmers together to cultivate fifteen hectares, which appears to be the norm for a typical joint operation, the consolidated block of land may still be too small to use farm machinery efficiently in a technological sense. It has been argued that mechanical energy applied to relatively small holdings is less efficient than human energy because of its relative indivisibility and tendency to be underutilized in terms of its total horsepower capacity. The clear advantage of human labor is its almost complete divisibility and the fact that it is utilized fairly close to its capacity level.

Clearly, the current major objective in Taiwan's agricultural development is to converge on an institutional setting and a technology that would permit output to grow at a rate substantially higher than that of population growth in the light of a continuing dwindling labor input. The problem is particularly complex because the government perceives that farm income has worsened relative to nonfarm income, thereby creating political pressures from farmers. Even though it is difficult to document unambiguously that such a relative worsening in farm income did, in fact, occur, some indicators might tend to confirm that the relative income position of farmers did not imporve vis-à-vis that of nonfarmers.

The key queston as Taiwan proceeds to move rapidly from a developing to a developed country is whether its agriculture, which had previously been squeezed, should not be helped, as almost all developed countries have done through price-support programs and various subsidies and other measures. There is general agreement that Taiwan's agriculture is at a crossroad. It is likely that the two objectives of increasing agricultural output and improving the relative income standards of the farmers, given the present institutional setting, may well be in conflict.

At the present level of per capita income in Taiwan, the income elasticity of demand for most common crops (in particular, rice) is bound to be very low, if not negative, as already

From Erik Thorbecke. "Agricultural Development," in Walter Galenson (ed.), *Economic Growth and Structural Change in Taiwan*, (Ithaca, New York: Cornell University Press, 1979), pp. 193-198. Copyright 1979 by Cornell University. Used by permission of the publisher, Cornell University Press. Footnotes omitted.

happened for sweet potatoes. On the other hand, livestock and diary products, which face the highest income elasticity, require very large imports of feedstuffs that cannot be economically produced in Taiwan. The prospects for identifying new successful export products such as asparagus and mushrooms which were successful in the last decade appear slim. It is clear that, given the new demand situation, a deceleration in the growth of agricultural output and a continuing shift in the compositon of output is needed. In the light of increasingly inelastic price and income elasticities of demand, as per capita income continues to rise, high growth rates of agricultural production, in particular of rice, might well be counterproductive in terms of farmers' income—at least under a regime of relatively free prices. Alternatively, a continuation of the present price-support policy for rice in the face of bleak export prospects and limited internal demand is bound to result in a regime of large rice surpluses (these stocks reached almost one million metric tons in 1976).

The real question appears to be whether Taiwan can continue to provide enough food—the composition of which is changing—to a still-expanding population without affecting negatively the relative income positon of farmers. There is a real risk that under the present institutional setting (very small farms and increasing mechanization and use of intermediate inputs) and the maintenance of a market economy (freely determined prices) the farmers would be subjected to a double squeeze. Any success on their part to increase output of rice and other crops facing inelastic price and income elasticities would result in lower prices for these commodities, while on the input side, the necessity of adopting an increasingly capital-intensive technology would continue to increase their costs of production. On the other hand, shifting from rice production to higher-valued crops for which demand is expanding, such as vegetables, fruit, and livestock, is difficult beyond a certain point and could be undertaken only at rising costs of production. It might be suggested that, subject to the constraints faced by the government, products for which demand is expanding should be protected instead of rice. The constraints in following such a policy are the desire for self-sufficiency in rice and the overwhelming importance of rice as a cash crop that has a major effect on most farmers' income. Supporting the price of rice is the closest the government can come to a nonselective income-support policy in agriculture.

The government has apparently not undertaken a systematic analysis of the costs and benefits of alternative agricultural policies on the major objectives (growth, improved income situation for farm households relative to nonfarm households, and self-sufficiency). Thus, for example, the type of question to explore relates to the weighing of the budgetary costs of the rice price-support policies and resulting increased storage costs as against the benefits in terms of improved farm income and self-sufficiency. It is conceivable that alternative agricultural policies of supporting products that face a stronger growth in demand than rice—such as livestock, dairy products, fruits, and vegetables—might achieve greater benefit-costs ratios in terms of growth and relative improvements in farmers' incomes and yet not be inconsistent with a strong desire for self-sufficiency in rice. This would be the case once stocks have been built up so as to take care of any emergency situation that could occur as a result of, for example, a severe drought. Once stocks have reached such a level, any further rice accumulation might be clearly counterproductive, and production should be scaled down to meet domestic consumption needs. Judging from the present size of stocks, Taiwan appears to have reached the point where any further increase in rice production should be discouraged, and, consequently, where equity objectives with regard to farm income could be achieved better through means other than a price-support program for rice.

In trying to reconcile the apparent conflict between the output objective and that of improving the relative income position of the farmers, it is essential to explore how the structure of the whole agricultural sector could be rationalized. Three alternative models have been suggested, mainly with respect to the farm size, which might be considered in the future development of the country: (1) at one extreme would be the U.S. approach which would require wide-scale land consolidation and the adoption of even more capital-intensive techniques than at present in order to increase labor productivity; (2) at a polar extreme would be the Japanese model which can be characterized as a system of part-time farmers; and (3) an intermediate positon would separate ownership from mamagement and land operation and, either as an alternative or as an additional element, involve a concomitant significant increase in the average farm size.

The first alternative would have major implications by causing a massive exodus out of agriculture and consequent urbanization. Nor is it likely to be acceptable to the Taiwanese farmers—and therefore feasible—given their very strong attachment to and identification with their own land. The process of land consolidation in the narrow sense of combining together adjacent landholdings of different owners into a larger land unit has not taken place in Taiwan. Rather, the term "land consolidation' in the Taiwanese context applies at best to the consolidation process of different scattered landholdings of the same owner and a variety of measures to provide more efficient drainage and irrigation facilities, land leveling and filling, and the improvement of road system.

The second alternative, the Japanese model, appears to be the easiest one to follow from an institutional standpoint because it would presumably emerge gradually from the present system. But, it may, in the process, entail major inefficiencies if the farmers are heavily protected or create a real farm income problem if they are not.

The third model appears to be the most reasonable one from an economic standpoint, but would require tremendous innovative thinking as to how ownership can actually be divorced from operation within the realities of Taiwan agriculture and, alternatively or additionally, how the average farm can be raised to a more efficient size. The new structures and forms of farm management discussed previously, such as joint operations, joint management, and specialized production areas, are attempts to effect a separation between ownership and operation. It is probably fair to say that so far this attempt has met with only limited success. The total number of farmers affected is still quite small (on the order of less than 10 percent of the total number of farm households) and is likely to be very difficult to spread more widely in the future.

With regard to the average size farm, T. H. Shen argues that "it is generally accepted that the ideal size of a family farm in Taiwan should be about thre hectares, with which it would be able to buy a power tiller and other farm machines for its use." Since the average size of the farm at the present time is about one hectare, the total number of farm families would have to be reduced by two-thirds to achieve this target. In other words, agricultural population would have to decline from its present level of approximately 5.6 million to 1.87 million—entailing a physical migration to the cities and rural centers of more than 3.7 million people. Such a transformation is not conceivable in less than a couple of decades. Thus, realistically, an increase in the average size of the family farm can be expected to occur gradually over at least the next two decades. In the meantime, imaginative new structures may have to be conceived and designed which would allow for a de facto, if not de jure, significant increase in the operating land unit. The average age of farmers in Taiwan has gone up, however, and with the ultimate retirement of this cohort land consolidation should meet with less resistance and mechanization might spread more rapidly.

The new agricultural policy tries to walk a tightrope between the objectives of continued efficient agricultural growth, increasing the farmers' relative income, and self-sufficiency (particulary in the case of rice). In this connection, most of the nine new measures listed by the government in its Accelerated Rural and Agricultural Development Program in 1972 appeared to favor these last two objectives through the elimination of the rice-fertilizer barter program and a reduction in the land tax. In contrast, the new Six-Year Plan for Economic Development, 1976-81, appears to emphasize efficiency relatively more than improvement in farmers' relative income, probably because measures to achieve the latter had already been implemented.

I have argued that there appears to be a limit as to how far joint operations and joint management can be pushed, particularly in the light of the highly fragmented and scattered nature of holdings and the consequent difficulty of bringing together farmers to cultivate jointly a larger unit. A prior step to the expansion of joint operations and management probably should consist of land consolidation at both the intrafarm and interfarm levels. At the intrafarm level, this would necessitate traditing scattered lots in different locations until all the fragmented holdings had become one unit. At the interfarm level, the objective would be to work out exchanges among farmers so as to create adjacent pieces of land that could be cultivated as a larger common unit. Both of these exchange processes are extremely difficult to implement because farmers are reluctant to trade their holdings for others in different locations. Unless progress takes place on both of these fronts, however, a continuation of the present trend toward part-time farming would entail high efficiency costs resulting from two factors: (1) the use of suboptimal mechanical technology on extremely small farms because of the difficulty of consolidating land into larger units; and (2) the consequent need for subsidizing agricultural income to retain a minimal number of farmers on the land at farm income levels not drastically different from those obtained outside that sector.

3. Industry and Changes in the Structure of Employment

Industrial Development

Jan. S. Prybyla

Industrial growth has been spectacular. From 1952 through 1978 industrial output grew at an average annual rate of about 16 percent. The general index of industrial production stood at in 1978 (1952 = 100). In twenty-five years (1952-77) Taiwan increased industry's share of net domestic product by 21 percentage points, a transformation that is almost without parallel in the history of development. The shift is reflected in the change composition of the labor force (Diagram 1). Much the greater part of industrial output growth to-date is attributable to increases in labor productivity. Direct labor productivity in manufacturing (which accounts for roughly 80 percent of total industrial employment) increased at an average annual rate of about 14 percent in the years before derecognition (1973-76). In 1978 it jumped by 24.8 percent, the sharp rise being traceable in part to higher capacity utilization rates.

DIAGRAM 1:   Changing composition of the labor force

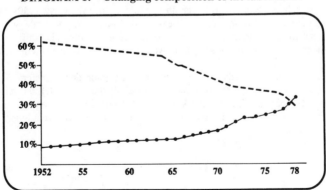

Source: Ministry of Economic Affiars, ROC.

Jan S. Prybyla, "Some Reflections on Derecognition and the Economy of Taiwan," in *Taiwan: One Year After United States—China Normalization,* A workshop sponsored by the Committee on Foreign Relations, U.S. Senate, and Congressional Research Service, Library of Congress, June 1980 (Washington, D.C.: U.S. Government Printing Office, 1980), pp. 73–74, 82.

The statistical growth record of industry serves here merely as a backdrop to a more significant aspect of Taiwan's industrial development: the profound and continuing change in the structure of industry. Until the early 1960's Taiwan pursued an important substitution strategy of industrialization, with focus on textiles, chemical fertilizer, and cement, especially the first. Beginning in the early 1960s this strategy gave way to export-led industrialization (development of export industries) focusing on higher grade textiles, processed foods, and fishery and wood products. In the late 1960s other industries were added to the export promotion list: chemicals (including plastics and man-made fibers), electronic equipment (television sets), general machinery and household durables. These export-oriented industries were noted for labor intensity and the moderate quality of their products. Beginning in the early 1970s a major policy reorientation began to be implemented. The new industrialization strategy compromised three major decisions:

(a) A decision to upgrade the quality of industrial products; (b) a decision to shift attention to the develoment of "heavy" industries (steel, shipbuilding, petrochemicals, nuclear power development) and infrastructural facilities (trunk highways, railroads); and (c) implicit in the first two decisions, a decision to move from labor-intensive to capital- and skill-intensive industries. The first phase of the new policy (the construction of the "Ten Major Development Projects" costing U.S.$6 billion) was completed by early 1979. The second phase, begun in 1979, is both a continuation and a modification of the first.

Continuation means the enlargement of facilities built during the first phase (e.g., expansion of the Kaoshiung steel mill and petrochemical complex; enlargement of power generating capacity, including the construction of two additional nuclear power plants; completion of major railroad projects). Modification implies a more dramatic shift toward high technology engineering industries (including metal manufacturers, electrical and non-electrical engineering industries (including metal manufacturers, electrical and nonelectrical machinery and precision engineering products) characterized by higher than heretofore knowledge and skill intensity, sophisticated technological content, value added, and stronger interindustry linkage effects but relatively lower capital intensity than phase one industries (steel, petrochemicals). The modification phase is exemplified by (i) some of the "Twelve New Development Projects"; (ii) adaptation of some of the existing ten major development projects (e.g., the Kaoshiung shipyard) to changed international market conditions (slump in the demand for tankers); and (iii) various arrangements (e.g., establishment of the Hsinchu Science and Industry Park) intended to encourage high level technology transfers from abroad. The policy shift is timely because Taiwan is no longer a labor surplus economy and its competitive low cost labor advantage is being lost to other countries in which wage rates are lower. In summary, since the early 1950s Taiwan has pursued a judicious, well-timed, and well-executed industrialization strategy designed to shift resources from lower to higher productivity employments. The shift of industrial policy has been made possible in large part by a continuing expansion and improvement of education.

In the light of the politically controversial, military imprudent transfers of advanced American technology to Communist countries (especially the U.S.S.R.), the existence of a permanent and expanding Taiwan market for such technology is a positive factor that should be taken into account in an analysis of U.S.-Taiwan economic relations.

Retrospect and Prospects of Industrial Development in Taiwan: The 1980s

T. L. Yu

1. RETROSPECT OF INDUSTRIAL DEVELOPMENT AT THE BEGINNING OF 1980's

At the turning point when the decade of 1980s is coming in on the heels of 1970s and when the world situation is changing rapidly filled with uncertainties, it is considered fit and proper to review in retrospect the development of industries in the last five years and at the same time to take a prospective look into the future. At the outset, the status of economic development of the last five years is presented as follows:

Status of Economic Development of the Last Five Years
In the latter half of 1970s, the impact of oil crisis which occurred during 1973–1974 had not wholly subsided. The world economy was then sunk into the gulch of stagflation. Every country, developed or underdeveloped, took measures in order to try to bottom out the recession as quickly as possible. During that time, our country through the adoption of positive measures achieved fruitful results and was fortunate to have been enabled to maintain a continued growth in economic development. In 1978, the economic growth rate accounted for a record high of 12.8 percent. Due to the turmoil in Iran, the situation of Middle East became even worse and the world is on the brink of another oil crisis. The economic achievement made in Taiwan for the last five years are enumerated as follows:

(1) *The economy maintained rapid growth*
In 1975, the country's economic growth rate declined because of the world economic recession, but it gained momentum in the subsequent years. The economic growth rates of the last five years are given below:

Year	1975	1976	1977	1978	1979
Growth Rate (%)	2.4	11.5	8.5	12.8	8.03
Average	8.6				

(2) *Prices were stabilized*
Prices declined 5 percent instead of going up in the ensuing year after oil crisis. During the period from 1976 to 1978, wholesale prices rose 3.1 percent and retail prices 6.4 percent. In 1979, both prices rose only 13.8 percent and 9.7 percent respectively.

(3) *Foreign trade continued to expand*
In 1979, the foreign trade of the Republic of China amounted to US$30.8 billion, nearly tripled the amount of 1975 which was US$11.26 billion. This increase accounted for 30 percent compared with US$23.7 billion recorded in 1978. In 1979, total imports amounted to US$14.7 billion, or up 30 percent over preceding year while total exports amounted to US$16.1 billion, up 35 percent over the last year.

(4) *Full employment was maintained*
In the past five years, the average rate of employment in Taiwan was 98 percent. As of June 1979, it reached a record high of 98.8 percent of which the employment in manufacturing industries took a share of 32.93 percent.

(5) *Ten major construction projects completed*
The ten major construction projects began in 1973 and all had been completed with the Suao-Hualien railroad opened for traffic at the end of 1979. Of the ten projects six are related to infrastructure facilities, namely: 1) North-South Freeway, 2) Railroad Electrifica-

T. L. Yu, "Retrospect and Prospect of Industrial Development in Taiwan in 1980's" *Economic Review* (Taipei: The International Commercial Bank of China), July-August, 1980, pp. 6-13. Some tables omitted.

tion, 3) Suao-Hualien Railroad, 4) Taichung Port, 5) Suao Port, 6) Airport at Taoyuan. The other four belong to industrial establishments which are: 7) Integrated Steel Mill, 8) Petrochemical Industry, 9) Kaohsiung Shipyard, 10) Nuclear Power Plants. The enormous investment made in the ten major construction projects has contributed greatly to promotion of economic stabilization and recovery, acceleration of economic growth and creation of employment opportunities. In addition, the government also endeavored to improve the life of low income people, which has resulted gradually in a more equitable income distribution. At the same time, positive measures were taken in promoting social welfare for the purpose of making Taiwan a peaceful and wealthy society. It can not be denied that the country attained great achievements over the past five years.

Status of Industrial Development in the Last Five Years
The strategy for industrial development in Taiwan in the 1970s was to elevate industry to higher level by establishing captial- and technology-intensive industries. For the last five years, the efforts in this direction have begun to show some results. Despite the adverse condition under the world economic recession caused by the oil crisis, industry in Taiwan still maintained a steady growth. The status of industrial development during this period is indicated as follows:

(1) *Industrial production continued to grow*
The general indices of industrial production in the recent five years, with the year of 1976 as base, are given in the following:

Year	1975	1976	1977	1978	1979
General Index	80.4	100	112.9	141	153.1
Growth as Compared With previous Year		24.4	12.9	24.9	8.6

(2) *Heavy industry gradually gained weight in industrial production*
In 1952, production value of heavy industry accounted for only 24.8 percent of the total value of manufacturing industry whereas the light industry 75.2 percent. In 1979 production value of heavy industry rose to 43.8 percent. The change in structure of light and heavy industry in shown in the following table:

Year	1952	1975	1976	1977	1978	1979
Heavy Industry	24.8	46.9	50.8	52.9	56.2	56.2
Light Industry	75.2	53.1	49.2	47.1	43.8	43.8

(3) *Industry became the main force of external trade*
Before 1953, Taiwan products for export consisted mainly of agricultural products and processed agricultural products. In 1952, export of industrial products accounted for US$9.5 million of 8.1 percent of the total export of US$116.5 million. Since the implementation of the first Four-Year Economic Plan beginning from 1953, the composition of imports and exports has significantly changed. The total import and export trade in 1979 recorded US$30,874 million, about 95.4 percent of the gross national product (GNP) which totaled US$32,337 million. The export of industrial products (US$14,565.9 million) and the import of capital goods and industrial raw materials accounted for 91.9 percent of the total export and import in 1979.

(4) *Investments by foreign national kept increasing*
During the period from 1975 to 1979 investments by foreign nationals kept increasing every year. Foreign-owned firms now number more than 1,000; among them about 400 are engaged in making electrical and electronic appliances of one kind or another. Many of the internationally renowned firms have also invested in the industries of Taiwan either in the

form of complete ownership or joint venture, or enter into technical cooperation with local firms. These renowned firms include Ford, Gulf Oil, General Instrument, Goodyear, IBM, Philips, Pfizer, RCA, Singer, etc. Foreign investments in the last five years are indicated in the following table:

				Unit: US$1,000	
Year	1975	1976	1977	1978	1979
Value	70,940	102,032	95,186	136,719	181,483

Major Industrial Development Projects

In the past five years implementation of the major industrial development projects have been carried out in accordance with the established schedule of progress. These projects fall mainly under the categories of energy, basic metal, machinery, petrochemical, and textile industries, and are outlined below.

• *Energy industry*

1) Electric power—In 1979 the installed capacity of Taiwan Power Company totaled 7.7 million kilowatts consisting of 5 million kilowatts of thermal power, 1.4 million kilowatts of hydro power, and 1.3 million kilowatts of nuclear power.

2) Petroleum and natural gas—In 1979 production of natural gas was recorded as 1,425,600 KL of oil equivalent and production of petroleum products from imported crude oil totaled 19,674,000 KL.

• *Basic metal industry*

Construction of the first stage of the integrated steel mill was completed in 1977 with annual production capacity of 1.5 million metric tons of liquid steel. Second stage construction is now in progress.

• *Shipbuilding industry*

In 1976 Kaohsiung Shipyard was completed for operation with a capacity of 1.5 million tons of construction and 2.5 million tons of repairs annually. Presently the total annual capacity of shipbuilding of Keelung and Kaohsiung shipyards combined reaches 1.8 million tons and repair capacity up to four million tons.

• *Automotive industry*

Currently there are altogether seven companies engaged in the manufacture of automobiles which turned out 103,000 units of cars and trucks with local content rate of 70 percnet in 1979.

• *Heavy machineries industry*

1) The first unit of marine diesel engine of 28,000 HP, under the prime mover manufacturing project sponsored by Taiwan Machinery Manufacturing Corporation in technical cooperation with Sultz Brothers Limited of Switzerland, was completed in February 1980.

2) Project for cold work shop for bridge and structural steel fabrication was completed in 1979 with annual output of 18,000 tons.

3) Tatung Company has already begun production of 161KV transformers.

4) Air compressors, boilers, heat exchangers, etc., have been in production by private companies, which contribute greatly to the development of whole plant machinery and equipment manufacturing industry.

• *Precision industry*

1) Precision electronic industry—The Electronics Research and Service Organization of the Industrial Technology Research Institute has completed research and development for the manufacture of more than 40 items of integrated circuits for electronic watches. Other items such as electronic micro-processors, minicomputer, quartz oscillators, light emitting diodes, etc., are being produced.

2) Precision machinery industry—Precision machine tools, precision molds and dies, precision instruments, and precision gear are now being produced or developed by private firms.

• *Petrochemical industry*
  1) With the completion of the second naphtha cracking unit in 1975, the third naphtha cracking unit in 1978 and the xylene separation unit in 1979 by the Chinese Petroleum Corporation, the annual production capacities of basic raw materials for petrochemical industry reached:

	MT / YEAR
Ethylene	568,000
Propylene	257,000
Butadiene	70,000
Benzene	260,000
Para-xylene	200,000
Ortho-xylene	60,000

• *Intermediates produced by downstream petrochemical plants include:*

	MT / YEAR
Plastics Raw Materials (VCM, Styrene, Polyethylene, Polypropylene, etc.)	730,000
Synthetic Fiber Materials (Caprolactam, DMT, PTA, EG, AN, etc.)	610,000
Rubber Materials (SBR, Carbon Black, etc.)	100,000
Detergent Materials (Alkyl Benzene)	20,000
Others (PO, PA, DOP)	90,000
Total	1,550,000

• *Textile industry*
  Currently there are altogether about 3,200,000 spindles for cotton spinning and 400,000 spindles for wool and synthetic fiber spinning. Recently, a program for accelerated improvement of the textile industry has been launched in order to promote automation, to improve dyeing and finishing facilities, and to strengthen personnel training. In addition, modern equipment and machinery like shuttleless looms have been introduced from aborad so that production capability can be greatly improved.

2. PROSPECT OF INDUSTRIAL DEVELOPMENT IN 1980's

The 1980s is a decade of great challenge, an epoch during which the Republic of China will join the club of developed countries. In order to reach the target of maintaining economic growth of 8.0 percent annually and 10 percent growth in the industrial sector in particular, the Republic of China will adopt the strategies as given below for future industrial development and will also carry out various projects which are developed based on these strategies.

Strategies for Future Industrial Development

The strategies for industrial development in the coming ten years are:
  (1) *Continued development of heavy and precision industries*
  Development of heavy industries and petrochemical industries will be continued in order to lay a solid foundation for the industrialization of the nation. With the natural energy resources imported from abroad or exploited at home, essential raw materials and interme-

diates will be produced to feed the processing industries in the country for multi-processing of finished products so as to increase value added to the products. And at the same time, precision industries of high technology will be developed with technologies introduced from other advanced countries.

(2) *Improvement of traditional light industries and small and medium industries*

Since the traditional light industries are the main force of the exports and small and medium industries account for 95 percent of the total number of units of industry in the Republic of China, it is considered necessary to assist the industries of these categories to help them improve management and operation and upgrade product quality so as to achieve overall advancement of the industry as a whole.

(3) *Intensification of research and development of science and technology and development of strategic industries.*

Greater importance will be attached to research and development of basic and applied science as well as industrial technology. Research organizations and universities and colleges will be allocated sufficient funds to engage in special research projects. In addition, industries of the public and private sectors will be encouraged to intensify research and development relevant to their own fields so as to develop new processes or new products. Those industries that are low energy intensive and high technology intensive will be actively developed as strategic industries to produce materials and resources in meeting the requirements for national security and elevating national strength.

Major Industrial Investment Projects in 1980s

Major industrial investment projects in 1980s will include the following:

• *Electric power*

1) No. 2 and No. 3 nuclear power plants—altogether 4 units totalling 3.9 million KW, all under construction.

2) No. 4 nuclear power plant—two units totalling 2.4 million KW.

3) Thermal generation will increase 13 units of 500,000 KW and 750,000 KW respectively, totalling 8.0 million KW.

4) Hydro power generation project—altogether four units with capacity of 250,000 KW each; of the Minghu pump storage generation totalling one million KW, and eight units of Mingtan pump storage power generation with capacity of 200,000 KW totalling 1.6 million KW.

• *Petroleum and natural gas*

Exploration and exploitation of oil and natural gas on land and offshore will be stepped up. In addition, plans for cooperation with foreign countries to invest in exploration of oil resources have been underway and more refining installations together with storage capacity and distribution facilities will be constructed.

• *Basic metal and heavy machinery industry*

1) When the second stage of the first phase expansion project of the integrated steel mill is completed, the annual production capacity of liquid steel will reach 3.25 million metric tons. In addition, construction of a cold rolled steel sheet mill is being planned. It is estimated that in the mid-1980s annual production capacity of liquid steel will reach eight million metric tons.

2) Stainless steel manufacturing projects are being planned to produce annually 50,000 tons of stainless steel sheet.

3) Production of general purpose low-valued carbon steel by small electric arc furnaces will be shifted to production of special alloy steel.

4) The second stage expansion of the copper refinery plant will be completed in 1985 with annual production capacity of 50,000 metric tons of electrolytic copper.

5) Expansion project for aluminum ingot production to increase annual production capacity to 130,000 metric tons and another project for producing high intensity aluminum alloy is being implemented.

6) Subsequent project for manufacture of prime mover is scheduled to be completed in 1983. When completed, the annual production capacity of marine diesel engine will be

increased to 12 sets with an increase of local content rate from 30 percent to 60 percent.

7) Manufacture of high pressure boilers, heat exchangers, cranes, on-deck machinery for use by ships is being planned. Repair shipyards in Taichung and Hualien harbors will be established. These two shipyards will be further developed to have ship construction capacity of 260,000 tons.

8) Project for the manufacture of 550 MW steam turbinegenerators is scheduled to be completed in 1982.

9) A large scale automotive plant with annual production capacity of 200,000 units is being planned, and implementation of a heavy duty truck and bus manufacturing project is also being stepped up.

• *Petrochemical industry*

1) Plan for the establishment of the fourth naphtaha cracking unit has been completed and construction, which is scheduled to be completed in 1983, is now underway. This naphtha cracking unit will produce annually 385,000 tons of ethylene, 200,000 tons of propylene and 60,000 tons of butadiene. Coupled with the production of the fourth naphtha cracking unit, 24 downstream plants will produce various petrochemicals by using principal raw materials produced by this upstream plant. The additional annual production capacity of petrochemicals will exceed one million tons.

2) Development projects in the 1980s

The guidelines for allocation of petrochemical building blocks to the industries will be given to those products that have high value added and are essential to the whole economy. Under this principle, plants for the manufacture of the following materials are to be selected as first stage of development and planned for operation before 1985:

A. Phenol and phenol derivative complex—It is expected that the requirement of phenol for the manufacture of bispheonl-A, phenol resin, and caprolactam will reach 73,000 MT a year in 1985. Therefore, the establishment of a plant with annual production capacity of 100,000 MT of phenol is being contemplated, so as to supply the requirement and develop derivatives.

B. Maleic anhydride—It can be foreseen that by 1985 the requirement of maleic anhydride will reach 12,500 MT a year, therefore, construction of a maleic anhydride plant with annual production capacity of 20,000 is being planned.

C. TDI (Toluene-2, 4-diisocynate) and Phosgene—In 1985 the requirement of TDI will increase to 8,800 MT annually. In view of this, plan is being made for the establishment of a TDI plant with production capacity of 10,000 MT a year.

D. Acetaldehyde, aniline, and coal tar chemicals—Plants for the production of aniline and acetaldehyde and fractional distillation of coal tar into naphthalene, anthracene, cresol, and pyridine are contemplated. Downstream products derive from these products will also be further developed.

3) Fifth Naphtha Cracking Unit—after 1985, when growth in petroleum refinery capacity and petrochemical market demands warrant an additional naphtha cracking unit, the fifth naphtha cracking unit with a capacity of 400,000 MT of ethylene per year will by planned and established.

4) Specialty Chemicals

Construction of plants producing white carbon, rubber accelerators, and latex is in progress. In addition, under the special project sponsored by Ministry of Economic Affairs, Union Industrial Research Laboratories of the Industrial Technology Research Institute have been delegated to undertake research and development for new products.

• *Precision electronics and machinery industry*

1) Technical know-how for the manufacture of 40 different kinds of integrated circuit is being transferred to a company formed by privately-owned firms to produce electronic elements. The second-phase computer research and develoment project is also being carried out.

2) Precision machinery industry

Preparation for manufacture and development of precision machine tools, numerically controlled machine tools and precision instruments is being launched with the continued introduction of precision industrial technology from abroad.

• *Promotion of automation*—An automation laboratory is being set up for the promotion of design and engineering of automation systems and the manufacture of automation facilities.

3. PROSPECT FOR THE FUTURE

Since the government has made efforts to change the structure of industry, to promote development of technology-intensive industry, to allocate funds of sufficient amount for the research work of industrial technologies, and to intensify development of strategic industries, heavy industries as well as high technology will continue to grow at a rapid pace. In the petrochemical industry, the fourth naphtha cracking unit and its downstream plants are being developed as an integrated system. With completion of this system, raw materials and intermediates for petrochemicals required by the processing industries will be adequately supplied. The products thus produced will maintain competiveness in the international market. In the field of metal industry, the production of special materials, such as high intensity aluminum alloy, special steel alloy and stainless steel, will meet the needs of the machinery industry in general and industries related to national security in particular. Active promotion for the development of precision and sophisticated industries such as electronics and precision machinery which are low energy-intensive will not only increase the efficiency in the use of energy but also increase the value added to their sophisticated products.

III.   Income Distribution

Income Distribution in the Process of Economic Growth in Taiwan

Yuan-li Wu

Economic Benefits—Distribution and Growth

Analysis of economic development in quantitative aggregates would be woefully incomplete if one were to ignore the distribution of benefits of development. If we compare the GNP, a frequently economic development will make the pie larger, as has been amply demonstrated in the case of Taiwan. However, since a growing "pie" is not produced merely as an object of wonderment, to be admired in the abstract but not to be touched by anyone, how the pie is sliced and how and when the slices are made available to individual members of the society are an inalienable part of economic development. Success or failure of the development process must, therefore, be judged from the points of view of both production and distribution.

Distribution by Income Class—A Preliminary International Comparison with Developed and Less Developed Countries

According to an IBRD study on income distribution in less developed countries (LDCs), the typical pattern to be found in an LDC is as shown in Table 1.

Table 1.   Income Distribution in LDCs

Percent of total households Arranged in Descending Order of Income	Percent of Total Income
Highest 20%	53
2nd 20%	22
3rd 20%	13
4th 20%	7
Lowest 20%	5
Total	100

Sixty-six developed and underdeveloped countries that had data on income distribution were examined by the author and classified into three groups: (1) "high inequality" (income share of the lowest, i.e., poorest, 40 percent of all households being less than 12 percent); (2) "moderate inequality" (income share of the lowest 40 percent, between 12 and 17 percent); (3) "low inequality" (income share of the lowest 40 percent, 17 percent and above). Each of the three groups was further divided into three subsets according to the level of per capita income. See Table 2.

Of the 66 countries included in the IBRD study, ten are in East, Southeast and South Asia. In terms of GNP per capita, Japan is the most developed of these ten while Sri Lanka, India, Pakistan and Burma, all in South Asia (Burma also straddling Southeast Asia) are the poorest. The remaining five, including Taiwan, Korea, Thailand, Malaysia, and the Philippines, fall within a relatively narrow range and are all in East or Southeast Asia. For comparison, the respective income distribution patterns of these Asian countries can be seen in Table 3.

Yuan-li Wu, "Income Distribution in the Process of Economic Growth in Taiwan," in Yuan-li Wu and Kung-chia Yeh (eds.), *Growth, Distribution, and Social Change: Essays on the Economy of the Republic of China, Occasional Papers/Reprints Series in Contemporary Asian Studies*, (University of Maryland, School of Law), No. 3-1978 (15), pp. 67, 72-92. Footnotes omitted.

**Table 2. Number and Percent Distribution of
Selected Countries in Terms of
Income Distribution**

	Total	High Inequality	Moderate Inequality	Low Inequality
		(1) 26 Countries with per capita GNP up to US $300 a year		
Number	26	10	8	8
Percent	100.0	38.4	30.8	30.8
		(2) 21 Countries with per capita GNP of US $300-750 a year		
Number	21	10	6	5
Percent	100.0	47.6	28.6	23.8
		(3) 19 Countries with per capita GNP above US $750		
Number	19	3	8	8
Percent	100.0	15.8	42.1	42.1
		(4) All 66 Countries		
Number	66	23	22	21
Percent	100.0	34.8	33.3	31.8

Source omitted.

**Table 3. Patterns of Income Distribution in
Selected Asian Countries**

	Year of Data	GNP per Capita (US $)	Relative Shares of Income by Income Class		
			Lowest 40% of All Households	Middle 40% of All Households	Top 20% of All Households
High Inequality					
The Philippines	1971	239	11.6	34.6	53.8
Malaysia	1970	330	11.6	32.4	56.0
Moderate Inequality					
Burma	1958	82	16.5	38.7	44.8
India	1964	99	16.0	32.0	52.0
Low Inequality					
Sri Lanka	1969	95	17.0	37.0	46.0
Pakistan	1964	100	17.5	37.5	45.0
Thailand	1970	180	17.0	37.5	45.5
ROK (South Korea)	1970	235	18.0	37.0	45.0
ROC (Taiwan)	1964	241	20.4	39.5	40.1
Japan	1963	950	20.7	39.3	40.0

Source omitted.

Table 4. Comparative Income Growth Rates

		Annual Rates of Income Growth in Percent by Class of Income Recipients			Annual Increase in Welfare for the Country as a Whole		
	Period	Upper 20%	Middle 40%	Lowest 40%	GNP Weights	Equal Weights	Poverty Weights
Korea	1964-70	10.6	7.8	9.3	9.3	9.0	9.0
The Philippines	1961-71	4.9	6.4	5.0	5.4	5.5	5.4
India	1954-64	5.1	3.9	3.9	4.5	4.1	4.0
Taiwan	1953-61	4.5	9.1	12.1	6.8	9.4	10.4

Source omitted.

"Equal Weights" implies a weight of 0.2 for the upper 20% of the income recipients, and 0.4 for the middle and lowest 40% respectively. "Poverty Weights" are 0.1 for the highest 20%, 0.3 for the middle 40%, and 0.6 for the lowest 40%.

Although the "poverty weights" are clearly arbitrary and could just as well be replaced by other weights, the effect of their use in the case of Taiwan is especially illuminating.

As far as Taiwan is concerned, especially noteworthy are (1) the virtually identical pattern of its income distribution with that of Japan, (2) the close approximation of the Taiwan and Japanese patterns to that of the United States, and (3) the slightly larger share of the lowest 40 percent on the income ladder in the Taiwan and Japanese distributions as compared with the other Asian countries of low inequality, or, for that matter, as compared with the United States.

The fact that income distribution has become increasingly equitable over a lengthy period of rapid growth in GNP per capita has made the Republic of China on Taiwan one of the few developing countries whose growth is "distributionally biased" in favor of persons with low incomes. A comparison with three other Asian countries can be seen in the estimates of Chenery et al., given in Table 4.

Table 5. Changes in Income Distrubition in Taiwan

Distribution in Quintiles	1953	1961	1964	1972
Lowest quintile of all households	3.0	4.5	7.7	8.6
Second quintile	8.3	9.7	12.6	13.1
Middle quintile	9.1	14.0	16.6	17.0
Fourth quintile	18.2	19.8	22.1	22.2
Highest quintile	61.4	52.0	41.0	39.1
Second highest 15%	28.8	26.4	24.8	24.8
Top 5%	32.6	25.6	16.2	14.3
Gini Coefficient	0.56	0.46	0.33	0.30
Ratio of Income Share				
Top 10% to bottom 10%	30.4	19.3	8.6	6.8
Top 20% to bottom 20%	20.5	11.6	5.3	4.6
Index of Decline Inequality	0.46	0.37	0.26	0.24

Source omitted.

The Trend of Increasing Equality in Income Distribution by Household

The cross-section comparison presented in Table 2 shows the Taiwan economy as one of low income inequality on the basis of 1964 data. A closer examination can be made by looking at the same statistics in several benchmark years both before and after 1964. These figures show a progressive decline of inequality during a 20-year span in terms of several alternative measures (Table 5).

Several phenomena are most interesting from the point of view of economic policy, and politically most significant from the perspectives both of the Republic of China and of other countries. One is the combination of a progressive movement toward greater equality by income class with a sharp increase in GNP and in average household income over the same period. At constant 1972 prices, per capita GNP in Taiwan rose from NT$10,875 in 1964 to NT$19,122 in 1972, while average household income rose from NT$32,452 in 1964 to NT$61,032 in 1972. This means that the groups at the lower end of the income ladder enjoyed an accelerated rate of absolute and relative improvement, which is what some development economists have advocated as most desirable. The narrowing of the income gap between the rich and the poor in the course of economic growth through the faster improvement of those in lower income intervals is bound to affect mutual perceptions of one another by people of different incomes, making the establishment of consensus for major policies easier. Given the wide distribution of television sets in Taiwan and the great visual impact of differences in living standards and life styles due to income differences, this is an important stabilizing and unifying influence not to be lightly ignored.

A second interesting phenomenon is the continuation of the trend toward greater equality over the entire 20 year period. The first decade of economic development was accompanied by a sharp decrease in income inequality: 18 percent between 1953 and 1961 in terms of the Gini income concentration ratio. This was followed by a further decrease in terms of the same index of 28.3 percent in 1961-64 and of another 9.1 percent in 1964-72. How did these progressive and continued improvements in distribtuion come about simultaneously with rapid increases in total output and several significant shifts of Taiwan's development strategy during the two decades?

Income Differentials between Farmers and Non-Farmers and Sectoral Distribution Patterns

If changes in income distribution in Taiwan have resulted in greater equality in terms of various measures based on income classes cutting across different economic sectors, what changes in income differences have occurred both between and in individual sectors? An answer to this question will go a part of the way in answering the question raised at the end of the last section. Growing differences in this respect could also create antagonisms detrimental to economic and political stability and the national consensus in policy making.

Let us attempt to answer this question with respect to farm and non-farm families, about which considerable statistical information is available. Using the DGBAS data for 1970-72 adjusted to include the city of Taipei, Kuo Wan-yong shows that while income equality increased in the entire economy during 1964-72, the degree of equality increased more— that is, the Gini coefficient decreased more—for non-farm families than for farm families (Table 6). In 1972, the Gini coefficient showed a greater degree of equality for the former than for the latter although their relative standings had been the reverse in 1964. The "cross-over" occurred between 1970 and 1971. Given these patterns of distribution within the two sectors, respectively, it is not surprising that the rapid expansion of the industrial sector in the late 1960s and early 1970s contributed to greater overall equality rather than inequality.

Contrary to the preceding favorable distributive effect of rapid industrial growth, to be explained below, an unfavorable development during 1964-72 was the widening discrepancy between farm and non-farm incomes although both were rising. Average income per farm family rose by 53.3 percent between 1964 and 1972, from NT$32,013 to NT$49,090, at constant 1972 prices. On the other hand, average non-farm family income rose by 97 percent, from NT$32,740, virtually at par with farm family income, in 1964 to NT$64,497 in 1972, 31.5 percent higher than the corresponding farm figure. This factor is probably

Table 6. Gini Coefficients of Income Concentration by Sector

Year	Farm	Non-farm	Both Sectors
1964	0.315	0.336	0.328
1968	0.292	0.338	0.335
1970	0.283	0.285	0.299
1971	0.297	0.292	0.301
1972	0.291	0.288	0.295

Source omitted.

among the most serious potential threats to income equality if it is allowed to continue unchecked.

Economic Policy and Income Equality

The changes in overall and sectoral income distribution in Taiwan can be explained in terms of (1) sectoral emphasis and shifts in development strategy over time, (2) the open economy and foreign trade orientation of the island, (3) the initial state of asset distribution and subsequent changes effected by government intervention, and (4) other governmental measures that have improved access to education and technology and redirected investment in favor of certain groups and sectors that might otherwise have been at a disadvantage in comparison with the rest of the society.

The 1950s and Early 1960s

Two basic facts should be borne in mind. First, since the ratio of labor to capital in agricultural production, given Taiwan's small-farm, labor-intensive economy, was a priori greater in agriculture than in the non-agricultural sector during the 1950s, a larger share of factor income should go to labor in the agricultural sector than in the non-agricultural sector as production in both sectors increased. (The reverse may be true in the case of the labor-land ratio other than urban housing construction.) How the relative shares of labor to capital (or labor to land) in factor income might change in the aggregate would depend upon the relative rates of growth of the two economic sectors during a given period. Second, as shown in Table 7 the contribution of agriculture to net domestic product per capita grew at about the same rate during 1952-60 as did the non-agricultural sector. Thus, if other things had been equal, the expansion of agricultural and non-agricultural production at a virtually

Table 7. Contribution of Agriculture to Net
Domestic Product per Capita

	1952	1960	1972
Total population (in thousand persons)	8,128	10,792	15,289
Agriculture	4,257	5,373	5,947
Non-agriculture	3,871	5,419	9,342
Net Domestic Product (NT$ million)			
Agriculture	5,233	16,528	38,121
Non-agriculture	9,424	34,305	190,217
Per Capita Value-added (NT$)			
Agriculture	1,229.3	3,076.1	6,410.1
Non-agriculture	2,434.5	6,330.5	20,361.5
Ratio of Non-agriculture: Agriculture	1.98:1	2.06:1	3.18:1

Source omitted.

equal pace during 1952-60 should not alter the proportion between factor income earned by labor and factor income that went to owners of property, i.e., both land and capital. The benefit of increased production would then be shared by labor and property owners in the same proportion as their respective income shares were at the beginning of the period.

However, other things did not remain equal during this period. One of the most important economic events in the early 1950s, if not the most important single event, was the implementation of land reform in Taiwan in 1953 (one of the benchmark years previously selected), preceded during 1949-52 by sale of public land and reduction of land rent paid by tenant farmers. The rent reduction had the effect of reducing the rate of return to property in the agricultural sector, thereby increasing the relative share of labor in a period of rising agricultural output and income (Table 8).

Table 8. Distribution of Agriculture Income by Factor (in percent)

	Land	Capital	Labor
Before Land Reform (Under Japanese Rule)			
1941	52.20	11.48	36.32
1942	51.99	11.44	36.57
1943	45.65	10.04	44.31
Post Land Reform			
1953	37.39	8.23	54.38
1956	36.28	7.98	55.74

Source omitted.

Under Land Reform, the conversion of many tenants into owner farmers and wider dispersion of land ownership, with limitation on the size of individual holdings, had the effect of further spreading property income among a larger number of farm families. The net effect of rent reduction and land reform together, therefore, was to increase sharply the degree of equality in income distribution in the agricultural sector.

It goes without saying that these beneficial effects of asset redistribution through land reform could have been at least partially nullified had agricultural production declined. The actual increase in production after land reform enabled the recipients of property income in the agricultural sector also to enjoy rising income from property ownership. One must therefore also examine why agricultural output actually increased after land reform, a point to be discussed elsewhere.

The overall equalizing effect of greater income equality in the agricultural sector during 1952-60 was not offset by developments in the non-agricultural sector where income distribution was more unequal. Several factors contributed to this outcome. First, the discrepancy between agricultural and non-agricultural per capita income which developed later did not widen significantly during this period. Second, the expansion of production in the non-agricultural sector during this period was probably brought about by an increase mostly in relatively small businesses, many of which were established by new immigrant entrepreneurs from the China mainland. Even in the beginning of the 1970s small firms employing less than 100 persons each were still responsible for 35 percent of gross production in manufacturing. Private capital ownership was not highly concentrated. A number of large industrial enterprises previously owned by the Japanese had been taken over by the ROC government and were run as public enterprises so that income which would have accrued to property owners of these enterprises went to the Treasury. Third, outside the economic infrastructure which was expanded by the government and government enterprises, industrial production in Taiwan during this early phase of the island's postwar economic development stressed consumer goods production using products from the agricultural sector as

168 THE TAIWAN EXPERIENCE

inputs. Thus expansion in the non-agricultural sector had the effect of stimulating production in the agricultural sector where income distribution was more equal. At the same time,
production in the industrial sector was not capital intensive; the initial asset distribution did
not seem to be highly concentrated; the small-scale enterprises tended to spread the benefit
of increased production more widely among owners of industrial property. Also, the most
important industrial inputs used by the agricultural sector at that time, viz., chemical fertilizers and pesticides, were mostly imported. Their purchase did not constitute a source of
demand for the domestic industrial sector. Finally, greater industrial employment and the
relative case of business formation by enterprising persons of low income were obviously
helpful in raising the earnings of the lower-income groups in the non-agricultural sector.

To sum up, (1) the ROC government's initial emphasis on agricultural production,
(2) asset redistribution through land reform, (3) the consumer goods and small business
emphasis in the industrial sector, and (4) certain characteristics of asset distribution of the
postwar and post-1949 period were responsible for the improvement in income distribution
in Taiwan during the 1950s and the beginning of the 1960s.

From the 1960s to the early 1970s

Although further improvement in income equality slowed down during the 1960s and early
1970s, a remarkable phenomenon was that the movement toward greater equality continued
in both the farm and non-farm sectors. This occurred in spite of a widening gap between
farm and non-farm family incomes due to the failure of agriculture production to keep pace
with the accelerated expansion of industrial production. Several factors are involved in
explaining what happened to income distribution in the second decade.

First, the crux of the development strategy adopted during this period was the expansion
of foreign trade. In the light of the preceding expansion of the agricultural sector, export
expansion began very naturally with increased export of agricultural and processed agricultural products. This was helpful in sustaining agricultural income.

Second, because of the paucity of its natural resources, Taiwan's foreign trade orientation involved an expansion of both exports and imports. By eschewing self-sufficiency as
an objective, the rapidly expanding exports were based on progressively increasing imports
which included many capital-intensive products. Any attempt to achieve self-sufficiency
by stressing import substitution at this point would doubtless have reduced the rate of
expansion considerably. The export orientation of Taiwan's economic development not
only increased the rate of economic growth, but also reduced the rate at which capital's
share of factor income was to increase.

Third, much of the export expansion during this period took place in the form of labor-
intensive products. Imported raw materials and intermediate goods were processed into
finished goods for export through the concentrated application of labor which was much
cheaper in Taiwan than in the countries where Taiwan exports were marketed. The several
Export Processing Zones established to attract foreign capital were especially illustrative of
this practice. The effect on income distribution was twofold. Within the industrial sector,
the very rapid expansion of labor-intensive exports in the late 1960s and early 1970s, prior
to the 1974 world-wide recession induced by the oil cartel's price hike, reduced the initial
labor surplus and raised wages and employment. The result was to raise the earnings of non-
farm families at the lower income levels. For farm families, participation in the rapid
expansion of the industrial sector took place partly through access to the new employment
opportunities offered. Many women employees of foreign businesses in the Export Processing Zones came from farm families. The net effect was to increase the proportion of
non-agricultural income for farm families, especially those with smaller land holdings.
This in turn served to reduce the income discrepancy between farm and non-farm families,
in spite of the lagging growth of the farm versus the non-farm sector, while simultaneously
increasing income equality in the farm sector.

In short, a very rapidly expanding industrial sector oriented to export that was based on
processing of imported materials by highly labor-intensive methods was instrumental in

raising wages, which also benefited farm families. The latter were progressively becoming less dependent on agriculture as their sole source of labor income. Under these conditions income equality was able to improve further, albeit at a slower rate than before.

Distribution of Wealth between Pre- and Post-1945 Settlers

Aside from the distribution of income between farm and non-farm families, a related distributive factor of major interest is the relative economic status of the pre-1945 ethnic Chinese settlers of Taiwan (often loosely referred to as Taiwanese by Westerners) versus that of the post-1945 settlers (often referred to as Mainlanders). Since the "Mainlanders" came to Taiwan in 1945 to take over the Japanese administration, political power was initially vested entirely in their hands. During the past 30 years, they have progressively broadened the participation of government so that more and more members of the pre-1945 settler group are now included in the government hierarchy. This progressively more equal distribution of political power, more advanced at the provincial and local government levels than at the central government level, should be considered in conjunction with the distribution of economic benefits between the two groups. An interesting point that concerns us in this paper is whether the relative economic status of the two groups corresponds to their relative political positions or whether a different relationship prevails.

Although income distribution data are not available on the basis of the dates of immigration of family heads to Taiwan, the problem can be approached indirectly by examining the distribution of wealth between the two groups. Two major points need to be borne in mind in this connection. First, the 1953 land reform which took place not very long after the transfer of the central government of the Republic of China from the mainland to Taiwan effectively precluded the existence of absentee landlords. The earliest group of post-1945 settlers from the mainland consisted primarily of government officials, members of the armed forces, officers of public corporations and some businessmen. Few of them, if any, had either the inclination or time, before the land reform, to become farm land owners. Thus, land, a form of physical asset of dominant importance during the early years of Taiwan's post-World War II economic development, has remained entirely in the hands of the pre-1945 settlers. Some of the public land taken over by the ROC government from the Japanese was also sold to the farmers as a part of the land reform program. While the government and public corporations, such as Taiwan Sugar, still own some of the land, there has not been any redistribution benefiting the post-1945 settlers. Only to the extent that land has been transferred from crop cultivation to non-agricultural or other agricultural uses could ownership of landed wealth outside the urban areas become vested in the hands of post-1945 settlers.

In view of the above, unless the distribution of wealth outside the agricultural sector were in favor of the post-1945 settlers, the distribution of wealth as a whole would tend to favor the pre-1945 settlers who are owners of virtually all private farm land. A most important factor to bear in mind in this connection, therefore, is the distribution of ownership of large enterprises in the civilian sector of the economy. In 1975 there were 35 businesses in Taiwan whose annual sales exceeded NT$1 billion each. In addition, another 66 firms had annual sales exceeding NT$400 million each (see Table 9). Altogether 132 firms had annual sales exceeding NT$200 million each. If these firms are grouped according to whether the Chairman of the Board of Directors and the President of the firm are from pre- or post-1945 settler families, 59 percent of the aggregate capital of all the firms is accounted for by enterprises headed by pre-1945 settlers as against 41 pecent by post-1945 settlers. Furthermore, if a line is drawn at the level of NT$300 million in capitalization, there are 47 firms above this line. Of these larger firms, which are further divided into five intervals (see Table 10), those headed by pre-1945 settlers account for an overwhelmingly larger proportion of invested capital than the post-1945 settlers in four groups, the single exception being the group of firms with capitalization from NT$500 million to NT$1 billion. In contrast, for firms capitalized below NT$300 million, a larger proportion of invested capital is accounted for by enterprises with post-1945 settler heads, the only exception being the group of firms with capitalization of NT$100 to NT$200 million.

Table 9. Business Enterprises in Taiwan
with Annual Sales Exceeding NT $200 Million

Heads of Firms	No. of Firms	Aggregate Annual Sales (NT $ million)								Total
		Over 6,000	5,000 to under 6,000	4,000 to under 5,000	3,000 to under 4,000	2,000 to under 3,000	1,000 to under 2,000	500 to under 1,000	Under 500	
Pre-1945 Settlers	69	6,147.5 (1)	10,947.3 (2)	9,162.7 (2)	6,163.0 (2)	4,559.2 (2)	12,692.8 (10)	22,203.7 (32)	6,162.1 (18)	78,038.3 (69)
Post-1945 Settlers	63	9,859.5 (1)	0 (0)	4,080.1 (1)	3,225.4 (1)	7,477.7 (3)	13,970.5 (10)	10,480.0 (14)	11,995.8 (33)	61,089.0 (63)
Total	132	16,007.0	10,947.3	13,242.8	9,388.4	12,036.9	26,663.3	32,683.7	18,157.9	139,127.3
Percent										
Pre-1945 Settlers	52	38	100	69	66	38	48	68	34	56
Post-1945 Settlers	48	62	0	31	34	62	52	32	66	44
Total	100	100	100	100	100	100	100	100	100	100

Figures in parentheses are the numbers of firms in each group.
Source omitted.

Table 10. Business Enterprises in Taiwan with Annual Sales Exceeding NT $200 Million

Heads of Firms	No. of Firms	Total Capitalization (1,000,000 NT $)								
		Over 2,000	1,000 to under 2,000	500 to under 1,000	400 to under 500	300 to under 400	200 to under 300	100 to under 200	Under 100	Total
Pre-1945 Settlers	69	2,040.0 (1)	5,379.3 (4)	5,077.0 (8)	4,493.7 (10)	2,425.3 (7)	2,717.0 (12)	2,581.5 (19)	429.3 (8)	25,143.1 (69)
Post-1945 Settlers	61*	— (0)	2,120.0 (2)	7,430.9 (11)	810.0 (2)	680.0 (2)	3,521.8 (15)	1,907.6 (14)	667.8 (15)	17,138.1 (61)
Total	130	2,040.0	7,499.3	12,507.9	5,303.7	3,105.3	6,238.8	4,489.1	1,097.1	42,281.2
Percent										
Pre-1945 Settlers	53	100	72	41	85	78	44	58	39	59
Post-1945 Settlers	47	0	28	59	15	22	56	42	61	41
Total	100	100	100	100	100	100	100	100	100	100

*Two of the firms are without data on capital
Figures in parentheses are the numbers of firms in each group.
Source omitted.

Similarly, one can use annual sales as the criterion. On this basis, of 10 firms each with annual sales in excess of NT$3 billion, 7 are headed by pre-1945 settlers and only 3 by post-1945 settlers.

In contrast, of 122 firms each with annual sales below NT$3 billion, 62 are headed by pre-1945 settlers as against 60 by post-1945 settlers. Furthermore, within each sales interval above the NT$3 billion mark, firms headed by pre-1945 settlers account for an overwhelmingly larger proportion of total sales, there being only a single exception. In all the sales intervals below the NT$3 billion mark the reverse is true, again with the exception of a single interval.

An earlier survey in 1969 which divided business firms in Taiwan on the basis of financial groups shows that of 337 firms which can be clearly identified in terms of ownership by pre- or post-1945 settlers, 60 percent were accounted for by the pre-1945 settlers while the post-1945 settlers controlled 28 percent (95 firms), with 12 percent (41 firms) representing combined ownership. Furthermore, the firms of the pre-1945 group were responsible for 61 percent of invested capital on the basis of capitalization and 59 percent of business revenue in that year. On the other hand, the firms of the post-1945 group were responsible for 30 percent of invested capital and 31 percent of total business revenue. The mixed group accounted for 9 percent of capitalization and 11 percent of revenue. These earlier statistics point to the larger ownership of the pre-1945 settlers in business outside the agricultural sector, but there was no noticeable disparity in size between the enterprises of the two groups. Hence the growth of the relative importance of the pre-1945 settlers in the control of the larger enterprises in the 1975 survey appeared to be a phenomenon of the early 1970s.

Both the 1969 and 1975 statistics lend support to the conclusion that the larger Taiwan enterprises are headed by pre-1945 settlers while the smaller firms have a larger proportion of post-1945 settler heads. The more recent growth was in favor of the pre-1945 settlers for the larger enterprises and the post-1945 settlers for the smaller ones. The exceptions to the rule are relatively few. Although the 1975 data deal with only the larger firms, while the 1969 data include a wider spectrum of businesses, comparison of the more recent findings with the 1969 statistics suggest that there may have been a trend during the first half of the 1970s for the post-1945 settlers to move up in their relative economic standing while some members of the pre-1945 settler group forged even further ahead. In view of the fact that the post-1945 settlers were late comers and few of them had settled in Taiwan with vast personal wealth, it is quite understandable that they have had to compete very hard in the private economic sector and are not in a dominant position. This can be contrasted with the more favorable political position the post-1945 settlers enjoyed. We have already noted the movement toward greater equality in the distribution of political power in favor of the pre-1945 settlers. The present statistical analysis indicates that there may have been a slight and slower shift toward greater equality in the distribution of industrial and commercial wealth in favor of the post-1945 settlers. Fortunately for Taiwan, therefore, the redistribution of political power and material wealth can move in opposite directions, thus serving to compensate each other. A priori, one is inclined to conclude that this is a situation favoring greater social stability.

Future Prospects
We have put the preceding discussion on income distribution in the past tense, although many of the conditions of the 1960s and early 1970s continue to hold today, because several circumstances now exist that could significantly alter the course of development. First, Taiwan is trying to shift toward more capital-intensive and technology-intensive production. It is also trying to supply domestically more of the manufactured industrial raw materials it needs. The relative rates of growth of the agricultural and non-agricultural sectors will change further and the relative share of capital as factor income will probably also rise. There is a latent tendency, therefore, toward less rather than greater equality in income distribution unless capital ownership can become progressively more equally distributed, and unless other corrective measures are undertaken. Thus the role of government intervention may have to, and probably will, increase in order to forestall a reversal of the previous

trend toward greater equality in income distribution. Both existing and new measures, fiscal and otherwise, will have to be expanded, but greater government intervention could stifle productivity and economic growth if adequate safeguards and judicious restraint are not provided.

Within this context some of the measures adopted in recent years deserve mention. In the first place, the progressive income tax, although a part of the ROC's long-standing taxes, has been implemented much more vigorously in recent years as a result of technical reforms in data collection and reporting. Income tax collections increased noticeably between 1966 and 1972, especially for the higher income brackets. Secondly, among the more recent measures, reduction of various hidden taxes levied in the form of rice collection since 1964, and particularly since 1969, has contributed to greater income equality, especially in reducing the disparity between farm and non-farm incomes. These two categories of measures are clearly focused on income transfers.

In the third place, expansion of the stock exchange, which can be seen in an increase in the number of listed stocks betwen 1962 and 1973, has been a welcome development in promoting the dispersion of property ownership. This development could be extended if institutions can be developed in the near future so that farm families can progressively participate in industrial expansion by becoming owners of stocks in industrial enterprises just as they have already participated by providing labor to the expanding industrial sector. It may be necessary for the government to step in by organizing intermediaries in the form of "mutual funds" which can collect rural savings for investment in industry, thus altering the distribution of industrial assets which are growing rapidly.

Another set of government measures has had the effect of especially accelerating development in the lagging agricultural sector. Special funds over and above the level of private investment have been earmarked in recent years for investment in the accelerated development of agriculture. Central government funds totalling NT$2.43 billion have been provided for this purpose in the 1977 fiscal year. As of 1975 year-end, projects totalling NT$2.58 billion (including central government and other funds) in expenditure had been approved out of the 1976 fiscal year program. A portion of the expenditures is channeled through programs for irrigation, flood control, etc. under the jurisdiction of the provincial authorities. The bulk of these expenditures is aimed at expanding the infrastructure of the agricultural sector. Efforts such as this are aimed at modifying sectoral balance and income disparity between sectors. There may be some question about the rate of return obtained from such special efforts. The issue clearly is one of balancing growth against distribution and touches upon the central question that economic development, not to mention that overall development of a society, may have multiple goals.

Finally, there are two important sets of measures that have begun to be implemented in 1976. One is the ruling that the heads of government-related banking institutions must henceforth be rotated so as to avoid the emergence of financial fiefs. The second development is the progressive implementation of the law limiting urban land ownership and taxation of large capital gains derived from such ownership. This is both to avoid overconcentration of ownership of urban property and to discourage land speculation and wealth accumulation based on large "unearned" increments. Thus the authorities are evidently coming to grips with emergent issues affecting distribution.

Distribution of Educational Opportunities

Yung Wei

In 1946 when Taiwan was restored to China, there were only four colleges, 215 middle schools, and 1,130 primary schools on the island. Since that time, a phenomenal growth has occurred at all levels of education. The 1972 educational survey revealed that there were 81 universities and colleges, 842 middle schools, and 2,193 primary schools on Taiwan. The ratio of school age children and youths in educational institutions at various levels has also witnessed a drastic increase. In 1972, 12.5 percent of college age groups, 57.8 percent of the middle school age groups, and 98.13 percent of the primary school age groups were enrolled in educational institutions of their levels.

One of the important practices of Taiwan's educational system that has helped maintain an equal opportunity for education has been the entrance examination system. Not only does admission into colleges and universities require participation in a highly competitive examination supervised by the Ministry of Education, entrance into senior high school also requires passing an examination. The entrance examination system has created something of an "examination hell" for thousands of candidates eager to get into the more prestigious educational institutions. It has been criticized for years as one of the basic problems in the educational system of Taiwan. Yet little has been done to change the examination system. The major reason is that this system, though taxing on the physical and mental strength of the students, is still the fairest device for guaranteeing equal opportunities for entry into the educational institutions at various levels. The extension of compulsory and free education from six to nine years has partially solved the problem at the junior high level. But unless a great many more colleges and universities are established in Taiwan, there is no solution in sight to satisfy the endless demand for higher education among an increasingly affluent population.

Other than the numerical increase of educational opportunities, there are indications that the opportunities for education have increased substantially for the tenant farmers. According to the data provided to this author by the Land Reform Insitute of Taiwan, the number of former tenant farmer's children attending primary schools has increased 257 percent between 1948 and 1971; those attending middle school, 2,827 percent; and those enrolling in college, 16,820 percent. These facts are made more significant when one realizes that between 1952 and 1971, the population employed in agricultural activities in Taiwan has increased only 128.45 percent.

Yung Wei, "Modernization Process in Taiwan: An Allocative Analysis," *Asian Survey,* Vol. XVI, No. 3 (March, 1976), pp. 262-263. Copyright 1976 by The Regents of the University of California. Reprinted by permission of The Regents.

Part II

Economic Development: External Aspects

by Yuan-li Wu

The economic development of Taiwan during the past three decades has depended to a large degree upon its external economic relations. The nature of these relations has changed with Taiwan's emergence from post-World War II economic reconstruction and stabilization to export-oriented economic take-off, and then to further transition into a developed economy. The story of these changing external economic relations mirrors the successive stages the Taiwan economy has undergone. The following selections have been made with a view to offering the reader an insight into this evolution as a continuing process.

When the seat of the ROC government was first moved to Taiwan, a heavy burden was thrust upon the island's economy, and it was hard to see how the latter could have sustained this burden for very long. But for the outbreak of the Korean war in 1950, U.S. aid to Taiwan, which had been held in abeyance with minor exceptions (notably the JCRR), might not have been resumed. The resumption of U.S. aid, therefore, signalled the beginning of a new hope. Restoration of price stability and rebuilding of the economic infrastructure were the first obvious economic objectives of the country which commodity and project aid was to help attain. Yet what began as a respite eventually turned out to be an unprecedented success story, both for Taiwan and for the post-war U.S. foreign aid program. It is fitting, therefore, that Selection 1 in our section should be taken from Dean Jacoby's assessment of U.S. aid to Taiwan which he undertook for the Agency for International Development when termination of the Agency's program on Taiwan had been ordered. It appears that some of Dean Jacoby's conclusions on the lasting benefits of U.S. aid in terms of the cultivation of a capability for the effective use of limited public resources to channel the much greater potential of private entrepreneurs and workers in specific directions are shared by key ROC officials. Evidence of this may be found in Minister K. T. Li's ideas on the strategy of Taiwan's technological development (Selection 9).

Preoccupation with the country's persistent balance of payments disequilibrium and low foreign reserves and the desire that the country should be able to supply the bare essentials of livelihood domestically—an important political priority—were among the underlying reasons for an initial policy of import substitution. Only when the first objectives of economic stabilization has been accomplished, toward the second half of the 1950s, did the country dare to abolish multiple exchange rates and simplify for-

Yuan-li Wu, editor of this part of the Economic Section, is Professor of Economics, University of San Francisco (San Francisco, Ca.).

eign trade controls. Export promotion, including the establishment of export processing zones, and import liberalization then followed in the 1960s and 70s. These developments are described in Selection 2, by Maurice Scott.

The 1973–74 oil shock ushered in a new period with serious threats of imported cost-push inflation, unemployment, loss of competitiveness on the world market, export stagnation, and cessation of growth. The nature of these problems and how Taiwan has managed thus far to keep on top of them are discussed in Selections 3, 4, and 5. Not all the problems, of course, are the direct outcome of OPEC actions. Structural changes in Taiwan's foreign trade is a logical outcome of economic development, while the growing volume of foreign trade necessarily calls for its partial redirection. Steps to (1) minimize the risk of foreign protectionism, (2) redress large bilateral trade surplus/deficit with the United States and Japan, respectively, and (3) open up some hitherto forbidden markets in Eastern Europe, are among the topics discussed in Selections 3 (Wu and Yeh) 4 (Sun), 5 (Holbrooke), and 6 (AIT).

Selections 5 and 6 also provide an official U.S. assessment of Taiwan's economic position in mid-1980, eighteen months after the U.S. severance of diplomatic relations with the ROC government on Taiwan in favor of the Communist PRC government on the Chinese mainland. These assessments provide a fitting commentary on the end of an era that had begun with the resumption of U.S. aid to Taiwan.

Taiwan's transition to a developed economy seems to be continuing its inexorable course. Greater technological maturity, growing economic and technological interdependence with its neighbors in Southeast Asia and with the world's develped economies, including the United States, the European Community, and Japan, and an increased ability to break out of the constraints of an island economy, are predicated upon expanding flows of capital, technology and human resources in multiple directions. These topics, therefore, constitute the focus of the remaining selections. Selection 7 (Van Gessel) provides an American investor's view of Taiwan's climate for foreign capital and technology export. Selection 8 (Wu and Yeh) looks at the beginning of what promises to be a long-term trend of overseas investment by Taiwan. Selections 9 (K. T. Li), 10 (Denis F. Simon) and 11 (Simon) discuss Taiwan's strategy for technological transfer, including both its successes and its shortcomings to date. Selection 12 (Li) then shifts the focus of scientific and technological development back to education and the structure of the domestic science community and its relationship to industry. The last two, Selections 13 (Li) and 14 (Wu & Yeh), discuss certain instances of technology transfers between Taiwan and the United States, as well as between Taiwan and Southeast Asia. Kinship among ethnic Chinese in different countries serves as a potential catalyst in producing deferred returns for large Chinese exports of human capital in previous years. In many respects, the reader is thus reminded of the interrelationship between economic development and foreign policy.

I.   The Role of U.S. Aid

1.   An American Evaluation

N. H. Jacoby   ◆

Reasons for Success in Taiwan

The primary features of the U.S. economic aid program for Taiwan that accounted for its high degree of success may be recapitulated as follows:

(a) *A mutual focus on development.* Both the Chinese and the U.S. governments increasingly focused upon development as the major policy objective during the final two-thirds of the aid period. Both U.S. aid and local resources were used to increase output, rather than for relief, social welfare, spreading employment, political influence, or other purposes.

(b) *A sound developmental strategy.* The Chinese and U.S. governments agreed upon a productive strategy of development, which emphasized solutions to the salient problems in chronological order: monetary and price stability, agricultural production, infrastructure building and human resource development, and, finally, industrial growth.

(c) *A high level of aid.* Given a clear mutual objective, a relatively high level of aid was provided. This "saturated" Taiwan's absorptive capacities, produced manifest evidence of progress, and gave the U.S. Mission strong influence upon Chinese policies.

(d) *Avoidance of overplanning.* The Chinese government did not produce detailed plans for development, but left a maximum scope for market guidance to investment. AID wisely refrained from pushing the government into more elaborate planning.

(e) *Concentration of public investment in infrastructure and human resources.* Most U.S aid went into sectors that were the proper province of government, leaving a fairly open field for private enterprise in agriculture and industry, where it is generally more efficient.

(f) *Pursuit of comparative advantange in investment.* Private investment was free to concentrate upon those labor-intensive processing industries in which Taiwan had the greatest comparative advantage in international trade. This principle, rather than the dubious concepts of "balanced growth," or "import saving" guided private investment. Capital-intensive industrial investment was avoided.

(g) *Treatment of savings as an effect instead of a cause of higher incomes.* The Chinese government, which maintained an ample level of taxation in relation to national income, did not attempt to force savings by higher taxation, or by price inflation, but allowed savings to emerge naturally out of higher real incomes. This policy gave strong and pervasive incentives to people to raise their incomes and, later, their savings.

(h) *Active use of U.S. influence on Chinese economic policy.* AID followed an activist policy in using its influence upon the Chinese government to inaugurate a favorable climate for private investment and enterprise. It rejected the fallacious view that aid should have "no strings."

(i) *Avoidance of using U.S. aid as a lever to induce political reforms.* AID wisely refrained from using economic assistance as an instrument to "democratize" the Republic of China or to force political changes. Thus, it underwrote the stable political framework for economic progress provided by an authoritarian government, and let political reforms come later.

(j) *Focus on development of the private sector.* Both through its allocations of aid funds to investment projects, and through its influence on Chinese policies, AID helped to make private enterprise flower. It did not "build socialism" in the Republic of China.

(k) *Extrabudgetary administration of aid.* AID administered assistance to the Republic of China through semi-autonomous Chinese institutions outside of the government budget. It jointly controlled with them U.S. dollar projects, NT dollar projects, and imports. This

N. H., Jacoby, *U.S. Aid to Taiwan* (New York: Praeger, 1966), pp. 243–245 and 232–234. Copyright 1966 by Praeger. Used with permission of the publisher.

administrative process improved resource allocation in Taiwan. AID did not write the Chinese government a check and walk away.

(l) *Competent staffing of the U.S. Mission*. Throughout the aid period, the U.S. Mission of China was directed by men of exceptional ability whose terms of office were relatively long. Adequate housing and other amenities were provided to attract and retain competent staff members.

Economic Prospects in 1965

The Republic of China had excellent prospects of continuing its rapid development without American aid. Late in 1964, the Economic Commission for Asia and the Far East of the United Nations published a forecast of the economic growth of countries in the region up to 1980. It projected an annual growth of Taiwan's GNP between 6 and 7 percent—the highest of any country—compared with a rate of 3.9 to 4.7 percent of the ECAFE region as a whole. This growth would involve an expansion of Taiwan's economy during the fifteen post-aid years, but little slower than the 7.6 percent maintained during the fifteen years of U.S. aid. ECAFE's forecast was confirmed by the target growth rate of 7 percent a year contained in the Chinese government's own Four-year plan for 1965–68. Although this rate was a target rather than a forecast, the fact that the targets of all three previous Four-Year Plans were realized gave it more than usual credibility. Indeed, in an unpublished econometric study, the Council on International Economic Cooperation and Development projected an expansion of Taiwan's economy at that rate over the entire decade 1965–74.

There is abundant evidence that the Republic of China occupied a promising economic position in 1965, given freedom from involvement in active warfare, and a continuance of liberal policies of international trade in the non-Communist world. Its strength derived from an ample supply of efficient labor, and a cost structure in both agriculture and industry that was markedly lower than in any other country of the Western Pacific basin. A rapid increase in wage rates and manufacturing costs in Japan and Hong Kong during the 1960s had widened the differential in favor of Taiwan. It made the island a much more attractive site for labor-intensive manufacturing industries. The size of the differential is indicated by the fact that in 1965 Taiwan factory laborers worked for about $1 a day, compared with $2 a day in Hong Kong, and $4 a day in Japan.

Low labor costs, combined with the establishment of tax- and duty-free industrial processing zones and the attractive investment policies of the Republic of China, were accelerating the rate of foreign private investment in the island. Taiwan offered the foot-loose international businessman tax incentives, stable government, and strategic location, as well as low costs. With protection of the island by the U.S. Seventh Fleet, political risks were low. Little wonder that firms engaged in light manufacturing operations, such as electronics, toys, pharmaceuticals, clothing, and food processing, were planning to establish or to expand plants in an environment so congenial to profit-making. Capital-intensive heavy industries were attracted by the relatively low plant construction costs and a central location that minimized transport costs.

The favorable competitive position of Taiwan in international markets appeared likely to persist for many years. The sizable unemployment rate of 1965 would more probably rise than decline, as a result of huge accessions to the labor force during the next decade from a young population. Although the industrial worker lacked many of the fringe benefits found in more advanced economies, his living conditions had improved. Independent and militant labor unions were unlikely to develop under the government of the Republic of China.

Above all, the Chinese government clearly understood that Taiwan's progress depended upon maintaining a competitive "edge" in international trade. Its leaders were determined to generate larger exports; they were committed to private enterprise as the best instrument for this purpose. The urgency of governmental needs for revenue to replace U.S. aid would probably accelerate sale of its shares in industrial enterprises to private investors. For all these reasons, the favorable climate for private investment created during the U.S. aid era was unlikely to deteriorate. It was quite possible that, within a few years, annual foreign investment in Taiwan could reach the $100 million annual level attained by Hong Kong.

II.   Foreign Trade and Exchange

2. Developments up to the Mid-Seventies
Maurice Scott

My concern is with foreign trade and the balance-of-payments, and the most important development here was the resumption of U.S. aid in June 1950. This took a year or so to build up to a rate of about U.S.$90 million a year, when it financed about 40 percent of Taiwan's imports of goods and services.

Apart from U.S. aid, no effective measures were taken to deal with the foreign exchange stiuation until April 1951. The large balance-of-payments deficit nearly exhausted the government's gold and foreign exchange reserves, and no stringent and effective system of exchange control was put into force until 1951. By that time the exchange rate, which had been initially fixed at N.T.$5 = U.S.$1 when the New Taiwan dollar was introduced in June 1949, had become N.T.$10.30 = U.S.$1 for certain official transactions and N.T.$15.65 for imports by private enterprises.

Strict Import Controls, 1951–1957
The strict import controls imposed in April 1951 were accompanied, as the figures given above imply, by a multiple exchange rate system. Changes were made in the system from time to time, with the exchange rates being repeatedly devalued. Broadly speaking, the effect of these measures was to give a much stronger financial inducement to import substitution than to exporting. There were high tariffs on a great many imports, and importers were required to make advance payments for imports equivalent to their full value for most items until 1965. Last, but probably most important, imports were severely restricted by license.

Nevertheless, there were some worrying features. First, the balance of payments on current account remained heavily in deficit. . . . Second, the growth rate of the GDP was decelerating . . . , and there had been a pronounced decline in the absolute amount of private-sector gross investment after 1954. . . . Neil H. Jacoby attributes this stagnation to "the 1954 Communist Chinese attack on Tachen, an offshore island north of Quemoy." . . . Other reasons were the limited size of the domestic market and failure to make a decisive break into foreign markets. . . . Thus by 1958 there were many indications of a need for measures to promote private investment and exports of manufactures.

These measures undoubltedly increased the profitability of import substitution and must have been partly responsible for the doubling of manufacturing production between 1952 and 1958.

These measures undoubltedly increased the profitability of import substitution and must have been partly responsible for the doubling of manufacturing production between 1952 and 1958.

The 1958–1960 Reforms and Some Earlier Ones
The 1958–60 reforms were preceded by two important sets of measures, most of them taken in 1955. The 1958–60 reforms permitted the "fuel" to flow into the tanks without which exports could never have taken off in the way they did. The 1955 measures, however, made the "fuel," crew, and other costs cheap enough for the flight to be a worthwhile proposition. This elliptical metaphor must be explained.

Prior to 1955 there was no general system of rebating either import duties or commodity taxes for exports. As an article in *Industry of Free China* remarked, "Fragmentary mea-

Maurice Scott, "Foreign Trade" in Walter Galenson, (ed.), *Economic Growth and Structural Change in Taiwan* (Ithaca, N.Y.: Cornell U. Press, 1979), pp. 314–315, 321, 324–325, 327–328, 330–333, 336–337, and 359–363. Used by permission of the publisher, Cornell University Press. Footnotes omitted.

sures had been taken in the past to refund tax to raw materials used in producing export products. But they were disorganized and not well coordinated." Accordingly, the "Regulations for Rebate of Taxes on Export Products" passed by the Executive Yuan in July 1955 were widely welcomed. They provided for the rebate of commodity tax, import duty, and defense tax. In fact, exporters did not need to pay the first two taxes at all, merely giving an undertaking that they would be paid if the materials concerned were not used for making exports, this bond being redeemed at the time of exportation.

The second important measure taken in 1955 was the devaluation of the exchange rate applicable to private-sector exports of manufactures from N.T.$15.55 to around N.T.$25 per U.S. dollar, which, by reducing the cost of nontrade inputs (chiefly wages) in exportable products, increased the potential profitability of exporting.

The reforms initiated in April 1958, and spread out over the next two years, made three important changes.

First, and in my view by far the most important change, quantitative restrictions on imports were removed in many cases and the allocation system was much improved in others. It was this freeing of imports (especially materials) from control that I characterized as "allowing the fuel to enter the tanks."

Second, the multiple exchange rate system was gradually collapsed into a single rate system.

Third, the exchange rate applicable to the bulk of imports and to exports by private enterprises was devalued from around N.T.$25 to close to N.T.$40 per U.S. dollar.

Apart from the three main sets of measures discussed above, the 1958–60 reforms assisted exports by removing export controls from more than two hundred items, simplifying the procedures for tax rebates, waiving the 2 percent harbor dues on exports, and providing easier credit terms for exporters.

Import Liberalization

Import Restrictions. It is not easy to assess the changes in the restrictiveness of the import licensing system. There is no easily obtainable number, like the rate of import duty, to measure their effect. Data on price comparisons are not readily available. We must therefore fall back on less satisfactory indicators.

One such indicator is provided by Table 1, which shows the number of imported items classified as being "prohibited," "controlled," or "permissible" from 1968 to 1976. A short explanation of the last two categories is given at the foot of the table. The figures seem to suggest that there was a substantial freeing of imports after 1970, as the numbers included in both the "prohibited' and "controlled" categories were then drastically reduced. Lin gives similar figures to show that from 1957 to 1969 not many more items were shifted from the "controlled" to the "permissible" category than were shifted the other way— although the balance definitely was in favor of liberalization from 1964 onward following the very favorable balance of payments achieved in 1963 as a result of a doubling of the sugar price in that year. The main conclusions these figures suggest are that liberalization did not really get under way until about 1964, that most controls were not swept away until after 1970, and that, by 1976, few remained. Although this probably is the broad picture, it is not altogether accurate.

In the first place, as was mentioned above, the restrictions on imports of materials and, to only a slightly lesser extent, equipment, for manufacturers who wanted to export were very substantially eased from 1958 onward. The items concerned were not formally decontrolled, but in practice exporters could get what materials they wanted. In fact, the allowances were deliberately generous so as to provide an incentive to export. The exporters were, in effect, subsidized through their ability to sell surplus foreign exchange entitlements to other manufacturers, such sale being legally permitted. This system lasted throughout the 1960s, but became redundant in the early 1970s, when nearly all items were liberalized, and partly because of this and partly because it was in conflict with the principle of a unified exchange rate, it was abolished in January 1971.

Second, even for nonexporters there was some liberalization during the 1960s as the

Table 1.   Numbers of Imported Commodities According to Their Status Under Import Control, 1968–1976

	Prohibited	Controlled	Permissible	Total
1968 (Dec.)	209	4,551	6,240	11,000
1970 (July)	208	4,780	6,431	11,419
1972 (July)	5	2,822	12,531	15,358
1974 (Feb.)	4	453	14,605	15,062
1976 (June)	13	531	14,822	15,366

Sources omitted.

criteria used to justify the banning of imports of a commodity were progressively tightened. In 1960 domestic manufacturers seeking protection had to show that the quantity and quality of their products were adequate to satisfy domestic demand and that their prices did not exceed the prices of comparable imports (inclusive of all duties) by more than 25 percent. In 1964 this was reduced to 15 percent and in 1968 to 10 percent. In 1964 a time limit of three years was set for restricted items. These rules were probably not applied strictly—to do so would have required the collection of a great deal of data on price comparisons every year. Nevertheless, their existence helped the import liberalization lobby and made the task of those seeking protection more difficult.

The above two qualifications show that there was more liberalization in the 1960s than the numbers in Table 1 suggest. Three further qualifications show that the degree of liberalization finally achieved by 1976 was not as complete as that table makes it appear. First, the fall in the number of "prohibited" or "controlled" items was partly caused by a change in the method of classification. Thus is in 1960s, imports of alcoholic drinks and tobacco products were classified as "prohibited," whereas in 1976 they were not so classified and were not even classified as "controlled," but their status was just the same, that is, they could be imported only by the state monopolies.

Second, although the items remaining "prohibited" or "controlled" in 1976 were nearly all in these categories for reasons that clearly had nothing to do with protection and little to do with saving foreign exchange (at least on current account), there were other items, subject to control over their origin, for which protection remained an important motive. Thus, most garments (apart from military uniforms) were not classified as "prohibited" or "controlled" and are, therefore, counted in Table 1 as "permissible." Yet they could be imported only from Europe or America, thus effectively excluding the most competitive sources of such products—Hong Kong, Japan, and South Korea. The same was true of some yarns, artificial fibers, and fabrics, with the further restriction that only approved manufacturing plants could import many of the yarns and artificial fibers. Some manufactured foodstuffs, chemicals, toilet preparations, machinery, and electrical apparatus were subject to similar restrictions. Imports of ordinary passenger cars, with few exceptions, were banned, although no mention of this fact is made in the Board of Foreign Trade's *Classification of Import and Export Commodities*.

Many of these restrictions (including the ban on imported cars were aimed at Japan, and here the reason was not just protection. Taiwan had a large bilateral trade deficit with Japan. In a rational world this would not matter since the deficit could be offset by surpluses in trade with other countries. Unfortunately, the world is not so rational. Taiwan was under pressure from her other trading partners to reduce her bilateral surpluses with them by importing more from them or by restricting her exports to them. She in turn was therfore under some compulsion to transmit this pressure to Japan, since a reduction in her surpluses with other countries would necessitate a reduction in her deficit with Japan. A further reason sometimes given from restricting imports from Japan was that it was alleged that Japanese exporters were sometimes dumping, although this was difficult to prove.

As a third and final qualification, the regulations governing the manufacture of certain products laid down minimum percentages of total costs that must consist either of value-added within the factory itself or of inputs produced in Taiwan. The objective was to

**Table 2.   Products Manufactured in Taiwan and Subject
to Minimum Percentages of Domestic Content in 1976**

Products	Minimum percentages in 1976*
Black and white television set	90
Color television sets	50
Telephones	90
Switch exchangers: manual and step by step	80
Automobiles†	60
Motorcycles	90
Power tillers	90
Crossbar exchanger components	85
Crossbar exchanger frames	90
Crossbar exchanger switches	70
Crossbar exchanger wire spring relays	60
Registers	50
CR-7 terminal boards	100
CR-6 terminal boards	90

*The minimum percentages refer to: $\dfrac{\text{Total costs} - \text{imported components}}{\text{Total costs}}$. "Imported components" means those directly imported by the manufacturer. The import content of inputs bought from other manufacturers is ignored.

†Automobile manufacturers must choose to make at least one of the following six parts in their own factories: engine body, cylinder head, piston connecting pin and rod, camshaft, crankshaft, main spring.

Source omitted.

encourage the formation of "backward linkages," and the regulations usually required a progressively increasing percentage of "domestic content." New manufacturers had to meet the same requirements as those who had started earlier, so that there was no "unfair" advantage. This meant that the government was under no pressure from two different directions. Some manufacturers had more than satisfied the minimum percentages and wanted them raised to squeeze out their competitors; others who had not wanted them lowered. Table 2 shows the products affected in 1976 and the relevant percentages.

Export Promotion

Exports were promoted following the 1958—60 reforms by the setting up of Export Processing Zones and bonded factories, cheap credit for exporters, some private schemes, and a group of miscellaneous measures.

The original idea for setting up export processing zones in Taiwan was put forward by the Economic Stabilization Board in 1956. Establishment of such zones was also recommended in 1958 by an American port expert when reviewing the Kaohsiung Harbor extension plan (partly financed by U.S. aid) and was investigated in connection with the drafting of the Statute for Encouragement of Investment in 1963. Finally, a special law was promulgated in January 1965. The Kaohsiung Export Processing Zone was formally opened in December 1966, although exporting from the zone had begun before. Subsequently, in 1969, as applications from investors to set up in the zone flooded in in excess of the space available, the government decided to set up two more zones: one in Nantze, which is also Kaohsiung City, and a smaller one in Taichung.

The Reasons for Taiwan's Export Success

My approach to answering the questoin, "Why did Taiwan's exports grow so fast?" is to look for reasons that made exporting very profitable and then to discuss why high profitability in turn encouraged rapid growth.

Profitability can be high if costs are low relative to prices. The relative importance of different costs in three major categories of Taiwan's exports—textiles, apparel, and electronics—are shown in Table 3, where a comparison is made with the structure of costs for similar industries in her principal export market, the United States.

Table 3. **The Structure of Costs in Textiles, Apparel and Electronics in Taiwan, 1971 and the United States, 1967 (percentages of gross output)**

Country and Industry	Traded inputs (1)	Nontraced inputs (excl. value-added) (2)	Wages (3)	Indirect taxes (4)	Gross profits (5)	Total (6)
A. *Taiwan*						
1. Textiles	70.1	7.8	8.3	2.3	11.6	100.0
2. Apparel	70.1	8.4	16.2	0.6	4.7	100.0
3. Communication equipment	65.7	8.5	11.3	3.8	10.8	100.0
B. *United States*						
4. Textiles	58.8	11.3	21.2	0.5	8.4	100.0
5. Apparel	53.8	9.2	30.2	0.4	6.4	100.0
6. Radio, Television communication equipt.	40.5	14.5	36.4	0.6	8.1	100.0
7. Electronic components and accessories	40.7	14.6	38.3	0.6	5.9	100.0

The overwhelming importance of traded materials and components in total costs in Taiwan is clear. Exportation is possible only if these inputs can be purchased by the export manufacturer at a price close to or below those paid by his main competitors. Any appreciable taxes on these inputs or any premiums resulting from import controls (assuming the manufacturer must buy or can sell at premium-inclusive prices) are likely to make exporting unprofitable. Thus for the industries shown in Table 3, a tax or premium of only 17 percent on all traded imports would eliminate the average gross profit margin on all three industries, assuming that prices could not be increased nor other cost elements reduced. Since the gross profit margin must cover the rent of land and depreciation before it starts contributing to interest and profit, a much small tax or premium would knock out most exports of these products. This underlines the importance of the tax rebate system and of the free availability of imported materials and components to would-be exporters.

Transport costs could also be important. Although these may add only a few percentage points to the cost of imported materials, that is still a large proportion of the available profit margin. There is thus a real advantage in being able to buy locally, if local producers' costs are as low as those of an overseas supplier (f.o.b.). As Taiwan's industrial base widened and as costs came down, the scope for local purchase at competitive prices increased. Increasing competitiveness in one sector therefore helped to increase it in others.

The share of traded inputs in total costs is much higher in Taiwan than in the United States, perhaps because of differences in the product mix, but probably at least partly because of lower ex-factory prices for the same goods in Taiwan than in the United States. Indeed, unless those prices were lower, it is difficult to see how exports could have increased so fast. It was precisely because Taiwan's goods were cheaper that U.S. buyers switched to them in preference to U.S. goods. Furthermore, ex-factory prices of exports in Taiwan had to be lower to bear the transport costs to the United States. If one makes the bold assumptions that prices of traded inputs for export goods were the same in Taiwan as in the United States, that the cost structures in Table 3, which in reality are for the whole production, apply to that part of it destined for export, and, finally, that the same quantities of traded inputs per unit of output were needed in both countries, then it follows that prices in Taiwan were about 16 percent lower for textiles, 23 percent lower for apparel, and 38 percent lower for electronics.

After traded inputs, the next largest category of costs is wages, and here the contrast between Taiwan and the United States is even more striking. The proportion of wages in total costs is only half or a third as high in Taiwan as in the United States. Using the same assumptions as in the last paragraph, and so allowing for lower prices in Taiwan, wage costs per unit of output in Taiwan work out at from 18 percent (for electronics) to 41 percent (for apparel) of their levels in the United States. *Wage-rates,* however, are a good deal lower than this. I reviewed the available evidence on hourly earnings in Taiwan, the United States, and some other countries in 1972. Such comparisons are difficult to make, and the results are correspondingly uncertain. The following figures give the orders of magnitude for typical hourly earnings, including fringe benefits, for workers in textiles and electronics in 1972 (since then all the other countries' wages have risen relative to those of the United States):

	U.S. $/hour
United States	2.75
Germany	1.90
Japan	1.20
South Korea	0.22
Taiwan	0.20

Thus wage rates were perhaps only 7 percent as high in Taiwan as in the United States in 1972. The difference between relative wage rates and wage costs per unit of output presumably reflects higher productivity resulting from better skills and more and better equipment in the United States, but undoubltedly in some particular process the productivity of Chinese workers was just as high as that of U.S. workers. In some electronics operations, for example, it does not pay to design and build expensive equipment to save labor because the technology is changing so fast that such equipment would be obsolete before it had recouped its costs. Consequently, for these processes the cost advantage in undertaking them in Taiwan, rather than in the United States, is equivalent to virtually the whole of the wage-rate difference. There are then substantial profits to be earned by shifting such processes to Taiwan, as many U.S., Japanese, and other electronics companies have done. More generally, Taiwan's low wage rates gave her a comparative advantage in labor-intensive products and processes, with the result that she specialized in the production and export of these goods.

Another relevant factor regarding labor costs is hours and intensity of work. Obviously, the harder one works for a given hourly wage, the lower is one's labor cost. A survey of electronics firms undertaken in 1972 concluded that, in the judgment of the industrialists operating factories in various Asian countries and the United States, labor efficiency ("the time required to manufacture a specific product") was highest in Japan and Hong Kong and next highest in Taiwan, which ranked above the United States and South Korea. The Phillipines, Singapore, Indonesia, Malaysia, and Thailand were placed lower still. Taiwan's laborers work long hours, especially by comparison with those in North American and European countries. While this does not reduce hourly labor costs, it does reduce average capital costs per unit of output because it permits fuller utilization of capacity.

Two other categories of costs on which some comments may be given are nontraded inputs and capital. The lower share of the former in Taiwan than in the United States may mainly reflect lower wages, since most of these costs consist of services (such as wholesaling) with a big wage element. The availability of power and water was, of course, essential, but their relative prices were probably not important because they represented a small fraction of costs for these industries.

Capital is a more complicated problem. A distinction must be made between the cost of physical capital goods (machinery, equipment, buildings, and the like) and interest rates. As regards the former, building costs were certainly lower, but imported machinery would cost more, even if duties were exempted (as they were for "approved" projects or in the Export Processing Zones). On balance, these costs were probably a bit lower in Taiwan than in the United States, but there is no hard evidence.

I would also classify as capital costs, on a par with the costs of physical capital, all other costs of *change*, including, for example, costs of migration and training of workers. The youthfulness of the Taiwan labor force and its good standard of education must have increased its adaptability and speed of learning and kept these costs low. Furthermore, the expansion of exports was heavily concentrated in particular industries where the techniques soon became familiar—clothing, textiles, canned foodstuffs, and plywood, for example. This concentration, in effect, reduced the cost of change since businessmen, managers, and technicians did not have to learn new and unfamiliar techniques—it was a case of "more of the same.'' In the electronics industries, where the techniques were new, the knowledge was to a great extent supplied by foreign investors, and so the cost of learning (and discovering) was not borne by the Taiwan economy. All this is an exemplification of the gains from specialization made possible for foreign trade. Had an inward-looking strategy been pursued, such specialization would not have been possible, and the capital costs of growth (properly defined to include both physical capital and all other costs of change) would have been much higher.

Interest rates were, of course, much higher in Taiwan than in the United States or Europe, but this should be regarded as a reflection of the generally high rate of return to investment and not a subtraction from it. A business that was entirely self-financed would receive the whole of the ''interest'' as part of the return on its investment, and there seems no reason to suppose that a business that could borrow would earn any less on that part of the capital it had subscribed itself. Indeed, given the high average real rate of return, ''gearing'' of this kind would generally increase the owner's return.

Study of the relative costs of inputs in Taiwan and the United States thus makes it appear that they either cost about the same or else were cheaper in Taiwan—and very substantially so for direct and indirect labor. Of course, we are not treating the rate of return on capital as a cost here but rather are subtracting all other costs from revenues in order to deduce something about that rate of return. The entrepreneur is not merely someone who combines all other inputs, including capital, which he hires, and who receives ''pure'' profit as a result. He is an investor as well as an organizer, and I am trying to explain the return on his investment.

3.   The Foreign Trade Structure—
Changing Markets and Goods

Y. L. Wu and K. C. Yeh

Problems in the Post-Oil Crisis Period

At the time the worldwide energy crisis broke out, Taiwan ranked among the highest of the developing countries in the rate of economic growth and per capita income. But its very success of development through trade also created serious problems because Taiwan was now so dependent on trade that the economy became increasingly sensitive to abrupt changes in the outside world. The following ratios exports and imports to gross domestic product in selected years since 1952 show the extent of Taiwan's dependency on external markets and sources.

	Exports / GDP	Imports / GDP
1952	8	14
1959	12	21
1965	18	21
1973	49	43
1976	52	50

The problem of high trade-GDP ratio is further compounded by heavy reliance on trade with Japan and the United States, as demonstrated by the following figures showing exports to and imports from the United States and Japan as percentage of Taiwan's total exports and imports:

| Year | Exports | | Imports | |
	To U.S.	To Japan	From U.S.	From Japan
1953	4.2	45.6	38.7	30.7
1959	8.6	41.5	36.1	40.3
1965	21.3	30.6	31.7	39.8
1973	37.4	18.4	25.1	37.5
1975	34.3	13.1	27.8	30.4

Y. L. Wu, and K. C. Yeh, ''Taiwan's External Economic Relations'' in *Occasional Papers / Reprints Series in Contemporary Asian Studies*, No. 3-1978 (15) (U. of Maryland: School of Law), pp. 189-196.

Taiwan's exports to these two countries accounted for about 50 percent of its total exports. The degree of heavy reliance on these two markets as a whole has remained unchanged in the last two decades. However, the share of exports to the United States rose sharply since the 1960s, while that to Japan declined for the reasons given above.

Taiwan's dependence on these two countries for imports was even greater than its dependence for exports. About 70 percent of total imports came from these two countries in the period up to 1965. The proportion fell to about 60 percent in the early 1970s. The decline was due to a reduction of the U.S. share after the termination of the U.S. aid in 1965. Japan's share, however, remained fairly high. The concentration of trade with Japan and the United States means that Taiwan's economy would be highly vulnerable to changes in these countries.

The immediate effect of the oil crisis on Taiwan was an enormous trade deficit of US$1.3 billion in 1974. Taiwan's deficit with the oil-producing countries (Kuwait, Saudi Arabia, and Iran) totalled US$0.7 billion, actually much less than its deficit with Japan, US$1.4 billion. In 1975, both total exports and imports declined for the first time since 1969. The total trade deficit was reduced to US$0.6 billion but the deficit with Japan remained as high as US$1.1 billion.

In fact, for decades before the oil crisis, Taiwan had persistent deficits with Japan, for various reasons. Taiwan's exports to Japan consist largely of agricultural products, partly because the geographical proximity of the two countries lowers the transportation costs for bulky agricultural products, partly because of the similarity in the Chinese and Japanese diets, and also because of Japan's restrictive policy toward its imports of manufactured products. The growth of such imports has been slow despite Japan's rapid economic growth, because the income elasticity of demand for these products was rather low. Taiwan's demand for imports of capital goods (steel, machinery, chemicals) however, expanded by leaps and bounds. Again because of lower transport costs and the sizable Japanese investment in Taiwan, together with the traditional ties between the Japanese and the Taiwanese business community, imports of these capital goods were largely from Japan.

Another serious problem in the post-1973 period was the effect of worldwide inflation on domestic prices. Wholesale prices in 1974 rose by 35 percent and the consumers price index by 47 percent over 1973. The sharp increase in prices inevitably forced the labor costs to go up despite the rise in unemployment.

By 1976 the situation had improved. The rate of inflation was greatly reduced. Exports and GNP turned upward again, and the rate of unemployment was much lower. However, the economic recovery does not necessarily mean a return to the smooth sailing of the last decade, for Taiwan now faces some new economic and political challenges. Competition from Hong Kong and South Korea has become keener as these countries have moved into textiles and electronics. Wages in Taiwan rose faster than in other countries so that Taiwan lost some of the advantages in low labor cost. Moreover, in the developed countries, the slowdown in economic growth and high rates of unemployment gave rise to protectionist sentiments. More serious still, changes in the relations between Peking and Washington in recent years renewed fears about Taiwan's future. The political uncertainty could have adverse effects on the economy. In the first place, insecurity on the part of Taiwan might force the government to divert more resources from investment to defense preparations. Second, economic viability and growth depend heavily on foreign investment, which is apparently very sensitive to changes in the political climate. The rate of U.S. and Japanese investment in Taiwan dropped in 1971 and 1972 probably as a result of the ROC's international setbacks during those years and investors' concern over its future status. Another decline in new Japanese investment in Taiwan occurred in 1974 and 1975 following Japan's transfer of diplomatic recognition from Taipei to Peking in 1972, although the cause of the decline is somewhat ambigious because it coincided with the worldwide recession. Without the continued inflow of foreign capital that brings in new technology and marketing skills, it would be difficult to sustain high rates of export growth. Once again Taiwan has reached a critical stage, as it did in the late 1950s and early 1960s; however, the conditions are different, but so is Taiwan's economic capability. The economy's productivity and capacity to save and the stock of physical and human capital have grown tremendously over the last two decades. Of the ten major investments now under construction, seven are new additions to the infrastructure, which, when completed, will greatly increase the power-generating capacity and transportation facilities needed for future export growth. Above all, the government and the business community have accumulated substantial experience in adapting themselves to changing conditions. At each critical juncture in the past, the government had been able to take appropriate measures to promote the transition from one stage of growth to the next. Although Taiwan now faces many problems, the central question remains essentially the same as in the past: how to identify, develop, and exploit new areas of comparative advantage in the future international environment. In the search for solutions, political, economic, and strategic issues are inevitably involved.

Long-term Expectations

As an economy develops, the commodity composition and country distribution of its external trade are bound to change. In the case of Taiwan, the rate of adjustment required is enhanced by the speed of economic change inherent in the continuation of fairly rapid economic growth that the ROC authorities plan to maintain. There certainly are strong noneconomic reasons calling for steady economic growth at an at least moderately high rate. Given Taiwan's island economy, this means continued large imports that must be paid for. Thus, exports must continue to rise, and it would be necessary, not merely desirable, to have a given amount of resources devoted to exports to earn an increasing amount of imports. Exports based on low wage, labor-intensive production methods will increasingly lose their edge in competition with the products of other countries as wage rates rise in Taiwan and as other countries with a much larger labor supply—e.g., South Korea and several countries in Southeast Asia—expand their manufacturing and export industries further. Taiwan's import demand for intermediate products can be progressively reduced through domestic production in what is sometimes described as the backward linkage process. However, both the production of intermediate products at home and expansion of more capital and technology-intensive exports of higher unit value will still require the inflow of technology from overseas and of some foreign capital in the case of "embodied technology." In addition, there will be a need to expand other sources of foreign exchange earnings than current exports. This need will still be there even if raw material imports become relatively more important as the proportion of intermediate industrial products in imports recedes. In light of the world's recent experience concerning the pricing and availability of primary commodities (including both raw materials and energy products), security of imported raw material supply is one aspect of its future trade pattern that Taiwan cannot ignore.

Changes in the direction of Taiwan's foreign trade are also becoming increasingly necessary as the volume of trade increases. In some commodities, such as low-priced footwear and textiles and black-and-white TV sets, Taiwan products now account for a very large portion of certain markets, e.g., the United States. This phenomenon has evoked the usual outcry from local producers demanding import tariffs and quotas, countervailing duties, "voluntary" restraint on the part of Taiwan exporters, etc. To some extend, this roadblock to Taiwan's export expansion can be bypassed through limiting sales of any specific commodity in any one market to a share of the total supply that would be regarded as tolerable by local competitors. (What would constitute such a share is another question.) This can be done by trying to sell in more markets and by selling a larger number of exports in any given market. Diversification by commodity and by market must, therefore, be regarded as a most urgent task facing Taiwan's foreign traders.

4. Outlook in 1979—a Taiwan Perspective

Chen Sun

Although the general price level has risen more rapidly in early 1979 than in the four or five years since the 1973-74 inflation, Taiwan's exports have remained competitive pricewise on the international market. The situation today is quite different from that of the recession years following the 1973/74 oil crisis. In 1973 and early 1974 domestic prices rose more rapidly than prices on the world market and, as a consequence, Taiwan lost much of its competitiveness in the U.S. market. This can be shown in the following table prepared in 1977.

Changing Position of Exports from Taiwan in the U.S. Market, 1970-76 (US$ million, %)

	1970	1971	1972	1973	1974	1975	1976
Total	549	817	1,293	1,784	2,098	1,938	2,989
As % of total U.S. imports	1.37	1.79	2.33	2.57	2.09	2.02	2.48
As % of U.S. imports from developing countries	5.26	7.07	9.01	8.78	5.32	4.94	5.68
As % of U.S. imports from Asia	5.69	6.92	8.54	9.81	7.65	7.16	7.58
As % of U.S. imports from East & South Asia	16.16	20.73	24.56	25.33	20.48	18.96	20.41

Source: Chen Sun, "Prospects for Sino-American Trade," *Industry of Free China*, July 1977.

I can think of no good reason why the Republic of China should fail in the foreseeable future to maintain its past trend in productivity improvement. In fact, it would be reasonable to expect the rate of increase in productivity to rise after the completion of the 10 major projects. If a six to seven percent annual growth rate in labor productivity can be maintained in the future as it was in the decade ending 1971-73, then a potential GDP growth rate in the neighborhood of nine percent could be achieved without much difficulty.

Let's take a look at the matter from the demand side. Although the total volume of world imports may expand at a lower rate than before 1973, competitively priced exports from Taiwan can grow at a more than proportional rate by gaining a foothold in new markets and enlarging their shares of old ones. Even if export expansion falls short of expectations, an increase in the domestic value-added per unit of export still could induce higher economic growth, given the pace of export expansion. In fact, the development of the second-phase import-substituting industries in the 1970s in Taiwan was at least partly aimed at an increasing in the domestic value-added proportion or, what amounts to the same thing, a decreasing in the import content proportion of exports.

As the substitution of domestic for imported intermediate products continues, import controls will be gradually relaxed and tariffs reduced. This will encourage imports, thereby reducing the huge trade surplus, and promote production efficiency by introducing competition from abroad which, I understand, has long been the policy of the government.

Another source of growth from the demand side is enlargement of the domestic market. Rising per capita income can be expected to spark a rapid increase in demand for services, housing, and consumer durables as well as a strong desire for improvement in the quality of life. As a result, the domestic market will become even more important to the future development of the economy.

Chen Sun, "Prospects of the Taiwan Economy," in *Industry of Free China*, Vol. LII, No. 5, (November 1979), pp. 10-11.

5. Developments in 1979-80

Richard C. Holbrook

An Official U.S. Assessment

The Economy: Performance Since Normalization

Taiwan's Gross National Product advanced 20.3 percent in current prices in 1979, to $32 billion. Total trade with 120 partners increased 31 percent to nearly $31 billion, and United States and other foreign investment reached a record $329 million as compared to $213 million in 1978.

In the first quarter of this year the total value of Taiwan's imports increased 44 percent to $4.5 billion, of which 21 percent—nearly $1 billion—was crude oil. Imports from the United States during the quarter—mainly farm products, fertilizer and machinery—were up 65 percent over the same period in 1979, to $1.1 billion.

The value of Taiwan's exports in the first quarter reached almost $4.5 billion, an increase of 34 percent over January—March 1979. The United States absorbed $1.5 billion of the total, mainly textiles, footwear, and electronic items and electrical machinery.

Globally, Taiwan had a trade deficit (rare for Taiwan) of about $64 million in the first quarter. It is now too early to predict whether or not the traditional trade surplus will emerge by year's end.

Special Factors Underpinning the Economy

Taiwan's broad-based economic development rests on a strong private sector and enlightened economic policies hospitable to foreign as well as domestic private investment and designed to foster high levels of savings, employment, and vital public services. The services include universal education designed to meet the needs of the economy. Budget surpluses and favorable trade balances are the rule rather than the exception in Taiwan. As a result, over the last two decades Taiwan has become a stable industrial economy. Per capita income has grown from subsistence level in the 1950's to nearly $1,900 in 1980.

Taiwan's Role in the World Economy

Taiwan's economy is heavily export oriented and is overly dependent on the United States and Japanese markets, which together absorb about 50 percent of Taiwan's exports. The United States took 39 percent of Taiwan's exports in 1970 and 35 percent in 1979, but the value rose in 9 years to $5.65 billion from $567 million. The U.S. trade deficit was $2.3 billion in 1979, slightly less than the $2.6 billion in 1978. The implications of a downturn in the world economy can be seen in the worldwide recession in 1974-75: Taiwan's real growth plunged to 1.1 percent in 1974 from 13 percent in 1973, and reached only 3.1 percent in 1975.

Taiwan's GNP grew at an annual rate of 6.2 percent in real terms in the first quarter of 1980, low by Taiwan standards but remarkable by world standards. It reflects mainly soaring costs of the 380,000 barrels of oil imported each day. At present prices the year's oil bill will total $3.8 billion, 74 percent higher than in 1979. Taiwan's growth, however, is based not only on a vibrant export sector, but also on strong consumer demand, booming housing and industrial construction, and progress on a number of railway, harbor, highway, nuclear power, and other infrastructure projects. Inflation in 1980 will be about 15 percent. Wages will probably increase an average of 20 percent.

Prospects

Despite worldwide stagflation at present, the long term prospects for Taiwan's economy are excellent. Exports and markets are being expanded and diversified, and economic policies remain conducive to investment and development.

U.S. Congress, House, Committee on Foreign Affairs Hearings before the Subcommittee on Asian and Pacific Affairs, *Implementation of the Taiwan Relations Act.* 96th Cong., 2nd sess., June 11, 17, and July 30, 1980. *Statement by Richard C. Holbrooke,* Asst. Secretary, Bureau of East Asian and Pacific Affairs, Dept. of State.

6.   An "Unofficial" U.S. View of New Development

American Institute in Taiwan

Trade and Foreign Economic Relations

Undoubtedly the most important determinant of Taiwan's economic growth over the last twenty years has been the pull of foreign demand for Taiwan's exports. In terms of constant 1971 prices, Taiwan's exports between 1960 and 1978 grew at a compound rate of 20 percent per annum. The fall in that real growth in 1979, to a level of 13.4 percent, is one of the major reasons that GNP growth was so much below average. The dim outlook for stronger export growth in 1980 brings the conclusion that GNP growth this year will probably be as low as previously estimated, around 5 percent for the year.

In order to reduce the impact on its economy of a downturn in the United States' demand for its products, Taiwan is diversifying its markets. OPEC members are a prime target in this diversification program, because they are the countries with the stronger balances of payments. However, another group of countries targeted to receive more of Taiwan's exports are the east European nations.

Until late 1979, Taiwan's businesspeople were forbidden to trade with any Communist countries. Now they are permitted to trade directly with Yugoslavia, Czechoslovakia, Hungary, and Poland. They are allowed to trade through third parties with Romania, Bulgaria, Albania and the Soviet Union. At present, trade consists largely of man-made fibers and other textile inputs from Taiwan, and coal and some machinery from Eastern Europe.

Officially, Taiwan prohibits all trade with the People's Republic of China. However, it is well known, and discussed in the international press, that Hong Kong traders have bought a number of goods in Taiwan—again largely textile inputs—and resold them on the mainland. Furthermore, in mid-1979 Taiwan eliminated prohibitions on a number of imports from Japan, Korea, Hong Kong, Singapore, and Malaysia which are known to be produced almost exclusively in China. These movements indicate there is a basic compatibility between the two economies which could permit a mutually profitable expansion of trade should a political thaw occur.

On a worldwide basis, Taiwan's major exports are still primarily labor-intensive consumer goods. Textiles are still the number one export, followed closely by electronic goods. These same products are Taiwan's leading exports to the United States.

Trade with the United States

The pattern of trade with the United States has not changed significantly in the past couple of years, and is not expected to in the immediate future. Over the coming decade, however, one can expect there will be a gradual shift in the composition of Taiwan's exports to the United States which will reflect the shift in worldwide exports. A smaller percentage of goods will be low-cost consumer textiles and consumer electronics. High fashion textiles, electronic components and computer electronic equipment, and more machinery and household appliances will be large ticket items in Taiwan's 1989 sales to the United States.

One of the aspects of the Taiwan-U.S. relationship which did have a noticeable change in 1979 was the portion of Taiwan's total exports going to the United States. That portion was nearly 40 percent in 1978, but was down to 35 percent in 1979. Gradually over the decade, Taiwan hopes to reduce its share of exports going to the United States to something below 25 percent. If it realizes this target, the value of Taiwan's exports to the United States in current terms in 1989 will be about $50 billion, and imports will be about $49 billion. Stated otherwise, Taiwan expects to have a trade surplus with the United States through the decade, but one which will decline significantly in both real terms and as a percentage of total two-way trade. At present, the surplus is equal to about 24 percent of two-way trade, whereas in 1989 it is expected to be only 1 percent.

In 1979, the United States exported more than $1 billion of agricultural goods to Taiwan. The 1980 total will again be over $1 billion. Taiwan will remain one of the larger markets

American Institute in Taiwan, *Taiwan* (Foreign Trends and Their Implications for the United States series) (Washington, D.C.: U.S. Department of Commerce, September, 1980), pp. 9-11.

for U.S. agricultural exports through the decade. However, as a percentage of total exports to Taiwan, agricultural products will probably decline steadily.

The real growth markets for U.S. exports to Taiwan will be inputs for those industries which are expanding most strongly in Taiwan, e.g., inputs for electronics, precision instruments, general machinery, trucks, autos, and steel. Taiwan will also be a good market for selling technological information, licensing agreements, financial services, and marketing expertise. It is quite likely that the sale of such services—which will undoubtedly be closely linked to investment ventures in Taiwan's demonstrably safe and improving economic environment—and the repatriation of profits by American investors in Taiwan during the latter half of the decade will completely offset Taiwan's surplus on the trade account. If so, the United States could well have a small surplus on the bilateral current account.

U.S.—Taiwan Financial Relations

With the strong likelihood that there will be balance in the U.S. bilateral current account toward the end of the decade, whatever financial arrangements are entered into on the capital account will actually represent an exchange of assets and mutual portfolio diversification. Such diversification should give Taiwan's financial market more stability and permit it to develop more depth. There is great potential for growth in such financial diversification, stablization and deepening; but it is also believed that this potential will only be realized if Taiwan permits American-owned banks to participate more fully in normal banking activities in Taiwan. Similarly, Taiwan's banks need to expand their direct participation in American money markets.

If American banks were permitted to accept NT dollar time deposits which curent policy prohibits, they would be able to contribute to the development of a term-loan market on Taiwan for funding of plant and equipment purchases. If American banks were permitted normal access to the Central Bank's rediscount facilities, they could better adjust their portfolios to meet the changing needs of Taiwan's development. With minor adjustments to foreign exchange regulations, U.S. banks could offer merchant banking services and would undoubtedly be able to improve the terms, conditions and amounts of funds lent to Taiwan's borrowers. And by expanding the range of services which they could offer in Taiwan, American banks would, automatically, contribute to the development of Taiwan's economy through the training of personnel who, in the normal course of time, would circulate through both the private business sector and the indigenous banking sector. At the same time, with official controls on the amount of capital which American banks can bring into Taiwan, it is highly unlikely that collectively they would ever control more than 4 or 5 percent of the market. At the present time, capital restraints would prevent them from controlling even 3 percent of deposits were they immediately given the right to accept time deposits.

Taiwan's banks should also be encouraged to set up more branches in the United States. At present there is only one bank from Taiwan, the International Commercial Bank of China, which operates in Chicago. If Taiwan opened more branches, the names of Taiwan's banks and their credit ratings would become better known. They would then be able to gain better access to U.S. funds, and they would be better positioned to manage Taiwan's sizeable and growing assets on deposit in American institutions.

Recent Developments

The break in formal diplomatic relations between the United States and Taiwan, which occurred at the end of 1978, had no significant effect upon Taiwan's economic stability. While there was a very small and short-lived outflow of capital that might have been related to the break, foreign investment over the year was stronger than ever. As previously discussed, domestic investment was, also, at an all-time high, unemployment remained very low, real wages rose 12 percent, and GNP growth was one of the best in the world.

In April 1980, Taiwan lost the China seat in the International Monetary Fund to the People's Republic of China. In May, it lost the one in the World Bank. At present, no deleterious effect on Taiwan from these losses has been detected. Private bankers voice strong support for lending to Taiwan, pointing to Taiwan's trade account, to Taiwan's low debt-service ratio, and to Taiwan's large net holdings of foreign assets as the underpinnings of its credit rating.

To underline bank confidence in Taiwan, three additional American banks have recently opened branches in Taipei, and another one has opened a representitive office. There are now eleven American banks with branches and five with representative offices in Taiwan. Furthermore, five European banks have been granted permission to open branches, and another four have pending applications.

With rates of return on capital which appear generally to be in the vicinity of 20 percent per annum, most American businessmen in Taiwan are confident that they will more then earn back all that they have invested in Taiwan. To advise businessmen contemplating investments in Taiwan, the American Chamber of Commerce maintains offices in Taipei. The Overseas Private Investment Corporation (OPIC), an organization established by an act of Congress, also offers insurance for firms investing in or financing projects in Taiwan.

III. Two-Way Foreign Investments and Technological Transfers

7. The Investment Climate

Marinus von Gessel

In order to put the subject in perspective, let me first give you some numbers on the total amount of foreign investment in the Republic of China. As of March 1980, the total accumulated foreign investment amounted to US$2,309 million—of which the Overseas Chinese had the largest portion with $756 million closely followed by the U.S. with $687 million, next by Japan with $385 million, then Europe with $250 million, and others with $231 million. When we rearrange these numbers by industry, it comes as no surprise that the largest categories are in electronics and electric appliances, chemicals, and machinery equipment. Foreign investment still keeps coming in at a rapid pace . . . from January till March of this year some $56 million has already been approved.

One quick way to assess the quality of the investment climate in this country is to take a quick look at what companies have already made investment decisions. Our membership list—some 250 corporate members—includes such well known names as Zenith, RCA, Ford, Gulf, Du Pont, IBM, Grundig, General Electric, Philips, Eli Lilly, GTE, and Goodyear. And to my knowledge, no foreign company has ever withdrawn its investment—except of course in the form of royalties, interest, and dividends—which is what the game is all about anyway. At any rate, the quality and quantity of foreign investors already on location in Taiwan speaks well for the investment climate.

Another way to assess the quality of the investment climate is to list the incentives and guarantees currently available. If I did that I would be guilty of plagiarism, since exactly the same speech was given about a year ago by Lawrence Lu, Director of the ROC's Industrial Development and Investment Center (IDIC), to the AMA "Taiwan Update" Seminar in April of 1979. The IDIC is an organization established specifically for providing investment services to investors and potential investors. I have known Lawrence Lu for many years and can presonally attest to his organization's willingness to assist you in a professional manner. I recommend his April 1979 speech as further reading, should you be considering an investment in Taiwan.

Marinus von Gessel, "American Businessmen's Views on the Investment Climate in Taiwan, ROC" in *Industry of Free China*, Vol. LIII, No. 4, (April, 1980), pp. 6-12.

Anyway, rather than duplicating Lawrence Lu's work, I believe a more useful way to address the subject is for me to raise a series of questions one should ask before making any investment in any country. Then it is my intention to answer each question specifically as it relates to Taiwan.

The first question is fundamental—*What is Taiwan's political stability now and in the future?*

Much has been reported on the political changes between the U.S. and the R.O.C. over the past-eighteen months. At midnight on December 31, 1978, the United States terminated official diplomatic relations with the Republic of China on Taiwan, and on January 1, 1979, established diplomatic relations with the People's Republic of China on the Mainland. New legislation (the Taiwan Relations Act) was signed by President Carter on April 10, 1979, under which all but one agreement (the Mutual Defense Treaty) were continued in force on an "unofficial" basis. In addition, this new legislation includes a security resolution which is a definite improvement over the language of the since-expired Mutual Defense Treaty.

First, the Defense Treaty spoke in terms of an armed attack on the territory of Taiwan and pledges the U.S. simply to take action in accordance with its constitutional processes. The Taiwan Relations Act speaks not only of an armed attack on the territory, but any attempt to resolve Taiwan's future by other than peaceful means. This would include any form of military coercion as well as any form of economic coercion, specifically including boycotts and embargoes. It goes on to pledge the United States to take exactly the same kind of action, that is to act and to meet this threat in accordance with its constitutional processes.

But, it also specifically requires the United States to maintain the capability to do such and obligates the United States to continue to provide defensive arms to the Republic of China on Taiwan.

Second, it is important to realize that the defense treaty was 25 years old. There could not have more than a dozen people still in the U.S. Congress who actually voted to approve this treaty back in 1954. Many people have taken the position that the Defense Treaty was out of date and that it was concluded under a different set of circumstances and really did not apply to the situation which exists today. On the other hand, the Taiwan Relations Act security provision has recently been voted on by virtually every Congressmen and Senator with an approval of close to 90 percent. That means that those members of the Congress, the ones whom Taiwan would have to turn to for action if any threat to the peace really arose, have a sense of personal commitment to Taiwan's security.

We believe that the Republic of China has weathered the political changes very well. We have been encouraged by the strong continuing interest of the U.S. Congress in Taiwan's welfare—strong economic growth has continued—and thus far, Communist China has made little trouble for the R.O.C., probably since they have had their hands full with their own economic development, ironically somewhat based on the Taiwan model.

On balance, confidence has returned to Taiwan, and the new "American formula" is expected to have some indirect benefits for the R.O.C., as Japan and some European nations are now in the process of upgrading their unofficial relationships to the new U.S. standard.

Let me add some comments on our perception of internal political stability, particularly as related to people's welfare. Most of these points were described in a recent speech by K. S. Chang, Minister of Economic Affairs of the R.O.C.

The standard of living in Taiwan is rapidly increasing—per capita income in 1979 reached US$1,720 and is forecasted to reach US$6,107 by the end of the eighties. The gap between rich and poor has steadily narrowed—the ratio of per capita income between the top 20 percent and the bottom 20 percent of the population has been reduced from 15:1 in 1953 to about 4:1 in 1979. Compare this to Mexico's ratio of 20:1 and even the United States' of 9:1, and you will have to agree that Taiwan is distributing its wealth equitably.

School is compulsory for nine grades and illiteracy has virtually been eliminated. Electric power is now available to 99.7 percent of all households, and home appliances such as television, refrigerators, air conditioning, and rice cookers are common items. Average calorie intake per day is 2,800 with some 80 grams of protein.

The upshot of these points is that when people can earn a decent living, eat well, can afford some luxuries, can read and write, and most important, can see most of their friends and neighbors benefitting in the same manner, they are not interested in upsetting the social order—which in turn breeds strong internal political stability.

The second question I would pose is *"What is the risk of Government appropriation or nationalization?"*

Protection against government appropriation or requistion is specifically covered in article 16 of the R.O.C.'s Statute for Investment by Foreign Nationals. Provided that a foreign investor contributes at least 45 percent of the total capital of an enterprise, the enterprise will not be subject to expropriation for 20 years. In addition, Article 15 of the same Statue states that investments with under 45 percent foreign participation can be expropriated only on the grounds of national defense needs. I believe the Statute answers the question quite well.

The third question is one of special interest to all businessmen— *"Are there any restrictions on the repatriation of capital and profits?"* Again, the answer is very straightforward. The Statute reads that all net profits and interest earnings can be converted and remitted. Annual repatriation of 20 percent of the total invested capital is allowed beginning two years after project completion. Exchange controls are comprehensive and all transactions require Central Bank approval, but generally the process is workable.

So far so good . . . However, there is one measure which restricts the ability of foreign manufacturers to maximize their returns. Specifically, sales or service branches of foreign invested companies are not allowed to repatriate profits earned on Taiwan. The present situation requires a foreign seller to choose between either relying on a local agent to sell and service his products, or establishing a local office that cannot remit or convert its NT dollar profits. Effective penetration of the market is thereby hindered. In addition, this policy discourages foreign companies from using Taiwan as a regional sales and servicing center for other Asian countries, which is unfortunate since Taiwan is in an ideal position to do business with the overseas Chinese in Southeast Asia.

Moving on to the fourth question, *"Does Taiwan have a sound economic system and responsive economic policy?"* Certainly the results over the last 28 years indicate a very positive answer. Since 1952, when the R.O.C. first started its six successive economic development plans, the R.O.C. achieved the following results:

• GNP rose from US$1 billion to $32 billion, an average annual growth rate of 8.3 percent.
• Per capita income went from US$148 to $1,720.
• Foreign Trade increased from US$300 million to $30 billion.

Taiwan basically has a free enterprise system guided by planned programs. Its development objective is to seek the ultimate industrialization within the shortest time span economically and socially possible. The R.O.C. Government has been consistent in its past actions and therefore is predictable in its future policies. For example, economic growth is stressed, but not at the expense of price stability. Consequently, Taiwan has suffered less from this international virus in the past than its competitor countries, and it is reasonable to predict that it will suffer less from this malady in the future.

There is now a call for diversification of industry into the areas of capital intensive heavy and chemical industries and technology intensive precision industries. These are not meant to replace the light manufacturing industries, but rather to complement them. But such a diversification is not without its problems—foremost among these is the need to acquire and efficiently use advanced technology. However, a number of inhibiting factors presently exist which could slow the process. I am referring to factors such as inadequate protection of industrial property rights (patents and trademarks) as well as restrictions on trademark licensing.

For the most part, though, the R.O.C. Government has had an enlightened policy attitude toward foreign investors. We can own our own business—100 percent equity. We can own the land on which our factories are built. We can bring in our technology, manufacture to U.S. quality standards and export our products with little difficulty. We are able to employ or discharge employees as our business conditions demand. We can train people, and we are able to export as well as import trained technicians. Basically, we are allowed to operate as we see fit in creating economic opportunity. As long as our operations have economic value and generally conform to national economic goals, they can progress unimpeded. And even on the occasion we meet with what seems like a insoluble problem, it is easy to arrange a meeting with cabinet level people—right up to Premier Y. S. Sun—and receive a responsive audience.

The next question is *"What are Taiwan's special incentives and guarantees?"* Here the answer is fairly simple as it can be checked by reading the pertinent statutes. Some of the major incentives include a five-year tax holiday, accelerated depreciation, a duty drawback system, special accomodations in industrial estates such as the Kaohsiung export processing zone, plus an indexing mechanism to adjust depreciation to compensate for higher replacement costs caused by inflation. All in all, a very acceptable package at present—a package which the R.O.C. Government is continually improving.

The sixth question relates to Customs— *"What are Taiwan's policies on customs and tariffs?"* Considering that customs duties account for the major part of the Government's revenue, it should come as no surprise that Taiwan has high tariff levels, plus levies on cost and freight value plus 15 percent. We believe that if dutes were lowered, it could help economic development as foreign investors would find it easier to import additional equipment to make their factories more efficient.

Protectionism initiated in Taiwan as well as in other Asian countries breeds protectionism in the U.S. and in the EEC, and could threaten market access abroad. Some small progress is being made, however, as the Government has agreed to phase out the 15 percent surcharge over 4 years. Hopefully, the Government will also change its method of customs valuation to the FOB basis.

The seventh question of *"Does Taiwan have a well-planned infrastructure?"* is easily and positively answered by just taking a drive through the countryside. The first ten infrastructure projects have recently been completed—which include transportation, utilities, heavy industry, and nuclear power generation. Another twelve projects have now been initiated—which include expansion of harbors, development of new towns, farm mechanization, and additional highways and railroads. An added benefit of these infrastructure projects is that it buffers the economy in times of recession.

The eighth question is *"Does Taiwan have as sound energy policy?"* Again, a very positive answer to this question. The Government-owned Tai Power Company has carefully laid out plans from now to the year 2000. Nuclear power is stressed, as are good relations with Middle East oil suppliers, such as Saudi Arabia and Kuwait.

The net result of these policies is that energy in Taiwan cost less than in its competitor countries such as Japan, South Korea and Hong Kong. For example, heavy oil prices and industrial electric power prices are lower in Taiwan than in these countries.

The next question is *"Does Taiwan have an effective banking system?"* Not yet—thus far Taiwan has been able to get by with its money and credit system, but it is quite apparent that the system needs to be modernized. It has been difficult to borrow NT dollars, and foreign currency funding needs Central Bank approval. Notwithstanding the condition of the banking system, Taiwan has an excellent credit standing internationally.

One positive point of interest is the ability of the expatriate to deal with familiar banks from his home country. There are branches of eleven U.S. banks on Taiwan and five European banks will establish offices here in 1980. Again, their full service is restricted since they have limited capacity to provide local currency financing both short and long term. We hope that the R.O.C. Government will rectify this situation by allowing them to pay interest on local time deposits, which would provide the funds necessary to make NT dollar loans.

The tenth question— *"Does Taiwan have a good labor environment?"* is a complicated one to answer. On the positive side, the workforce in Taiwan is well motivated, well skilled and educated, diligent, and by law cannot strike. Unions do exist, but for the most part are a constructive part of the process. On the negative side—periodically there are not enough people to fill the jobs, particularly in the young female assembler category. What appears to happen is that these workers move into service type employment or temporarily return to their homes or farms during certain periods of time. But intensive recruiting and higher wages seem to bring them back so that the manufacturers can meet their production schedules. Nevertheless, the excessive labor turnover is an unnecessary cost which both Government and industry together should try to eliminate.

As mentioned earlier, the Government has perceived this and has embarked on a new route leading to more sophisticated high technology industries as a complement to light manufacturing. Meanwhile, this change will take some time, and the labor turnover will continue to exist. An additional challenge will be faced as the higher technology industries require more skilled technicians and better-trained managers. I understand the Government is about to initiate programs to raise the level of such training.

The final question which is particularly important to the families of expatriates is *"How is the quality of life for expartriates in Taiwan?"* I can personally state that there are good living conditions for our families. The R.O.C. Government has cooperated to continue many of the social and educational facilities associated with the former U.S. diplomatic and military presence in Taiwan. American type "education" through the high school level is available for expatriate dependents. There are Boy Scout and Girl Scout troops. The American Club in China has some of the finest facilities for family recreation and social activities in Asia. An English language radio station is on the air 24 hours a day with sophisticated programs. I can go on and on, since I am somewhat subjective in my opinion on this subject, as I like living in Taiwan.

In conclusion, I believe that it is no accident that the OECD has termed the Republic of China as one of the 10 newly industrialized nations. The investment climate in Taiwan is one of the best in Asia and with the few needed improvements mentioned earlier, it can even be better. As we say in the U.S.A., "Come on in, the water is fine."

IV.   Augmenting Natural Resources Supply from Overseas

8.   Investing Overseas and "Farming the Sea."

Y. L. Wu and K. C. Yeh

Like the Japanese, businessmen in Taiwan who have developed certain enterprises and technical expertise have begun to establish similar undertakings in foreign markets. For instance, this has been done through investment in outlets and facilities for foreign sales. Manufacturing facilities have also been located overseas to promote sales in local foreign markets, in industries in which the investors have already gained considerable experience at home—e.g., textiles, petrochemicals, and construction materials. In addition, overseas investment to provide for the supply of resources for domestic use in the future has also started, as yet only on a very small scale. For example, timber land in Indonesia, corn-growing farms in Thailand, etc. have been developed by Taiwan-based investors. In due course, such acquisitions will help assure Taiwan producers and consumers of continuity of supply and access to raw materials on potentially more advantageous terms. Most such direct investments will also present possibilities of exporting to third countries from overseas locations.

From 1959 through 1975, 91 applications by ROC businessmen for investment in foreign countries, totalling $26.5 million, were officially approved. Their distribution by sector and by country is shown in Table 1. Forty percent of such investments are in various manufacturing industries; 19 percent in construction and construction materials; 13 percent in textiles; 10 percent in foreign trade; 8.5 percent in machinery and metal products. Only a little over 3 percent are for the development of mineral and agricultural resources.

The accompanying data represent only officially approved investments from Taiwan. Some investments, however, have been made in the form of joint ventures in partnership with business interests in the host countries or third countries. Some "third" country (e.g., Hong Kong) interests conceivably may also be beneficially owned by Taiwan investors. At any rate, Taiwan exporters are permitted to retain, in foreign exchange, a small amount of their export proceeds for purposes of their overseas business operations. With annual exports currently (1976) running at the rate of about $8 billion, even 5 percent would come to $400 million.

There is some evidence that Taiwan investments abroad are substantially larger than those shown in Table 1. Obviously, one important source of such capital consists of residual export earnings retained abroad, as shown in Table 2.

If the data in Table 2 are correct, actual investments are at least 14-15 times the value of approved investments that have been made directly by Taiwan investors in four of the ASEAN countries during 1959-75. Since investments in Singapore and Hong Kong are bound to be sizable in view of the close relations maintained by businessmen in the three areas, one might hazard the guess that $200 million would be the minimum value of Taiwan's direct foreign investments in Southeast Asia to date (1976).

Since the official data on approved investments indicate a predominant concentration in light manufacturing and foreign trade, activities in overseas resources development accounting for a very small share, the majority of these investments appear to have been motivated by efforts to support and supplement external trade activities, as well as to extend established manufacturing to production in foreign markets. Investments for resource development, however, present an opportunity that Taiwan can ill afford not to exploit, and more should be expected in the future, the present small beginning notwithstanding.

Geographically, Taiwan's existing approved foreign investments are concentrated in Southeast Asia, where manufacturers from Taiwan frequently enjoy a technical advantage

Y. L. Wu and K. C. Yeh, "Taiwan's Economic Relations," in *Occasional Papers / Reprints Series in Contemporary Asian Studies*, No. 3-1978 (15), (U. of Maryland, School of Law), pp. 196-201.

Table 1. Overseas Investment by Taiwan Investors, Distribution by Country and Industry, 1959-75
(Value in US $ thousand based on approved investment applications)

	Construction Material and Engineering		Lumber		Mining and Refining		Textiles		Machinery and Metal Products		Petro-Chemicals		Agriculture and Fisheries		Miscellaneous Manufacturing		Foreign Trade		Total		Percent
	No.	Amount	No.	Amount	No.	Amount	No.	Amount	No.	Amount	No.	Amount	No.	Amount	No.	Amount	No.	Amount	No.	Amount	
Southeast Asia																					
ASEAN																					
Malaysia	3	179	1	201	1	160	1	129	4	412	1	80	1	13	—	—	1	16	13	1,190	4.6
Thailand	—	—	2	379	—	—	—	—	4	1,154	2	460	—	—	10	2,098	1	96	19	4,187	16.30
Singapore	1	956	—	—	1	80	5	1,272	2	251	1	408	—	—	1	374	—	—	10	3,261	12.7
Philippines	—	—	—	—	—	—	1	60	1	180	1	69	—	—	1	250	1	100	5	559	2.2
Indonesia	1	354	—	—	—	—	1	215	1	194	1	270	—	—	1	1,500	1	225	6	2,744	10.7
Other	—	—	—	—	—	—	2	180	—	—	—	—	—	—	2	838	—	—	5	1,212	4.7
Hong Kong	1	2,128	—	—	—	—	1	34	—	—	—	—	—	—	1	82	2	103	5	2,347	9.1
Japan	—	—	—	—	—	—	—	—	—	—	—	—	—	—	—	—	1	50	1	50	0.2
Okinawa	—	—	—	—	—	—	—	—	—	—	—	—	—	—	1	5	—	—	1	5	0.02
Republic of Korea	—	—	—	—	—	—	—	—	—	—	—	—	—	—	1	25	—	—	1	25	0.09
Australia	—	—	—	—	—	—	1	90	—	—	—	—	—	—	—	—	—	—	1	90	0.3
U.S.A.	—	—	—	—	—	—	1	500	—	—	—	—	—	—	4	240	1	900	6	1,640	6.4
Guam	3	1,336	—	—	—	—	—	—	—	—	—	—	—	—	2	187	—	—	5	1,523	5.9
Canada	—	—	—	—	—	—	—	—	—	—	—	—	—	—	1	25	—	—	1	25	0.9
Latin America	—	—	—	—	—	—	1	500	—	—	—	—	—	—	2	1,063	2	1,050	5	2,613	10.2
West Germany	—	—	—	—	—	—	—	—	—	—	—	—	—	—	—	—	1	22	1	22	0.08
United Kingdom	—	—	—	—	—	—	—	—	—	—	—	—	—	—	—	—	1	35	1	35	0.1
Middle East	—	—	—	—	—	—	1	375	—	—	—	—	—	—	1	3,125	1	113	3	3,613	14.1
Africa	—	—	—	—	—	—	—	—	—	—	—	—	—	—	1	463	1	21	3	484	1.9
Total	9	4,953	3	580	2	240	15	3,355	12	2,191	6	1,287	1	13	29	10,275	14	2,731	91	25,625	100.0
Percent	19.3		2.3		0.9		13.1		8.5		5.0		0.05		40.1		10.5		100.0		

Table 2. Other Foreign Investments by Taiwanese (US$ million)

Host Country	Period and Remarks	Investments Reported by Host Country as Taiwan Investments	Approved Investments in 1959-75 as Reported by the ROC
Indonesia	Approved investments cumulative to 1975	16.0	2.7
Philippines	Investment by Board of Investment approved firms, 1968-75	85.1	0.5
Thailand	Total registered capital, 1960-May 31, 1975	22.6	4.2
Malaysia	1974-75 only	2.8	1.2
		126.5	8.6

over local enterprise and where joint ventures with local ethnic Chinese interests are quite common practice. The ASEAN countries, for example, accounted for 46.5 percent of such approved investments through 1975, while Hong Kong took another 9.1 percent. Since Southeast Asia is a logical source of raw materials for Taiwan, as it is for Japan, it will probably take precedence over other areas as Taiwan businessmen increase their investments for resource development in the future. However, other major exporters of resources, such as Saudi Arabia, Taiwan's principal source of crude oil, and Bahrain, have also attracted Taiwan businessmen. Expanding bilateral trade and economic relations have arisen as a result of Taiwan's need to secure an oil supply from the Middle East, and growing trade relations have in turn fostered investment. (However, no investment in Middle Eastern oil has been attempted so far.)

The Potential of Ocean Fishing

A second method for an island nation to expand its supply of natural resources is to increase it access to the surrounding waters. "Farming the sea" in an ever-widening area, a natural development in these circumstances, is a function of the development of the fishing industry. Taiwan's fishing fleet today is no longer confined to the island's coastal waters or even the South China Sea. The Indian Ocean, the waters near Australia, and the American Pacific fishing grounds are frequented by fishing vessels from Taiwan. Perhaps the farthest these vessels have ventured is the exploratory shrimping trip to the South polar region undertaken by an experimental vessel in 1977, which used Capetown as its staging point. The potential of ocean fishing can be illustrated by the data in Table 3.

Table 3. Composition of Taiwan Fishery Production

	Total Production (thousand metric tons)		Index
	1976	1965	1965 = 100
Deep Sea	325,327	135,949	239.3
Inshore	317,327	160,924	197.4
Coastal	31,961	30,655	104.2
Aquaculture	135,450	54,160	250.0
Total	810,475	381,688	212.3

Of the total volume reported in Table 3, 157,800 tons, valued at $314.2 million, were exported. Between 1965 and 1976, the increase in production was more than 2 times while that of export was nearly 28 times in volume and 11.4 times in value.

9. A Strategy for Technological Development

K. T. Li

To a developing country, the building up of science and technology becomes a twofold quest that is both complex and urgent. On the one hand, there is always a severe constraint in resources. Whether it is human resources, natural resources, or fiscal resources, or any combination thereof, a developing country tends to find that the scarcity of resources results in limited options and difficult trade-off calculations. This usually dictates a strategy based on a highly selective approach to emphasis and priorities, which in turn demands careful planning. At the same time, one still must face the necessity of a trial and error process in decision-making. On the other hand, a developing country is always racing against time, hence the urgency in technological development. There usually is not enough time for decision-makers to test alternative propositions, to reflect adequately on all contingencies in tradeoffs, or even to explore and experiment with secondary impacts in a larger socio-economic context. There is the permeating fear that the technological gap between one's country and others will widen. Benign neglect is a luxury which decision-makers in a developing country can ill afford.

Systematic and serious work on economic development in my country can be traced back to 1952 when we adopted our first four-year plan. In the following quarter century, there emerged a number of salient features in our experience. These features may be relevant to similar situations in another country and another time. To put it succinctly, these features can be described as:

1. A prudent approach to technological sophistication
2. Balance between industry and agriculture
3. International cooperation and an inducive investment climate for self-help
4. Heavy educational investments
5. Overseas feedbacks for planning and review
6. Fiscal conservatism and balanced budget.

First and foremost, I believe we have adopted a prudent approach in our strategy for technology, even though from time to time we have moved swiftly. In the early 1950s, our initial efforts at industrial development were directed toward the rehabilitation of then-existing facilities with priority assigned to the infrastructure, agriculture-based industries, and import-substituting industries, such as chemical fertilizers and textiles. These industries were principally those having to do with the needs of the people for clothing, food, shelter and transportation. Subsequent efforts were turned to the production of more durable goods and industrial intermediates. As we progressed further, increasing sophistication and diversification took place as evidenced by the manufacture of synthetic fibers, plastics and electronics. In the meantime, export expansion rather than import substitution has become the dominant factor in the allocation of resources. During the last 10 years, in fact, our economy has become increasingly export-oriented. In 1976 the total of our international trade, at close to US$15 billion, slightly surpassed our GDP. The country has thus become increasingly aware that economic interdependence is now far more important than economic independence. To maintain our economic ties with over a hundred nations, we have adopted a series of new measures, including the Ten Major Projects designed to remove the bottlenecks in the infrastructure and to promote petrochemical and heavy industries. Furthermore, efforts are being made to build up innovative industries involving high technology.

This very brief account of our recent history of industrialization bespeaks of an evolutionary approach to technology. While the target technologies may not have been acquired

K. T. Li, "Strategy for Technological Development," in K. T. Li, *My Views on Taiwan Economic Development,* August, 1980, pp. 65-72.

at an even pace, they were pursued in a step-by-step manner. What is more, the methodology of technology transfer went through an evolutionary cycle of its own. In the 1950s, the basic reliance was on our own experience from the China mainland or on turnkey contracts. In the 1960s, more emphasis was given to licensing arrangements. In the 1970s, new thrusts are being made in improved technology by our own industries or in joint ventures with foreign investors, particularly in petrochemical and engineering industries. We have had difficulties at every turn in this strategy for technology development. But looking back, the route we traversed was a safe and prudent one. Without the guiding spirit of prudence, we could perhaps have done much better in certain aspects, but we probably would also have fared less well in terms of overall development.

In the second place, we have always placed a high premium in the process of our industrialization on agriculture as well as industry. This even-handed approach has had a far-reaching impact on our social structure. In the past three decades, our farming population has declined from more than two-thirds of the total to less than one third. Agricultural products, which once occupied a predominant position in our exports, now account for only 10 percent or so. However, our agricultural productivity, particularly on a per hectare basis, has improved so much that it has more than made up for the loss of farming population, and that by and large we can still manage to pay for our imported grains with money earned from our exports of an ever increasing variety of cash crops and processed foods. The nutrition standard of our people has risen steadily, and we now enjoy the highest per capita intake of calories in all of Asia. Total protein per capita availability is comparable to that of Japan. We have found, indeed, that a sound agricultural base is a very effective social and economic shock absorber and also helps to prevent excessive urbanization. A most dramatic experience we had was to see agriculture coming to the rescue of industry during the worldwide recession of 1974 and 1975. Some 200,000 urban workers laid off by industry were quietly absorbed by agriculture without any serious social problem.

To keep agricultural practices abreast with the modern world naturally will require massive efforts in science and technology, in rural extension work, and in organization and management. In basic research, through experimental stations to practical extension service, our agricultural sector is more sophisticated than our industrial sector. In the past three decades our agricultural people have mastered the art of identifying their problems and of mapping out valid strategies to deal with them. There has been close cooperation between research scientist and farmer.

A third feature I would like to mention is the genuine atmosphere of international cooperation we have maintained and the genial investment climate we have created. First and foremost among our international cooperation programs was, of course, the U.S. AID program between 1950 and 1965. In this period we received about US$1.5 billion in loans and grants, mostly in the form of farm products and industrial supplies. Looking back today, I feel strongly that the most significant contribution of the AID program was not the material aid per se, but rather the program's spin-offs. In coordination with the AID program we ourselves developed the basics of economic planning and programming methodology. Directional planning and objective budgeting, among others, were introduced into the country and firmly took root. The most dramatic evidence of this was that, two years before our graduation from the AID program, the Chinese agency handling AID funds was reorganized and integrated into our economic planning and implementing machinery. Another important spin-off was the confidence instilled into our private sector through our land reform program and AID loan operations. As a result, we have witnessed the booming of our private sector in the post-AID years because the Chinese government created a favorable investment climate in the early 1960s. Last but not least, the AID program put down seed money for the improvement of our universities, technical and vocational institutions, particularly in sciences, engineering and medicine. Now that we have developed a healthy graduate education system in the last 10 years, which I will discuss further later, we have been able to cope with the "brain drain," and to start a new pattern of a two-way international flow of talent.

Closely connected with international economic cooperation is the creation of a climate favorable to domestic and foreign investment. In this respect we have adopted a number of measures, in law as well as in practice. In addition to non-expropriation guarantees and liberal provisions permitting foreign investors to transfer their assets abroad, we also insist on no statutory limitation on the share of non-Chinese ownership and no restriction whatsoever on remittance of earnings. At first glance, this policy may seem to violate the so-called basic national interest. Our experience, however, tells an opposite story. Under this policy, a large amount of desirable technology has been introduced as investors sought to take advantage of our social stability and skilled manpower. This has in turn stimulated our local industry to strive for greater sophistication and higher quality standards. I need only to mention a few actual cases for illustration. The Singer Sewing Machine Company was among the earlier American investments in Taiwan, and was perhaps the prime mover in upgrading our technology in machine parts and precision machinery produced by its satellite plants. Philips, the giant Dutch firm, has had a large subsidiary in Taiwan for the last 10 years. In the beginning, quality control equipment and testing instruments were all imported. Soon a wave of what might be called "machine shop innovation" started to flourish. I understand that the Taiwan subsidiary is now selling a number of machine tools designed and made in Taiwan back to the parent company. Taiwan Polymers, a subsidiary of the National Distillers and commonly known as the USI, was established in Taiwan in 1965 for the production of polyethylene. In the beginning, our total domestic demand for PE was only one-third of the plant's initial capacity of 34,000 tons. Twelve years later, the annual production of PE by Taiwan Polymers had increased to 90,000 tons and could not fill domestic demand. It now counts more than 1,400 firms as its downstream customers and has extended new applications of its products over a wide range, from greenhouses to packaging and insulating materials. A few months ago, I visited a local battery plant and was surprised to find that it is on the verge of putting out a high-quality, maintenance-free battery similar to what is now advertised in America as the "Freedom Battery." The manager told me that this innovation is developed simply to supply all Ford Motor Company cars made in Taiwan! Stories like these are too numerous to cite, and we are convinced that, at least from the viewpoint of technology, we have gained much more than we have lost as a result of our liberal investment laws and practices.

The fourth feature in our developmental strategy is an all-out commitment to education. This is perhaps as much a dictate of our traditional respect for education as it is a policy choice. At present, over a quarter of our population is in schools. Illiteracy has been practically wiped out. In 1969 we extended our free education from six to nine years. On a per capita basis, our university and college population is on a par with West Germany and Japan. Our local governments sometimes must allocate over 50 percent of their budgets for education. The result has been basically beneficial, even though new problems have emerged. A most vexing problem among developing countries is the difficulty in building up a critical mass of technical manpower. This is in turn compounded by the "brain drain." We had suffered from it until the late 1960s, but then the tide gradually began to turn. In the last five years, we have been attracting back, mostly from the United States, over 5,000 technical and professional people, 40 percent of whom are at the Ph. D. level. Since we still lose about 2,000 college graduates for advanced training abroad each year; at least we can clearly perceive a two-way flow of talent. With the disappearance of low-cost labor, we now have a concentration of low-cost scientists and engineers. This is as much an opportunity as it is a challenge. We must create meaningful employment markets for these highly trained young men and women. This is one of our most basic reasons for moving into innovative industries involving higher technology.

To promote science and technology in a small economy has many inherent difficulties. One of these is the difficulty in establishing a viable, independent and effective peer review system for R & D planning and evaluation. In a small, tightly-knit R & D community, where everyone knows nearly everyone else in his own field, it is almost impossible to ensure that personal bias is kept out of review opinions. Fortunately we can tap the service of a much larger R & D community of our compatriots abroad. The National Science Council, for instance, has engaged over 300 top-notch scientists and engineers of Chinese ancestry and residing overseas as its unpaid reviewers and consultants. For all major project proposals, both in-country and out-country reviews are made. This not only gives us assurance that the work is not duplicating something that has already been done elsewhere, but also gives us the confidence in the objectivity of the review opinions.

In addition, we have also institutionalized consultation with overseas Chinese specialists on technological strategy. Participation is by no means limited to overseas Chinese, but includes experienced experts wherever we can find them. Topics cover a broad spectrum, including earthquake and landslide engineering, electronics, computer usage, land use research, remote sensing, nuclear power reactor technology manpower research, industrial innovation and product development, and machine tools, just to mention a few. This pattern of intensive and extensive interaction is most valuable to our technology planners, given our insular geographic position.

The sixth and last special feature in our experience is our fiscal conservatism in technological development. Throughout both good and lean years, the government has maintained a strong policy of living within its means with a balanced budget. This has been accomplished in spite of the fact that defense expenditures have necessitated over 40 percent of our national budget. As a result, we must be highly conscious of borrowing as well as meticulous in our revenue estimates. Although harsh criticism has often been leveled by businessmen at our tight money policy, we did achieve our purposes. Inflation has long been under control, except for the years of worldwide inflation in 1973-74. And our credit rating with international bankers has also been high. The basic assumption has been that real progress for the masses is possible only on the basis of stability.

Our new problems are many. The most pressing ones include:

1. Energy
2. Environmental quality
3. Transformation of our economic structure
4. Competing for new niches in the world market
5. Reorientation of manpower utilization

Energy would be a serious problem in Taiwan even without the 1973 crisis. The projected demand for energy in my country will almost triple our present capacity by 1990, and we have little indigenous energy left to develop. For the next 10 years or so, we must rely heavily on nuclear power, for which we have contracted six light-water reactors to be installed in three plants, with one nearing completion, one under construction, and one in the final stages of design. By 1985, our three nuclear power plants will generate a total of more than 5,000 megawatts, which will be about 40 percent of our generating capacity at that time. At present, we are holding up plans for further expansion in nuclear power. For one thing, the world's deposit of uranium, like fossil fuels, is also finite. Secondly, there may be tight political constraints on the development of newer and more efficient reactors. We have always been a faithful member of NPT, and we will stay that way under any circumstances, certain irresponsible reports from the news media notwithstanding. We must therefore chart a very careful course in nuclear technology, namely, how to operate our contracted nuclear facilities with optimum efficiency.

To meet our rising energy demand, we must look into alternative energy sources. At present, geothermal energy and wind energy look most promising; we estimate that these two sources may eventually contribute up to 20 percent of our energy needs. R & D groups have been formed by the government to investigate these alternative sources.

Energy substitutes and energy conservation are also formidable topics that must be dealt with. In the area of energy substitutes, I would like to mention our decision to develop single-cell protein as animal feed for partial replacement of the energy-intensive soybean meal and fish meal. At this stage of the game, methanol and agricultural wastes seem to be most promising carbon sources for the single cell protein because of their availability. Consequently great progress is needed in enzyme technology and fermentation technique. As far as energy conservation is concerned, we realize that it cannot be achieved by thrift alone. We are in fact hindered by a number of our cultural hangups. For one thing, our industry is operated on a one shift or a two-shift basis. For thousands of years the Chinese believed that one should be asked to work only between sunrise and sunset, and we are now faced with a question of excessive power production during off-peak hours. A series of measures have been launched to deal with this problem, ranging from reverse-pumping reservoirs (aided by modern windmills) to the development of an electric battery car with central stations for battery recharging at night. Other conservation measures are under consideration, the most important of which is the recycling of industrial waste heat through cogeneration.

The foregoing is a partial list of our new energy program. It represents a highly selective approach. We also have our decisions on what not to do in energy development. For example, we will not experiment with fast breeders, nor will we touch fusion reactors, nor will we seriously work on solar energy for direct power generation. The choice of our do's and don'ts is again guided by a sense of prudence.

Our environmental concerns have been late-blooming flowers, but are growing rapidly. These concerns go far behind air and water and noise pollution. We are now acutely aware to two aspects of environmental degeneration. First, there is the problem of over-crowding. Second, there has been a sharp change in our soil chemistry resulting from years of excessive use of chemical fertilizers and pesticides. We are therefore resolved to work harder than ever on family planning and population diversification, as well as on pest control management systems. In biological control of pests we already have had some budding success, and the campaign is being carried on to the microbiological level. At least one project of using mass-cultured, aerobic bacteria as suppressants for pathogens in the soil is showing great promise.

The transformation of our economic structure poses serious problems as it brings great expectations. Our industry must be converted from a labor-intensive one to a technology- and capital-intensive one. Needed also are a new pattern of university-industry interactions, a massive effort to establish a few industries which can hold on to a number of relatively safe niches in the world market, a concerted move to build up our domestic market, and a determined effort to upgrade our standards, services and patent practices. A concrete example of our determination in this direction was the recent decision to set up a Science Industry Park in Hsinchu, some 75 kilometers south of Taipei. This is merely a first step, and we hope it will be a short-cut to higher technology in my country.

Our agricultural community is also anticipating drastic transformations. The goal used to be maximum output per hectare. In the future we must give most consideration to the demand of maximum output per farmer. Consequently, massive efforts are being made toward farm mechanization, intensive culture of cash crops, commercialization of farming, and location of certain industries in rural areas.

There is a new awakening in my country that science and technology must be fully integrated into national policies. Recently our President, Mr. Chiang Ching-Kuo, appointed a ministerial committee to assure that this is done. The task force is known as the Coordinating Committee for the Application of Science and Technology to National Objectives, and I was asked to serve as the Chairman of this Committee. I see the work as posing a great many new challenges. The job is a continuous one. I hope that a younger generation of decision-makers will face these challenges with vigor and that I do not make too many mistakes so as to create more problems for them to solve. I also see splendid opportunities for people in different countries to work together on problems of common concern. The world is certainly becoming smaller day by day, and we all know in our hearts that we are not only one family, but are also in the same boat.

10.   The Hsin-chu Science Industry Park

Denis Fred Simon

The development of the park has been conceived in three stages. During Stage One, the primary participants in the park will be foreign firms. These firms will set up operations in one of four areas: (1) first-line industries such as energy exploration and communications; (2) innovation design and improvement of production techniques; (3) information generation for direct use in the industrial sector to design new products; and (4) development of alternative raw materials for key sectors in the Taiwan economy. During Stage Two, the park will attempt to involve the local economy through joint ventures and closer cooperation with existing scientific institutions. In Stage Three, local firms will be allowed to establish operations in the park and to employ the techniques and skills that they have secured from their experiences with foreign firms already based in the park. As of April 1980, five major companies had received government approval to begin Stage One of the project, including: Wang Laboratories (CRT monitors); RCA (integrated circuits); and Texas Instruments (assorted electronics components). The National Science Council on Taiwan has affirmed its invitation to 56 American companies to set up operations in the park.

In order to attract foreign firms within high technology industries, the government has offered the same special incentives available to other foreign investors. Moreover, tax rates and duties have been adjusted to accord with the requirements for establishing a high technology-based industry. To qualify, firms must fit into one of the four key areas specified in Stage One and must offer a high level of competitive technology with a stable and possibly growing international market. Firms must indicate how they will contribute to the local economy either through sourcing practices, worker training in Taiwan or abroad, or utilization of research facilities in Taiwan. Although there was initial disagreement about whether the park should be oriented to applied or to pure research and development, applied research was favored. Firms within the park will work closely with the nearby universities, as well as with ITRI, the government-sponsored industrial technology research institute also located in Hsinchu.

Denis Fred Simon (National Foreign Assessment Center), "Technology Transfer and Technology Policies in Taiwan," (unpublished paper), pp. 38-39.

11.   Technology Transfer to Taiwan

Denis Fred Simon

The development and application of technology in Taiwan has been governed by Taiwan's particular political setting. Generally speaking, Taiwan has adopted a bimodal strategy to meet its technology needs and to enhance its S&T capabilities. One objective has been to expand and extend the island's interdependence within the world economy. Taiwan has attempted to move away from a position of technological dependency toward a position of interdependence. In some ways, this goal has been reflected in attempts to expand the "dependence" on Taiwan of others, such as transnational corporations. This does not imply that symmetry can ever be attained, but only to note that Taiwan has tried to increase its importance to others. Through government promotion of various policies to increase the attractiveness of Taiwan as an investment site, as a sourcing site for technology parts, components, and final products, and, most recently, as a partner with developed country firms in third country projects, Taiwan has begun to shift away from an economy dominated by labor-intensive production activities toward one increasingly oriented toward the manufacture of more and more technically complex and sophisticated products and parts. By relying on prior experiences with simpler assembly-oriented production operations and on its well-educated skilled labor force, Taiwan has attempted to hurdle over the technology gap that has separated the advanced industrialized nations from the developing countries of the world.

Taiwan's policies towards technology applications and transfer have also been informed by considerations of self-reliance. Increasing raw materials prices and supply considerations in such key industries as petrochemicals have made a more active role imperative for the state in the allocation, distribution, and pricing of needed raw materials and intermediates. Decreasing dependence on external suppliers is to be accomplished through the acquisition and local development of an assortment of critical production technologies. By moving toward greater backward integration in such areas as petrochemicals, the government can alter prices and control supplies in order to improve local firm competitiveness in the international market for such products as plastics, synthetics, and assorted textiles. By reducing import costs, the government hopes to ease partially the strain on the balance of payments being caused by rising oil prices. The movement towards greater local self-reliance involves other industries as well. Efforts to enhance technological capabilities in the machinery industry reflect the desire to decrease reliance on imports as the economic structure shifts towards more precision industries. Acquisition of design and construction capabilities in the nuclear engineering field is intended to develop and meet self-reliance objectives in the energy area. Through a combination of policies aimed at increased cost competitiveness and quality improvements in production processes and products, the government on Taiwan hopes to deal more effectively with the economic and political challenges facing the island.

Both these objectives, technology upgrading and greater self-reliance, are joined together by Taiwan's decision to use imported technology to achieve these goals. In many respects, Taiwan's policies in this area are a reflection of the Japanese experience. Japan's technology strategy was basically absorptive in nature: it emphasized borrowed technologies. The local infrastructure was designed to help absorb imported technologies . . . because desired technologies were often readily available. The same considerations seem to underlie Taiwan's current actions in this area. The island has had almost unimpeded access to foreign technologies across a wide spectrum of industries. For Taiwan, the introduction of technology from abroad has been a stimulus for breaking down domestic technological stagnation. From a long-term perspective, use of foreign technologies has had a catalytic effect—that is, it has set off a search for new intermediate or appropriate technologies that are better able to capitalize on the existing indigenous set of factor endowments,

---

Denis Fred Simon, (National Foreign Assessment Center), "Technology Transfer and Technology Policies in Taiwan," (unpublished paper), pp. 4-7, 13-22, and 45-47.

including the local skill mix.

Between 1952–79, in addition to U.S. AID-sponsored technology transfers and technical assistance, the Taiwan government has approved over 1,300 technology cooperation
agreements. Although a sizeable number of these have been between foreign and state-
owned firms, the majority have involved private Taiwan companies and foreign corporations. Statistics from the Investment Commission, Ministry of Economic Affairs, indicate
that most technology transfer and cooperation agreements have been between Japanese and
local firms.

As of 1979, the number of agreements with Japan totaled 926 cases, or 70.3 percent of
all technology transfer cases (Table 1). Agreements with U.S. firms have accounted for 254
cases, or 19.3 percent of all agreements. Transfer agreements with European firms have
numbered 115 cases. (8.7 percent), while agreements with firms from other nations have
accounted for 23 cases (1.7 percent). The late 1960s seems to mark the period when technology cooperation agreements began to steadily increase. In 1978 and 1979, the number of
cases equaled 18.4 percent of the total number of cases (1,318), the highest proportion over
any two year period.

Table 1
APPROVED TECHNOLOGY COOPERATION AGREEMENTS BY SOURCE
(1952-1979)

Unit: Cases

YEAR	U.S.A.	JAPAN	EUROPE	OTHER	TOTAL
1952	—	1	—	—	1
1953	—	—	—	—	—
1954	1	6	—	1	8
1955	1	2	—	—	3
1956	2	2	—	—	4
1957	4	10	—	—	14
1958	—	8	2	—	10
1959	3	5	—	—	8
1960	3	7	2	—	12
1961	3	9	—	1	13
1962	3	15	1	1	20
1963	5	10	2	—	17
1964	3	11	4	—	18
1965	5	23	—	—	28
1966	8	28	5	—	41
1967	2	41	1	1	45
1968	8	68	1	2	79
1969	12	72	8	1	93
1970	10	101	3	3	117
1971	19	79	4	—	102
1972	17	36	9	1	63
1973	18	38	7	2	65
1974	24	43	8	1	76
1975	14	40	5	1	60
1976	18	59	9	2	88
1977	18	59	10	3	90
1978	22	69	17	2	110
1979	31	84	17	1	133
Total	254	926	115	23	1,318
% Share	19.3	70.3	8.7	1.7	100.0

According to the Central Bank of China in Taipei, Taiwan firms paid these amounts for patent royalties and licensing fees between 1973–77:

Copyrights and Patent Royalties		Licensing Fees (after taxes)
(Millions of U.S. Dollars)		
1973	36.7	28.0
1974	45.0	35.0
1975	35.3	29.8
1976	38.6	24.5
1977	42.0	24.2
Total	197.6	141.5

These amounts have constituted only a small percentage of Taiwan total imports, averaging from 1 percent to 2.5 percent over the five-year period. A recent study by the Investment Commission (1979) suggested that, out of a sample of 206 firms which have arranged technology transfer agreements, only 35 (16.99 percent) have relied on the purchase of patents to secure technology (Investment Commission, August 1979). An additional 25 firms reported that technology transfer arrangements contained both patent agreements and the purchase of technology designs and blueprints. The majority of cases involving technology transfer into Taiwan do not seem to involve patent arrangements. Only within the chemicals industry in general, and the petrochemicals industry sector in particular, are patents an integral part of the transfer agreement. It is thus safe to conclude that technology has been brought into Tawian through other methods—the most popular being training, consultation, and other forms of technical assistance and cooperation on a person-to-person and company-to-company basis.

One of the primary vehicles for technology transfer into Taiwan has been the transnational corporation. Foreign firms are attracted to the Taiwan economy not because of the general science and technology climate but because the investment climate is conducive to the exploitation of their particular production technologies. Taiwan possesses an attractive set of investment incentives, a stable political environment, and a skilled labor force. Technology is transferred and diffused through the backward and forward linkages associated with investments by foreign firms. Some foreign firms participating in joint ventures have used their technology as capital in arranging investment agreements with local firms. According to Taiwan's investment statutes, a foreign-invested company can capitalize up to 15 percent of its technology and 20 percent of its patent technology as part of its investment. In the past, foreign firms have infrequently chosen this option due to tax considerations. This pattern may change, however, particularly as the complexity and the value of imported technology increases.

In recent years, the process of foreign investment has been one of the primary stimuli behind the growing number of formal technology cooperation agreements. As Table 1 indicates, technology cooperation agreements appear to be a lagged function of foreign investment. Comparing the number of approved technology cooperation agreements with the number of approved foreign investment cases from 1952 through 1979, operation of this lag becomes quite clear. In addition, both foreign investment and technology cooperation have been concentrated in the same industries: electronics, petrochemicals, and machinery. In many respects, foreign investment and the linkages generated by these investments have provided key incentives for a particular local firm to manufacture a needed part or component.

In some respects, political factors have led to the "unbundling" of the TNC package and have made licensing and technology cooperation increasingly more desirable. However, this "unbundling" could have some potentially negative effects since the success of a technology transfer agreement is very much dependent upon a sustained company-to-company relationship. In addition, equity commitments are often useful in encouraging foreign partners to stand by their technology commitments. Taiwan has also continually stressed the need for close technical relationships involving personnel training and exchange. This type of interaction appears to be conducive to successful absorption. Any indication that foreign firms were reluctant to make equity investments in Taiwan would almost surely have a negative effect on future flows of technology to the island.

An indication of the importance of technology cooperation is best illustrated by the distribution of agreements across industries (Table 2). As of 1979, the largest number of agreements have been in the electronics sector, with 337 cases—25.6 percent of the total. The electronics industry is Taiwan's most rapidly growing industry. The majority of cases involve firms from Japan, which accounted for 236 cases (70.0 percent). Next to electronics is the chemicals industry. The development of the synthetic fiber industry in Taiwan owes much to the chemical processing technology acquired from foreign firms. Since 1952, there have been 253 cases of cooperation (19.2 percent). Here again, Japanese firms outnumber both American and European firms, accounting for 58.5 percent of the cases. Part of the reason for the much larger number of agreements with Japanese firms is the geographical proximity between Japan and Taiwan, and the relative ease with which Taiwanese and Japanese work with each other. Another reason is the nature of the technology itself. Frequently, Japanese firms will utilize a cooperation agreement as a structure to facilitate the sale of parts and raw materials to local firms or to become involved in the marketing of a locally-produced item. The cooperation agreement may also provide a means for the Japanese firm to gain some influence over the production process in the host country firm. Moreover, the goal of technology transfer among Japanese firms has not been to stimulate greater technological independence on the part of the local partner, but to promote "trade" and to insure that these firms help to accommodate the needs of other Japanese firms producing in Taiwan.

Table 2
APPROVED TECHNOLOGY COOPERATION AGREEMENTS
BY INDUSTRY (1952-1979)

Unit: Cases

PRODUCTS	U.S.A.	JAPAN	EUROPE	OTHER	TOTAL
Food	7	32	3	—	42
Textiles	12	24	3	—	39
Clothing	6	6	—	2	14
Wood	—	3	—	2	5
Paper	5	10	1	—	16
Leather	1	3	—	—	4
Plastics	6	56	5	1	68
Chemicals	65	148	32	9	254
Non-Metals	10	39	6	—	55
Basic Metals	26	145	12	1	184
Machinery	25	151	26	4	216
Electronics	80	236	18	3	337
Construction	1	15	3	—	19
Fisheries	—	1	—	—	1
Services	7	13	—	1	21
Other	3	34	6	—	43
Total	254	926	115	23	1,318

As of January 1, 1977, a considerable proportion of technology cooperation agreements had already expired, been cancelled, or discontinued. Out of a total of 985 agreements, only 421 were still in effect as of the beginning of 1977. The United States had the most agreements still in effect (59 percent) while the Japanese had the least (37 percent). This reflects the fact that most agreements with Japan are generally shorter than those with the Americans. Moreover, the government tends to grant more renewals to American and European firms than to Japanese companies. As one government official remarked, "the government has been trying to decrease its reliance on Japanese imports, especially in the area of technology."

One of the frequent explanations provided for this policy is that local firms have complained about the tie-in agreements that often accompany technology cooperation agreements with the Japanese. In mid-1978, an editorial in the *Economic Daily News* (June 20, 1978) in Taipei suggested that 70 percent of the technology cooperation agreements with Japan had resulted in little actual technology transfer. Many Taiwan firms claim that Japanese companies and business agents come to Taiwan only to sell machinery and equipment to local manufacturers. However, the Japanese usually reserve an important component in the machinery or the production process as the basis for a technology cooperation agreement. In the case of one local iron and steel company, the manager claimed that Japanese businessmen encouraged his firm to expand its product mix in order to increase local sales. Initially, all the materials for the new products were supplied by imports from Japan, and the local firm simply assembled the parts into finished products. Later, the firm was able to source more of its own parts and materials from the local market, but the final products were of lower-level quality and quantity. The Japanese firm refused to provide the Taiwan company with the necessary technology to upgrade its production levels. With no other course available, the local firm embarked upon its own product improvement program and, within a short time, was able to significantly upgrade the quality of its products.

Generally, it can be said that the Taiwan economy exhibits a high level of dependence on foreign technology to support its economic activities. Most of the technology used in the key areas of the production system has been acquired by licensing agreements, imitation and copying, and technology cooperation. Most local firms consider reliance on foreign-made products and process technologies as the most viable way to accommodate production needs. Utilization of foreign technology often brings with it the opportunity to use foreign brand names and trademarks. These tend to provide Taiwan products with a stamp of good quality and thus help to increase the marketability of Taiwan-made manufactures both overseas and at home. With most local firms in the small- to medium-size category, and without sufficient capital and experience to undertake a research and development program, the absence of a formally recognized engineering function in Taiwan remains conspicuous.

Recognizing these advantages and local constraints, technology cooperation agreements have been given a high priority by certain Taiwan companies. According to a 1975 report on Taiwan's precision industries by the Industrial Technology Research Institute, the most successful local firms in Taiwan tend to be those with technology linkages with foreign firms. A sizeable number of firms within Taiwan's 106 largest business groups have either a capital or technology relationship with a foreign firm. Most of the major products manufactured by Tatung Electronics Company, one of the largest local firms in Taiwan, are produced under licensing agreements with foreign firms. In fact, Tatung's emergence as a major producer of consumer and uplifting of the science and technology environment in Taiwan include investments in the Computer Industry Development Center, which received a US$16.3 million grant in 1979 from the Executive Yuan to purchase equipment and to improve research facilities. Arrangements were also made to send 30 Chinese engineers to Hewlett-Packard in the United States for training to make the Computer Center a major source of computer design on the island. In addition, an Institute of Information Industry was established with the assistance of K. T. Li, Minister without Portfolio for Science and Technology Applications. Altogether, a total of US$3.5 million was made available to fund research at the Institute. The key feature of the new Institute is that it was organized on the basis of both public and private capital. Rather than seeking to develop a fully-integrated, widespread computer industrial electronics items started via a licensing agreement with a Japanese firm to produce watt-meters for industrial and residential use. The watt-meter project, which was begun in the early 1950s, received financial support from the U.S. AID mission in Taiwan.

An August 1979 study of 206 Taiwan firms conducted by Taiwan's Investment Commission revealed that in 1978 83 of the surveyed firms (40.3 percent) depended upon licensing and technology cooperation agreements for 50 percent or more of their production.

Within the same survey, 63 firms (30.6 percent) reported that they depended on licensed technology for 100 percent of their production operation. Within the metal industry, which includes basic metals, mechanical parts forging, machine tools, and foundries, most of the technology employed is imported. The same holds for the petrochemicals sector, whose growth is derived from a combination of state capital and foreign technology.

The Hsinchu Science and Technology Park is one example of a project designed to forge closer links between science and technology-related institutions and productivity-yielding organizations. Other activities engineered by the state to effect a general capability, research and development efforts at the Institute concentrate on more specialized projects, in particular, mini-and micro-computer development. The Institute will also try to promote cooperation with foreign firms to develop Chinese language business machines. An Industrial Technology Transfer Corporation was formed in late 1979 with the assistance of the government and private capital. The firm is a joint venture, with 60 percent of its capital coming from the Industrial Technology Research Institute, a government-sponsored organization, and 40 percent from four local firms, each holding 10 percent of the shares. The corporation will try to link up potential suppliers with possible users to help facilitate the transfer of technology to Taiwan. The government has also become a catalyst in two major technology transfer agreements, one between RCA and ITRI for integrated circuit design capabilities and the other with Taipower Company and Bechtel Corporation for nuclear engineering technology.

All these activities are characterized by three features: (1) extensive government planning and investment; (2) foreign technology as the catalyst behind government efforts; and (3) close cooperation with local firms by the government or government-sponsored organizations. Heavy government intervention not only will mean mandatory government approval, but also will involve much more direct relations with the government by local firms, since the government will play the role of partner, buyer, and possibly licensor. Government investment will mean more state control, but it will also help to promote improved relations between the government and the private sector. The need for closer cooperation in the economic sector, and now in the technology area, may indeed indirectly contribute to better political relations between the two groups. It will also facilitate an increase in the bargaining position of both local and state firms vis-a-vis foreign companies, especially in those cases, such as electronics, where access to the Taiwan economy becomes more important for particular foreign firms.

12.   Research & Development (R&D) and Education

K. T. Li

In July 1979, the government formally authorized establishment of the Hsinchu Science-Based Industrial Park. The Park is 45 miles southwest of Taipei and will ultimately include 210 hectares. It is adjacent to the North-South Expressway, and 34 miles from the Chiang Kai-shek International Airport. The Industrial Technology Research Institute, next door to the Park, can provide contract research in many technical areas. The National Tsing Hua University and the National Chiao Tung University, two of our leading institutions in science and engineering, are located nearby. The National Taiwan University, the National Central University, and several other colleges and specialized research institutes are also conveniently accessible to the Park. We believe these institutions and their experienced personnel can provide increasingly effective R&D support to qualified high-technology companies which set up their operations in the Science Park.

First stage development of the Park is already underway, in an area of 30 hectares. Roads, utilities, standard factory buildings and residential units will be ready within the next two months. The Park will operate as a bonded, duty-free area, with a computerized inventory control system rather than a physical wall at the boundary. Special incentives are available to qualified investors, including duty-free import of sophisticated machinery and of raw materials for export products, other tax incentives, streamlined procedures for entry and exit of personnel, rental of land and buildings to reduce capital expenditures, and modern communications facilities, including real time computer access to data banks in Taiwan and the U.S. The administrative personnel of the Park sincerely desire to meet all reasonable needs of investors; they welcome constructive suggestions.

Five projects for the Science Park have already been approved, for enterprises which will make mini-computers, integrated circuits and laser optics. The ground-breaking ceremony for one of the IC factories was held on May 24, 1980. Seven other companies have applied to set up factories in the Park, for software development, precision instrument, silicon chips, micro-computer systems, electronic printers, and other high-technology items.

A key element in our science and technology program will be the education and training of an adequate supply of people. Our studies of manpower needs and resources show that during the decade of the 1980s we must prepare more than one million people for work in scientific and technological positions, including researchers, specialists and managers with advanced degrees, engineers, technicians, analysts, craftsmen, and skilled and semi-skilled labor. This will present a difficult and exciting challenge to our educational system. Several of our universities already offer master's and doctoral degrees in science and engineering. These programs are being expanded and strengthened. We are also moving to establish postgraduate programs and special courses in which our graduate engineers and scientists can participate, on a part-time basis, for higher degrees and further training which will directly increase their professional competence. We are also expanding, diversifying and modernizing our vocational schools and training centers to prepare young men and women for productive service and periodic retraining in technology-related industries. A separate Vocational Training Bureau is now being established in the Ministry of Interior to coordinate the supply and demand of technical personnel in response to the changing needs of a high-technology economy.

We have already made encouraging progress in the gradual upgrading of science and technology. Private companies in Taiwan, with the cooperation and technical support of such original equipment manufacturers as IBM, are now making computer printing heads, hybrid circuits, and similar sophisticated precision products. High-technology foreign firms, such as Mostek with its US$5 million project for integrated circuits, have already come to Taiwan. We believe that further measures to improve our climate for science and

K. T. Li, "Address to the Joint Conference of ROC-USA and USA-ROC Economic Councils," in K. T. Li, *My Views on Taiwan Economic Development*, August, 1980, pp. 158-160.

technology, which I have briefly outlined, will stimulate a continuation of this trend.

Technology transfer is a very important part of our science and technology program as we accelerate the transition from mass production of labor intensive consumer goods to the manufacture of sophisticated capital equipment, special materials, and scientific grade instruments and components. The United Asia Electric Company, established on May 15, 1980 as a US$40 million joint venture of the General Electric Company, the Taiwan Power Company and the Central Investment Holding Company, will manufacture 550 MW steam turbine generators, initially for operation in Taiwan and later for export. The project provides for continuous transfer of technology, so that ultimately the local company will have full design capability, and be able to contribute to further advances in TG technology. At first, a limited number of parts and components will be manufactured locally, but this soon will increase to all items which can be made profitably in Taiwan. Similar ventures are under way in other sophisticated manufacturing technologies. Three of the leading engineering firms in the US, Gibbs & Hill, Bechtel and Ebasco, have established joint ventures with local engineering firms under which complete technology transfer will be effected for design and construction of fossil and nuclear power stations, in Taiwan and other developing countries. A committee for review and evaluation of technology transfer, chaired by Minister K. S. Chang, Ministry of Economic Affairs, has been established to monitor the rapid and effective transfer of technology under current and future agreements.

13. Scientific & Technological Exchanges with the United States

K. T. Li

In the early days of our economic development in Taiwan, technology came in from other countries, mainly the U.S., and entered largely through the industrial sector. We imported increasingly large and sophisticated machines to produce a high volume of consumer goods. We encouraged foreign investors to bring in their technology to manufacture export products in Taiwan. Our own manufacturers signed technical assistance agreements with foreign companies, and we sent our engineers and production people abroad for training in overseas factories. In the meantime, our best young people were leaving Taiwan and not returning. This outflow of our most precious resource had to be reversed in order for the nation to survive and prosper.

In response to this problem, several Sino-American joint ventures were organized to encourage a two-way flow of technology and talent between Taiwan and the U.S. In 1964, the U.S. National Academy of Sciences and our Academia Sinica established a program of scientific cooperation and formed a Joint Committee to identify and resolve the most pressing problems of science development in the Republic of China. It was agreed that to counter the brain drain a viable graduate program must be established in Taiwan. This was started in 1965-66 by five of our leading universities with the formation of five graduate research centers. The initial capital investment was largely provided by the Council for International Economic Cooperation and Development. The program has grown and broadened. In July 1978 the National Taiwan University alone awarded 295 master's degrees and 7 doctorates in the fields of science, engineering, agriculture and medicine.

The two academies have also sponsored a series of Sino-American workshops in various scientific subjects, beginning in 1965. The Joint Committee has consistently furnished first-class American experts to assist in planning, consultation and review. This coopera-

K. T. Li, "Two-Way Technology Transfer between the United States and the Republic of China," in K. T. Li, *My Views on Taiwan Economic Development,* August, 1980, pp. 74-79.

tive program between the U.S. National Academy of Sciences and Academia Sinica was so successful that it was used as a model for 30 similar programs between The American Academy and its counterparts in foreign countries.

As a result of the visit of former Vice President and Premier C. K. Yen, President Johnson asked his Science Advisor Dr. Donald Hornig to lead a delegation to Taiwan in 1967, which helped to work out a master program of science development in the Republic of China. The Hornig mission also recommended that an inter-governmental Science cooperation program be established. This led in early 1969 to a government-to-government agreement under which the Chinese National Science Council and the American National Science Foundation undertook a joint program of scientific and technological cooperation. This program is now the second largest of some 40 bilateral scientific programs in which the U.S participates. Since 1970 the Sino-American joint venture has sponsored 61 long-term visits—up to two years—by outstanding scientists, two thirds of whom were Chinese-American; and 363 short-term scientist visits of up to three months. The two agencies have also promoted cooperative research, binational seminars and the free flow of scientific information and ideas. I would emphasize that these programs have not been simply a one-way flow of people and information to Taiwan. In most respects our level of science and technology is lower than in the advanced nations, but we have made impressive achievements in some areas, including the agricultural and biological sciences. In the first cooperative research program under the bilateral agreement, our Chinese scientists played a prominent role in the artificial propagation of the grey mullet. As time goes by, we are gradually establishing a position of equality in other areas of basic and applied research and technological development.

The Chinese Institute of Engineers in Taiwan and the Chinese Institute of Engineers in America have jointly contributed to a stimulating technological interchange between the United States and the Republic of China. Starting in 1966, Modern Engineering and Technology Seminars have been held every two years in Taipei to examine the suitability of various technologies for the present stage of our industrial development and engineering construction. Each meeting is preceded by careful preparatory work to chose relevant subjects and select the most qualified speakers. The first seminar had 24 speakers and 300 participants and covered only the fields of chemicals, electronics, mechanical and civil engineering. The seventh seminar (July 1978) will present 65 speakers in eleven fields, including one for management and one for interdisciplinary discussions. More than 2,000 participants are expected.

In 1972 a series of National Reconstruction Seminars was established under the sponsorship of the Ministry of Education, the Youth Commission and other agencies. These seminars are held annually, with about 120 specialists from the United States, Canada, Europe, Japan and Australia. Also participating in these seminars are people from local universities, business and government.

The National Science Council and the Ministry of Education, either singly or jointly, sponsor additional programs of visiting professors, visiting specialists, special professorial chairs and recruitment of overseas scientists, under which a total of more than 2,500 specially selected individuals, virtually all with doctorate degrees, have visited Taiwan since 1967. Most of them were Chinese in America and about one third decided to stay on and work permanently to upgrade education and technology in the Republic of China. The Youth Commission is carrying out a program of assistance for recruitment of Chinese scholars which since 1971 has recruited almost 4,000 scholars holding at least a MA, MS or equivalent degree. Several times a year, we send a number of senior professors to seminars and conferences abroad. They are encouraged to meet, interview and recruit outstanding scientists and scholars for the various programs in Taiwan.

Most of the visiting professors, scholars and scientists under these programs are from 35 to 40 years old, compared to an average of over 50 for the college professors in Taiwan. The visitors thus bring in new ideas and new teaching methods. Gradually traditional teaching by lecture and examination is giving way to more discussion, experimentation and intellectural interchange between professor and student and among students and professors. We must move strongly in this direction in order to encourage the creativity and leadership ability needed in a free technological society. There must be greater efforts to increase the number of highly qualified professors and teachers, permitting a reduction in class size and more direct teacher-student communication.

Over private industries are now showing more interest in obtaining Chinese scientists and engineers from America and other countries to conduct research and upgrade technology and quality. Most of these companies are unwilling to search directly overseas, but the National Science Council and the universities in Taiwan welcome on-campus talent searches and readily release any of the visiting professors and scientists recruited by a private company. Several firms have found and employed valuable people through their on-campus talent searches.

The Republic of China encourages its outstanding overseas scientists and inventors with managerial talent to return permanently to Taiwan and set up enterprises based on the technology they have developed. Space has been reserved in the new Science Park in Hsinchu for such enterprises and our government has set up a venture capital program through China Development Corporation to bring promising ideas to the production stage.

The more progressive foreign-invested companies in Taiwan have also discovered that the scientists, engineers and technicians here, under competent management, can obtain impressive results in applied research and advancement of technology. One of the foreign plastics manufacturers have developed a method of injecting additives directly into the extrusion hopper, eliminating a separate remelting and mixing step in the process with significant saving in energy and investment. This improvement has now been adopted by the parent company's manufacturing units throughout the world. The same company has used Chinese technical personnel to upscale the design of its catalyst injection pumps, and has worked with a local manufacturer to develop an efficient gas compressor. A number of foreign-invested electronics companies in Taiwan have launched aggressive programs of productivity improvement carried out mostly by their Chinese personnel. In this way, innovations have been put into effect, not only in the factories here but also in those overseas. Thus technology transfer is increasingly a two-way flow between Taiwan and the rest of the industrialized world.

The Chinese-American community residing in the United States also contributes indirectly to the outward flow of technology from the Republic of China. The latest U.S. census, conducted in 1970, recorded 48,000 Chinese Americans in the professional, technical and related fields, including about 5,000 college and university teachers and professors, 9,000 engineers, 4,000 physicians, dentists and related practitioners, 4,000 technicians, and 3,000 research workers. These people, some of whom were a part of the "brain drain" from Taiwan, have made significant contributions to science, technology and education in the U.S. Several of the large American companies, including Boeing, IBM and Bell Laboratories, have large "Chinese communities" in their engineering and research departments. Some U.S. companies offer Chinese food in their cafeterias, mahjong for the wives, and Chinese lessons for the children in order to provide an attractive employment package. Despite such allurements, many of these Chinese Americans have, as I previously mentioned, already returned temporarily or permanently to Taiwan. Their past performance in the American professional environment gives us confidence that we can, with appropriate effort, establish a strong technological base in the Republic of China.

We must, however, guard against the development of technology simply for the sake of technology. The only justification for better technology is its ability to improve the welfare of the people. All of the programs and goals I have mentioned should be evaluated in the light of their ability to provide goods and services which are genuinely useful to our people, to improve the environment, and to preserve and enhance social institutions and relationships conducive to personal freedom and fulfillment. Changes in the past have been rapid and this trend will continue. It is supremely important that we honestly and competently assess the total impact of past and future changes, and insist on direction and goals which will maintain and strengthen our free society.

14.   Investing in Human Resources Overseas
and Deferred Returns

Y. L. Wu and K. C. Yeh

Any upgrading of exports by increasing their technological content will require a continuous increase in the supply of technicians, engineers, scientists, and modern managerial personnel. Better coordination of vocational, scientific and managerial education with (a) the specific manpower requirements of development, (b) domestic research and development, and (c) technological imports is extremely important. This topic is usually discussed in connection with education and manpower planning for economic development. Our concern at this point is, however, with investment in human resources overseas, which could subsequently rebound to the economic benefit of Taiwan.

During the past 25 years, large numbers of Chinese graduate students have left Taiwan for advanced training abroad. The majority have chosen to specialize in the physical sciences and engineering, and many have subsequently remained abroad instead of returning to Taiwan. This phenomenon is generally thought of a "brain drain" to Taiwan.

Distribution of Chinese Students in the
United States by Field of Study 1970

Field of Study	U.S. Graduate Students 1973 (in percent)	Chinese Students 1970 (in percent)
Engineering	7.94	27.25
Natural sciences	9.39	33.59
Social sciences	11.91	8.57
Health professions	1.74	3.59
Business	10.72	6.96
Agriculture	1.06	2.35
Humanities	4.60	11.44
Other (including law, education, etc.)	52.64	6.25
	100.00	100.00

Sources omitted.

Between 1950 and 1974, 30,765 Chinese students were approved for advanced study abroad by the ROC Ministry of Education. The annual figure reached a peak of 3,015 in 1969 and averaged about 1,900 persons in the first half of the 1970s. An overwhelming majority of these students came to the United States, so that, as shown in the table, a comparison of their distribution by field of study with the corresponding distribution of U.S. graduate students as a whole would be illuminating.

Thus, the United States is the principal focus of overseas investment in human resources in the technological fields by Taiwan investors. Utilization of this reservoir of human capital as its productivity increases with appropriate "maturing" will, therefore, be of vital importance in the long-run evaluation of Taiwan's comparative advantage. Understandably, if a person educated in Taiwan at considerable private and public expenditure emigrates, earns his living abroad, sends no money home, and otherwise contributes little to the Taiwan economy, the resources invested will be a loss to Taiwan. In general, a university graduate from Taiwan who moves to a foreign country spends additional funds on education, and the total investment he represents is even larger. However, whether there will be a

Y. L. Wu and K. C. Yeh, *Growth Distribution, and Social Change. Essays on the Economy of the Republic of China, Occasional Papers/Reprints Series in Contemporary Asian Studies,* (U. of Maryland: School of Law), No. 3-1978 (15), pp. 201-207.

waste of resources is by no means a foregone conclusion. Analogous to the installation of a valuable piece of equipment in a factory located abroad in an overseas investment project, such an overseas investment in human resources leads ultimately to waste from Taiwan's point of view only when there is little or no return. The crucial question, therefore, is whether a number of the graduate engineers and scientists might not at some future date become channels of communication in introducing new technology as well as managerial and business know-how into Taiwan that would not otherwise be available. They may not have returned in the past to participate in the island's regular labor force; they could, however, return in the future as investors and partners in joint ventures with resident Taiwan interests in new industries.

Its effect on production and increase in productivity through technological upgrading has only just begun. One is probably correct in assuming that the effectiveness of this process is contingent upon the attainment by the Taiwan economy of a stage in economic development at which it will no longer be dependent in every case upon external sources for both financing and technology. This would seem to be the same condition under which licensing agreements with foreign businesses can begin to be effectively used to expand and upgrade production in any developing country. It is a variant of the technological inflow process that takes advantage of the "brain drain."

Still another often-ignored aspect of ROC external economic activities is the technical training Taiwan offers to students of Chinese origin from foreign countries, mostly from Southeast Asia. Where advanced technical training is denied to ethnic Chinese by certain foreign governments through a quota system, as in Malaysia, the availability of such training in Taiwan is a boon to those who cannot go to Europe or the United States for their advanced education and technical training.

Taiwan's role as an intermediary in conveying technological know-how and experience in economic development to Southeast Asian countries began in the 1960s. At its peak in 1967, 114 persons were involved in the program of overseas technical cooperation and teams of specialists from Taiwan were found in Vietnam and Singapore. Two years earlier, similar teams from Taiwan were also found in Malaysia and the Philippines. By 1974, however, Vietnam was the only Southeast Asian country that still had a Taiwan technical cooperation team. With the fall of Vietnam in 1975, Taiwan's role in providing technical aid was sharply curtailed in Southeast Asia. Consequently, training of students from Southeast Asian contries has become a much more important source of contact with the future technological *cum* business elite of Southeast Asia than it was ten years earlier. It is more than likely that upon return to their own countries, many of these students will become active businessmen and professionals. The contacts they have gained in Taiwan will be an asset that could lead to a preference for Taiwan products and opportunities for joint venture with Taiwan interests. Their assistance in foreign marketing and an expanding investment horizon in Southeast Asia are advantages of vast importance to Taiwan's future export growth.

What is peculiarly Chinese in the Taiwan case is the specific opportunities presented by the many large and economically active—in some instances, even dominant—ethnic Chinese communities in Southeast Asia, together with the importance of Southeast Asia as a source of raw material supply. Joint ventures between ROC and Southeast Asia business interests have vast potential. At the same time, the educational, training, and business opportunities that Taiwan offers to the ethnic Chinese elsewhere are attractions that the latter can hardly ignore. Future expansion of trade and investment relationships that take advantage of these facts and ultimately use Taiwan as an intermediary in the infusion of technological know-how from the West (and Japan) to Southeast Asia, along with direct infusions from the West to Southeast Asia, offer a challenge to business entrepreneurs everywhere who are interested in the region.

Section 4

Social Conditions & Social Change

Edited by Yu-ming Shaw

Section 4
Social Conditions & Social Change

by Yu-ming Shaw

As the Republic of China on Taiwan has changed from an *underdeveloped* nation in the late 1940s to a country that is very close to becoming a *developed* nation in 1981, the transformation of Taiwan's society has been profound and far-reaching. This editor grew up and lived in Taiwan for nearly two decades (1948-1965) and has made frequent trips there during recent years, and has personally observed and experienced the rapid transformation of Taiwan's society. Taiwan's economic progress has brought about changes in the non-economic sectors. Take for example the change in the discipline methods used by elementary-school teachers in the 1950s and today. This editor can never forget the experience that once all of his classmates in the sixth grade were spanked with a baseball bat by their Japanese-trained teacher, simply because some of them had engaged in private conversations during a session for quiet reading. But today, any teacher who indulges in such cruel physical punishment of his students will definitely be fired, if not subjected to legal prosecution.

To do full justice to our study of the transformation of Taiwan's society in the last three decades, we should include the following subjects: social stratification, mobility, community development, bureaucratic organization, small groups, social disorganization and deviant behavior, social control and social changes, and also professional practice. But dictated by the limits of space, the editor can only include six contributions in this section to show some major aspects of the island's social transformation.

The first contribution is selected from a much longer study, *Socio-Economic Change in Rural Taiwan, 1950-1978*, by Professors Cheng-hung Liao and Martin M. C. Yang. This study consists of two parts, with Part I giving an overall view of Taiwan's rural socio-economic change, and Part II offering a case study of the changes that took place in Ta-yuan Hsiang, which is a rural township 24 miles southwest of Taipei—the capital city of the ROC. The two parts are thus complementary to each other and provide a very clear picture of the impressive progress that has been made in Taiwan's rural areas. Since both scholars have been involved in the work of agricultural extension in Taiwan for many years, their findings are particularly worthy of consideration.

In Part I, before giving their findings on socio-economic changes in the rural areas, the authors point out the agents for these changes: the land

Yu-ming Shaw, editor of this section, is on the faculty of the History Department at the University of Notre Dame, South Bend, Indiana. He is indebted to Professors C. Martin Wilbur (Columbia University), Kuo-shu Yang and Ch'ung-yi Wen (both of National Taiwan University and Academia Sinica), and Hsiao-yung Yang (Soochow University, Taipei) for their advice and the provision of materials.

reform program from 1949 to 1953; the popularization of education; the agricultural extension program; the introduction of new farm technology and the development of industries; the development of transportation and communication systems; and lastly, the arrival of people with "new" culture from the Chinese mainland in the late 1940s. Our selection deals with only the changes that actually occurred and omits the discussion of the change agents. Part II of the Liao-Yang study, which is too lengthy to be included here, is also omitted.

Major Changes in Rural Taiwan

Among the major changes in Taiwan's countryside, there is first the change in the people's mentality and behavior pattern. Previously, they listened passively to their kinship elders, gentry leaders, and other local notables for advice and guidance. But now they have become more autonomous and do their own thinking on matters of concern. They have also developed the habit of participating in group discussions with other villagers and farming experts about solutions to their problems. In short, the mind-set or thinking pattern of these farmers has changed from passivism to activism.

A second major change is in family life. Previously, the father or the head of the family usually made all decisions; now decisions are made through mutual consultations between parents and children. Children today are much better educated and more articulate with regard to their wishes and aspirations.

Another change is seen in community structures and relations. In place of kinship elders, landlords, gentry leaders, and other local worthies, new sources of leadership have now appeared. The arrival of the agricultural extension workers, and the existence of the village people's assembly and the village government have gradually brought changes in the management of local affairs. Since the composition and functions of the village assembly and the village government are very much decided by the wishes of the villagers, and these organizations manage their affairs more in a democratic than in an authoritarian manner, they have performed some very useful services to the people. Therefore, Liao and Yang conclude that the rural community is "changing rapidly from the traditional folk or kinship community to an associated society," and, in structure, it is "changing from a hierarchy set-up to a horizontal network." The authors further note that the meetings between farmers and outside farming experts and officials from governmental agricultural agencies are conducted like the agricultural extension meetings in the United States.

Daily life in the rural society has also changed from monotony and stagnation to liveliness and excitement, as a result of modernization and the increase of wealth. As each peasant family enjoys more modern amenities, more contact with the urban sectors of the country, and more extra income to spend, village life now sports more sound and sight, not to mention the frequent, joyful, and boisterous *pai-pai* feasts, which have both religious and social connotations.

The last major change is the shift from self-sufficiency to interdependence in local agricultural development. The availability of credits and loans from both governmental and commercial sources has enabled the farmers to expand their individual cultivation into group farming and even to set up product marketing cooperatives. All in all, the life of the traditional Chinese farmer as described sympathetically in Pearl S. Buck's novels or negatively in Lu Hsun's short stories is a thing of the past in Taiwan. For the farmers in Taiwan, their life is no more an object of pity, but a bright spot in comparison with many of their counterparts in other developing nations.

The second selection is an article by Professor Albert R. O'Hara of National Taiwan University, who has lived in China and taught in Chinese universities for many decades. His article is based on many surveys he conducted between the 1950s and the 1970s among Taiwan's college students in regard to their attitudes toward marriage and the family.

Toward marriage, he finds in one survey that nearly half of these students (41 percent) prefer to choose their own mate and also to live in separate houses from their parents. While they prefer marriage based on romantic love, more of them favor having three children, which is rather high compared to the college students in, say, the United States. This shows that the old Chinese emphasis on having more children (so as to have a better chance of having at least one son) dies hard even among the modern-minded Chinese college students of today.

Another example of their "more traditional" behavior toward married life is that most of the male students would not like their wives to work outside on a full-time basis. Whether this is due to their male chauvanism or their concern for their children is a question to which Professor O'Hara's article has given no answer.

Closeness in Family Ties

As for the relationship between these college students and their families, that is, the families in which they were brought up, it is a very close one. Their parents, as well as other members of the family, have helped them in their studies, and also taught them about moral values. Furthermore, their family life is full of group recreational activities such as singing or watching movies or television together. Another proof of this closeness in family ties between grownup children and their families is that they always find their homes a source of warmth and support even after they have left the home for college for many years.

From the O'Hara article we can draw some firmer conclusions. The Chinese families in Taiwan today, even those that have youngsters in college (who have a tendency to eventually move out of their parents' homes), have in general remained as closely-knit social units and have not been seriously affected by the modernization process. The family bond is still very strong, and the family still remains a rich source of comfort and support. All of these phenomena are consistent with the old Chinese family tradition. Because of this strong tradition, one may speculate that despite the effects of Taiwan's modernization, the traditional spirit and features of the Chinese family system will probably have a better chance of survival than those of most of the families in the modern West.

The next selection is Professor Nancy J. Olsen's study of Chinese child-rearing patterns, based on her research done in 1967-68 in Taipei and in the village of Lu-shang in Chang-hua County.

Her research indicates that high-status urban mothers are most likely to use the "love-oriented" techniques of discipline in raising their children; the rural women use "power-assertive" techniques of discipline; and the lower-middle and working class urban groups use techniques that fall in between the other two groups. Olsen further points out that these patterns are similar to those found in the United States, Greece, and Lebanon. Olsen's major conclusions are that "social structure influences socialization values as well as practices," and that "the patterning of social class and rural-urban differences in family socialization has been found to be so similar from society to society."

In her article, Olsen also tries to offer some explanation for these conclusions. "Educational level," she explains, "was the primary determinant of socialization values, and of those patterns of maternal behavior surrounding the expression and manipulation of affection, but that occupation position had the greater impact on punishing patterns." While she finds that the social position of parents has "predictable" effects on the patterns of child-rearing, she cautions against "drawing general conclusions about the functioning of the society as a whole, much less that of other societies inhabited by people sharing a distinctively Chinese culture." For lack of space, however, our selection does not include her explanation or caution.

If we can accept Olsen's findings, then it seems safe to predict that with the increasing advancement on the educational level of the people of Taiwan, the child-rearing patterns of the parents will also be increasingly "love-oriented," rather than "power-assertive." In light of the Chinese cultural emphasis on filial piety and traditional belief in the efficacy of a more rigid form of child-rearing, however, this editor doubts very much whether the middle class, urban, and well-educated Chinese parents will in the future go so far as their American counterparts in applying the "love-oriented" techniques of discipline to their children.

Social Mobility in Taiwan

The next selection concerns social mobility in Taiwan, a question that is very important in evaluating the degree of egalitarianism existing in Taiwan's society. Taiwan's economic progress and its equitable distribution of wealth are generally recognized. But is the Taiwan society also equitable and egalitarian in its social mobility? No society is equitable or egalitarian if its social mobility is stagnant or unfair for its members. This question is addressed in Professor Charlotte Wang's piece on Taiwan's social mobility.

Relying upon various existing data, Wang compares Taiwan's social mobility with that of Haiti, Costa Rica, Great Britain, and the United States. Wang's conclusions are as follows.

First, the direct effects of the father's occupation on that of the son in Taiwan is the smallest, except for the United States. Second, a large part of one's occupational achievements is based on educational qualifications, and it is almost as large as that in Great Britain. Third, the effect of the father's occupation or status on the son's educational attainment is relatively high. Based on these findings, Wang concludes that "there is more equality in the social mobility process in Taiwan than other countries, considering the levels of industrialization." But why is this so? She attributes this to the probable result of the Chinese cultural tradition emphasizing the importance of education. She also credits the Nationalist Government in Taiwan for the preservation and promotion of this cultural tradition.

The next two selections deal with the change of social values among the Chinese people in Taiwan. The first, by Professor Sheldon Appleton, is a study of the differences in values held by men and women, and the second, by Professor Kuo-shu Yang, deals with overall value changes among the Chinese people as a whole.

Professor Appleton's study reaches several conclusions. The first is that both men and women have placed values such as "family security," "a world at peace," and "inner harmony" as most important, while "religion" and "a happy afterlife" are at the very bottom of their value scale. The marginal differences in their perception of these values are that men give higher priority to matters outside of the home, and women to home and family—a phenomenon that is consistent with the traditional sex-role expectations and the distinction between *nei* (inside) and *wai* (outside).

Appleton's second conclusion is that women's status in Taiwan has gained in stride, and women have obtained more egalitarian relations with men in the family, at school, and in society as a whole. This change is particularly striking in the educational sector. Just to cite two statistics to illustrate this significant change: In 1965, fewer than 3,200 women graduated from colleges and universities; but in 1972, 17,800 graduated. In 1964, women faculty at the college and university level constituted 18 percent, but in 1973 it grew to 25 percent.

The third major conclusion is that Chinese men and women consider the various social relations in their society superior to those in the United States. Appleton divides social relations into nine categories: husband-wife, father-children, mother-children, siblings, boys-girls, neighbors, teacher-student, employer-employee, and people in general. While both men and women consider the Chinese patterns in these relations superior, only women feel less enthusiastic than men about their superiority in the category of husband-wife relations. Appleton also agrees with a finding that "there has been a . . . displacement of the most intensive relationship in the family from father-son (ideal) or mother-son (actual) to husband-wife." This shows an increasing modern orientation in Chinese conjugal relations.

Some Uneasiness with Social Trends

In the last section of his study, Appleton points out one "disquieting" factor in the course of social change in Taiwan, that is, the best-educated and the most elite segment of the population feels "uncomfortable" with the social changes achieved so far and with the prospect of future changes. These elites are now experiencing some of the negative aspects of Western social life, such as the disruption of family ties, uncertainty in social relations, the perils of urban life, general alienation from traditional moorings, and the difficulty in fulfilling their "self-actualizing" values.

At the end of his study, while affirming the general Chinese preference for these changes, Appleton drops a guarded note about the future development of the Taiwan society: "Whether the island's people will be able to work out a distinctive and viable response to the clash of Chinese and Western values—and whether the vicissitudes of international politics will permit them to do so—remain very much open and fascinating questions as the decade of the 1980s comes into view."

In contrast to Appleton's more reserved attitude toward certain effects from value change in Taiwan's society and to his more guarded reading of the future, Professor Kuo-shu Yang's article offers much hope. His article not only reaffirms many of the positive changes in value as described in Appleton's study, it also evinces his confidence that these changes are so solid and so healthy that they will insure Taiwan's inevitable advancement into a real modern and democratic society in the future. This article is based not only on his many scholarly studies on Taiwan's society, but also on his experiences of personal involvement in social and political affairs in Taiwan for many years.

Yang's article is both sociological and historical. While his is a study of the changes in Chinese mentality and behavior as a result of modernization, all these changes are examined in the context of modern Chinese history. He notes these positive changes: (1) humanistic attitudes—such as emphasis on egalitarianism as opposed to authoritarianism, man's mastery of nature, present and future oriented outlooks, mutual tolerance, and positive personality traits; (2) individualistic orientations—such as self-respect, assertiveness, personal exertions rather than reliance on external factors, and equal treatment in social relations; (3) increasing ability to adapt to changes; and (4) increasing sense of happiness in life.

Yang believes that these value changes not only have created the "modern man," but also will gradually lead to the appearance of the "world man." In affirming their positive effects, he nevertheless serves a warning that these modern changes should not go unrestrained and should be harnessed within the bounds of law and the accepted social norms; otherwise, the public interests of society might be impinged upon and the equal chances for the self-actualization of individuals might also be jeopardized.

Yang also points out the importance of the further development of modern social values, if Taiwan is to reach a higher level of political, economic, and social advancement. In his analysis, governmental policies play a very important role in the initial stage of the modernization process; but once the country has achieved some progress, the development of these positive social values will be essential for further progress in modernization.

Yang's projection of the future development of Taiwan's society is very positive. He believes that the value changes so far have gone beyond the level of *yung* (application) and reached *ti* (fundamental). In conclusion, Yang predicts with great confidence that as long as these healthy trends continue, further modernization will bring a bountiful harvest to everyone in the Chinese society.

No Desertion of Rural Areas

The last selection is Professor Alden Speare, Jr.'s study on demographic changes in Taiwan's urbanization and migration in the 1960s. While there is a net migration from the rural to the urban areas and large urban towns, it has not caused a massive desertion of the rural areas. The reasons for this phenomenon are that Taiwan's impressive agricultural development has absorbed a substantial number of the rural population; Taiwan's industrialization has permeated the countryside; and the farming population has also found, besides work on the land, other gainful employment in or near their rural residences. Another factor contributing to the stability of the rural population is the trend of "return migration." According to Speare's study, for every four migrants to the major cities, there were three who left the cities for the countryside.

With regard to migration from rural to urban areas, Speare gives a favorable reading of its overall effects and considers it to be in general "a rational response to changing economic conditions."

Since Speare's study deals only with Taiwan's migration patterns in the 1960s, it needs updating. From all available information, the rural areas are known to have had a shortage of manpower in recent years. If this is indeed the case, it seems that forced repatriation of the rural migrants or further spread of industrialization into the countryside would be logical solutions. Since, however, forced repatriation of the rural migrants would be both unfeasible and in violation of the people's freedom and right to choose their work and residence, the real solution seems to lie in spreading industries into the countryside. Another helpful solution is to modernize the rural areas so as to make these more attractive places in which to live. Dr. Sun Yat-sen once set a goal of China's simultaneous development of urban and rural areas: to urbanize the countryside and to ruralize the urban areas. While it may not be wholly achievable, the vision contained in the goal may prove to be compelling to the people in Taiwan, as they have reached a high level of industrialization.

1. Socio-Economic Change in Rural Taiwan: 1950-1978

Cheng-hung Liao and Martin M. C. Yang

Changes in People's Minds

Outward changes, especially sophisticated ones, are usually consequences or extensions of people's inner changes. Therefore, we take up changes in people's minds first.

After a people have lived a long time in physical and cultural isolation, their minds become static. Ways of life and work tend to become fixed. One can just mechanically follow them without the danger of making any serious mistakes. So, there is hardly any need for the mind to work at all.

New things disturb the status quo. People begin to question. Questioning is the first stage of the action of mind. This may lead to the second stage: asking questions, searching for answers to questions, and on to the formulation of ideas and concepts about those most important things. The final stage of the action of the mind is generalization with evaluations for making conclusions or decisions.

Two decades ago, the rural community in Taiwan was an undisturbed tradition-bound society. Today, there are three manners of thinking in Taiwan. First, individual thinking. Second, thinking with family members. Many rural families have been taught or advised by agricultural extension workers to consider important family matters at meetings attended by all grown-up family members. They make plans together and decide on the role to be played by each member, etc. Third, joint thinking with the other people of the same village of the same rural community. This is often conducted in village-level farm study classes, joint cultivation teams, and other similar groups.

Emphasis is not on the group per se. There were group gatherings before. Emphasis is on the fact that in the new group, the participating members, every one of them, are actually thinking. In the old days, such a group was always dominated by one, two, or a few of the leading members. It was actually the few leading members who did the thinking. The rest of them just sat there. The best that these other people could do was to listen. It was assumed that they were not able to think. Actually it was because they were bound by the tradition that they were not supposed to say anything, let alone argue, debate, or discuss. Now practically every one who takes part in such a group meeting has learned to speak and he is encouraged to speak. If one is to speak in public, he has to do some thinking before he stands up.

Another important point in regard to today's thinking is that it is no longer fragmentary, disorderly and wandering. Many of the farm people who have participated in study or discussion groups have been trained to think and speak with considerable rationality and organization.

The subject-matter is also different from the old days. Today, the rural people think mostly of the ways and methods of improving agricultural production and the marketing of farm produce. They think of the non-farm jobs which they themselves or their young people wish to get. They also think of local politics, which is increasingly involved in their daily life and work.

Changes in Family Life

The first observed changes are changes in family structure or organization. Structurally, the traditional extended family is definitely and rapidly disappearing. But the Western type of family is not yet welcome, even among younger people. It is doubtful that it will ever become a universally accepted pattern. A majority of the college students and graduates prefer a family of grandparents, parents and unmarried children.

The size of the family has decreased and it continues to decrease. One way of reducing its size is to separate the family soon after all the sons get married. The other way is to

From *Socio-Economic Change in Rural Taiwan,* (Taipei, Taiwan: Dept. of Agricultural Extension, National Taiwan University, 1979), pp. 11-21. Professor Liao is with the Department of Agricultural Extension, National Taiwan University; and Professor Yang is with the Department of Sociology, Soochow University, Taipei.

reduce the number of children by practicing family planning. It is surprising that a majority of the common people, including farmers, industrial workers and store keepers, have all accepted this kind of birth control, against the long tradition of honoring ancestors by having many children.

Relations between husband and wife have changed from inequality to equality. Privileges and responsibilities are shared on a equal basis but with due regard to differences in strength, capability, temperment, interest, time, etc. As a whole, the women's position has been raised considerably. This change should be attributed mostly to mainlander families.

In power structure and in the exercise of authority the family has changed from the authoritarian type to a moderately democratic type. The father no longer has and exercises all authority. Parents and grown-up children often consult with each other on family business, relations with other families, any significant planning for something new, etc. Both sons and daughters express their opinions on their own education, marriage and career. The traditional tension between an authoritarian father and a submissive son has been eased a great deal. The immediate reasons for these changes are, first, the sons and daughters now have more education and more knowledge in new things than do their parents and, consequently, they can contribute more economically to the family. Second, sons and daughters can now get jobs for themselves. They can be independent of the family if necessary. Third, the general social trend is antiauthoritarian. This is true in every place and in every social class. Any father who still tries to cling to traditional authority will certainly be ridiculed by his neighbors.

In functions the family has also changed. It may still perform those universal and intrinsic duties, but it is no longer the individuals' only sanctuary from society at large. The grown-up children of a family must stand on their own in their relations with the outside world. The family has not willingly relinquished this function. But many new economic, social, cultural and legal conditions have made it do so.

Many of the families, especially the most modern, have youth-centered culture. This means the children's wishes and activities occupy the center of the family's life and destiny. Parents yield to their children on almost everything. Permissiveness is widely practiced. The degrees of this practice are different in families of different social classes, of different occupations and of different cultural standards. There are two interpretations of this youth culture. One interpretation sees the family's chief function as the production of good children. The other claims that according to modern, democratic and scientific education and child training, children should be allowed to express their own wishes and interests. They should be allowed to have their own activities; inhibiting discipline is no longer appropriate.

Changes in Community Structures and Relations

The community, including the rural community, is changing rapidly from the traditional folk or kinship community to an associated society, or from *Gemeinschaft* to *Gesellschaft*.

In structure it is changing from a hierarchical set-up to a horizontal network. The trend is far from complete, but it is going on at a high speed. Traditionally, the structure has been a line, consisting of, from top to bottom: (a) the village or community gentry which included the heads of families of any significance, persons who have education high enough to be gentlemen or school teachers; (b) the official community head and his lieutenants; (c) the *pao* and *chia* heads; (d) the land or neighborhood lay leaders; and (e) the common citizens. Power and leadership come from the gentry on top, through all the levels, and lar.ded on the common civilians. Practically all other social or kinship organizations were also by and large built in such a structure.

This hierarchical structure is collapsing, or being leveled down. Under the pressure of the leveling down, the structure spreads out horizontally. It is already common for community affairs to be taken care of by two parallel organizations: the village people's assembly, *tsun min* (or *li min*) *ta hui,* and the village government, *tsun kung shueh* (or *li kung shueh*). In a township, which is one level above the village, the two organizations are assembly of township representatives, *hsiang min* (or *chen min*) *tai piao ta hui,* and the township government, *hsiang* (or *chen*) *kung shueh*. The village people's assembly and the assembly of the township representatives are organizations responsible for consideration and discussion of community affairs and for making suggestions or proposals. In other words, they are legislative organizations, while the village government and the township government are executive organizations.

In both organizations the present manner of handling public affairs is much more horizontal than hierarchical. The chairman of a village people's assembly, for example, periodically calls all the villagers, or representatives of all the families, into session one evening to discuss some important issues concerning the whole village's well-being. Ad hoc committees may be organized to make investigations into certain matters. Either formal or informal suggestions or proposals are made with all participants' agreement or consensus. A similar process is used in the assembly of township representatives. In the executive branch, or the village and township governments, the process is that the chief of the government periodically calls all his staff members, or if the staff is too big, only the senior ones, to a conference to make plans or programs according to suggestions or proposals presented to them by the village people's assembly or the assembly of town representatives. Program committees may be organized. All these processes show that the flowing of power or authority and the communication of thought and information are horizontal rather than vertical. The old way of passing orders from top to bottom is less and less practiced.

With the new kind of community structure and the new manner of conducting the community affairs the social relations in a community must also change from vertical to horizontal. More associations are formed on common or similar interests, or on belonging to the same professions. Social relations based on mutual, equal friendship, or on mutual taste are becoming more and more common. Those based on respect for paternalistic affection or seniority are now limited to only close kinship circles and a small number of student-teacher relations. In government offices one may also still find some junior officers holding respectful or sentimental relations with their long-time senior superiors.

It is interesting to note that the traditionally prestiged intellectuals are now coming down from the high platform to sit with the common people on the same floor in the same hall. On numerous occasions the authors have witnessed and participated in personally discussion meetings organized by groups of younger citrus fruit farmers, horticulture professors from agricultural colleges, and senior officers from the department of agriculture. They talked and discussed problems of citrus orchards in a very free atmosphere; questions and answers flew back and forth not only smoothly but also intelligently between farmers and the professors. The whole situation has become like what we saw in agricultural extension meetings in the U.S.A. twenty-five or thirty years ago. On the township level, or the front line, quite a few extension workers are college graduates and their number is increasing. They work directly with the farm people and share with them most of the hardships and problems.

In this period of transition not all the changes in a community are encouraging or desirable. There are new forces which serve only to disintegrate the unity of the community. For instance, many of the new political interests or political relations have divided a community into numerous rival and contending factions. The division has seriously weakened the power for constructive undertakings. Not a few of the village elders wish that the new ideas and things had never come. The breaking down of the traditional hierarchical structure and the disregard for social relations based on respect for paternalism, kinship and seniority have made it very difficult for village elders trying to keep young people's behavior within the moral code.

Changes in Community Leadership

Traditionally, public leadership in a village or a community was in the hands of the village gentry or the community gentry. As mentioned previously, the village gentry consisted chiefly of heads of the strong clans, heads of wealthy families and big landlords. In many cases these three categories described the same individuals. One or two Confucian academicians and a couple of smart and persuasive personalities might also have been included. Now, with the disappearance of the landlords through land reform, the decline of kinship influences, and the dying out of the old Confucian academicians, the traditional village gentry has practically collapsed. Thus the community's public leadership has had to change hands.

It is still too early to say into whose hands the leadership will evolve. But the general trend is to a joint leadership or a federation of leadership. It will most probably be a federation of successful business people, well-know professionals, school superintendents, farmers' association managers or board members, local politicians, and community affair experts. There is no need to list the qualifications of being a community leader, for the people who are able to be in these categories have their own qualifications.

The new leadership will not be the traditional gentlemen who had a lot of leisure and performed very few positive functions. The new leadership will have a great many activities, good and bad. The new leadership will be much younger than the traditional one. For one reason, older people will not be able to endure all the activities and demands. Women will gradually be included in the public leadership. The new leadership has become elective and it will stay this way.

Changes in the Countryside as a Whole

The whole countryside has changed from a state of quiet to a state of movement. In the movement there are orderly actions and disorderly commotions. We are not concerned with commotions in the big cities but rather in those recent actions in the rural communities.

Practically all the farmers are busily moving around looking for new and more profitable crops, better land utilization, better cultivation methods, etc. That they are doing so is indicated in their participation in the various and numerous agricultural extension programs such as farm study groups and farm observation tours.

Because of the commercialization of the farm business most of the farmers are busy transporting their farm produce to the local towns, big city markets, processing factories, and the collecting stations of the marketing cooperatives. In return they buy and take back materials to be used on the farms and at home. In these trips the farmers are also busy seeing and absorbing new things in the towns and cities. In the evenings or other unoccupied times they tell the tales of what they saw or heard to family members or neighbors.

The township farmers' associations have really become going concerns since their reorganization and revitalization. Each conducts daily a number of services and a large volume of business for the farmers with other rural people, rural organizations and government agencies. Relations between the farmers and the township farmers' associations are growing rapidly. In addition to farmers' associations there are a number of other private and public agencies which also have business with the farm people. So, the farmers have to go to these agencies too.

Rural electrification has made the countryside both seemingly active and really active. By seemingly active, we mean that when all the lights in the houses and on the streets are on, the whole village seems to be alive. This is especially true when the older villagers make a comparision between the present evenings and those before electricity. In the old days one felt the village was covered by death in the darkness. By really active we mean that with the presence of this electric power all the villagers can turn on their radio loud and so the place is full of sound and noise. After all, the roads in the countryside have been paved, motor vehicles are coming and going, the whole village is in motion.

Another new phenomenon is the movement of students on the roads between their village homes and the schools in the towns. Every morning between six and eight o'clock there are thousands and thousands of young people, both boys and girls, going to middle schools on bicycles. At these hours all the main roads leading to the rural towns are very crowded. The same is seen at the hours from four to six in the afternoon when the students are coming home from school. Now practically every village has a primary school, therefore, the primary school students no longer need to travel on roads to school. In the morning between eight and nine o'clock every village is filled with laughter, shouting and singing by hundreds of the youngsters gathered on the field of the primary school.

Because the economic conditions of the people as a whole have been greatly improved and because most of the people who have just come out of long poverty like to do some show-off spending, the traditional *pai-pai*, a religious festival, has especially flourished in recent years, notwithstanding the fact that both the government and the far-sighted community leaders have tried to persuade to people to celebrate it moderately. In the villages, towns, cities and religious sites there are *pai-pai* almost every month, if not every day. In every one of them there are at least several thousands of people involved. The Matsu Temple in Pei-kong, a big rural town, has become the busiest religious site in Taiwan in recent years. Pai-pai is conducted here several times a year. In each of the big ones half million people gather and the town is filled with crowds.

From Self-sufficiency to Interdependence

Formerly, a great majority of the rural people were self-dependent in their life and work and depended on natural forces. They did not ask and they did not expect much from the others. They did their best to get things done and to enjoy the fruits of their own efforts. If they failed or had to endure poverty or hardship, they blamed themselves. It is true that within the family and to a certain extent within the local community there was some mutual dependence. Dependence on natural forces means that rural people, after having done their own duties, waited patiently and expectingly for the natural elements to play their parts. They always hoped that nature would bless their work and make it fruitful. If the result was failure, they blamed it on fate or their own bad luck. They seldom blamed other people for the failure and seldom expected other people to help, except those in the closest kinship network.

This kind of attitude has changed a great deal in the past twenty-five years. First, if the land reform has really been a good thing for the farmers as a whole, the credit must go to the government. No power or authority other than the state can conduct such a program and have it satisfactorily completed. Besides, there are still a number of things closely related to land reform which are still a number of things closely related to land reform which ought to be done or to be dealt with if further benefits of this nature are to be expected? Who will be surprised if one finds that the cultivators place their hope in the government?

Second, most of the farmers who have followed the teaching or information of the extension workers saved a lot of labor and costs in their farm operation while harvesting greater and better crops. Or, if they still had to use the same amounts of labor and costs, their per unit production has increased considerably. The same thing has happened in the raising of hogs and chickens. All these facts have convinced the farmers that merely depending on their own traditional farm experience is no longer adequate or effective. They had come to realize that for any wholesome new knowledge in the farm business they must have relations and cooperation with people in the agricultural extension service.

Third, as soon as farm business was directed toward a market, or no longer operated on a self-sufficiency basis, the level of operational capital needed to be considerably increased. A great majority of the ordinary farmers were not able to make the increase by themselves and it was not at all realistic or advantageous for them to borrow money from professional, private money lenders or commercial money agencies. The government came to help. It established both the general farm credit system and the special commodity loans in the state banks, the government owned Food Bureau (an agency in charge of food administration and the promotion of food production), the Taiwan Sugar Corporation and the Tobacco and Wine Monopoly Bureau. For any emergency, public loans could be negotiated through the township farmers' associations. Once convinced of the government's true purpose of rendering service, the farmers' reliance on the state for securing badly-needed farm credit has increased considerably.

A fourth example of the change in the rural people's traditional attitudes is the fact that a joint cultivation system and a number of farm product marketing cooperatives have been established in rural districts. A joint cultivation system means a number of farm families whose farms are adjacent to each other do important jobs in the cultivation of a certain important crops together. They pool labor, farm implements and materials in order to make the operation much more efficient. Another great advantage is that it makes the utilization of modern and big farm machinery and techniques possible and economical. Although accomplishment or results of these two kinds of efforts have thus far not been conspicuous, the farmers have at least begun building business interrelations among themselves. They are learning interdependence between neighbors and among people in the local communities.

2. Actual Changes Follow Attitudinal Changes Toward Marriage and the Family in the Republic of China

Albert R. O'Hara

Upon my arrival in Shanghai in 1933, I was highly surprised and interested by the numerous and deep differences between Americans and Chinese in marriage and home attitudes and practices. One of my students asked for leave to get married in early May. I suggested that he wait a month for the summer vacation and was told he could not because his father had ordered him to come home now. And "How about the bride?" I asked. "It's the same for her," he replied. "Therefore you have no say about whom, when and where you marry?" I asked. "No, that's the way it is," he replied.

However, there had commenced to be slow and uneven changes from traditional to modern styles in marriage and family life. Patterns of the family and marriage in traditional (i.e. pre-twentieth century) China are relatively documented in the sociological literature. The following six traditional patterns are pertinent.

1. Parental control of the selection of a spouse.
2. Separation of the sexes, from puberty to marriage, in formal education and other spheres.
3. Absence of dating, courting and engagement.
4. Irrelevance of romantic love as an institutionalized basis of selection. It might be developed later as such between a man and his wife or a man and his concubine.
5. Patrilocal residence as an ideal.
6. Subordination of the wife to the husband's parents or family and especially of the wife to her mother-in-law.

The contrasting patterns, found in the United States and other Western industrialized societies, which will be referred to as "modern," are:

1. Greater freedom from parental control in the choice of spouse.
2. Increasingly frequent and open interaction between the sexes.
3. Dating, courtship, and engagement and their diffusion to progressively younger groups.
4. Romantic love institutionalized as the basis of marriage.
5. Separate local residence of each couple, both ideally and actually.
6. The couple's relatively greater independence of the husband's parents and family, and the wife of the mother-in-law.

Earlier empirical studies show the contemporary Chinese family as neither fully traditional nor fully modern in the above senses. For example, the large extended and the small nuclear families have existed side by side for some decades of years. The basis for the above data is found in P'an Kuang-tan's *Problems of the Chinese Family,* Olga Lang's *Chinese Family and Society,* Marion Levy's *The Family Revolution in Modern China,* etc.

The *Journal of Sociology* (National Taiwan University), No. 3 (July 1979), pp. 83-96. The author is Professor of Sociology, National Taiwan University.

Method and Sample
To test whether Chinese society had been slowly moving in the direction from traditional as outlined above toward a more modern one, Robert Marsh and I worked out a questionnaire type of both poll, open ended concerning the six aspects of marriage listed above. It was administered to undergraduate classes in two universities in Taipei. A total of 651 students filled out the questionnaire. We were not able to control the sample because it was drawn from a somewhat biased section of the curriculum, namely, Western Literature, Labor Problems and Sociology. A second possible bias was the noted bias overrepresenting the number of females in the two universities (27 percent). By eliminating every second female respondent, we reduced the proportion of females in the sample to 28 percent. Reanalyzing our finding with this corrected sample, we found no important difference was introduced by the overrepresentation of females in the original sample and therefore reported our findings on basis of the full sample of 651 students. We classified the respondents by their own and their parents' geographic origin as shown in the accompanying tabulation.

	Per Cent
Respondent and both parents both born on Mainland China	44
Respondent and both parents born in Taiwan (Formosa)	35
Respondents and both parents born in Hong Kong, Macao or South East Asia (Overseas Chinese)	7
Mixed (Respondent and parents born in different places	7
No answer	7
Total	100

Here a few words of explanation are required to understand the origin of the following charts. The opening paragraphs of this report come from random and unrecorded observation. When the author came to Taiwan and was invited to teach sociology in the National Taiwan University random observation seem to indicate that there had been a heavy shift in university students attitudes toward marriage and the family. In 1956, the writer made the survey mentioned above and with the cooperation of Robert Marsh analyzed the data and wrote a report which was published in the *American Journal of Sociology*, July 1961.

Ten years later the same type of survey was made in Taiwan and reported in a Twentieth Anniversary Review of the National Taiwan University. Shortly after the time of the first survey, Robert Marsh returned to the United States and administered the same survey to 238 undergraduate students in the University of Michigan. The results in the early reports are given as percentages of the total number of respondents in each case and the later report which was gathered and made out in 1971 from the same Taiwan universities is given in a numerical summary of the results.

The first report from Taiwan students showed a general but uneven shift of attitudes from the traditional patterns toward the modern ones. In the two later Taiwan surveys in most questions there was an increasing shift toward the modern patterns. However, many conditions peculiar to Taiwan may hinder the particular social class to do what they now desire to do. For example, a survey modelled on the ones of this author was administered to government employees where large numbers of the female employees work in a great crowd of women and hence have little chance to meet men. In the survey made by *New Life Daily*, a vernacular newspaper (Taipei, March 16, 1959), 32 percent of the men and 75 percent of the women declared that they found "no suitable or ideal partner" and in fact very little opportunity to even meet persons of the opposite sex. In another survey based on that of the author but given to higher middle school students, to the question "Will you be able to choose your own mate?", a relatively small number said they thought they could do so. The results of the above mentioned surveys will be given in table type outlays on the following pages.

One may see a number of reasons for some of the older marriage and family practices which cling together such as parental choice of a mate for a daughter-in-law for their sons. The bride will come to join the family of the father and hence both mother and father in that family are quite insistent that they have the say in what type of woman shall enter their family circle. However, if the young people don't want to live with the parents, then the question of what type of girl or woman will enter their family circle doesn't enter into the problem. However, another short survey threw new light on this problem, for it seemed that these four types of relationship didn't work out that way in the survey. Ranking four logically possible responses according to the frequency with which they are given gives the following results:

1. Choose mate independently and live in a
   separate house   230-41%
2. Parents choose mate but live in a separate
   house   139-25%
3. Choose mate independently but live patrilo-
   cally   110-20%
4. Parents choose mate and live patrilocally   77-14%

The fully modern pattern (1) is considerably more prevalent than the fully traditionally (4) among our sample of Chinese students. But the combination of the two compromises (2 and 3) is slightly more prevalent than is the fully modern.

There is no doubt that the question of how many children they hope to have in their family is somewhat affected by the family planning efforts which lately have been blessed and approved by both provincial and national governments. The motto for national consumption for the last several years has been that two children are ideal for the modern family. Since the birth rate has dropped from 45.29 per thousand in 1955 to below 25.64 in 1971 and has gone even lower since then, the birth control program must have had some effect on this change. However, the attitudes of the university students toward the desired number of children seems to work independently of the propaganda, for the latest returns show that out of 382 answers, 184 wanted three children, 93 wanted four or more babies and 105 wanted two. The birth control workers themselves admitted that many adult Chinese said, "We are still Chinese and we would like to have male children to carry on the family name and some remembrance by the members of the family of their ancestors. Therefore it is safer to have at least four so as to have a good chance to obtain at least two

Table 1
Attitudes of Taiwan U. and Michigan Students Toward Marriage and the Family

Percentage of total	Place of survey Mich. Univ.	Taiwan Univ 1956	1965
1. Marriage should be based on love and there should be love before marriage	98%	92	92
2. I want to choose my mate independently	—	87	94
3. The new style marriage is better than the old	—	87	90
4. Sexes should not be separated at social affairs	96	87	92
5. Sexes should not be separated in universities	94	87	90
6. Sexes should not be separated in primary schools	94	84	90
7. Young people should be engaged before marriage	93	84	—
8. Newlyweds should not live with parents	99	59	80
9. I expect to be able to choose my mate independently	93	58	82
10. Sexes should not be separated in middle schools	95	45	25
Numbers responding for each question	238	651	410

"—" means not asked of American students

Table 2
Attitudes of Taiwan U. Students Toward Marriage and the Family Numbers—
not Percentage. (1971)

QUESTIONS	ANSWERS		
	YES	NO	
1. You wish to marry?	381	1	
2. Do you wish to choose your own mate?	375	7	
3. Should love be the basis for marriage?	370	12	
4. Do you approve coeducation in the schools?	367	15	
5. Do you want a mate who likes children?	381	1	
6. Is the possibility of divorce dangerous to marriage stability?	345	37	
7. Is the possibility of divorce harmful to your family?	334	48	
8. Is dating among university students good?	251	31	
9. Should there be an engagement before marriage?	297	35	
10. Is full employment for wives desireable?	65	317	
11. Is neolocal residence desireable?	309	73	
12. How many children would you like to have?	TWO	THREE	4 or more
	105	184	93

male children. If you limit the total number to two children, you will have difficulty to get even one male and if he dies, it will be too late to get another one.''

It has been the impression of non-Chinese in the past that Chinese people, both male and female, love their children and like to care for them. It is also the impression of Westerners that they too like to have children in the home and that it makes life happier. However, a fellow Professor of mine in the Sociology Department made a small survey of married people in Taipei after my first large survey. It was done by mail to a number of young married people and one of the questions was, "Do you have any children and if you have none are you unhappy without children in the house?" He recorded that there were a number of couples which had no children and they were as happy as anyone else. The result seems to be highly atypical and I think the survey should be repeated at intervals, for it seems to contradict what the university students wrote down in the three surveys that I made of their attitudes. Of course, there is the possibility that the childless couples replied this way defensively.

Industrialization and Urbanization

The increase of industrialization and urbanization in the Western world seems to bring on the following changes in society: (1) more divorces, (2) residential mobility, (3) emancipation of women and their increased entry into the labor force, and (4) diminshed responsibility of the children for their parents in old age and for their grandparents.

Within the last ten to fifteen years we have witnessed rapid industrialization and urbanization with most of the above mentioned phenomena becoming quite apparent. A government employee, complaining about industrial accidents both in factories and mines and his inability to reduce their incidence said, "I have 25 men for this work but within the last two years we have started 10,000 new factories." The attraction of youth, both male and female, from the agricultural areas to the city has been much as mentioned in the beginning of this paper, that is, seven out of ten farm youths were preparing to go to the cities for jobs.

The rapid urban population increase made new housing a very urgent need. Space needs required the change from one-story small Japanese-type houses into many-storied apartment houses that rose high in the city skylines. One important result was that those who moved to the city for industrial or other work usually came alone. If they already had a wife in the country areas, they left her with their family of origin. However, even if they returned home for occasional visits, they often struck up relations with another woman in the city, with divorce a frequent result. However, if the whole family moved to the big city, it was still a nuclear family and for the most part remained that way since housing was very hard to obtain and new buildings had to take care of the inflow from the country as well as natural increases. While the five largest cities of Taiwan all grew rapidly, Taipei was the fastest growing. It grew from a city of about 800,00 in 1956 to 1,500,000 in 1971. Of course, the new housing was mostly apartment-type, and complaints about this type of housing were that living quarters were too crowded, there was no garden space, and noises from other apartments reverberated throughout the whole building or at least into the next apartments. There were special complaints about the noise of those who kept dogs. A few questions were added on to the fundamental questions in the last survey of students attitudes and are included below.

Table No. 3

	Live in an apartment		Like it as well as previous housing	
	Yes	No	Yes	No
	Number		Number	
Taiwanese	63	185	37	26
Mainlanders	41	73	25	16
Overseas	44	37	27	17
TOTAL	148	295	89	59

Table No. 4

	Too Private		Too Closed in		Expensive	
	Yes	No	Yes	No	Yes	No
	Number		Number		Number	
Taiwanese	44	42	29	37	26	40
Mainlanders	21	22	22	22	19	23
Overseas	27	16	22	21	27	16
TOTAL	92	80	73	80	72	79

Table No. 5

A Month's Rent	Under NT$500	–NT500 to 1000	–$1000 to 1500	$1500 to $2000	to Over
			NUMBERS		
Taiwanese	47	0	1	2	9
Mainlanders	33	0	1	2	5
Overseas	25	7	2	4	6
TOTAL	105	7	4	8	20

Functions of the Family

The brief sub-title given above refers to the functions the family performs for its members. While different authors chose different numbers and names, I concur here with Ogburn and Nimkoff and choose the seven that they name and explain: economic, social status, educational, protective, religious, recreational and affectional.

Sociologists, the two above named included, judge that these family functions have greatly decreased in recent years. After having explained these functions of the family to the students of the National Taiwan University and the National Taiwan Normal University, I decided to find out how much these functions of the family had changed and decreased among the Chinese families in the Republic of China. To do this I made out a questionnaire about practical matters, the answers to which would indicate how much or how little was still being done for members of families in modern Taiwan. Therefore during May, 1964 random sampling was made among the 9,000 students of the National Taiwan University. Since reply to the survey was voluntary, out of 835 questionnaires distributed, 727 respondents turned in papers fully answered. The place of origin of the students was 36.2 percent from Taiwanese families, 37.4 percent percent from families which had come from the Chinese mainland, and 26.4 percent from families of overseas communities.

Closely connected with the changes in the functions of the family is the change in the occupation of the fathers and mothers and the planned occupations of the sons and daughters. Hence in the beginning of the questionnaire respondents were asked about the occupations of their parents and their own planned occupation. Those who proposed to take positions in the commercial field were but 8.1 percent of the total sample, and practically the same percentage looked forward to government employment. But nearly 30 percent prepared for work in the educational field, some 15 percent desired positions in the professions, 5 percent chose miscellaneous jobs, and, strange to say, 31 percent gave no answer. This high percentage of "no answer" on the question of "planned occupation" may indicate that these respondents, who for the most part came from the sophomore and junior years of university, really have not yet made up their minds as to what they want to do; it may also mean that the students are quite willing and able to answer questions of fact such as the occupations of their fathers, in which only 6.8 percent gave no answer.

Here we shall first take up the data supplied by the survey on the economic function of the family, and in doing so we should note that there still exists a strong distinction between the rural and urban families in Taiwan. By this is meant that the economic function of the families has yielded to the encroachments of government agencies and the like far more than it has done in the agricultural areas. There are two more points to keep in mind here: the first is that both in Taiwan and in other countries, many families in Asia move from the country to big cities and yet retain their rural customs and folkways to a very large extent. This point is more fully developed by Professor Philip M. Hauser in *Urbanization in Asia and in Far East*. From personal observation, I would say that in my early days in Taiwan it applied here. A second point to note is that almost none of the respondents reported their fathers as employed in agricultural pursuits. The questions asked the respondents may seem simple, but they are practical in that they seek what families do for their members economically. I asked how many members of the family contribute to the support of the family, also how many worked outside of the family, how many worked at home and a closely connected question, "How many people support the family in any way?" The students were also asked whether clothes such as sweaters, underclothes and dresses were made at home or bought outside of the home. It was not thought useful to ask whether the remote and the immediate preparation of food was done outside the home or at home, since in China most of the remote preparation is done outside of the home and even much of the immediate preparation is done outside in shops near the home or by hawkers who travel up and down the streets calling out their products—such as, for breakfast, the *Yu-t'iao, Shao-ping,* and *Tou-chiang.*

A typical urban family in which the members depended on the income of one of its members was found in 46.4 percent of the families of the total respondents. This pattern was especially true of Mainland respondents' families which accounted for 55.3 percent of the total respondents. Families depending on two persons for total income accounted for 30.1 percent of the sample, while 11.4 percent depended on three persons. 6.9 percent depended on more than 3 persons. Of the total sample 5.2 percent said they depended on "none" which may be explained by recalling that their income may be from property, pensions or some other form of non-personal income.

Part of the economic function of the family was the making of clothes for its members. Formerly, in the agricultural areas, the family often produced all the items of clothing for both male and female members, but now in the cities many items of clothing are machine-made and supplied in large quantities at low prices. Therefore, the following question was asked of the students respondents, "Are the following items of clothing made at home: sweaters, women's dresses, and underwear?" Answers to this question were as follows: Sweaters–11.7 percent, women's dresses–32.6 percent, and underclothes–34.1 percent. Knit wear at that time was small because of the difficulty of getting wool yarn.

Since most of the respondents came from a non-agricultural background, we already knew that much of the technical teaching of the father and mother is missing from the educational function of the families but we may inquire as to whether the respondents learned anything either formally or informally at home. In order to make this general question more specific, the students were asked whether they learned to read or write at home, simple mathematics, did they receive aid from parents, brothers or sisters with their lessons and whether they received any moral instructions at home. This question was phrased in the Guttman scale at "much, little or none." As a little side issue, the author was interested in finding out whether the students were receiving any moral instructions in the schools, so the question was repeated for primary, secondary or high schools and universities.

In the survey it was found that 60.4 percent of the respondents claimed to have learned to read and write at home, 55.2 percent of the students had been helped with their studies by other members of their families, and 60.7 percent said they had been taught simple mathematics at home. In regard to the second large question, whether the students had been taught about right and wrong at home, 67 percent said they had been taught "much" at home, 28.3 percent said they had been taught a "little" at home, while only 1.8 percent reported that they had been taught "nothing" at home about "right and wrong."

As for the recreational function for the family both in the city and the country in earlier days, outside of festivals and special holidays there was not too much to attract the family members. There were such enjoyments as the family singing together at home for 34.4 percent of the respondents, listening to music together 47 percent, 28.9 percent going on picnics together as a family and 64.6 percent said they went to the movies "as a family." A relatively small percentage admitted to playing Mah Jong at home, for Chinese thought it was gambling and they thought that gambling was a vice and would not like to admit they did it at home. More recently, television sets have been introduced to about 90 percent of the homes of a city like Taipei, and most often the respondents listen and "watch" as families. At an even later date than the above cited survey, it is quite clear from random observation that life in the cities draws crowds of both young and old to the "movies," to entertainment in eating houses, bowling alleys, swimming pools, Chinese operas, sporting contests, public lectures and meetings.

In regard to the religious function of the family, matters are more complicated since the variables are numerous, that is, we have the religion of the father, of the mother and of the respondents, who are university students. Moreover the questions had to be suited to the various religions such as Bible reading for the Protestants, attending religious services, offering of incense, foodstuffs at home and then the breakdown of the respondents ito Taiwanese, Mainlanders and Overseas. There are two very noticeable trends as we go from the religious beliefs of the children. The first is that there is a very noticeable trend in some belief in the parents to no religious belief in the children. The second trend is that there is a heavy loss in Buddhism to no religious belief. There is some gain toward belief in Protestantism and Catholicism but it is not a startling one. This trend is borne out in other surveys made by the authors, Robert Marsh and Albert O'Hara, in "Attitudes of University Students toward Marriage and the Family in Taiwan," *American Journal of Sociology,* July 1961.

However, there is a new trend, stronger is the countryside but still visable in the cities, of rebuilding temples and refurnishing them. The temples are not strictly Buddhist, Taoist, etc., but indicate an eclectic interest in folk religion as well as fixed beliefs. The interesting point in this development is that the necessary funds are not supplied or sought by the monks or nuns, but by the people who live in the area of the temples and by those who frequent them. It is also interesting that government officials and prominent members of political parties make generous contributions, and folk festivals find the temples crowded.

The question of prayer in commmon as a family practice was placed on a reduced Murphy-Likert scale so that 10 percent said they "often" prayed together at home, 37.8 percent reported that they sometimes prayed together at home, while 46.4 said they never prayed at home together. The making of offerings of incense, foodstuffs, etc., has long been a traditional practice in Chinese homes and it is a practice that is not easily dropped. In this case 17.5 percent of the students reported making such offerings in the homes as a family practice; at the same time 37.9 percent reported other types of religious practices at home. Outside of statistical data on the religious function of the family we may well agree with C. K. Yang in his book, *Religion in Chinese Society,* when he states, "Examining the religious characteristics in the light of diffused religion, we shall see that it was a pervasive factor in all major aspects of social life, contributing to the stability of social institutions and that institutional religion, although important in its own way, lacked organizational strength to make it a powerful structural factor in the over-all Chinese social organization."

General Summary

To now take a sweeping glance at the Chinese family as it finds itself today in the midst of sweeping and rapid industrialization and urbanization, we may note the following.

It is true that the extended families have in general changed into nuclear families and a great number of them find shelter in apartment buildings, but therein they find the conveniences of modern living. They reap the advantages of running water, electricity for machine applicances such as electric fans, air conditioners, bread toasters and cookers. Almost every home in Taipei has a television set and the lesser cities are not far behind them. Within the last few years, wages and salaries have been raised, due to both heavy demand and new labor laws.

While it is true that there may be more television sets than telephones, the number of phones is great and each year is increasing. The number of private cars, taxis and motorcycles in Taipei is bewildering. The bus service is both reasonable in price and well planned for communication. The postal service in China, earlier on the mainland but now here in Taiwan, is very reliable and offers frequent daily deliveries.

As indicated above the desire for romance and love in seeking a mate for marriage and for married life itself has grown stronger and has become a more widespread fact that seems to make many people happier. Professor Martin M. C. Yang, in his report about the changes in the countryside about choosing a mate, reported that even the older women said that they felt it was a good change and they only wish it had started in their youth.

With universal education for children of both sexes, companionate marriages are more possible and enjoyable. It also makes possible some work outside the home for the wives. However, the surveys of university attitudes toward marriage and the family made it quite clear that they felt full employment for the wife was not a desireable matter, since 316 out of 381 students voted against it and only 65 were for it. Since the Government has made education free and required for nine years of schooling, children under 14 years of age are over 98 percent of the total in schools. And the latest reliable figures report that of the total population of the Republc of China, one out of four are in some level of education. This factor influences the average of marriage and hence affects the birthrate. The average age of marriage of women has now risen above 24 years; since the high fertile period for women is from 18 to 24, the family planning association grants that this factor has had a decided effect on the decrease in the birth rate in Taiwan.

While the attractions of urban life have had a decided effect on the large-scale migration of the young to the cities, rural life seems to still have an attraction for a large part of the youth of the Republic of China. Before the recession in the U.S.A., and therefore when the products of the Republic of China's industry were in great demand over there, young labor was in great demand here. There was almost complete freedom from parental control and industrial employment brought weekly wages which gave the young the possibility of the price of taking part in the cities "bright life" and buying the new and colorful clothes which seemed so attractive. Life on the farm did put money in one's pockets in the same way, and parents did not easily give children enough money to look for new amusement and modern clothes.

However, when the recession in American set in and factories in Taiwan closed down due to a lack of demand for their products, unemployment became widespread. Even though the youthful workers very reluctantly returned home, they still found parents who gave them the warmth of family life and security from debts and hunger. Moreover, the family and religious festivals were much more comforting that the high-priced cold pleasures of the cities' "bright lights." Moreover many students returned to university professors after graduation and said, "The socialization that has taken place in our families, primary and middle school and universities has had some warmth and sympathy in it but that socialization we have met in the social and economic life after graduation is unfeeling and cruel. Moreover, it is good to belong to a family for we have some status and protection but when we have to go it alone our life is cold, lonely and uninteresting."

3.   Social Class and Rural-Urban Patterning of Socialization in Taiwan

Nancy J. Olsen

Method of Study

The research was conducted in the capital city of Taipei, and in the village of Lu-shang, located in Chang-hua County, on the island's central plain. In both locales, the study was limited to families of Taiwanese descent. Since Mainlanders are disproportionately represented in the higher status urban groups, including them might have introduced systemic bias into the results.

At the time of the study (1967-68), Taipei's rapidly growing population was one and one-quarter million, crowded into an area of 67 square kilometers. Two-thirds of these inhabitants were Taiwanese. Taipei was chosen for the research because the diversity of occupations, both traditional and modern, meant that a full range of types of Taiwanese families could be found there.

It was precisely its unusually large size, approximately 6200 people arranged in over 1000 households, that made Lu-shang especially attractive as a rural research site. The sampling scheme, which will be described below, called for an initially large group of families from which a smaller number could be carefully selected according to several criteria. The village's size does not mean that it is a marketing center in any sense. The several shops and small businesses cater only to the people of Lu-shang, and over 90 percent of the men are farmers. Because the land is poor and irrigation uncertain, peanuts and sweet potatoes are the dominant crops, although rice is grown whenever possible. Many men cannot support their families on the amount of land they own, and must occasionally take on part-time work, either as laborers in town or in the sugar cane fields. Some, in fact, spend more time as agricultural laborers than they do in cultivating their own land, but only the families of men whose main occupation was "owner-cultivator" were studied for the research reported upon here.

In order to find suitable families, over 2000 sixth grade school children were surveyed with regard to their family backgrounds. In Taipei these children came from two very large public elementary schools, Hsi-men and Chung-shan, selected because they draw from heterogeneous Taiwanese neighborhoods. In Lu-shang, the children were enrolled in the Lu-shang village school, which also serves some very small villages nearby. Sixth grade children were chosen for study because they are maximally literate within the age group where universal education is expected.

In each of these three schools, all children in all sixth grade classes completed a questionnaire dealing with parental occupation and education, household composition, etc., and from their responses, 107 Taiwanese families were selected so as to meet rigid sampling requirements.

Social class within the urban sample was measured by the general level of prestige accorded the occupation of the family's main wage earner, since in American research, at any rate, this dimension has been found to be the one most highly correlated with all other aspects of social class. The use of occupational position as an index also follows theoretically from a common definition of social stratification: "The structure of differential evaluations of and rewards attached to roles in the division of labor." While American socializatoin studies have often found it possible to use two occupational categories (white- and blue-collar), this did not seem a very realistic breakdown in Taiwan. No simple scheme could do justice to the complexity of the occupational structure there, but preliminary research suggested that it would be possible to delineate three fairly homogeneous groups. Given labels only for the sake of convenience, there are an "upper-middle" group composed of professionals, high governmental officials, and owners of large businesses; a

Journal of Asian Studies 34, No. 3 (May, 1975), pp. 663-68. The author is on the faculty of the University of Santa Clara, Santa Clara, California. Footnotes omitted.

"lower-middle" group made up of minor government officials, shopkeepers, primary school teachers, and other poorly paid white collar workers; and a "working-class" of peddlers, factory workers and laborers.

The sample was chosen so that there were approximately equal numbers of families from each of these three urban classes and from the village. The four groups were equated on a number of possibly confounding variables—average number of children per family, sex and ordinal position of the sixth grade sample child, household composition (whether nuclear or extended), employment status of the mother, and (for urban families) average length of time in Taipei.

The cooperation of each of the 107 families was solicited through a letter signed by the child's school principal, and there was only one refusal (a substitution was made). The family was then visited by a young Taiwanese women who, using a structured schedule similar to that designed for cross-cultural work by the Six Cultures Project, interviewed the mother about her socialization practices and values.

The questionnaries were examined for items which could be used to index the six dimensions which seemed important both because of their relevance to the patterning of family socialization in Taiwan and because of their more general theoretical significance. Operational definitions and examples for each of these variables are as follows:

Affection (6 items): the mother reported many instances of affectionate, consoling, and rewarding behavior. Example: "When your child comes to you feeling sad, what do you do?"

"Power-Assertive" Discipline (7 items): the mother indicated frequent, mostly physical, punishment for all sorts of infractions. Example: "When your child gets a low mark on a school examination, what do you usually do?"

"Love-Oriented" Discipline (5 items): the mother said that she responds to the child's misbehavior with methods that aim at making him feel guilty or ashamed. Example: "When reprimanding their children, different mothers say different things. Do you ever tell your child that his behavior has made you very sad and disappointed?"

Conformity Values (4 items): the mother expressed the opinion that learning to obey those in authority was more important than learning self-control. Example: "From the following list of qualities, which do you think are the most important for a sixth grade child to learn?" Included on the list were "obedience" and "politeness" which were weighted positively on this scale, "self-control" and "responsibility," which were weighted negatively.

Self-Reliance Values (5 items): the mother believed that it was good for children to do things on their own rather than to depend on adults in the family. Example: "In general, do you think that a child ought to try to do things that are hard for him, or do you think it is best for him to ask adults for help?"

Aggression Control (4 items): the mother indicated that controlling children's fighting was very important, and punished infractions. Example: "Some mothers have told us that there are circumstances when a child would be justified in hitting back. What do you think about this—are there ever times when a child should be allowed to hit back?"

The items chosen to index each of these six dimensions were inter-correlated, and those which were positively related to the other items were retained. The number of items composing each index ranged from four to seven. A mother's responses to each item were scored from 1 (low) to 3 (high), and a women's score on each dimension was simply the sum of her scores on the component items. For a dimension indexed by four items, for example, scores could range from a low of 4 to a high of 12.

In order to compare the socialization values and practices of women in the three urban social classes and in the village, mean scores were calculated for each group on each dimension. Furthermore, so as to give a clearer idea of the importance of social class and rural-urban residence as determinants of family socialization, a measure of association (Kendall's τ) was used to measure the strength of the relationship.

For the purpose of statistical manipulation (and particularly in order to be able to apply the partial correlation analysis described below), the rural sample was ranked as a fourth social class. The justification for doing so is not completely straight-forward. In terms of occupational prestige *per se,* "owner-cultivators" are not viewed by Taiwanese urbanities as inferior to the urban working class, although farm laborers are regarded very poorly indeed. However, in terms of other dimensions of social class—the *rewards* attached to social position (income, education, consumption patterns, and so forth)—farmers are definitely far below the lower status urban groups. In any case, the reader should keep in mind that this ranking is for the sake of statistical convenience and is not meant to imply that farmers constitute a social class in the same sense as do the urban samples.

Results: Social Structure and Socialization

From Table 1 it can be seen that social class and rural-urban residence are significantly related to all of the six selected socialization dimensions. Ethnographic accounts of Taiwanese family life had suggested that affection and disciplinary techniques would vary among the social groups being studied, and this is indeed the case. High status urban mothers are the most affectionate and the least punitive. They do not, however, ignore their children's misbehavior, for they are the group which is most likely to use the "love-oriented" techniques of discipline—trying to make their children feel guilty or ashamed. Rural women are at the opposite extreme on these dimensions, with the lower-middle and working class urban groups ranged in between.

**Table 1.   Scores of Mothers in the
Three Urban Social Classes,
and in the Rural Village**

	Upper Middle (n = 29)	Lower Middle (n = 30)	Working (n = 26)	Rural (n = 22)	Degree of Association**
Affection (6–18)*	15.17	14.17	12.62	9.91	+ .44
"Power-Assertive" Discipline (7–21)	13.21	15.97	15.58	16.18	− .21
"Love-Oriented" Discipline (5–15)	12.52	11.90	11.85	11.05	+ .17
Conformity Values (4–12)	8.48	9.13	9.62	10.86	− .28
Self-Reliance Values (5–15)	10.07	10.07	9.77	8.41	+ .19
Aggression Control (4–12)	7.89	8.20	9.39	9.81	− .32

 * Indicates possible range of scores.
 ** Kendall's τ. Positive correlations indicate that high scores are associated with higher social class. Correlations of ± .10 are significant at .05 (one-tailed test).

The present data indicate that social structure influences socialization *values,* as well as practices. The figures presented in Table 1 clearly show that the traditional values of aggression control, conformity to parental authority, and interdependence rather than self-reliance are *not* equally emphasized by all social groups. It is the rural mothers who are most likely to subscribe to these goals, the high status urban women who find them least important.

It is true that the effects of social position are more pronounced for some of these variables than for others. Affectionate behavior in particular, is noteworthy for the very strong relationship it bears to social class, and especially to rural-urban residence. Other variables, such as "Love-Oriented" Discipline and Self-Reliance, are less influenced by social position. Nonetheless, for all of these dimensions, those involving child-rearing values as well as disciplinary techniques, social class is systematically and significantly related to family socialization. The position one occupies in the social structure of Taiwan makes a definite difference to the way one approaches the child-rearing process.

Although these results are only partially consistent with the differences suggested by ethnographic accounts of Taiwanese family life, they correspond very closely to those obtained in similar studies in the United States and elsewhere. For example, Bronfenbrenner's review of several American studies showed higher status parents to be more affectionate and rewarding, and to more often employ the "love-oriented techniques of discipline in preference to physical punishment. This pattern has also appeared in more recent research, and in studies done in other countries—Greece, Lebanon, England, Norway, and Germany. Similarly, an emphasis on self-reliance and self-direction rather than conformity to authority has been found to characterize higher status parents in the United States, Italy, the Philippines, England, Greece, Java, Norway, and in a study of eleven industrialized nations. Finally, aggression control seems to be more characterisic of lower status parents in the United States, a finding which has been replicated in Greece.

Most of these studies have confined themselves to social class differences within urban and/or suburban populations. The only ones to have also included rural parents are those conducted in Greece and Lebanon and one American study of socialization values. In these few studies, however, the pattern of results was similar to that found in Taiwan, the high status urban parents being at one extreme, the rural parents at the other, with the lower status urban parents falling at an intermediate position. Thus, for example, Prothro's study showed Greek peasants to be very strict about controlling expressons of aggression, an urban laboring group somewhat less strict, and an urban white-collar group quite permissive in this respect. Similarly, Kohn found that obedience to authority was valued most by American men living in rural areas, somewhat less by urban working-class fathers, and least of all by fathers from the urban middle-class.

It is significant that the patterning of social class and rural-urban differences in family socialization has been found to be so similar from society to society. Taken together, these various studies suggest that, depite general cultural differences, there are features of the social structure of all differentiated societies that might be expected to have similar effects upon patterns of family socialization.

4.   Social Mobility in Tawian

Charlotte Shiang-Yun Wang

Comparative studies on social stratification, especially on the social mobility process, are considerably meager compared to the abundance of occupational stratification studies in the United States. Adequate theories explaining differences in the social stratification systems of various societies ought to be based on empirical cross-cultural studies. Chinese people are often considered culturally different than Western people. Comparative studies of the Chinese stratification system with the Western systems seem to be indispensable to the task of building an adequate stratification theory.

There are numerous books and articles comparing Chinese societies to Western societies. Unfortunately, there is only a handful of empirical studies on the Chinese stratification system that are scientifically conducted. Of these studies, most investigated the occupational distribution and ignored social mobility. However, social mobility is an equally important, if not more important, issue in stratification. In order to know whether a society is equal, it is essential to investigate whether people from different family backgrounds have the same opportunity to achieve certain statuses. Among those whose analyzed Chinese social mobility, few have utilized multivariate techniques as a strategy for analyzing the process of stratification. Due to the complexity of the social mobility process, vis-à-vis the lack of multivariate analysis for the Chinese system, the Chinese stratification process remains a vague and somewhat contradictory picture.

On the one hand, students of Chinese studies are often impressed by the great Chinese imperial examination system which was in operation more than a thousand years ago. There was a strong belief and practice of 'meritocracy,'' that the administrators should be chosen by ability and talent. The statement, ''Poor families produce *chuan-yuan's'' (Han men chu chuan-yuan)* was not only a folklore but often a reality in Chinese history. *Chuan-yuan's* who passed the imperial examinations with top performance often came from poor families. Despite his poor family background, whoever was the *chuan-yuan* would be endowed with high official power, prestigious status, and wealth. People who passed the civil service examination at other levels would also be endowed with appropriate reward, regardless of their family background. Empirically, Hsu's analysis of biographies and District Gazetteers showed that a fairly high degree of social mobility existed in Chinese society during the last thousand years. He found that in the majority of cases prominence did not last over one generation, and that of the families which did maintain themselves a little longer, the vast majority did not last over two generations. Kracke reached the same conclusion from entirely different lists of civil service graduates.

The 1911 Republican revolution abolished the imperial examination, yet the emphasis on education and merit was not reduced at all. On the contrary, it probably was increased. The abolition of the imperial examination does not mean the abolition of education. Rather, it only means the change of style and content of education. Formal education takes the place of traditional tutorial education. The nationalist government in Taiwan first institutionalized compulsory public education for the first six grades, and recently the government extended compulsory education to the ninth grade. Appleton pointed out:

> Enrollments at every educational level have expanded rapidly over the past generation. From 1954 to 1974, the percentage of the total population enrolled in secondary schools increased nearly five times, and the percentage in institutions of higher education almost twelve times. Three times as many students were working toward advanced and graduate degrees in 1974 as had received such degrees over the entire preceding decade.

This demonstrates the increasing importance of education in the Republic of China. Above

Papers in Social Sciences (Nakang, Taipei: Academia Sinica), No. 80-3 (1980). The author is Fulbright Visiting Associate Professor at the National Taiwan University. Footnotes omitted.

all, it may also be indicative of the fact that there is even more emphasis on qualification and ability in Taiwan than in traditional China.

On the other hand, some scholars adhere to a different view. They find Chinese society extremely stratified. Eberhard identified "inequality" as one of the three principles inherent in the "Chinese" features of social structure throughout history. There was a clear ranking among Chinese people according to age, social status and sex. The ranking criteria dominate the "Five Cardinal Relations of Humanity": father and son; sovereign and minister; husband and wife; older and younger; and friend. In addition, it is well-known that the structure of occupational status in traditional China is basically classified into four strata: scholars *(shih)*, farmers *(nung)*, artisans *(kung)* and merchants *(shang)*. One of the major themes of Confucius' teaching is that everybody should always be aware of his/her position in the ranking hierarchy in all circumstances and behave accordingly.

Since families had a very vital role in traditional China, it would be understandable that an individual's achievement would influence his family member's status, especially his son's. Wittfogel's study indicates that social mobility in traditional China is considerably influenced by *yin* privileges through which the son of an official could enter the bureaucracy and obtain a high status without passing the regular examination.

Although the Republican revolution of 1911 disintegrated the traditional system of central political control, many scholars feel that there was no sweeping introduction of any new pattern of the social system, and that inequality prevailed in China after 1911. The alleged inequality under the Nationalist Government is often claimed to be one of the causes of the Communist Revolution. Since the government in the Republic of China (Taiwan) is the Nationalist Government, we would expect to find the same inequality in Taiwan. In fact, it is no secret that family background or social contacts facilitate one's accessibility to certain job opportunities.

However, there is no known society, including the United States, in which family background or social contacts do not more or less influence one's job opportunities. The important question is *to what extent* and *how* does one's family background affect his achievement. If the effect in the Republic of China is indeed larger than that of Western societies, another question has to be asked as to whether this is expected according to the level of industrialization. Ferdinand Toennies pointed out that the *Gesellschaft* Western societies were also developed from *Gemeinschaft* societies. Maine indicates that one uniform respect of the movement of progessive societies has been a movement from "status" to contract. That is, in all societies there is a gradual dissolution of family dependency and the growth of individual obligation in its place. The role of the family was, at one time, very important in the history of Western societies as well. In fact, even in the present Western societies, an individual's family status still exerts its influence on the individual's status attainment, although perhaps to a lesser extent than in the past. It is the purpose of this study to use a status attainment model to compare the occupational achievement process in the Republic of China to that of other countries, considering their levels of development.

Treiman and Terrell studies the process of status attainment in the United States and Great Britain. Lin and Yauger compared the process of occupational status attainment in Haiti and Costa Rica to that of Great Britain and the United States, considering the level of development of these societies. The major purpose of this study is to compare the findings of these two studies and the occupational achievement process in Taiwan.

Models and Propositions

The model to be tested in this study is illustrated in Figure 1 which is the same as that of Lin and Yauger. It represents a simplified version developed from the famous Blau and Duncan occupational status attainment model, in that the influence of father's education on son's occupation is omitted. Father's education was omitted from the model because the information was not available in either Lin and Yauger's study or in Treiman's British analysis. For the sake of comparison, the same simplified model is used for the study, although the information on father's education is available for Taiwan. In addition, since the main interest of these studies is in the process of *inter*-generational status attainment, the distinction between son's first job and occupation of destination is omitted from the model. Thus,

Figure 1. A Model of the Process of Occupational Status Attainment

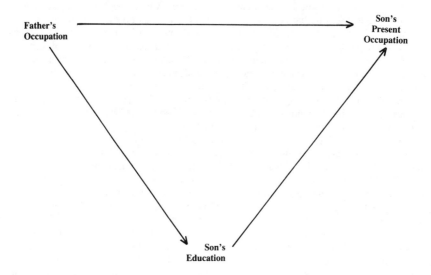

Figure 1 illustrates a process in which father's occupation affects son's education, and that both of these variables affect son's occupation.

The model provides us with a synthesis of the opposing theories on social stratification in China. It indicates that an individual's occupational achievement may be partly due to his own educational attainment and partly due to his father's occupational status (the individual's family influence.) Above all, the model allows us to assess both the direct and the indirect effects of father's occupational status on son's occupational achievement. On the one hand, the direct effect indicates that an individual may obtain a desirable job simply because of his father's prestigious status, e.g., *yin* privileges. On the other hand, the indirect effect indicates than an individual from a family with high status achieves high occupational prestige which may be due to the fact that the aspiration and/or wealth from his family enables him to attain a high level of education which in turn provides him with the ability and qualifications for his occupational achievement. These are certainly two different social mobility processes for family status to have an effect on son's occupation. The two processes have totally different meanings in stratification. Most likely both processes are operating in Taiwan. the model allows us to assess the magnitude of each effect illustrated in Figure 1. Then these effects can be compared with corresponding effects in the models for other countries.

In a utopian society where there is total equality, one would expect the effect of son's education on son's occupation to be extremely high and the other effects in the model would be expected to be insignificant. On the other hand, in an extremely unequal society, we would expect to find a very strong effect of father's occupation on son's occupation, while the other effects become very weak. Of course, in reality none of these ideal types exist. Thus, comparative study is essential, for it can determine the extent of inequality in a society, relative to the other countries.

Industrialization not only changes the economic structure but it also changes the structure of other social institutions. Three propositions relating social mobility to industrialization were derived by Treiman from the existing literature.

Proposition 1. The more industrialized a society, the weaker the direct effect of father's occupational status on son's occupational achievement

Proposition 2. The more industrialized a society, the stronger the direct effect of an individual's own education on his occupational achievement.

Propositon 3. The more industrialized a society, the smaller the effect of father's status on son's education attainment.

Lin and Yauger tested the propositions with data from four societies — Haiti, Costa Rica, Great Britain, and the U.S. The data does not seem to fit the propositions. Lest not enough points were identified along the continuum of societal development, Lin and Yauger created three subsamples from the data for Costa Rica and added them to the study as if they represented three distinct societies on a scale of development. With the additional data points, the following modified propositions were suggested:

Modified Proposition 1. The direct effect of father's occupational status on son's occupational status is curvilinearly (convex) related to the degree of industrialization.

Modified Proposition 2. The direct effect of an individual's education on his occupational achievement is cuvilinearly (concave) related to the degree of industrialization.

Modified Proposition 3. The effect of father's occupational status on son's educational attainment is positively and linearly related to the degree of industrialization.

Data

The Taiwan data consist of an island-wide survey of household which was conducted in 1970 by Wolfgang Grichting. The population of the study contained all of the households in Taiwan, excluding mountain people, Caucasians and Negroes, and all those living in public institutions (prisons, army, etc.). Those living in private institutions (convents, monasteries, etc.) as well as professional military and retired soldiers housed in military compounds that are publicly accessible are also included in the survey. It is a carefully designed stratified sample of 1,882 respondents drawn from four strata according to the degree of urbanization: provincial cities, prefectural cities, townships, and rural areas. Since the total city population is considerably smaller than the country population, the cities were oversampled. This bias can be corrected by using weights inversely proportional to the stratum probability. After the weighting procedure, the original sample size was 1,879. All of the statistics reported in the present study are the weighted results.

Although one usually does not doubt the reliability of data collected from a well-designed probability sample, it is always a comfort to know that the statistics of a sample match the findings of other data sources, especially those of the census. Where the statistics from a sample can be checked against available census data or church statistics, the Grichting data seem to be consistent with results from independent sources.

Since one of the major purposes of the present study is to compare the Taiwan data to those of the other countries, it is important that the samples of these studies are comparable. The Treiman and Terrell analysis is restricted to male heads of households aged 25-64 in the civilian labor force. Thus, the sample of the present study excludes all female household heads, those who are younger than 25 and older than 64 years, and those not in the labor force.

During the interview, it was randomly predetermined that the respondent would be the head of the household, the wife of the head of the household, or "Other." "Other" refers to situations where the head's wife was to be interviewed and there was no wife because the household consisted of two or more adults not related by marriage. In this situation, the head of household was interviewed by coded "other." The cases in which the respondents are either head's wife or "other" are excluded from our sample. Some preliminary analysis of the data raised some doubt as to whether the information on "respondent's occupation" consistently denotes the "household head's occupation." Sometimes when the heads' wives were interviewed, they may have reported their own occupations. Besides, the information on head's occupation given by his wife may have some reliability problems. Wives do not always know the details of their husband's jobs. Therefore, the cases in which respondents are heads' wives are excluded from this study. Since it was randomly predetermined whether the respondent should be the head of the household, or the wife of the head, the exclusion of wives from the sample would not introduce any systematic samply bias. In order to preserve the randomness of the selection, "others" are also excluded from the study.

Finally, a small number of respondents who did not have formal education, or whose data on educational attainment, occupational achievement, or father's occupation are not available are further excluded from the sample. This results in a sample size of 681.

Measurement of Variables
Basically, there are four variables in this study: father's occupation, respondent's education, respondent's occupation, and Index of Societal Differentiation. The respondent's education in the Taiwan data was grouped into seven categories according to the number of years of school completed. In order to obtain an interval scale in this study, education is assigned with the midpoint of each category. The only exception is in the last category — "graduate training" — for which no numerical limits are indicated in the original data. A value of 19 is assigned for this group with the assumption that graduate training is equivalent to 17–21 years of schooling.

The variable of education in the data for Haiti and Costa Rica are also measured with the number of years of school completed. The British and U.S. data had two measures for education: "school-leaving age" and "effect proportional scale." Because the latter was based on the average occupational status of the individuals in each educational category, it tends to increase the effect of education on occupation. To be conservative in measuring the effect of education, and above all, for the sake of comparability, school leaving age is used as the measure of education in the U.S. and British data. Since most children attend first grade at the age of six, subtracting six from the measure of education (school-leaving age) in the U.S. and British data will be equivalent to the measure for education (number of years of schooling) in the other data.

Both the respondent's and the father's occupation data in all data sets in Treiman-Terrell's and Lin-Yauger's studies are coded according to Treiman's Standard International Occupational Prestige Scale (hereafter referred to as the Standard Scale) in order to obtain comparable occupational prestige scores cross-nationally. For comparative purposes, it is essential to convert occupational information for the Taiwan data into Treiman's Standard Scale. The Standard Scale was based on a collation of data from occupational prestige studies conducted in 55 countries around the world. The scores from each foreign data were converted to a standard metric, i.e., the United States metric. Then a summary score for each of the 509 occupations was constructed by averaging the converted scores from all the prestige data sets for that particular occupation. Standard Scale Scores are available for both the first edition (International Labour Office, 1958) and the 1969 edition (International Labour Office, 1969) of the International Standard Classification of Occupations.

Generally speaking, Grichting's occupational classification coincides more closely with the first edition of the ISCO than with the 1969 edition. However, for certain occupational groups, his classification is similar to the 1969 ISCO where detailed information on occupational units is provided.

Since the occupational scores are extremely important for the present study, extra caution is exercised in matching code categories between the Grichting classification and the Standard Scale categories. The matching procedure was carried out twice, once by an American graduate student and again by a Chinese graduate student. Later, Treiman provided me with another list of Standard Scale Scores which he and his research assistant assigned to the Taiwan data. Finally, three lists are compared. Whenever there is a discrepancy among the three lists, one of the Standard Scale Scores is chosen by this author through careful deliberation based on both the Chinese and the English versions of the Taiwan occupational classification.

There are different methods of measuring levels of societal development. Lin and Yauger used Marsh's Index of Societal Differentiation, which is constructed according to gross energy consumption and the percentage of males in nonfarm occupations. For the sake of comparability and convenience, the same measure is used for this study.

Table 1 indicates the Index of Differentiation Scores for the five relevant countries that are constructed by Marsh.

Table 1. Index of Differentiation Scores for Levels of Societal Development

Societies	Index of Differentiation Scores
Haiti	11.0
Costa Rica	24.1
Republic of China (Taiwan)	32.4
Great Britain	84.6
United States	109.4

Note: The Index of Differentiation Scores was constructed by Marsh for 114 countries by coverting the percentage of males in nonagricultural occupations and gross energy consumption per capita into t-scores according to the formula $t = 50 + 10(X - \bar{X}) / s$. The scores were then summed to obtain values on the index.

The table indicates that Haiti is the least industrialized and the U.S. the most industrialized among these countries. The Republic of China is somewhere in the middle of the continuum, although closer to the lower end; its developmental level is higher than Costa Rica but lower than Great Britain.

Data Analysis and Findings

Path analysis which applies the Ordinary Least Square regression techniques is used to assess the status attainment model illustrated in Figure 1. Statistics for the U.S. and British data are based on the published version of the Treiman and Terrell study. Since the U.S. and British statistics used in Lin and Yauger's study are in accordance with an earlier version of the Treiman and Terrell paper, there are some slight differences between the corresponding figures in this study and those in Lin and Yaugers's.

Table 2 presents the correlation coefficients among the variables in our status attainment model and the means and standard deviations of these variables for the Republic of China (Taiwan) compared to Haiti, Costa Rica, Great Britain and the U.S. The average level of education in each society seems to coincide with the order of societal development, where the higher the development, the higher the mean education. However, the variation of education in Taiwan seems to be very high compared to the other four countries. This could be due to the insufficient facilities for higher education prior to 1970 when the survey was conducted. The extension of compulsory education (from the first six grades to the ninth grade) started in 1968 and the increasing number of institutions for higher education would certainly increase the mean and perhaps decrease the standard deviation of education in Taiwan.

The mean scores for both father's and respondent's occupational prestige scores in Taiwan are relatively high compared to the other countries. This may be due to long existence of bureaucratization and specialization. To facilitate systematic comparisons, Figure 2 plots the correlation coefficients in various countries by the Index of Differentiation Scores for the respective societies. Table 3 presents regression coefficients of the variables in the equations constructed according to the status attainment model illustrated in Figure 1. First, respondent's education is regressed on father's occupation. Then, respondent's occupation is regressed on father's occupation and the respondent's own education. The various standardized regression coefficients in the five countries are plotted by the level of societal development in Figure 3.

Table 2.
Correlations, Means and Standard Deviations Among Variables in a Status Attainment Model for the Republic of China (Taiwan) Compared to Haiti, Costa Rica, Great Britain and the United States.

	Education	Occupation	Mean	Std. Dev.
Haiti (N = 455)				
Father's occupation	.127	.263	14.8	13.4
Education		.258	1.2	2.7
Occupation			18.3	15.0
Costa Rica (N = 366)				
Father's occupation	.130	.423	28.8	10.9
Education		.268	3.8	2.4
Occupation			30.9	10.6
Republic of China (N = 681) (Taiwan)				
Father's occupation	.348	.292	39.8	8.6
Education		420	5.9	4.2
Occupation			39.9	11.3
Great Britain (N = 536)				
Father's occupation	.254	.352	35.3	10.5
Education†		.451	14.5	1.3
Occupation			38.8	11.5
United States (N = 10,479)				
Father's occupation	.266	.255	41.0	10.3
Education†		.532	17.1	3.4
Occupation			43.1	12.1

†School-leaving age. Thus, for example, approximate means for years of school completed are 8.5 and 11.1 for British and U.S. data, respectively.

Figure 2.
Correlation Coefficients Among Variables in Status Attainment Models by Societal Level of Development

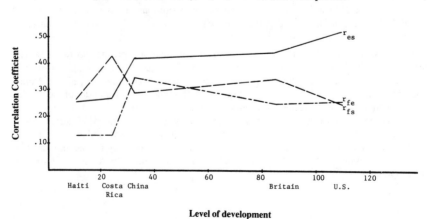

Level of development

Table 3.
Regression Coefficients of a Model of the Status Attainment Process in the Republic of China (Taiwan) Compared to Haiti, Costa Rica, Great Britain and the United States.

Independent Variables	Dependent Variables			
	Metric Coefficients		Standardized Coefficients	
	Education	Occupation	Education	Occupation
Haiti (N = 455)				
Father's occupation	.003	.261	.127	.234
	(.001)	(.050)		
Education		1.290		.229
		(.251)		
Intercept†				
$R^{2\dagger}$				
Costa Rica (N = 336)				
Father's occupation	.003	.384	.130	.395
Education	(.001)	(.047)		
		.980		.217
		(.220)		
Intercept†				
$R^{2\dagger}$				
Republic of China (N = 681)				
(Taiwan)				
Father's occupation	.172	.217	.348	.165
	(.018)	(0.48)		
Education		.968		.363
		(.098)		
Intercept	−0.964	25.502		
R^2	.121	.201		
Great Britain (N = 536)				
Father's occupation	.032	.278	.254	.254
	(.005)	(.042)		
Education		3.38		.387
		(.336)		
Intercept	13.3	−20.0		
R^2	.064	.274		
United States (N = 10,479)				
Father's occupation	.089	.143	.266	.122
	(.003)	(.010)		
Education		1.76		.499
		(.030)		
Intercept	7.47	17.6		
R^2	0.71	.296		

Note: Numbers in parentheses = standard errors.
† The figures for Intercept and R^2 in the models for Haiti and Costa Rica are not available.

Figure 3.
Regression Coefficients in Status Attainment Models by Societal Level
of Development

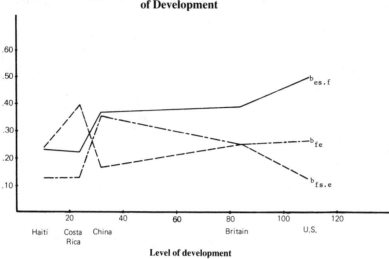

Level of development

1. Effect of Father's Occupation on Son's Occupation:

Table 2 indicates that the correlation between father's and son's occupations in Taiwan is .292. This is the total effect of father's occupational status on son's occupational achievement in standardized scores which amounts to a total effect of .384 in metric scores. That is, an increase of 10 points of prestige scores of father's status will result in a total increase of about 4 points of son's occupational prestige. In Table 3 where respondent's occupation is regressed on both father's occupation and son's own education, the effect of father's occupation on son's occupation is reduced to .165 in standardized scale and to .217 in metric scale. These regression coefficients indicate the direct effect of father's occupational status on son's occupational achievement. In other words, an increase of 10 points of prestige score of father's status leads directly to an increase of 2 points on son's occupational prestige without having to raise his son's educational level. The difference between the total and the direct effects indicates that half of the effect of father's status on son's occupation is mediated by son's education.

Proposition 1 expects a decline of the direct effect of father's occupation on son's occupation, as industrialization increases. Among the direct effects of father's occupation on son's occupation in the five countries compared, the effect in Taiwan is the smallest, except for the U.S. In Figures 2 and 3 the total effect (r_{fs}) as well as the direct effect ($b_{fs.e}$) of father's occupation on son's occupation in Costa Rica, Great Britain and the U.S. seem to indicate a decreasing effect as industrialization increases. However, the correlation coefficients for Taiwan and Haiti are almost as low as that for the U.S. After education is controlled, the effect of father's occupational status on son's occupational achievement drastically decreased for the U.S., Taiwan, and Great Britain, especially the former two. The direct effect for Taiwan becomes the second lowest among all the countries compared.

The findings indicate that there is more equality than expected in Taiwan. The pattern is more obvious for the direct effect. More importantly, the process of social mobility in Taiwan is similar to the U.S. where about half of the effect of father's status on son's occupational achievement is mediated via education, while father's status in the other countries exerts a larger proportion of its effect on son's occupational status directly.

The zig-zag pattern of the effect of father's occupation on son's occupation is not consistent with Proposition 1 which predicts a linear pattern of decreasing effect corresponding to industrialization. Above all, the pattern certainly is far from Lin and Yauger's Modified Proposition 1 in which there is a *convex* curvilinearity in the relationship of the effect to the level of development. If it was a convex pattern, according to the level of Taiwan's industrialization, the effect of father's occupation on son's occupation would be somewhat at the peak of the curve, rather than at the bottom. However, our data clearly demonstrate that the direct effect of father's occupational status on son's occupational prestige in Taiwan is the lowest among the five countries, except the U.S.

2. Effect of Education on Occupation:
Since there is no intervening variable between education and occupation, the regression coefficients of education in the occupation equation is the total effect as well as the direct effect of education on occupation. The regression coefficient ($b_{es.f}$ = .968) in Table 3 indicates that in Taiwan, one more year of schooling would increase one's occupational prestige by about one point. After the coefficient is standardized, it shows that one standard deviation (4.2 years of education) of increase in education will raise the individual's prestige by .363 of standard deviation.

When the metric coefficient of education for the Taiwan data is compared with those for the other countries in Table 3, we find an irregular pattern in which the Taiwan coefficient is the lowest while the British is the highest. The low coefficient in Taiwan is partly due to its extremely high standard deviation of education, and the high coefficient in Great Britain is partly attributable to the low standard deviation of British education (see Table 2).

After the coefficients are standardized, and juxtaposed in Figure 3, a general pattern substantiates Proposition 2, in that the effect of education on occupation increases as societies develop. The pattern of the standardized regression coefficients is similar to that of the correlations. Although the pattern does not fit a perfect linear line, it by no means supports the *concave* curvilinear line that is suggested by Lin and Yauger. Based on the concave curvilinearity, the effect of education on occupation for Taiwan would be predicted to be lower than the linear line. On the contrary, the Taiwan effect is considerably above the linear line. An individual's education has a stronger effect on his occupational status in Taiwan than the linear prediction according to its level of industrialization. It indicates that a very large part of an individual's occupational achievement is based on his educational qualifications; it is almost as large as that in Britain.

3. Effect of Father's Occupation on Son's Education:
Since education has only one independent variable, i.e., father's occupation, in the model, the correlation coefficient is equal to the total as well as the direct effect of father's occupation on son's education, in standardized scores. The metric coefficient in Table 3 indicates that a son of person A whose occupational prestige is 10 points higher than person B, will have 1.7 more years of schooling than the son of person B. In other words, an increase on one standard deviation of son's education.

Both the metric and standardized coefficients for Taiwan are highest among all the corresponding coefficients. Comparing Taiwan to the countries with higher levels of industrialization, the data seem to support Proposition 3 that the effect of father's occupational status on son's educational attainment decreases as industrialization increases—a negative relationship. It does not appear to be consistent with Lin and Yauger's modified proposition of positive linear relationship between the effect and the degree of industrialization.

Figure 3, juxtaposing the coefficients for all five countries, suggests that the effect of father's occupation on son's education is related to industrialization in a convex pattern. In the underdeveloped countries, the effect of father's occupational status on son's educational attainment is expected to be minimal, since the mean education is low (high illiteracy rate) and since there is lack of educational variations. However father's occupational status gains influence on son's educational attainment, as educational opportunities for those who can afford it increase in more developed societies. The limited number of institutions for higher education widens the variation among educational attainment. It is evident in the extremely high standard deviation of education in Taiwan. Due to the low level of farm mechanization and the pervasive non-skilled manual labor, children from families with low occupational status are either un-motivated psychologically or unable to economically afford to attain higher education. When societies reach a higher level of industrialization, e.g. Britain and the U.S., availability of higher education increases. Social origin reduces its dominance over the son's educational opportunities.

Conclusion

The present study has systematically examined the social mobility process in Taiwan and compared the Taiwan data with those of Haiti, Costa Rica, Britain, and the U.S. To assess the social mobility process, a simplified version of Blau and Duncan's status attainment model is used. Thus, the direct effect of father's occupation on son's occupation, the effect of father's occupation on son's education, and the effect of son's education on son's occupation are estimated simultaneously.

The findings seem to indicate that there is more equality in the social mobility process in Taiwan than other countries, considering the levels of industrialization. The direct influence of father's status on son's occupational status is very weak in Taiwan. A large part of father's influence on son's status works through son's education. That is, father's status affects son's educational attainment which in turn influences son's occupational achievement. In fact, the data indicate that both the effect of father's status on son's education and the effect of son's education on son's occupation are relatively high in Taiwan.

The equalitarian feature of the social mobility process in Taiwan is probably the result of Chinese culture which stresses the importance of education throughout history. The Nationalist Government in Taiwan makes special efforts to preserve the traditional Chinese values. Especially Confucianism, which emphasizes the significance of education, is upheld in Taiwan. The ideology may have resulted in the impressive pattern of the social mobility process in Taiwan.

The pattern of the effect of father's occupation on son's occupation is neither consistent with the linear prediction of Proposition 1 nor with the convex prediction of Modified Proposition 1. The data suggest that culture may influence the social mobility process in a society. However the present study does not refute that industrialization has a relationship with the direct effect of father's occupational status on son's occupation. Nor does it resolve the issue as to whether the relationship in linear or curvilinear. Therefore, there is no reason to reject Lin and Yauger's modified proposition which suggests a convex curvilinear relationship.

The data on the effect of education on occupation seem to fit Treiman's linear prediction better than Lin and Yauger's concave curvilinear line. However the effect in Taiwan is even stronger than that expected from a linear prediction. Again, this is probably due to culture.

The relationship of the effect of father's occupation on son's education to the degree of industrialization was predicted to be a negative linear line by Treiman and a positive linear line by Lin and Yauger. However, the data in this research suggest a convex curvilinear relationship. In underdeveloped countries, the effect of father's occupation on son's education is minimal, due to the low level of education in the general population. As societies progress, father's occupation gains influence on son's educational attainment when limited opportunities for higher education appear. Social origin reduces its dominance over son's educational attainment, due to the extension of compulsory public education and the increasing availability of higher education.

The curvilinear finding may be considered as a synthesis of the seemingly contradictory propositions suggested by Treiman and Lin and Yauger. It seems that Treiman was examining the change in societies from middle levels of development to advanced levels. On the other hand, Lin and Yauger's proposition appears to be meant for societies progressing from underdeveloped to middle levels. They considered Great Britain and the U.S. as societies at middle levels of industrialization, and thus proposed a positive linear prediction.

In short, this study suggests the following propositions.
1. Adoption of Lin and Yauger's Modified Proposition 1:

The direct effect of father's occupational status on son's occupational status is curvilinearly (convex) related to the degree of industrialization.

2. Adoption of Treiman's Proposition 2:
The more industrialized a society, the stronger the direct effect of an individual's own education on his occupational achievement.

3. Synthesis of Treiman's Proposition 3 and Lin and Yauger's Modified Proposition 3:
The effect of father's occupational status on son's educational attainment is curvilinearly (convex) related to the degree of industrialization.

4. Culture has a significant effect on all of the above three effects in the social mobility process.

The comparative analysis in this study can only be considered exploratory. It by no means makes any definitive conclusion about macrotheories of social mobility. However the finding has cast some doubts on previous propositions about the relationship between social mobility process and the degree of industrialization. In addition, it suggested some possible cultural effects. Further comparative research is in order. A wider range of data points should be included in the study. Different measures of levels of industrialization may be used to test whether the same patterns persist. More rigorous methods should be used in assessing the patterns. Until then, the propositions can only be considered tentative. Nevertheless, the present study carries us one step further toward an empirically based global theory of social mobility.

5.   Sex, Values, and Change on Taiwan

Sheldon Appleton

Despite the world-wide surge of interest in the social roles and values of women, very little data-based work has appeared on the values held by men and women in Taiwan. The reasons for this are not difficult to find. Because survey research is in its infancy in Taiwan, surveys dealing with the values of individuals have been conducted relatively infrequently. Since even these were designed primarily to probe ethnic (that is, Taiwanese-Mainlander) or status differences rather than sex differences, value differences between men and women often have not been reported at all or have been merely mentioned in passing. Some of these surveys, moreover, suffer from a number of methodological deficiencies.

Methods

In this study an effort will be made to take another look at some of the studies relevant to values which have been carried out on Taiwan, to see what they can tell us about the relationship between sex and values among the island's residents. This will be done both by reviewing and reinterpreting previously published data, and, in some cases, by reprocessing the original data sets in search of further insight into the changing values of men and women on Taiwan. These techniques of analysis have advantages as well as disadvantages. The principal disadvantage, of course, is that the surveys cited were not designed specifically to explore sex-based differences in values, and therefore did not include a number of questions that would have been very helpful to the present analysis. The main advantage is that by using a number of independently conducted surveys findings emerging from one survey can often be tested against those from another. Especially in view of the methodological problems involved in these surveys, it is necessary to look for patterns supported by more than one survey whenever possible, and to view with caution interpretation sug-

From Richard W. Wilson, Amy Auerbacher Wilson, and Sidney L. Greenblatt, (eds.), *Value Change in Chinese Society* (New York: Praeger, 1979), pp. 185-201. The author is on the faculty at Oakland University, Rochester, Michigan. Copyright 1979 by Praeger. Used with permission of the publisher.

gested by only a single survey. Some of the surveys involved — virtually all of them conducted over the decade from 1966 to 1975 — focus on Taiwan's student population, constituting more than a quarter of the island's more than 16 million residents, or on residents of the capital city alone, rather than on the population of the island as a whole.

The only available survey that attempted to inquire about the values of almost all of the residents of Taiwan was conducted by a missionary, Wolfgang Grichting, in 1970. This was an islandwide stratified sampling of household rather than individuals, which probably underrepresents some population groupings — notably soldiers and young people. Since it was carried out with government cooperation, the responses given by those interviewed no doubt reflected a good deal of caution. Few of the responses that will be reported, however — mostly those dealing with simple demographic information and with values — seem so politically sensitive as to be susceptible to major distortion on this account. In any event, the results can be compared with responses to paper-and-pencil questionnaires administered by several investigators to students whose anonymity appears to have been credibly guaranteed.

TABLE 1
Rankings of Values by Men and Women in Taiwan

	Average Rank	
Values	Men	Women
Family security	2.6	2.3
A world at peace	2.7	3.1
Inner harmony	3.4	3.2
A comfortable life	4.1	3.7
True friendship	4.7	5.3
Social recognition	5.7	5.9
Faith	7.0	6.8
Religion	7.0	6.8
Happy afterlife	7.7	7.8

Notes: The highest possible ranking is 1; the lowest is 9, Rho = .98. The sample consisted of 973 men and 901 women. Source omitted.

Probably the most direct question regarding values posed to this islandwide household sample utilized an adapted version of Rokeach's "terminal values" inventory. Respondents were asked to rank nine values in order of how important each was a guiding principle in their lives. The results are given in Table 1. From this table can be inferred two main themes that will appear repeatedly in the data. First, the stated value preferences of male and female Taiwan residents are very much alike — more so, for instance, than the preferences of those in differing ethnic or level-of-education groupings. Second, such differences as do appear seem to involve the traditional *nei/wai* (inside/outside) distinction in sex roles among Chinese: the women's role centering on home and family and matters within the household; the man's on matters outside of the home. Thus, the women in Grichting's sample assigned a marginally more important role to "family security," and the men to "a world at peace." Men also ranked "friendship" and "social recognition" slightly higher, though in these cases the differences are too small to be conclusive.

Findings
Young men — as might be expected, since many of them are unmarried — place less emphasis than their elders on "family security" and more on "friendship" and "inner harmony." (Only 2 percent of the women in this household sample, as compared to 7 percent of the men, had never been married.) Both young men (under 30) and old (over 55) put greater stress on "social recognition" than do the middle-aged. Younger women, too, value "fam-

ily security'' a bit less than their seniors, but for them, unlike the men, this value comes first at every age. Younger women also put more value (though still less than young men) on ''friendship'' and give less priority to ''a comfortable life'' than do older women, more heavily involved in family raising. Beyond these relatively small variations, differences in value rankings by age group for each sex are not large (though they are a bit greater than the differences between the sexes). The limitations on the data available make it possible to discover to what extent these differences may be attributed to generational or ''life cycle'' effects, respectively.

Responses to a different version of the Rokeach terminal and instrumental values inventories, administered to college and vocational high school students on Taiwan by the author, are quite similar to those of Grichting's sample (see Tables 2 and 3.) Again, especially among the high school students, who are less atypical then the college students of the

TABLE 2
Rankings of Values by Vocational High School
Students in Taiwan

	Average Rank	
	Men (N = 249)	Women (N = 146)
Terminal values [1]		
A world at peace	3.5	3.6
National security	3.8	3.6
Freedom	4.2	4.1
Equality	5.0	5.5
A meaningful life	5.5	5.5
True friendship	5.8	5.6
Wisdom	6.4	6.1
Respect for others	7.5	7.3
Respect from others	7.8	7.1
A comfortable life	8.5	9.0
Maturity	10.0	10.5
Salvation	10.1	10.0
Instrumental Values [2]		
Responsible	4.4	4.6
Clean	5.1	5.5
Honorable	5.6	5.3
Trustful	5.7	5.8
Polite	6.2	5.6
Broadminded	6.3	7.0
Cooperative	6.4	7.1
Courageous	6.8	6.3
Forgiving	7.1	6.5
Self-Disciplined	7.4	7.8
Tender	7.8	7.3
Intellectual	9.1	8.9

1. Defined as ''an idealized goal or end-state of existence.''
2. Defined as ''an idealized mode of conduct.''

Notes: Data are for combined groups of students from the same school surveyed at two different times, three years apart. The sample consisted of 249 men and 146 women. The highest possible ranking is 1; the lowest is 12. For the terminal values, Rho = .98; for the instrumental values, Rho = .91. Sources omitted.

population at large, the value rankings assigned by male and female students correspond closely to one another. There are somewhat greater differences between the rankings of high school and college students of the same sex, and between those of two groups of students at the same high school surveyed three years apart. The main differences in terminal values between the two sexes are the slightly higher rankings assigned to "equality," "a comfortable life," and "maturity" by the men, and to "respect from others" by the women. The last of these may have a sex-related connotation for these young women — that is, it may include respect for their conformity to traditional sexual mores which are strongly affirmed on Taiwan.

Among the college students, women again value "respect from others" slightly more, while men clearly place a higher value on "equality" and "a comfortable life." Some other differences show up as well. The male students put a higher value on "national security" and "freedom," consistent with the *nei/wai* distinction. The women's higher ranking of "wisdom" and "friendship" seems related less to sex-role differences than to their particular position in life — what is sometimes called the "life cycle" effect. Many fewer women than men get as far as universities in Taiwan.

TABLE 3
Rankings of Values by College and University Students in Taiwan

	Average Rank	
	Men (N = 450)	Women (N = 304)
Terminal Values [1]		
National security	4.1	4.9
Freedom	4.2	4.5
A meaningful life	4.6	4.4
A world at peace	5.0	5.3
Equality	5.5	6.3
Wisdom	5.5	4.4
True friendship	5.5	4.8
Respect from others	7.2	6.2
Respect for others	7.5	7.6
A comfortable life	7.5	8.3
Salvation	10.4	9.8
Maturity	10.8	11.1
Instrumental Values [2]		
Responsible	3.8	3.9
Honorable	4.7	4.9
Trustful	5.1	4.9
Clean	6.3	6.2
Forgiving	6.8	6.5
Polite	6.8	6.5
Cooperative	6.9	7.3
Self-Disciplined	7.1	7.4
Broadminded	7.2	8.2
Courageous	7.3	8.5
Tender	7.4	6.0
Intellectual	8.4	7.6

1. Defined as "an idealized goal or end-state of existence."
2. Defined as "an idealized mode of conduct."
    Notes: The highest possible ranking is 1; the lowest is 12. For the terminal values, Rho = .79; for the instrumental values, Rho = .77. Sources omitted.

The following table, computed from Grichting, shows the levels of education of respondents in his household sample:

	Under 35		Over 35	
	Men (N = 139)	Women (N = 278)	Men (N = 834)	Women (N = 623)
Percent with more than 6 years schooling	44	25	32	14
Percent with more than 12 years schooling	12	4	8	1

Women who do get as far as the university are likely to be from higher status families, and to put a special value on learning (note also their higher ranking of "intellectual" among the instrumental values). They also may have a special need for friends (usually fellow students) to help them navigate their way through the basically male university world. The high school women also valued "wisdom," "friendship," and "intellectual" slightly more than their male counterparts. After they have married and become involved in raising families, however, Grichting's data show that women put a lower value on "friendship" than men, and report having fewer friends as well. After age 55, this difference on the value assigned to "friendship" diminishes.

The higher rankings assigned to "tender," "polite," and "forgiving" by both college and high school women, and to "courageous" by the college males are certainly consistent with traditional sex roles. The greater male preference for "broadminded" is largely a function of Mainlander/Taiwanese differences rather than sex differences per se. Mainlanders ranked "broadminded" last among these twelve instrumental values, while Taiwanese ranked it eighth, and at both the high school and college levels a much greater proportion of the female than of the male students were Mainlanders. The self-selection process involved in the choice of the high school women to attend a vocational school may be reflected in the relatively high value they put on "courageous." The higher rankings of "a comfortable life" by *male* high school and college students and by the *women* in Grichting's islandwide sample are not as inconsistent as they seem. For this value, the key explanatory variable is socioeconomic status (SES). The higher the SES, for both students and the general population, the lower the ranking of "a comfortable life." Women, as noted, have higher status than their male fellow-students at the high school and college levels, but somewhat lower status in the population at large. Finally, women, especially higher-status Mainlander women, are more likely than men to be Christian. Thus the greater emphasis on "salvation" among the college women.

Other findings from surveys of adult Taiwan residents seem consistent with the pattern described above. There are a close correspondence between the responses of men and women to Grichting's questions on the goals of a college education and the meaning of success. Both groups were likely to cite specialized skills as the main thing to be gained from college, though women were a bit more likely to mention earning power and men to cite personal qualities or good citizenship. Similarly, both groupings defined success primarily in terms of education itself, with women more likely to refer to career success, while men were a bit more likely to mention development of individual talents, good citizenship, and independence. The differences in each case, however, were very small, and are accounted for largely by the generally higher status and educational levels of the men. In accordance with Maslow's theories, lower-status groups on Taiwan seem to put more emphasis on lower-order needs (money, career, family security, a comfortable life), while higher-status groups, having achieved a greater measure of these, put more emphasis on "self-actualizing" values (world peace, inner harmony, citizenship, personal development). The greater emphasis by men on good citizenship, however, remains even when education is controlled.

Ronald Inglehart reports similar findings for the United States, Western European nations, and Japan. Men are more likely to have "post-industrial" values, such as protecting freedom of speech, and women to have "materialist" values, such as fighting crime and inflation. The differences by sex are smallest in the United States, largest in Japan. Except in the United States, women were also found more likely than men to vote for conservative political parties.

These findings seem related to the tendency previously noted for women to be somewhat more traditional than men in their outlooks. Thus the women in Grichting's islandwide sample were more likely to say that obedience should be emphasized most in child rearing, while men were more likely to stress independence. Analysis of the data shows that this difference is a function of educational differences, however, and is virtually eliminated when level of education is controlled.

Studies of schoolchildren point in the same direction. Richard Wilson found minimal differences in the value orientations of third, fifth, and seventh grade boys and girls with respect to autocentricity (inner-directedness) versus heterocentricity (other-directedness). Girls were slightly more inner-directed, but differences were very small. Analyzing the responses of a large, randomly drawn, islandwide sample of 11-to 19-year old students, Gerald McBeath found women students less likely to identify failure to recover the mainland as Taiwan's most urgent national problem, and more likely to cite social disorder. The responses of lower-status women students less likely than men to follow public affairs in the media or discuss them with others. Grichting found the same to be true among his islandwide household sample. These behavioral differences reflect the *nei/wai* distinction referred to earlier.

Mechanisms
The pattern noted here — very similar responses by men and women, except for differences in attitudes toward appropriate sex-role behavior — appears also in responses by residents of the city of Taipei to Robert Mitchell's questions concerning what gives them the most satisfaction, what people must have in order to be looked up to and admired, and what they worried about most. Thus, though both sexes said their children gave them the most satisfaction, women (39 percent) were more likely to give this response than men (27 percent), and to mention their spouse (25 percent of the women; 14 percent of the men). Men more often (17 percent, to 3 percent of the women) said that work gave them the most satisfaction. Men worried most about jobs and money, women about their children. And though both men and women agreed (44 – 45 percent) that being willing to help others was most important in winning the admiration of others, men more often mentioned having a respectable job (15 percent, to 6 percent for women), and women being a good family person (12 percent, to 5 percent of men).

Some of Mitchell's questions to Taipei residents help in understanding something of the consequences of these differences in values. Women were much more likely to hold lower-status jobs, and to earn less. But they were no more likely than men to say they were unhappy, or to score high on an index of hostility. Men were more likely to feel it was personally important to them to be successful, and to be dissatisfied with their present living situations and with what they have achieved in life. Thus the very fact that they seemed to set higher goals for themselves than did women seemed to lead men to greater disappointment. Women, on the other hand, appeared to internalize their frustrations. They were more likely than men to feel they could not control the course of their own lives (57 percent of the women and 41 percent of the men expressed this feeling), to withdraw from both home and work roles, to have low self-esteem, to worry, and to report poorer physical health and symptoms of emotional strain.

Behavioral Evidence
Behavioral evidence of the influence of traditional sex roles in Taiwan can also be found in government-issued statistics on educational enrollments and employment. At every educational level, more males than females are enrolled as students and employed as teachers. The higher the level, and in the universities, the higher the rank, the greater the ratio of males to females. Thus, in 1973, 49 percent of primary-school students, and 45 percent of

the teachers were women, while at the college and university level only 37 percent of the students and 25 percent of the full-time faculty (9 percent of the full and associate professors) were women. Of the small number of graduate degrees (fewer than 1,000) awarded in 1972, only 12 percent were received by women. It is also worthy of note than unemployment has been higher among women than among men at every educational level. Table 4 shows the percentage of women enrolled in various subject fields in colleges and universities and in vocational high schools. Women were grossly overrepresented in the humanities, nursing, home economics, and commerce (often secretarial), and grossly underrepresented in the natural sciences and engineering and in industrial programs.

However, the same educational statistics that give evidence of the continuing strength of traditional sex roles yield evidence as well of gradual change. Over the nine years from 1964 to 1973, the percentage of enrolled female students increased from 37 to 43 percent in high schools, from 29 to 37 percent in colleges and universities, and from 28 to 40 percent in the prestigious national universities. Over the same period the percentage of women teachers went up from 38 to 45 at the primary level, from 23 to 39 at the secondary level, and from 18 to 25 at the college and university level. In absolute terms, the number of women obtaining higher levels of education is even more dramatic. In 1965, fewer than 3,200 women graduated from colleges or universities. In 1972, just seven years later, 17,800 graduated.

This change in educational and job opportunities for women is reflected also in responses to the surveys previously cited. The younger respondents in Grichting's islandwide sample, for instance, were more likely to discuss a variety of matters with their spouses and to share in the making of family decisions. Both men and women considered level of education an important factor in choosing a wife as well as a husband; and both sons and

TABLE 4
Women Enrolled in Various Courses of Study in College and Universities and in Vocational High Schools, 1973

Course of Study	Percent Women
College and university	
Humanities	64
Education	42
Social sciences	34
Law	29
Agriculture	29
Fine arts	25
Medical science	21
Natural sciences	16
Engineering	2
All courses	37
Vocational high school	
Home economics	100
Commerce	88
Nursing and midwifery	79
Agriculture	21
Marine products	9
Industry	4
All courses	45

Source omitted.

daughters were widely expected to play an important role in selecting their own marriage partners.

Even in personality characteristics, change was apparent. Kenneth Abbott administered the California Personality Inventory to samples of adolescents and their parents in a district of Taipei. On almost every scale, males of both generations scored higher than females. But the differences between adolescent men and women were in almost every case smaller than sex differences in their parents' generation on scales measuring poise, self-assurance, personal adequacy, sense of responsibility, achievement potential, intellectual efficiency, and so on.

Attitude Toward Social Change

Table 5 shows the responses of men and women in Grichting's islandwide sample to a series of questions asking them, first, to assess the changes in a number of relationships over the last ten years; second, to indicate their view of expected further changes in these relationships over the following decade; and, finally, to compare Taiwan with the United States with respect to each of these relationships. For each of these nine relationships, more people thought there had been some change than felt that matters had remained the same; and a majority of those who saw a change believed it to have been a change for the better. The same was true for expectations of future change. And in every case, about two-third to five-sixths of those reponding said Taiwan was superior to the United States with respect to these relationships.

TABLE 5

Attitudes of Taiwan Men and Women toward Changes in Social Relationships

Relationship	Attitude Toward Change Over Past 10 Years [1]		Attitude Toward Change Over Next 10 Years [2]		Comparison of Taiwan to the United States [3]	
	Men	Women	Men	Women	Men	Women
Husband-wife	22	27	18	27	70	65
Father-children	9	20	17	22	74	75
Mother-children	14	24	20	24	75	77
Siblings	11	22	17	20	73	74
Boys-girls	14	18	12	16	63	63
Neighbors	4	10	10	14	66	70
Teacher-student	3	8	11	13	60	63
Employer-employee	10	10	3	15	55	58
People in general	−1[4]	5	7	11	61	63

1. Percentage seeing favorable change in relationships, minus percentage seeing unfavorable change.
2. Percentage predicting favorable change in relationships, minus percentage predicting unfavorable change.
3. Percentage rating Taiwan better on relationships, minus percentage rating the United States better.
4. Minus sign indicates a plurality of negative responses.
   Note: Sample consisted of 843 men and 738 women. Source omitted.

In almost every case, women were more positive than men about the changes that had taken place over the past ten years, and more optimistic about the changes expected over the next decade. Both men and women were most positive — women even more so than men — about changes in the relationships between husbands and wives; and the women, but not the men, were more hopeful about likely future changes in this relationship. The other relationships viewed most positively and hopefully by women also involved the family — relationships between mothers and children, fathers and children, and among siblings. In particular, men were far less positive than women about both past and anticipated changes in relations between fathers and their children. There were actually slightly more men who felt that relations among "people in general" had changed for the worse than for the better — the only negative entry in the entire table — whereas at least a small plurality of women believed the reverse. Since this was the most general relationship inquired about, it is perhaps the one most likely to tap vague misgivings over the trend of developments. Only a very small plurality of men were hopeful about expected future changes in relations among "people in general."

In all but two cases, women were at least slightly more likely than men to feel, on balance, that Taiwan is superior to the United States with regard to these relationships. The two exceptions are boy-girl relations, where there is no sex difference in the responses, and husband-wife relations — the only instance in which women show more receptivity to the American model than men. Men were also more likely than women to believe that the United States had something to offer Taiwan in every one of the ten areas inquired about by Grichting: morality, art, law, religion, medicine, education, industry and technology, economics, political ideas, and social welfare. Though consistent with a greater *wai* orientation on the part of men, these differences are large attributable to men's higher educational levels.

An interpretation consistent with these figures would suggest that some change is taking place in relationships between men and women on Taiwan and among other family members — change in the direction of the more equalitarian Western model. This change seems to be received fairly well, though perhaps with some misgivings, by men, and for the most part quite favorably by women.

The surveys of Martin M. C. Yang in rural Taiwan, and the studies by Mitchell and Abbott already cited, have documented some of these changes in the structure of the Chinese family under the impact of modernization. "There has been a . . . displacement of the most intensive relationship in the family from father-son (ideal) to mother-son (acutal) to husband-wife," Abbott reported. The change in class status of many familites also leads to changes in family influence and communicaiton patterns, since these seem to be class-based. The traditional misery of young women's situations is somewhat mitigated, and the emotional distance between fathers and sons lessens, leaving more room for emotional warmth between them. Nevertheless, these changes have created some problems for the personality development of Chinese young people, somewhat akin to those felt by Western youth.

A similar set of questions asked of a group of vocational high school students by the author offers some striking support for this interpretation. In the same year that Grichting's survey was conducted, these students were asked to compare contemporary Taiwan with the United States and traditional China on a number of dimensions. Table 6 gives men's and women's reponses to these questions. As noted earlier, the women in this group are somewhat more "select" than their male fellow students, simply because it is less likely that a women will continue her education as long as a man. These students, both men and women, are above average in educational attainment for their age group (less than sixth of Grichting's sample [a fifth of those under 35] had received *any* senior high school education), though, as vocational high school students, they are scarcely candidates for membership in the island's socioeconomic or educaitonal elite. Their value choices have been discussed above in some detail (see Table 2). The main difference between the value rankings of these students and those of a group surveyed at the same school three years before was the greater emphasis placed the later (1970) students — and especially the women — on "a meaningful life" and "broadminded" at the expense of such traditional virtues as "polite" and "courageous." Note that a meaningful life was rated even higher by the college students surveyed (Table 3), and highest of all — at the top of their rankings — by college women.

Perhaps the most striking difference revealed in Table 6, consistent with the analysis of Grichting's data, is the tendency of women to be more positively oriented to the present, and less positively oriented toward the traditional model, on 10 of the 11 dimensions included (the single exception in commercial abilities). For a number of the dimensions, including human relations and life aims, the size of the difference is quite large.

TABLE 6
Vocational High School Students' Comparisons of Their Own
Society (Taiwan) with Traditional China and the United States

Dimension	Taiwan Compared with Traditional China		Taiwan Compared with the United States	
	Men	Women	Men	Women
Father-son relations	−28	−3	86	90
Teacher-student relations	−61	−28	38	20
Friendship relations	−34	−16	49	42
Superior-subordinate relations	11	29	−24	−9
Commercial abilities	63	54	−30	−59
Ability to manage large organizations	69	77	−65	−78
Life aims	46	74	18	−11
Civic-mindedness	−3	16	−45	−29
Human relations	−43	3	51	41
Group cooperation	5	28	−25	−21
Relations between government officials and the people	14	37	−36	−22

Notes: for each dimension, figures show percentage preferring contemporary Taiwan, minus percentage preferring traditional China or the United States, respectively. Minus signs indicate a plurability of reponses favoring traditional China or the United States. The sample consisted of 183 men and 78 women.
Source: Survey data collected by the author.

In comparing their own society with that of the United States, both men and women preferred the Chinese pattern of interpersonal relationships (father-son relations; teacher-student relations; friendship relations; and human relations in general). Both preferred the Western (U.S.) model in business-related and civic areas (commercial abilities; abilty to manage large organizations; superior-subordinate relations; civic-mindedness; group cooperation; and relations between government officials and the people). All of this is consistent with the *ti yong* model of nineteenth-century Chinese reformers: Western values for practical use, Chinese values for fundamentals. One of the sharpest divisions shows up on the dimension most relevant to values — life aims. A majority of the male students felt that life aims on Taiwan today are better than what they believe those aims to be in the United States. A majority of the women, on the other hand, believed that American life aims were preferable to those in their own society.

Similarly, women were likely to feel even more distant from traditional China's life aims than men. Two-thirds of the men, but almost nine-tenths of the women, believed that life aims in Taiwan today were better than those in traditional China, and women were almost twice as likely (39 percent to 22 percent) to say contemporary life aims were *much* better. This is particularly interesting because, as noted, survey responses show women to be generally most traditional and less "Westernized" or "modern" than men. For this reason, it seems quite probable that the responses described in the last several paragraphs are indications of a positive response on the part of many women — especially the young — to the gradual opening-up of greater educational and career opportunities for women on Taiwan, and to the development of somewhat more equalitarian relations between the sexes in familial and personal relationships in general.

Summary and Discussion

A review of available empirical studies and educational statistics has led to a number of inferences and interpretations concerning the relationship among sex, values, and change on Taiwan. The expressed values of men and women on Taiwan were found to be very similar, with such values as "family security," "a world at peace," and "inner harmony" near the top of their value hierarchies. Marginal differences were largely consistent with traditional sex-role expectations and the distinction between *nei* and *wai:* women gave higher priority to home and family, men to matters outside the home — friends, the community, the nation, the world at large.

There were some indications that the results of these value differences and the social context in which they are embedded created emotional strains of somewhat different types for women and men. While neither sex seemed clearly happier than the other, the higher value put by men on the achievement of success outside the home appeared to make them more subject to disappointment in themselves and feelings of failure. Women, in contrast, seemed more likely to resign themselves to the difficulties inherent in their role expectations to turn their frustrations inward in the form of low self-esteem, poorer physical health, symptoms of emotional strain, withdrawal from home and work roles, and feelings of inability to control the course of their lives. Some evidence was presented, however, that sex roles have been gradually changing in Taiwan in the wake of rapid economic growth and Westernization. These changes have opened up somewhat greater — though still far from equal — economic opportunities for women, and have led to more equalitarian relations between the sexes in the family, at school, and in the society as a whole. Especially among young people, there were indications that women were more receptive to these changes than men and more hopeful of continued change in a positive direction — that is, in the direction of Western models of relationships between the sexes. The young also showed some tendency, with increasing education, to emphasize self-actualizing values ("inner harmony," "a meaningful life") more, and material values less, than their elders.

One disquieting factor in the course of social change in Taiwan has been the more negative response to social change on the part of the best educated, most elite (and disportionately male) segment of the population. This elite seems uncomfortable not only with the prospect of future changes, which might jeopardize their places at the top, but even with many of the changes that have already taken place, and, in fact, often have been instrumental in their attainment of elite status. This group seems to have passed through the initial states of Westernization, when rising living standards, growing career opportunities, and the loosening of rigidly hierarchical social ties bring new satisfactions. They have begun to experience some of the negative aspects of Western social life as well — disruption of family ties, uncertainty in social relations, the perils of urban life, lessened "respect" from others, and some general alienation from traditional moorings. At the same time, in accordance with Maslow's theories, their achievement of basic material needs has led them, as noted, to place a new emphasis on "self-actualizing" values that involve states of inner being and are less readily fulfilled on Taiwan. As women increasingly gain entry to this elite, the form their reaction to this dilemma will take remains to be seen.

In the longer run, the gradual changes in relations between the sexes that have been described here are bound to continue to affect the dynamics of the family system, the personality development of children, and the attitudes of Taiwan's residents toward their political system. These changes, in turn, are likely to pose serious social and political problems for Taiwan, its government, and its people. Material needs, after all, are more easily met by governmental and social action than the "self-actualizing" values that seem to emerge in industrializing societies.

All that is certain is that these changes are already in motion, and that given the unwillingness of the populace to return to the living standards and personal constraints of traditional times, the old ways cannot be expected to return. The impact of Western modes of interpersonal relations on Taiwan's society and values are only beginning to be felt. Whether the island's people will be able to work out a distinctive and viable response to the clash of Chinese and Western values — and whether the vicissitudes of international politics will permit them to do so — remain very much open and fascinating questions as the decade of the 1980s comes into view.

6.   Transformation of the Chinese People

Kuo-shu Yang

For ethnic, geographic and historic reasons, the Chinese have been a people possessing unique characteristics. These characteristics are expressed not only in obvious *objective* culture such as literature, arts, architecture, implements, laws and institutions, but also in *subjective* culture such as recognition, thought, attitudes, values, needs and character. The former is a "dead" culture, whereas the latter is a "live" one. The Chinese people's peculiar "live culture" has led to this unique behavior and activities, and finally produced their peculiar "dead culture." That is to say, the unique subjective culture of the Chinese people causes their unique objective culture. From this point of view, the characteristics of the subjective culture seem to be more fundamental than those of the objective culture. Furthermore, material culture dies out easily, whereas spiritual culture can last for generations through the process of social change. In other words, the culture which can continually show the Chinese people's uniqueness is the spiritual one, not the material one.

In the last several thousand years, China has encountered numerous upheavals, but its people did not change much in the domain of subjective culture. Major changes occurred only in the last two hundred years, when China encountered unprecedented crises, during which the Chinese people responded to humiliations and setbacks with a stream of modernizing efforts. Despite the twists and turns, the tide of modernization has drastically changed some specific aspects of Chinese society and the people's way of life, especially in Taiwan. No matter in what society it takes place, modernization is a whole process, in which changes not only affect every social stratum but individuals as well; not only objective culture, but also subjective culture. In the Chinese modernization process, the changes affecting the social strata and objective culture are more perceptible, but we lack a systematic understanding of the changes affecting the individuals and our subjective culture. What are the changes that have been made in the thoughts, concepts, manner, motivation, and dispositions of the Chinese? Do the Chinese people at present still keep their original characteristics in their subjective culture? What are the advantages and disadvantages of these changes for the livelihood of the Chinese? What gains or losses did these changes bring to the development of the Chinese society, economy, politics, etc.? These important questions are worthy of serious study.

First of all, let us discuss the first two questions I raised in the previous paragaph: What changes have the Chinese made in their mentality and behavior in the course of modernization? Do they still maintain their original characteristics? Numerous studies have been made in Taiwan and Hongkong in the behavioral sciences, to explore the effects of modernization on the individual's mentality and behavior. Beginning in 1969, several of my colleagues and I have conducted almost 20 such empirical studies with Chinese adults in Taiwan. From the results of these studies, we can infer that modernization has at least caused the following changes mentality and behavior:

1. The Chinese now care less about what other people think of them and increasingly value and follow their own views.

2. The Chinese have become less indecisive, modest, and subservient, and are more self-assertive.

3. They show less authoritarian attitudes, including conventionalism, blind obedience, belief in fatalism, lack of imagination, identification with authority, and suspicion and even antagonism toward others, and have moved toward egalitarianism.

4. They now believe that their well-being is determined less by external factors (fate, opportunities, personal connections, powerful groups, etc.) and more by controllable factors (ability, efforts, and other personal conditions).

Abbreviated translations from *Taiwan Hsin-sheng Pao*, May 3, 1976. The author is Professor of National Taiwan University and Research Fellow in the Institute of Ethnology of Academia Sinica, Taipei, Taiwan.

5. They believe that, in man's relationship with nature, "man should harness nature" instead of that "man should follow nature."

6. They think equality and individualism are more important than subordination in human relationships.

7. They now put more emphasis on the present and the future than on the past.

8. In terms of one's values in life, they attach more importance to achievements and activities than to meditation and moral cultivation.

9. They are now more tolerant toward different creeds, opinions, and values.

10. They are more adaptable and flexible in thought and behavior and also more curious.

11. They are more active, easy-going, and more open-minded, and less timid, shy, and suspicious.

12. They tend more than before to blame other people and things for their failures.

13. They are happier and more satisfied and have fewer worries.

Of course, modernization has caused more changes in the mentality and bahavior of the Chinese than those mentioned above. But these preliminary results of the studies show the major trends of the changes. First, we notice that several of the changes (especially numbers 3, 5, 7, 9, 11) are related to humanistic attitudes. They show that the Chinese emphasize more and more man's intrinsic worth, equality, and the importance of man's potentiality, desires, and happiness. In other words, in the process of modernization, the Chinese are not paying more attention to humanistic values. Another important direction of change is the emphasis on individualistic orientations, which can be seen in changes 1, 2, 4, and 6. The major characteristics of this trend are individual dignity, honesty in personal feelings, and self-realization. People are less likely to yield to pressures and neglect their own importance. The third major trend is the Chinese people's increasing ability to adapt to changes (see number 10). Change is one of the most important characteristics in modern life, and in the course of modernization the Chinese people seem to be more malleable and willing to change. Another trend is that the Chinese feel happier. The more a society is modernized, the more its people can adjust their emotions and their state of mind to the outside world.

The above trends of change among the Chinese are similar to the findings in other countries, for instance, A. Inkeles' findings about Chile, Argentina, Israel, Nigeria, India and Pakistan; K. A. Kahl's about Brazil and Mexico; L. W. Doob's about African countries; and J. L. M. Dawson's about Western African countries and Australia. The results of these studies reveal that, in the course of modernization, despite the differences in geographical locations and people's traditional cultures, the major trends of change in people's mentality and behavior are almost the same. That is to say, the more the society is modernized, the more the people emphasize individualistic orientations and humanistic values, and the greater the degree of happiness and adaptability. The changing trends in the Chinese people's "subjective culture" show no significant difference from those of other peoples in the world. We can also say that in the course of modernization, all the peoples in the world manifest greater commonalities, while their differences gradually fade away. In fact, in "subjective culture," the contemporary Chinese people possess less and less of their original characteristics, and the effects of modernization have quietly paved the way for the emergence of a new "world man."

We have discussed changes of the Chinese people but have not made any value judgements on these changes. Since we Chinese have experienced something in the process of modernization and its results have directly affected our interests, we need to dwell more on a further question: Are these changes beneficial to the Chinese people? As we all know, any form of change can be either beneficial or harmful. In the course of modernization, the strengthening of our humanistic spirit, behavioral malleability, and mental health is, of course, helpful to us. But the ascent of individualistic orientations is not necessarily an advantage to us. For instance, if we continue to stress individualistic orientations, law and norms may eventually lose their effectiveness, and people may eventually seek only personal gains and neglect their social obligations and impinge upon the rights of others. In other words, extreme forms of individualistic pursuits will harm the larger interests of society. Therefore, democracy and the rule of law for the benefits of the majority need be promoted in a modern society, and individualistic pursuits should no be allowed to go against the interests of the public. All in all, only under democracy and the rule of law will the changes derived from modernization benefit the individuals and the public alike.

I would like to emphasize that in the course of modernization its overall effects have been beneficial for the Chinese people, and the Chinese people have felt happier in their daily life. Inkeles draws the same conclusion from his studies of six countries: modernization can promote one's social adaptability and mental health. People often say that the more the society is modernized, the more difficult it is for the people to adapt to it. This is not true. Judging from the results of the studies we have done, we should at least be optimistic about the consequence of modernization.

One last question: In the process of modernization, what are the effects of our changes in thought, manner, motivation and disposition on social, economic and political developments? Before we answer this question, we need to know the roles that social and personal factors play in the course of modernization as well as the relationship between these two factors. Generally speaking, in the beginning stage of modernization in a society, usually the well-planned political, economic, and educational policies of the government play a more important role. But after modernization has developed to a certain degree, further modernization calls for appropriate psychological and behavioral reorientations for its citizens. Therefore, if, due to certain reasons, the initial phase of modernization has failed to produce the kind of individual characteristics that are helpful to further the modernization process, than no great modernization can be finally achieved.

As stated throughout this essay, modernization has greatly changed the mentality and behavior of the Chinese people in Taiwan and these people have adapted well to modern life. With a modernized citizenry, there will be ample room for further development of the entire society. In psychological and behavioral changes, we stand to gain from a further strengthening of the following ages:

1. Motivation for achievement
2. Concept of "harnessing nature"
3. Sense of "deciding one's own fate"
4. Concept of stressing the importance of the present and the future
5. Adaptability to changes and reforms
6. Emphasis on egalitarian attitudes as opposed to authoritarianism
7. Need for independence and self-reliance
8. Emphasis on equality in human relations
9. Tolerance of different opinions and creeds

The above psychological and behavioral characteristics are beneficial to the further development of our nation and society. Among them, the first four are especially advantageous to economic and scientific developments, and the latter four to democracy.

To sum up, the first stage of modernization of Taiwan has formed a new type of "subjective culture" for the Chinese people. Chinese modernization has already passed the level of "*yung*" (application) and advanced to the level of "*ti*" (fundamental). Therefore, there is every reason to believe that, if we continue to make progress in our political, economic, and social developments, the Republic of China on Taiwan will become a fully modernized nation in the very near future.

7. Urbanization and Migration in Taiwan

Alden Speare, Jr.

In the first part of this paper we shall make use of published data from the household and migration records to examine briefly the history of city growth in Taiwan and to analyze the pattern of urbanization. In the second part we shall discuss the major streams of migration relevant to urbanization and study the characteristics of migrants in different streams using data obtained from a relatively large sample of migration and household records. We shall pay particular attention to the questions of how the nature of economic development in Taiwan affects the selectivity of migrants.

A Summary of Population Growth and City Growth 1920–70

Between 1920 and 1970, the population of Taiwan grew from 3.7 million to 14.7 million. Most of this increase was due to the natural increase of the Taiwanese who were living in Taiwan before the Japanese arrived in 1895 and who now comprise 85 percent of the population. During this century there has been very little migration to or from Taiwan. The main exception to this rule is the 1945–50 period when the Japanese who were living in Taiwan were repatriated to Japan, and Nationalist Chinese moved to Taiwan in the wake of the Communist takeover on the mainland.

The influx of the mainland Chinese in the late 1940s did not result in a substantial increase in the civilian population. Many replaced the Japanese who departed or persons who died as a result of World War II. Thus, the population growth rate during the 1940s was similar to the growth rates for the two preceding decades.

The rapid increase of the Taiwanese population has been primarily the result of a high birth rate and a falling death rate. The birth rate fluctuated between 40 and 45 births per 1,000 up to 1960, after which it declined, reaching 27 births per 1,000 in 1970. During the same period, the death rate declined from about 25 deaths per 1,000 in the period 1920–25 to above five per 1,000 in 1970. As a result, the Taiwanese population has grown at a rate of 2 or 3 percent per year since 1920.

In 1920, most of the available land in Taiwan was already in use, and in the following 50 years the total cultivated land increased only from 749,000 hectares to 905,000 hectares. Since few of the new additions to the labor force were able to obtain new lands to cultivate, the population growth has resulted in both an increase in the ratio of rural population to land and a shift toward nonagricultural employment. The proportion of the labor force employed in agriculture and fishing declined from 70 percent in 1920 to 35 percent in 1970.

The result has been that the cities have grown considerably faster than the countryside. Between 1920 and 1970 the population of the five major cities increased almost tenfold in comparison with the rest of Taiwan, which increased fourfold.

The average annual growth rates for each decade, shown in Table 1, indicate a continual flow of people to the cities. The city growth was greatest in the 1940s and 1950s when the internal rural-to-urban flow was augmented by the registration of migrants from the mainland of China who settle mainly in the cities. However, even in this period the bulk of the city growth was due to the natural increase of the city population and the migration of Taiwanese into the cities.

Migration has been greatest to the largest cities. For example, between 1961 and 1966 the average annual net migration rate was 15.9 per 1,000 population for the five largest cities, 12.5 for the other five cities over 100,000 and 4.9 for urban townships between 50,000 and 100,000. Smaller urban townships and rural townships lost population, on the average.

An examination of net migration rates for individual townships indicates that most of the net migration can be explained as a shift from agricultural to nonagricultural areas. In Table 2 we have shown the relationship between net in-migration during 1961–66 and various

Economic Development and Cultural Change, Vol. 22, No. 2 (January, 1974), pp. 302-319. The author is a professor at Brown University. Footnotes omitted.

TABLE 1
Population and Average Annual Growth Rates for Taiwan and Five Major Cities, 1920 – 70

Year	ALL TAIWAN		FIVE MAJOR CITIES*	
	Total	Taiwanese Only	Total	Taiwanese Only
	Population			
1920	3,655	3,467	356	253
1930	4,593	4,314	517	360
1940	5,872	5,510	751	575
1950	7,554	7,029	1,337	1,017
1960	10,792	9,513	2,237	1,600
1970	14,676	12,361	3,450	2,441
	Average Annual Growth Rate (%)			
1920 – 30	2.3	2.2	3.7	3.5
1930 – 40	2.5	2.4	3.7	4.7
1940 – 50	2.5	2.4	5.8	5.7
1950 – 60	3.6	3.0	5.1	4.5
1960 – 70	3.1	2.6	4.3	4.2

*Kaohsiung, Keelung, Taichung, Tainan, and Taipei. The 1970 population of Taipei has been adjusted to represent the population within the boundaries prior to the annexation of several townships in 1968. Source omitted.

charcteristics of townships of Taiwan. Although the zero-order correlations indicate that net in-migration is related to several variables such as distance to the nearest large city, density, and the percentage of males who had completed primary school, when all of these variables are entered into multiple regression the percentage of the male labor force in agriculture and fishing is the only variable with a substantial net relationship to migration. This variable alone accounts for 25 percent of the variance in the net migration rates. The addition of the four other variables increases the explained variance by only 2 percent. This fact is clearly reflected in the size of the β coefficients. The β coefficient for the percentage of the male labor force employed in agriculture and fishing is $-.51$, while all of the other β coefficients are .08 or smaller.

TABLE 2
Correlations of Selected Variables with Net Migration Rate for 260 Areas in Western Taiwan, 1961 – 66

	Zero-Order Correlation	Multiple-Regression β Coefficient
Percentage of male labor force 15 and over in agriculture and fishing, 1961	−.50	−.51
Percentage of males 12 and over who completed primary school, 1961	.29	.08
Log of density, 1961	.19	−.07
Total population, 1961	.15	−.08
Distance to nearest large city	−.21	−.08
Multiple R	...	.52
Multiple R^2	...	.27

Source omitted.

The average level of education of a township has little net effect on the net migration rate because the educational level is highly correlated with the proportion in agriculture and fishing ($r = -.49$). This does not mean that education has no effect on migration at the individual level. We shall show later that those people who leave a given township tend to be better educated than those who stay behind.

The failure of distance from major cities to show a significant independent relationship to net migration may be due to the excellent transportation facilities in Taiwan which make it relatively easy to travel from even the more distant areas. Few townships along the west coast of Taiwan are more than 2 hours' travel time by public transportation from one of the major cities. This means that the difference between towns close to a city and those farther away in either the costs of migration or the availability of information about opportunities in the city are relatively small.

Although we have clearly documented a pattern of migration from rural to urban areas, we cannot yet conclude that the major cause of this migration has been the growing population pressure on the limited land resources in rural areas. While there has been little increase in the amount of cultivated land since 1920, agricultural yield per acre has more than doubled. The more uniform distribution of land that resulted from the 1953 Land-to-the-Tiller Act increased the attractiveness of farming for small farmers. Many of the small farmers, who might otherwise have moved to the city when their limited land became insufficient to feed their growing families, may have been encouraged to remain on the land. Furthermore, some of the industrial growth occurred outside the largest cities. Approximately 44 percent of all men in Taiwan who were registered as employed in manufacturing lived outside the 10 largest cities in 1965. While some of these probably commuted to the city to work and others were employed in small-scale food processing, many were employed in industries located outside the cities.

An alternative to the rural push hypothesis which seems equally tenable is that people from rural areas have been attracted to the cities because they are able to earn higher wages and obtain types of employment which are more enjoyable than farming. To resolve this question, we shall turn to the analysis of the characteristics of migrants.

The Migration Record Sample

The Taiwan Provincial Civil Affairs Department, which maintains the household register, in 1967 began to collect routinely a random sample of approximately 2 percent of the migration record for persons who registered moves across township boundaries each month. This sample was representative of all migration in Taiwan with the exclusion of the migration of men serving in the military, the migration of a bride to the home of the groom (or the groom to the home of the bride) at the time of marriage, and the migration to or from the townships inhabited by aborigines.

The Civil Affairs Department also obtained a sample of household records for approximately 0.3 percent of the households in Taiwan, irrespective of migration status, in December 1967. The household record sample was collected in such a way as to make it highly comparable with the migration record sample. For both samples, a two-stage sampling plan was employed. In the first stage 57 townships were selected with probability proportional to size from 27 strata which controlled for level of urbanization, total fertility, and level of female education. the same 57 townships were used for both samples. In the second stage, sampling was carried out by applying sampling fractions to the townships selected in each strata in such a way as to equalize the overall selection probabilities across strata.

These two samples provide a valuable source of migration data. Since these two samples yield comparable data for migrants and the general population, we can compute migration rates for people with specific charcteristics by using the migration data for numerators and the general population data for denominators and applying appropriate weights. Because the samples are large, migration rates can be calculated for detailed subgroups of the population.

The analysis reported on in the remainder of this paper is based on original tabulations of the migration records for 1967 and 1968 and the household records collected at the end of

1967. These sources yielded a total sample of 28,297 migrants and 41,276 residents.

For many of the tabulations we have chosen to divide all migration into nine streams, representing all possible flows between the three major types of areas: cities, urban townships, and rural townships. The urban and rural townships are minor administrative units which typically consist of an urban area surrounded by a rural area. The townships which are designated as urban tend to be larger and more urban than the rural townships, although there is no clear dividing line. The small cities, with populations between 64,000 and 220,000, have been grouped with the urban townships because they could not be separated in the coded data. Although precincts of the large cities are separately identified, we have treated the major cities as single units and have excluded migration between precincts of the same city.

Out-migration rates for each migration stream and each subgroup of the population were calcuated as follows: $R_{ijk} = (M_{ijk}/P_{ij}) \times (F_p/F_m) \times 1,000$, with i = type of place of origin (city, urban township); j = type of place of destination; k = subgroup (e.g., age category, education category); R_{ijk} = migration rate for persons in the kth subgroup who moved from place type i to place type j; M_{ijk} = number of migrants in the kth subgroup who moved from plate type i to place type j; P_{ik} = Number of residents in the kth subgroup living at place type i; F_p = sampling fraction for the resident population; and F_m = sampling fraction for out-migrants.

Similar equations were used for other types of migration.

In addition to sampling errors, our rates are affected by errors in the migration records. These errors are of two types: coverage errors and errors in the characteristics reported on the records. The major source of coverage errors is the tendency of many people to delay migration registration, which results in the failure to count many migrants who moved during a specified period of time within the same period of time. If the volume and direction of migration and the average delay in registration do not change rapidly, then the effects of these delays tend to cancel out. In this case the only group of migrants not adequately represented in the migration records are those who remain only a short time at the destination and then return or move to another place. These migrants have no effect on measures of net migration.

Another source of coverage errors are migration records which correspond to legal transfers of residence where not actual migration took place. While these legal transfers tend to compensate numerically for those migrants who never register because they do not stay at the destination for a long time, the persons on these records do not necessarily have the same characteristics as those who never register.

The errors in reported characteristics vary considerably with the characteristic. Age is reliably reported because date of birth is copied from the original household record. The quality of data on educational attainment approximates that of the U.S. census. However, the reliability of the occupation and employment status data is very poor because these items tend to be copied from the household record and are not updated unless a special request is made. Thus, many men who move to the city from farms remain registered as farmers on the household record in the city and are recorded as farmers in any subsequent moves.

Migration Streams

In 1967 and 1968, an annual average of about 772,900 moves across city and township boundaries were reported to the registration offices. If each migrant moved only once during a given year, this would mean that about 6 percent of the population moved each year. However, since some migrants reported two or more moves during a year, the actual percentage of registered migrants in the population was somewhat lower.

The major net flows were from urban or rural townships to the cities. In addition, there was a smaller net flow from rural townships to urban townships, compensating in part for the net flow from urban townships to cities. This is similar to the stepwise migration observed by Ravenstein. Stepwise migration can occur either when rural migrants move to urban towns and later proceeed to the major cities, or when rural migrants move to urban towns to fill positions vacated by migrants from urban towns to the cities, or through a combination of these processes.

Because the designation of townships as either "urban" or "rural" no longer conforms to any clear rules, the use of this classification can provide only a crude measure of the degree of urbanization. A more precise measure based on the size of place would be desirable. This is possible for the 1968 migration record data where the exact place of origin and destination were coded rather than simply the type of place.

In classifying the origins and destinations of migrants in the 1968 sample, we have chosen to retain the urban town-rural town distinction, but to distinguish large urban towns from small urban towns and large rural towns from small rural towns. This results in a classification scheme with five levels of urbanization: large cities (all over 250,000); large urban townships and small cities (50,000 – 250,000); small urban townships (under 50,000); large rural townships (over 25,000); small rural townships (under 25,000). The urban townships over 50,000 can be considered to be primarily urban, whereas the smaller ones are more mixed urban and rural. The large rural townships are essentially in the same size category as the small urban towns. Only six of the 45 small urban towns were smaller than 25,000, and only three of the 98 large rural towns were larger than 50,000 in 1967. However, since the proportion of the labor force engaged in urban occupations was originally taken into consideration in designating towns as "rural" or "urban," the small urban towns are still somewhat more urban in character than the large rural towns.

The 25 migration streams between the five types of places are shown in Table 3. The net flows between pairs of place types are positive for all flows toward greater urbanization. This is true even for the flow between large rural towns and small urban towns, although this flow is a very small one.

The distinction between large and small urban townships proves to be an important one with respect to the total net migration (see the last column of panel B in Table 3). The large urban townships have a net gain due to migration, whereas the small urban towns have a net loss. The small urban towns are much more similar to the rural towns, both large and small, than they are to the large urban towns. This is most evident in panel C of Table 3, which shows the ratios of estimated migration to the migration which would be expected if migration were proportional to the population in the class of places of origin and the population in the class of places of destination. With the exception of the ratio for migration between small urban towns and other small urban towns, the ratios are close to those for the rural towns. The relatively high ratio for migration between small urban towns cannot easily be explained and may be due to the fact that this estimate was based on a relatively small number of cases.

In summary, the estimates of gross migration in various streams based on tabulations of individual migration records tend to confirm the conclusions drawn from calculations based on published sources. The major net migration flows in Taiwan are in the direction of greater urbanization, particularly toward the five largest cities and the small cities and urban towns with populations over 50,000. However, these net flows account for a small proportion of the total migration in Taiwan. For instance, the major cities received 245,200 migrants in 1968 and sent out 185,000, while the small cities and urban towns received 236,000 migrants and sent out 219,300. This means that the ratio of net in-migration to total in-migration was about one in four for the major cities and one in 14 for the small cities and large urban towns. Although the major population shift due to migration is toward greater urbanization, this process is not a very efficient one.

Much of the so-called inefficiency in migration is probably due to the return migration of many migrants who move from small urban towns and rural towns to cities and large urban towns. Since the migration records contain no prior moves, we have no way of identifying return migrants. However, it might be reasonable to assume that most migrants moving from major cities to rural towns were returning to their previous homes. If we make this assumption, the estimates in table 3 indicate that approximately half of all migrants from rural towns to the city return to the rural towns. This figure may well be an underestimate, as many persons who return to their place of origin within a year of their original move fail to register either move and thus are not counted in the migration register.

TABLE 3
Selected Measures of Migration between Five Types of Places in Taiwan, 1968

	DESTINATION					
Origin	Major City	Large Urban	Small Urban	Large Rural	Small Rural	Total
A. Estimated Gross Migration (in Thousands)						
Major city	48.1	66.2	16.5	35.9	18.9	185.6
Large urban	74.8	49.7	23.0	51.8	20.0	219.3
Small urban	33.7	27.9	19.5	20.6	9.1	110.8
Large rural	54.0	60.3	22.5	32.6	17.2	186.6
Small rural	34.6	31.9	10.9	20.2	8.1	105.7
Total	245.2	236.0	92.4	161.1	73.3	808.0
B. Estimated Net Migration (in Thousands)						
Major city	...	−8.6	−17.2	−18.1	−15.7	
Large urban	8.6	...	−4.9	−8.5	−11.9	
Small urban	17.2	4.9	...	−1.9	−1.8	
Large rural	18.1	8.5	1.9	...	−3.0	
Small rural	15.7	11.9	1.8	3.0	...	
Total	59.6	16.7	−18.4	−25.5	−32.4	
C. Ratio of Estimated Migration to Expected Migration*						
Major city	1.35	1.38	0.66	0.71	0.71	1.00
Large urban	1.63	1.03	0.89	1.00	0.73	1.10
Small urban	1.40	1.09	1.48	0.76	0.64	1.06
Large rural	1.13	1.17	0.83	0.61	0.60	0.89
Small rural	1.37	1.17	0.77	0.71	0.54	0.96
Total	1.37	1.18	0.88	0.76	0.66	1.00

Based on a 2 percent sample of migration records.

*Expected migration if migration were proportional to the population at the origin and the population at the destination: $M_{exp} = M_{tot} \times (P_i P_j{'}) / [P_{tot}(P_{tot} - P_i / n_i)]$ if $i = j$, $P_j{'} = P_i - P_{i n_i}$; otherwise $P_j{'} = P_j$, P_i = population in the class of places at the origin; P_j = population in the class of places at the destination; P_{tot} = total population; n_i = number of places in the ith class of places; M_{tot} = total number of migrants.

TABLE 4
Migration Rates by Age and Sex for Taiwanese and Mainlanders

	Taiwanese			Mainlanders		
Age Group	Males	Females	Male Rate / Female Rate	Males	Females	Male Rate / Female Rate
0–14	41.8	40.7	1.03	83.0	85.5	0.97
15–29	78.1	75.0	1.04	69.8	116.7	0.60
30–44	58.6	46.4	1.26	151.6	73.1	2.08
45–59	35.6	33.2	1.07	100.5	57.9	1.74
60+	21.2	22.2	0.96	76.5	58.5	1.31
Total	52.2	48.5	1.08	101.2	89.8	1.13

Characteristics of Migrants in Particular Streams

In addition to providing data on the origin and destination of each move, the migration records provide data on the birth date, education, occupation, and domicile for each migrant. The term "domicile" refers to the place of origin of a person's family. It provides a means of distinguishing native Taiwanese from the Chinese who moved from the mainland of China since World War II and their descendants.

As in most other places in the world, internal migration in Taiwan is highly age selective, with the highest rates of migration occurring between the ages of 15 and 44. Taiwan, however, has one peculiarity due to the fact that the mainlanders have an age distribution which is skewed toward the older ages. Since mainlanders tend to be more mobile than native Taiwanese, their inclusion leads to higher mobility rates for the older age groups than one observes elsewhere. When the two groups are separated the migration rates for Taiwanese show the normal relationship to age (see Table 4). With the exception of ages 30 – 44 when male migration rates exceed female rates by 29 percent, there is little difference between migration rates for males and females among Taiwanese. The similarity of rates in the 15 – 29 age range when many of the migrants are single indicates that both sexes are responding equally to the changing economic conditions. While males are differentially attracted to transportation, construction, and heavy industry, some of the newer industries attract more women than men.

Mainlanders differ considerably from Taiwanese in the variation of migration rates with age and sex. The highest migration among mainlanders is for males aged 30–44. The migration rate for this group is nearly double that for mainlander females and about two and a half times greater than that for Taiwanese males in the same age group. The same is true of the migration rate for mainlander males aged 45–59. The explanation for these differences is related to the fact that many of the mainlander males in these two age groups are single men who have retired from the army, having moved to Taiwan in 1949–50 under Chiang Kai-shek. With no family and no previous civilian residence, these men tend to be highly mobile.

Because a large part of the variation in migration rates of the mainlanders is related to unique historical factors rather than more general social and economic factors, we shall confine the remainder of our analysis to the native Taiwanese.

The relative educational level of migrants and nonmigrants is of considerable interest in a developing country. Because educational attainment is a clearly defined concept which can be reliably measured, it is perhaps the best available indicator of both the socioeconomic status of migrants and their qualifications for work at the destination.

Studies in developed countries have found no consistent relationship between migration and educational attainment. Freedom and Hawley found that educational selectivity varied from stream to stream for migration in the United States during the depression and that when controls were introduced for age, occupation, and other variables, there was no significant difference in the migration rates for different education groups. Suval and Hamilton found that migrants to and from the South were positively selected with respect to education. Four recent studies in underdeveloped countries have all shown migration to be selective of the better educated.

In general, migrants in Taiwan tend to be drawn disproportionately from the better educated. Both male and female migration was selective of the better educated in seven of the nine streams between types of places. In all seven of these streams those who had completed senior school had the highest migration rate, and those who had not completed primary school had the lowest rate. In most of these streams, there was very little difference between the rates for primary school graduates and junior school graduates.

The selectivity was greatest in the three streams toward greater urbanization (rural towns to cities, and rural towns to urban towns). Selectivity was almost as high in the three streams between areas of the same degree of urbanization (cities to cities, urban towns to urban towns, and rural towns to rural towns). There was less evidence of selectivity in the streams toward lesser urbanization (cities to urban towns, cities to rural towns, and urban towns to rural towns).

TABLE 5
Migration Rates per 1,000 Population, by Age, Sex, and Education for
Taiwanese, 1967–68

Sex and Age Group	Highest Level of School Completed				
	Senior	Junior	Primary	None	Total
Males:					
15–29	105.6	63.4	78.1	68.5	78.6
30–44	113.2	62.2	58.9	40.4	58.8
45–59	103.5	44.7	42.4	25.5	35.6
Total ...	107.5	62.0	66.2	41.4	64.0
Females:					
15–29	93.1	67.8	79.4	66.5	75.1
30–44	141.2	68.9	53.2	37.6	46.5
45–59	136.8	104.6	59.5	26.7	32.9
Total ...	101.7	68.7	70.4	42.7	57.9

Educational selectivity in migration could be merely a reflection of age selectivity. Since young adults are more likely to migrate and since they also have more education than older adults, migrants could have more education that nonmigrants even if there were not educational selectivity. However, when age is controlled, much of the educational selectivity of migration remains (see Table 5). For males and females in the age groups 30–44 and 45–59, migration rates increase considerably with education. In both age groups for both sexes, the migration rate for senior school graduates is more than double the rate for those who did not complete primary school.

In the 15–29 age group, neither the male nor female migration rates show as clear a relationship to education. Migration rates are uniformly highest for senior school graduates. However, among both males and females, the migration rates are higher for primary school graduates than for either junior school graduates for those who did not complete primary school. The migration rates for junior graduates may be somewhat depressed because some of the junior graduates are attending senior school. We would expect a smaller proportion of persons classified as primary graduates to be in school if they were in school they would be in junior school, and most students complete junior school by age 15 or 16.

The question of the relative educational attainment of migrants in different streams can best be answered by looking at the educational distribution of migrants in each stream. In Table 6 we have shown the percentage of migrants in each stream who are junior graduates or higher. These percentages show a regular progression with respect to both type of place of origin and type of place of destination. Migrants from cities are better educated than migrants from urban towns, who are, in turn, better educated than migrants from rural towns. Similarly, among migrants leaving a particular point, those who go to the cities have the most education; those who go to the rural towns have the least education.

In all streams except those from cities to rural towns and from cities to urban towns male migrants have more education, on the average, than male residents at the place of origin. Female migrants also have more education than female residents at the place of origin in seven of the nine streams. These findings are consistent with the differences in migration rates discussed earlier.

Although migrants tend to be better educated than the residents at the place of origin, they are not necessarily better educated than the residents at the place of destination. In the streams toward greater urbanization, migrants tend to be intermediate in education between the residents at the place of origin and those at the place of destination. This is true for

TABLE 6
Percentage of Migrants in Each Stream and Percentage of Residents at Origin and Destination Who Completed Junior School, Taiwanese, 1967-68

Migration Stream	Males Aged 15–59			Females Aged 15–59		
	Residents at Origin	Migrants	Residents at Destination	Residents at Origin	Migration	Residents at Destination
Cities to:						
Cities	42.1	50.0	42.1	23.9	29.4	23.9
Urban towns	42.1	41.1	26.9	23.9	27.9	15.1
Rural towns	42.1	32.5	21.3	23.9	19.3	8.0
Urban towns to:						
Cities	26.9	42.9	42.1	15.1	23.2	23.9
Urban towns	26.9	33.4	36.9	15.1	20.4	15.1
Rural towns	26.9	30.6	21.3	15.1	15.3	8.0
Rural towns to:						
Cities	21.3	32.8	42.1	8.0	17.6	23.9
Urban towns	21.3	29.7	26.9	8.0	14.6	15.1
Rural towns	21.3	24.1	21.3	8.0	7.5	8.0

females in the streams from urban towns to cities, rural towns to cities, and rural towns to urban towns. It is also true for males in the rural-towns-to-cities stream. However, in the streams from urban towns to cities and from rural to urban towns, male migrants are slightly more likely to be junior graduates than males at the destination.

Migrants who move in the direction of lesser urbanization have more education than the residents at the place to which they move. In fact, the proportion of migrants who are junior graduates differs little between the major flow and the reverse flow between two types of places. For example, 32.8 percent of the male migrants from rural towns to cities are junior graduates, and 32.5 percent of the male migrants from cities to rural towns are junior graduates. This means that if we assume that a large proportion of the persons in the reverse flows are return migrants, the probability of a migrant returning must depend very little on his education.

It is hard to reconcile the lack of educational selectivity in the return streams with the high degree of selectivity in the major streams. If educational selectivity in the streams toward greater urbanization is due to greater opportunities of finding satisfactory employment for the better educated, we would expect the return streams to be disproportionately drawn from the poorly educated who would have less success in finding satisfactory employment. However, eduation may have little effect on one's chances of obtaining satisfactory employment in the city since what one defines as satisfactory may vary with one's education. Taiwan has a high proportion of junior and senior high school graduates relative to its level of development, and it may be harder for them to find jobs commensurate with their education than it is for someone with less education. Thus, while many highly educated persons may be motivated to leave rural areas because there is little opportunity for them to find work which utilizes their skills there, they may be no more successful in finding such work in the cities than the poorly educated migrant who seeks unskilled employment.

Another explanation is that many migrants improve their education in the city and some come primarily to gain further schooling with the intention of returning. If we could first separate out those migrants who initially intended to return and then compare the current educational level of the other return migrants with those who stayed in the city, we might well find that those who returned had less education than those who stayed.

Finally, despite the similarity in average educational attainment between migrants in the

TABLE 7
Selected Characteristics of Migrants and Nonmigrants

	Migrants before Move	Nonmigrants
Graduated from junior school (ninth grade) (%)	38.0	20.5
Employed as salaried professionals, managers, or clerks (%)	20.6	8.9
Employed in production or construction (%)	17.8	11.6
Employed as farmers or farm laborers (%)	18.7	43.5
Not employed (%)	4.7	3.5
Living in farm families (%)	38.3	56.8
Those living in farm families whose imputed farm income exceeds $900 per year (%)*	33.3	19.1
Ever lived on a farm (%)	82.7	83.9
N	321	370

*Base of percentage is number living in farm families.

primary and return migration streams between rural townships and cities, there is still a selective loss of the more educated persons by the rural areas because more migrants leave than return. Thus we may still speak of the net migration between rural townships and cities as selective of the better educated.

Additional Evidence from a Survey of Rural to Urban Migrants

A clearer understanding of the factors associated with the selectivity of rural to urban migration in Taiwan can be obtained from the results of the Taichung Migration Survey—conducted in 1967. The survey consisted of intensive interviews with two samples: one a sample of 321 Taiwanese men aged 23–42 who had registered a move to Taichung City from one of the for surrounding countries in 1966–67; the other was a sample of comparable men living in rural and urban towns within these four counties. This survey enables detailed characteristics of recent migrants to be compared with nonmigrants at the place of origin.

The survey results confirm the finding of the migration record analysis that migrants are positively selected with respect to education (see Table 7). Migrants were also less likely than nonmigrants to have been employed as a farmer or to have lived on a farm just prior to moving. However, there was little difference between migrants and nonmigrants in the proportion who had ever lived on a farm. This indicates that for many migrants the move to the city was the last step in a series of moves away from farming.

Twenty-one percent of the migrants said they had been employed as professionals, managers, or clerks (excluding the self-employed who mostly have very small retail businesses) compared with 9 percent of the nonmigrants. The high proportion of white-collar occupations is due in part to the inclusion of some large urban towns and the seat of the provincial government in the sample area. Many of the white-collar workers were government employees, although the majority of these worked for local governments or government enterprises. Employment in the Chinese civil service has traditionally involved a considerable amount of geographical mobility. The old principle was to rotate the higher officials to keep them from developing local ties which might mitigate against their loyalty to the central government. We have not ascertained the extent to which this principle is still adhered to by the Nationalist Chinese, although the fact that a large percentage of the moves of government employees were job transfers requested by the government implies that this principle may still be followed.

Migrants from farms tended to be selected more from the large farms than the smaller farms. In order to control for differences in the quality of landholdings, we have standardized the data on family landholdings by converting them into imputed monthly income based on the average total income (including income in kind) for different types of land obtained from agricultural surveys. Among those who had lived on a farm, more migrants than nonmigrants lived on farms with imputed yearly incomes of $900 or more.

The greater migration from larger farms is a function of two factors. First, members of families with larger holdings have a greater opportunity to obtain advanced education than members of families with smaller holdings. The data show that they do in fact have better education and that when educational level is controlled there is little difference in the migration rates by farm size.

Second, members of poorer families who do not move to a large city have other alternatives to work on the family farm. They can work as agricultural laborers, perhaps filling in for labor shortages created by out-migration from some of the larger farms. They can also take up nonagricultural employment in the village or commute to one of the factories located outside the city. A survey by T. L. Lin and H. H. Chen shows that the alternative which is chosen is related to education. The higher the education, the more likely one is to seek employment away from home. When all the alternates are taken into account, they find that the number of persons leaving family work has the expected negative correlation with farm size.

Summary

Since World War II, the cities of Taiwan have grown at an average rate of close to 5 percent per year. Although a small part of this growth was due to the influx of migrants from the mainland of China around 1949, the effect of this migration on city growth was small compared with the migration of Taiwanese from the countryside. In fact, the postwar growth of cities was shown to be only slightly greater than the growth earlier in this century.

The rate of net out-migration was found to be the highest in areas where a high percentage of the males were employed in agriculture. With the exception of a relatively small movement to the east coast of Taiwan where some new land has been put to cultivation, recent net migration in Taiwan can be explained as almost entirely a move from agricultural areas to cities and large urban towns (over 50,000). While it is easy to point to the fact that virtually all available land in Taiwan has been intensely cultivated for some time and that the rural population has been growing rapidly during this period, these facts do not necessarily imply that the rural urban movement has been primarily due to a rural "push."

While the rural population has been growing, the population growth has been more than offset by increases in agricultural yield resulting from the introduction of new seed, fertilizer, and improved irrigation. Land reform, by dividing the land more equitably, may have made farming more attractive for many who otherwise would have left the rural areas. Furthermore, some of the industrialization in Taiwan has permeated the countryside, and there has been increased opportunity for nonagricultural employment both within rural areas and within commuting range of these areas.

With a few exceptions, rural-to-urban migration in Taiwan can be viewed as a rational response to changing economic conditions. The growing rural population has adjusted to the pressure of population on limited resources by sending to the major cities those members of the rural population who are best qualified for urban employment. The migrants have been drawn disproportionately from the young adults, from the more highly educated, from those working most recently in nonagricultural employment, and from the larger farms.

Other members of the rural community have responded in other ways. Those with less education or from smaller farms have tended to seek other employment nearby either through seasonal employment as an agricultural laborer or in local nonagricultural employment or by daily commuting to nonagricultural employment in a smaller urban place.

Although the major net flow of migration was from rural areas to the major cities, this net flow was only a small part of the total internal migration in Taiwan. On the average, for every four migrants who entered the major cities there were three migrants who left these cities, most of them probably returning to their original places of residence. The finding that these "return migrants" were approximately equal to the primary-stream migrants in education could not be completely explained. There is a clear need for more detailed studies of return migration and its relationship to economic development.

Section 5
Law and Justice
Edited by Hungdah Chiu
with Jyh-pin Fa

Section 5
Law and Justice

Edited by Hungdah Chiu, with Jyh-pin Fa

The goal of the Nationalist Revolution led by the Kuomintang (Nationalist Party), beginning in the late 19th and early 20th centuries, was to transform China from a traditional, agricultural and authoritarian society into a modern, democratic, and industrial society within the context of Chinese cultural tradition. In pursuing this goal, the modernization of Chinese law has been a very important process. Although the law reform movement started in the late Ch'ing Dynasty (1644–1911) and continued in the early Republican period (beginning 1912), it was not until the Nationalists had achieved national power in 1927–1928 that a systematic law reform was launched. The National Government established by the Kuomintang achieved considerable success in modernizing Chinese law between 1927 and 1937, when the Sino-Japanese War broke out and interrupted the Chinese reform efforts.

The legal modernization resumed by the National Government after the end of the war in 1945 was highlighted by the promulgation of the Constitution of January 1, 1947, which entered into force on December 25, of the same year. Since then, the National Government has been renamed the Government of the Republic of China (ROC). The implementation of the 1947 Constitution and the accompanying law reform was severely marred, however, by the widespread civil war between the Government and the Chinese Communists, until the removal of the ROC Government from the mainland to Taiwan on December 8, 1949. The ROC Government brought with it, nevertheless, the Constitution, the laws, and the legal system intact, and these have been in force within the present territories under the ROC's jurisdiction.

In view of this historical context, it is necessary to begin the survey of the ROC legal development in Taiwan with its experience in the mainland. After that, this study describes the system of law and justice in Taiwan up to about 1966. The final sections present a more thorough study of certain specific important issues on law and justice, some of which are briefly described in the earliest part, with special emphasis on developments since 1966. Limitations of space confine the discussion of the law and justice in the ROC primarily to the criminal justice system and its related problems; it has not been possible to cover the broad and important areas of civil, commerical, administrative and trade and investment laws.

Hungdah Chiu is Professor of Law at University of Maryland School of Law; Jyh-pin Fa is Associate Professor of Law at National Chengchi University, Taipei, Taiwan.

I. THE MODERNIZATION OF CHINESE LAW
UNDER THE NATIONAL GOVERNMENT 1927–1949

A. Law Reform between the Late Nineteenth Century and 1937

Under the traditional Chinese legal system, the written law was predominantly penal, and the traditional society was not legally oriented. Matters of a civil nature were either ignored almost entirely (for example, contract law), or were given only limited treatment within the penal system (for example, property rights, inheritance, marriage). There was neither an independent judiciary, nor professional lawyers or formal legal education in the modern sense. The legal system evolved to meet needs of an isolated agricultural society.

Before the period of the French Revolution (1789), the legal system and the administration of justice in China were superior to those of the West, as were many other features of Chinese institutional and cultural life. [1]

However, beginning at the end of the eighteenth century, the European countries underwent a series of social, political and legal reforms which made their legal systems much more advanced and humane than that of China. As a result, since the early 19th century, Europeans in China had sharply resisted the exercise of Chinese legal jurisdiction over their affairs.

With the defeat of China by the British in the 1839–42 Opium War, the humiliating system of extraterritoriality, which excluded foreigners from Chinese legal jursidiction, was imposed on China. The Imperial Government, however, steadfastly denied the need for undertaking a complete reform and reorganization of the Chinese legal system until 1880. Nevertheless, throughout the period between the Opium War and the first legal reforms, the Chinese people increasingly came to realize that a thorough reform of the legal system was a prerequisite for ending extraterritoriality and developing China into a modern state. Moreover, Japan's success in throwing off the yoke of extraterritoriality by modernizing its legal system at the end of the nineteenth century inspired China to seek a similar path. Furthermore, beginning in 1902, the major Western powers provided China with a substantial incentive to undertake the vast effort "to reform its judicial system and to bring it into accord with that of Western nations"; in a series of bilateral treaties they stated that, if China did so, they "will also be prepared to relinquish extra-territorial rights when satisfied that the state of the Chinese laws, the arrangements for their administration and other considerations warrant it . . ." [2]

The following excerpts describe the law reform from the period of late Ch'ing Dynasty to the outbreak of the Sino-Japanese War in 1937.

NOTES

1. See, e.g., E. Parker, *China: Her History, Diplomacy and Commerce* 308 (1917).

2. The quotations are from Article XV of the Treaty between China and the United States Respecting Commerical Relations, October 8, 1903, in 1 *Hertslet's China Treaties* 575 (1908).

1.   Early 20th-Century Law Reform in China

Jyh-pin Fa

The Imperial Law Codification Commission was established in 1904. It included Dr. Wu Ting-fang, a member of the English Bar and former Minister to the United States, and Shan Chia-pan, an eminent jurist in Chinese jurisprudence. Japanese advisor Mutsuoka Yashitada was associated with the Commission, and it is not surprising to find that a number of draft codes of procedure and of criminal and civil law were considerably influenced by the Japanese code, which in turn was based upon Continental Codes, primarily the German and the French.

There was considerable wisdom in the appointment of Japanese experts since Japan had recently solved the difficult problem of adapting Western legal principles to Eastern requirements. Moreover, there also was plausible reason for the reproduction in the Chinese code of the chief characteristics of continental rather than Anglo-American law. It is said that "Anglo-American law emphasizes that individual at the expense of the family, while continental law inherits something of the old 'familia.' The family being the unit of Chinese society, anything which weakens the existence and power of that institution must be as unacceptable in principle as it would be unworkable in practice." The more important consideration was that Anglo-American law existed not only in statutes but also in judicial as well as administrative decisions which were too complex and too little systematized at that time. To a country which had to borrow foreign codes, a ready-made code of comprehensively rules clearly and consicely set forth article by article was not only simpler and more systematic, but a more promising method of obtaining satisfactory results. As one eminent Chinese jurist once said to G. Keeton, a keen English observor of extraterritoriality in China, "We like your law and for some reasons we would have preferred them as a model for our own, but we cannot codify your own laws for you."

The first modern code ever drafted by the Codification Commission was the Kung-ssu-lu (Company Law) of 1904. The Code was a hybrid of Japanese and English company laws in an abridged form. The Anglo-American influence was, however, limited to that particular field. In addition to this, a number of codes on civil law, maritime law, bankruptcy law, and civil and criminal procedure were also drafted. Of those early efforts, however, only the "Provisional Regulations of the Organization of the Courts and Subordinate Courts" (1907), the "Law of the Organization of the Judiciary" (1909), and the Criminal Code ever came into operation; the rest remained only on paper, because they were generally the result of hasty drafting and because the sponsoring Ch'ing government fell within a few years. According to these organic laws, a hierarchy of modern courts of four classes — the Local Court, the District Court, the High Court and the Supreme Court — was created. Subsequently, the Local Court was abolished. Since then the District Court has become the court of first instance, where the trial is conducted by one judge. An appeal may be made to a High Court where three judges sit, and the last appeal is usually heard by five judges without oral argument and is limited to questions of law in the Supreme Court.

To every modern court, a procurator of corresponding grade is attached. The Chinese procurator has no exact equivalent in American legal terminology. His authority is quite extensive and powerful. He is the combination of prosecutor, coronor, or grand jury under American system; that is, he has the power to hold a preliminary examination of the accused, and the witness so as to decide whether the case should be prosecuted or not. In exercising this power he may summon, arrest, and detain the accused without first getting approval from a judge; he may also compel a witness to appear and make such searches and investigation as may serve to throw light on the case. This structure of the modern courts continues to function today even though related laws have been revised several times.

Jyh-pin Fa, *A Comparative Study of Judicial Review Under Nationalist Chinese and American Constitutional Law,* Baltimore, Maryland: *Occasional Papers / Reprints Series in Contemporary Asian Studies,* U. of Maryland, School of Law, No. 4-1980 (33), pp. 30-39. Footnotes omitted.

The drafted Criminal Code was promulgated by an imperial edict at the end of the Ching dynasty. The republican government, by a presidential mandate of March 3, 1912, adopted the said Code, with the exception of those provisions pertaining to the royal family of the late regime. Several revisions were made in 1914, 1921, and 1928 to bring it in line with most recent developments in criminal jurisprudence. This code provided, for the first time, that no person could be held guilty of an offense unless it was expressly provided for. It also ended the principle of collective responsibility of the family and clan for the crimes of members, and torture was abolished. These revised codes were again drafted by the Codification Commission, now with different members after the establishment of the Republic. Dr. Wang Chung-hui, a graduate of Yale and a deputy-judge of the Permanent Court of International Justice as well as the famous translator of the German Civil Code into English, was among them. In addition, Tung Kang, the Chief Justice of the Chinese Supreme Court, later Minister of Justice and the last living authority on ancient Chinese law, and Lo Wen-kan, an Oxford M.A. and procurator-general of the Republic, were also members. In addition to two Japanese advisors, Itakura Matsutaro and Iwata Shin, the Frenchman M. G. Padoux was also associated with the Commission. The latter had been responsible for modernization of the Siamese codes which led to the eventual abolition of extraterritoriality in that country.

The work of this Commission was quite impressive. It published the following volumes within ten years: The Regulations Relating to Criminal Procedure, The Ordinance of the General Regulation of Traders, The Trade Mark Law, The Regulations Relating to Civil Procedure, The Chinese Supreme Court Decisions, Chinese Prisons, and many others. Nevertheless, the external political turmoil which has resulted from the incessant civil wars among warlords and the continued interference by the military seriously impeded the progress of legal reform, particularly in the area of the administration of justice. In other words, the whole system of Chinese law at the time, satisfactory in theory, was inefficient and arbitrary in practice. Therefore, it is natural that the report of the Commission sent to China by the resolution of the Washington Conference of 1922 to inquire into the present practice of extraterritoriality in China, and into the laws and judicial system and the methods of judicial administration of China, was a disappointment to the Chinese.

Although the existing system of extraterritoriality was still desirable, according to the survey of Chinese law made by the Commission, this disheartening fact did not discourage the continuance of the law reform movement. Between the establishment of the National Government in 1928 and the outbreak of the war of resistance against Japan in 1937, the work on codification came to fruition and constituted the most significant domestic achievement by the National Government. The Commission of Codification of Law was transformed into a legislative commission headed by Sun Fo, son of Dr. Sun Yat-sen, and the President of the Legislature. The Commission produced the Criminal Code (1935), the Code of Civil Procedure (1935), the Code of Criminal Procedure (1935), the Civil Code (1929), the Law of Insurance (1929), Company Law (1929), Maritime Law (1929), Bankruptcy Law (1935), the Negotiable Instruments Law (1929), and the Trademark Law (1936).

Without exception, the Criminal Code was largely a product of various foreign codes. One particular feature may be illustrated. This code was based on the equality of men. No privileged group was entitled to exemption or mitigation as the traditional codes provided. Even today, however, family relations still play a part in the determination of punishments. In offenses such as profaning the dead, homicide, causing bodily harm, restraining personal liberty, and abandonment, the existence of family relation between the offender and the victim increases the punishment. On the other hand, in offenses such as theft, fraud, and receiving stolen property, the presence of a family relationship either requires the judge to remit the sentence or to limit the sentence or limit judicial cognizance to cases where the injured party himself starts a private prosecution.

As civil matters were largely regulated by custom in traditional China, the codification of civil law was not as aggressive as criminal law. The Civil Code of 1929 also affirmed the principle of the equality of man and women. Sons and daughters now shared the estate equally on the father's death intestate, and in order to prevent the exclusion of daughters by will, the Code even instituted the system of the "legitimate compulsory portion." As a result of the admission of women to the rights of succession, a woman might now have separate estate; the Code introduced the system of "union of goods," which originated in Switzerland, to regulate the position of the woman during marriage in the absence of a special agreement. Under this, the woman retained as her separate estate property for personal use, the products of her labor, and certain other types of property.

Perhaps the most conspicuous characteristic of the Civil Code was the unification of civil and commercial law, commonly separated in other societies. The basis for such a distinction between civil and commercial law is rooted in continental legal history. Since there was a separate class of merchants in the Middle Ages with their own customs, special courts were created to try commercial cases. No such reason existed in China; thus, no useful purpose was served by the separation. In addition, as Dean Roscoe Pound observed, "It [the distinction] requires difficult questions of jurisdiction, procedural distinctions and distinctions of application of law which are simply anachronisms." Therefore, the "abrogation of the separate commercial law and commercial jurisdiction was a real step forward."

However, some of the important aspects of commerical law were left to be covered by special laws later implemented; negotiable instruments,insurance, commercial companies and maritime commerce were dealt with in four special laws promulgated in 1929. The underlying reason for this might be that it was easier to make amendments to a single statute than to the code. By doing this, the general tenor of the law would be less likely to be disturbed during the development process in China.

In regard to criminal trials, Chinese procedure followed the normal continental form rather than the Anglo-American one. Following a preliminary investigation by a procurator, a preliminary examination was held to decide whether the accused is to be committed for trial. Then the public prosecution followed. A necessary corollary of this type of procedure was that lawyers played an insignificant role. Since pretrial interview of witnesses was forbidden for fear they may be influenced by the lawyers, a lawyer's pretrial investigation was largely confined to interviewing his client, possibly members of the client's family, and examining the documents and any real evidence under the client's control. During court trials, the customary rule of lawyers was not that of courageous fighters for the rights of their clients. It is said that their advice to the criminal defendant was often not to deny guilt, but to plead mitigating circumstances in order not to irritate the presiding judge.

Since the judge received and studied the records and dossiers of the police and procurator in advance of the trial, this practice inevitably influenced his attitude towards the disposition of the case. In sum, the trial was actually dominated by the civil law principle of "judicial prosecution," which means that the judge alone controls the proceeding of the trial rather than the "party prosecution" in the American system. In other words, speaking generally, criminal procedure in the civil law countries is "inquisitorial," while that in the common law countries is "accusatorial."

Another important feature in the adoption of the continental legal system was that in rendering a judgment the court was not bound by strict rules regarding the probative force of evidence, but rather was guided by its own conviction.

Although these codes were quite advanced according to the then Western standard, one thing could not be ignored: they were totally alien to the general public in China. Since the country was not only facing continuing threat from foreign powers, but was also undergoing incessant military actions against the remaining warlords and the Chinese Communists, and since it had only achieved nominal unification under the central government in Nanking, it was impossible to create an efficient, nation-wide system for the administration of justice. In the rural areas, the inquisitorial methods of the imperial regime, together with portions of the old codes and moral practices, were still enforced. Because the command of the central government was not carried far enough to reach every part of the country, many modern rules which ran counter to traditional practices were simply put aside. This unfortunate condition would have been temporary and would not have been hard to overcome if China had had more time to develop its legal system.

B. Law Reform between 1937 and 1949

The Sino-Japanese War of 1937–1945 severely disrupted the law reform movement as well as other aspects of Chinese society. The National Government nevertheless continued to carry out the law reform during this difficult period and immediately following the war. The following excerpts from an article written by Roscoe Pound, Former Dean of the Harvard Law School, concisely analyze the problems faced by the National Government during this period. Dean Pound carefully studied the Chinese legislation, codes and system of legal education between 1935 and 1947. Between 1946 and 1947, he was an adviser to the ROC Ministry of Justice and directed a team of 15 lawyers in an on-the-spot study and survey of the Chinese administration of justice in order to make recommendations to the Chinese Government.

2.   Law Reform During 1937–1949
Roscoe Pound

The Chinese Legal System and the War

Administration of justice in China in the past ten years has had to go on under many and serious difficulties. First of them is the general disruption brought on by the war and hostile occupation of the greater and richer part of the country. An account of the re-establishment of the courts at Shanghai on the evacuation by the Japanese in Spetember of 1945, to be found in the report of the Chief Procurator of the District Court covering September 1945 to September 1947, is revealing. At the Japanese invasion the judges and officials of the courts were scattered. The President of the High Court had to hide and was pursued relentlessly by the puppet regime set up by the invaders. The Chief Procurator of the District Court had to flee and went to Chungking. As soon as possible after the Japanese evacuation, on September 19, 1945, the Chief Procurator arrived in Shanghai. He had no baggage and no facilities for work, but at once set about the task of reconstruction. Everything was in disorder. The officials who had acted under the Japanese puppet regime could not be utilized. Indeed many of them had to be prosecuted. The original staff was largely out of reach and competent new officials to take their places were hard to find. The volume of prosecution growing out of the disorder following the collapse of the Japanese regime was enormous. On September 25 the lawful judges were at hand and the prosecuting machinery had been set up and had begun to function. Between September and December of 1945 the procurators handled 4,987 cases with a depleted staff, and only 975 cases were undisposed of at the end of December. From January to December of 1946 there were 17,570 prosecutions, and at the end of the year only 520 cases were not disposed of. From January to December of 1947 there were 19,708 prosecutions, and at the end of the year only 246 had to been concluded. There was not a full staff of procurators, clerks, and clerical assistants until the latter part of 1946.

In more than one city the court records were destroyed or dissipated. Often the buildings and furniture of the courts were gone or in great part destroyed. In Nanking the High Court still has to make use of part of a Confucian temple, the rest being used for a school. In many places the prisons and houses of detention were destroyed in whole or in part, and where not destroyed the equipment was removed and has had to be replaced. Often the courts are

Roscoe Pound, "Progress of the Law in China," *The Washington Law Review*, Vol. 23 (1948), pp. 346-356.

working with deficient equipment, and money is lacking as a rule to supply what has been lost. The efficiency with which courts are operating in spite of this condition speaks eloquently for the energy, ability, and devotion to duty of the judges, procurators, and clerks.

A like story to that told in the report of the Chief Procurator of the District Court at Shanghai can be told for the High Court and for civil causes and indeed for the District Courts and High Courts throughout the regions occupied by the Japanese.

Traffic in and use of opium had been effectually stopped by 1937. It came back during the Japanese occupation. The Japanese actively fomented its use. Now it is a prolific breeder of crime, and the criminal courts, already overburdened with prosecutions growing out of conditions of disorder created by the war, are much occupied with opium prosecutions, and the prisons, especially the women's prisons, are filled with opium convicts. Also, since the Japanese evacuation, prosecution of "collaborators" (those who took active part in the Japanese puppet regime) has taken up much of the time and activities of procurators and crowded the dockets of the courts. I have read many complaints as to the way the "collaborators" are treated. I talked with many of them in the prisons of the High Court at Nanking and at Shanghai. Some of them were well educated, not infrequently in American universities, and had held good and even high positions. I found them well treated, given, if they desired it, work in teaching fellow convicts, and translating or copying if their education had fitted them for such work. They were furnished good books to read, given a special diet if they were not used to Chinese food, and put in comfortable cells. I could see no reason for complaint as to their treatment in prison.

Communist activities, too, give the prosecutors and courts much additional work. It is not general advocacy of communist ideas or preaching of abstract communism that is prosecuted but direct stirring up of disorder, rioting, and destruction, even hiring children to set fires. Prosecution of these overt acts is often represented as political persecution. But I am satisfied, after having the records examined, that the authorities are discriminating and cautious beyond what we have been in the United States in time of war.

Difficulties of Administration

A very great hindrance to reconstructing the administration of justice has been and is lack of money. After eight years of occupation of the greater and richer part of the country, with widespread destruction of the means of communication, of court houses and government buildings, and of the buildings and equipment of edcational and penal institutions, and of libraries and court records, of the disruption of the judicial, administrative, educational, and correctional systems, with the exigencies of civil war taking a heavy toll of its revenues, the government is hard-pressed to meet even the minimum requirements of reconstruction of the administration of justice. The progress which has been made since the return of the Ministry of Justice from Chungking in the summer of 1946, under such circumstances, is truly marvelous. One of the most serious effects of lack of money is to be seen in the low salaries which the government can afford to pay the judges, procurators, and officials of the Ministry of Justice. Taken with the depreciation of the national currency ad the mounting cost of living, they are a serious handicap to reconstruction. Yet the progress goes on steadily notwithstanding.

Want of unified teaching, interpretation, and application of the codes has also been a hindrance, though to less extent than one might have anticipated. There has been a certain clash of ideas and techniques between teachers trained in different systems and modes of juristic thought, in France, Germany, England—either in the Inns of Court or in the Universities—the United States—in universities in different parts of the country with more or less different traditions—in Japan, or in China by teachers with a like diversity of training. The tendency of much of this training abroad has been to bring about fixed ideas derived from some foreign system of the doctrines and techniques of the system as the legal order on nature. While many law teachers whom I have met are able to rise above this, it remains something with which law teaching and so law must reckon until teaching of Chinese law as such, and not as declaratory of comparative law or of some other system, becomes well established.

Another difficulty in interpreting and applying the constitution and codes is the need of finding out how to adapt provisions borrowed from Anglo-American law to a Continental legel system and reach a balance of comparative law and historical Chinese traditions and modes of thought which have entered into both the constitution and the codes. In the Constitution, in particlar, need of adjusting Anglo-American legal rules and methods to systematic ideas derived from the Continental modern Roman law, will require judges and teachers of wide knowledge of comparative law and clear grasp of the technique of both systems and their possibilities of adaptation. Happily such jurists are to be found in China in larger proportion than in countries where no such adjustments have to be made.

An example of the difficulties made for courts by hasty importation of rigid provisions, without considering their accord with the system in which they are to operate and adjusting them thereto, may be seen in one of the clauses in Article 8 of the Constitution. As it has been translated it reads: "No person shall be tried or punished except by a court of law in accordance with procedure prescribed by law." To the Anglo-American ear this sounds very well. But to the Chinese, accustomed to the French regime of police handling of petty police offenses informally, and to general convenience and satisfaction, if the words of the original are rightly translated "court of law," the result will be awkward. The inconvenience to the public of the American system of traffic courts for petty cases in large cities— Shanghai, 6,000,000 people; Nanking, 2,000,000; Hangchow, 1,000,000—in comparison with the French system, which I have seen in operation in France and in those cities, is obvious to the critical observer. Moreover, the traffic courts in the United States for such things as parking in the wrong place or wrong way and like minor infractions of traffic regulations are by no means satisfactory. If the Chinese text can be translated "judicial authority" and legislation can be enacted describing the limits of the offenses cognizable and prescribing the procedure in case of minor infractions of police regulations, the customary practice can be brought within the Constitution. This is not the only problem of the sort raised by the Constitution. In places the Constitution suggests over much the work of abstract political scientists, in places where lawyers should have been turned to, which will require molding by constitutional law.

Another difficulty, especially awkward in legal education but with marked effect in many connections, is lack of a fully developed Chinese juristic and legal terminology. Such ideas as "administration of justice," the distinction between "law" and "a law," the conception of "a right" and the many distinctions developed in the latter part of the nineteenth and in the present century by analysis of "a right," the distinction of legal precepts as rules, principles, precepts defining conceptions, and precepts establishing standards, and the distinctions of "justice" as an individual virture, as the ideal relation among men, as the end of law, and as a regime of adjusting relations and ordering conduct, are very hard to bring home to Chinese students in words with which they are familiar and make the teaching of the science of law and hard task. Indeed despair of putting such fundamental ideas in Chinese led an eminent Continental jurist, who served for some time as legal adviser to the Chinese government, to the mistaken conclusion that the Chinese did not have the idea of justice. The modern science of law in Chinese is a matter of fifty years as compared with its long development in the West from the classical Roman jurists to the present. Moreover, when in English and in the Continental languages we are confronted with new ideas or a new phenomenon we can always fall back on Greek and Latin for the material from which to coin a work. The Chinese lack that resource and have to turn to paraphrases and to analogical uses of familiar words or combinations of them. Juristic development in China will gradually find how to meet this difficulty as a unified juristic method is worked out and the results of diversified training in the legal systems and juristic methods of other lands are eliminated.

Immediate Needs for Improvement

Needs of the administration of justice, some of them urgent, but all of which must await improvement of the financial position of the government, which is pressed with demands of reconstruction on every side, are: More complete equipment of all the agencies of justice, adequate libraries — court libraries, bar libraries, and law school libraries — adequate salaries, Chinese treatises and textbooks applying the more recent methods of doctrinal development and exposition to the codes, an adequate system of reporting judicial decisions, development of constitutional law to go along with the interpretation and application of the Constitution, and improvement of the position of the bar. Each of these needs calls for some explanation or consideration.

Few courthouses escaped partial destruction. Some were razed and all rendered untenantable. In the shortage of buildings due to widespread destruction the best has had to be made of such quarters as have been available. The furniture and equipment was destroyed or carried off, and in some important courthouses I have visited courtrooms which have the barest of furnishings and in others essential furniture is still being made. This is even more true of penal and correctional institutions and causes crowding which is undesirable but necessary. Nowhere are the records adequately protected against fire. Temporary wooden cases are all that has been available.

Law libraries were either destroyed or greatly impaired. In Nanking and Shanghai the agencies of criminal investigation have built up good working libraries, but everywhere there is little more than a beginning of restoring the necessary libraries. This has specially bad effect upon the law schools.

Need of adequate salaries in every part of the administration of justice, as in all the agencies of government and education, is an outsanding drawback.

Also the judges, overburdened with work of writing out judgments and orders, need secretaries such as we have learned to give them in America. But even if there were money for this the law schools are hardly yet in a position to supply the needed men.

Since even the best of codes will not administer themselves, there is much need of Chinese doctrinal treatises, such as are well known in Continental Europe, not only as the basis of law teaching but for the assistance of courts and legal advisers. When we remember that the system of codes was not complete until 1930 and the Code of Civil Procedure was revised in 1935, that the Japanese were in control of Manchuria from 1931 and of the greater part of China from 1937 to 1945, it can be understood why there has been no more than the beginning of a Chinese legal literature. Commentaries on the codes noting the decisions of the Supreme Court applying their articles is about as much as has been possible. There are in China many well-trained, learned, able jurists, some of them of world-wide repute. But doctrinal treatises on the interpretation and application of the codes will require (1) consideration of the history and course of development of the texts taken or adapted from other recent codes and the course of doctrinal exposition and judicial interpretation of them and of analogous texts or texts on the same point in other codes, and (2) consideration of the conditions, customs, and modes of thought in China in the light of which and of Chinese ethical philosophy the codes must be interpreted and applied. This will call for libraries which have to be restored, for money to restore them has mostly been lacking, and leisure, which the teacher, who has to eke out a meager salary by taking on other work, is seldom able to find.

There is need of a better system of reporting judicial decisions. Thus far only syllabi of the points of law are published. But such reports are not adequate. There ought to be a full statement of the facts and of the application of those facts of the articles of the code interpreted. There is no need of the elaborate discussions of facts or elaborate citations and discussions of authorities to be found in American judicial opinions, although the former operate as a check on the courts and satisfy the public that the facts have been thoroughly considered, and the latter are valuable in estimating the value of a decision as a precedent. But there should be enough reported to enable assured understanding of what the court decided and to have its application to the facts clearly brought out.

A great and immediate need is the development of a true constitutional law. Like the American Constitution the Chinese Constitution is both a legal and a political document. But teaching and writing on the Chinese Constitution have tended to be from the standpoint of political science rather than of law, and a tendency to treat constitutional questions, which under the Constitution should be legal, as political, and to attempt to adjust jurisdictional lines by compromises at conferences of party leaders and of representatives of departments, instead of by law, has been noticeable. However, some of the leading men of China are aware of this, and I hope to see a real text book of Chinese constitutional law set constitutional development in the straight path at the outset.

Not the least need is the place of the bar in the administration of justice, which needs to be better understood and the profession needs to be better appreciated. The position of the bar in public esteem in China is much what is was in America after our Revolution and in the beginnings of our independent polity and in large part for like reasons. It is enough to say in the present connection that when we reflect on the conditions of admission to and conduct and discipline of the profession and the consequences as they were manifest in our large cities down to the change which began only in the last decade of the nineteenth century, we have no cause to reproach China for not, in the generation since her Revolution of 1911–1912, getting as far as we did in the fifty years after 1890. At any rate, the Chinese system of admission insures educated, trained, and reasonably competent practitioners.

Features of the Chinese System

Of the noteworthy good features of Chinese administration of justice we may put first the organization of courts. On the whole, the courts are organized on the French model except that the judiciary is independent of the executive instead of being a part of the executive as in France. At its head is the Judicial Yuan, one of the five departments of government provided by the Chinese Constitution. It has general jurisdiction over the administration of justice and disciplinary punishment of public functionaries. The Grand Justices, nominated by the President of the Republic and confirmed by the Control Yuan, have the duty of interpreting the Constitution and unifying the interpretation of laws and ordinances. Laws and executive ordinances in conflict with the Constitution are declared null and void, and the jurisdiction to give effect to these provisions is in the Grand Justices. At the head of this body is Dr. Wang Chung-hui, D.C.L. of Yale, barrister of the Middle Temple, deputy judge of the Permanent Court of International Justice at The Hauge, 1923–30, judge of the court, 1930–35, former Minister of Justice, translator into English of the German Civil Code, known all over the world as a jurist of the first rank.

The court system provides a Supreme Court, sitting at the capital, modelled on the French Court of Cessation. Its jurisdiction is appellate from the High Court and its proceeds by examination of the records transmitted to it and written arguments of counsel accompanying the grounds of appeal. Like the highest court of France it does not as a rule hear oral argument and passes only on questions of law. In each province there is a High Court with some original jurisdiction (*e.g.*, in cases of treason) but primarily it is a court of appeal from the District Courts, modelled on the French Courts of Appeal. In provinces where business requires it has a number of branches. The courts of general jurisdiction of first instance are the District Courts, provided for districts in each province. Where business requires it they may have civil and criminal branches. There are no separate courts for small causes. The flexible organization of the District Courts makes it possible to handle them well with a simple procedure. The judges are appointed for life, removable only for misconduct (upon conviction or disciplinary judgment) or inability to function, and may not be superseded, transferred, or have their salaries reduced except in accordance with law.

Another outstanding feature is the Ministry of Justice. It is part of the executive Yuan. It has general powers with respect to the administrative side of the courts very like those of the office administration of our federal courts. Also it has the power exercised by the Home Secretary in England of reprieves and commutation of punishment in capital cases. But its most important work from an American point of view is to study the functioning of legal institutions, the application and enforcement of law, the cases in which and reasons for which it fails to do justice or to do complete justice, the new situations which arise continually and means of meeting them, what legislation achieves its purpose and what not and why, and thus to give expert and intelligent guidance to those who frame and those who administer the laws. The Minister of Justice, Dr. Hsieh Kwan-sheng, is a *docteur en droit* of the University of Paris and a scholar and wise administrator with vision as to the future of Chinese law. He has held the position since 1937 and did notable work in keeping the machinery of justice going during the Japanese occupation and in restoring the disrupted organization and system since the close of the war. One of the most useful acts was the setting up of an experimental court at Chungking to try out features of procedure and observe the possibilities of procedural simplifications and devices.

China has excellent codes. They will compare with the best of the recent codes which have been framed and enacted since 1896. The Civil Code is exceptionally well done. It has made good use of the Swiss Civil Code of 1907, revised in 1912, and has introduced some notable improvements, particularly the giving up of the historical distinction between civil and commercial law, which grew up on the continent of Europe in the Middle Ages when the merchants were a distinct class, trading from land to land, with their own customary law and their own courts. The distinction has no rational claim to perpetuation in a modern code but had persisted until China gave it up. Also the Civil Code is well adapted to Chinese conditions, since it makes ample provision for the local customs which have been long established in different parts of China's vast domain. The Code of Civil Procedure is very well framed also. It follows largely the Austrian Procedure and is advanced, flexible, and simple.

Another excellent feature of the Chinese polity is the examination system. The Constitution provides (Article 85) that no person shall be appointed to a public office unless he is "qualified by examination." It provdes also (Article 86) for examinations as to "qualifications for practice in specialized professions and as technicians." The Examination Yuan is a separate and independent department of the government. It is based on an old traditional institution in China and the system has the confidence of the public. Such complaints of it as I have heard grow out of disturbed conditions during the war and at the beginning of reconstruction or else are what President Eliot used to call the wail of the unfit. The system assures training and competence from the top to the bottom of the judicial and administrative personnel.

In all the courts the record system and the compiling of statistics are admirable. Everything is well indexed and one can ascertain readily the exact state of the business of the courts and of the procurators, what each judge and each procurator has done and is doing, and the condition and progress of each case.

Legal education is fundamental in a country governed by a consitution which is the supreme law of the land, to be interpreted by judges an prescribing government by law. But legal education in China has had but a short time and little chance to develop. It is a matter of the present century. In 1904 the imperial regime perceived that it would be needful for China to transform her law fundamentally in order to keep pace with the rest of the world. A commission was appointed to compile a commercial code. In 1906 a codification commission was appointed. Universities founded by missionaries from abroad began to teach law, but not Chinese law, however, which was only at the beginning of its formative era, but French or Anglo-American, according to where the teachers came from. Chinese students began to go to Europe, to America, and to Japan to study law. After the Revolution in 1911-1912, codification went forward, culminating in 1930 in the present system of codes. In 1927 the establishment of the central government at Nanking began a period of rapid growth of education and establishment of insitutions of higher and professional learning. Some strong law schools had already grown up and others were set up and a general high level of legal education was aimed at. But the Japanese invasion upset the whole program. Most of the institutions of higher learning had to move to the interior and often many times more further. Their buildings were often destroyed and largely damaged. Their libraries and equipment were destroyed or looted and their teachers scattered. They carried on notwithstanding and have made a remarkable recovery in the last three years, though sorely hampered by lack of means to restore buildings, equipment, and libraries. The Ministry of Education has prescribed a standard curriculum. The goals are excellent. But want of textbooks, want of libraries, necessary low salaries in a time of high living costs, difficulty of finding qualified teachers, and necessity of large use of part-time teachers, joined to the pressure to turn out, as quickly as reasonable, men qualified to become judges and procurators, to enable the courts to cope with the tide of litigation in a time of reconstruction, make the task of the law schools very hard. Nevertheless, there are some very good law schools, and all of them are doing more and better than might have been expected under the circumstances. I have lectured before ten of them and met members of the faculties of many. On the whole, the teachers are well-trained, learned, diligent, and zealous. The Minister of Education has a sound ultimate program in view, and we may be assured progress will go forward as fast as circumstances will permit.

There are some excellent legal scholars among the law teachers. Some of them have written good doctrinal expositions of particular provisions of the Civil Code. But there is need of a whole systematic legal literature of which, on account of the war and destruction of libraries, there is only a beginning. To meet this need I have advised an organization analogous to the American Law Institute and a complete doctrinal exposition of Chinese law as a whole, to do what has been done in the United States by the Restatements of the Law.

C. The ROC Constitution of 1947

Modern constitutionalism was unknown in traditional China, where the emperor possessed all legislative, executive, and judicial powers. However, imperial rule was not absolute, and there were some limitations on the emperor's authority in practice, usage, and the teachings of the ancients, particularly Confucius. Beyond that, the censorial institution formed another check on the Chinese emperor. The censors had the duty to watch and criticize any member of the entire official system, including the emperor. Thus the Chinese tradition embodied a counterpart to the modern constitutional limitation on the government.

Modern western constitutional concepts were introduced to China in the late nineteenth century. After decades of efforts by the Nationalist Party, a modern constitution was adopted on December 25, 1946. This constitution is still in effect in Taiwan. The following excerpts describe the tortuous road to the adoption of the constitution in China.

3. Adoption of the ROC Constitution of 1946

Herbert H. Ma

China's first attempt to emulate Western political and legal institutions dates back to the last years of the last dynasty, the Manchu reign, in the 1800s. However, serious efforts to make a permanent constitution began only after the founding of the Republic of China in 1912. As a result, a number of drafts were introduced leading to the May 5th Draft Constitution of 1936, which in turn formed the basis of the present Constitution of 1947.

Both the May 5th Draft Constitution and the present Constitution are founded on the unique political theory of the Three Principles of the People and the doctrine of separation of five powers as taught by Dr. Sun Yat-sen, founder of the Chinese Republic. However, Western influence has always been present. . . .

When Japan first defeated China in 1894 and then Russia in 1905, the Manchu rulers of the Ch'ing dynasty were convinced by loyal political reformers that a constitutional government was the only way to be strong again. A concrete step was taken in 1908 when the Emperor Kuang-shü declared the 23-article General Plan of the Constitution aiming at transforming the body politic into a constitutional monarchy patterned after the Meiji Restoration in Japan. However, it was a time when the revolutionaries led by Dr. Sun Yat-sen had determined to bring down the dynasty as a prerequisite to the successful reconstruction of China. As a last attempt to survive, the Manchu imperial house further promulgated in 1911 the Nineteen Constitutional Principles to take effect immediately as a temporary constitution. These Principles were obviously meant to copy the British cabinet system, with the Emperor as mere figurehead. But it was too late to turn the tide. The next year saw the fall of the last dynasty in China's long monarchical history, and the first Chinese republic came into being.

In late 1911, the governors of Kiang-su and Chekiang provinces called upon all other provinces which had declared independence to send delegates to a meeting in Shanghai to form a provisional government.

Delegates from ten and later seventeen provinces did meet in Shanghai and elsewhere, and the result was the 24-article General Plan for Organization of the Provisional Government. Though quickly drawn up and short-lived, these articles are nevertheless fruits of the first attempt at constitution-making of the first Chinese Republic. These articles bore some striking similarities to the original United States Constitution. Among other things, they made the provisional President the real chief executive, and there was no mention of the people's basic rights and duties.

It was most unfortunate that the Chinese Republic had to face in her infancy successive crises of internal disruptions, to repeat the words of the above-quoted joint proposal used to describe the United States of America in her initial stage. The fact was, shortly after the installation of the provisional government, there arose warlordism, which kept the country divided and irresolute. It started with Yuan Shih-kai, the most influential figure during China's transition from a monarchy to a republic. When Sun Yat-sen, the revolutionary leader, was made the provisional President, no one feared he would abuse that powerful position. But the members of the Senate did have grave concern over the ambitious incoming President, Yuan Shih-kai—so much so that the Senate strongly proposed a Provisional Constitution of fifty-six articles, which replaced the General Plan for Organization of the Provisional Government and changed the American type of presidential system to the cabinet system based on the French model.

When an elected Congress worked out a draft for a permanent constitution in 1913, it adhered to the cabinet system, which requires all the President's acts to be countersigned by a member of the government. This greatly angered Yuan Shih-kai, who had by then become

Herbert H. Ma, "Republic of China," in Lawrence Ward Beer, (ed.) *Constitutionalism in Asia*, (Berkeley: University of California Press, 1979), pp. 39-49. Copyright 1979 by The Regents of the University of California; Reprinted by permission of the University of California Press. Footnotes omitted.

dissatisfied with his already dictatorial presidential power. After disbanding the Congress by force, Yuan Shih-kai sought to put himself on the throne. In this he failed. But great damage was done to the cause of republicanism in China, because, although the Congress was soon reassembled and the constitution-making efforts were made to continue in the following ten years, warlords began to vie with one another for control of the central government in Peking. Since they were not genuinely willing to see China embrace constitutionalism, which would threaten their own positions, the constitutional drafts drawn up in 1919, 1923, and 1924, respectively, were either abortive or never enforced. These drafts all adopted the French cabinet system, but each time in a more elaborate form.

At the time when the warlords battled against each other in the north, Dr. Sun Yat-sen, the founder of the Republic, rallied the revolutionary forces of his Nationalist Party in South China to oppose them. He was not to see China unified before he died in 1925. The unification of China was left for his devoted disciple, Generalissimo Chiang Kai-shek, to complete when in 1926 he successfully carried through the northern expedition which wiped out the major warlords. The capital was moved to Nanking, and a new epoch began in China's efforts to make a permanent constitution, this time on the basis of the theory of Dr. Sun Yat-sen's Three Principles of the People and the doctrine of separation of five powers.

Often translated as the Principle of Nationalism, the Principle of Democracy, and the Principle of People's Livelihood, these Three Principles provide the theoretical bases for the cause of revolution and national construction. Since so much has been written about them, it is sufficient for our purpose to say that they aim at national unity and independence, a government of popular sovereignty and the general welfare of the people. The separation of five powers as a direct guideline for constitution-making is meant to implement the three principles. While this theory and doctrine are unique in many senses, they are not cut off from the main currents of political thought underlying any democratic form of government. Indeed, it has been asserted that Dr. Sun Yat-sen's Three Principles of the People were in the main of American origin. The immediate inspiration of the three principles was said to be Lincoln's Gettysburg Address, particularly his "government of the people, by the people and for the people." However, since Dr. Sun Yat-sen in elaborating his Three Principles obviously resorted to many sources, Eastern as well as Western, European as well as American, the above assertion is only true to the extent that Lincoln's words probably gave a powerful impetus to Dr. Sun's forming the idea of three principles of the people.

On the other hand, the separation of five powers as a foundation of China's constitutional structure is not a departure from, but an improvement on, Montesquieu's doctrine of separation of powers. The ingenuity of separating the powers of examination and impeachment, traditionally highly developed in China, from the executive and legislative powers and according them independent status marks the uniqueness of the doctrine. In this way, a government of qualified persons chosen by means of competitive civil service examinations may be ensured. On the other hand, the power of impeachment may no longer be used to achieve partisan purposes in parliament, but may be exercised independently to help bring about a clean and efficient government. Dr. Sun Yat-sen believed, however, that a five-power government plan would not be able to substantiate popular sovereignty as advocated by him unless the demarcation of political powers and administrative (government) powers were realized. In short, Dr. Sun Yat-sen would push the idea of direct democracy to the extent possible by installing a popularly elected National Assembly armed with the political powers of election, recall, initiative, and referendum, so that the five-power government would function according to the will of the people. On the basis of these doctrines, the Organic Law of the National Government was formulated in 1928 to create the first five-power national government under the leadership of the Nationalist Party (Kuomintang).

In the subsequent years constitution-making efforts continued steadily. In 1931 a Provisional Constitution was adopted, consisting of eighty-nine articles to be divided into eight chapters. This document recognized the supremacy of the Kuomintang during the period of political tutelage in that "the National Congress of the Kuomintang delegates shall exercise the powers on behalf of the National Assembly." But this period of party rule was supposed to be of short duration. Hence, after 1932, drafts of the permanent constitution began to be proposed and released to the public for comment and criticism. It was only after six revisions that the draft became final on May 5 in 1936. Hence the popular name, "May 5th Draft Constitution."

Unfortunately, the constitution-making task was interrupted, first by the Sino-Japanese war, which broke out the next year and lasted for eight years, then by the political crises started by the Chinese Communists who, taking advantage of the war, had been made so strong as to threaten the existing government and its determination to introduce a permanent constitution. To keep the country united the government agreed to a Political Consultation Conference to settle the differences of all major political parties with regard to constitution-making. Although certain agreements were reached, the Communists and leftist parties still refused to participate. The National Assembly finally met to pass a revised version of the May 5th Draft Constitution as guided by the agreements, on December 25, 1946.

Since the present Constitution differs from the May 5th Draft Constitution in both form and substance, it is pertinent to point out the highlights of that draft before dealing with the present Constitution in more detail. The May 5th Draft Constitution is by and large in conformity with the guidelines bequeathed by Dr. Sun Yat-sen. As far as government structure is concerned, it entrusted the four political powers with a popularly elected National Assembly, which elects and recalls, among other officials, the President and Vice-President of the Republic. The President of the Republic, on the other hand, possesses actual power, and the office resembles to a large extent that of the President of the United States of America. He appoints all the top officials of the executive department of the central government, who are individually responsible to him. Though his acts must be countersigned by the president of the Executive Yuan, the fact that the President of the Republic chairs the meetings of the Executive Yuan Council gives him every opportunity to exert his influence.

The Constitution in its present form consists of 175 articles divided into 14 chapters. It was meant to cover all the major points of Dr. Sun Yat-sen's constitutional theories and the principles agreed upon at the Political Consultation Conference participated in by leaders of the then existing political parties. For this reason, some deviations from the May 5th Draft Constitution were unavoidable. Consequently, there has been much argument as to whether as a result the present constitution is not less conformative to Dr. Sun Yat-sen's teachings than the May 5th Draft Constitution.

Under the chapter on Rights and Duties of the People there are articles corresponding to the Bill of Rights in the United States Constitution. For example, the people are guaranteed (1) freedom of speech, lecturing, writing, and publication (Article 11, first amendment), (2) freedom of religious faith (Article 13, first amendment), (3) freedom of assembly and of association (Article 14, first amendment), (4) freedom of person (Article 8, fourth amendment), (5) right to present petitions, to file complaints, and to institute legal proceedings (Article 16, first amendment). Article 22 of the Chinese Constitution is strikingly similar to the Ninth Amendment to the U.S. Constitution. That Article provides that "all other freedoms and rights of the people that are not detrimental to social order or public welfare shall be guaranteed under the Constitution."

However, while the Chinese Constitution, like its American counterpart, guarantees individual freedoms and rights without qualification, restriction of them is allowable under conditions set forth in Article 23, namely: (1) to prevent infringement upon the freedoms of other persons, (2) to avert an imminent crisis, (3) to maintain social order, (4) to advance public welfare.

The governmental structure as found in the present Constitution is based in general on Dr. Sun Yat-sen's demarcation of political and administrative powers and the separation of five administrative powers. There are a National Assembly, a President, and five Yuan: the Executive Yuan, the Legislative Yuan, the Judicial Yuan, the Examination Yuan, and the Control Yuan. Compared with the National Assembly as defined in the May 5th Draft Constitution, the present National Assembly is so limited in its powers that in practice it only elects the President and Vice-President of the Republic. For this reason, it has been derogatively likened to the American presidential electoral college.

Of particular relevance to our purpose is the frequent question whether the central government structure adopted by the Chinese Constitution is modelled on the American presidential system or on the British cabinet system. This question can best be answered in light of the triangular relationship between the President, the Executive Yuan, and the Legislative Yuan. Article 57 reads:

1. The Executive Yuan has the duty to present to the Legislative Yuan a statement of its administrative policies and a report on its administration. While the Legislative Yuan is in session, Members of the Legislative Yuan shall have the right to question the President and the Ministers and Chairmen of Commissions of the Executive Yuan.

2. If the Legislative Yuan does not concur in any important policy of the Executive Yuan, it may, by resolution, request the Executive Yuan to alter such a policy. With respect to such resolution, the Executive Yuan may, with the approval of the President of the Republic, request the Legislative Yuan for a reconsiderations. If, after reconsideration, two-thirds of the Members of the Legislative Yuan present at the meeting uphold the original resolution, the President of the Executive Yuan shall either abide by the same or resign from office.

3. If the Executive Yuan deems a resolution on a statutory, budgetary, or treaty bill passed by the Legislative Yuan difficult of execution, it may, with the approval of the President of the Republic and within ten days after its transmission to the Executive Yuan, request the Legislative Yuan to reconsider the said resolution. If, after reconsideration, two-thirds of the Members of the Legislative Yuan present at the meeting uphold the original resolution, the President of the Executive Yuan shall either abide by the same or resign from office.

If the above provision gives one the initial impression that the system contained therein appears to be both cabinet and presidential, a closer look indicates that it is neither the one nor the other. While the President of the Executive Yuan (the Prime Minister) is made responsible to the Legislative Yuan, Article 57 expressly prohibits members of the Legislative Yuan from holding government posts concurrently, and the President of the Executive Yuan is not given the power to dissolve the legislature. On the other hand, while the President of the Republic, subject to the consent of the legislature, does nominate and appoint the President of the Executive Yuan, his power of appointment ceases there and does not reach down to the Vice-President of the Executive Yuan and the various heads of the ministries and commissions. And unlike the American system, where the President is the ultimate decision maker, the Executive Yuan meeting, which the President of the Yuan himself chairs, makes the decisions on all important matters of the State. Article 57 does adopt the veto power, the prerogative of the American President, but it is exercised by the President of the Executive Yuan. The President of the Republic only reserves the power of approval. So analyzed, the Chinese government system is of a unique type taking after both the British cabinet system and the American presidential system.

One may next ask whether the American judicial review system, which has been adopted by many countries, obtains in the Chinese Constitution. If by judicial review is meant the power vested in the judiciary to interpret the Constitution and to repudiate the applicability of laws inconsistent with the Constitution, it has its counterpart in the Chinese Constitution.

According to the provisions of Articles 78, 79, 171, and 173 of the Constitution, the Council of Grand Justices, a component part of the Judicial Yuan, is vested with the exclusive power of judicial review and the power of interpreting the Constitution and unifying the interpretations of laws and ordinances. Among other things, the Council alone is to determine whether a law or an ordinance is in conflict with the Constitution. However, interpretation can be given only upon request by governmental organs or the people and not of the Council's own initiative.

On the other hand, the ordinary courts, unlike their American counterparts, have no power of judicial review as to whether a law is in conflict with the Constitution. Only if a judgement is deemed to be in conflict with the Constitution does the litigant concerned have the right to state this in the reasons for his appeal to a higher court while the proceedings for the case are still in progress.

Finally, a few words about the Control Yuan may be in order. Although based on the traditional Chinese censorial system, the Control Yuan as found in the present Constitution is to a certain extent in its organization modelled on the United States Senate. For example, members of the Control Yuan are basically elected by provincial and municipal councils, the number being five from each province and two from each municipality. They are prohibited from occupying any other public office during the time for which they are elected. One of the major functions of the Control Yuan is to exercise the power of consent in the appointment of the President, Vice-President, and Grand Justices of the Judicial Yuan, and the President, Vice-President, and Members of the Examination Yuan. In fact, it was on the basis of its similarity to the upper house of a Western parliament or congress, such as the United States Senate, that the Control Yuan, the National Assembly, and the Legislative Yuan jointly were regarded by the Council of Grand Justices as being equivalent to a "parliament" of a Western democracy.

Two years after the promulgation of the Constitution of 1947, the Chinese Communists overran the country and the Nationalist government retreated from the mainland to the island province of Taiwan. It brought with it the Constitution, the laws, and the legal system intact, and they have since been in force within the present territories of the Republic of China. In other words, there is a continuation in the Constitution proper since it was framed in 1947, but the interpretation and application of the Constitution are limited to the experiences after the Nationalist government moved to Taiwan in 1949.

The promulgation of a constitution did not bring China into the era of constitutionalism. On the contrary, the civil war between the ROC government and the Chinese Communists accelerated to an unprecedented level. Amid the war, the first session of the first term of the National Assembly convened at Nanking in 1948 and elected Chiang Kai-shek as the President of the ROC. It also adopted "Temporary Provisions for the Duration of Mobilization to Suppress the Rebellion" (hereinafter referred to as the "Temporary Provisions") through the procedure for constitutional amendment. The Temporary Provisions strengthened the President's emergency powers (see *infra*) and restricted certain freedoms of the people.

II. LAW AND JUSTICE IN TAIWAN, 1950-66

In the fall of 1949, Communist forces occupied Fukien Province and were threatening to launch a massive attack on the island of Taiwan across the strait. In late October, a Communist force landed at Quemoy, but to the surprise of Western observers, the ROC defense force wiped out all the 20,000 or so invading troops and temporarily halted the Communist attempt to seize Taiwan. While the Communists consolidated their control of the mainland in 1949-1950, more than one million government forces and civilians were evacuated to Taiwan. During the period, the United States adopted a hands-off policy toward Taiwan and refused to provide military assistance to the ROC government. It was amid this bleak and seemingly hopeless situation that the ROC government reestablished itself in Taiwan in late 1949.

Despite the difficulties caused by its defeat on the mainland and the constant threat of a Communist invasion, the ROC government continued its strenuous efforts to administer law and justice within the framework of the 1947 Constitution and the legal system established while it was on the mainland. The following excerpts are a survey of the operation of the legal system during the period from 1950 to 1966.

4.   Public Order and Safety in Taiwan

Frederick H. Chaffee, et. al.

In the years immediately following the removal of the government to Taiwan, the influx of thousands of refugees fleeing the mainland and the constant threat that the Communist revolution would spread to the island created problems of public order in which considerations of national security were paramount. Martial law was in effect, and there was a tendency to look upon any public disturbance as essentially subversive or connected with national security in one way or another.

A special security force, known as the Peace Preservation Corps (PPC) and operating under the Ministry of National Defense, virtually replaced regular police forces as the major instrument of law enforcement, and military courts were more active than their civilian counterparts. Interference in the daily life of citizens was common, and its arbitrary nature fostered much resentment among them. The Chinese, however, are traditionally law-abiding people; they are accustomed to obeying legal restrictions and have a deeply ingrained respect for constituted authority. The greater part of them also were mindful of the necessity for strict controls to ensure national survival, so that the nation as a whole remained under remarkably good control.

When it became evident that invasion by Communist forces was not imminent and that subversion could be controlled, the situation began to return to more normal procedures. Martial law continued, but efforts were made to phase the PPC out of most police operations in favor of regular forces. As early as 1952 the jurisdiction of military courts over routine criminal offenders was abolished, except when espionage or insurrection was involved. Police activities, which had been carried out through a number of independent forces that included separate agencies dealing with criminal, railroad, port, traffic, and other operations, were consolidated under the Taiwan provincial government. The Taiwan provincial Police Administration established a single coordinated Provincial Police Force and also founded two academies to train officers and enlisted personnel to man it. In 1967 this force had full responsibility for all conventional police operations.

Violations of public order are covered and proscribed by the enlightened Criminal Code, promulgated in 1935 and maintained in force ever since. The code is based on European concepts and provides penalties and punishments for offenders but it is aimed primarily at rehabilitating offenders rather than retaliating against them. It also exempts mentally incompetent persons from liability for their acts and provides for lighter punishment, but not remission of guilt or criminal responsibility, for juveniles under 18 years of age.

The prosecution of violators is conducted under the Code of Criminal Procedure and may be carried through as many as three levels of courts on appeals. There are no provisions for juries, but cases are heard and decided by a panel of three judges in all but trials of first instance that concern relatively simple violations. Defendants in trials are entitled to legal defense counsel and are provided with court-appointed public defenders when they cannot retain their own.

The Republic of China is a participating member of the United Nations Conference on the Prevention of Crime and the Treatment of Prisoners, to whose conclusions and recommendations it is committed. Convicted criminals undergo much political indoctrination, as well as regular vocational training, to enable them to return to society fully capable of earning a living. While they are in custody they engage in productive work on prison farms or in prison-owned factories and can be remunerated for their labor. A premium is placed on good behavior, and after specified lengths of time cooperative and tractable prisoners may be released on parole.

Frederick H. Chaffee, George E. Aurell, Helen A. Barth, Ann S. Cort, John H. Dombrowski, Vincent J. Fasano and John O. Weaver, *Area Handbook for the Republic of China*, (Washington, D.C.: U.S. Government Printing Office, 1969), pp. 373-392.

Since 1960 there has been a noticeable increase in the incidence of crime attributable to two factors—a rather large increase in the size of the population, particularly in urban areas, and a definite increase in the police efficiency in detecting crime and apprehending criminals. There is no evidence that the increase of crime is caused by a mounting disrespect for law; on the contrary, the Chinese remain generally law-abiding, and the police appear to be well in command of routine disorders.

Much of this high regard for authority is inherent in the Chinese character, but in modern Taiwan much is also the result of a widespread campaign of legal education carried out by the government among the general public. There is a lingering-tendency, nevertheless, among a large part of the population, especially in villages and rural areas, to avoid involvement in the courts and to settle differences among themselves, usually through the services of a respected elder who acts as arbitrator.

ORGANIZATION FOR LAW AND ORDER

Responsibility for the administration and maintenance of law and order is vested in three agencies of the government. At the national level the state by the Constitution, is concerned with a determination of the constitutionality of laws and actions taken by government officials, departments, or agencies. At this level also, the Executive Yuan, through its Ministry of Justice, administers all courts below the Supreme Court, supervises the nation's penal institutions, and operates the Bureau of Investigation, which is the Chinese counterpart of the American Federal Bureau of Investigation. The third governmental agency involved in law and order is the Taiwan provincial government that raises, trains, and administers regular police forces.

The Judicial Yuan

The Judicial Yuan, whose president and vice president are appointed by the President of the Republic, directs the activities of the Council of Grand Justices, the Supreme Court, the Administrative Court, and the Committee on the Discipline of Public Functionaries.

The Council of Grand Justices is a body of 15 senior members of the Judiciary appointed by the President of the Republic for terms of 9 years each. It sits in continuous session under the chairmanship of the president of the Judicial Yuan. The Council is not a trial court but concerns itself with interpreting the Constitution, with determining the constitutionality of final decisions rendered by lower courts or government departments, and with unifying interpretations of law.

The function of unifying interpretations of law is required whenever two or more branches of the government are in dispute as to the meaning and application of a law or an executive order. If the problem cannot be settled between or among the agencies concerned, it is submitted to the Council for consideration. After due deliberation, in which the intent of the Constitution receives major attention, the Council issues an interpretation that becomes official and binding on all sectors of the government.

The Supreme Court is the highest tribunal for the adjudication of both civil and criminal cases. As far as can be determined, it has no original jurisdiction but acts as a court of second instance to hear appeals from decisions of lower courts. In addition to its appellate function, that court has a Precedents Compilation Committee, which is charged with the selection and publication of exemplary trial decisions for the guidance of lower courts. In 1967 the Committee had issued a total of five volumes of Synopses of Precedents that were in general use.

The Administrative Court is a special organ that hears appeals from decisions in which an individual claims he was injured by an unlawful court judgement or by an illegal administrative act by some government agency. It is not concerned with criminal or civil aspects of the case but only with whether or not the basis for judgement was legal.

The Committee on the Discipline of Public Functionaries is the agency within the Judicial Yuan that determines disciplinary action against any public official for malfeasance or improper conduct. Its disciplinary action stops short of impeachment, which is the exclusive prerogative of the control Yuan.

The Ministry of Justice

The Ministry of Justice is the largest and most active national agency involved in the administration of law and order. It runs the Bureau of Investigation, supervises and administers all courts below the Supreme Court and is responsible for the nation's penal institutions. It also operates the Judicial Personnel Training Center (JPTC) and carries on an extensive information program for disseminating legal knowledge among the people.

Below the Supreme Court, which is in the Judicial Yuan but acts completely independent from it, the judicial system, administered by the Ministry of Justice, consists of two types of lower courts known as district and high courts. Each of these, regardless of type, has jurisdiction over both civil and criminal cases and often hears them in separate tribunals. In addition, four new juvenile courts were established at Taipei, Kaohsiung, Tainan, and Taichung in July, 1967.

District courts are the base of the legal structure as courts of first instance for all cases except those involving state security or friendly relations with foreign states. Under the Constitution district courts were authorized to be established in each county or municipality, but in practice this was not always followed. In some areas several municipalities or counties may be grouped under a single district court; where jurisdictions are large and contain sizable population concentrations, however, the usual practice is to establish branch district courts to help lighten the work-load. In 1967 there were 12 district courts in the province of Taiwan and 1 on Quemoy (Kinmen), which is considered legally to be part of Fukien province. The Taiwanese district courts were located at Taipei, Tsinchu, Taichung, Chiayi, Tainan, Kaohsiung, Pingtung, Keelung, Ilan, Hualien, Taitung, and the Pescadores (Penghu). The tribunals at Taichung and Chiayi had branch courts at Chunghua and Yunlin, respectively.

Each district court or branch operated under a president, who did not sit on the bench but was concerned exclusively with its administrative affairs. Each court also had a panel of judges, whose number varied with the anticipated work-load, and an assigned procuratorate of attorneys-at-law, who acted as state prosecutors. If the number of assigned judges exceeded six, they usually were organized into separate divisions for criminal and civil cases. In most cases, however, only one judge sits for a particular case.

High courts are superior tribunals organized in identical manner to district courts except that the division of their judges into criminal and civil panels is mandatory. The basis for their establishment was one per province, although branches were set up for Taiwan where the jurisdictional area was too extensive to be handled conveniently by a single court. In 1967 the Republic of China had one high court, located at the national capital, with branches at Taichung, Tainan, and Hualien to relieve the parent tribunal of cases arising in central, southern, and eastern Taiwan, respectively. Since the mainland was a denied area, there was only an Amoy-dialect branch of the Fukien High Court at Quemoy serving that province.

A high court has jurisdiction in all criminal cases that involve offenses against the internal or external security of the state and those that affect friendly relations with foreign states. It also acts as a court of second instance to hear appeals against criminal and civil judgement of district courts or their branches. Habitually, three judges sit for a particular case. Judgements of a high court are considered final when it sits as a court of second instance or when its decision in an original trial involves a case that is routine or of relative unimportance. In either situation, however, provision is made for litigants on either side to submit appeals to the Supreme Court for final judgement.

The new juvenile courts were the nation's first. Each was manned by a staff of 10 to 12 judges and procurators trained especially to handle cases involving minors. Their procedures were identical to those of adult courts, but their judgements usually called for vocational training at reformatories rather than incarceration for punishment.

Under the law the *Bureau of Investigation* is the major government agency concerned with investigating offenses against national security and interest. Its agents have legal status as judicial police whose job is to investigate crime and identify criminals on a national basis. They are empowered to act on their own initiative, but much of their service is in support and at the request of the regular police forces. In order to discharge its responsibilities, the Bureau maintains complete criminal files at its headquarters, including a large section devoted to fingerprint classification and storage and a complex of 24 chemical, electrical, audio, and optical crime laboratories for the scientific examination and identification of evidence.

The Judicial Personnel Training Center (JPTC)

The Judicial Personnel Training Center is of great significance because it is the primary source of manpower for both the judicial and the penal systems. Persons who aspire to become judges are selected and recruited by the Ministry of Justice from graduates of law colleges or from others who take a special examination administered by the Examination Yuan. Few nongraduate personnel are recruited because the examination is so difficult that only about 3 percent of those who take it score high enough to matriculate at the JPTC. Judicial courses cover a year and a half and include about 1,300 hours of classroom instruction in theory of law and judicial practice, as well as much practical training in the conduct of mock trials. Graduates of the course are appointed directly to judicial posts by the Ministry.

In addition to courses for judges, the JPTC conducts training of similar duration for court clerks, bailiffs, criminal investigators, prison wardens, and other judicial and penal personnel to provide a constant flow of qualified people for these duties. The JPTC curriculum also includes numerous short courses in specialized subjects for those already on duty who require refresher training, who seek qualification in new skills or who simply wish to improve their chances for promotion.

A special section within the Ministry has been established to reduce crime through the dissemination of knowledge about laws and their application. It produces a variety of tracts, brochures, and pamphlets for distribution to the general public through the Government Information Office (GIO). It also makes extensive use of radio to reach the broadest possible segment of the population.

The major radio effort, carried by 33 government and private radio stations, consists of a series of short, 3-to-5-minute programs inserted strategically in regular musical programs throughout the day. Material usually consists of examples of common legal problems and a discussion of the laws governing their solutions. The programs received such wide acceptance among listeners that several stations instituted separate and additional offerings of their own as featured presentations during prime listening time.

Most of these independent programs are conducted by female announcers who have gained wide reputations and have become distinct radio personalities with loyal followings of their own. Among the more popular of them are Miss Wu Chuan, whose "Evening Chat at the Provincial Capital" is carried by the Chung Hsing station at Nantou; Miss Huang Min, whose "Law Knowledge for the People" is aired by the Hua Sheng station of Taipei; Miss Chen Chao-an, whose "Law Education for the Public" is scheduled by the Cheng Hua station at Keelung; and Miss Pai Chien-ju, whose "Our Family" is broadcast over the Broadcasting Corporation of China (BCC) network.

The Provincial Government of Taiwan

The Ministry of the Interior of the Executive Yuan establishes policy and exercises general supervision over police affairs for the entire country, but their actual administration is the responsibility of the Taiwan provincial government. In the early days of the regime's removal to Taiwan the many activities normally carried out by Chinese police, such as fire and ambulance service, railroad and highway patrol, forest and mine police, marine and harbor police, and other specialized services, operated through separate forces. Gradually, however, they were all consolidated as branches of the regular police force under unified control of the Taiwan Provincial Police Administration.

Control of police is vested in a central provincial police headquarters at Taipei and is exercised through 21 police bureaus established in each country and major city or special police district. These bureaus supervise the activities of some 90 branch bureaus, over 200 police stations in larger cities, and about 1,250 substations in smaller towns and villages.

Police Headquarters is organized into three major departments. The Central Department controls police operations as a whole and runs the Senior Police Officers' Training School. The Provincial Department controls various specialized divisions of the force, such as the forestry, highway, harbor, and railroad police, and administers the Taiwan Police Academy for training nonofficer personnel. The Town and City Department deals with the various bureaus and stations to coordinate and control their activities at the basic operating level.

THE CRIMINAL CODE

The Criminal Code first was enacted on the mainland in 1928 but was revised and put into force in 1935. Its revised form was declared in effect for Taiwan when the island was returned to Chinese sovereignty after World War II and has been in force ever since. Its provisions are based on the continental rather than the Anglo-Saxon legal system. As a basic principle, the Code emphasizes individual, not collective, responsibility in a criminal case. It also states that no person shall be held guilty of an offense not expressly covered in the Code. Modern Chinese jurisprudence does not tolerate the practice of collective responsibility and does not hold a family or a village responsible for the guilt of any of its members.

Several categories of offenders are granted immunity from criminal liability. An unpremediated or negligent act is not punishable except when specifically made so by law. In regard to capacity to commit a premeditated crime, the Code provides that an act committed by a person under 14 years of age is not subject to punishment. If an offender is over 14 but under 18, the sentence may be reduced. Similarly, a person judged to be insane is not held accountable for his acts, and one who is feeble-minded usually receives a reduced sentence.

The Code recognizes that the prevention of a crime is more important than its punishment, and the penalties it prescribes are directed more at the reformation of the wrongdoer than at retaliation against him. Accordingly, it requires that juvenile delinquents be detained in reformatories for rehabilitation; that insane persons be kept in some appropriate institution for their own protection as well as for that of society; that opium addicts and habitual drunkards be sent to hospitals for cure; and that vagrants be rehabilitated through work. With the same goal in mind the Code also permits suspension of punishment and conditional release on fairly easy terms. When a person shows evidence of repentence during the execution of a sentence of imprisonment, he may, after having served 10 years of a life sentence or half his term for lesser offenses, be granted conditional release upon recommendation of prison authorities.

Chinese jurisprudence adopts a modern doctrine of criminal law requiring a judge to consider not only the crime committed but also the nature of the person committing it and all extenuating circumstances that may have prompted the act. The Code directs the judges to pay special attention to such factors as motive, provocation, the character and intelligence of the offender, the relations normally existing between the offender and the injured party, and the conduct of the offender after the offense.

THE POLICE SYSTEM

The Chinese police system is made up of three broad categories of forces: the regular police organization administered by the Taiwan provincial government; the PPC, a force concerned with the detection and suppression of Communist subversive activities; and a number of other security agencies primarily engaged in counterespionage operations.

The Regular Police

The regime has displayed a great reluctance in releasing information about its police forces because, technically, the nation is still in a state of martial law, and, like the armed forces, police are vital elements of national security. According to best informed estimates, however, the regular forces, including specialized elements, such as those for traffic, forest, mining, and harbor patrol, have a combined strength of approximately 20,000 officers and men.

According to the published Taiwan Police Law, their basic mission is to preserve public order by enforcing the criminal and civil codes and routine police regulations. The Police Law also charges them with issuing police orders; punishing contraventions of police regulations; assisting in the investigation of crimes; searching, detaining, and arresting suspects; and executing administrative orders. The regular police, further, have responsibility for regulating traffic; protecting health; taking the census; guarding against fire, disaster, and moral turpitude; and protecting private and public property. Except for infractions of police regulations, they have no punitive powers and even then are limited to the imposition of fines of NT$100 (NT$40 equal US$1) and detention not to exceed 14 days. Criminal violators apprehended by the police must be turned over to an appropriate law court for prosecution within 24 hours of arrest.

Among other functions the enforcement of various antinarcotic laws has engaged considerable attention of the police because narcotic addiction, traffic, and sales are prohibited in the Republic. Rewards for information leading to the detection of illegal use and traffic in narcotics are relatively high and have proved effective in reducing their incidence on the island.

Virtually all members of the regular police, except senior officials and some of the older men, are recruited into the force after graduation from one of the two schools operated by Police Headquarters to train police personnel. From time to time experienced officers and men repatriated to Taiwan from such places as Hong Kong, Macao, or Indochina are added to the force, but even they must undergo short refresher and orientation courses at one of the schools before being assigned permanent posts. All officer personnel are trained at the Taiwan Police Academy.

Any Chinese national between the ages of 19 and 30, male or female, who can meet certain requirements may apply for admission to either school. In addition to passing a rigid competitive examination and a thorough physical checkup, those who aspire to the Senior Police Officers' Training School must be graduates of some institution of higher learning; those who seek to enter the Taiwan Police Academy must be at least high school graduates.

Courses for officers vary from 2 to 4 years, depending on the student's previous education. Courses include instruction in criminology, penology, law, politics, foreign police systems, electricity, photography, fingerprint analysis, mathematics, biology, police-dog handling, and practical work or exercises in criminal procedure. Courses for enlisted personnel last from 6 months to a year and involve training in politics, law, history, police duties, geography, military training, self-defense, and physical culture. Graduates from both schools are assigned to permanent posts immediately after completing their courses.

Although no figures are available to indicate the proportion of mainlanders and Taiwanese in the police, it is likely that the latter constitute the major portion in the ranks and junior-officer posts. The prospect of a career in the police force helping to preserve law and order at home seems to have more appeal for young Taiwanese than one in the armed forces.

Generally speaking, the regular police force appear to be well trained and disciplined. They display high morale, good efficiency, and a deep sense of duty. Most police are stern but considerate in handling violations of police regulations and seem to exercise care in avoiding undue interference in people's daily lives and affairs. There is some evidence of graft and corruption, particularly in efforts to ensure desirable assignments and in accepting bribes to refrain from imposing restraints on gambling or vice, but its prevalence is unknown; only occasionally has a case warranting prosecution been uncovered.

In normal times the police are believed capable of preserving local order. In time of great mass excitement, as in large organized riot or demonstration, they probably would have to invoke assistance from units of the armed forces.

The Peace Preservation Corps

The maintenance of local law and order is well controlled and poses no problem or challenge to the national government. The main threat to national security comes from subversive activities by Communist underground agents. The PPC is a specialized force of semisecret elements established in 1949 and incorporated with other agencies into a combined Taiwan Garrison Command in 1958 to deal with the problem.

The governor of Taiwan province is the ex-officio commander of the PPC, but the actual work of directing and supervising it is performed by a deputy commander, who is always a military officer. The incorporation of the PPC into the structure of the provincial government, however, appears to be one of convenience and appearance only for its real control is exercised by Lieutenant General Chiang Ching-kuo, the Minister of National Defense and chief of all Nationalist Party (Kuomintang) organizations concerned with internal security.

Among the functions of the PPC are the issuance of entry and exit permits, protection of public utility installations, prevention of smuggling, and control of shipping. Its major task, however, is counter-espionage. According to official releases, Communist underground agents were most active to Taiwan just before the Korean War. Since the launching of a continuing counterespionage campaign, Communist activities have declined and in 1967 were not considered critically out of hand.

The headquarters of the PPC at Taipei has been extremely successful in keeping details of its work from becoming public knowledge; consequently, there are conflicting reports and much speculation about the number of arrests and persons involved and the identity of the PPC's principal agents. Detailed information was given out in 1950 concerning the break-up of an underground Communist organization in Taipei whose membership included a deputy chief of staff, the wife of the general in charge of Army training, and the managing director of the Taiwan Sugar Corporation. Since then reliable information has been scant and usually consists of an occasional isolated newspaper account of the arrest of a Communist agent or of a raid on some suspected center of Communist activity.

The most spectacular incident, perhaps, was one that occurred at the Taipei railroad station in 1959. The plaza around the station is wired with loudspeakers over which the BCC's official newscast is relayed during busy hours for the edification of waiting commuters and travelers. On this occasion the loudspeakers blared forth with a Communist propaganda commentary from the mainland instead of the regular program. In was some minutes before authorities could switch the system back to normal. The PPC conducted a thorough investigation, but its findings were never made public. The official explanation offered in the newspapers were merely that some technician at the intercept receiver had gotten his connections crossed.

In addition to counterespionage, the PPC conducts propaganda drives designed to win surrender of Communist agents. In 1951 the government promulgated the set of Procedures for the Voluntary Surrender of Communists and Communist Sympathizers, which called upon these people to come out into the open and renounce their Communist affiliation. In return their life and property would be protected and their employment guaranteed. The Procedures were still in effect in 1967 and had accounted for the surrender of hundreds of confessed Communists over the years.

The PPC also is concerned with persons who escape from the mainland and make their way to Taiwan. The PPC maintains a register of these individuals and keeps track of their movements and activities, as well as providing them with protection against possible reprisals by Communist agents. The greatest influx of such people was the group of 14,209 Chinese prisoners of the Korean war who elected to go to Taiwan rather than return to their homeland.

Units of the PPC, which are organized in companies as in the army, are stationed at strategic points for the protection of bridges, waterworks, power stations, mines, and industrial plants. Entrances into mountain areas of the aboriginal tribes are guarded to prevent the infiltration of Communist agents. Officers of the PPC also provide training for aboriginal groups in methods of self-defense to improve their capability for overcoming possible clandestine attack by Communist elements and to reduce the likelihood of infiltration.

Part of the PPC's work is to check the arrival and departure of passengers at airports, seaports, and railroad stations. To guard against smuggling and infiltration of Communists at these points, each traveler has to deposit the name of a guarantor at PPC headquarters before an entry or exit permit is issued. Since the improvement of public safety conditions there are indications that these requirements have been relaxed since 1963 and that the procedures for applying for such permits have been simplified. In 1967 technicians, students returning from foreign schools, Overseas Chinese who intended to make investment in Taiwan, and people whose loyalty was known to the government no longer had to obtain exit and entry permits in advance.

Other Security Agencies

A number of other security agencies, such as the Files Office attached to the President's household and the various investigation bureaus in the government and the military establishment, are charged with counterespionage activities.

The government takes the position that disruptions to normal life caused by the activities of such agencies are unavoidable and that tight security control and severe penalties for espionage are necessary to ensure the safety of the island and its people. At the same time the regime is sensitive to criticism of its agents, and it has taken measures to eliminate as far as possible any interference with personal freedom and to reduce the incidence of unwarranted arrest.

The jurisdiction of military courts has been restricted to offenses committed by military personnel or by civilians who act directly against military interests. Accused persons are provided with public defenders in all courts, civilian and military, and are awarded compensation if they can prove false arrest. Security agents are instructed to be certain of actual guilt before they make an arrest and are subject to disciplinary action if they act too rashly.

CRIMINAL PROCEDURES

The Code of Criminal Procedure was promulgated at the same time as the Criminal Code. It includes provisions for public and private prosecution as well as for trials and appeals.

Public Prosecution

The highest officer in the procurator system is the procurator general, who has his office in the Supreme Court. In each of the lower courts there is a chief procurator and several subordinate procurators. These officers have no independent control hierarchy but are individually responsible to the court which they serve.

An officially designated procurator represents the state in courts at all levels. He institutes public prosecution when the evidence obtained during a preliminary investigation appears sufficient to warrant legal action. A procurator need not prosecute cases involving offenses which he considers obviously trivial or pardonable.

Private Prosecution by Complaint

A private person may introduce criminal prosecution on his own initiative or when he feels the procurator has erred after preliminary investigation in not lodging charges against an offender. To facilitate the process, a complaining bell is located beside the outer door of every district court. Any person who has suffered damage and feels justified in seeking redress through the court can use the bell to call for immediate attention to his complaint. Once the bell has been rung, procurators and court officials are bound to continue action, regardless of their own opinions about the case.

In cases of private prosecution responsibility for the investigation rests upon the aggrieved individual. If the procurator has already completed a preliminary investigation on the same case, private prosecution may not begin. If there has been no official action, however, investigation must be undertaken by the plaintiff. The procurator may not initiate an official investigation since two complaints cannot be filed in a single case.

The court, upon receipt of a private petition for prosecution, immediately must send a copy of the complaint to the accused and notify the procurator of the date set for the hearing. The procurator then must appear in court and express his official opinion. The trial then proceeds in accordance with the provisions of the Code of Criminal Procedure. There is no jury trial.

Advocate and Public Defender

Upon the institution of charges against an individual the accused may employ one to three lawyers. If no counsel has been retained by the accused, the judge must assign a public defender in cases that are punishable by imprisonment for more than a year and those that constitute trials of first instance in a high court.

Trial and Appeal

Criminal cases may go through as many as three courts—the District Court, the High Court, and the Supreme Court. In cases involving trivial offenses the court of first instance, upon application by the procurator, may order the sentencing of the offender without observing the usual trial procedure if the accused has confessed during the preliminary investigation or if sufficient evidence for conviction has been offered the court. Sentences imposed in such cases, however, are limited to a fine, detention, or not more than 6 months' imprisonment.

A party who is not satisfied with the judgement of a lower court may appeal to the next higher level. The procurator, advocate, statutory agent, or spouse of the accused may also appeal. A party who is not satisfied with the verdict of a high court, sitting either as a court of first or second instance, may direct his appeal to the Supreme Court. No appeal, however, will be accepted by the Supreme Court for a third trial if the case involved is a trivial one.

Retrial and Extraordinary Appeal

When the period for filing an appeal has elapsed or judgment has been rendered by a high court in routine cases or by the Supreme Court, the judgment is final. There is no other remedy for the person convicted except application for retrial or an extraordinary appeal filed in the Supreme Court by the procurator general.

After a final judgment is handed down, an application for retrial may be made in the interest of the person sentenced only if the original judgement was based on evidence that can be proved to have been altered or obtained under duress or where new incontrovertible evidence has been discovered to prove the innocence of the convicted person.

If it is discovered after the judgment becomes final that the conduct of the trial was contrary to law, the procurator general may file an extrordinary appeal in the Supreme Court and demand a new trial.

Martial Law and Trial by Military Court

The Republic of China has been subject to martial law ever since 1948 when the government was still on the mainland. The implementing measure, known as Temporary Provisions Effective During the Period of Communist Rebellion, was continued on Taiwan and, after minor amendments made in 1960 and 1966, is still in force. Regulations in support of martial law provide that military courts have primary jurisdiction over offenses against the internal and external security of the state and against public order, public safety, forgery, counterfeiting, interference with personal liberty, theft, robbery, piracy, intimidation, kidnapping, and malicious mischief. If these provisions had been enforced strictly, military courts would have replaced civil courts of law, but this, however, is not the case in practice.

Formal action to restrict the jurisdiction of military courts was taken as early as 1952. An Executive Yuan order issued in October 1954 was especially significant and has determined the division of authority ever since. It specified that military courts had jurisdiction only in cases involving espionage and insurrection and that all others fell within the purview of civil courts.

In order to guard against unwarranted arrest and imprisonment by the military, the Executive Yuan decreed that public defenders be provided in military courts to defend persons accused of violating martial law in cases where the minimum punishment for conviction was not less than 5 years' imprisonment. A spouse, lineal blood relative, collateral blood relative within third degree, or a statutory agent was authorized to be present at such trials and testify on behalf of the accused. In this way the danger of summary trial and punishment, carried out under the guise of national security, has been minimized.

THE PENAL SYSTEM
Penal Policies
The Republic of China is a participating member of the United Nations Conference on the Prevention of Crime and the Treatment of Prisoners and has based its administration of penal institutions on the findings and recommendations of that body. The Ministry of Justice, which administers the system, reflected these guidelines in an official statement of policy that described a prison as a place for the reeducation of lawbreakers. In practice, this has resulted in the adoption of measures that eschew ideas of retaliation in favor of rehabilitating a convict and returning him to society as a useful and productive citizen. Some of these measures have to do with the improvement, expansion, and development of prison facilities; others deal with more enlightened treatment of inmates.

Penal Institutions
The penal system consists of three types of custodial institutions—prisons, detention houses, and reformatories. Prisons are used to confine convicted criminals whose sentences involve terms greater than 1 year. Detention houses are employed to keep persons awaiting trial in temporary custody or to accommodate offenders sentenced to terms of less than 1 year. Reformatories are utilized as institutions to hold and rehabilitate juvenile criminals between 14 and 18 years of age,who, under the law, may not be jailed with adults.

Each district court has an associated prison and a detention house so that the total number of these institutions, including those on Quemoy, is 13 each. Figures on their individual or collective populations are not released by the government. Prisons and detention houses usually, although not always, are located in or near the city of the district court which they support. The Taipei prison, for example, has been relocated in newly built, modernized facilities at Taoyuan, about 10 miles west of the capital. In 1967 there were three reformatories, located at Taoyuan, Changhua, and Kaohsiung, serving north, central, and south Taiwan, respectively. In 1966 there was a total of 1,609 inmates in the three reformatories, and plans for others were under consideration.

The administrative organization of penal institutions is similar for all types. Under a warden appointed by the Ministry of Justice, it consists of five divisions: education and reform, work, health, guard, and general affairs. Many of the wardens are older men, experienced in prison administration, who received their jobs largely through political influence. As they reach the age of retirement, they are replaced by younger officials who must be graduates of the JPTC. Lower staff personnel, including guards, also receive training at the JPTC before receiving permanent assignments.

Facilities at penal institutions are quite extensive and include well-staffed medical sections and dispensaries, workshops for training inmates in a variety of trades, classrooms, and recreational areas of various types. Each has one or more farms; in addition, prisons usually have full-scale factories run by the inmates, the products of which are sold on the civilian market. The Taipei prison, for example, operates a plastics factory; the one at Taichung, a shoemaking plant. In 1967 the system owned and operated 22 farms and 95 factories or plants of various sorts. The proceeds derived from the sale of their products are subject to strict accounting in quarterly reports to the Ministry of Justice. Under the law 25 percent of all profits are distributed to the convicts in return for their labor; 40 percent is set aside for working capital; 10 pecent is deposited in the National Treasury; and the rest is put into a fund for improving conditions in the prison, such as the 1966 purchase of X-ray equipment for the medical section at Taipei prison.

There are no specialized penal institutions reserved exclusively for female prisoners, but each regular one has segregated and equal sections for housing the different sexes. Female prisoners who are mothers are permitted to bring all their children under 3 years of age to live with them. While the mothers are at school or work during the day, the children are kept in nurseries under the supervision of nurses and kindergarten teachers provided at each institution for that purpose.

Treatment of Prisoners

Every convict, upon entering a prison, is given a thorough physical examination. He then undergoes an intensive psychiatric examination conducted by a qualified staff doctor. The psychiatrist investigates the convict's character, education, physical and mental condition, family background, and other personal matters. The results are forwarded to the warden, who uses them to determine the type or grade of treatment to be meted out.

In the Chinese system convicts are categorized initially into one of four grades. Grade four is the lowest and is reserved for the most dangerous criminals. It involves confinement of the strictest sort, which may include solitary confinement for periods as long as 3 months. A man in grade four has no privileges while he is in solitary confinement and virtually none at other times when he is held under maximum security, except that he may be required to undergo instruction in the Three Principles of the People.

Convicts of the third grade are slightly better off. Their quarters, usually a room accommodating four persons, have better beds (two double-decked iron cots) and usually a stool and an all-purpose desk-table. Convicts of the third grade attend classes in academic subjects in which they are deficient as well as political indoctrination, which is a requirement placed on all convicts except those in grade four. They also are trained in various shops of the prison to develop useful skills or a trade that will help them find work after release. They are further permitted a limited amount of free time to engage in sports or other recreational activities. Those who already have some skill work during the daytime on the prison farm or in one of its factories.

Prisoners in the second grade are housed in better quarters and have many more privileges. They are allowed to mix with one another during the day time and may participate in the full range or recreational activities. Convicts of the first grade are comparable to what are commonly called "trusties" in Western countries. Their quarters are of good quality and are shared with no one. They are required to work in a factory or on a farm, but their free time is their own. There are no locks on the doors of their cells, and they may move about within the confines of the prison, wearing ordinary clothes, without restriction.

The system of grading convicts is a device to encourage prisoners to behave and cooperate with the administration. Men may move up the ladder, progressively earning better quarters and more privileges for better performance, and through their willingness to cooperate and learn demonstrate that their repentance is genuine. Its effectiveness is considerable and is proved partially by the fact that guards who maintain order within the walls do not carry arms.

As part of the rehabilitation and training process, convicts are given opportunities to practice self-government. In regular elections, in which candidates deliver campaign speeches to their fellows during recreational time and balloting is done in secret, they elect a slate of officers and representatives to act as intermediaries before prison officials and to form a council that administers a self-disciplining program among the inmates.

Convicts of the second grade and higher are permitted to receive visitors in special visiting rooms in which they are screened off from those visiting them. As a morale factor also, prison officials from time to time schedule family reunion parties in which the prisoner is able to get together with his entire family at one time. These usually are held in a large hall, unobtrusively guarded, and fitted out with long tables and chairs capable of accommodating numerous family groups simultaneously.

INCIDENCE OF CRIME

The incidence of crime is classified as a security matter; its statistics have never been released to the general public. Some ideas of its extent, however, may be gained from the number of criminal cases handled by the district courts in 1966; according to the official *China Yearbook,* these totaled 94,413. The source did not categorize them by type so that the prevalence of robbery over homicide, for example, is unknown.

Well-informed estimates based on experience and past performance would indicate that the most common offenses are theft, fraud, forgery, assault and battery, and homicide, in that order. Smuggling and traffic in narcotics also are believed to be quite common. The small number of cases involving divorce, obscentity, and public morality is attributed to the still-powerful influence of traditional Chinese thinking in regard to family and sex.

As a result of the enormous growth of population since 1949 and the strong tendency toward urbanization that has accompanied the industrialization of Taiwan, the rate of juvenile delinquency seems to be on the rise. Juvenile authorities attribute this to a general relaxation of traditional family controls. Normally, Chinese children were permitted on the streets only when going to and from school or when accompanied by an adult. Under modern urban living conditions this has been difficult to enforce. Youngsters, especially older teenagers, tend to go out and congregate in groups that often get into mischief. Delinquency has not yet, apparently, reached the high proportions or organized nature noted in some big cities of the United States. The relatively low number of juveniles in the three reformatories would indicate it so far has not become alarming.

PEOPLE'S ATTITUDES TOWARD LAW AND ORDER

In general, the Chinese attitude toward law and order is one of passive acquiescence rather than one of active acceptance. For those who live under Japanese rule, the memory that minor noncompliance with police order, not to say any major violations of the Criminal Code, would bring swift and sure reprisal is still fresh and tends to induce obedience. On rare occasions when the government has abused its power to an intolerable degree or when certain incidents have caused a mass emotional upheaval, they have not hesitated to protest and even to resort to riots. The 1947 riot, caused by discontent with the new Chinese administration, and the general mass excitement of the 1957 anti-American demonstrations, protesting the decision of a United States court-martial in acquitting a United States soldier accused of killing a Chinese national, are cases in point.

The latter instance has some attitudinal overtones that are significant in illustrating the difference between popular Chinese and Western concepts of law. Chinese stress the element of reasonableness in any court action, government decree, or general law. They believe that these things should be based on common sense and human feelings rather than on technicalities or strict literal definitions. Accordingly, they find it difficult to accept the fact that any person who has caused the death of another legally could be declared not guilty.

As a whole, the Chinese people are not litigious or contentious. They dislike the complexity and procrastination of court procedures. They are most reluctant to bring their quarrels, particularly those concerning family or money matters, to court for fear that their own affairs might be disclosed to the public.

Moreover, the severe penalties imposed by the Japanese police conditioned the Taiwanese to feel that any entanglement with law enforcement officers could bring only trouble. In towns and villages the people perfer mediation of their disputes by elders to adjudication in courts. In 1967 the education process was inducing them to use the courts more often, but a reluctance to take disputes to court was still strong.

III. LAW AND JUSTICE SINCE 1966*

In 1965, the United States terminated its economic aid to the ROC and also signed a Status of Forces Agreement to govern the jurisdictional problem of U.S. military forces in Taiwan. Because ROC criminal procedure differs from that of the United States in several important aspects, during the negotiation of the Agreement, the United States side insisted on the inclusion of certain procedural safeguards which were not provided in ROC Criminal Procedure Law. The conclusion of the Agreement also prompted the ROC to revise its Criminal Procedure Law to provide more safeguards to an accused in a criminal case.[1]

In 1966, the National Assembly adopted a Temporary Provision to revitalize the three national elective bodies—the Assembly itself, the Legislative Yuan and the Control Yuan[2]—which started a series of political reforms in Taiwan.

Since 1966, with the ROC government more solidly established in Taiwan and with rapid economic progress under the guidance of the government, the ROC has further accelerated its improvement of the quality of law and justice in Taiwan. The following study analyzes four major issues in the administration of justice in the ROC, and assesses the progress made in the last fifteen years.

A. Temporary Provisions of the Constitution and the President's Emergency Power

In 1948, the National Assembly adopted Temporary Provisions annexed to the 1947 Constitution, granting extensive emergency power to the President during the period of Communist rebellion.[3]

According to these provisions, the President may, for the period in question, by resolution of the Executive Yuan Council,[4] make any emergency measure necessary to prevent the state or the people from facing immediate dangers or to cope with serious financial or economic crises as prescribed in articles 39 and 48 of the Constitution, without being subject to the procedural restrictions of the Legislative Yuan. These two articles provide the first of the President's emergency powers. Article 39 provides that the President may declare the institution of martial law (similar to a stage of siege in other constitutions) but must secure prior or subsequent approval from the Legislative Yuan. Article 43 provides that during a natural calamity, epidemic, or a serious financial or economic crisis, when the Legislative Yuan is in recess, the President may issue emergency decrees by resolution of the Executive Yuan Council, but that such decrees must be confirmed by the Legislative Yuan within a month. Under the Temporary Provisions, the above stated procedural requirement was removed. However, the Legislative Yuan, under Article 57, can still modify or annul Presidential emergency measures by a resolution. Such a resolution, however, is subject to Presidential veto, which in turn can only be overridden

---

*This section of the commentary was jointly written by Hungdah Chiu and Jyh-pin Fa.

by a two-thirds majority of the Legislative Yuan—an unlikely situation.

Despite the extent of the President's emergency power, the experience in the last three decades has unequivocally demonstrated that the President has exercised maximum restraint in exercising his power. In fact, the President has invoked his emergency powers on only four occasions. In the first case, the power was invoked to declare the application of martial law in war areas in 1948-1949, and in the second it was invoked to announce monetary reforms during the same critical stage of the civil war. The third case enabled the President to deal with serious floods which occurred in the central and southern part of Taiwan in 1958. The last occasion was announced by the President on December 16, 1978 to put the armed forces on full alert, take necessary measures to maintain economic stability and development, suspend the pending election of national elective bodies when the United States abruptly announced its decision to terminate diplomatic relations with the ROC on January 1, 1979, and to abrogate the US-ROC mutual defense treaty a year later.

*   *   *

Subsequent to the enactment of the emergency powers provisions, several further Temporary Provisions were enacted by the National Assembly to solve the problem of election of three national elective bodies—the Assembly itself, the Legislative Yuan and the Control Yuan.

After the removal of the government to Taiwan, the election of these bodies was temporarily suspended on the grounds of national emergency and the members elected in 1948 have continued to serve indefinitely. Of the 2,961 National Assembly members elected in 1947, only 1,393 were still serving in 1971; of the 759 members of the Legislative Yuan, 434 remained; and in the Control Yuan, membership declined from 180 in 1949 to 69 in April, 1971.[5] Several Temporary Provisions of the Constitution were adopted to meet this problem. The 1966 Temporary Provisions authorized the President to hold elections to fill offices which had become vacant for legitimate reasons, or when additional representation was called for because of population increases in areas that were under government control.

In accordance with these provisions, a partial national election took place on December 20, 1969, during which 15 new members were elected to the National Assembly, 11 to the Legislative Yuan, and 2 to the Control Yuan. More extensive Temporary Provisions were adopted in 1972 authorizing the President to create additional seats in the three national elective bodies. As a result, 53 new seats were created for the Assembly, 36 for the Legislative Yuan, and 7 for the Control Yuan.

Based on the 1972 Temporary Provisions, on June 11, 1980, the Government announced the further expansion of the number of new members for the above three bodies. In total 204 new members will be elected in Taiwan—76 to the National Assembly, bringing the total to 1218, 96 to the

Legislative Yuan, bringing the total to 412, and 32 to the Control Yuan, bringing the total to 74.[6] The election was held in December, 1980. Among the three bodies, the most important one is the Legislative Yuan. The election of 96 new members to this body would significantly revitalize that body. Moreover, many remaining members are too old or ill to be active. As a result, less than half of the remaining members regularly attend the meetings of the Yuan. So, in practical terms, after the recent increase of the membership, approximately half of the active members of the Legislative Yuan will be elected in Taiwan.[7]

B. Judicial Organization, Administration of Justice and Compensation to People for Wrongful Acts of the Government

Although the Judicial Yuan is the highest judicial organ of the state and retains authority over civil, criminal, and administrative cases and over cases concerning disciplinary measures against public functionaries,[8] its actual authority until 1980 had been confined to supervising the Supreme and Administrative Courts and Disciplinary Committee, which are under its jurisdiction. Since each tribunal is supposed to exercise its functions independently, there is little work for the Judicial Yuan itself. Even authority to engage in constitutional interpretation, which in most nations is the exclusive right of a highest judicial organ, was entrusted to the Council of Grand Justices,[9] whose members are confirmed and appointed by the same procedure as the President and Vice-President of the Judicial Yuan.[10]

Along with the Supreme Court, High and District Courts constitute the three-tiered judicial hierarchy in the ROC.[11]

Unless otherwise provided,[12] the district court is the court of the first instance for all civil and criminal cases. In principle, the trials are before one judge without jury, but three judges sitting in council may be assigned to handle important cases.[13] Cases appealed to the High Court are decided by a panel of three judges. Five judges may sit when the Supreme Court is in session.[14]

Because both fact and law may be fully reconsidered as a matter of right before the High Court, appeal to the tribunal obviously provides for much broader review than an American appeal. However, the Supreme Court, which stands over the High Court in the judicial hierarchy, is supposed to review only issues of law.[15] This more broad scope of appeal on the second tier is common to other civil law countries.[16] On the other hand, the ROC system also permits the procurator to appeal from a judgment of acquittal or not guilty. The common law concept of the prohibition of double jeopardy has not been recognized because the appeal is regarded as a continuation of the proceeding and the case is not completed until the time for appeals has expired.[17] The possibility of increasing the sentence in criminal cases can only occur when the procurator appeals against the defendant. In the case of an appeal by the defendant himself or by the procurator for the benefit of the defendant, the appellate court may not increase the sentence.[18]

The Chinese procurator has no exact equivalent in American legal terminology. His authority is quite extensive and powerful. He has not only the power to prosecute a criminal action, but also an important power incidental thereto which is exercised generally, under the continental system by a *judge d'instruction*[19] and under the American system by an examining magistrate, a coroner or grand jury—namely, the power to hold a preliminary examination of the accused and the witnesses so as to decide whether the case should be prosecuted or not. In exercising this power he may summon, arrest, and detain the accused, compel a witness to appear, and make such searches and investigation as may throw light on the case.[20]

A serious controversy which until recently remained unsettled involved governmental jurisdiction over the courts. Two of the three grades of courts, namely, the High Court and the District Court, together with the whole hierarchy of procurators, had been under the jurisdiction of the Ministry of Justice, which is in turn under the control of the Executive Yuan; only the Supreme Court was directly under the Judicial Yuan. The judicial system was not only split, but its freedom from interference by the executive branch was questionable. Even if it seemed unlikely that the Ministry of Justice would interfere directly with judicial decision-making, there is little doubt that the power of the Ministry with respect to judicial appointments, promotions and transfers made the judicial branch vulnerable to outside influence.[21]

This jurisdictional problem evolved into a heated controversy among Yuans and led to an Interpretation rendered by the Council of Grand Justices which held that the District and High Courts should be under the jurisdiction of the Judicial Yuan.[22] This interpretation was not implemented, presumably due to the government's preoccupation with other domestic and international crises, until 1979 when the ROC government decided to implement it and set an effective date on July 1, 1980.

Following the French model, administrative adjudication is separated from the ordinary courts.[23] An Administrative Court has been established along with the Supreme Court under the supervision of the Judicial Yuan. The court has a number of judges divided into several chambers. The judges are required to have had at least four years of previous service in subordinate positions of due rank.[24] Among the five judges of each chamber, two must have had prior judicial service.[25] These requirements were devised to ensure that the judges would be familiar with the subject matter of the disputes before them.

On the other hand, as many as three judges within a chamber of five may by chance lack legal training, or trial experience. Moreover, there is a widespread perception that the assignment of judicial officers or high-ranking administrative officials to the Administrative Court has generally not been looked upon with favor in terms of career advancement. For these reasons, the caliber of the Administrative Court cannot be compared favorably to that of the Supreme Court.

Administrative suits are divided into three stages. Any individual who feels that injury has been done to his rights or interests through an unlawful decision or illegal administrative act on the part of a government organ may bring an action against that authority to the authority immediately higher.[26] If the ruling is unsatisfactory, the petitioner may make a re-appeal to an authority one step higher than the one which rendered the ruling. If he still is not satisfied with the decision of re-appeal, the last organ he may resort to is the Administrative Court.[27]

To safeguard the petitioner's rights further, if the government agency does not act upon a petitioner's appeal or re-appeal within three months, the law presumes the denial of the demand and the proceedings of re-appeal or administrative litigation automatically follow.[28] This is a salutary provision in view of the delays that frequently characterize the work of government agencies.[29]

The system of administrative appeal and adjudication is not without its weaknesses, however. For example, some degree of institutional bias in favor of the decision or act appealed from must be expected since the appeal is heard by the supervising administrative authority, and each official tends to defend his subordinates from criticism.[30] Moreover, the appeals and re-appeals are generally handled by ordinary administrative officials who may not have formal legal training. Finally, petitioners are not entitled to an oral hearing, although the reviewing agency might conduct an oral hearing in its own discretion.[31]

Two recent decrees of the Executive Yuan on June 28, 1979 mark the beginning of improvements in the administrative review system. In the decree entitled "Projects of Improving the Appeal System," those agencies handling not fewer than 15 appeals or 8 re-appeals monthly are required to appoint as a specialist within the review structure a law graduate who possesses the necessary qualification for civil service. The chairman and members of the Appeal Review Committee, which decides appeals, are required to be familiar with law. The decree entitled "Attentive Points of Handling Appeal Business" emphasizes that the petitioner's request for oral hearing must be given due consideration.[32]

Defects remain in the Administrative Court in spite of these decrees of the Executive Yuan. First, the court is unicameral, precluding the possibility of a further appeal. Heowever, some have argued that because all cases before the Administrative Court must have first gone through the appeal and re-appeal procedure and are thus doubly filtered, a court decision in favor of the plaintiff is unlikely. The situation is similar in other civil law countries.

Second, the Administrative Court has rarely conducted an oral hearing while deciding a case, despite the statutory provision allowing for such hearings when the Court deems it necessary or in response to the request of the parties.[33] Recently, however, it has appeared that the Court's reluctance toward oral hearings is waning. On August 16, 1979, the Administrative Court held oral hearings in a case which was ultimately lost by the government.[34] In a major recent speech, Shao-ku Huang, the President of the

Judicial Yuan since 1979, specifically encouraged the Administrative Court to conduct oral hearings.[35.] The need for establishing lower administrative courts, as was done in France after 1953, to hear cases before they are appealed to the final Administrative Court, thus giving litigants an additional opportunity to test their cases, has also been under serious consideration recently.[36]

Closely related to the Administrative litigation is the problem of government liability for the acts of its employees upon the private citizen. Article 24 of the ROC Constitution provides that any injured person may, in accordance with law, claim compensation from the state for damage sustained. The antique maxim that government can do no wrong seems to have been abandoned by the ROC government thirty years ago. In addition, the Administrative Proceedings Law also provides that compensation may be claimed incidentally when a case is brought to the Administrative Court.[37] In spite of the Constitutional and statutory authority, it remains the case that the Administrative Court has never in its history granted an individual claim for compensatory damages.[38] In defense of this situation, it has been asserted that legislation implementing Article 24 of the Constitution has never been enacted.[39] In order to fill this gap, the Research Commission of the Executive Yuan began a thorough study of the question in 1978; as a result the State Compensation Law was enacted on June 20, 1980 and with an effective date of July 1, 1981. The Law is composed of 17 articles, or which the major ones are as follows:

- The state shall assume the responsibility of compensation when a national's freedom or rights are illegally infringed on deliberately or by fault of public functionaries on duty. The same responsibility for compensation shall be applied to the infringements caused by neglect of duty by public functionaries.
- The state shall compensate those whose life, body and/or property are damaged because of flaws in installment and management of public facilities. The principle of liability without fault was adopted in the case of damage caused by defects of construction or maintenance of public works.
- The compensation shall be made in monetary payment, but restitution may be granted in certain circumstances or at the request of the individuals concerned. Government sectors at all levels are required to budget for the costs of compensation or restitution.
- As a statute of limitations, an individual's right to claim for compensation must be exercised within two years after he knows the occurrence of the damage, and no claim for damage may be allowed more than five years after the occurrence of the damage.
- Rights of foreigners are based on reciprocity

As a measure of its liberality, the ROC State Compensation Law provides more effective relief by its terms than does the U.S. Tort Claims Act, especially since the U.S. Congress in 1978 failed to pass the Justice Department's proposed Tort Claims Act amendments which would have narrowed many deliberate exceptions and ambiguities thereby broadening its limited scope.[41]

It is reliably reported that the ROC government has appropriated approximately the equivalent of U.S. $16,000,000 as funds to implement the law between fiscal year July 1, 1981–June 30, 1982. Additional funds, if needed, is also available from the reserved fund of the budget.

C. Criminal Procedure

In criminal cases in the United States, the first encounter between the police and the private citizen generally ends in an arrest, based on a standard of probable cause, whether the arrest is with or without a warrant. Contrary to the American practice, this coercive application of police power has never been looked upon with enthusiasm by civil law countries. A summons to the police station for interrogation is extensively used as the beginning of the criminal process, and an arrest is generally considered only as the last resort.[42] Before an arrest may be permitted, the defendant must be "strongly suspected" of being guilty.[43] Even where strong suspicion is present, an arrest without a previous summons for interrogation is permitted in only four situations: the suspect has no fixed residence; the suspect has taken flight or facts exist sufficient to suggest this possibility; facts exist to suggest that the suspect may destroy, forge, or alter evidence, or conspire with a co-defendant or witness; or the offense is punishable by death, life imprisonment, or not less than five years' imprisonment.[44] Even when these factors are present, ROC law requires an arrest warrant as well. Apart from the serious interference with personal inviolability caused by an arrest, the public in the United States has generally—and wrongfully— come to believe that an arrest is virtually conclusive evidence of criminal wrongdoing because arrest information has to be placed on the public record, even if arrests in the vast majority of cases do not lead to conviction in the United States.[45] Recognizing this bias or deficiency, the use of a citation or summons[46] in the United States has become more visible recently.[47]

Only under two conditions may an arrest be effected without a warrant in the ROC: when a circular order is issued or when the suspect is discovered *in flagrante delicto*.[48] Furthermore, a person is considered to be *in flagrante delicto* when he is being pursued with implements used to commit the crime, or with clear traces of guilt upon his body or dress.[49] This clause enlarges the concept of "flagrante offense," and broader authority is thus vested in the hands of the police. Although the possibility of abuse exists, there has been no discussion of this problem in the ROC press or the academic community.

After an accused is arrested, the ROC Constitution explicitly provides that he "shall be turned over to a competent court for hearing within 24 hours."[50] Because the Chinese procurator not only conducts the preliminary examination, but also determines whether to prosecute, the word "court" has been interpreted to include the procurator.[51] However, the

Code of Criminal Procedure only requires that the accused be sent "immediately" to the place designated without a specific time limit.[52] Moreover, following the American writ of *habeas corpus,* article 8 of the ROC Constitution further provides that an arrested or detained person may apply to the court that a writ to surrender him be served within twenty-four hours on the arresting agency and that the court *shall not reject* the application (emphasis added), nor shall it order the agency concerned to make an investigation and report first. The agency concerned may not refuse or delay the execution of the writ.

This detailed provision provides the Chinese people with unprecedented protection against governmental abuse of power. However, the Habeas Corpus Act, which specifies the procedural details of this privilege, authorizes the court to consider the application before issuing its order and to dismiss the writ if there is an obvious absence of cause.[53]

Unlike arrest, the issuance of a search warrant concerning the accused does not require any objective standard of proof. The Code of Criminal Procedure only provides: "If necessary, the person, property, dwelling house or other premises of an accused may be searched."[54] Although this abstract, subjective standard is very vague on its face, civil law countries tend to view the freedom of the person and property rights as different in nature.[55]

On the other hand, three situations may justify the warrantless search of a dwelling house: an actual arrest, the pursuit of a flagrant offender or escapee, or the existence of sufficient facts to show that a crime is being committed and circumstances are urgent. However, such cases must be reported to the procurator or the judge within twenty-four hours after the warrantless search is made.[56]

Several interesting provisions in the Code of Criminal Procedure are worthy of mention here. In the absence of prior consent or urgent circumstances, the night-time search of a residential house is prohibited.[57] If a search is executed in an occupied house, the occupant, watchman, or his representatives must be present; otherwise a neighbor or an official of a nearby self-governing body may be ordered to be present.[58] Search of the person of a female must be by a woman unless it is impossible.[59] These commendable devices are designed to protect the dignity and privacy of the individual.

In spite of these safeguards, there is no clear-cut answer to the effect of an illegal search and seizure. Some argue that the effect depends on the outcome; if incriminating evidence is discovered, the police are not held liable.[60] But others disagree. Pu-sheng Cheng, former President of the Supreme Court and now a Grand Justice, for example, has suggested that there is no general rule to be applied. Evidence discovered as a result of a warrantless search in a situation where a warrant is required, in his view, cannot be introduced before a court.[61] However, except in the case of night-time search or the search of a woman by a man, the admissibility of evidence is not deemed to be tainted by any procedural irregularity.[62]

Chinese law provides: "an accused may be detained if necessary after examination if it is discovered that one of the conditions specified in article 76 [arrest without sevice of summons] exists."[63] The subjective standard of necessity again appear, although it was originally designed to reduce the possibility of abuse by a procurator or judge. The words "sufficient facts exist" were new, added in the 1967 revision to ensure more objective application of pre-trial detention. This 1967 revision of the Code of Criminal Procedure further elaborated the period of preventive detention. Detention of an accused may not exceed two months during investigation and three months during trial and the extension must be approved by the court itself. Furthermore, each extension may not exceed two months and only one extension during investigation, three extensions during the first and second trials and one for third trial may be permitted if the maximum punishment carries less than ten years' imprisonment.[64] These are major improvements in the protection of individual rights.

As in other civil law countries, a defendant may bring a claim against the state for compensation as to his pre-trial detention if he is cleared in the trial,[65] and, on the other hand, time spent in detention may be credited against sentence in the event a judgement of guilty is handed down.[66] These are highly commendable provisions and it has been urged that the United States should follow this continental system.[67]

An analysis of ROC criminal procedure would not be complete without a discussion of the controversial Law for the Punishment of Police Offenses (hereinafter cited as the Police Offense Law). This law provides police with substantial powers to investigate crimes by circumventing the more rigid procedural requirements provided in the Code of Criminal Procedure.[68] It covers a wide variety of petty offences ranging from spitting in a public place to vagrancy.[69] Although most of these offences are also handled by police in other countries, the major controversy concerning the Police Offense Law centers on its enforcement procedures. Police may take custody of the individual for seven days and even up to two weeks under certain conditions. Moreover, there is no review of procedures under the Police Offense Law, and an aggrieved individual has only one opportunity for appeal to the higher police authority. The individual is thus deprived of the right of re-appeal and administrative suit before the Administrative Court as provided in other administrative enforcement procedures.[70]

As the current legal system of the ROC was derived directly from Japan and indirectly from Germany, so this Police Offense Law was borrowed from these two countries. Before World War II, Japan and Germany had similar enforcement procedure. Through the use of a minor administrative law, Japanese police were able to hold persons for months and even years before formally booking them as criminal suspects, and the supervision of the court as well as the procurator was absolutely excluded.[71] The power to mete out penalties for petty offenses was formerly in the hands of the German police[72] who could detain people up to two weeks, the detained person was entitled to request a trial before the *Amtsrichter* or district court.[73]

The procedure under the ROC Police Offense Law raises troublesome questions of constitutionality in view of Article 8 of the ROC Constitution. Because of this concern, on August 20, 1961 the Control Yuan applied to the Council of Grand Justices for a ruling on the constitutionality of the law. Finally, on November 7, 1980, the Council of Grand Justices decided that Article 8, paragraph 1 on the Constitution requires that the detention of individuals and the imposition of other sanctions under the Police Offense Law may be imposed only following legal proceedings within the jurisdiction of the Court.[74] The delay in the decision was understandable because most people in the ROC thought that adequate maintenance of the public order required the existence of summary extra-judicial mechanisms. On the other hand, the Law clearly violated Article 8 of the Constitution.

Another reason for the Council's delay in rendering its interpretation may be the inflexible requirement of three-fourths of the members for a quorum and that decision on interpretation of the Constitution has to be reached among three-fourths of those present.[75] In fact, one of the Grand Justices explained the reason for delay in this way.[76] Responding to some criticism of the Police Offense Law, the ROC government initiated the revision process in 1979. It is reported that a new law to replace the Police Offense Law will soon be enacted and will require the establishment of a police offense division in each district court to deal with police offenses.[77]

In regard to the conduct of the trial itself, the Chinese criminal procedure follows the continental rather than the Anglo-American form. After the preliminary investigation, the procurator conducts a preliminary examination to decide whether the accused is to be committed for trial. A superficial comparison indicates that the Chinese procurator possesses more authority than the American prosecutor. Although this comparison is not without foundation, it should be pointed out that the American prosecutor enjoys considerably more freedom from regulation or restraints than his Chinese counterpart. There are several reasons for this difference. Chinese procurators, as is usual in other civil law countries, are hierarchically organized. They are career civil servants and are under the supervision of the Ministry of Justice through the Procurator-General, which is attached to the Supreme Court. Their day-to-day operation is closely watched and directives are often issued from above.

Besides this administrative supervision, victims of crimes may bring a "private prosecution" to the court without going through the procurator, unless the prosecution is directed against a lineal relation or a spouse.[78] A private prosecution may even suspend a preliminary examination by the procurator if that examination is incomplete at the time the private prosecution is initiated.[79] Therefore, unlike the case under French law, a private prosecution is not conditioned upon the procurator's refusal to act, nor does the completion of the procuratorial investigation require the denial of private prosecution.

Most importantly, the Chinese Code of Criminal Procedure affords the individual the rights of reconsideration if the procurator decides not to prosecute. After receipt of a ruling not to prosecute, the complainant may file with the original procurator an application for reconsideration.[80] If the application is rejected for lack of grounds, the procurator is required to transmit the record, documents and evidence of the case to the chief procurator of a higher court for decision. In addition, the chief procurator of the original court may, if necessary, intervene before delivery is made; if the chief procurator of the original court also finds against prosecution, the case is immediately forwarded to the higher court.[81] Therefore, an internal review and appeal procedure is naturally instituted, when an application for reconsideration is filed. This process no doubt operates as a restraint upon the procurator's discretion. In fact, between 1973 and 1977, decisions to prosecute following a petition for reconsideration have consistently averaged about 30 pecent,[82] indicating that the system of reconsideration is an operational success and not an empty right conferred by law but denied in practice.

Because the right to counsel does not attach in the ROC system until a prosecution is initiated, the defendant may be interrogated during the whole process of investigation without the presence of a counsel.[83] It can hardly be denied that the protection provided to him is inadequate. Not only are scholars and judges in favor of revision; in fact, suggesting that the truth may be more easily revealed if counsel were allowed during investigation. Although the government has not considered this revision to be a priority among other judicial reforms, a detailed and comprehensive research is now under study.[84]

The effect of the failure to provide counsel during investigation has been minimized somewhat by the general civil law practice of granting counsel an unlimited right of access to the entire investigative dossier, including all the materials to be introduced in the forthcoming trial.[85] This is designed to avoid conviction by surprise, which sometimes occurs under American criminal procedure. Under ROC law, the procurator can restrict defense counsel's access to the investigative record only in regard to reasonable limitation on the time and place of making these materials available.[86] Traditionally, any liberalization of the rules of criminal discovery in the United States has been viewed with suspicion for fear that the defendant may be enabled to fabricate evidence or intimidate witnesses.[87] However, the Federal Rules of Criminal Procedure have moved slightly toward the continental model by allowing the defendant to have a copy of his previous confession, if any, or of recorded grand jury testimony given by him.[88] Nevertheless, any statements made by government witnesses, the most vital material for defense counsel, remain beyond the reach of discovery. In fact, the United States may stand virtually alone in this respect. England, with its great depth of common law tradition, has long abandoned the tradition of trial by surprise by enabling counsel to fully familiarize himself with the government's evidence before the trial through a combination of procedural devices and informal arrangements.[89]

After the procuratory has brought a case to court, another major diffence between common law and civil law appears. The entire records and dossiers are forwarded to the judge and he is expected to study them thoroughly in advance of the trial in order to carry out the responsibility of interrogation. Article 264 of the ROC Code of Criminal Procedure requires not only that criminal facts and evidence be included in the indictment, but also that the record and exhibits be sent to the court. Although in theory the procurator may retain the burden of proving each element of a criminal offense, and although the criminal judgment is in theory based on the record at trial,[90] nevertheless the impact of the procuratorial dossier on the judge's mind can hardly be disputed,[91] although it has been asserted that this system does not necessarily lead to bias.[92]

As a rule, trials in the ROC are public.[93] The proceedings begin with the interrogation of the accused by the presiding judge regarding his personal circumstances, which cover not only his identity generally, but also any previous convictions he may have incurred. The procurator then reads the accusation. A dialogue ensues between judge and defendant, during which, as is usual in continental criminal procedure, the judge inquires at length about the details of the incident.[94] However, unlike the common law practice, the defendant may not take the witness stand and testify under oath, because civil law practice considers the requirement that the defendant testify under oath to be undesirable, unfair, and even "inhumane." It has been said that sworn testimony imposes

> unfair pressure on the guilty defendant either to convict himself out of his own mouth by telling the truth, or else to suffer punishment for perjury by lying. In view of the incentive to testify so as to avoid possible unfavorable inferences from his failure to take the witness stand, the defendant often has little opportunity to avoid these "agonizing" alternatives.[95]

Does this mean the defendant has no privilege against self-incrimination? Legally, a defendant's silence may not be construed as evidence of his guilt under the ROC law.[96] The fact that a judge is likely to draw an unfavorable inference, consciously or unconsciously, from a defendant's silence has served as a psychological pressure on defendants to speak as well as respond; consequently, this right to remain silent has rarely been exercised. This is the general practice in civil law countries,[97] and the ROC is no exception. Furthermore, there is no requirement in ROC criminal procedure that a defendant be informed of his right to silence. This seems consistent with the traditional Chinese view that interrogation is not only a device to provoke an incriminating statement, but also an opportunity to air exculpating evidence and therefore an aid to determining the final truth of a particular case.

Witnesses are put on oath; they testify in response to questions to questions by the judge. Although the Code of Criminal Procedure allows parties to examine a witness following the judicial interrogation,[98] this procedure is rarely invoked in the ROC.[98] Too often, after reading the indictment the procurator remains silent during the rest of the proceeding and the customary role of defense counsel is to present his prepared argument for the defendant or to plead mitigating circumstances; even if the defense may occasionally request cross examination, the response from the bench is seldom encouraging.[99] However, the relatively insignificant role of the privilege against self-incrimination and of cross-examination in Chinese criminal procedure may have certain advantages vis-à-vis common law practice. Under common law procedure, the purpose of the examination by parties is to elicit one-sided statements or prevent incriminating evidence from surfacing, the atmosphere is wholly adversarial. Under the civil law practice of examination by the presiding judge, the adversarial aspect of the court proceedings is less evident, and the commitment to discovering the full facts is paramount. It is for this reason that a witness is required under civil law to give a detailed narrative of what he knows without interruption[100] instead of giving brief replies to questions, as the case in common law countries.

After the last witness is heard, the procurator presents his arguments. The defendant and his counsel follow with the arguments for the defense. If the procurator replies to the defense, another opportunity to speak by defense may be provided.[101] The most important respect in this order is that the defendant himself always has the last word.[102] The rule that the closing argument of the defense is always made after that of the prosecution serves the interest of the defense because in this way the defense can contest the whole argument of the opposite party. The psychological effect of this privilege upon the court is obvious and need not be explained further.

The system of evidence in the civil law countries is perhaps the biggest surprise for common law lawyers. In rendering a judgment the court is not bound by strict rules regarding the probative force of evidence, but rather is guided by its own conviction. The work of examination of evidence is enormously extensive and all pertinent evidence can be considered in light of its probative value; the court's examination may cover any matter deemed relevant to the issues or the credibility of the witness. The ROC Code of Criminal Procedure explicitly states: "Evidence shall be evaluated by the court according to its free conviction."[103] Nevertheless, the standard of free evaluation does not mean a Chinese judge may convict on whim: "Evidence given by an incompetent witness, having not been lawfully investigated, obviously contrary to reason or inconsistent with established facts shall not form the basis of a decision."[104] However, it cannot be denied that Chinese courts have wide and almost unlimited discretion with regard to the consideration of evidence.

The underlying reason for this liberal attitude towards the admissibility of evidence in civil law countries is that they believe that only by placing all the available information before the court can the truth be discovered.[105] In addition, cases are universally tried before trained judges, sitting without juries. There are few exceptions to this rule. Hearsay evidence is not admissible.[106] There is generally no exclusionary rule with respect to irregularly obtained evidence, *e.g.*, that obtained by the *ultra vires* actions of a police officer.[107] However, the confession of the defendant is excluded if it was obtained by coercion, fraud, illegal detention, or other improper means.[108] Furthermore, even if a confession was secured legally, other evidence against a defendant must still be presented to the ROC court. In other words, "Confession of an accused shall not be used as the sole evidence of conviction and other necessary evidence shall still be investigated to see if the confession coincides with facts."[109] Therefore, the American "guilty plea" is totally alien to the Chinese, who regard such a plea as contradicting the basic principle that the court must ascertain the full truth for itself.

Perhaps because the judge usually plays such a dominant role at trial and because there are fewer means for the defendant to delay the wheels of justice, issues can be clarified within a more shorter period. This, coupled with the unlimited pre-trial discovery, generally makes criminal trials shorter than in the United States. The averge number of days needed to handle a criminal case in the District Court has been reduced substantially from 13.92 in 1973 to 7.56 in 1977 for the procurator and 40.26 in 1967 to 31.03 in 1978 for the judge.[110] Sixty percent of the serious criminal cases, such as homicide, or other crimes that may carry penalties of death, life imprisonment, or ten or more years of imprisonment, are concluded within six months after the beginning of the investigation.[111] The Ministry of Justice even goes further to meet the popular demand to reduce administrative delay, within the permissable scope of the Code of Criminal Procedure, by issuing "Attentive Items of Speedy Trial and Conclusion of Serious Criminal Cases."[112] The problem of serious delay of criminal procedure in the United States has been the subject of criminal reform for years. Although placing firm deadlines on courtrooms is a popular practice, the result has not yet been encouraging. For example, one study showed that the median cases in Chicago took 267 days rather than the legislatively mandated 160.[113] The New York standard that defendants must be brought to trial within six months of the filing of their indictment was also largely ineffective.[114] As a whole, three months has been always the median time interval from filing to disposition for criminal defendants in U.S. District Courts.[115]

ROC courts are notably lenient in their sentencing, and imprisonment for less than one year is common. In the United States, 69 percent of sentences imposed by the U.S. District Courts are of one year or more,[116] while only 13 percent of the total sentences in the ROC were for one year or longer in 1976.[117] In the United States the average sentence of imprisonment is 47.2 months,[118] whereas 69 percent of Chinese defendants sentenced to prison receive terms of less than six months.[119] Therefore, Chinese courts are demonstrably less severe in their treatment of those convicted than are American courts. Perhaps this leniency makes people less concerned about the procedural fairness between parties at trial.

In addition to sentences of death, imprisonment and fine, there are several "peace preservation measures" provided in the Code of Criminal Law. These include reformatory education for juveniles, custody and protection of the insane or feebleminded, compulsory cures for alcoholics and opium, cocaine, morphine users, and compulsory labor for habitual or occupational criminals. The length of the prescribed period in these cases ranges from three months to three years.[120] However, the compulsory labor provision has been overshadowed by the Statute of Peace Preservation Measures dealing with Criminals of Larceny and Receiving Stolen Property during the Period of Suppression of Rebellions. These two types of criminals may be sent to compulsory labor for a period of seven years, which period may be extended once by another three years only.[121] The length of the period is decided by the court, and judicial approval has to be secured before granting extension.

Finally, there is another feature that is altogether alien to common law lawyers: when a court is trying a criminal case, a subsidiary civil action brought by the victim for damages sustained may be entertained at the same time. This system originated in France and has spread to other civil law countries.[122] Because it usually takes two actions to accomplish the same thing in the United States while the Chinese are able to settle them in one action, the economic advantages are obvious.

Martial Law and Military Trials

As Taiwan has been declared under martial law since May 20, 1949,[123] offenses relating to sedition or military affairs are normally tried before a military court. The state of "martial law" in the ROC is in fact similar to a "state of siege" in the civil law countries and is different from the concept of martial law in common law countries. This point needs further explanation.

The difference lies essentially in the divergent attitudes between the common and civil law systems toward the origin of this emergency measure. The "state of siege" emphasizes the suspension of certain normal rules of law, whereas "martial law" emphasizes the emergency as an effective threat against public safety and order. Thus, the prerequisite for martial rule in the United States is either that the civilian courts are closed or they can no longer perform their functions properly.[124] This condition does not apply to the civil law state of siege, under which the civilian courts may still function and only those crimes against national security, the constitution, and the public safety and order are under the jurisdiction of military courts. The civil and military powers within the government work side by side in a spirit of cooperation and do not have to be substituted one for the other as in the case of a common law country.[125] Another major difference should not be ignored. The executive and/or the legislature in civil law countries has the final word as to whether an emergency situation has arisen; the courts assume this function under the common law.

All these features of the state of siege have been apparent in the Republic of China since 1949. The President has the power to initiate the application of martial law, *i.e.*, state of siege, although this power is subject to confirmation by the Legislative Yuan. The latter by resolution may ask the President to terminate the application of the martial law. [127] Despite the existence of the martial law, the structure and functions of government and the way of life of the people in the ROC are left almost unaffected by the imposition of martial law. Citizens who primarily mind their own business may hardly known that martial law has been declared. It is interesting to note that contemporary Americans have had the similar experience. Until 1976, the United States had four national emergencies in effect and there were 470 laws granting the President emergency powers by the Congress; [128] even so, only a few people were aware that the United States was operating in a state of emergency.

Moreover, non-military personnel in the ROC are subject to a military trial only if they commit one of three types of crimes: sedition and espionage, theft or unauthorized sale or purchase of military equipment and supplies, or theft or damage of public communication equipment and facilities. These restrictions upon the enforcement of military trial are expressly provided in Article 2 of the "Measures Governing the Classification of Cases to be Tried by the Military Judicial Organs Themselves and Those Which are to be Turned Over to the Courts in the Region of Taiwan during the Period of Martial Law." [129] Significantly, the jurisdiction of the military judicial organs has gradually been reduced under a series of revisions in April, 1954 and September, 1967. [130] A fair consideration of martial law in the Republic of China should never fail to take account of these special "Measures."

The government had expanded the scope of military trial to include nine serious crimes in 1976. These were homicide, robbery, intentionally killing the victim after rape or robbery, kidnapping, etc., and the expansion was intended to deter then prevalent crimes of robbery and snatching. The popular demand for swift and severe punishment was genuine and the government merely acted upon it. Nevertheless, not all those types of cases were automatically under military jurisdiction; a decision by the Executive Yuan was required on a case-by-case basis before such crimes were referred to the military court. [131]

Moreover, the crimes and robbery and snatching did reduce substantially following the imposition of harsh treatment. The number of cases in this area had been gradually increasing from 200 in 1968 to 255 in 1972 and became alarming when it reached 435 in 1975. Perhaps this is the reason behind the introduction of military trial in the early months of 1976. [132] The result seems to be exactly what the government and people expected: the number of cases dropped to 288 in 1976 and further down to 278 in 1977. [133] The deterrent effect no doubt has been realized and, consequently, in the two most recent years there has not been a single case of robbery or snatching under military trial. [134]

Trials in the military courts generally follow the model of the civilian courts. The most controversial aspect is that judgment must be approved by a commanding officer before delivery. [135] However, this is not only a general practice of military trial in other countries, but, contrary to the American practice that no limitation is imposed, [136] the commanding officer in the ROC may express his disapproval only once. [137] Another problem related to the military trial is that a defendant may be sent to reformatory education because of mitigating circumstances, [138] or because he surrendered himself to the authorities. [139] The maximum period for reformatory education is three years and may not be extended. [140] Upon the expiration of the term, he must be released immediately, although two guarantees may be required to assure his later behavior. [141]

Whether the Government should declare the termination of martial law in the Taiwan area has frequently been debated among the legislators or scholars. A few have favored its termination in order to restore normal constitutional rule. The majority, however, have considered that Taiwan has remained constantly under military threat from the People's Republic of China (PRC) since 1949. In 1954 and again in 1958, the PRC prepared to launch large-scale invasions of the island. In recent years, while the PRC has taken a somewhat conciliatory attitude toward Taiwan, it has continued its political campaign and subversive activities against the ROC. Internationally, it has stepped up its campaign to isolate the ROC and thereby facilitate its ultimate goal of taking over Taiwan by force, if necessary. The PRC has also actively supported the violent subversive activities of the Taiwan Independence Movement. Despite the PRC's well-known opposition to Taiwan independence, the PRC's interests are aligned with the independence movement since an overthrow of the present government is beneficial to unification as it is to independence. The PRC might hope that by actively supporting the Taiwan Independence Movement it may create chaos in Taiwan so as to facilitate its intervention, or that some groups in Taiwan might invite it to intervene for fear of being persecuted by the Taiwan Independence Movement elements or for the cause of Chinese nationalism. Under these circumstances, the majority view has been that the lifting of Martial Law in Taiwan is a luxury Taiwan can hardly afford.

The Government is fully aware of the conflicting view on the question of continuation of Martial Law in Taiwan and has worked out a compromise solution. While nominally maintaining Martial Law in Taiwan, it has only exercised less than 10 percent of the power granted under the law, primarily in the area of military trials for civilians in a case of sedition or espionage. It also enacted the Military Trial Law in 1956 to make the procedure as similar as possible to that of the ROC Criminal Procedure Code.

NOTES

1. See generally Hungdah Chiu, *Status of Force Agreement with the Republic of China: Some Criminal Case Studies*, 3 *Boston C. Int. & Comp. L. R.* 67-88 (1979).

2. See *China Yearbook* 1979, at 94.

3. For text, see *Id.*, 651-652.

4. The Council is composed of the premier and vice-premier of the Executive Yuan, heads of the ministries and commissions with the premier as chairman. It is responsible for discussion and finalization of statutory or budgetary bills and other important matters to be submitted to the Legislative Yuan.

5. See generally, Wei, *Political Development in the Republic of China on Taiwan*, in *China and the Question of Taiwan* 74-111 (H. Chiu, ed. 1973).

6. *Parliamentary Seats Added*, 21 *Free China Weekly* 1 (No. 23 June 15, 1980).

7. See Hungdah Chiu, *The Future of Political Stability in Taiwan*, in *Taiwan: One Year After United States–China Normalization (A Senate Foreign Relations Committee Workshop)* 40-41 (June 1980).

8. Constitution of the ROC, art. 77.

9. Article 79, para. 2 of the ROC Constitution provides: "The Judicial Yuan shall have a certain number of Grand Justices to take charge of matters specified in article 78 of this Constitution (The Judicial Yuan shall interpret the Constitution). . . ."

10. They are nominated and, with the consent of the Control Yuan, appointed by the President of the Republic, art. 79, para. 1 of the Constitution. Although the President or the vice-President of the Judicial Yuan is the president *ex officio* during the meeting of the Council of Grand Justices, he can neither participate in the argument nor vote after debate. Moreover, the Council itself even created a Reviewing Bench, under which all the substantive matters are discussed without the participation of the President of the Judicial Yuan. For details, *see* J. Fa, *A Comparative Study of Judicial Review Under Natoinalist Chinese and American Constitutional Law* 88 (1980).

11. In principle, a District Court is to be established for each municipality or country and each province or special area must establish a High Court. A branch may be added if the jurisdictionary territory is widely extended; *see* arts. 9, 16 of the Law of Organization of the Court. There are now 15 District Courts; a High Court and its three branches in Taiwan; *see A Brief Introduction to the Judicial System of the Republic of China* (hereinafter cited as INTRODUCTION) 19 (1976). A hierarchy of four had existed in the early years of the Republic, but those Primary Courts were abolished within a short period. T. Ch'ien, *The Government and Politics of China* 253 (1967). However, the reestablishment of the Primary Court has been extensively discussed recently because of the heavy workload of the courts and to deal with the forthcoming additional business of deciding police offense cases, which used to be handled by the police department itself under the Police Offense Law; *Chung-kuo-Shih-Pao* (China Times), May 6, 1980; *Lien-Ho-Pao* (United Daily), May 16, 1980.

12. Criminal cases relating to offenses against the internal or external security of the state, and the election disputes are under the exclusive jurisdiction of the High Court, *see Introduction to Judicial System . . ., supra* note 11.

13. Law of the Organization of the Court, art. 3, para. 1. Those important cases include cases involving money exceeding $56,000, ten years or more, life imprisonment, and death sentences as well as complicated cases. *See* The Implementation Points of Sitting in Council and Strengthening Supervision of Division Chief in District Courts of Taiwan, arts. 2, 3.

14. Law of the Organization of the Court, art. 3, paras. 2 and 3.

15. Code of Civil Procedure, art. 467; Code of Criminal Procedure, art. 377.

16. Dainow, *The Constitutional and Judicial Organization of France and Germany and Some Comparisons of the Civil Law and Common Law Systems*, 37 *Ind. L. J.* 13, 31 (1961).

17. The preemptory periods of twenty or ten days after the service of the civil or criminal judgment are provided in arts. 438 and 349 of the Codes of Civil and Criminal Procedure.

18. Article 370 of the Code of Criminal Procedure. This is derived from the German system; *see* Harris & Schwarz, *Comparative Law: Important Contrasts in the Administration of Justice in the United States and Western Germany*, 30 *Tex. L. Rev.* 462, 478 (1952). Since the question of double jeopardy is linked to the jury system, its absence in civil law countries is conceivable.

19. For the functions of this French institution, *see* A. Sheehan, *Criminal Procedure in Scotland and France* 43-66 (1975).

20. Yang, *Powers of Chinese Courts*, 1 *Vand. L. Rev.* 16, 23 (1947); Pound, *Progress of the Law in China*, 23 *Wash. L. Rev.* 345, 357 (1948). The issuance of warrants of arrest or detention by procurators instead of a judge was the practice in Japan before World War II, which might be the model for the Chinese; *see* A. Oppler, *Legal Reform in Occupied Japan* 137 (1976); Appleton, *Reforms in Japanese Criminal Procedure under Allied Occupation*, 24 *Wash. L. Rev.* 401, 408 (1948).

21. As a judge is deemed to be a civil servant in some respects, the law governing the suspension, transfer or salary reduction of civil servants may therefore be applied.

22. Shih-tzu No. 86 Interpretation, August 15, 1960.

23. This separation originated in France. Before the revolution, France had an unhappy history of judicial interference with the administrative process in general and obstruction of necessary administrative reforms in particular, and judges attempted to conserve their own privileges and prerogatives. This resulted in fixing in the French mind a deep-rooted antipathy for judicial expansion and a strict interpretation of the theory of separation of powers. A specialized administrative court independent of the regular judicial hierarcy and possessed of the exclusive power of adjudication with respect to administrative acts has thus been established. For details, *see* B. Schwartz, *French Administrative Law and the Common Law World* 1-18 (1954).

In addition to the existence of such attitudes as revulsion and distrust on the part of the administrative hierarcy toward the judiciary, there also are some fundamental differences between administrative and regular civil or criminal adjudication.

Therefore, it is claimed that administrative suits should be heard by those who are intimately versed in matters of administration. In fact, when the United States recognized the merit of the administrative court system, the Court of Claims was established in 1855 and the Tort Claims Act of 1946 was passed which, under certain circumstances, made the government responsible for the actions of its servants.

24. The Organic Law of the Administrative Court, art. 6.

25. *Id.,* art. 4, para. 1.

26. The [Administrative] Appeal Law (hereinafter referred to as Appeal Law), art. 3.

27. A similar procedure also exists in other civil law countries. A prospective plaintiff in West Germany has to follow a "remonstrance" procedure, or an "appeal" (Widerspruch), to the administrative agency before applying to an administrative court; this takes place before higher administrative authorities. See Z. Nedjati & J. Trice, *English and Continental Systems of Administrative Law* 46 (1978).

28. One extension of two additional months is permitted, *see* art. 21 of the Appeal Law and the Law of Adminstrative Proceedings, art. 1.

29. France has the same system but the time limit for action is four months; *see* Nedjati & Trice *supra* note 27 at 43.

30. In reference materials provided by the Ministry of Justice for the second session of the Seminar of National Construction in November 1979, the rate in favor of plaintiffs in cases of taxation in 1978, which constituted the major body of appeals, was 20% and 21% upon cases of re-appeal; *see Chia-Chiang-Szu-Fa-Ke-Hsin P' ei-Yang-Fa-Chih-Ching-Shen (Strengthening Judicial Reform and Cultivating Spirit of Rule of Law)* 8 (1979).

31. The Appeal Law, art. 19.

32. *Chung-Yang-Jih-Pao* (Central Daily), June 29, 1979.

33. Law of Administrative Proceedings, art. 18. The lack of space was given as the basic reason for not conducting oral argument.

34. *Chung-Yang-Jih-Pao* (Central Daily), August 19, 1979.

35. *Chung-Yang-Jih-Pao* (Central Daily), July 2, 1980.

36. *Id.*

37. Article 2.

38. Y. Weng, A Study of Modernization of Administrative Proceedings, is *Hsing-Cheng-Fa-Yu-Hsien-Tai-Fa-Chih-Kuo-Chia (Administrative Law and Modern Country of Rule of Law)* 405 (1979).

39. There are some individual statutes providing compensation in their specified areas, e.g., Land Law, arts. 68, 70; Statute of Utilization of Police Weapon, art. 10.

40. See *Lien-Ho-Pao* (United Daily), June 21, 1980 and *The China Post,* international air mail edition, June 21, 1980, p. 1. The original draft exempted the government from liability if due attention had been paid to prevent the occurrence of damage. Because this exception could destroy the spirit of state compensation by providing an excuse to a government agency, it was cancelled in the Legislative Yuan; *see Lien-Ho-Pao* (United Daily), May 13, 1980. Government liability for acts of omission was also added in the legislative process.

41. Bell, *Federal Tort Claims Act,* 31 *Va. L. Weekly* 12:1 (Nov. 17, 1978).

42. G. Mueller & Fre le Poole-Griffiths, *Comparative Criminal Procedure* 17 (1969).

43. Some suggested that the standard of strong suspicion is tougher than American probable; see *id.,* at 15.

44. Code of Criminal Procedure, art. 76.

45. For a detailed comparison of American and civil law practice, *see* Cohn, *"Criminal Records"* — *A Comparative Approach,* 4 *Ga. J. Int'l & Comp. L.* 116-56 (1974).

46. The difference between a citation and a summons is that while the former may be given by a police officer in traffic cases the latter is usually issued by a judge or other court official.

47. *See* R. Carlson, *Criminal Justice Procedure* 19-21 (1978); LaFave, *Alternatives to the Present Bail System*, 1965 *U. Ill. L. F.* 8-19.

48. Code of Criminal Procedure, arts. 87 & 88, para. 1.

49. Code of Criminal Procedure, art. 88, para. 3.

50. Article 8 which is the most lengthy article in the ROC Constitution.

51. Pound, *Progress of the Law in China*, 23 Wash. L. Rev. 345, 357-58 (1948). *Contra* Chi-tung Lin, one of the most authoritative constitutional scholars, who adopted a narrow construction by excluding the procurator; see C. Lin, *Chung-Hua-Ming-Kuo Hsien-Fa Chu-Tiao Shih-Yi* (A Detailed Study of Articles of the Chinese Constitution) 120 (1975).

52. Article 91.

53. Article 4. Because the Act was enacted before the Constitution, this contradiction is conceivable. Nevertheless, it is inexcusable to allow this situation to continue for such a long period without amendment.

54. Article 122.

55. In German law, a mere suspicion is enough for a search, whereas arrest requires strong suspicion. Meuller, supra note 42, at 18.

56. Code of Criminal Procedure, art. 131.

57. Code of Criminal Procedure, art. 146.

58. Code of Criminal Procedure, art. 148.

59. Code of Criminal Procedure, art. 123.

60. Tao, *Reform of the Criminal Process in Nationalist China*, 19 Am. J. Comp. L. 747, 765 (1971).

61. P. Chen, *Hsing-Shih-Cheng-Chu-Fa* (Law of Criminal Evidence) 259 (1970).

62. *Id.*, at 260.

63. Code of Criminal Procedure, art. 101.

64. Code of Criminal Procedure, art. 108. The former article provided for three extensions during trial regardless of its level and three years' imprisonment as the baseline.

65. Law Governing Compensation for Wrongful Conviction, art. 1, para. 1.

66. Code of Criminal Law, art. 46.

67. Mueller, *supra* note 42, at 106.

68. Several examples were offered to show how the police invoke this Law to pursue criminal investigation by Lung-sheng Tao, in *supra* note 60, at 757-59.

69. For text, *see The Law for the Punishment of Police Offenses of the Republic of China* (L. Fuller & H. Fisher trans. 1960).

70. Articles 46 & 47.

71. Blakemore, *Post-War Development in Japanese Law*, 1947 Wis. L. Rev. 632, 650.

72. This practice was not unique under Nazis; it existed even under Weimar. The Nazis only expanded and abused it; *see* Loewensteon, *Law and the Legislative Process in Occupied Germany: II*, 57 *Yale L. J.* 994, 1018-19 (1948).

73. *Foreign Office, Manual of German Law* 155 (1952).

74. 22 *Szu-Fa Yuan Kung Pao* (Gazette of the Judicial Yuan) 3-4 (No. 11, November 15, 1980).

75. Organic Law of the Judicial Yuan, art. 6.

76. This is reported by Pu-sheng Chen, one of the current Grand Justices, in *Chung-Kuo-Shih-Pao* (China Times), May 14, 1970.

77. *Chung-Kuo-Chih-Pao* (China Times), April 6 and October 12, 1980.

78. Code of Criminal Procedure, arts. 319 & 321. For the practice in other civil law countries, *see* Hall, *The Role of the Victim in the Prosecution and Disposition of a Criminal Case*, 28 *Vand. L. Rev.* 951, 978-80 (1975).

79. Code of Criminal Procedure, art. 323, para. 2.

80. Code of Criminal Procedure, art. 256, para. 1.

81. Code of Criminal Procedure, art. 257, For a more detailed comparative study, *see* Sullivan, *A Comparative Survey of Problems in Criminal Procedure*, 6 *St. Louis U. L. J.* 380, 382 (1961).

82. *Research Center of Crime, Ministry of Justice, Fan-Tsui-Chuan K'uang Chi Ch'i-Fen-Hsi* (The Condition and Analysis of Crimes) (hereinafter cited as Condition and Analysis) 316-19 (1979).

83. Code of Criminal Procedure, art. 27.

84. *Chung-Kuo-Shih-Pao* (China Times), May 5, 1980.

85. Code of Criminal Procedure, art. 33.

86. C. Ch'u, *Il Hsing-Shih-Su-Sung-Fa-Lung* (A Study of Code of Criminal Procedure) 68 (1978).

87. See objections to pre-trial discovery made by Chief Justice Vanderbilt of the New Jersey Supreme Court in State v. Tune, 98 A.2d 881 (N.J. 1953), which has been quoted extensively. Ironically, American military law is much closer to the civil law practice by providing free access to the defense; *see generally*, Kent, *Practical Benefits for the Accused—A Case Comparison of the U.S. Civilian and*

Military Systems of Justice, 9 *Duq. L. Rev.* 186, 195-97 (1970).

88. *Fed. R. Crim. P.* 16 & 18 U.S.C. 3500.

89. Schlesinger, *Comparative Criminal Procedure: A Plea for Utilizing Foreign Experience*, 26 *Buffalo L. Rev.* 361, 373 (1977); Leigh, *Liberty and Efficiency in the Criminal Process—The Significance of Models*, 26 *Int'l. & Comp. L. Q.* 516, 528 (1977).

90. *See* Jescheck, Germany, in *The Accused: A Comparative Study* 246, 247 (J. Coutts, ed. 1966).

91. *See* generally, Damaška, *Evidentiary Barriers to Conviction and Two Models of Criminal Procedure: A Comparative Study*, 121 *Penn. L. Rev.* 506, 517 n. 16, 544 (1973).

92. Professor Damaška suggested a "scientific" theory by saying, "He the judge is, *mutatis mutandis*, like a scientist who, by having formed tentative theories about the object of his exploration, has not thereby surrendered his claims to impassivity. Only when he has a personal stake in the decision, or when his mind is closed on the case, may there be a ground for disqualification." To justify this continental practice, *see* Damaška, *Presentation of Evidence and Factfinding Precision*, 123 *Penn. L. Rev.* 1083, 1105 (1975).

93. Law of Organization of the Court, art. 65 provides: "All cases shall be debated on and all decisions pronounced in open court, provided, that if it is apprehended that it may be detrimental to public order and good moral, such cases may be held *in camera* by a resolution of the court."

94. Code of Criminal Procedure, art. 287.

95. Damaška, *supra* note 91, at 516, n. 13.

96. Code of Criminal Procedure, art. 156, para. 3.

97. Damaška, *supra* note 91, at 527; Clemens, *The Privilege against Self-Incrimination under Foreign Law: Germany*, 51 *J. Crim. L. C & P. S.* 172 (1960); Pieck, *The Accused's Privilege against Self-Incrimination in the Civil Law*, 11 *Am. J. Comp. L.* 585 (1962).

98. Code of Criminal Procedure, art. 166.

99. Han, *The Development of the Anglo-American Rules of Evidence and Their Possible Influence on the Continental Legal System*, 13 *She-Hui-Ko-Hsueh Lun-Tsung* (Journal of Social Sciences) 53, 75 (1963).

100. Code of Criminal Procedure, art. 190.

101. Code of Criminal Procedure, art. 289.

102. Code of Criminal Procedure, art. 290. The order of argument also applies to other civil law countries; West Germany is an obvious example. *See* Jescheck, *supra* note 90, at 250-51.

103. Code of Criminal Procedure, art. 155, para. 1.

104. Code of Criminal Procedure, art. 155, para. 2.

105. Judge Marvin E. Frankel summarized his nine years on the federal trial bench by warning "that our adversary system rates truth too low among the values that institutions of justice are meant to serve." Frankel, *The Search for Truth: An Umpireal View*, 123 *U. Penn. L. Rev.* 1031, 1032 (1975). A statement made by an eminent scholar after long and careful study is instructive: he said that if he were innocent, he would rather be tried by a civil law court, but if he were guilty, he would prefer to be tried by a common law court. This indicates that criminal procedure in the civil law country is more likely to distinguish accurately between the guilty and the innocent. *See* J. Merryman, *The Civil Law Tradition* 139 (1969).

106. Article 159 of the Code of Criminal Procedure provides: "Unless otherwise provided by law, statements made by a witness not during the trial shall not be admitted in evidence." However, the legislative history indicates the exclusion of hearsay evidence was not the mind of legislators; it was designed against written testimony rather than oral statements made by prospective witnesses before the trial. *See* Chen, *supra* note 61 at 134; Lee, *Theory and Practice of Newly Added Law of Evidence in the Criminal Procedure*, 13 *Fa-Hsueh-Tsung-Kan* (China Law Journal) 3:15, 19-21 (1968). However, in conformity with the current spirit and trend in the ROC to provide more protection to the defendant in criminal procedure, the provision has received a more liberal construction. *See* Chou, *A Study of the Hearsay Rule in Criminal Evidence Law*, 15 *Chengchi L. Rev.* 153, 183-84 (1977).

107. This is not only the practice of other civil law countries; both England and the Commonwealth system also refuse to follow the American precedent. *See* Symposium, *The Exclusionary Rules Under Foreign Law*, 52 *J. Crim. L. C. & P. S.* 271 (1961). In addition, it should be noted here that during the American post-trial pre-sentence procedure, the technical rules of evidence are not generally applicable. Williams v. New York, 337 U.S. 241 (1949); U.S. v. Shipiani, 435 F.2d 26 (2d Cir. 1970).

108. Article 156 provides that a confession of an accused not extracted by violence, threat, inducement, fraud, unlawful detention or other improper devices and consistent with facts may be admitted in evidence. Both France and West Germany have the same exception to the general rule of admissibility; *see* Sheehan, *supra* note 19, at 29; J. Langbeing, *Comparative Criminal Procedure: Germany* 69 (1977).

109. Code of Criminal Procedure, art. 156, para. 2.

110. Condition and Analysis, *supra* note 82, at 321. Data on judges were provided by the Ministry of Justice.

111. Condition and Analysis, *supra* note 82, at 344.

112. Those items include, e.g., consecutive sessions, investigation of evidence in person, the requirement that those cases involving possible death or life sentences must be forewarded within two days to the Supreme Court regardless of whether the parties have so petitioned, concentrating on serious cases without being allocated other cases, etc. *Lien-Ho-Pao* (United Daily), Jan 29, 1976.

113. J. Einsenstein & H. Jacob, *Felony Justice* 291 (1977).

114. *New York Times,* Sept. 26, 1979.

115. U.S. Dep't of Justice, *Sourcebook of Criminal Justice Statistics*—1977, 545 (1978).

116. *Id.,* at 552.

117. Condition and Analysis, *supra* note 82, at 330.

118. U.S. Dep't of Justice, *supra* note 115, at 552.

119. Condition and Analysis, *supra* note 82, at 330.

120. Code of Criminal Law, arts. 86-99.

121. Article 7.

122. *See* Larguier, *The Civil Action for Damages in French Criminal Procedure,* 39 *Tul. L. Rev.* 686 (1965); Pugh, *Ruminations re Reform of American Criminal Justice (Especially our Guilty Plea System): Reflections Derived from a Study of the French System,* 36 *La. L. Rev.* 947, 965, (1976). Germany imported this system during World War II and maintained it even after the war, but it has become dead letter for a variety of reasons; *see* Langbeing, *supra* note 108, at 111-15.

123. This proclamation automatically carried into operation the whole body of Martial Law. Article 8 specifically provides that during the period of enforcement of Martial Law the military organ may try, by itself, certain offenses including those against the internal and external security of the state and those against public order and public safety.

124. Traditionally, the fact that civil courts are open has precluded the use of martial law. However, the doctrine has undergone a revision, because the nature of modern war has changed; it is still possible for the civil courts to be open even in the actual fighting zone. Therefore, whether the function of the courts is obstructed or not should not be the real criterion. *See* Warren, *Spies, and the Power of Congress to Subject Certain Classes of Civilians to Trial by Military Tribunal.* 53 *Am. L. Rev.* 195, 201 (1919); Robert Rankin also cited a list of supporting articles on this point; *see* R. Rankin, *When Civil Law Fails* 181-84 (1939).

125. For details, *see* C. Rossiter, *Constitutional Dictatorship* 86-87 (1948).

126. C. Friedrich, *Constitutional Government and Democracy* 240 (1941).

127. Constitution, art. 39.

128. For details, *see* Fay, *Restraints on Executive Emergency Power in the United States and Canada,* 3 *Hastings Int'l & Comp. L. Rev.* 127, 143 (1979).

129. There would be more than 100 kinds of crime to be tried by military court if the government strictly followed the provisions of Martial Law.

130. For a fairly detailed investigation of the causes of these revisions, *see* I. Wang, *The Delimitation of Criminal Jurisdiction among Military and Civilian Judicial Organs in the Region of Taiwan during the Last Twenty Years,* in *Fa-Lin-Yueh-Kan Erh-Shih-Chou-Nien-Lun-Wan-Chi* (Symposium in Honor of Twentieth Anniversary of Law Monthly) 423-37 (S. Yu ed. 1970).

131. *Chung-Yang-Jih-Pao* (Central Daily), Jan. 25, 1976.

132. Condition and Analysis, *supra* note 82, at 108-09.

133. *Id.*

134. *Chung-Yang-Jih-Pao* (Central Daily), Jan. 8, 1980.

135. Military Trial Law, art. 133, para. 1.

136. Para. 88, *Manual for Courts-Martial, United States* (1969 rev.).

137. Military Trial Law, art. 133. para. 2.

138. Statute for Denunciation and Suppression of Rebels, art. 8.

139. Statute for Punishment of Rebellion, art. 9, para. 1.

140. Statute for Punishment of Rebellion, art. 9, paras. 2 & 3; Measures of Sending Rebels to the Reformation during Period of Suppression of Rebels, art. 2, para. 2.

141. Measures of Sending Rebels to Reformation during Period of Suppression of Rebels, art. 15, para. 2.

IV. OVERALL EVALUATION AND OUTLOOK

After the defeat of the ROC Government on the mainland by the Chinese Communists and its removal to Taiwan, President Chiang Kai-shek maintained that, while there were many factors beyond the control of the ROC leading to its defeat, one of the major causes for the Nationalist Party's defeat was its failure to fully implement Dr. Sun Yat-sen's Three Principles of the People. On Taiwan, the ROC began seriously to implement these principles. So far as law and justice are concerned, this has meant the continuation of constitutional rule and continued modernization of the Chinese legal system. Without a stable and secure legal environment, President Chiang maintained, it was not possible to carry out economic, social and political development.

In general, in the last three decades, the Government has established at least the foundation of a modern constitutional and legal system in Taiwan and planted the seeds for its future growth. While Taiwan's economic growth is well-known, its legal development is usually ignored by Westerners. Some even get the impression that Taiwan does not have a sophisticated modern legal system. Without a modern legal system, a country's economy can never achieve the level of economic development reached in Taiwan. This is especially clear from watching the experience of mainland China under Communist rule and that of many other developing countries.

In evaluating the legal development in Taiwan in the last three decades, one must remember the environment in which the ROC legal system operated. The ROC government and people are constantly facing invasion from the People's Republic of China only about a hundred miles away and cannot forget the international isolation resulting from the PRC's increasing acceptance in the diplomatic community. The fundamental concern of the people and the government in Taiwan is the security and the human rights of the entire 18 million people there. As an American law professor observed after her recent visit:

> national security consciousness runs high, marked by officially expressed fears that criticism in the political realm might be read as a sign of weakness and disunity, encouraging aggressive moves by the PRC. When we asked abut the . . . restrictions on antigovernment expression, we were told repeatedly: Do not compare us with the United States; a strong enemy lurks at our door. The point, if not a complete answer, was well made. One need only recall reactions in this country in times of stress, for example, the hardships imposed on Japanese-Americans during World War II and on a broad spectrum of Americans in the McCarthy era.[1]

Moreover, it should be always remembered that China has its own legal tradition. Despite the fact that the Nationalist Party has decided to introduce a Western legal system to China, it can never be expected to depart from certain vital values embodied in the Chinese legal tradition such as severe punishment for those who committed murder, rape and armed robbery and for those who advocate the separation of part of Chinese territory. In addition, some undesirable parts of the Chinese legal traditions, such as presumption of guilt and the combination of executive and judicial functions in one organ, cannot be repudiated instantaneously.

Furthermore, to evaluate the ROC legal system on the standard of advanced Western democracies is simply unfair because the country has had fewer than fifty years experience, of which almost fifteen years were in a period of external or civil war and the remaining thirty years have been under the constant military threat of a nuclear power—the People's Republic of China. An eminent American legal scholar, Roscoe Pound, had made an illuminating comment on this point:

> It is wholly unreasonable to expect the administration of justice in China to be one hundred percent perfect. Certainly American administration of justice is far from perfect, although it has had three centuries to develop in colonial and independent America, and has had no such disruption to contend with as that brought about by eight years of Japanese occupation of China, has had behind it the fully developed legal literature of the common law, well-organized legal education, a people brought up on belief in law and courts, and a bar with traditional organization, ethical traditions, and agencies of discipline. To measure administration of justice in China by standards of an abstract legal Utopia or to assume that not adopting wholesale American legal institutions, methods, and doctrines is proof of failure to comprehend the task of adjusting relations and ordering conduct through the systematic application of the force of a politically organized society is not merely grossly unfair. It argues ignorance of the machinery of justice in more than half of the world.[2]

The above observation does not mean that the legal system under the ROC government is perfect. Neither the government leaders nor the general public would so contend. There have been many criticisms and suggestions in the press and legal periodicals in Taiwan for further improvements of the legal system. In the future, if the United States would guarantee to provide Taiwan adequate defensive weapons and other security arrangements and if the PRC would be willing to compete with Taiwan peacefully and to forego the threat of the use of force and subversive activities, then the ROC on Taiwan would live in a more secure environment. Under those circumstances, one could expect that the ROC's constitutional rule and legal system would rapidly move to a higher stage of development.

NOTES

1. Ginsburg, *A Study Tour of Taiwan's Legal System*, 66 Am. Bar Assoc. L. J. 166 (1980).
2. Pound, *Progress of the Law in China*, 23 Wash. L. R. 362 (1948).

Section 6
Domestic Politics
Edited by John F. Copper

Section 6
Domestic Politics

by John F. Copper

The political system of the Republic of China traces its origins to Chinese politics on the mainland during the early part of this century. It was transplanted to Taiwan in 1945, when Japan's defeat during World War II brought to an end Taiwan's status as a part of the Japanese empire, which it had been for fifty years.

This political system is a blend of China's traditional government and Western political types. The five *yuan* or branches of government represent the three main functions of government in Western systems; two additional *yuan* represent important functions of government in pre-revolution China. The former are the Executive Yuan, the Legislative Yuan, and the Judicial Yuan. The latter include the Examination and Control Yuan. In the first selection in this section Han Lih-wu describes the structure of the government of the Republic of China.

The reader is advised to keep in mind that, while critics may claim the system is democratic in theory more than in practice, native-born Chinese, or "Taiwanese," in Taiwan played an insignificant role in politics while Taiwan was part of the Japanese empire. Taiwan was ruled by the Japanese as a colony. Thus in 1945 the political experience of the local Chinese was wanting. Moreover, they had almost no contact with the government of China on the mainland and had little understanding of that political system.

Consequently, the central or national government was controlled by those Chinese called "Mainlanders" who went to Taiwan after World War II, most of them in 1949, when Chiang Kai-shek and the Nationalist Chinese lost the mainland to the Communists. Local government is largely in the hands of the Taiwanese, who comprise about 80 percent of the population. The political system being a unitary one, however, the national government has greater prerogatives and it is here that political power resides.

Critics of the Republic of China polity often point out the fact that the system is controlled by a minority of mainland Chinese and that the system is neither representative nor democratic. And many that advocate change see little hope that this will occur. This view, however, misses the important fact that local politics in Taiwan involves the widespread use of democratic practices and in general Taiwan's citizens are more aware and more concerned about local political institutions and problems than their coun-

John F. Copper is Professor of Political Science, Southwestern University (Memphis, Tenn.)

terparts in many Western democracies. Clearly this is true, considering their knowledge of local political issues and their turnout at election time.

In fact, one might say that there is more democracy practiced at the local level in Taiwan than in most advanced countries where there is typically a problem of transience on the part of the residents (both due to commuting and to frequent changes of residence) and therefore lack of knowledge or understanding of issues and people. In this context, one might certainly speculate that democracy in Taiwan may be growing from the bottom up (see our first selection, by Han Li-Wu).

Furthermore, the Republic of China is technically still at war with the People's Republic of China (Peking), referred to by the government in Taipei as "Chinese bandits." Since it is official policy that the Nationalist government will return to the mainland someday, the structure of government and representation of all of the provinces on the mainland is preserved. This may be unrealistic to a Westerner, but it does rationalize the peculiar quality of the political system, while the Constitution suggests a working democratic system.

On the other hand, the "return to the mainland" theme also had the effect of stunting excessive demands for representative government and full democracy which would transform the ruling elite into a minority. If recognizing the possibility of what deToqueville calls the "tyranny of the majority" this group might become a suppressed or discriminated against minority if democracy is implemented too quickly—thereby suggesting a situation where majority rule should be accomplished gradually to avoid violence. The "phasing out" of the policy of reconquering the mainland, which more than a decade ago was said to be seventy percent political and thirty percent military and is now seldom cited except occasionally in any serious context, may suggest that this gradual transition is happening.

Both the first two selections in this section deal with the political structure of the Republic of China. The first selection, by Dr. Lih-wu Han, addresses governmental retrenchment and reorganization after the relocation of the ROC Government in Taiwan following the loss of the mainland in 1949, and provides an over-all view of the political structure as it has emerged in the ensuing years. Ralph Clough, in the second selection, discusses the political system in the context of the so-called mainlander-Taiwanese problems that have often been a favorite topic for Taiwan's critics. These problems, now on their way out, were more visible during the years immediately after the island's return to the ROC by Japan in 1945 at the conclusion of World War II. A large part of the cause for them was rooted in misadjustments and misunderstanding between the indigenous population and the most recent arrivals from the mainland in the late 1940's, as can be evidenced by the unfortunate February 28, 1947 riot. For his mishandling of the incident, Governor Ch'en Yi was removed by President Chiang Kai-shek and later executed.

In reading the first part of Selection 2, the reader is advised to bear in mind that the so-called Taiwanese and mainlanders are all Chinese; they are racially the same. Their culture and language are also of the same origin. One should also bear in mind that the two groups have a somewhat different past and therefore may see the world somewhat differently. The mainlanders, while certainly not a homogeneous group since they hail from all parts of China (though there are fewer from the Northern or Western provinces and an inordinately large number from east and central China), are more aware, and therefore more conscious of and proud of, Chinese history. The Taiwanese, on the other hand, may think more in terms of Taiwan's future as an island entity.

In recent years the two groups have manifested less separateness. In fact, some say there is now a larger generation gap in both groups than differences between the young people of the two. In other words, given a few more years and a setting of peace and prosperity, differences between the two groups will disappear.

It should also be noted that the threat of Communism, arising from Peking's claims upon Taiwan, has been a unifying factor in Taiwan. Both Taiwanese and mainlander Chinese know that they are better off autonomous or independent, and that they must stick together to protect the good life they have attained in recent years.

Clough also discusses, though briefly, the relationship between the government and the Kuomintang (KMT), or Nationalist Party. Clearly no analysis of the political system of the Republic of China would be complete without taking into consideration the role of the KMT. The present structure of the KMT goes back to the 1920's, when Soviet advisors in China played a role in renovating the system. And the KMT has found this kind of structure and organization efficient and workable and has therefore not altered it very much.

More so even than the government, the Party until now at least has remained dominated at the top by mainland Chinese. In recent years, though, the KMT has recruited many Taiwanese—in fact, in larger numbers than they are a percentage of the population. Thus, an "affirmative action" program may be said to be in effect. This has been done behind the leadership and initiative of Chiang Ching-Kuo. These efforts are gradually being felt at all levels of decision making.

While the KMT does not exercise the pervasive influence over the population that the Communist Party does in China, it is more a mass party than the Chinese Communist Party (CCP) in terms of the percentage of the population that holds membership. It has also been a better integrating force as well. The KMT has been quite successful in maintaining political stability, in generating economic growth, and in managing succession. Thus it is a party with widespread popular support for its program. The ROC under the KMT does allow some measure of political competition. There are two other small parties, though they do not constitue effective competition, and the formation of new parties is prohibited by law (via the "temporary provisions" added to the Constitution "during the period of Communist rebellion"). On the other hand, independent candidates are allowed to run for office and many elected officials are independents. Some describe Taiwan's political party system as a "one-party plus independents" system.

In addition to the Party, the military and the China Youth Corp constitute two other important seats of political power in Taiwan. The military is discussed in another section of this work. So suffice it to say here that Chiang Kai-shek, when he was alive, always maintained a close relationship with the army. And when his son, Chiang Ching-Kuo, came to power after his death in 1975, he also had close ties with the military.

Having learned a lesson from their defeat on the mainland, Nationalist Chinese leaders have paid special attention to the youth. The China Youth Corp, a second locus of political authority, is therefore not only a training organization for the KMT and future leaders of the Republic of China, it is in itself a center of not inconsiderable political power. It was once headed by Chiang Ching-kuo, and it remains a recognized base of political power and an organization with political influence.

Clough also notes the importance of the security police network in politics in the Republic of China. On the negative side, the police system on occasion has had to suppress political dissent and thus has impeded fuller development of democracy. On the positive side, it has helped create an atmosphere of peace and stability which has been conducive to rapid economic development as well as to personal security for citizens of the nation. People in Taiwan generally reply, when foreigners broach the subject of civil and human rights, that Chinese don't feel a need to criticize their leaders in crude terms as do many Westerners; it is a difference in political culture. They also point out that personal safety is of utmost importance and one can walk the streets in any city in Taiwan late at night without fear of being raped, mugged or murdered; this is true of few Western cities and probably no large city in the U.S.

When crime increases precipitously or is perceived to be a problem (though a rise in crime or a high crime rate in Taiwan would be a very low rate by U.S. standards), "temporary provisions" are often enacted making it possible to send civil cases to military courts and mete out stiff penalties including the death penalty for crimes of violence (which to the Chinese are in a different category). This has always resulted in a drop in the crime rate and public support for the government in using harsh measures to maintain public order. Dissidents have frequently charged that the police have used a rise in the crime rate as justification to eliminate legitimate dissent, but they get little public support for this complaint.

In the next contribution, by John F. Copper, the subject of political development is examined through an analysis of the way political power is actually exercised and by noting the extensive economic, and only to a slightly less extent social, change Taiwan has experienced in the past two to three decades.

It is suggested that the reader pay special attention to the point that certain organs of the ROC government have experienced considerable growth in terms of their power relative to the other organs of government. This is especially true of the Executive Yuan. And whereas this organ of decision-making authority is not popularly elected, it is probably the organ of government that is most sensitive to public opinion. This is true because of the increasing number of younger, more progressive officials that have been recruited to this branch of government, which has been the center of decisions relating to economic development. Most of the high officials in this branch of the government realize the importance of what Western social scientists call interest aggregation, interest articulation, feedback in the political system, and public support.

The Executive Yuan is therefore the generator of social and political change in Taiwan. Because it is not an elected body and it maintains a generally low profile (though it does advertise the fact to the public that if there are complaints about government or suggestions, it is the place to which they are to be addressed), it is not given much credit for its accomplishments. Perhaps at the present time there is no feasible alternative to its monopolization of political power and its mode of operation, since the other organs of government are staffed by older officials who are less disposed to change.

The question, of course, arises: Will the other branches of government follow the lead of the Executive Yuan? Or will they impede and reverse the progress made by this "vanguard" organ of government? The answer seems clearly to be the former. Pressure for change is already evident in other branches of government and the majority of the citizenry is ready for change, or so the polls taken on political attitudes suggest. Exactly how this will be done is not clear. One guess is that the election process will help bolster this prestige and authority of the Legislative Yuan and perhaps the Control Yuan. Similarly, the need for and the use of judicial solutions is likely to boost the position of the Judicial Yuan, as is happening in other developing countries and as happened in advanced countries during their periods of political development.

The point to be underscored is that structurally there has been almost no change in the ROC's political system—and, therefore, it is easy to see no progress if progress is simply equated with structural change. But change there has been within, and despite, the continuing structure. Those who criticize the polity of Taiwan generally make this error.

Another point that deserves to be stressed is the relationship between political development and economic growth. Taiwan's economic progress is analyzed in depth in another section of this book and the reader's attention is directed to that section. Here it is necessary to take cognizance of the fact that economic development usually engenders, or requires, political develoment. Sometimes there is a gap between economic and political progress, in which case pressure for change, sometimes of the quick or revolutionary kind, may exist. On the other hand, even Marxist historians advise us that revolutions are unlikely in the context of rapid economic growth—especially growth with equity. Therefore the gap between economic growth and political change in Taiwan must be seen as a gap which is not nearly as large as may critics contend. The reason is that they fail to understand the progress in political development noted above and look to elections, changes in the political structure, and constitutional revision as evidence of change. The gap as it exists is normal in a country experiencing the rapid economic growth that Taiwan has made and continues to experience.

In terms of a final remark on this subject, it should be noted that Taiwan's economic progress is self-generated. That is, it is not the product of selling raw materials (such as oil) in a favorable market as is the case of a number of formerly underdeveloped countries of the world that are now experiencing rapid progress in terms of economic statistics. Since Taiwan is poorly endowed in resources, especially on a per capita basis, its economic miracle must be attributed almost completely to its human talents, including organizational abilities. This suggests that even if there is a serious gap between the economic and political sectors, which is doubtful, the talent and the understanding exists to quickly rectify the problem.

The last selection in this section by John F. Copper on the recently held election may shed some light on the political succession question. In December, 1980, an election was held in Taiwan which was, in a variety of ways, unprecendented. Technically, it was the first national election in Taiwan. It was also an exercise in political choice done in a milieu of some considerable uncertainty and apprehension, but with the determination on the part of top national leaders, especially Chiang Ching-kuo to increase political participation and move in the direction of making the Republic of China's political institutions work democratically.

The election, however, may have much greater significance. Clearly, it satisfied outside observers in terms of the campaigning being hindered by few restrictions and the election procedures being fair. Indeed, an overwhelming majority of commentators saw it as a step forward toward democracy. Thus there may be less pressure on the ROC political leadership from Western countries who continue to support Taiwan's autonomy and independence, but want to see progress toward democracy and expect it as compensation. Also the election identified right and left extremists and made the government appear a force of moderation. Similarly, in view of the persistence of ethnic voting, it may offer proof that Taiwan is not ready for a two-party system.

Perhaps even more important, the government seemed to appraise the election in retrospect as reflecting an enlightened electorate and more moderate political views and behavior than expected. Thus the "establishment" has come away with more confidence in democratic processes, perhaps signaling a phasing out of the period of tutelage. The election no doubt will pave the way for even broader elections in the future. Finally, it will further erase differences between Taiwanese and mainlander Chinese, giving evidence that there can be a smooth transition of power.

Finally, some closing words need to be said in the realm of summing up and broaching future questions. Clearly the political system of the Republic of China has experienced progressive change in the time it has ruled Taiwan since 1945. This change is not obvious; but it is easily visible for the analyst to see. Moreover, it should be given much applause: for its efficiency in getting rid of corruption (a serious problem three decades ago), for dealing with ethnic problems (particularly if seen in the context of the events of February 1947), and for engineering rapid economic growth in the context of a population problem (Taiwan is more densely populated than any major nation on earth with the exception of Holland). Also, it has successfully managed to deal with criticism from Western countries that have little understanding of Chinese political culture and with pressure from outside for reform and democratization. In some senses, then, the political system of the Republic of China may be seen as a model. In fact, Taiwan has been cited recently as a model for the People's Republic of China. However, this has significance only if leaders in mainland China can be so persuaded.

Lastly, the Republic of China's polity has developed and changed in many ways that resemble the Japanese model. Western political culture has not taken root completely in Taiwan, and, like Japan, perhaps it never will. It is likely Taiwan is better off that this is the case. After all, a number of East Asian countries have political system, albeit influenced by the West, which seem in many ways more stable, more orderly, and more tolerant of the majority than a majority of Western states.

1.   Political and Social Conditions

Lih-Wu Han

With the occupation of mainland China by the Chinese Communists in 1949, the Central Government was moved to Taiwan and, in December of that year, Taipei became the temporary capital. The Central Government is composed of the National Assembly, the President, and the Executive, Legislative, Judicial, Examination, and Control Yuan. The administrative machinery combines the major features of the cabinet and presidential systems of government.

There has been a drastic retrenchment and streamlining in all government agencies, resulting in the merger of various units and a corresponding reduction of personnel. The authority of the local government is clearly separated from that of the Central Government. With the exception of the Ministries of Foreign Affairs, National Defense and Justice, the ministries, commissions and other national agencies in the Cabinet exercise only supervisory and planning functions over their corresponding provincial and county levels. The Constitution stipulates that any matter shall fall within the jurisdiction of the Central Government if it is national in nature, and of the county or city if it pertains to that area. In case of dispute over the demarcation of authority, the Legislative Yuan has the deciding voice.

Han Li-Wu, *Taiwan Today* (Taipei: Institute of International Relations, 1974), pp. 17-27.

Central Government

The National Assembly is the repository of the political power of the whole people. It is composed of delegates elected once every six years on the basis of both regional and occupational representation. Its functions are the election and recall of the President, amendment of the Constitution, and the alteration of the boundaries of the country.

The President is the head of state and all acts of state are conducted in his name. His term of office, as well as that of the Vice President, is six years and he may be re-elected once.

However, according to a constitutional provision enacted during the period of the Communist rebellion, the President and Vice President may be re-elected without regard to the two-term restriction. The late President Chiang Kai-shek was elected for his fifth term in March, 1972.

Each of the five Yuan has a specific and separate apparatus. The Executive Yuan, or the Cabinet, is the highest administrative branch of the Government. It consists of a premier, a deputy premier, a number of ministers, chairmen of commissions and ministers without portfolio. The president of the Executive Yuan is nominated and appointed, with the consent of the Legislative Yuan, by the President of the Republic upon the recommendation of the president of the Executive Yuan.

There are at present eight ministries and two commissions under the Cabinet. They are the Ministries of the Interior, Foreign Affairs, National Defense, Finance, Education, Justice*, Economic Affairs, and Communications, the Commissions of Mongolian and Tibetan Affairs, and the Commission of Overseas Chinese Affairs.

The Legislative Yuan is the highest legislative branch of the Government. Its members are elected for a term of three years on the basis of both geographical and occupational representation. The members elect a president and vice president as presiding officers.

The Judicial Yuan has charge of civil, criminal and administrative cases, and of cases concerning disciplinary measures against public functionaries. It interprets the constitution and has the power to unify the interpretation of laws and orders. The Judicial Yuan has a president, a vice president and a number of grand justices—all nominated and appointed by the President with the consent of the Control Yuan.

Under the Judicial Yuan, there are: (1) the Supreme Court for the adjudication of civil and criminal cases; (2) the Administrative Court for administrative suits; and (3) the Committee on the Discipline of Public Functionaries.

The main function of the Examination Yuan is to ensure the selection by competitive examination of the best qualified persons and to provide fair and equal opportunity for all to enter government service. Its president, vice president and commissioners who make up the Examination Council are all appointed by the President with the consent of the Control Yuan for a term of six years.

The Control Yuan has the power to impeach and censure public functionaries of the central and local governments and to propose, corrective measures for executive action. There is also a Ministry of Audit that supervises all budget preparations and approves final budget reports.

The Control Yuan is composed of representatives elected by the provincial assemblies, special municipal councils, border areas, and minority people for a term of six years. Members of the Yuan elect a president and vice president.

It should be noted that members of the National Assembly, the Legislative, and Control Yuan have been holding office since they were first elected on the mainland and elsewhere in 1947. However, for Taiwan and overseas Chinese, fresh elections have been held according to regulations since 1972.

Provincial Government

The first Taiwan Provincial Government was composed of 15 Commissioners, of whom seven were local. In December, 1948, a new Governor was appointed. In May, 1972, the

---

*Since the time of this writing, the Justice Ministry has been placed under the Judicial Yuan in order to maintain an independent court system, separate from the prosecuting functions of the State—General Editor.

ninth reorganization was effected with the appointment of 21 Commissioners of whom 11 are local, including the Governor.

To Commissioners, of whom one is designated Chairman, are appointed by the Central Government. This Chairman serves as the Provincial Governor and is considered the chief executive. He is subject to national laws and regulations and the Provincial Assembly and has not relation to the judiciary branch. As the executive, the Governor administers more by delegation of power to the various departments than by direct control, and makes major policy decisions only after meetings of the Commissioners. Only the Secretariat, the Information, Personnel, and Accounting and Statistics Departments are under his care with the assistance of a Secretary-General. The following departments are basically independent bodies which answer to the Governor: Civil Affairs, Finance, Reconstruction, Education, Agriculture and Forestry, Social Affairs, Police Affairs, Communications, Public Health, and the Food Bureau. The agricultural, forestry and aquatic products experimental stations formerly under the direct control of the Governor are now under the Department of Agriculture and Forestry. All schools have been turned over to the Department of Education. The harbors and meteorological stations, together with the railways and highways, are under the Conservation of Communications. The Bureau of Water Conservancy and the Institute of Industrial Research have been shifted to the Department of Reconstruction.

Provincial Assembly

As a preliminary step, the People's Political Council (PPC) was convened in May, 1946, less than six months after the takeover. It was an elective body of 37 members with a restrictive scope and whose resolutions were not binding.

In December, 1951, the PPC was replaced by the Provisional Provincial Assembly, consisting of 55 members indirectly elected by the country and city councils which themselves were popularly elected. This in turn became the Taiwan Provincial Assembly. The first Assembly was elected in August, 1959 and new elections were held in 1960, 1963, 1968, 1973, and 1977.

The Assembly has wide powers in the consideration of administrative policies and the Provincial budget. The Provincial Government has to abide by the decision of the Assembly unless it wants to appeal the decision to the Central Government, which has the last word. When the Province has full self-government, there will by only one final check: its decisions shall be within the sphere of national laws and regulations.

Local Government

Local self-government was suppressed by the Japanese for many years. As a first step after the takeover, provisional councils for nine cities and eight countries were elected by popular vote. Their functions were identical to those of the PPC, with one addition: the power to bring the mayor or magistrate before a supervisory body.

These city and county councils elected in 1946 were due for re-election in 1948, but it was decided that the life of the provisional councils be prolonged until they could be replaced by full-fledged ones. However, owing to unsettled conditions, the promulgation of general regulations pertaining to provincial, city and country self-government were postponed by the Central Government.

In 1949, the Provincial Government took the initiative by establishing a Committee for the Planning and Study of Local Self-Government in Taiwan. This Committee prepared and forwarded to the PPC for consideration a set of regulations pertaining to the general principles of city and council self-government, organization of city and county governments, election and recall of mayors and magistrates, organization of city and county councils, election and recall of city and county councillors, etc.

They also recommended the redemarcation of various cities and counties to be effected simultaneously with the plans for self-government. According to the Provincial Department of Civil Affairs, this was necessary because there were large differences in size and wealth between the various areas which would hinder the efficient operation of any governmental structure introduced. For example, Taichung county was twice as large as Taitung county and much more prosperous and Tainan county's population of 1,428,440 was almost nine times that of the county of Hualien.

After joint study by the Provincial Government and the provincial PPC, a plan for the rezoning of cities and counties and the election of local officials was submitted to the Central Government and approved by it in August 1950. Under this plan, the original eight counties and nine cities were transformed into sixteen counties and three cities. It was decided that three separate elections would be held for councillors, mayors and magistrates.

In order to insure the smooth transition to local government, the Government mobilized its educational agencies to enlighten the public about the basic ideas and regulations relative to self-government. The Department of Civil Affairs gave short training courses to local officials in charge of elections, and sent experts to various districts to train those charged with the enforcement of election regulations.

Hualien and Taitung, two eastern countries, have the distinction of being the first two self-governing counties. Their county councils were elected on July 2 and 6, 1950, and were convened in August. The second group held elections in September and October of the same year and the third group completed election of their councils in January, 1951. The elections for mayors and magistrates were also held in three groups during 1951, thus completing the system of self-rule for cities and counties.

In all, eight elections for mayors and magistrates and nine for council members have been held, the latest in November, 1977.

Mention should be made that Taipei became a special municipality (when its population reached one million) on July 1, 1967. While the mayor of such a municipality is appointed by the Central Government, the city council is still elected by popular vote. The latest election of Taipei City Council members was in November, 1977. Kaohsiung, Taiwan's second largest city, also became a special municipality on July 1, 1979. The members of the new provisional council are composed of the original 53 members of the Kaohsiung City Council and the three members of the Kaohsiung County Council elected from Hsiao Kang district, a nearby area annexed by Kaohsiung City when it became a special municipality.

Administration of Mountain Areas

Occupying a significant place in the civil affairs of Taiwan is the administration of the tribesmen, or aborigines, in the mountainous districts. There are nine tribes, the Ami, Tyla, Paiwan, Bunnum, Puyuma, Rukai, Saiset, Tsuo, and Yami. The first three are the largest tribal groups. Out of a total population of about 280,000, those still living in the mountains number 152,000.

The responsibility for administering mountainous districts belongs to the Civil Affairs Department. Schools are run by the Department of Education and the Department of Public Health attends to the prevention of disease and provides health care facilities. The aborigines are exempt from taxes and duties.

To promote self-rule among them, thirty village administrative units have been established. Village chiefs are elected by popular vote as are village councils. As a temporary measure, a lowland man is appointed as executive secretary by the magistrate of the county in which the village is located to assist the chief. Mountaineers are allowed one Provincial councillor for each village instead of the general arrangement of one representative for each 10,000 persons. They are also given special representation in the Provincial Assembly, with one member representing those living on the plains and two members representing those living in the mountains, while in the Provincial Government there is one Commissioner who is a tribesman.

Kinmen (Quemoy) Islands

Quemoy, or Kinmen, is part of the Kinmen complex comprising Kinmen, Little Kinmen, and 12 islets which block the mouth of Amoy Bay. The total area is 175 sq. km. Its shortest distance from the mainland is 2,310 meters and it is 198 nautical miles from Keelung in northern Taiwan. As of December, 1979, Kinmen had a population of 53,944.

Kinmen is a county of Fukien Province. A political affairs commission was established in June, 1956 to administer the islands under the Kinmen Garrison Headquarters. The county government has its seat in Kinmen, while the Fukien Provincial Government has its temporary office in Taipei.

Although the 12 satellite islands are low and flat, Kinmen is hilly and over 50 percent of the land is cultivated. Farming is the main occupation and Kinmen is self-sufficient in all foods except rice. There are 20 kindergartens, 18 primary schools, five junior high schools, one senior high school and one technical high school with students constituting 34.5 percent of the population. The island has a general hospital, three public health centers and 18 public health substations.

Matsu Islands

The Matsu Islands comprise 19 islets which form the northern anchor of an offshore defense line and seal the mouth of the Min River. The main island is Nankan, more commonly known as Matsu. It is 114 nautical miles west of northern Taiwan and the same distance north of Kinmen. As of December, 1979, the population was 9,809, most of whom earn their living by fishing. There are one kindergarten, 9 primary schools, 5 junior and one senior high school.

2.   The Political System of Taiwan

Ralph N. Clough

The ROC has been exceptional among developing countries for its political stability. With the exception of the Taiwanese uprising in 1947, before the Nationalist government had moved from the mainland to Taiwan, the island has not been plagued with the political disorders, insurgencies, and military coups common among developing countries. The question is how a government whose corruption and inefficiency had permitted the Chinese Communist party to win on the mainland managed to establish effective control and to gain a wide degree of popular acceptance in Taiwan.

The Nationalist government, headed by Chiang Kai-shek, and arrived in Taiwan in 1949 purged and chastened. Although the number of government and party officials who fled to Taiwan was large in relation to the territory that remained for them to govern, they were only a small fraction of all Chinese officials. The flight to a refuge that most of the world expected would soon be overrun by the victorious Communist armies automatically purged the Nationalist party, army, and government of large numbers of corrupt, wavering, and ineffective officials. Most of those who had the money to do so fled to Hong Kong or more distance places of safety. The officials who chose Taiwan had either strong personal loyalty to Chiang or no place else to go. Many of the less competent senior officials who reached Taiwan were shunted into sinecures that gave them a modest living but little influence. Chiang and his principal lieutenants, recognizing that they bore a significant share of responsibility for the debacle on the mainland, knew that their only hope for the future was to make radical improvements in their methods of governing. Taiwan was their last chance.

Conditions in Taiwan favored a new start. It was a small area with good transportation and communications. Its population was relatively well educated and accustomed to authoritarian rule. There was no entrenched provincial leadership that had to be catered to, for the Japanese had kept the reins of authority firmly in their own hands. Taking advantage of the absence of the kind of connections between landlords and government officials that had prevented land reform on the mainland, the government redistributed agricultural land,

Ralph N. Clough, *Island China* (Cambridge, Mass.: Harvard University Press, 1978), pp. 33-52.

thereby weakening the local political power of landlords and making large numbers of farmers beholden to the new government for title to their land and improvement in their economic position.

From mid-1950 on, the government also benefited from the support of the United States. The amount of economic and military aid per capita was much larger than that received by other countries getting U.S. aid. Perhaps even more important to the ability of the government to administer the island effectively during the early years was the U.S. commitment to prevent a Communist attack. The public confidence in the security of the island engendered by U.S. protection gave the government the breathing spell it needed to create an effective economic and political system. The deep involvement of the United States in the defense and economic development of the island also gave the modernizing technocrats in the government, many of whom were American-educated, for more influence on decisions than they had possessed on the mainland.

Although conditions in Taiwan were relatively advantageous for the Nationalist government, its political system has been beset by severe strains, arising particularly from Taiwanese resentment at mainlander domination and from the restiveness of intellectuals under the tight security controls imposed to prevent Communist subversion and Taiwanese opposition activities. The methods used by the government to cope with these political strains in the system, which have proven successful so far, must now prove their effectiveness in the face of the international uncertainties of the future.

It is difficult to reach judgments on the political system in Taiwan, for data on political attitudes are scanty, and conclusions must be based to a considerable extent on scattered impressions derived over the years from interview dealing with sensitive political subjects not freely debated in the press or scholarly journals. The effectiveness and stability of the political system must be evaluated from the viewpoint of the people of Taiwan, whose attitudes toward authority, civil rights, and democratic processes differ from those of the average American. Many tolerate or even approve of government behavior that most Americans would find unacceptable. For the people of Taiwan, comparisons with their own past are likely to be more meaningful than comparisons with the United States.

The Structure of Government

The national government of the ROC was established in accordance with a constitution adopted on the mainland in 1946. The constitution provides for a National Assembly to elect the president and vice-president and amend the constitution, a Legislative Yuan to pass the laws, an Executive Yuan to carry out the laws, a Judicial Yuan to interpret the constitution and serve as a court of last resort, a Control Yuan to supervise officials, and an Examination Yuan to conduct civil service examinations. Members of the three elective bodies— the National Assembly, the Legislative Yuan, and the Control Yuan—were elected on the mainland in 1947 and 1948 from all the provinces of China.

All these government bodies moved to Taiwan in 1949, although some of their members remained behind. Because the government of the ROC has never relinquished its claim to be the legitimate government of all China, the constitution and government structure have been retained essentially unchanged. The membership in the elective bodies has gradually declined, because over the years as members died, it was not possible to hold new elections throughout China, so the terms of the original members were extended for the duration of "the period of Communist rebellion." By 1969, it was evident that new members would have to be added. Consequently, special elections were held in Taiwan in 1969, 1972, and 1973, adding new members to all three bodies as follows:

National elective body	Original membership	Remaining original members	Members elected 1969	Members elected 1972–1973	Total membership 1974–1975
National Assembly	2961	1281	15	53	1349
Legislative Yuan	760	376	11	51	438
Control Yuan	180	57	2	15	74

The original members of all three elective bodies are old, and their death rate is continuing to rise. Consequently, more new members will have to be elected before long. With each new election, these bodies will become increasingly representative of Taiwan province. Even in 1976, the new members elected in Taiwan were more influential than their numbers would indicate, for many of the original members were too old or ill to be active. For example, in the Legislative Yuan only about 200 of the 438 members attended sessions regularly, and of these, 63 were new members elected since 1969.

Far more important than the Legislative Yuan is the Executive Yuan, the principal decision-making body of government. Because its members are appointed, not elected, its membership has been continually renewed. The president of the Executive Yuan, or premier, and the ministers and heads of commissions who constitute the Executive Yuan are all appointed by the president of the nation.

In addition to the national government, with its panoply of ministries and commissions responsible for the entire range of governmental functions, from defense and foreign affairs to finance, economics, education, and justice, there is a Taiwan provincial government, which has a variety of subordinate functions under the direction of the national government. The provincial government is headed by a governor appointed by the president. There is also an elected provincial assembly, which approves the budget of the provincial government and has other limited, mostly advisory, powers.

County magistrates, city mayors, and country and city councils, all of which are elected, have wide powers in local affairs. The city of Taipei is an exception, having been made a special municipality under the Executive Yuan in 1967. Its mayor is appointed by the president, but the Taipei city council is still elected by popular vote.

The electoral process in Taiwan is dominated by the ruling party, the Kuomintang (KMT), established by Sun Yat-sen in 1919 as the successor to earlier revolutionary parties which he had also founded. The KMT moved its headquarters to Taiwan along with the government. The party was headed by Chiang Kai-shek until his death in 1975 and subsequently by his son, Chiang Ching-kuo. It is a pyramidal structure, topped by a 130-member Central Committee elected by the Party Congress, which convenes at approximately six-year intervals. A 22-member Central Standing Committee serves as executive body between plenary sessions of the Central Committee. Below the Central Committee are provincial, county, and district committees, heading the party cells of 3 to 15 members each.

A large proportion of government officials and local politicians belong to the party. The KMT has a wide range of functions, including backing candidates for national, provincial, and local office, monitoring the press and cultural activities, sponsoring youth and women's organizations, and maintaining the ROC's connections and influence among overseas Chinese. It operates a number of profit-making enterprises and also has access to government funds to support its operations.* The two minor parties in Taiwan, the Young China party and the China Democratic Socialist party, have little prestige or influence. The political system in Taiwan is essentially a one-party system.

A prominent feature of government in Taiwan is the security system, designed to protect the government from subversion by Communist agents or by Taiwanese opponents of KMT rule. Since 1949 martial law has been in effect, suspending constitutional guarantees for those accused of political crimes and empowering the Taiwan Garrison Command, a military organization responsible for internal security, to try political suspects secretly in military courts. Although the Taiwan Garrison Command has the primary responsibility for internal security, the KMT, the military forces, and the Ministry of Justice all have investigative units that supplement it in particular areas.

Animosity between mainlanders and Taiwanese has been a principal cause of political strain in Taiwan. The ill will arose partly because of differences of language and customs, but primarily because the minority mainlanders had reserved to themselves the controlling position in the government, party, and military. Mainlanders clung to the myth that the government of the ROC was the legitimate government of all China, while Taiwanese

---

*ROC government sources maintain that the KMT does not have access to government funds *today*—General Editor.

inclined toward separatism for Taiwan. The PRC threat to Taiwan compelled mainlanders and Taiwanese to cooperate in the face of the common peril, but it also resulted at times in the imposition of excessive controls by both the KMT and the security agencies, which tended to heighten political strain. The protection extended to the island by the United States has moderated the impact of the PRC threat, but it has also stimulated resentment at Tawian's dependence on the United States and fear that the U.S. support might one day be withdrawn. Lesser strains, which may become more severe in the future, have arisen from the social changes brought about on the island by the process of modernization.

Mainlander-Taiwanese Differences

Of Taiwan's population of 17 million, about 14 percent, or more than 2 million, are those who came over from the China mainland since 1945 or their descendants. There are marked differences of dialect and custom between these recently arrived Mainlanders and the Taiwanese. But there are also divisions within each group. The ancestors of most Taiwanese emigrated from Fukien Province on the mainland during the eighteenth and nineteenth centuries, but there is a large minority, the Hakkas, whose forebears came from Kwangtung Province during this same period and who speak a distinctive dialect. The so-called Mainlanders, who come from various parts of China after 1945, speak a variety of other dialects. Thus, although the division between Taiwanese and Mainlanders is the most important one for political purposes, the differences within each group, not only in spoken dialect but also in social and economic status, tend to blur and soften the clash of interests between the two major groups.

    Friction and tension between Mainlanders and Taiwanese developed early. The newcomers were initially welcome by the Taiwanese, who expected that the reunion of Taiwan with China and the departure of their Japanese colonial rulers would give them a greater part in running the island. Unfortunately, the first wave of Mainlanders under Governor Ch'en Yi, a corrupt and inept Nationalist general, was more interested in making fortunes out of the assets confiscated from the Japanese than in restoring the island's war-damaged economy. Instead of moving up into administrative and technical positions vacated by the departing Japanese, the Taiwanese saw these positions taken over by mainland officials and their relatives. Some Taiwanese were even ousted from their jobs and houses by arriving "carpetbaggers." The rising resentment of the Taiwanese boiled over on February 28, 1947, when the arrest by government agents of a Taiwanese woman accused of peddling untaxed cigarettes set off sporadic rioting against Mainlanders which soon spread throughout the island. The Taiwanese hastily organized to demand reforms, but Ch'en Yi temporized until large numbers of troops had arrived from the mainland and brutally suppressed all opposition. Thousands of Taiwanese were killed, including many of the island's political elite.

    The February 28 uprising left behind a lasting legacy of hostility and suspicion between Mainlanders and Taiwanese. Although Ch'en Yi was replaced soon afterward by Governor Wei Tao-ming, who made a serious attempt to repair the damage, the collapse of the Nationalist government on the mainland and the arrival of a flood of refugees in Taiwan made the improvement of relations between Mainlanders and Taiwanese difficult. A few of the Taiwanese who had been active in the uprising escaped to Hong Kong, where they founded the Taiwan independence movement, which advocated an independent state of Taiwan governed by Taiwanese and drew on the memory of the uprising to stimulate Taiwanese antipathy to KMT rule.

    Aside from the February repression, the primary source of tension between the two groups was the dominant position of Mainlanders on the island. All the higher level positions in the government, party, and army were initially occupied by Mainlanders, except for a few token positions held by Taiwanese who had spent much of their lives on the mainland and had returned to Taiwan with the Mainlanders. The Mainlanders constituted the great majority in the elective bodies, since they were chosen to represent all the provinces of China. By holding tenaciously to recovery of the mainland as the government's primary objective, Chiang Kai-shek perpetuated the unrepresentative character of the national government on Taiwan. To make the national government representative of the majority of people on Taiwan—the Taiwanese—would have amounted to abandoning this cherished national goal. Moreover, personal interests strongly motivated the Mainlanders to hold on to their positions in the national government. Most had no other way of making a living. They owned no land or businesses in Taiwan. Thrust into an environment where they lacked the local personal ties and connections so essential to making one's way in Chinese society, they clung to the only means of livelihood they had, government jobs.

Thus, personal and national objectives intertwined. For the Mainlanders, the goal of mainland recovery, however illusory it might come to seem as the years passed, justified the perpetuation of a national government that represented all China and therefore should not be dominated and staffed by Taiwanese. So long as Mainland recovery seemed a credible possibility, the policy also held potential benefits for Taiwanese, through the return of the national government to the mainland, the departure of large numbers of Mainlanders from Taiwan, and the elimination of the military threat posed to the island by the PRC. But as mainland recovery increasingly appeared to be a mirage, the policy came to be viewed by most Taiwanese as principally a device for ensuring the retention of power in Mainlanders hands.

The handful of Taiwanese exiles who had fled to Hong Kong after the February 28 uprising soon split into two factions, pro-Communist and anti-Communist. The pro-Communists went to the China mainland after the Communist victory there, while the principal anti-Communist leaders moved to Tokyo. The Taiwanese in mainland China organized a Taiwan Democratic Self-Government League, which took the view that Taiwan was an integral part of China and should be "liberated" from the control of the Nationalist government and brought under Peking. The Tokyo group, however, called for overthrowing the Nationalist government and setting up an independent state of Taiwan to be governed by Taiwanese. Their publications elaborated the historical and legal arguments for regarding Taiwan as a political entity separate from China.

In 1956, Taiwanese exiles in Tokyo announced the establishment of a Provisional Government of the Republic of Formosa, with Liao Wen-yi (Thomas Liao) as its first president. There was much internal bickering and factionalism among the Taiwanese exiles, however, and in 1965 Liao himself abandoned the movement to return to Taiwan, soon followed by others active in the movement. Other organizations advocating independence for Taiwan sprang up in Tokyo, including the Formosan Association, first headed by Ong Jok-tik and later by Richard Koo, and the United Young Formosans for Independence, led by Ng Yu-zin. In 1970, a more broadly based organization appeared, known as the World United Formosans for Independence. It has a chapter in the United States headed by George T. Chang, which has solicited members mainly among the large community of Taiwanese students, as well as chapters in Japan and Europe.

All organizations favoring Taiwanese independence were strictly proscribed by the government in Taiwan which, not unreasonably, regarded actions aimed at its overthrow as treasonable. Secret supporters of the Taiwan independence movement were sought out just as assiduously by security agencies as were agents of the PRC. In fact, ROC officials charged that the Taiwan independence movement was backed by the PRC, despite the obvious inconsistency between the goals of that movement and the PRC's insistence on "one China." The PRC, in turn, accused the United States of backing the Taiwan independence movement, perhaps in the hope of creating friction between the United States and the ROC. The weakness of the independence movement and its tendency to split into warring factions suggested that it had no powerful backer. Its limited funds probably were provided principally by Taiwanese or Japanese businessmen in Japan.

The Taiwan independence movement was unable to create an effective underground organization in Taiwan, but occasional arrests of Taiwanese for carrying on antigovernment activities in support of Taiwan's independence demonstrate that the concept has had enough attraction for some Taiwanese to inspire them to take grave risks to promote it. The relatively few arrests on security charges reported in the press (although most such arrests are not so reported) indicate that Taiwanese were more likely to be arrested for Taiwan independence activities than for acting as agents of the PRC. A case which attracted international attention was that of Professor Peng Ming-min, former chairman of the political science department at National Taiwan University, who in 1965 along with two associates was sentenced to eight years in prison for having had secretly printed a manifesto calling on Taiwanese to unite to overthrow "Chiang's dictatorial regime." Peng's sentence was subsequently commuted, and he escaped from Taiwan via Sweden to the United States. Although the vast majority of Taiwanese have not been directly affected by the government's suppression of the Taiwan independence movement, the constant surveillance by mainlander-dominated security agencies of Taiwanese suspected of engaging in such activities and the arrests of some of these have contributed in Mainlander-Taiwanese tension.

Other causes of tension have grown out of the differing status and outlook of Mainlanders and Taiwanese. Corruption in government, although far less pervasive than in some other Asian developing countries, has created resentment among Taiwanese, as has favoritism toward Mainlanders by Mainlander bureaucrats. Taiwanese are more likely than Mainlanders to take exception to the size of the tax burden to support the military forces and the requirement of military service for all young men. Even land reform, which created a large group of new landowners beholden to the national government for their gains, incurred costs for the government in the alienation of many of the influential local gentry who were forced to give up their land. This group of former landlords recall most fondly the "good old days" under the Japanese.

Internal Security and External Dependency
The ever-present PRC threat to Taiwan is a fundamental source of political strain. Although the military threat has seemed less imminent since the offshore island crisis of 1958, the danger of infiltration and subversion has not receded. This danger is associated in the minds of ROC security officials with Taiwanese disaffection, but it has a broader compass, potentially affecting Mainlanders as well. In fact, Mainlanders are more susceptible than Taiwanese to being recruited by the PRC because of their past association with the mainland and the presence of their relatives there.

To cope with the subversive danger, the government declared martial law in 1949, which remains in effect today. The Taiwan Garrison Command and other agencies responsible for internal security maintain an extensive network of informants and watch carefully for any suspicious activities. Political officers in each unit of the armed forces are responsible for the detection of any evidence of disloyalty there. The KMT, through campus cells of the Youth Work Committee and the China Youth Corps, as well as the military instruction personnel, or *chiao kuan*, at the universities, monitor student attitudes and behavior. The KMT also supervises the media to guard against the appearance of material helpful to the enemy. So extensive a security system inevitably commits errors and abuses. Consequently, there is a constant tension between the need for security measures that nearly everybody recognizes are necessary and the tendency to carry them to excessive lengths resulting in the arrest of innocent people and the smothering of healthy debate on government policy.

The government of the ROC had ample reason to be worried about Communist subversion when it withdrew from the mainland to Taiwan in 1949. The civilian bureaucracy and the army on the mainland had been riddled with Communist agents, and the number and importance of defections to the Communst side rose rapidly as it became increasingly evident that the Nationalists were losing the civil war. In late 1948, Chiang Kai-shek sent one of his most competent and trusted generals, Ch'en Ch'eng, to take over as governor of Taiwan, assisted in the field of internal security by Chiang's older son, Chiang Ching-kuo. An American observer, writing from the perspective of 1952, described the actions they took to weed out the subversives:

> The Nationalists acted hurriedly and sometimes ruthlessly to stamp out Communist activities, arresting and interrogating some thousands of suspects. They captured and executed some real Communist agents and frightened others off the island, but they also intimidated and imprisoned many individuals who appeared to be innocent. At present several thousand persons are in jail, where may of them have been held for more than a year and a half without benefit of public trials.

For the great majority of Chinese on Formosa the fearful feature of this situation is the lack of legal protection for the ordinary citizen. He can be arrested at night by a squad of military police, tried by a military court-martial and sentenced, without the opportunity for appeal. Once taken into custody, the ordinary Chinese is in effect at the mercy of the garrison headquarters. A person may be arrested because he actually is subversive. He can also be picked up because someone who wants his job or property has denounced him as a Communist to the authorities.

As confidence grew that Taiwan would not come under early Communist attack, security measures were eased somewhat and procedures regularized. In 1952 security regulations had already been modified to require a civil police warrant for the arrest of a civilian, to allow defense counsel in military courts, and to permit the accused the presence of family and material witnesses during trial. Nevertheless, close surveillance of suspects and arrests and trials continued. A recent official publication states: "the tasks of searching for Communist agents and uncovering their plot [have] been vigorously pursued and a number of arrests and executions have taken place over the years."

The workings of the security system brought about the downfall of several prominent mainlanders. Wu Kuo-Shen (K. C. Wu), an Amreican-educated, liberally inclined politician who had been mayor of Shanghai, succeeded Ch'en Ch'eng as governor of Taiwan in 1949, when the latter was made premier. Wu found the political atmosphere in Taiwan stifling and the security agencies abusive of their powers. Resigning in 1953, he left for the United States where he denounced Taiwan's lack of democracy and security excess in open letters to the National Assembly and Chiang Kai-shek. Sun Li-jen, commander-in-chief of the army, was removed from his position in 1955, charged with responsibility for the demands presented to Chiang at a military review by disaffected officers under his command. He was placed under house arrest, where he remained in 1977. Lei Chen, editor of the political journal *Free China*, who attempted to organize an opposition party in 1960, was charged with harboring a Communist agent on his staff and sentenced to ten years in prison. As these cases indicate, opposition to the leadership or attempts to bring about fundamental change in the political system were severely repressed, even when there was no evidence that the individual was a Communist agent. Although over the years the balance gradually shifted within the government from those who favored harsh and strict security measures to those who were more lenient, the problem of striking the right balance between the demands of security and the requirements of a modernizing society remains a principal source of political strain in Taiwan.

Overdependence on any outside power over a long period of time cannot fail to produce resentment. Taiwan is no exception to this rule. As early as 1957, resentment boiled over in the sacking of the U.S. embassy by a mob infuriated by the acquittal in a U.S. military court of an American serviceman who had shot and killed a Chinese. The government quickly presented apologies and repaired the physical damage. But the knowledge that Taiwan's security and prosperity are so much at the mercy of the United States will continue to cause strain.

The submerged feelings of the people of Taiwan came to the surface from time to time in bitter comments in the Taipei press about the United States, particularly since President Nixon's 1971 announcement of the changes in U.S. policy toward the PRC. The government's dilemma has been how to reconcile its reliance on the United States for the principal support for Taiwan's survival as an autonomous political entity with its need to satisfy the people that it is acting in a manner that upholds the national dignity and self-respect of the ROC. The strain imposed by this dilemma will inevitably increase as the United States moves closer to the normalization of its relations with the PRC. And Peking will no doubt do its utmost to increase the strain by its accusations that the government in Taiwan is a U.S. puppet.

One-Party System

The KMT has also played an important role in maintaining political stability in Taiwan. It has had the primary responsibility for establishing and controlling the limits of public debate, for broadening political participation, especially by integrating the Taiwanese into the poltical system, and for providing a link between the leadership and the people.

The view of the leaders and party ideologues have been disseminated principally, although not exclusively, through KMT channels. The party owns and operates the Central News Agency with its worldwide network for collecting and distributing news, the *Central Daily News (Chung Yang Jih Pao)* in Taipei and other newspapers, the Broadcasting Corporation of China (operating seventy transmitters and broadcasting six hundred hours daily in seventeen languages), the Central Motion Picture Corporation, and the Chung Cheng Book Company. The party organs for disseminating information are supplemented by the Government Information Office, and official body under the Executive Yuan.

The party does not hold a monopoly on the dissemination of news and opinion, having to compete with numerous privately-owned newspapers, magazines, book publishers, radio and TV stations, and motion picture studios. But the party has a special responsibility for monitoring the output of these private companies to ensure that subversive material is excluded. News management in the ROC is rather sophisticated, in that a wide range of material appears, some of it quite critical of government officials, agencies, and policies. Dispatches from foreign news agencies supplement those of the Central News Agency to provide the reading public with a broad coverage of international news. Certain topics, however, are taboo, such as personal attacks on the leader, favorable comments on the PRC, and any questioning of the baisc political system in the ROC or its mainland recovery policy. Over the years, a number of political journals have been suspended, shut down, or forced to change management for having overstepped the permitted bounds.

Since the introduction of local self-government in Taiwan in 1950, the KMT has had the responsibility of putting forward and supporting candidates for election as city mayors, county magistrates, provincial assemblymen, city and county councilmen, and village and township chiefs. Candidates backed by the KMT have had a substantial advantage over independents or those KMT members who sometimes ran without party approval. During the elections held between 1964 and 1968, for example, the proportion of KMT-backed candidates elected at all levels ranged from 78 percent to 92 percent.

Because only Taiwanese candidates stood any chance of being elected in those local elections by the predominantly Taiwanese electorate, it was essential to bring Taiwanese in large numbers into the KMT party organization. Initially, Taiwanese occupied only the lower rungs of the party hierarchy, but as their numbers in the party increased, they moved up into the middle grades and few senior positions. Although party jobs generally carried less prestige than government appointive or elective positions of an equivalent level, they did provide a means of co-opting thousands of Taiwanese into the political system. Taiwanese now constitute 70 percent of the party membership, although the top positions remain in Mainlander hands. Of the twenty-two members of the Central Standing Committee in 1976, only five were Taiwanese.

Another major function of the KMT is to provide a link between the leadership and the people. Professional party workers work closely with and have significant influence on leaders of farmers' associations, fishermen's associations, labor unions cooperatives, and women's organizations. They operate 400 service centers throughout the island, providing assistance to people ranging from free medical care to vocational training and job procurement. They direct the China Youth Corps, which carries out recreational and educational programs for 200,000 participants each year, and through party cells on college campuses they keep in close touch with student opinion and activities. They maintain contact with overseas Chinese around the world. Thus, the KMT touches the lives of the people in many ways. The leadership relies on the party's intricate network of connections with mass organizations throughout the country as an important means of indoctrinating and influencing people and winning sufficient support to enable them to go on governing effectively.

Although the KMT seems omnipresent in Taiwan, it is not dominant as the party is in Communist countries. As an organization, it has relatively little influence on military, economic, and foreign policy decisions. Except in those areas where it has primary responsibility, such as the management of local elections and the monitoring of the media, it does not normally initiate action. In most areas, action is initiated by the government department concerned or by the leader himself, and decisions are made by the leader in consultation with his principal economic and military officials. Major decisions are then ratified by the Central Standing Committee of the KMT, of which the leader and the chief economic and military officials are members.

In Taiwan, unlike the practice in Communist states, few party careerists have made their way into the top ranks of government. One reason may be that the KMT is not a small, elite organization with stiff requirements for admission, designed to train future leaders. Anyone can join who is at least twenty years old, subscribes to KMT principles, and submits to party discipline. As of 1976, membership was 1,570,000, or about 20 percent of all persons over nineteen years of age. Party members probably number over one-third of all adult males, since as of 1970 only about 10 percent of party members were women. Samuel Huntington argued that one indicator of the strength of a one-party system is the premium placed on party membership, and that if membership becomes universal, it becomes meaningless. Thus the KMT's mass membership policy has probably tended to weaken the influence of the party.

3. Political Development in Taiwan

John F. Copper

If one were to take a public opinion poll in almost any Western country or even query their intellectual classes, one would be impressed by the fact that the majority view is that there has been astonishingly little political change in the territory under the control of the government of the Republic of China (Taiwan, the Pescadores Islands, and the "Offshore Islands" of Quemoy and Matsu) and among its 17 million inhabitants.* Rather the response would be that the Republic of China is a regime that has resisted change, and that little has happened in Taiwan politically despite the rapid economic and corollary social development that the nation has experienced in the last two to three decades. In fact, many regard the ROC as outstanding for its qualities of being able to resist political modernization in the midst of economic and social change and a vastly altered internationl environment. Many reasons can be cited to explain why this is commonly espoused.

Hungdah Chiu, *China and the Taiwan Issue* (New York: Praeger, 1979), pp. 37-73. Copyright 1979 by Praeger. Used with permission of the publisher.

*It is necessary to point out in the way of background information that the large majority of the population under the control of the ROC live on the island of Taiwan. The population of the Pescadores is about 120,000 and all of the offshore islands about 75,000 (excluding the military). About 2 percent of the population, called aborigines, are related to the Malay people of Southeast Asia. The rest of the population hail from China, but there are distinctions based upon the time of migration to Taiwan and the area of China from where they came. Slightly over 85 percent of the population, those called Taiwanese, came from China from several generations to several centuries ago. Most of these came from Fukien Province just across the Taiwan Strait and speak the Fukien dialect of Chinese. There is a historical cleavage in this group between those who came from the Changchou area west of Amoy and those from the Chuanchou area northeast of Amoy. This separation was more meaningful in the past than it is today, but differences are still noticeable and can be observed in politics, where the former group is much more active. Another group of Taiwanese hail from Kwangtung Province and speak a dialect called Hakka, which is generally incomprehensible by the other Taiwanese. They constitute about 13 percent of the population. In some parts of Taiwan there are serious frictions between Hakka Taiwanese and Fukien Taiwanese. The remaining 15 percent of the population is comprised of "Mainlander" Chinese who came to Taiwan with Chiang Kai-shek in 1949 when the Nationalists were defeated on the mainland. They hail from various parts of China and speak a variety of dialects, depending upon the part of China where they were born, though all speak Mandarin. There are a great number of cleavages among this group. Even as late as 1970 the Central Committee of the ruling Nationalist party was comprised primarily (60 percent) of persons from the three provinces: Chekiang, Kiangsu, and Hunan. Mainlanders from northern China are almost excluded from government positions, especially those from Manchuria, an area that remained outside of Nationalist control in the 1930s and whose leaders were accused of cooperating with the communists.

First, in terms of both the structure and the operation of the government in Taiwan there has been little change. The basic framework of government has not been altered in any significant way since before the regime moved to Taiwan in 1949. The five branches of the government remain, as does the single-party system; and political power is still monopolized by the Kuomintang or the Nationalist party. Provisions in the constitution that provide for changes in that document and for the means to institute democracy and implement human rights have been circumvented by temporary emergency provisons and martial law, which has been in effect for the approximately 30 years since the government moved to Taipei.

Second, not only has the structure of the government not change, neither has the ROC's political ideology or the attitudes of most of those who hold top seats of power. Its political ideology is based upon Sun Yat-sen's *San Min Chu Yi* (Three Principles of the People), which have remained virtually unrevised since he formalized them in the 1920s. Meanwhile the regime claims to be the sole repository of Chinese culture and tradition. And it still takes an adamant anticommunist stand on global issues as it did during the period of intense struggle between East and West in the 1950s.

Third, as further evidence for resistance to change, many observers point to the fact that the death of Chiang Kai-shek produced no visible political change in Taiwan, not even debate regarding the future without him, and that Chiang was succeeded by his son—after the fashion of succession in imperial China. What appears to have happened is that another dynasty has been established and Chiang Ching-kuo will rule in the matter and style of his father.

In addition to the above, what change that has occurred has not garnered much attention from the rest of the world. For example, Taiwan's land reform program—one of the world's most successful—never got the attention it deserved from planners in other countries or even Western scholars and now is largely forgotten. Meanwhile the People's Republic of China flaunts a competing model of political, economic, and social development that is new and revolutionary. Its land reform attracts world acclaim even through it was a failure. Hence, even where the ROC should be regarded as a model of economic and social progress it has gotten little acclaim.

This phenomenon is in part a result of the fact that the West draws attention to Peking because it has long been regarded an enemy. Also, mainland China was closed to most Western observers for so long. Now it is at the forefront of detente, and that is exciting. Conversely the ROC is often labeled as "reactionary" as a form of rationalization by those governments that voted for Taipei's expulsion from the United Nations, or that have given diplomatic recognition recently to the PRC. Many of them perceive that Taiwan's days are numbered and they would prefer to feel that this is Taipei's fault (for being resistant to change and inflexible).

The image that the ROC polity is ossified and its leaders resistant to change, however, cannot go unchallenged. The streamlining of the decision making processes that economic development has brought is very evident upon even superficial examination. Political corruption, still endemic in most of Asia, is less prevalent in Taiwan that in many Western countries. In recent years the average age of those in government had decreased significantly, and the role of the military has diminished. And whereas the basic ideological tenets of the ROC have not changed, the emphasis has: there is more pragmatism and less regard for ideology in the abstract. Then, albeit social progress in some realms has been tempered by the government's conservatism, surveys show considerable change in citizens' views and aspirations, while one of the most important domestic problems in terms of the future of the country—the differences between mainlander Chinese and Taiwanese—is rapidly diminishing in importance.

Finally, while Chiang Ching-kuo has indeed followed in his father's footsteps in many ways, particularly in his style, he has in subtle ways revolutionized politics in Taiwan and has started new trends that reflect that Taiwan is adjusting functionally to problems both internal and external. He has put more Taiwanese and young people in important positions in the government; he has made the government more honest and responsive to the public; and he has enhanced the influence of civilians in government.

In answer to the critic who may reply that these things are merely facade, or are of minimal importance, one can simply cite some statistics that usually—some say inevitably—relate to political change and modernization. Most obvious is Taiwan's economic growth. It is hard to conceive of a nation with close to the world's best record in terms of economic growth not engineering political change in advance to make that growth possible, or experiencing political change as a result of economic progress. Similarly it seems unfathomable that the sharp rise in the number of educated people has not had manifold and political effects. It is also hard to believe that the large number of citizens who go abroad for study and the many foreigners who reside in the Republic of China or visit the country as tourists have had no impact. Finally the rapid urbanization of the population, and until recently a high birth rate accompanied by markedly longer life expectancy, must be considered. All of those factors have produced political change; it is only a matter of asking how much.

The important question to be asked then are: What is the lag between economic and social change and change in both of these realms and political change? There does seem to be one. But is it bigger than in other countries? Is political modernization occurring at a sufficiently rapid rate to accommodate other changes, or is the political system impeding change to the point that it will endanger the government's ability to maintain control at some time in the future? Will this in turn threaten the nation? Is political change taking place in such a way that the government can resolve the problem of its legitimacy to the rest of the world? In other words, is the progress in democracy and human rights sufficient so that the ROC can claim global support for its continued right to exist in the face of Peking's claims that Taiwan is a part of China? Will the government be able to adjust to internal antagonisms: for example, those who demand Taiwanese independence or self-government without the Chinese who came from the mainland in 1949, and the "diehards" in the party and government who resist any concessions to the Taiwanese majority and who want to keep them out of positions of political power on the grounds that they do not sufficiently understand the Communist threat? Or will Tawian become another Rhodesia?

With these questions in mind the author in the following pages will consider the following: changes that have taken place in the structure and use of political authority in Taiwan; the impact of rapid economic development upon the ROC polity; the nature and scope of social change and its impact upon protest and reform; and the rule of the ROC's new leader, Chiang Ching-kuo. In all of these sections there is one common theme objective: ascertaining the rate or scope of political change while assessing the functional and dysfunctional aspects of this change in the context of Taiwan's modernization and the legitimacy of its government, present and future. In the concluding section efforts will be made to sum up and give some final answers to the question whether the ROC, or Taiwan, will survive as a nation-state into the next decade.

It must be remembered that the ROC government had been under the constant threat of Communist infiltration and subversion since it moved to Taiwan, and twice, in 1954 and 1958, it was faced with armed invasion. It should also be kept in mind that Peking has repeatedly vowed to "liberate" Taiwan "by military force if necessary" and has by its own admission sent saboteurs and other agents to Taiwan. Finally the ROC government has since 1971 faced the problem of a steady erosion of its diplomatic influence and the steady loss of diplomatic recognition by other nations. This has to some degree threatened the government's legitimacy and thus its authority. Thus the continuance of martial law must be seen in a situation where the government is aware of outside criticisms but has weighed this against the risks. It should also be noted that although there is opposition to the Temporary Provisions, this is not as intense as it might seem, while many support them as both necessary and desirable.

In 1975, for example, a special section of the martial law provisions was invoked in order to deal with the problem of a marked increase in crime, especially violent crime. Criminal defendants in cases where violence was used were sent to military courts and the offenders dealt with quickly and efficiently, usually ending with the firing squad. Even through some of the cases where the death penalty was imposed entailed only petty robbery,

Figure 1.
ROC Government Organization (at end of 1975)

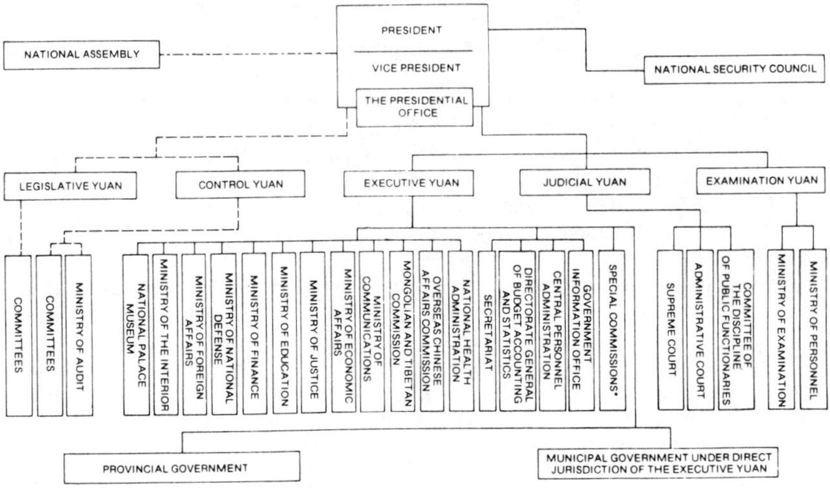

*Economic Planning Council, National Science Council, Atomic Energy Council, Administrative Research and Evaluation Commission, Commission for Youth Assistance and Guidance, Vocational Assistance for Retired Servicemen, Coordination Council for North American Affairs (functional substitute for former ROC Embassy and consulates in U.S.)

Source: *China Yearbook 1976* (Taipei: China Publishing Co.), p. 86.

public reaction clearly supported the government.* Moreover, high officials noted that a majority of U.S. military personnel and tourists in Taiwan had made favorable comments about the efficient justice that made it possible to walk in any part of Taipei at night without fear, quite in contrast to most large cities in the United States.

Political power in the ROC resides chiefly in the hands of the president, the head of the party (Nationalist party or Kuomintang), and the military.† It is manipulated or implemented through the five branches of government (or *Yuan*) and the National Assembly they control—although the latter in theory is elected by the people and grants the president his political power. (See Figure 1 for a diagram of the ROC government organization.) Chiang Kai-shek until his death in 1975 held all of the important seats of power, and this is true of his son Chiang Ching-kuo at the present time—though there has been some shifting of positions and seats of power since the elder Chiang's death, which will be discussed in later pages.

The National Assembly, which, according to the Constitution, represents the people and therefore could be thought of as the bastion of democracy, is in reality little more than a sounding board. Since the body is designated to have a representative from every 500,000 persons (including Chinese on the mainland) as well as delegates from occupational groups, racial minorities, and the overseas Chinese, and now has less than 100 representatives from Taiwan Province, it does not in reality represent a voting electorate. After the government moved to Taiwan in 1949, elections, which were to be held at six-year intervals, became impossible and delegates remained in their positions by an interpretation of the Council of

---

*A news reporter in Taiwan did a survey with a number of taxi drivers at the time and the overwhelming majority supported the harsh penalties that were being meted out under martial law. Although their responses should not be seen as necessarily typical, the author asked a number of people informally about the use of martial law in this way and most of the agreed with government policy. Most of those who disagreed noted that it should not have been applied to one case where a theft using violence did not involve the use of any weapon and the thief got only NT$20, or the equivalent of U.S.$.50.

†The president and the premier have generally not been important at the same time, though this did occur during the transition of Chiang Ching-kuo to power.

Grand Justice of the Judicial Yuan (though in 1969 and 1972 elections were held to elect 69 additional delegates from Taiwan to the Assembly*).

The office of the president, an elected position according to the formal structure of the Constitution (by the National Assembly), is in reality independent of the Assembly and for that matter any other branch or organ of government. The president, except for the period 1975-78, has controlled the Legislative Yuan and other organs of the government through his leadership of the Nationalist party and has ruled the country with almost plenipotentiary powers. In 1975, when President Chiang Kai-shek passed away, Vice-President Yen Chia-kan became president. For the next three years the vast powers of the president resided in the hands of Chiang Ching-kuo who was premier and who became chairman of the KMT after his father's death. The younger Chiang as former defense minister also held sway over the military. In view of his power bases in the party and the military as well as his position as premier, plus the fact that President Yen had been clearly a figurehead when he was vice-president, Chiang Ching-kuo's leadership of the country was not seriously challenged. In May, 1978 he was accordingly elected president, replacing C. K. Yen who had already announced his retirement.

Three of the branches of the government—the executive, legislative, and judicial—are similar to their counterparts in Western political systems. The Examination and Control Yuans are a carryover of Chinese tradition. The Examination Yuan is responsible for giving exams for governments jobs and serves as a personnel agency. Members of this yuan are appointed by the president (with the consent of the Control Yuan) and they reflect his wishes. The Control Yuan nominally holds the powers of consent, impeachment, censure, and auditing. Its members are elected indirectly by each provincial assembly and overseas Chinese representatives. Clearly neither the Examination Yuan nor the Control Yuan exercises any political power independent of the president or the Kuomintang but rather are manipulated from above.

The Legislative Yuan and the Judicial Yuan are similar to the two branches of government described in the previous paragraph in that they exert little or no authority independent of the president, premier, or party. The Legislative Yuan, according to formal procedures, decides on budgetary matters, passes bills on war, peace, treaties, and martial law, directs the Executive Yuan to alter policies it does not agree with (by a two-thirds majority), and initiates constitutional amendments. It meets twice a year in two- to three-month sessions. The Legislative Yuan, however, like the Control Yuan, is composed of members elected from all of China's provinces, municipalities, border areas, minority groups, and overseas Chinese, and for this reason it does not justly represent the people of Taiwan. It also has suffered from old age and attrition. In 1948, 760 legislators were elected, but by 1966 only 457 were taking their seats in regular sessions. The problem of attrition was overcome to some extent by a special election in Taipei that brought in 11 new members to serve "indefinite terms" and the creation of 52 new three-year seats in 1972. Notwithstanding, the Legislative Yuan does not reflect public opinion in Taiwan; nor has it become an active and important part of the government.

The Judicial Yuan interprets the Constitution as well as all laws, adjudicates civil, criminal, and administrative suits, and is responsible for the discipline and punishment of government officials. Members of the Judicial Yuan are appointed by the president (with the approval of the Control Yuan) and thus reflect the thinking of the president and the party with little or not interpretation or dissent.

The Executive Yuan, in contrast to the other four branches of government, however, is not simply a rubber stamp agency. It is an administrative branch of government and one that carries out or executes policy, in theory made by the Legislative Yuan but in reality made by the KMT or itself with party approval. The head of the Executive Yuan is the premier, who is appointed by the president with the consent of the Legislative Yuan. He presides over the ministries, commissions, ministers without portfolio, and a large administrative staff, as well as the Government Information Office, Director General of Budgets, Office of Ac-

---

*Only 1,204 members of this body, including the 69 Taiwanese, were present in March, 1978 to vote for Chiang Ching-kuo's nomination to the presidency.

counts and Statistics, and other smaller or temporary agencies. The ministries are: interior, foreign affairs, national defense, finance, education, justice, economic affairs, and communications. Two committees have cabinet status: the Overseas Chinese Affairs and Mongolian and Tibetan Affairs. There are also several important commissions with subcabinet status such as the National Science Council and the Research, Review and Evaluation Commission. The ministries and commissions generate policy internally and are important and efficient organs of government that are generally responsive to current problems. Hence, while officials of the Executive Yuan are not chosen by a democratic process, the Executive Yuan has been very sensitive to public opinion and to the needs of the country and its citizens. And it is here that business leaders, civic and other organizations, and even private citizens communicate with the government.

Below the national government organization are the provincial, county, and municipal governments. Outside of their jurisdiction the offshore islands of Quemoy and Matsu are governed by the Ministry of Defense and thus are administratively under the Executive Yuan, as is the city of Taipei since July, 1967 when it was declared a special municipality to bring the temporary captial under the contol of the central government. This was done nominally so that Taipei could keep its own tax revenue and thus improve city services sorely needed due to the population growth of the city. The decision, however, also made the mayorship of Taipei and appointed position and ended political campaigns for the mayorship, which accentuated dissension between Mainland and Taiwanese Chinese.

The provincial government, whose capital is 100 miles southwest of Taipei, rules over 16 countries plus the larger cities that are classified as municipalities—with the exception of Taipei (since 1967) and Kaohsiung (since January 1, 1979). According to the Constitution, the governor of Taiwan, who heads the provincial government, is elected along with members of the Provincial Council. The position of governor now, however, is an appointed position—by the president from a list of nominees furnished by the Executive Yuan. Notwithstanding the incorporation of some important positions of local government by the central government, political participation has increased as is reflected in the elections for Provincial Assembly seats, and Taiwanese holds a majority of these four-year elective jobs as well as the positions of speaker and deputy speaker. The Provincial Assembly has broad legislative powers, though the central government has been careful not to allow this body too much power. In short, the top leadership has allowed the Assembly enough prerogatives to prevent an image of mainland Chinese dominance in provincial affairs, but it has maintained sufficient control to prevent the growth of native Taiwanese nationalism.

The next tier under the provincial government is comprised of the county and municipal governments. County governments are run by county magistrates and a popularly elected assembly; municipal governments are headed by a mayor who works with an assembly or council. Neither the municipal nor the county-elected bodies can be dissolved by higher authority, though both are under the supervision of the Provincial government. In 1964 more than 1,500 candidates (including 230 women) filed for 907 seats. In 1977, 1,600 offices were contested, though a small amount of the increase came from consolidating local and provincial elections.

Both provincial and local elections bring out the voters in large numbers. And voter turnout has been increasing: in 1964 over 76 percent voted; in 1977, 80 percent. It is an interesting phenomenon, especially in contrast to most Western countries, that the voter turnout in local elections is higher than in national elections. This, of course, reflects the fact that there is more participation and thus more democracy at the level of local government in Taiwan. In fact, when Taiwan's political system is criticized by Westerners for being undemocratic, the response is often that this is true of national, not local, government, and the democracy is more meaningful at the local level because issues are more personal and less complicated. Some Taiwanese even contend that local elections in Taiwan are more democratic than in most Western countries, because the newness of the democratic process has fostered an intense interest in government as well as a positive attitude toward politics even compared to Western countries. Also, they note there are few entrenched local bosses and a large number of independent candidates supported by "grass roots" movements, while there is less transience among the voting electorate, which does not force candidates to appeal to the public through a political party or the media as in most Western democracies. Democracy at the local level is also enhanced by the growth of a host of farmers' organizations, businessmen's groups, and so on, that generally function as professional or public service organizations rather than lobbies. In short, there is a high level of interest as well as participation in local politics in Taiwan and strong positive feelings toward government at the level.

Paralleling or shadowing governmental organization at all levels is the KMT. Thus understanding the Nationalist party's structure and its influence on politics at all levels is a *sine qua non* for understanding the political processes in Taiwan. The organization structure of the KMT is hierarchical or like a pyramid, starting at the bottom with local units of 15 or less members, up to subdistrict, district, county, provincial, and finally national headquarters. Each level above the local groups has a central committee and an advisory committee. Committees at the bottom or lower levels are elected by party members; at higher levels they are elected by party congresses. The Provincial Congress meets every two years and the National Congress meets every five years. The Central Committee of the National Congress meets every year and makes decisions that are generally approved *pro forma* by the latter. Real power, however, lies in the Standing Committee of the Central Committee, which makes policy when the latter is not is session. This committee is headed by the director-general of the party, who is given his authority by the Party Congress and thus has veto power over Central Committee actions. Chiang Kai-shek held this post from 1938 to his death in 1975; his son, Chiang Ching-kuo, holds the post now. Inasmuch as the KMT is tightly controlled from the top and because it is the only political part of importance, heading the party may be said to constitute running the nation.* If one judges the progress toward establishing a democratic system in Taiwan by the KMT's rules or decision-making procedures, or by the growth of opposing political parties, then one's conclusion must be a negative one. On the other hand, the majority of non-Western countries have one-party systems and in most where democratic procedures have been put into practice, this has happened within the party, more than through the growth of opposition parties.

The KMT, which was a party of Mainland Chinese and dominated by members from three provinces in east China when the ROC moved to Taiwan in 1949, has expanded its membership and now is fairly representative of Taiwan's population. Although it has not regularly published the size of its membership, in November, 1976 it was reported that is rolls had increased from 910,000 in 1969 to 1.5 million. Thus the party would qualify under the definition of "mass party." At this time 48 new members were elected to the Central Committee, bringing the total to 130, of which 16 were Taiwanese and 13 were women. The powerful Standing Committee was also increased in size to 22; two new members were Taiwanese, raising the total to five. The average age of the Standing Committee members has been steadily decreased. Although Taiwanese, who constitute a majority of the population, still do not control the party they do constitute from 60 to 70 percent of its membership and a number are in the top decision-making echelons. Moreover, the representation of the military has diminished while the number of women has increased. All of this reflects a trend toward fairer representation and may indicate that more democratic procedures in decision making and electing top leaders may soom emerge.

Recent elections also suggest increased political party competition in that more candidates have run as independents. In the November, 1977 election the KMT won an unprecedently low figure of 85 percent of the elective offices, with almost all of the rest going to independents. President Carter's human rights campaign undoubtedly encouraged independent candidates, though this was an already growing trend. If present trends continue one might speculate that the ROC's political system will evolve into a "one-party-plus-independents" system.

---

*There are two other political parties, the Chinese Youth Party and the Democratic Socialist Party, both of which had their beginnings on the mainland and continue to function. However, they remain small parties and generally insignificant in terms of their prospects to win an election or to solidify public opinion or votes on important issues.

By way of summary, neither the Constitution nor the structure of political authority has changed significantly in Taiwan since the ROC moved there in 1949. Political power remains concentrated at the top, and while there has been a considerable decentralization of governmental functions, ultimate authority is still held by a small select group plus one individual. And while there are provisions in the Constitution and in the law for the implementation of democratic practices and civil rights, this has been and remains circumvented by martial law and the Temporary Provisions. Improvements that have taken place in civil rights have largely been granted by the top and, as we will see in a later section, are qualified. On the other hand, there is a great deal of democracy practiced in local government, and municipal and county governments have expanded in terms of both functions and influence much faster than the national government, especially in the past few years—quite in contrast to political systems elsewhere. What democratization (modernization and streamlining of the political system would probably be better criteria) that has taken place in the national government has taken the form of reform or change by decree and is change in substance rather than organizational, ideological, or image change. Finally, much of the reform and improvement in government efficiency and responsiveness has been the work of one person—Chiang Ching-kuo.

In short, one can say then that political modernization in Taiwan has occurred not by changing the structure of the system but rather by other means. Reform from within has been accomplished by creating ministries and commissions that are more responsive to public, civic organization and interest group demand and are more representative of the Taiwanese and the youth. The central government has delegated power to local officials and has cautiously given increased prerogatives to local government. Here political participation is intense and the system works as democratically as in most Western countries. The KMT has changed very little in terms of organization or structure, though the party membership is now a majority of Taiwanese. Meanwhile, older members of the party leadership are often ignored by the new president or their influence circumvented by making decisions in the Executive Yuan without party concurrence. This, plus the increasing number of independent candidates in recent elections, seems to indicate that there is promise to reform the party and this may soon affect its top leadership.

Social Change and Political Modernization

Rapid economic growth makes social change inevitable in almost any society or culture. The same is true of increasing access to education by large segments of all society, the importation of new ideas from outside, and materialism—all of which appear to be strongly influencing the society in Taiwan at the present time. To comprehend the rapid social change that is going on in Taiwan one needs only to observe the number of people who see Western movies, their Western dress and buying habits, the decline in population growth, the number of tourists who visit each year, and the breakdown of traditional class barriers. Such manifold and deep-seated change can have vast stabilizing or destabilizing effects on the political system. It can promote political modernization, or it can create serious problems for the decision makers in power. In Taiwan social change is clearly having both effects.

The questions that appear to be most important and that will be entertained in the following pages are: To what extent has economic development created a materialist culture that espouses values that contradict the government's pursuit of stability and its efforts to conserve Chinese culture? And is the latter important? How has the growth of mass education affected political outlooks, and could this present a problem to the regime? In both cases is there an impetus to create democratic institutions and ideals faster than the government is prepared to give up many of its authoritarian practices? Has there occurred a significant rise in crime as a result of social change and is this threat to political harmony and the government's image? Did the expulsion from the United Nations give rise to an intellectual movement that might make threatening demands on the government, and what is the future of that movement? Finally, does the Taiwanese Independence Movement threaten the government and what is its future?

First let us look at the impact of economic development. Some data on the impact of increases in the standard of living need to be examined to comprehend the scope of its impact. The average yearly per capita income in Taiwan in 1952 was $148; in 1972 it was $1,079. During the same period the average daily caloric intake of the residents of Taiwan rose from 2,078 to 2,770, while the consumption of protein increased over 50 percent from 49 grams per day to 77. During this period the average life span increased from 58 years to over 71. In the realm of material comforts during this period the percentage of households with electricity increased from 35.4 percent to virtually all, or 99.7 percent, while the number of households with T.V. sets increased from zero to 94.5 percent. Citing further evidence, the number of radios increased 13 times during the period 1953–62, making it possible for virtually anyone in Taiwan who wanted a radio to have one. The same thing followed with T.V. sets, and to a lesser extent with telephones, which increased in number by more than 500 percent in the ten years after 1965. Most homes now have refrigerators, ovens, and a variety of kitchen and other appliances. Air conditioners are also common place. Most families also have a motorcycle or car. All of this suggests that consumerism, or materialism, has become a way of life in Taiwan. What are its effects?

Because of mass consumption the disparities between social class and other groups in Taiwan are rapidly disappearing. Although Chinese recently coming from the mainland still have an edge over Taiwanese in per capita income, the gap is quickly closing. The rural areas of Taiwan are poorer than urban areas and certain districts are richer than others, but those differences are rapidly diminishing. Other disparities in material wealth and possessions are also evaporating. This has given rise to a materialistic culture and with it secular and detached attitudes. Reflecting these trends a number of attitude surveys conducted in recent years indicate that there is little difference in perceptions on most issues (including political attitudes, confidence in the government, and so on) between the Taiwanese and mainland Chinese and among other groups on Taiwan, except for recent immigrants. If one thinks in terms of Taiwan's continued independent existence in the context of social problems that might cause instability or opposition to the government and that might in turn weaken Taiwan's unity, these are certainly positive trends.

On the other hand, materialism has also loosened almost all bonds in the society and has created a variety of problems such as generation gap, juvenile crime, and other such problems. This may cause difficulties for the government in the future, if other problems simultaneously become acute. At present, however, the main product of materialism in terms of social effects—in addition to those specific changes already mentioned—is the fostering of an atomization or individual self-dependence. If Taiwan follows the development patterns of other societies this will give the government more responsibilities and hence increased prerogatives. It will also make the citizenry more government dependent, and although not more satisfied with government certainly less likely to try to overthrow or change it.

This is not, however, to say that present social trends are contributory to democracy. Surveys, for example, show that notwithstanding the high voter turnout at the polls there is a declining interest in politics on the part of Taiwan's citizenry. One survey conducted in the early 1970s recorded that only 18 percent of students talk with their peers about politics once a week, and that only 24 percent of law students who are old enough to vote have actually voted. What is more, 93 percent responded that respect for elders is a "most important virtue," while only 13 percent agreed that majority rule, periodic elections, the protection of dissent, and more than one political party are important characteristics of democracy. One could argue, and a number of Western scholars have, that the explanation is simply that democracy is developing slowly in Taiwan. On the other hand, Taiwan seems to be going in the direction of Japan, more than the United States or Western Europe, where many authoritarian practices are not regarded as undemocratic and where individualism is considered less necessary (and sometimes even undesirable) to the growth of democracy. It may also be true that whereas certain facets of Western democracy have or are now taking hold, it is uncertain whether many others will or not because of Taiwan's citizens' negative attitudes toward many aspects of American democracy and Western culture.

One writer suggests that the people in Taiwan are not being taught democracy, and that what democracy the citizens of the ROC have seen has to a large extent given them expectations that have not been and cannot be fulfilled; therefore their enthusiasm for democratic values has diminished in some important ways. Others suggest that the complexities produced by urbanization, technology, and so on are producing the same trends in Taiwan as in the West, namely the feeling that the society is too complicated for democracy. Indeed material comforts and higher standards of living have fostered more concern with a "meaningful life," which includes such amenities as leisure time and artistic pleasure but has not produced any obvious attitudes or perceptions toward the government that can be categorically positive or negative.

The rising standard of living in Taiwan in contrast to producing new political attitudes directly, however, has made possible extremely rapid rises in the level of education, and this in turn has affected social changes as well as attitudes toward politics. The importance of this can be comprehended only after seeing the scope of the broadening of education in Taiwan. From 1954 to 1974 the percentage of the population in secondary schools inceased almost five times and the percentage in institutions of higher learning increased nearly twelve times. Three times as many persons were working on advanced degrees in 1974 as received degrees during the entire preceding ten years. At present more than one-fourth of the population in Taiwan are students—more than in England. Moreover, whereas at one time one-quarter of Taiwan's university graduates went aboad and few returned, now less than 8 percent leave and several times as many as once returned now come back. It is also a new phenomenon for there to be a high level of unemployment among the higher educated while some factories have difficulties hiring workers. This suggests potential intellectual disenchantment and unrest. Taiwan's educated thus might be expected to serve as a bastion of support or opposition to government or make certain demands for political change that the government may be compelled to meet or reject with force.

Another recent survey indicates that whereas there has been and continues to be a high regard for education, the gap in education level between mainland Chinese and Taiwanese is still large, with Mainlanders (who are about 15 percent of the population) constituting 40 percent of the enrollment in the best universities. This is juxtaposed beside the fact that both groups perceive that having an education is more advantageous to a Taiwanese than to a Mainlander, and that there is a larger portion of Taiwanese than their ratio of the population given government jobs. While there is still discrimination against Mainlanders in business (which is largely Taiwanese controlled), this suggests that there could be considerable disenchantment among young, educated Mainlanders. This is borne out by a number of observers who have talked to young Mainlanders in Taiwan in recent years. There is even evidence that some among this group may constitute opposition to the government. At this juncture, however, the top ruling hierarchy of the government does not seem to have cause for fear and many even see this as an advantage in that it would distract support from the Taiwanese Independence Movement and discourage Taiwanese from opposing the government that they see as granting them favorable treatment.

Still another survey of the higher educated in Taiwan indicates a low level of concern for national security compared to the less educated or average citizen. It is no doubt correct to assume that this suggets that future high defense exependitures may not have as much public support as in the past and there may even develop opposition to a large defense burden. This seems to agree with the observation often made that there has long been a decline in support for the "return to the mainland" policy. Although this contradicted by the reaction of Taiwan people to U.S derecognition (for example, they voluntarily donated U.S. $50 million to the national defense fund within two months), in the future most citizens may not be willing to fight or pay for what it costs to remain independent. On the other hand, this may simply suggest that they do not perceive a serious threat and may change their attitudes when and if a threat arises.

Another gap in terms of the educated population's outlook and government policy, and this is perhaps ironic, is that the more educated people do not give a high priority to equality as compared to those with an avarage level of education. This may reflect the fact that they perceive that the government's income leveling policy has gone too far or that the government bureaucracy has become too impersonal and doesn't give due recognition to the value of education. It is interesting that whereas this is a widely espoused position of the educated, activist intellectuals in Taiwan frequently complain of the "ravages of capitalism" and the evils of economic inequality. The conclusion would seem to be warranted that the activists do not have a strong base of support on these charges at least and the government may have already given the country as much equality, and perhaps more, than it wants. Two other differences indicated by survey research between the more and less educated that may be significant, but which at the same time are difficult to draw conclusions from, are that more education produces more interest in politics, but a lower voter turnout, and that higher education increases the probability of supporting the KMT platform as opposed to independent candidates.

This brings us to the problem of dissent and political opposition in Taiwan. With the exception of the Taiwanese Independence Movement there has been little organized public dissent or protest by ROC citizens—that is until 1971. Prior to that date a few political candidates would occasionally take a "Taiwanese" line in campaigning or would criticize the KMT for autocratic practices and human rights violations. Generally, however, they did not pass certain bonds and when they did they were "visited" by the police or were arrested. At times outspokenness would transcend the understood boundaries for a while, but this would be followed by a crackdown to serve as a warning to future mavericks or radicals. In 1971, however, two events occurred that changed this. First, the Senkaku Islands (Tiao Yu Tai in Chinese), 100 miles north of Taiwan, were promised to Japan along with Okinawa as part of the U.S. reversion agreement with Tokyo. These small, uninhabited islands were mentioned in early Chinese records, thus giving China a historical basis for a claim on them even though they were under Japanese sovereignty prior to World War II. In 1969 it was reported that there might be oil undersea near the Senkakus and the reversion of Okinawa (which included the Senkakus) to Japan gave Tokyo claim to the oil. Meanwhile, geological evidence had indicated that the islands were not part of the Ryukyo chain but were rather part of China's continental shelf. The second event was the ROC's expulsion from the United Nations. This was a blow to the ROC government's prestige, particularly in view of its uncompromising anticommunism and its willingness to do anything to prevent or soften this diplomatic setback and instead predicted incorrectly that UN members would "come to their senses." Both events evoked intellectual concern and thus a protest movement.

To what extent the movement to claim the Senkaku Islands was spontaneous is uncertain. In any case the government, rather than trying to stop the movement, organized its own demonstrations by gathering groups of college students to march in Taipei and protest at the U.S. and Japanese embassies. Demonstrations of sufficient size to attract attention were also held in the United States and Hong Kong, though the ROC soon put the lid on when it appeared that Peking might be able to infiltrate the demonstrations abroad. The movement soon fizzled out and little has been heard about the issue since. It did, however, set a precedent of open protest in Taiwan and it may have compounded the seriousness of what soon followed.

Shortly thereafter, when Taipei was expelled from the United Nations, a number of intellectuals formed study groups to discuss the problems of the ROC's deteriorating world position and methods to cope with Taiwan's image, including the problem of a government that was "weak, unaware of current problems, too old," and so on. Sometimes criticism was couched in even stronger language such as "reactionary, authoritarian, undemocratic, and self-serving." During this time a number of journals or magazines started publishing articles dealing with contemporary issues, especially problems that related to Taiwan's new predicament. Most notable of these was the *Taiwan Political Review*. However, the movement, which at first showed some signs of unity of purpose and spirit, soon began to split apart. Some leading members of the movement began to call for expression on issues that were either unrealistic or had no support among the masses. For example, a number of members of the movement called for reducing antagonisms between Taiwanese and mainlander Chinese. This may have been good idea, but it was clearly something that the movement could not accomplish. Some members also criticized the government for placing too much stress on economic growth and for allowing foreign exploitation and economic inequalities. Since economic growth had widespread support and since Taiwan's development was quite outstanding for producing a minimum of inequality, this tended to discredit the movement. Finally, personalities became an issue and the movement floundered.

To what extent the top hierarchy of the government was responsible for the failure of the intellectual movement is uncertain. There were certainly other causes than those just mentioned. However, one other factor that did serious damage to the movement, though this was probably important only after the movement was already on the skids, was the fact that, beginning in 1972, Chiang Ching-kuo appointed a number of young, American-educated Ph.D.s to important positions in the government—but none that had been or were leaders in the intellectual movement.

In any event in the last several years the thrust of dissent has once again focused on independent political candidates who take a stand against the KMT and official government policy. But this has not gotten out of hand and it may be seen by the top hierarchy of the government as a way of allowing more dissent (to please liberals in the United States and elsewhere) yet not allow it to go too far. Judging from what independent candidates have said in recent years, the government is able to tolerate charges of corruption and undemocratic practices, election fixing (when there is some substance to the comments), government policy on a wide range of domestic (especially local) issues, and the age of government officials. Even human rights can be discussed openly within certain limits. On the other hand, the top hierarchy of the government will not tolerate criticism that may be construed to mean changing or overthrowing the system, anything that might be pro-Communist or suggest negotiating with Peking, or anything aimed directly at individuals in the top leadership hierarchy. Similarly it will not tolerate Taiwanese who run strictly as Taiwanese or who advocate Taiwanese independence.

In the late months of 1977 leading up to the elections in November a marked trend toward more leniency can be perceived. A number of independent candidates openly charged KMT candidates with violations of electioneering practices and the police with interfering in the election. Some criticism was leveled at the KMT itself—though not specifically its top leaders—for allowing corruption and dishonesty. Comments were also made by independent candidates about the KMT being too conservative and controlled by the old and feeble-minded. The highlight of the campaign was a riot in Chungli, a suburb of Taipei. Young independent Taiwanese candidates had criticized the KMT for allowing ballot tampering and police interference in elections. In this context a disturbance flared when officials invalidated some votes. It then escalated into the gathering of a crowd of 10,000 and rioting that culminated in the burning of six police cars. The police did not intervene, as they had apparently been instructed not to. The incident was clearly anti-KMT and marked the first mass violence in Taiwan for 30 years.

On the other hand, the government after 1975 started taking a hard stand on crime, cracking down on violent crime in response to complaints of motorcycle gangs that terrorized people in the Taipei area, an increase in bodily crimes, and a number of violent crimes that became sensationalized, such as the gang rape of a noted Taipei singer. Contrary to past practice, some cases were sent to military courts under martial law provisions and stern sentences were meted out quickly. Although some protested that the sudden crackdown on crime was being used as a warning to potential dissenters, which is probably true, the move had the sympathy of the majority and did prove effective in reversing the rising crime rate and preserving Taipei's record as the safest city in the world of over 1 million population. In recent years the government has also maintained its guard against overt threats to its rule under the guise of vigilance against Communist infiltrators and spies. In January, 1978 a military court sentenced a group of three Taiwanese and three Mainlanders to stiff sentences up to life in prison for writing threatening letters to foreign businessmen and planning to kidnap the director of the United States Information Agency in Taipei and blow up his office along with a U.S.-owned hotel. The government also caught and sentenced the individual responsible for sending several letter bombs in October, 1976, one of which injured the governor of Taiwan. In late 1975 the *Taiwan Political Review* was banned and not long after one of its editors was sentenced to jail for sedition. In September, 1978 the Taiwan *Daily News* was brought under government pressure by pro-government Taiwanese businessmen; the apparent reason was that it had given too much attention to opposition within the Provincial Assembly.

These above-cited incidences of crackdown were probably more an effort to keep the lid on protest and keep the crime rate from escalating rather than eliminate dissent and opposition completely. However, they also served as a signal to potential opponents of the government that there were limits to what the government would tolerate. In any case they were balanced by an unprecedented statement by Chiang Ching-kuo in December, 1976 that since 1949 the government had convicted 254 persons on charges of sedition and that only one had been sentenced to death, and that there had been only 33 such convictions in 1976. Chiang went on to say that he would be glad to cooperate with an international organization that wanted to review human rights in the ROC. He also issued orders to Taiwan's police organizations, especially the Taiwan Garrison Command, which handles sedition cases, to use more orthodox investigating and enforcement techniques, and judging from their behavior this was carried out.

The Taiwanese Independence Movement (TIM) constitutes another sort of opposition to the ROC government: one not active in Taiwan, but organized abroad. The main centers of activity abroad are in the United States and Japan, areas where there are sizable numbers of Taiwanese with foreign citizenship. The organization has been active in both countries for some time and advocates a Taiwan ruled by Taiwanese and the overthrow by force if necessary—and it is generally assumed by members that it is necessary—of the ROC government. Some would also expel mainland Chinese from the island. During the 1960s the TIM got considerable publicity when the United States and Japan seemed to be moving toward a two-China policy, and also because of support allegedly given by the ruling Liberal Democratic party in Japan and the Central Intelligence Agency in the United States. Two incidents particularly gave the TIM notoriety: the escape of a TIM leader from Taiwan in 1968, after he had been released from prison and was under surveillance, and the attempt made on Chiang Ching-kuo's life by two of its members in New York in April, 1970.

Beginning in 1971, however, the TIM began to decline in importance, particularly in terms of the publicity it got abroad. A number of factors and events account for this decline. First, the movement is quite different (in addition to there being two main competing movements in Japan and factions in the United States) in the two countries where it has the largest following, with mostly older members in Japan (many members of the former aristocracy under Japanese colonial rule) as opposed to primarily a student membership in the United States. Second, the movements in the United States and Japan split over the Senkaku Islands issue in early 1971 with the Japan-based group opposing any protest. Third, the TIM suffered a major shock when President Nixon signed the Shanghai Communique in 1972, which said that there was only one China, since it was widely assumed that the United States was moving toward a two-China policy, meaning one China and one Taiwan. Soon after this, Tokyo recognized Peking and members of the ruling party in Japan as well as businessmen became cautious about their support of the TIM. Added to this the United States in 1971 failed to support the independence movement in Bangladesh (or anywhere else of importance) and was thus seen to give a lower priority to the cause of self-determination. The CIA then got involved in serious public relations problems that weakened the agency and put constraints on its covert activities (assuming this was important because it had supported the TIM or at least its membership thought so). Finally, a number of American intellectuals who wanted to ingratiate themselves with the Peking government abandoned the TIM. Perhaps more important than all of these reasons, many Taiwanese came to the realization that the Mainlander-dominated KMT might made a deal with Peking if they tried to overthrow the government and that they must cooperate with the Mainlanders if Taiwan were to survive efforts by Peking to "incorporate" it. In short the majority of Taiwanese came to perceive that they were in the same boat with the Mainlanders vis-à-vis resisting the People's Republic's efforts to force the United States and the international community to forsake Taiwan, and that this was the biggest threat that they faced.

For these reasons the Taiwanese Independence Movement has not been as active in recent years, and though it does not publish its membership rolls, membership figures are no doubt down. In any case, at present it has little hope of attaining its goals as an independent Taiwan Republic. On the other hand, some independent Taiwanese politicians in Taiwan secretly hope that the TIM will survive as it makes the KMT more understanding of their more "moderate" demands and puts the KMT "diehards" (those who resist Taiwanese participation in the party) in the same category as the "extremists" in the TIM who want to rid Taiwan of mainland Chinese.

At the time of this writing it is difficult to assure what impact U.S. derecognition will have on social change in Taiwan. Initial evidence suggests that it will further alleviate the differences between Taiwanese and Mainlanders and will foster greater unity aimed at preserving Taiwan's independence. Clearly all groups seem to be burying their differences and have become acutely aware of their future. This will undoubtedly affect many social trends in the near future.

Conclusions

The image that Taiwan is stagnant in terms of political change is far from the truth. Using the behavioralist approach to political change whereby modernization follows economic growth, increases in education, literacy, improved communications facilities, more consumerism and secularism, and the degree to which the society is penetrated by outside ideas, Taiwan has the foundations at least for a high level of political development. Compared to the PRC—a nation with less than half the per capita income, literacy, and urbanization, less than one-tenth the number of newspapers per capita, and only a tiny fraction of the T.V. sets per capita—the stimuli for political modernization are much more present in the ROC. Across the board, the factors that cause political change are much more present in Taiwan than in People's China.

When comparing the two countries on other realms one notes that the PRC has experienced in recent years efforts by local leaders to exert autonomy from Peking, intense social and political instability, and even leadership crises. In the PRC the problem of factionalism in the party and the "red versus expert" controversy seem to be lasting and perhaps constitute irresolvable problems. Such do not exist in the ROC. In Taiwan there have been no efforts by local leaders to challenge the center, except to request a little more autonomy and democracy. There is no "red versus expert" controversy, unless one wants to perceive the changing role of higher education as giving rise to a similar but clearly less serious problem. Certainly it is not a source of conflict as severe as exists on the mainland. And the ROC political leadership is stable as evidenced by the succession of Chiang Ching-kuo—achieved very smoothly and without having destabilizing effects on the society.

To the uninitiated observer, however, it appears that vast political development has been generated in the PRC while little or no change has occurred in the ROC. This image is fostered from looking at superficialities and what the leaders say they want to do or are going to do, while ignoring the real factors that underlie political modernization. ROC leaders have consistently opposed change in almost everything they say. After all they are the preservers of Chinese tradition. Just exactly the opposite situation prevails in the PRC: change for change's sake. But when looking at substance instead of rhetoric it becomes clear that Taiwan is a much more rapidly changing society and political modernization of the lasting kind is taking place at a much more rapid pace.

To cite just a few examples, the ROC government has demonstrated that it has the capabilities to engineer and manage economic growth. On the mainland, Chinese leaders are still experimenting, and their overall record in not good. Bureaucracy is a problem in Taiwan, but not as serious as in People's China. Education and technology have expanded to a degree in Taiwan that makes the PRC appear backward. Secular attitudes and individualism are present in Taiwan to a degree unknown in China. Elections are with little doubt more meaningful in Taiwan than in the PRC, and if public opinion polls could be taken, mass approval of and support for the government would indicate a much more popular and responsive government in Taiwan. Personal freedom and human rights are also much more prevalent in Taiwan.

Another reason that political development hasn't been noticed in Taiwan is that too much attention is given to political institutions and organizations that haven't remained as important as appearances would suggest. A number of ROC political institutions haven't modernized. What has happened is that they have simply become relics of the past and no longer have much influence on political decision making. For example, the naive observer is often led to believe that the Executive Yuan and the Legislative Yuan or the Control Yuan have equal power. Nothing could be further from the truth. Rather than changing the organizational structure of government, top leaders in Taiwan simply use much of the system as a rubber stamp. The same thing is done in other societies including the PRC. The difference is that Westerners recognize the branches of government (except the Examination and Control Yuans) as counterparts of their own system and see that they are not functional, whereas the rubber-stamp organs of government in the PRC are seen as exactly that without expectations that they should be anything else.

Finally, there is the issue of democracy and human rights. Westerners assume that a country headed by a Christian (Chiang Kai-shek was a Christian, although it is uncertain whether his son is or not), allied with the West, and receiving large quantities of U.S. aid (true until 1964) should establish democratic institutions, have free elections, and respect human rights. Americans also expect even more of the ROC since it is regarded as a historic ally and a nation closer to the United States than most other Asian nations. The populace of Taiwan, however, was not steeped in democratic traditions. Many Mainlanders, especially those in government, were brought up in the Confucian tradition—which has a democratic foundation yet is very different from Western democracy. The Taiwanese have not governed themselves and are not accustomed to doing so. From 1895 to 1945 Taiwan was a part of the Japanese Empire and was ruled by a Japanese colonial government, and no attempt was made to teach democracy or even self-rule. Furthermore both Taiwanese and mainland Chinese see much that they consider less than desirable about Western democracy and Western culture. Perhaps most important, they perceive hypocrisy and decadence. With few exceptions Western policies toward China as well as Taiwan were based upon commercial profit and exploitation. The Chinese have also been more aware than others of the waxing and waning of the West; they are more conscious of history. Today most people in Taiwan do not see democracy as necessarily the wave of the future, and they often associate democracy with hippies, drugs, and anarchy. They are very suspicious of the kind of freedoms that allow such social ills to develop. Also they have lived through years of weak and inefficient government and a drug problem the proportions of which the West has never known.

Westerners also fail to realize that the Chinese people are very pragmatic. This can be seen clearly when studying the role of the overseas Chinese, wherever they reside. And Westerners seldom criticize the overseas Chinese for not getting involved in local politics; in fact, they applaud it. But when people in Taiwan say that they are not interested in politics or they don't feel it important not to be able to criticize their leaders on a personal level, Westerners fail to understand. Americans especially fail to comprehend their greater concern with economic growth, security, and national survival rather than with tidy political procedures and institutions.

On the other hand, there is still good reason to apply Western standards to Taiwan's political modernization. After all the West will play a vital role in deciding whether the ROC survives or not, whether it evolves into an independent, autonomous government of Taiwan or is absorbed by the PRC. Westerners, and the rest of the world for that matter, don't give much thought to the question of whether the poeple in Taiwan want incorporation or not, or the blood bath and loss of human rights that would result if Peking incorporates Taiwan. Rather they are concerned with whether Taiwan deserves its independence and whether self-determination is appropriate. Thus Taiwan must be attentive to the views of the international community. Perhaps Chiang Ching-kuo has already realized this. He is cultivating an image of concern for the peasants and the common man. And he has convinced them. There is little doubt that Chiang and his government have mass support.

In short, the ROC government is now trying to publicize the modernization that has occurred in Taiwan in the past two to three decades rather than hiding it. This underscores Taiwan's nationhood status in the context of U.S. derecognition and a deteriorating diplomatic role in world affairs. And it is a race for time. It has to make the world know that Taiwan has joined the ranks of the modern nations and that its government, economy, society, and culture are different from those of the People's Republic to the point that regarding Taiwan as part of the PRC makes little sense. Only in this way can it preserve Taiwan's phenomenal progress and at the same time give its 17 million people their right to choose their own destiny.

4.   Taiwan's Recent Election: Progress Toward a Democratic System

John F. Copper

On December 6, 1980, the electorate of Taiwan went to the polls to vote in what was regarded by most observers as the most important election in recent years. In a sense it was the first national election in Taiwan. Previous "national" elections had been held only to fill vacant seats in the Legislative Yuan (branch of government) and the National Assembly. Other elections have been only "provincial" or local in scope.

It was an election that had been scheduled for December, 1978, but had to be cancelled due to the decision by the Carter Administration to derecognize the government of the Republic of China and transfer recognition to the People's Republic of China. It was also an election held in a milieu of more than just slight apprehension and nervousness. Less than a year earlier, political protest had turned into violence at a Human Rights Day demonstration in Taiwan's second largest city, Kaohsiung. Following this incident, a number of the instigators of the demonstration were put on trial for sedition, convicted and given stiff prison sentences. In addition, the last election, in 1977, saw violence in the city of Chungli, not far from Taipei, following a controversy resulting from the invalidation of some ballots.

Early in the year the government proceeded to write new election laws and promised elections for late in the year, while adding a number of new seats to the National Assembly and the Legislative Yuan. Before the election, security forces warned political elements on the right not to disturb the election process or intimidate liberal and independent candidates. (A warning had already been made to the left during the trials and they were made to understand that they could criticize the government—but within definite limits.)

The promise to hold an election reflected public demands to more fully implement the Constitution and thereby increase the scope of democratic processes in government, as well as efforts by President Chiang Ching-kuo to bring more Taiwanese into government. Pressure had also come from the United States and other Western nations who needed justification for supporting Taiwan morally and through trade and other contacts in its continued claim to represent "a China." Thus the election represented a turning point in Taiwan's efforts to democratize its political system at a crucial juncture. The success or failure of these efforts to some extent remain to be seen. However, the present effort seems to be a good start.

Asian Survey, XXI, No. 10 (October, 1981). Copyright 1981 by The Regents of the University of California. Reprinted by permission of The Regents. Footnotes omitted.

The Election and Taiwan's Political System

Taiwan's political system is founded upon the political philosophy of Sun Yet-sen and a Constitution written in 1947. Sun evisioned the implementation of a fully democratic system of government after a period of tutelage, taking account of the fact that the Chinese people had no experience with democracy and that democratic government had to be implemented gradually while the people were prepared for political participation. The Constitution of 1947 thus provides for general elections where the electorate picks representatives of one of the five branches of the government, plus the National Assembly that elects the President and Vice-President. Indirect elections provide for representation in another branch of the government, though the Legislative Yuan—the branch of government that was popularily elected—was to have considerable influence over appointments made to the other branches of government.

The 1947 Constitution gave the right to vote to citizens aged 20 and over and the right to run for office to anyone over age 23. Election disputes were to be handled by the courts, and the people were given the powers of initiative, recall, and referendum.

In 1947 an election was held in that part of China not under Communist control, and 2,961 delegates were elected to the National Assembly for six year terms. In 1948 another election provided for the selection of 760 representatives to the Legislative Yuan. Subsequently 180 members of the Control Yuan, an organ of government that supervises and controls public functionaries, were chosen by indirect election. Members of the Executive Judicial and Examination Yuans were appointed, though with certain checks and balances functioning in the making of these appointments.

In 1948 "temporary provisions effective during the period of Communist rebellion" were affixed to the Constitution thereby institutionalizing martial law while nullifying some of the civil rights sections of the Constitution. The "temporary provisions" also circumvented the requirement of having regular elections, thus "freezing" the elected bodies as they were. This situation prevailed when the Nationalist Chinese government move to Taiwan in 1949.

By 1966 the size of the National Assembly had been reduced through attrition to 1,488 delegates and the Legislative Yuan to about half of its original size even though some vacancies had been filled by appointment. In that year the "temporary provisions" were amended by giving the President the power to call for elections to fill vacancies. The next year additional power was given the President by the National Assembly to make appointments to fill empty seats. Subsequently "special elections" were held to give Taiwan added representation in a political system that was designed to represent all of China after the mainland was liberated from Communist control.

Despite these elections the national government remained controlled by "mainlander" Chinese who came to Taiwan in 1949 and who were a 15 per cent minority of the population. Local or "Taiwanese" Chinese began to play a role in local politics and became active in the Nationalist Party or Kuomintang (KMT); but few held positions of importance in the Central Government. In 1972, when Chiang Ching-kuo became Premier, six Taiwanese were named to cabinet posts and Taiwanese were aggressively recruited by the KMT—equal to or at times even above their ratio of the population. The National Assembly and the Legislative Yuan, however, remained dominated by mainlander Chinese.

Preelection Events

In 1978 national elections were planned to rectify the situation described above. However, this was not to be a revolutionary process: more local seats were to be added to two branches of government which had in the past two to three decades declined in authority and influence; political control was to generally remain in the hands of the KMT and the Executive Yuan. Also, standing members of the National Assembly and the Legislative Yuan did not have to stand for re-election. Nonetheless, it was seen as an important beginning.

Thus, Taiwan's first national election was scheduled for mid-December. But before it was held the Carter Administration announced the decision to derecognize the Republic of China and transfer recognition and the U.S. Embassy to the People's Republic of China.

The decision was naturally a shock for Taipei, the U.S. being Taipei's most important ally. Consequently, the elections were cancelled.

The government did not, however, take other emergency actions save to close the stock market for a short time and effectuate some measures mostly of an administrative nature to adjust to the new situation. In fact, during 1979 the government announced guidelines to allow for freer speech and publishing. This, plus the fact that the government's credibility had been undermined by the U.S. action, gave rise to protest which focused primarily on the unrepresentative nature of the political system, the existence of only one political party and unrealistic policy of retaking the mainland. There was also some criticism voiced concerning the fact that the government was still dominated by mainlander Chinese and that it might negotiate with the Communists rather than allow Taiwanese to come to dominate the political system as would happen naturally as the system becomes democratized.

Culminating a near year-long period of dissent during which the *Formosa Magazine* and its related organization was at center stage and behaving like a political party, a large demonstration was held on December 10, Human Rights Day, in Kaohsiung—Taiwan's second largest city. Violence broke out during the demonstration and 183 policemen were injured (though few demonstrators were hurt as the police had been instructed not to react with force). Some argued that the police were supposed to be martyrs to justify a crackdown on the movement. Others charged that the *Formosa Magazine* leaders had recruited opportunists and members of local gangs and had exceeded their authority by transcending the purposes of the movement in terms of the desires of their followers and supporters.

In any event, those responsible for organizing the demonstration and provoking the violence were arrested and put on trial for sedition. Quite inexplicable to many, the government allowed an open trial with access to news reporters, thus giving national and international attention to the case. During the trials, several of the defendants made a very cogent case for the need for political reforms while criticizing the government for being unrealistic (concerning the return to the mainland policy), undemocratic, and even conspiratorial (in the sense that the government was accused of negotiating with the Chinese Communists). Some of the defendants also pointed out that the government had violated the Constitution and the spirit of Sun Yet-sen's "Three Principles of the People."

Seemingly undaunted, the government proceeded, convicting most of the defendants of sedition. Prison sentences ranging from 12 years to life were meted out. Ironically, while the dissidents had considerable public support during 1979 and despite the fact that to many objective observers they made a very convincing argument in court (better than the government's, according to many) public opinion surveys reflected a large majority of the population supported the government's actions. The explanation is that the dissidents had by this time become viewed as a source of political instability that constituted a threat to public order and to the economy. Also, the government promised an election late in the year and the addition of new seats in the National Assembly and the Legislative Yuan. In fact, during the trials it was already in the process of writing new election laws.

The Election Laws
During 1979 and early 1980 debates were held on the promulgation of new campaigning and election laws. The government invited over 200 scholars, including experts on constitutional law, elections, and foreign political systems, to take part. The press also joined the process by making the discussions known to the public, thereby waking public concern and debate.

On May 14, "The Public Officials' Election and Recall Law" was officially adopted. It contained 113 articles specifying in considerable detail how elections were to be conducted, the rules pertaining to candidates, etc. Most important, the publishing of the new laws made clear the rights of dissident candidates. It also made lucid certain restrictions on candidates' activities and what they might not say in the process of electioneering.

The election laws, by making no provisions for other political parties, made it clear (since the formation of additional parties is prohibited under the "temporary provisions") that independent candidates could not organize or unite in an anti-KMT or anti-government platform. Thus, advocating a change from the one-Party system was in essence proscribed. This, however, independent candidates accepted as the "rules of the game."

Non-party candidates were nevertheless critical of certain provisions in the new election law. Specifically they disagreed with a part of Article 51 which specified that printed handbills and other written matter distributed by candidates had to bear the printer's name and address. They felt that this made the printers *de facto* censors, and, because of their fear of arrest, limited what the candidates could publish. They also opposed another section of the law which divided the campaigning into periods of candidate-sponsored meetings and election commission-sponsored meetings, with the latter to equal the former and which excluded the former during the last days of the campaign (Article 49). Similarly they objected to the fact that campaign assistants could not make speeches on behalf of candidates during the latter period.

Opposition candidates did, however, agree that the new election law made for a more honest campaign by tightening up the procedures and by forbidding certain practices generally seen as dishonest, such as candidates dropping out of elections for a bribe. They also generally agreed that more strict and clearly stated election laws were needed.

During the campaign some non-Party candidates accused KMT candidates of violating a provision of the new election law of which they were already suspicious, namely, a section prohibiting government functionaries from serving as campaign assistants. They also argued that some of the provisions of the election law were unconstitutional though they did not push this criticism very far. Nevertheless, they generally agreed to abide by the new law, and, with the exception of a few minor infractions, they did.

The Campaign

On November 21, 403 candidates began campaigning for office (408 had registered as candidates and five were disqualified). Private campaigning lasted until November 28. From November 29 to December 5 the public, or election commission-sponsored, part of the campaign began and candidates had to speak in line at government (election commission) arranged public rallies.

At stake were 97 seats in the Legislative Yuan and 76 in the National Assembly, or 23.3 percent of the former and 6.2 percent of the latter body. Of the candidates to the Legislative Yuan 55 percent were to be picked by the general electorate, 17 percent by women's groups and professional organizations such as farmers and workers, and 28 percent by the Overseas Chinese—i.e., by special appointment. Of candidates seeking seats in the National Assembly, 70 percent were to be chosen by the general electorate and 30 percent by women's and professional groups.

The KMT, the Young China Party and the Democratic Socialist Party all fielded candidates. But most exciting and controversial were the independent or non-Party candidates. The latter were larger in number and advocated the most important changes in the political system and in domestic and foreign policies. They were labelled the progressives or liberals, but were more often called simply the "without party" candidates.

Two of the non-party candidates were relatives—one a wife—of dissidents sentenced to prison for sedition in the spring. They were two of the most controversial, anti-government and provocative of the candidates. They appealed for what many called the "sympathy vote."

They and a number of other non-party candidates, almost all of whom were Taiwanese, voiced criticism of a type that had not been heard before in Taiwan. Some of the candidates' headquarters displayed large cartoon posters characterizing the government and the KMT as being corrupt, oppressive, practicing nepotism, having a bad human rights record and being undemocratic. In some instances the KMT was even compared to the Communist Party in China. Such criticisms were also voiced in public almost without exception to the astonishment of most of those present.

Yet noticeably, at least to alert observers, the non-party candidates did not assail the government's return to the mainland policy, which justifies the continued existence of a mainlander Chinese minority government. Nor did they advocate a two party system. Similarly, they did not say anything about the government negotiating with Peking or advocate becoming part of the People's Republic of China (which almost all if not all of these candidates and most of the electorate oppose, but which had been advocated by some dissidents earlier). Nor did the two relatives of dissidents put on trial and sentenced for sedition earlier in the year claim to represent the dissidents.

To the wonderment of many, a backlash was conspiciously absent. Many of the candidates complained about police and other official harrassment, but few offered any specific evidence. When questioned about why no right-wing groups had disrupted their campaigning or used violence against non-party candidates as would have been expected, they offered no real explanation. The reason, of course, was that the security and police force had admantly forewarned right wing groups and veterans against interfering in the election process. And the warning was effective: no anti-Communist or pro-KMT groups opposed the independent candidates collectively or on an individual basis.

Some new issues came out during the campaigning and some were given a new emphasis, notwithstanding the fact that personalities were more important than issues. Non-party candidates particularly, but KMT and other party candidates as well, expressed a deep concern about housing, labor, and welfare. Perhaps the reason these issues did not attract so much concern, even though they may be categorized as serious problems, was the fact that they were new issues, and that the government had already taken what appeared to be effective actions to deal with most of them.

The Election Results

Despite what was less than ideal weather just over 65 percent of the eligible voters went to the polls on December 6. There were no serious complaints of election rigging or irregularities. New ballot boxes were used that were transparent to be sure that they were empty when the balloting began. Every effort was made by election officials to be sure that no one voted twice or was intimidated or bribed before making a selection among candidates. The counting was done at most polls in the plain sight of spectators with results tallied on the walls and telephoned to election headquarters for announcement on national television.

In terms of pronouncing a winner the results were clearly mixed. All groups with some justification claimed victory. In the National Assembly contest the KMT took 63 of the 76 seats accounting for more than 82 percent of the victorious candidates. In the Legislative Yuan contest the KMT won 56 for a 80 percent win. The other two parties also claimed victory, but since their representation is so small this is difficult to judge. Non-party candidates also claimed a victory, although the percentage of non-party candidates that won was not high. On the other hand, several non-party candidates were among the top vote getters because they were the most controversial and most vociferous in their anti-KMT, anti-government criticism. Finally, independent candidates made a better showing than in past elections.

Most of the candidates, non-party and KMT alike, were Taiwanese. Similarly, most of the victorious candidates were Taiwanese, thus giving this majority group better representation in the two organs of government in question. Most of the candidates, and again including most of these that won, were better educated than politicians in the past. Of those elected to the National Assembly four hold the Ph.D. degree, six have M.A. degrees and 45 have earned the B.A. degree. In the Legislative Yuan, the figures are eight, nine and 42 respectively.

Perhaps more important still is the fact that most of the winning candidates are much younger than those currently occupying seats in the National Assembly and the Legislative Yuan. The average age of candidates elected to the National Assembly was 45, and to the Legislative Yuan 44. This compares to an average of 70-plus for those already holding seats.

Most of the winning candidates were businessmen, thus apparently guaranteeing continuing good relations between the government and the business community. To some observers this fact guarantees Taiwan's continued economic success. Yet many of the businessmen elected can not be categorized as espousing unqualified pro-business policies.

More than most officials they favor labor reform legislation, social welfare programs and environmental protection. As a group they reflect a high level of civic consciousness.

Ideologues did not fare well in the election. While they were few in number and not many candidates made ideology a central part of their platform, and therefore the election was not very ideologically in tone, the candidates known for their ideological positions either deemphasized political philosophy, or they lost.

Some regional preferences were noticeable. KMT candidates did best in Taipei, the capital city. Independent or non-party candidates did better in the south and the rural areas of the island. On the other hand, in some districts where there were heavily favored candidates, some candidates were elected without a sizable number of votes due to one popular candidate taking such a large portion of the ballots. This tended to blur regional as well as other preferences.

A number of candidates tried to employ unique and sensational techniques in campaigning, including the hiring of movie stars and other noted personalities to help them in advertising their campaign. Candidates, however, were not allowed to buy T.V. time, thus putting a limit on this kind of activity and perhaps making it less successful than it might have been. In any case, most of these using celebrities were not elected, suggesting that in the minds of the electorate this was not an accepted practice. Most candidates spent a large amount of money on the campaign, with the average in the vicinity of U.S. $500,000, and those that spent more money generally fared better.

Conclusions
The December, 1980 election has been called one of the most important events in Taiwan's recent history, and probably rightfully so. It has special significance for a number of reasons.

The election clearly indicates that the government of Taiwan, particularily Chiang Ching-kuo and the top echelons of the decision making hierarchy, are committed to the growth of democracy in Taiwan. Although the election itself represents but a small step in this direction, it is no doubt symbolic of what can be expected in the future. This is especially so in that the election can probably be taken as a precedent that will be followed by regular national elections in the future. Second, up to this time the process of making the government more responsive, efficient and representative had been accomplished by President Chiang Ching-kuo's initiative, with the Executive Yuan at the forefront of the modernization process. This election suggests political development will now be furthered by other organs of the national government as well, most importantly the Legislative Yuan.

Anything that can be said in terms of the election constituting a turning point in the democratization process and in mirroring political development must be underscored by the fact that it was conducted in an atmosphere of apprehension and some nervousness. During and before the election considerable concern was expressed by many that something might go wrong—meaning that extremists on the right or left might disrupt the election process, or that candidates may be tempted during the campaign to abandon certain tacit understandings and rules. This did not happen. The election was conducted as smoothly as could have been hoped and without any major incident. This reflects that while there was some disagreement about the rules (including the new election law) there was near unaninimity of feeling that some bad rules are better than none and that the political system must be changed in a legal fashion and peacefully.

The younger age of those elected suggests that both the National Assembly and the Legislative Yuan will be revitalized, and perhaps more: that they will become more important organs of government and function as they were originally intended under the Constitution. The "new blood" brought in by this election in effect doubles the active membership of the Legislative Yuan and will no doubt give it as well as the National Assembly new energy and leadership. The election also raised Taiwanese membership in both organs of government, in the Legislative Yuan to around 30 percent—a much larger figure if counting only active membership.

The fact that the KMT won a victory in spite of the government liberalizing campaign guidelines and the presence of a large number of independent candidates will no doubt give it confidence to allow competition in the future. Perhaps more important still, the fact that the majority of its victorious candidates were Taiwanese reflects that the Party is becoming more broadly representative. It can no longer be seen as a Mainlander-dominated party, or at least this is not its future. What may be implied for the future is a one-party plus independents competitive system with neither representing ethnic groups. This, in fact, may be the best system for managing interest aggregation that is possible at this time. (The prevalence of voting based on ethnic identification in this election clearly reflects that a two-party system at this juncture would be destabilizing.)

The election also mirrored the fact that government officials and the KMT can withstand criticism, even of a very provocative nature. They were confident—as they should be—based on their past successes in economic development and the fact that opinion surveys reflect a high level of trust and positive attitudes toward the political system. This confidence was duly rewarded during the election even though criticism of the government was rather strident at times. Extreme criticism was generally seen as that and in most cases alienated voters. Some criticism was also seen by the public to be contradictory: for example, some candidates asked for continued rapid economic growth, and more investment in housing and social welfare programs.

Finally, all factions and groups seemed to recognize that Taiwan is a comfortable place to live, free of crime and with living standards that have improved markedly in recent years. Most want more of the same and are suspicious of revolutionary solutions. In short, they realize that they are well off and that improvements must be made on the present political system rather than replacing it. It is also clear that Taiwan's economic system as well as its political system are working better than their counterparts in China. (While the elections were in progress parts of the trial of the "Gang of Four" were shown on T.V. in Taiwan.) All of this suggests that Taiwan's future is seen with optimism, and that political modernization and democratization are part of this future.

Section 7
Foreign Relations
Edited by Winberg Chai

Section 7
Foreign Relations

by Winberg Chai

The foreign relations of the Republic of China (ROC) on Taiwan during the past thirty years can be broadly classified into three distinct decades: a decade of survival (1950–60); a decade of expansion (1960–70); and a decade of consolidation and adaptation (1970–80).

A Decade of Survival (1950–60)

The survival period encompassed the first decade of the Presidency of Chiang Kai-shek after he resumed this office in Taipei on February 28, 1950. This was an era under which the principal objectives of the ROC's foreign policy were: first, to maintain its legitimacy as the sole legal government of China; secondly, to affiliate Taiwan with the anti-Communist defense alliance of the U.S. and the Free World; and finally, to prevent the U.S. and other friendly governments from recognizing the Communist government in Peking.

The national government on Taiwan, as noted from the sections on law and domestic politics, claims legitimacy within the framework of the Republic of China Constitution promulgated on January 1, 1947 in Nanking, China; its structure is an emergency model of the ROC government constituted in 1948, when it was still on the mainland.

When Chiang Kai-shek left Chungking for Taipei in August, 1949, his authority was limited to that of the Director-General *(Tsung-tsai)* of Kuomintang. Early in the year, he had "withdrawn" (or resigned) from the Presidency of the Republic; and the government was theoretically under the authority of Acting President Li Tsung-jen, who had refused to join Chiang in Taiwan and instead took refuge in the U.S. just as the Communists were taking over the China mainland.

Moreover, the U.S. government had considered Taiwan a "lost cause" and already formulated policy with the hope to "minimize damage to the U.S. prestige and others' morale by the possible fall of Formosa [Taiwan] to the Chinese Communist forces."[1]

Chiang Kai-shek's immediate actions in Taiwan were: to re-establish the legitimacy of his authority by the resumption of the Presidency; to personally contact leaders of his two strongest allies in Asia, South Korea and the Phillipines, to gain their support; to instruct his representative in the United Nations to prevent the accreditation of representatives from Peking in that

Winberg Chai is Professor of Political Science, University of South Dakota (Vermillion, S.D.)

world body; and finally, to submit a draft resolution requesting the General Assembly of the U.N. to do the following:

• To determine that the Soviet Union had violated the Charter of the U.N. and the Sino-Soviet Treaty of August 14, 1945;

• To urge all member states to desist and refrain from giving any military and economic aid to the Chinese Communists;

• To recommend to all member states not to accord diplomatic recognition to any regime organized by the Chinese Communists; and

• To call upon all member states to refrain from taking advantage of the present situation in China for any purpose that was incompatible with the political independence, territorial and administrative integrity of China.[2]

While the U.N. did not adopt that resolution, the General Assembly did pass a milder form of "condemnation" of the Soviety Union, and did reject the admission of delegates from the People's Republic of China (PRC). Thus, the world body pronounced a much needed moral judgment favorable to the frail ROC government in Taiwan and strengthened its legitimacy.

The turning point for the ROC in Taiwan, however, was the outbreak of the Korean War on June 25, 1950, which became a decisive factor for the U.S. to reverse its previous neutrality stand on Taiwan. President Harry S. Truman, in direct response to the Communist aggression in South Korea, ordered the dispatch of the U.S. Seventh Fleet to patrol the Taiwan strait, to prevent any Chinese Communist military attack on the island.

Thereafter, Taiwan's survival was assured as U.S. military matériel began to pour in. By May, 1951, the first U.S. Military Assistance Advisory Group was established in Taiwan to provide training for the Chinese Nationalist armed forces. This was followed by additional massive economic and military aid; and finally, a mutual defense treaty was signed in 1954 between the two countries to formalize the partnership. In accepting the treaty, the ROC had agreed not to take unilateral action against the Communists on the mainland.

Other important foreign policy accomplishments in this period included the conclusion of a peace treaty with Japan in 1952, and the resumption of diplomatic relations with a number of important countries in Asia, Europe, Latin America, the Middle East, and Africa. The ROC was able to retain its membership in the U.N. without interruption, as the PRC was at war with U.N. forces in Korea, and the question of Chinese representation was kept off the agenda of the Assembly for the period of 1951 through 1960.

The cornerstone of the ROC's foreign policy was nevertheless based upon the Mutual Defense Treaty with the U.S., which enabled the government to withstand and repulse several Chinese Communist military attacks on its Kinmen and Matsu offshore islands in 1954, 1955, and 1958. Furthermore, with the security of Taiwan guaranteed by the U.S., the ROC government was able to devote more energy and resources to agricultural, economic and political development and transformed Taiwan from a developing society into a modern industrialized country.

A Decade of Expansion (1960–70)

The second decade, from 1960 to 1970, was a time of rapid expansion, due to the unprecedented growth of the Taiwan economy. Survival was no longer a priority issue.

The ROC expanded its foreign relations by offering, for the first time, its own foreign assistance programs to other developing nations. The first such technical assistance program was extended to Liberia in 1961; and by the end of the decade, it had expanded its services to some 40 countries in Africa, the Middle East, Southeast Asia and, Latin America.

Africa became an important "card" in Taiwan's bid for international recognition as the sole representative of China. Each year, the ROC sent a ranking diplomat to tour the African continent and its client-states, which included: Botswana, Cameroon, Central African Republic, Chad, Congo (Kinshasa), Dahomey, Ethiopia, Gabon, Gambia, Ghana, Ivory Coast, Kenya, Lesotho, Liberia, Libya, Malagasy Republic, Malawi, Niger, Mauritius, Nigeria, Rwanda, Senegal, Sierra Leone, South Africa, Togo, Upper Volta, and Swaziland.

In Asia, Japan became the ROC's most important trading partner and political ally. Japanese investments in Taiwan and the technical and economic cooperation between the two countries reached an all-time high. But the balance of trade was in favor of Japan; for example, 1969 exports to Japan were $178.8 million, and imports, $489.2 million.

Taiwan was able to play an active role in the nine-nation Asia and Pacific Council (ASPAC), which it helped to form in 1966 with Japan, South Korea, Australia, New Zealand, the Philippines, Thailand, Malaysia, and South Vietnam as members. Efforts were made by the ROC to push the ASPAC in the direction of a political alliance.

The success of its foreign policy was evidenced by the fact that in 1966 the ROC was able to increase the votes opposing the seating of the PRC in the U.N. to 57 from a previous high of 47 votes in 1965. In fact, by the end of the decade, the world count totalled 71 countries in the ROC column and 48 for Peking.

In spite of its global success, the ROC was unable to prevent the U.S. from conducting direct negotiations with PRC representatives, which were first initiated through the efforts of the United Kingdom and India in 1955. Midway between the first and second sessions of the 86th Congress in 1961, the U.S. Senate Foreign Relations Committee released an important report, known as the "Conlon Report," in which it made a number of damaging assumptions:[3]

(1)"The Chinese Communist Government will have a lengthy tenure..."

(2)"Communist China is confident that within a decade her power and influence will demand acknowledgement..."

(3)"Either Taiwan will be joined with Mainland China or the process of Taiwanization will continue... to the Taiwanese."[3]

The ROC has always objected to any discussion of a "two-China" concept in international relations, although Washington had long accorded Peking a *de facto* recognition in their more than 150 bilateral negotiations, the U.S. disclaimer notwithstanding.

For President Chiang Kai-shek, mainland China remained the key to the ROC's destiny. Chiang knew that his own previous revolutions in 1911 and 1927 had been consummated only after years of failure. He believed that the wiles of ancient Sun Tzu, the first great Chinese philosopher of war, and the demonic patience of Mao Tse-tung's "protracted strategy" could not save Communism from ruin. Chiang did not intend to wait for Communist ruin to come of its own accord. He himself had to help bring about the downfall of the Communist regime.

A Decade of Consolidation and Adaptation (1970–80)

The past decade, from 1970 to 1980, was a period of adaptation and consolidation for the ROC's foreign relations. It was a painful decade wherein old assumptions were questioned, and new alternatives had to be developed.

The change began with Canada's recognition of the PRC in mid-October, 1970, under a formula which permitted Canada to "take note" of the PRC's claim to Taiwan without explicitly endorsing it. Using the same formula, thirteen governments previously friendly to the ROC on Taiwan switched sides.

The most intractable external problem continued to be the ROC's relations with the U.S. For over twenty years, the ROC had maintained close relations with the U.S., beginning with the Eisenhower Administration with John Foster Dulles as Secretary of State. After the election of John F. Kennedy in 1960, despite the damaging Kennedy-Nixon debate in which Kennedy questioned the validity of the Nationalist-held islands of Kinmen and Matsu, the ROC was able to adjust to the Democrats. Neither Kennedy nor Johnson had made any compromise with the Chinese Communists, and the ROC was able to advance economically and politically to a high level of growth.

When Nixon was elected President in 1968, with his strong anti-Communist credentials, there were high hopes that "better days are here again." Both Deputy Premier Chiang Ching-kuo and Vice-President C. K. Yen visited the U.S. in 1970 to put more pressure on the U.S. government to continue its one-China (Taiwan) policy.

Without prior consultation with the ROC on Taiwan or Taiwan's friends in the U.S., President Nixon told millions of surprised Americans on July 16, 1972 that he would visit Peking and seek "the normalization of relations with the PRC." The following year, accompanied by hundreds of reporters and television cameras, Nixon toasted Premier Chou En-lai in the Great Hall of the People in Peking, and the two men signed the "Shanghai Communique" on February 27, 1972.

The consequential damages were unprecedented for the ROC, as it was expelled from the U.N. in 1971, and Japan—Taiwan's most important partner in Asia—switched its recognition to Peking in 1972. Twenty-five other countries followed suit between 1971 and 1972, including Belgium, Greece and West Germany in Europe; Argentina, Ecuador, Peru, Mexico in Latin America; and Australia and New Zealand in Asia. Eighteen additional countries extended their recognition to the PRC in the next three years (1973–1975) includng Spain, the Philippines, and Thailand.

Amidst efforts to offset these dramatic setbacks which, if unchecked, would have led to its political and economic isolation, the ROC started a leadership shake-up in 1972, when Chiang Ching-kuo was named Premier. He made a number of important changes including the launching of an all-out diplomatic effort which stressed economic, technical, cultural, and educational ties with selected countries, regardless of each country's official relations with the ROC government. For example, after the severance of formal diplomatic relations with Japan on September 29, 1972, two nongovernmental agencies were established to continue their relationship. They are the "Association of East Asian Relations of the Republic of China" (for Taiwan) and "the Interchange Association of Japan".

The ROC government also greatly expanded the country's public-relations program overseas, under the guidance of a reorganized Government Information Office, and enlarged its various cultural, educational and economic exchange programs. In 1977, the Government Information Office alone invited guests from 47 countries, among them legislators, correspondents, columnists, writers, scholars, TV commentators and photographers. The Government Information Office also distributed some 4,500,000 copies of various publications telling Taiwan's story. In addition, numerous seminars and sightseeing tours were organized under the government's sponsorship.

For a while, the ROC leadership on Taiwan seemed to think that time was on its side, especially after mainland China's disastrous Cultural Revolution, the deaths of Mao Tse-tung and Chou En-lai, the discrediting of President Nixon after Watergate, and finally, the departure of Kissinger from active policymaking.

When President Carter, after his 1976 campaign pledge that he would "never let the friendship [with the PRC] stand in the way of the preservation of the independence and freedom of the people of Taiwan,"[4] announced on December 15, 1978 that the U.S. would sever diplomatic relations with the ROC and terminate the 1954 Mutual Defense Treaty, Taiwan went through a period of total shock. In fact, for the first time since the 1950's, the ROC felt that its security was threatened, as President Chiang Ching-kuo explained:

"The next two weeks after December 16 were the most unstable period. The stock market dropped, and the exchange rate between the U.S. dollar and the New Taiwan dollar on the black market rose to NT$43 to US$1 [official rate NT$36 to US$1]. Domestic and foreign investors seemed to be reconsidering their investments."[5]

Thousands of people in Taiwan went to the streets en masse to demonstrate against the U.S. Hundreds of the ROC's friends in the U.S. voluntarily went to Washington D.C. and lobbied on Capitol Hill on behalf of the ROC government. Conservative U.S. Senators also challenged their own President's decision, and some sued in American courts.

This pressure generated a wave of sympathy, and the U.S. Congress quickly enacted the "Taiwan Relations Act" (HR2479), which President Carter signed into law on April 10, 1979. The Act established a new relationship defined as "unofficial," for the handling of which an American Institute in Taiwan (AIT) was created. The ROC government created the Coordination Council for North American Affairs (CCNAA) to act as its counterpart to AIT.

Whether the Taiwan Relations Act can provide sufficient guarantees for Taiwan's security remains to be tested, but the U.S. action did jolt many in the ROC into considering a few latent but obvious alternatives, such as: "Independent Statehood;" "Nuclear Options;" "Soviet Option;" "Two Governments—One China," etc.

Meanwhile, the government expanded its overseas lobbying efforts and unofficial contacts encouraging other nations which do not recognize it to adopt the American or the Japanese formula. The campaign met with some success, as West Germany, France, the Netherlands, and Singapore all opened new trade offices in Taipei; and the ROC itself maintained commercial links with more than 140 nations. In fact, the Dutch government in 1980 approved a US$500 million deal with Taiwan, including the sale of two submarines and a nuclear power station, in spite of Peking's strong protests.

The government further moved to strengthen its formal ties with the remaining 22 nations, with the Republic of Nauru added to this small list on May 4, 1980. Premier U. S. Sun paid a state visit to Saudi Arabia in September, 1979, to insure the continuity of the oil supply. The ROC also provided the Saudis with agricultural, industrial, and medical assistance. Again, in March, 1980 the Premier was in South Africa, Malawi, Lesotho and Swaziland for a two-week official visit.

In May, 1980, Foreign Minister Chu Fu-sung also made a tour of Central America, visiting Guatemala, Honduras, Costa Rica, Panama, the Dominican Republic, and Haiti. The ROC's trade with Latin American countries rose 28.2 percent in 1979 over the previous year, to reach US$815,293,000.

But there were limitations to Taiwan's flexibility. The ROC has flatly rejected Peking's proposals for the establishment of air, postal, commercial and travel links, and has never forsaken its goal of defeating Communism.

NOTES

1. Dept. of State Policy Information Paper—Formosa. Special Guidance No. 28 (Dec. 23, 1949)

2. General Assembly, *Official Records*, 4th Session, A/1215, p. 234

3. "U.S. Foreign Policy in Asia" Study No. 5, *United States Foreign Policy: Compilation of Studies*, 87C1, S. Document 24, (Washington D.C.), p. 527, p. 535, 539

4. Quoted in Hungdah Chiu, ed. *China and the Taiwan Issue*, (New York, Praeger Publishers, 1979), p. 182

5. *Time*, May 28, 1979, p. 10

The following 10 selections, presented here in chronological order, were chosen for the purpose of illustrating the opportunities and problems encountered by the ROC during the past 30 years in foreign relations.

The first three selections highlight the country's struggle for survival and security during its first decade as illustrated by the fight in the United Nations (Selection #1), the conclusion of the peace treaty with Japan (#2), and the mutual security pact with the United States (#3).

The next three selections illustrates the ROC's confidence during the second decade from 1960 to 1970, as exemplified by a treaty with Niger (#4), a speech by President Chiang Kai-shek (#5), and a pro-ROC "lobby" at work in the United States (#6).

Finally, there are four selections which demonstrate the complexity and dramatic changes during the final decade from 1970 to 1980. Thomas Bellow's article introduces to the reader the changes adopted by the ROC (#7); and the article by Wei discusses some of Taiwan's options (#8). Also included are two official statements by President Chiang Ching-kuo and Premier Sun Yun-suan (#9); and, Victor Li's outline for future dilemmas (#10).

1. The Questions of Chinese Representation in The United Nations

[The problem of the representation of China in the United Nations began on November 18, 1949 when the newly established Central People's Government of the PRC requested that the United Nations immediately deprive the ROC delegation of the right to represent China in the United Nations; and the question was not resolved until 1971 in favor of the PRC. The following analysis, made by a study group of the Chinese Institute of International Affairs in Taipei, Taiwan, presents the views of the ROC.]

On 1 October 1949, the Chinese Communist party set up the Central People's Government of the People's Republic of China, to which the Soviet Union accorded recognition two days later. On 10 January 1950, at a meeting of the Security Council, the Soviet representative for the first time raised the question of Chinese representation in the United Nations and challenged the right of the Chinese representative, Dr. Tingfu Tsiang, to represent China. On 13 January the Security Council rejected the Soviet demand. Thereupon the Soviet representative, Mr. Y. A. Malik, walked out of the Security Council, stating that the USSR would not return until "the representative of the Kuomintang group . . . has been removed . . ." and that the USSR would not recognize decisions of the Security Council adopted with the participation of the delegate of Nationalist China. This began the seven-month Soviet boycott of United Nations organs. On 25 June 1950 North Korean forces invaded South Korea. On 27 June the Security Council recommended that the members of the United Nations aid South Korea to repel that attack. Had the Soviet representative been present at the meeting, he would certainly have vetoed this historic decision of the Security Council.

Chinese Institute of International Affairs, *China and the United Nations* (New York: Carnegie Endowment for International Peace, 1959), pp. 252-258. Footnotes omitted.

From this time on, the question of Chinese representation has been raised in all United Nations organs of which China is a member and at every session of the General Assembly. Up to the time of writing, the attempt to exclude representatives of the Republic of China from United Nations organs has utterly failed.

In the following pages the principal arguments that have been advanced for and against the seating of representatives of the Chinese Communist regime will be discussed.

Strange to say, Mr. Trygve Lie, then Secretary-General of the United Nations, was among the first to put forward a juridical argument in favor of seating the Chinese Communists. In February 1950 Mr. Lie circulated to various members of the Security Council a confidential memorandum on the legal aspects of the problem of representation in the United Nations. Some of the points contained therein have been and are still being used as a basis for arguments in favor of seating the Chinese Communists in the United Nations. The basic argument, in brief, is that when a new government exercises effective authority within the territory of the state and is habitually obeyed by the bulk of the population, the United Nations organs should accord such a government the right to represent the state in the organization, even though individual members of the organization may refuse to accord it recognition as the lawful government. According to Mr. Lie himself, he told President Truman that the China issue had to be solved on a basis that recognized the realities. Years after Mr. Lie's departure from the United Nations scene, the same argument is still being advanced. Recently one Asian delegate told the United Nations General Assembly that those who were opposed to the seating of representatives of mainland China shut their eyes to the historical changes in China and were acting unrealistically.

Political realism has been a pet argument in support of the seating of the Chinese Communists. In the words of the representative of one of the countries behind the Iron Curtain:

> A most important factor in the political development of Asia, and not only of Asia, is the establishment and consolidation of the People's Republic of China, a great Power representing a people 600 million strong. With a population which is thus double that of the United States, the United Kingdom and France combined with 10 million square kilometres of territory, an area equal to that of the whole of Europe, China is one of the greatest countries in the world. Not a single important political problem of our time, particularly where Asia and the Far East are concerned, can be solved without taking into account the interests of the People's Republic of China and without the participation of its representatives.

The principle of universality of United Nations membership has also repeatedly been brought into the discussion. Those who favor the seating of delegations representing the Peiping regime point out that there are both Communist and anti-Communist countries in the organization. From the outset the United Nations has included members having different political, social, and economic systems and ideologies. They see no reason why Communist China should be excluded.

Finally, there is the argument that the authority and effectiveness of the United Nations suffer considerably from the fact that representatives of the Chinese People's Republic are not allowed to take part in the making of decisions. It is emphasized that, in the absence of representatives of a government ruling almost one fourth of the population of the whole world, the organs of the United Nations are unable successfully to perform the tasks assigned to them in carrying out the purposes of the Charter.

But the majority of the United Nations membership is still strongly opposed to the seating of Chinese Communists or in favor of postponing discussion of the issue. The United States government has taken a strong lead in opposing the admission of Chinese Communists. The United States representative, Mr. Henry Cabot Lodge, Jr., declared in the General Assembly: "To admit the Chinese Communists would stultify the United Nations and thus destroy the usefulness of the organization." In these words he echoed a statement by Secretary of State John Foster Dulles at San Francisco on 28 June 1957 that the recognition by the United States of Communist China would make it probable that the Communist regime would obtain China's United Nations seat. That would not be in the interest either of the United States or of the United Nations.

The United States stand is widely shared and supported by members of the United Nations. One of the most respected representatives to the organization—Mr. Victor Belaunde—expressed the feeling of many of his colleagues when he addressed the General Assembly in these words:

We cannot forget that the Government of Communist China has been condemned by this Assembly for open aggression. In that clear and flagrant case of aggression, when the Assembly attempted to use its good offices and to establish, in conformity with a legal principle which we are proud to believe originated on the American Continent, a return to the *status quo*, the army, with the support of the Chinese volunteers, for which the Government of Communist China was fully responsible, far from respecting the Assembly's call for a ceasefire and a return to the *status quo*, rejected the Assembly's proposal, which we adopted in the full exercise of our rights and the full support of world opinion. That Government was therefore justly condemned for aggression.

The consequences of the aggression have not yet been repaired; Korea remains divided. There was similar action in Viet-Nam and that country remains divided. What gestures has Communist China made towards respect for the principles which the United Nations justly upheld and applied? What signs of repentance—for one can speak of repentance in the case of nations just as one can in the case of individuals— what tokens of at least objective reparation, of a change of attitude, of adaptation to the mentality, the goals and the spirit of the United Nations Charter has Communist China given us to justify a change in our attitude?

As votes indicate, a substantial majority of delegations has been in favor of postponing discussion on the question of Chinese representation, and these delegations regard the debate as purely procedural. The United Kingdom and Australia, for example, take the position that on this subject opposing views are so strongly held that discussion could greatly increase international tension and would not contribute to a solution. Delegations that support the motion for postponing discussion are generally anxious to dispose of the item as quickly as possible; and they make only terse and curt statements or remain silent. This has not, however, prevented the Soviet bloc or other delegations friendly to the Peiping regime from entering into the substance of the question or advancing political arguments in support of seating the Chinese Communists.

The main arguments in support of seating the Chinese Communists are that the regime has *de facto* control of mainland China, that exclusion of Communist China is contrary to the principle of universality, and that the absence of the voice of one quarter of the earth's people on a huge land mass profoundly affects the ability to deal realistically with and settle all major world problems.

China's representatives do not agree or accept the thesis that the regime in Peiping enjoys any reasonable prospect of permanency or commands the obedience of the mass of the population. The regime came to power through treachery and with the active assistance of a foreign power, and has been maintained by tyranny and terror. At the Assembly's twelfth session, Dr. Hu Shih, speaking in plenary meeting, said that the student unrest, protests, and riots and the tremendous volume of outspoken criticism against the regime are also clear and unmistakable evidence to prove that the Chinese Communist regime, which has had eight years of military and political control of the Chinese mainland, is as unstable and as shaky as was the Hungarian regime under Rakosi and Gero.

Representatives in favor of seating Communist China talk glibly of the mainland having either 475 million or 600 million inhabitants and accuse the West of lack of realism in trying to solve important political problems without the participation of one fourth of the world's population. The assumption is that the regime has the loyal support of the mainland's entire population and could represent its views on most political problems. The assumption is not warranted by facts. If we have any respect for the principle of "the consent of the governed," a small minority of Communists cannot be regarded to have the right to represent the political views of 450 million people. In the light of these facts, any person who still insists that the Peiping regime represents the voice and the vote of one quarter of the earth's population is shutting his eyes to political realities.

The Peiping regime is not only non-Chinese in origin; it is also non-Chinese in its nature. This is because Communism is an alien ideology, contrary to Chinese character, tradition and moral values; and indeed contrary to everything the Chinese people stand for. This basic fact makes the regime unpopular, unstable and precarious. The Chinese representative reminded the thirteenth General Assembly that at the end of the Korean War, fourteen thousand Chinese prisoners of war, or about 75 percent of the total, elected to leave their families and friends behind on the mainland and to go to Free China and Taiwan. "This is" declared the Chinese representative, "a sure indication of the true wishes of the Chinese people." Since 1949 vast numbers of Chinese people have fled the country for Taiwan or refugee camps in Hong Kong. They represent a cross section of the Chinese population: students, small traders, professional men, artisans, peasant workers and even a sprinkling of deserters from the Communist army.

The principle of universality has been frequently invoked in support of the seating of the Chinese Communists. One representative expressed the hope that before long all nations would be brought into the United Nations so that it might become a strong force for peace and goodness in the world. A careful study of the Charter will show that it advocates neither universality nor exclusiveness. When every potential member becomes truly peace-loving, one of the preconditions for an organization which will one day embrace all nations in the world and thereby fulfill the eminently desirable principle of universality will have been satisfied.

The true meaning of universality consists, however, not of a mechanical counting of heads. It must be a fellowhip of kindred minds and spirits sharing the same fears, hopes, and aims. If this dream should came true, the United Nations would be able to include in its membership every nation on earth. But if this great assemblage persists in incessant quarrel and endless recrimination, engendering bitterness, hatred, and wars, it will remain a house divided against itself. A United Nations that embraces all peoples, but is not imbued with a co-operative and peace-loving spirit, can lay no claim to the principle of universality.

2. Treaty of Peace Between the Republic of China and Japan

[The ROC was one of the first nations to declare war on Japan and fought the longest among allies against Japanese aggression (1937–1945). However, it was not invited to participate in the San Francisco Peace Conference on Japan, on September 8, 1951, because China became a divided nation with the mainland occupied by the Chinese Communists under a new government. However, under Article 2 of that Treaty, Japan renounced all right, title and claim to Taiwan and the Pescadores, or Penghu. In February, 1952, the ROC and Japan began to negotiate a bilateral peace treaty, which, with its accompanying notes and other documents, was signed on April 28, 1952. On August 5 of the same year this new peace treaty came into force.]

The state of war between the Republic of China and Japan is terminated as from the date on which the present Treaty enters into force.

United Nations Treaty Series, Vol. 138, pp. 38, 40, 42, 46, 48, 50 and 52.

Article II

It is recognized that under Article 2 of the Treaty of Peace with Japan signed at the city of San Francisco in the United States of America on September 8, 1951 (hereinafter referred to as the San Francisco Treaty), Japan has renounced all right, title and claim to Taiwan and the Paracel Islands.

Article III

The disposition of property of Japan and of its nationals in Taiwan (Formosa) and Penghu (the Pescadores), and their claims, including debts, against the authorities of the Republic of China in Taiwan (Formosa) and Penghu (the Pescadores) and the residents thereof, and the disposition in Japan of property of such authorites and residents and their claims, including debts, against Japan and its nationals, shall be the subject of special arrangements between the Government of the Republic of China and the Government of Japan. The terms nationals and residents whenever used in the present Treaty include juridical persons.

Article IV

It is recognized that all treaties, conventions and agreements concluded before December 9, 1941, between China and Japan have become null and void as a consequence of the war.

Article X

For the purposes of the present Treaty, nationals of the Republic of China shall be deemed to include all the inhabitants and former inhabitants of Taiwan (Formosa) and Penghu (the Pescadores) and their descendants who are of the Chinese nationality in accordance with the laws and regulations which have been or may hereafter be enforced by the Republic of China in Taiwan (Formosa) and Penghu (the Pescadores); and juridical persons of the Republic of China shall be deemed to include all those registered under the laws and regulations which have been or may hereafter be enforced by the Republic of China in Taiwan (Formosa) and Penghu (the Pescadores).

Protocol

At the moment of signing this day the Treaty of Peace between the Republic of China and Japan (hereinafter referred to as the present Treaty), the undersigned Plenipotentiaries have agreed upon the following terms which shall constitute an integral part of the present Treaty:

2. The commerce and navigation between the Republic of China and Japan shall be governed by the following Arrangements:

(d) In the application of the present Arrangements, it is understood:

(i) that vessels of the Republic of China shall be deemed to include all those registered under the laws and regulations which have been or may hereafter be enforced by the Republic of China in Taiwan (Formosa) and Penghu (the Pescadores); and products of the Republic of China shall be deemed to include all those originating in Taiwan (Formosa) and Penghu (the Pescadores); and

The Arrangements set forth in this paragraph shall remain in force for a period of one year as from the date on which the present Treaty enters into force.

Exchange of Notes

(I) Note from the Japanese Plenipotentiary to the Chinese Plenipotentiary No. 1.

Taipei, April 28, 1952

Excellency,

In regard to the Treaty of Peace between Japan and the Republic of China signed this day, I have the honor to refer, on behalf of my Government, to the understanding reached between us that the terms of the present Treaty shall, in respect of the Republic of China, be applicable to all the territories which are now, or which may hereafter be, under the control of its Government.

I shall be appreciative, if you will confirm the understanding set forth above.

I avail myself of this opportunity to convey to Your Excellency the assurance of my highest consideration.

(signed) Isao Kawada

His Excellency
      Monsieur Yeh Kung Chao,
      Plenipotentiary of the Republic of China

(II) Note from the Chinese Plenipotentiary to the Japanese Plenipotentiary No. 1.

                                                                Taipei, April 28, 1952
Excellency,
      In connection with the Treaty of Peace between the Republic of China and Japan signed
this day, I have the honor to acknowledge receipt of Your Excellency's Note of to-day's date
reading as follows:
                              [Text of Japanese note]
      I have the honor to confirm, on behalf of my Government, the understanding set forth in
Your Excellency's Note under reply.
      I avail myself of this opportunity to convey to Your Excellency the assurance of my
highest consideration.
                                                                (signed) Yeh Kung Chao

His Excellency
      Mr. Isao Kawada,
      Plenipotentiary of Japan

                        Agreed   Minutes
                              I

Chinese Delegate:
      It is my understanding that the expression "or which may hereafter be" in the Notes No. 1
exchanged to-day can be taken to mean "and which may hereafter be." Is it so?

Japanese Delegate:
      Yes, it is so. I assure you that the Treaty is applicable to all the territories under the control
of the Government of the Republic of China.
                                                                (signed) Yeh Kung Chao
                                                                (signed) Isao Kawada

3. Mutual Defense Treaty between The United States and The Republic of China

[This was considered to be a major victory and the corner stone of the
ROC's foreign policy during the first decade, because it guaranteed
Taiwan's security from Communist aggression.

[The U.S. was first reluctant to enter into such a formal agreement for
fear of being dragged into a prolonged internal Chinese conflict, although
it had previously signed several defense treaties with the Philippines
(August 30, 1951), Japan (September 8, 1951), and Australia and New
Zealand (ANZUS Pact, September, 1951).

[However, after the Korean Armistice Agreement was signed on July,
1953, the PRC began to initiate pressure to "liberate" Taiwan, including
the deployment of large military forces opposite Quemoy & Matsu, two
offshore islands held by the ROC. Finally, on September 13, 1954, PRC
commenced artillery attacks on the offshore island of Quemoy. Against

this background the ROC applied intensive diplomatic and political pressure upon the U.S. for a formal guarantee of its security as finalized in the following treaty of December 8, 1954.

[As a concession to the United States, the ROC agreed, in a separate exchange of notes, that it would not use force against the Mainland (PRC) without "joint agreement" with the United States.

[This important Mutual Defense Treaty was approved for ratification by the U.S. Senate on February 9, 1955, and came into force on March 3, 1955, after instruments of ratification were exchanged. However, it must be noted that when President Carter announced the establishment of diplomatic relations with the PRC on December 15, 1978, he served notice on the termination of the Treaty a year from that date.]

The Parties to this Treaty,

Reaffirming their faith in the purposes and principles of the Charter of the United Nations and their desire to live in peace with all peoples and all Governments, and desiring to strengthen the fabric of peace in the West Pacific Area,

Recalling with mutual pride the relationship which brought their two peoples together in a common bond of sympathy and mutual ideals to fight side by side against imperialist aggression during the last war,

Desiring to declare publicly and formally their sense of unity and their common determination to defend themselves against external armed attack, so that no potential aggressor could be under the illusion that either of them stands alone in the West Pacific Area, and

Desiring further to strengthen their present efforts for collective defense for the preservation of peace and security pending the development of a more comprehensive system of regional security in the West Pacific Area,

Have agreed as follows:

Article I

The Parties undertake, as set forth in the Charter of the United Nations, to settle any international dispute in which they may be involved by peaceful means in such a manner that international peace, security and justice are not endangered and to refrain in their international relations from the threat or use of force in any manner inconsistent with the purposes of the United Nations.

Article II

In order more effectively to achieve the objective of this Treaty, the Parties separately and jointly by self-help and mutual aid will maintain and develop their individual and collective capacity to resist armed attack and communist subversive activities directed from without against their territorial integrity and political stability.

Article III

The Parties undertake to strengthen their free institutions and to cooperate with each other in the development of economic progress and social well-being and to further their individual and collective efforts toward these ends.

Article IV

The Parties, through their Foreign Ministers or their deputies, will consult together from time to time regarding the implementation of this Treaty.

Article V

Each Party recognizes that an armed attack in the West Pacific Area directed against the territories of either of the Parties would be dangerous to its own peace and safety and declares that it would act to meet the common danger in accordance with its constitutional processes.

Any such armed attack and all measures taken as a result thereof shall be immediately reported to the Security Council of the United Nations. Such measures shall be terminated when the Security Council has taken the measures necessary to restore and maintain international peace and security.

Article VI

For the purposes of Article II and V, the terms "territorial" and "territories" shall mean in respect of the Republic of China, Taiwan and the Pescadores; and in respect of the United States of America, the island territories in the West Pacific under its jurisdiction. The provisions of Articles II and V will be applicable to such other territories as may be determined by mutual agreement.

Article VII

The Government of the Republic of China grants, and the Government of the United States of America accepts, the right to dispose such United States land, air and sea forces in and about Taiwan and the Pescadores as may be required for their defense, as determined by mutual agreement.

Article VIII

This Treaty does not affect and shall not be interpreted as affecting in any way the rights and obligations to the Parties under the Charter of the United Nations or the responsibility of the United Nations for the maintenance of international peace and security.

Article IX

This Treaty shall be ratified by the Republic of China and the United States of America in accordance with their respective constitutional processes and will come into force when instruments of ratification thereof have been exchanged by them at Taipei.

Article X

This Treaty shall remain in force indefinitely. Either Party may terminate it one year after notice has been given to the other party.

IN WITNESS WHEREOF, The Undersigned Plenipotentiaries have signed this Treaty.

DONE in duplicate, the Chinese and English languages, at Washington on this Second day of the Twelfth month of the Forty-third Year of the Republic of China, corresponding to the Second day of December of the Year One Thousand Nine Hundred and Fifty-four.

> For the Republic of China:
> (signed) George K. C. Yeh
> For the United States of America:
> (signed) John Foster Dulles

Exchange of Notes

I

The Secretary of State to the Chinese Minister
of Foreign Affairs
Department of State
Washington

December 10, 1954

Excellency:

I have the honor to refer to recent conversations between representatives of our two Governments and to confirm the understandings reached as a result of those conversations, as follows:

The Republic of China effectively controls both the territory described in Article VI of the Treaty of Mutual Defense between the Republic of China and the United States of America signed on December 2, 1954, at Washington and other territory. It possesses with respect to all territory now and hereafter under its control the inherent right of self-defense. In view of the obligations of the two Parties under the said Treaty and of the fact that the use of force from either of these areas by either of the Parties affects the other, it is agreed that such use of force will be a matter of joint agreement, subject to action of an emergency character which is clearly an exercise of the inherent right of self-defense. Military elements which are a product of joint effort and contribution by the two Parties will not be removed from the territories described in Article VI to a degree which would substantially diminish the defensibility of such territories without mutual agreement.

Accept, Excellency, the assurances of my highest consideration.

John Foster Dulles
Secretary of State of the United States of America

His Excellency George K. C. Yeh
Minister of Foreign Affairs of the Republic of China

II

December 10, 1954

Excellency:

I have the honor to acknowledge the receipt of Your Excellency's Note of today's date, which reads as follows:

[See note I]

I have the honor to confirm, on behalf of my Government, the understanding set forth in Your Excellency's Note under reply.

I avai' myself of this opportunity to convey to Your Excellency the assurances of my highest consideration.

George K. C. Yeh
Minister for Foreign Affairs
of the Republic of China

His Excellency John Foster Dulles
Secretary of State of the United States of America

4. Agreement for Economic and Technical Cooperation between The Republic of China and The Republic of Niger

[The ROC expanded its foreign relations during the second decade, from 1960 to 1970, because of the rapid growth of the Taiwan economy. It began to broaden its international support and cooperation. For example, the ROC began to render economic and technical assistance to other developing nations in Africa and Latin America, and extended it to some 40 countries by the end of the decade.

[The following agreement, signed by the ROC and the Republic of Niger on 1962, offers an example of the types of assistance rendered by the ROC during this decade.]

The Government of the Repulic of China and the Government of the Republic of Niger, desirous to maintaining and strengthening the friendly relations between the two countries and their peoples,

Considering that the encouragement of international economic cooperation by the two Governments is in the common interest of the two countries,

China Yearbook, 1963–1964, pp. 901–902.

Recognizing that such cooperation is advantageous to the two Contracting Parties,
Have agreed as follows:

Article 1. The Government of the Republic of China and the Government of the Republic of Niger shall, as equals, provide mutual help and cooperation in economic and technical fields.

Based upon this Agreement, the two Contracting Parties shall conclude specific protocols pertaining to certain projects within the scope of economic and technical cooperation.

Article 2. With a view to realizing the objectives of this Agreement, the Government of the Republic of China shall engage to:

a. Help training of Niger technical personnel;
b. Dispatch experts to Niger for certain projects;
c. Help Niger establish companies and enterprises of national interest within the scope of economic development plans.

Article 3. The Government of the Republic of Niger shall engage to:

a. Assure the experts and other personnel of Technical Assistance of the Republic of China dispatched to Niger of living conditions that will enable them accomplish their mission;
b. Assure the same living conditions to their families;
c. Provide them with furnished accommodations and ensure maintenance;
d. Support occasional traveling expenses of the experts and personnel of Technical Assistance necessary for their activities within the domain of Niger.

Article 4. The Government of the Republic of Niger shall assure the experts and other personnel of Technical Assistance of the Republic of China dispatched to Niger guarantees similar to those given to the members of the international technical assistance missions.

Article 5. The two Parties shall, within the extent of this Agreement, provide reciprocal information on the training and working programs concerned with execution of economic and technical cooperation.

Article 6. The present Agreement shall come into force on the date of signature by the two Parties and shall remain valid for a period of one year.

This Agreement shall automatically continue in force for another period of one year, unless either of the Contracting Parties expresses its intention to terminate the present Agreement four months prior to the date of expiration.

DONE at Taipei, on this Tenth day of the Eleventh month of the Fifty-first year of the Republic of China corresponding to the Tenth Day of November in the Year One Thousand Nine Hundred and Sixty-Two, in the Chinese and French languages, two texts equally authentic.

For the Government
of the Republic of China

SHEN Chang-huan

Minister of Foreign Affairs

For the Government
of the Republic of Niger

Yacouba DJIBO

Minister of the Rural Economy

PROTOCOL

For the enforcement of the provisions set forth in Article 2 of the Agreement for Economic and Technical Cooperation concluded at Taipei on November 10, 1962, between the Republic of China and the Republic of Niger, the Government of the Republic of China shall engage to:

a. Train Niger technicians in Chinese agricultural techniques, on the understanding that the number of trainees and the program of training shall be determined by the Government of the Republic of China with the consent of the Government of Niger.

b. Dispatch, in the immediate future, a mission of agricultural experts to the Republic of

Niger with a view to conducting a survey of agricultural conditions in general and the possibilities for cultivation of rice and sugar cane in particular.

c. Dispatch, upon recommendation of this Mission, an agricultural demonstration team to the Republic of Niger for experimentation in the cultivation of rice, fruit and sugar cane, the details of which shall be negotiated later.

d. Bear the round-trip expenses of the Niger trainees in China as well as those of the Mission and the Team to Niger, and also the salary of the members of the Mission and the Team during their service in Niger.

This Protocol shall come into force on the day of signature by the two Parties.

DONE at Taipei, on this Tenth day of the Eleventh month of the Fifty-first year of the Republic of China corresponding to the Tenth day of November in the year One Thousand Nine Hundred and Sixty-Two, in the Chinese and French languages, two texts equally authentic.

For the Government
of the Republic of China

SHEN Chang-huan

Minister of Foreign Affairs

For the Government
of the Republic of Niger

Yacouba DJIBO

Minister of the Rural Economy

5. Double Ten Message

Chiang Kai-Shek

[The history of the ROC is clearly inseparable from the personal history of its leader Chiang Kai-shek (1886–1975), who had led the early revolution against the warlords in the 1920s, and in the national resistance against Japanese aggression in the 1930s and 1940s. After the Communist take-over on the mainland and the retreat of the ROC Government to Taiwan, he regenerated his forces and held on to his unfailing hope of recovering the mainland of China.

[The following message, which Chiang delivered on October 10, 1963, illustrate his faith and sense of mission.]

My Fellow Countrymen:

As we commemorate today the 52nd anniversary of the founding of the Republic of China, the whole world is undergoing unprecedented changes that may determine whether mankind is to survive or perish. This is especially true for the Chinese people who, after five thousand years of historical and culture vicissitudes, have reached a turning point. It is going to be an era of renaissance for the Republic of China.

China Yearbook, 1963–1964, pp. 911-915.

By their long dedication, the father of our republic, Dr. Sun Yat-sen, and our revolutionary martyrs, had started our country on the path of the Three Principles of the People. For the past 51 years, we have endeavored to carry on their task not only to meet the tests of the times, but also to accept the responsibilities and duties inherent in our beliefs.

Our people's protracted revolutionary fight against Communism and aggression has enhanced the confidence of the free world in its own future. All those shut behind the Iron Curtain have derived courage in their struggle for righteousness and freedom from the example set by our mainland compatriots who have been pressing on in their determined resistance to the Communist regime.

Day and night our compatriots are engaged in ceaseless acts of direct and indirect resistance against the Communists both at the border and in the hinterland. These involve the use of explosives, the laying of ambushes and sabotage. All such undertakings have unnerved Mao Tse-tung and haunted him in his waking hours. He knows that the situation is totally hopeless for him and his regime.

Meanwhile, our forces have continued to reach the Chinese mainland by air and by sea to harass the enemy both at the front and in the rear. There is no way for the Communists to prevent such assaults as people on the mainland give cover and support to our forces the moment they land in their midst. The cooperation between our military forces and the civilians on the mainland, and between our revolutionary forces and the freedom fighters on the mainland, is creating a new opportunity in our efforts for national recovery.

My fellow countrymen: Faith is the foundation of our national restoration. Patience assures us of success in our revolution. We should remember that Dr. Sun Yat-sen and our revolutionary martyrs, despite 10 abortive attempts, finally succeeded in the Wuchang Uprising in 1911. This was followed by successes of the East River campaign to secure our revolutionary base in South China, the Northward Expedition to achieve national unification, the repeated drives to free the Central China provinces of Communists, and finally the war of resistance against Japanese aggression.

Our war of resistance lasted for 14 years. Now it has been another 14 years since the fall of the mainland. Thus it can be truthfully said that our righteous war against aggression and slavery has been going on for 32 years. During the lengthy period of time, our people have suffered immensely from massacres, bombings, privations, loss of dear ones, and damage to property. The persecution, starvation, and agonies experienced by the mainland people in recent years are without historical precedent. The over-all cause of this catastrophe was foreign aggression which began with the Mukden Incident. If it had not been for the Mukden Incident, the Chinese mainland would not have fallen and there would be no Communist threat to other Asian nations. Yet the people on the mainland have not ceased in their anti-Communist resistance. On the contrary, they are fighting with renewed courage and increased effectiveness.

My Fellow Countrymen: It is the reserve of Chinese resilience and toughness which has made possible for our people to survive the tests of the last 32 years. It is the same self-confidence, revolutionary patience, progressive spirit, and epic courage which has enabled our people to withstand the trails of such tragic experience. If a persevering people such as ours, resolutely opposed to depotism and standing firmly for independence, should fail to survive, to win freedom, and to achieve final victory, righteousness would disappear from the world and civilization itself would be doomed.

History bears ample witness to the fact that a revolutionary war fought for righteousness, justice, freedom, against tyranny and in answer to the unanimous wish of a people for survival and freedom, cannot fail. It has been so in the past and it will be so in the future.

Our counter-offensive and national recovery, therefore, is not a case of wishful thinking, but the consensus of aspirations burning in the hearts of our 600 million compatriots. Neither jibes nor jeers can dampen our spirit or weaken our resolve. They can only stimulate us to more determined action and goad us to move forward faster to earlier victory. One can not prove one's faith until he is tested. One can not prove his preseverance until he is tried. Similarly, light is appreciated only when it is in contrast to darkness.

Today the Chinese Communists are deeply mired in contradictions. Those outside the party oppose Communism while those inside it oppose Mao Tse-tung. Meanwhile, there are quarrels at the top and popular grievances at the bottom. There are also contradictions between those loyal to Khrushchev and others loyal to Mao Tse-tung, between the majority and the minority factions, and between the "Marxist-Leninist rebels," and the "disguised banner-bearers of Trotskyites." The whole situation is simply one of putridness. Furthermore, Mao has become so demented as to say that he would not hesitate to sacrifice 300 million of the mainland's people and half of the world's 2.7 billion population "to build a future upon the ruins of death." Can we allow such a lunatic and such a traitorous regime to persevere and do unending harm to the world and put into practice its monstrous ideas? Can the mainland people wait for a "posthumous freedom" built on the bodies of the hundreds of millions who would have died?

On our shoulders lies the heavy responsibility of delivering our compatriots, recovering the mainland, and destroying the Chinese Communist regime, that scourge of mankind. The desire to accept this responsibility is deeply engraved in the hearts of all our compatriots. Now the goal is not far to reach. Though some people abroad maintain that no important change will come to the Chinese Communist regime in the next three to five years, we firmly believe that both subjective and objective conditions for our return to the mainland are ripening so fast that we do not have to wait that long before we can bury Mao's regime.

Admittedly the world situation today is complicated and unpredictable and the revolutionary path is seldom smooth. In other words, it may not be possible for us to attain our goal in one leap. But the return to the mainland is what all of our people, military and civilian, at home and abroad, are awaiting. If we are united in deed and thought, and if we strive unceasingly, we shall reach our objective of national recovery in the near future.

Today I want to call upon all of you further to cultivate the traditional Chinese virtues of righteousness, perseverance, self-sacrifice, and compassion. Only thus can we triumph over adversities, attain justice, preserve freedom and insure survival. Only thus can we be equal to the responsibility of safeguarding peace and security for Asia and the world. In this spirit of humility which would preclude impulsiveness and imprudence we rededicate ourselves to the determined fight aginst Communism and its evils; to the destruction of the Mao Tse-tung regime; to the recovery of the mainland; and to the liberation of our enslaved compatriot. Such determination dominates our minds. Nothing else matters in our hearts.

My Fellow Countrymen: Some people in the free world have been mentally poisoned into believing that Mao Tse-tung can be influenced and changed, and that his regime can be persuaded to coexist with the free world. They believe they need not buy his principles but they can make a profit from training with him.

But they have failed to realize these points:

—If Khrushchev himself cannot exercise any corrective influence on the "adventurism" and "monstrous mentality" of Mao Tse-tung, how can others stay Mao's hand and escape the fate of "being baked in a thermo-nuclear war"?

—If Khrushchev cannot coexist with Mao on a father-son party basis, and has had to tear up hundreds of agreements he had signed with Mao, how can others hope to negotiate successfully with Mao on such matters as test ban and disarmament?

—If Khrushchev himself cannot settle old accounts with and collect bad debts from the "poorest and least developed" Communist-controlled Chinese mainland, how can others put their foot in the door and establish trade ties with Mao while Moscow is engaged in a bitter struggle with Peiping? This would be more than buying Communism at a higher price. It would be falling into the Communist trap, providing excellent opportunities for infiltration and subversion and inviting an obvious but endless disaster. Anyone doing so would be gambling with the future welfare of his nation and people.

This is to say that anyone who gives the Chinese Communists a chance to struggle for survival, to catch a second breath, or to bind up their wounds—in other words, anyone who does the enemy's bidding—will be making a direct investment in Mao Tse-tung's plan to sacrifice half of the world's 2.7 billion inhabitants. This is a fact which no Asian leaders, especially those of countries at the periphery of the Chinese mainland, can safely ignore or take lightly.

My Fellow Countrymen: We Chinese people have always based our conduct on compassion and benevolence, and have always regarded the safeguarding of human life, freedom, and justice as our own duty. We have never wanted to see a global war, much less a nuclear war. To us recovery of the mainland is a sacred mission and to end Communist aggression in Asia is to remove the danger of a nuclear war. It is our duty to launch a punitive expedition against the rebels, to deliver our compatriots from tyranny, and to recover the mainland. As this is our internal war against the Communist rebels, we need not, and will not, involve other nations.

From our revolutionary martyrs we have inherited not only their spirit but their traditions. Dr. Sun Yat-sen told us that "the Three Principles of the People provided the basic tenets for the revolutionary movement in China. A revolution based on these principles is the only course for the revolutionary movement in China." Thus a revolution for the realization of the Three Principles of the People is the only way for our people to obliterate the bane of mainland Communism.

My Fellow Countrymen: Success in the restoration and reunification of the nation can come only if we put our principles into practice. We should all be firm in our faith, and act according to our beliefs. This is the way to discharge our duty toward our nation and toward our principles. Our principles, our country, and our duty constitute the spiritual standards for all six hundred million Chinese people to observe. It is incumbent upon every Chinese to participate in, and support the national revolutionary movement based on the Three Principles of the people! Everyone has the right to participate in the counteroffensive and national recovery. This is especially true with our mainland compatriots, who are duty-bound to take part in anti-Communist activities and to provide cover for the freedom-fighters.

My Fellow Countrymen: The time to begin counter-offensive action may now come at any minute. Every bit of territory on the mainland provides a battle-field for our assault forces landing there either by sea or by air, and also for the freedom-fighters in popular uprisings in the enemy's rear. Our aim is to liberate every single compatriot on the mainland. All Communist soldiers and cadres who have realized their mistakes could become our comrades-at-arms by turning against Mao's regime.

As long as we all maintain the noble revolutionary spirit characteristic of our people, remain united in spirit and singular in purpose, and mobilize our resources for the sake of our national task, we shall be able to destroy the enemy's morale and overpower him with both frontal and flank attacks, thus shortening the duration of our war of liberation.

I have repeatedly called the attention of our people to the "Six Freedoms and Three Assurances," and the "Four Principles and Ten Pledges," which are solemn promises we shall fulfill without fail in the course of our supreme effort for mainland recovery.

My Fellow Countrymen: Our revolutionary martyrs are silently blessing us. The people on the mainland are waiting for us. The future of the free world, and especially Asia, will hinge upon our action for national recovery.

Today we dedicate the immense task of our national recovery to the cause of peace for mankind!

Let the Three Principles of the People, as bequeathed to us by Dr. Sun Yat-sen, light the way for the anti-Communist and freedom seeking world. Let all those who are enslaved and oppressed by the Communists be freed of their shackles to enjoy the blessings of a new era—liberty, equality, and welfare.

Now let us exclaim the cheers of the day:

Victory in our counter-offensive and mainland recovery!

Long live the Three Principles of the People!

Long live the Republic of China!

6. No Trade with the Enemy

Stanley D. Bachrack

[In the pursuit of its foreign policy objectives, the ROC had the help and support of a number of friends and organizations in the U.S., including "the Committee of One Million Against the Admission of Communist China to the United Nations." One Congressman in particular, Dr. Walter H. Judd, a former medical missionary in China, launched this group, which was joined by many other legislators. The Committee hired a New York public relations firm to solicit funds and popular support, and tried to exert its influence publicly and privately to support a favorable U.S. policy toward the ROC.

[The following excerpts provide an example of the Committee at work.]

Shortly after the presidential election and the General Assembly vote (postponing for another year consideration of the China seating question) the Committee got into print on another issue: the prospect of relaxation in the American trade embargo against the People's Republic. Responding to a declaration by the president of the U.S. Chamber of Commerce favoring resumption of trade in nonstrategic goods, Marvin Liebman released a statement warning against any expansion of trade. The whole front page of the Committee's fifth *Newsletter*, under the heading "Drive to Expand Red China Trade," dealt with the trade issue. The pro-recognition forces having "suffered a serious defeat" at the United Nations, "they have now embarked on a long-range program" (full trade relations with the mainland). This was "more dangerous than the overt drive to admit Red China to the UN because of its subtlety and because of the many well-known American individuals and organizations who favor such proposals." Named were the American Assembly and the U.S. Chamber of Commerce president. The article attacked the very concept of nonstrategic goods: "there are no goods which are nonstrategic to a nation dedicated to building up an aggressive military machine."

Trade would be taken on in earnest by the Committee in the spring of 1957, but its unfolding as a salient issue should be considered in the context of simultaneous developments bearing on Sino-American relations.

The sequence of events ran roughly as follows: When Secretary Dulles first was asked to comment on reports of possible changes in U.S. trade policies toward the Peking regime, he also was queried about the State Department's policy of denying American reporters travel access to the mainland. This issue mushroomed during the spring, understandably receiving considerable press attention, but the Committee apparently ignored it (insofar as can be determined) except for a fleeting mention in an important May memorandum to be considered below.

Then, on February 18, the chairman of the State Foreign Relations Committee, Senator Theodore Francis Green (D., R.I.), was quoted as saying that sooner or later the United States should recognize Red China: "We don't like their form of government, but the country is a great country and organized, and I do not myself see why we should recognize these other Communist countries and withhold recognition of China unless we are going to apply that to other Communist countries." Two days later, House Majority Leader John W. McCormack, the former steering committee member, inserted in the Appendix of the *Record* a long *Wall Street Journal* article which speculated that President Eisenhower might bow to pressure from various American allies and approve an easing of trade restrictions with the Communists.

In mid-March Secretary Dulles issued a statement on China policy from Canberry, Australia, where he was attending the third meeting of the Council of the Southeast Asia Treaty

Stanley D. Bachrack, *The Committee of One Million, "China Lobby" Politics,* 1953-1971 (New York: Columbia University Press, 1976), pp. 132-138. Footnotes omitted.

Organization. "The United States adheres steadfastly to the three main aspects of its China policy," the statement began, "which is to recognize the Republic of China; not to recognize the so-called People's Republic of China; and to oppose the seating of this People's Republic in the United Nations." Dulles said the policy was not merely "an expression of emotional dislike of Chinese communism," although this was "repugnant to us." Rather, the policy was based considerations both of national and international interest:

> United States diplomatic recognition of the Chinese Communist regime would serve no national purpose but would strengthen and encourage influences hostile to us and our allies and further imperil lands whose independence is related to our own peace and security . . .
> . . . We believe that United States policies are not merely in our own interest and in the interest of the free world but also that they are in the interest of the Chinese people themselves, with whom the American people have historic ties of friendship.

On the Senate floor two days after Dulles' statement, Committee supporter Senator Styles H. Bridges (R., N.H.), repudiated presidential assistant Meyer Kestnbaum for stating (March 7), then repeating (March 13), that the Chinese Communists should be recognized by the United States and admitted to the United Nations. "He said, of course, he was expressing his personal views," Bridges added, "but nevertheless, he is a presidential assistant and has this official capacity." Bridges, onetime New Hampshire governor, was troubled about a "Red China Lobby":

> Mr. President, at times in the past we have heard quite a good deal about the China lobby. Without going into the merits or demerits of such a so-called organization, it is quite clear that there now must be a Red China lobby operating in the United States and around the world. Various individuals have spoken but one of these individuals whose remarks I considered to be wholly out of place is Meyer Kestnbaum, as assistant to President Eisenhower . . .

On April 20, the State Department announced that the United States was prepared to discuss with the fourteen other allied nations participating in the multilateral trade control system certain modifications in the trade controls against Communist China and the Soviet bloc. In response to allied pressure on the issue, the statement said, modifications in certain items "for peaceful use" would be considered. Although these items would be removed from controls and given the status of similar items traded with the European Soviet bloc, "It was emphasized to our allies that there is no change in United States policy with respect to trade with Communist China. The United States will continue its unilateral embargo on all trade."

The Committee wasted no time. "The time has come," said a May 13 letter signed by the steering committee,

> when we must once again forcefully restate the opposition of the great majority of the American people to any deals with Red China . . .
> You will find attached a memorandum which presents the reasoning behind this point of view. It is, in substance, recognition of the dangers of appeasement and a refusal to join in strengthening the avowed enemies of our nation and the Free World.

Attached was a thirteen-page memorandum dated May 1957 entitled "Relations between the United States and Communist China." A later Committee pamphlet called this report a "scholarly paper," saying it was based on a "careful survey. . . of the strength and influence of pro-appeasement sentiment in the United States." Indeed, some passages in the polemic balanced the Committee's views against opposing arguments with uncharacteristic restraint (perhaps prompting former Ambassador Stanley K. Hornbeck to write Marvin Liebman that it was the best presentation of the situation and problem(s) he had seen anywhere.)

A "concerted effort" had gotten underway in the past few months, the paper began, "to convince the American people of the desirability of closer economic and diplomatic relations with Communist China." Pressures had reached "alarming proportions" since November; the new campaign seemed based primarily on two assumptions: because the

Communists firmly controlled the Chinese mainland there was nothing the United States or the "Free Chinese on Taiwan" could do to change the situation; because "Chinese Communism is somewhat different from that promoted by the Kremlin," the expansion of trade and cultural relations would "drive a wedge between the Kremlin and Peiping and perhaps even make a Tito out of Mao Tse-tung." These two assumptions were completely false, the document said. Comparing the current situation with the conditions of pre-World War II Europe and Asia, it claimed the lessons about "the fallacy of appeasement of tyranny" evidently had not been learned. Next, the paper took on "Some Advocates of This Point of View," hitting at several newly discovered targets: first, the reports of the American Assembly's November 1956 meeting at Harriman, N.Y., which had pondered the problem of "The United States and the Far East"; second, a speech on December 10, 1956, by Dr. John A. Mackay, at the National Council of Churches in Indianapolis; third, an article in the April 16, 1957, issue of *Look* magazine by Edmund Stevens, with photographs by Philip Harrington "(the two American newspapermen who recently toured Red China in defiance of the official policy of their Government)"; fourth, an article in the April 1957 *Atlantic* magazine entitled "China: Time For A Policy," by Professor John K. Fairbank; and fifth, a Foreign Policy Association pamphlet entitled "Should the United States Deal With Red China?" by Professor A. Doak Barnett. In essence, the memorandum came to the conclusion that the prestige of the People's Republic would be enhanced by any closer ties with the United States. The document's conclusion called for "strong counter measures" against "the campaign to condition the American people for a deal with Communist China," but did not specify what they should be. Considering the argument "that we must be 'realistic' and 'practical,'" the statement answered "that it is precisely because we must be realistic and practical that we must not recognize Red China or accept it into civilized society."

The "strong counter measures" began to unfold after the United Kingdom announced, on May 30, that the same restrictions on trade controls with the Soviet Union thereafter would be applied to the People's Republic. Official State Department reaction: ". . . most disappointed by this action." But the statement noted that security controls on strategic exports to Communist China would be continued on the same basis as then applied to the Soviet bloc.

Publicly, the Committee's response took the form of a full-page advertisement in the June 9 International Edition of the *New York Times,* distributed, in page proof, on June 6, with an accompanying brief memorandum from the steering committee.

The heading screamed **"An Appeal to All Free Men—No Trade with the Enemy,"** with the text following the arguments and sometimes the language of the long memorandum described above. The ad listed 224 "members"—95 representatives and 24 senators (including the regular legislative members of the steering committee, listed separately). On June 11, the steering committee released a statement to the American press opposing the lifting of trade restrictions.

Behind the scenes, the Committee worked quietly but energetically. On June 13, 1957, Liebman thanked Howard P. Jones, Deputy Assistant Secretary of State for Far Eastern Affairs, for seeing him and Treasurer McKee the previous day and enclosed a copy of both the June 9 advertisement and the May memorandum. Liebman said he had spoken to Mr. Harold Baynton of the Senate's Interstate and Foreign Commerce Committee about proposed trade hearings and had learned they would first be conducted as closed sessions beginning June 20, without a subcommittee to deal exclusively with Red China trade. The secretary then reminded the official that he was planning a trip, mainly to the Far East, and would like to discuss those areas on his itinerary where he might be of service. What type of service he did not elaborate. Several days before Marvin Liebman left on his world tour—in his official capacity, as he later would reveal, as the Committee's secretary—he wrote to President Eisenhower on behalf of the steering committee, enclosing a statement signed by 176 American business leaders. "We, the undersigned businessmen," it began, "hereby strongly express our opposition to any trade relations between our country and Communist China." Opposition was based on six points: 1) that the economy of Communist China would be strengthened; 2) trade relations would be the first step toward recognition and admission to the United Nations; 3) an economy based on free labor could not compete successfully in the world market with an economy based on slave labor; 4) Communist China was an avowed enemy of the United States "and the entire Free World"; 5) opening trade with the enemy would undermine America's allies' anti-Communist position and force them into the Communist orbit; and 6) trade with Communist China would have the same effect as did trade with the Axis Powers prior to World War II, building up the military power of the aggressor. "Just because some misguided nations are willing to make the same fatal mistakes of the past is no reason for the United States to follow suit in this road to national suicide."

Assistant to the President Sherman Adams responded to the Liebman letter on July 31, after the State Department had advised the White House that it "does not consider that a personal reply from the President is required. . . . However, *in view of the prominence of The Committee of One Million and of the signers to the statement transmitted by Mr. Liebman,* it is recommended that a reply be made by an appropriate member of the President's staff" (italics added). A suggested State Department reply, slightly revised, was sent by Adams:

> On behalf of the President, I would like to thank you for your recent letter and accompanying statement on trade relations with Communist China signed by one hundred and seventy-six leaders of the American business community.
>
> It is gratifying to receive this manifestation of support for the United States position on this vital subject.

7. Taiwan's Foreign Policy in the 1970s

Thomas J. Bellows

[The period of 1970 to 1980 was a decade of adaptation and consolidation for the ROC's foreign relations. It began with a series of diplomatic setbacks in the early 1970s, which included Canada's recognition of the PRC, the ROC's withdrawal from the United Nations, President Nixon's visit to Peking, and the danger of diplomatic isolation as many friendly nations began to switch sides.

[Professor Bellow's article describes how the ROC was able to meet the new challenges with fexibility and innovation in the early period in order to stablize the ROC's overall position.]

Unchanging Principles and Changing Strategy

The selection of President Chiang's eldest son, Chiang Ching-kuo, as Premier on May 16, 1972, signified important changes in the Taipei political scene, Within a few days, the popular Foreign Minister, Chou Shu-kai, was replaced by Shen Chang-huan. Ambassador Shen had served as Foreign Minister between 1960 and 1966 and immediately prior to his appointment was Ambassador to Thailand. A more cautious individual, he was less given to public comments. The new Foreign Minister at one time was the last President Chiang's interpreter and apparently is close to Madame Chiang.

Asian Survey, XVI, No. 7, (July, 1976); pp. 596–98; 599–601; 606–8. Copyright 1976 by The Regents of the University of California. Reprinted by permission of The Regents. Footnotes omitted.

TABLE 1: Countries Recognizing the People's Republic of China since October 24, 1971 (listed chronologically)

Belgium*	10/25/71	Chad*	11/28/72
Bhutan	10/25/71	Australia*	12/22/72
Peru*	11/02/71	New Zealand*	12/22/72
Ecuador*	11/09/71	Spain*	03/07/73
Lebanon*	11/09/71	Upper Volta*	09/15/73
Rwanda	11/12/71	Guinea Bissau	09/30/73
Iceland	12/14/71	Botswana*	03/25/74
Cyprus*	12/14/71	Malaysia	05/31/74
Malta*	01/31/72	Trinidad and Tobago*	06/20/74
Mexico*	02/14/72	Venezuela*	06/28/74
Argentina*	02/19/72	Niger*	07/16/74
Bahrain	04/10/72	Brazil*	08/15/74
Greece*	06/05/72	Grenada	10/10/74
Guyana	06/27/72	Gambia*	12/17/74
Japan*	09/29/72	Portugal	01/06/75
West Germany	10/11/72	Philippines*	06/09/75
Maldives	10/14/72	Thailand*	07/01/75
Gabon*	10/16/72	Bangladesh	10/04/75
Malagasy Republic*	11/06/72	Fiji	11/05/75
Luxembourg*	11/16/72	Comoro Islands	11/13/75
Jamaica*	11/21/72	Western Samoa*	11/13/75
Zaire*	11/24/72		

*Countries previously recognizing Republic of China.

For some time stories had been circulating that Taiwan was engaging in formal discussions with the Soviet Union and might expand relations to fill a vacuum should the Americans withdraw. On at least two occasions, an "unofficial" Soviet representatives visited Taiwan. Former American ambassador to Taiwan, Walter P. McConaughy, has publicly stated that in 1969 "a Soviet correspondent was allowed to visit Taiwan." Soviet correspondent and reputed KGB agent, Victor Louis, visited Taiwan in November 1971, and had informal talks with Foreign Minister Chou. Chou may have played a role in arranging for these visits and informally supported such contacts when talking to correspondents. Chou's replacement by Shen in 1972 was partly interpreted as a rejection of such policies at that time. There also were rumors and speculations that Taipei might enter into unofficial discusions with PRC officials. In order to end these speculations, Premier Chiang outlined four "unchangeable principles" of foreign policy to the Legislative Yuan on September 29, 1972. The unequivocally anti-Communist principles included "national recovery" of the mainland. The hard line in practice is implemented through a pragmatic strategy of survival and growth: 1) strengthen existing diplomatic relations; 2) encourage foreign trade and foreign investment in Taiwan; and 3) "all-out" diplomacy which stresses economic, technical, cultural and educational interaction with selected countries, regardless of whether or not the country officially recognizes the ROC.

During the 1970s, the ROC has emphasized strengthening diplomatic ties, cultural, and educational exchanges, and commercial relations such as trade and foreign investment, the latter not completely controlled by the official foreign policy institutions. This section analyzes those parts of Taiwan's global interactions which are entirely government controlled. The trend of official diplomatic relations has not favored Taiwan. Between 1963 and mid-1975, countries formally recognizing the ROC dropped from 66 to 26 while the number recognizing the PRC went from 50 to 112.

It is difficult to stop the current world trend toward recognition of Peking, but Taipei is making great efforts to reinforce existing relations and stablize the number of countries recognizing the ROC. This is a difficult objective. President Ferdinand Marcos of the Philippines visited the PRC in June 1975, and announced from Peking that as of that date diplomatic relations were established between the two countries. The joint communique stressed non-interference in each other's internal affairs. A trade agreement was signed the same day. Taipei worked diligently between Mrs. Marcos' ten-day visit to the PRC in September 1974 and the June announcement to dissuade the Philippines from recognizing Peking since ROC officials were convinced, correctly so, that Thailand would recognize Peking within a few days of the Philippine recognition. Thai recognition occurred on July 1, 1975, during a visit by Prime Minister Kukrit to Peking. Singapore may then, as its own leaders have predicted, be the last ASEAN nation to establish diplomatic relations with the PRC.

Continued American recognition is important if a respectable modicum of official diplomatic relationships is to be maintained. Premier Chiang recently enunciated what he regarded as the first practical objective of Taiwan's foreign policy: "We shall do our utmost to maintain bilateral relations with friendly countries and especially to strengthen our alliance with the U.S."

Taiwan opened two new consulates in the U.S. during 1973-74 (Atlanta and Kansas City) and reactivated the consulate in Portland. These offices publicize the ROC's political position and facilitate the expansion of commercial ties between the two countries. Official ROC policy for well over a year has been that Taiwan's favorable balance of trade with the U.S. should be reduced, and an effort is being made to import more American goods. In some cases importers are encouraged to place orders with American firms, even though Japanese or other countries of origin goods might be less expensive.

Trade also follows and stabilizes the diplomatic flag in other cases. The past year has witnessed considerable exchanges of dignitaries between Taiwan and Jordan, Saudi Arabia, and Central American countries recognizing the ROC, as well as efforts to expand trade with these friendly countries. Foreign assistance is also used to strengthen ties, though in the case of a donor nation such as Taiwan these must be selective and not require massive expenditures.

The first major technical assistance effort which proved politically successful began in the 1960s. This effort was stimulated by the 1960 U.N. General Assembly vote when the ROC lost two votes, dropping to 42, while the PRC gained five, up to 34. A diplomatic campaign began, with emphasis on Africa. During 1960, 17 states were admitted to U.N. membership, 16 of them in Africa. Between 1960-62, 23 African countries gained independence. Thirteen recognized the ROC; five recognized the PRC; and five recognized neither. Eight African nations which abstained on the U.N. China vote in 1961 voted against the PRC in 1962. At the time the Cultural Revolution drew to a close in mainland China in 1969, the ROC had diplomatic relations with 24 African countries. In part, this was a result of the PRC's diplomatic inepitude of the 1960s. It was also a consequence of Taiwan's export of an "agricultural revolution" to parts of Africa. This was not a case of aid leading to subversion, but aid, among other objectives, sustaining needed diplomatic support.

During the 1960s and through 1971, one political payoff of these missions was the support African nations gave the ROC. Another story was the incessant and relatively successful push of the PRC's "smiling diplomacy" during the 1970s to reduce the number of countries recognizing Taiwan in Africa and Latin America. Table 2 summarizes the ROC's exchange missions which remain important in maintaining a small nucleus of recognition for the ROC in Africa and Latin America.

Selected technical assistance then, is an important aspect of Taiwan's overall diplomatic effort. Because a majority of the countries recognizing the ROC are small, developing countries, a nation such as the ROC can have some economic and political impact, despite the inherent fiscal limitations on its efforts. A dependable albeit small base of countries will provide the minimum necessary for international legitimacy. Taiwan continues to hold memberships in at least 15 international organizations, including the Asian Development

TABLE 2: Number of ROC Personnel Participating Annually in Overseas Technical Missions (Unit: 1 person)

	1961	1964	1967	1970	1971	1972	1973	mid-1974
Africa	441	231	640	813	801	822	621	661
Latin America	—	6	22	48	23	52	82	107
Other	29	96	100	63	40	49	60	64

Bank, IMF, World Bank, and the International Development Association. Without a nucleus of formal recognition, official participation in international organizations would be rather difficult unless an official two-China recognition policy was followed by several countries and was tolerated by both the ROC and the PRC. Despite adverse circumstances, Taiwan's diplomatic policies have been surprisingly successful.

ROC Relationships With Countries Not Having Diplomatic Ties

ROC government officials regularly point out that Taipei has economic, cultural, and educational ties with over 140 countries. Premier Chiang not long ago reaffirmed ROC's intentions "to maintain relations with friendly countries." He did not limit friendly counties to those that did not recognize the PRC, but said: "more than a hundred countries continue to maintain economic, trade and cultural relations with us. We shall never permit the Communists to succeed in their sinister designs to isolate us."

Dating back to 1971, Taiwan adopted a more flexible foreign policy. One unusual example is the Libyan Arab Republic. Although Libya recognized the PRC in June 1971, ambassadors were never exchanged, and the ROC embassy in Tripoli remains open. Taiwan also reacts less immediately when a country recognizes the PRC. Gambia, for example, recognized the PRC on December 12, 1974, but it was not until December 28 that Taipei formally announced that it would suspend its diplomatic relations with Gambia. During the intervening two weeks it was possible for the ROC embassy to effect other unofficial ties which would not sever all contact between the two nations. The breaking of diplomatic ties does not mean the end of all substantive ties. In fact, as the following examples show, unofficial transactions may grow.

A rank-ordering of Taiwan's top ten trading partners in 1973—U.S.A., Japan, West Germany, Hong Kong, Indonesia, Australia, Canada, United Kingdom, Singapore, and the Netherlands (ranging from $2.63 billion to $131 million total trade)—reveals that only one among the "top ten," the United States, maintains formal diplomatic relations with Taipei. West Germany, for example, recognized the PRC in October 1972, yet this did not curtail ROC/West German interaction. West Germany is Taiwan's leading European trading partner.

Trade between the two countries tripled between 1972 and 1975, with a trade total of $690 million in 1975, and Germany enjoying a favorable balance of $55.4 million. Scholarships were exchanged between the two countries in 1973, and 300 nurses recruited from Taiwan are serving in German hospitals.

An interesting Asian case is Indonesia which has recognized the PRC for more than two decades. Following the decimation of the Parti Kommunis Indonesia in 1965–66, links between Jakarta and Taipei began to evolve. Trade climbed from a total of $100,000 in 1963 to $345.2 million in 1975. The largest trade increase (78.6 percent) occurred between 1972–73. Most ROC contracts in Indonesia are handled through the Chinese Chamber of Commerce. Figures on private ROC business investment in Indonesia are difficult to secure, but are substantial. Many of these investments are joint efforts with Indonesian military/business elites. This latter transnational movement of funds and ventures is a factor which has led some elements in the present Indonesian leaderships to oppose reopening ties with Peking, though formally Jakarta still recognizes the PRC.

Japan recognized the PRC in September 1972. Within two months, Taipei and Tokyo staffed organizations in the opposite capitals which were responsible for practically the identical work previously handled through the embassies. Taiwan opened the Association of East Asian Relations in Tokyo and Japan established the Interchange Association in Taipei. Key personnel in both organizations were either retired diplomats or diplomats on leave. Both the total volume of trade and Japanese investment have increased since 1972.

A 130-member Diet mission visited Taipei in October/November, 1974 to honor President Chiang Kai-shek on his birthday. A major point of discussions held then was a resumption of air links after they had been severed in April 1974. The ROC had terminated the air pact between the two countries eighteen months after Tokyo recognized the PRC, when then Japanese Foreign Minister Ohira had publicly declared that China Airlines was not "considered a carrier representing a state." Following extended negotiations, CAL air links with Japan were formally reestablished in an agreement signed on July 9, 1975. JAL has established a 100 percent owned subsidiary, Japan Asia Airways, which will be the Japanese airline on the Tokyo/Taipei route. The action which ultimately led to the resumption of flights was Foreign Minister Miyazawa's statement that the Nationalist flag is regarded as a national flag by those countries recognizing the ROC.

The Japanese case is the most notable example of linkages being sustained despite a political rupture which a few years ago would have led to opposite results. Similar arrangements have been made with the Philippines and Thailand. Taiwan's energetic foreign relations, which include the active participation of government departments such as the Ministries of Foreign Affairs, Economic Affairs, and Education, as well as many private groups, has been remarkably successful to date. Taiwan is not internationally isolated despite diplomatic setbacks which only a few years ago might have led to an inevitable and progressive political deterioration.

8. Unification or Confrontation

Yung Wei

[The ROC on Taiwan derives its legitimacy from the Constitution promulgated on the mainland on January 1, 1947; and its structure is an emergency model of the Nanking government of 1948. A large percentage of its leaders in the Central government are mainland Chinese. On the other hand, the great majority of the people are the so-called Taiwanese Chinese, Taiwan-born. Very few today would wish to reunite with mainland China under the PRC because of Peking's oppressive and backward economic and political system.

[Confronted with this dilemma, the ROC must seek a new policy vis-á-vis the mainland in order to continue its international standing and legitimacy. The following excerpts from an article, written by a prominent ROC government official when he was a professor in the U.S. some years ago, still commands attention.]

Having presented a brief review of the history of confrontation between the ROC and the PRC as well as identifying some of the unique features of PRC-ROC relations, some assessment of the possible developments between the two political systems is in order. Theoretically speaking, there could be at least four possible developments in the relations between

From Ray E. Johnston, (ed.) *The Politics of Division, Partition, and Unification* (New York: Praeger, 1976), pp. 73-77. Copyright 1976 by Praeger. Used with permission of the publisher. Footnotes omitted.

mainland China and Taiwan, including (1) a peaceful unification of mainland China and Taiwan into a single political entity, (2) military unification either through the conquest of Taiwan by the Communists, or through the repossession of mainland China by the Nationalists in a counterattack, (3) the emergence of a Taiwanese nation, separate from mainland China, and (4) the continuation of the status quo.

Let us first examine the possibility of a peaceful unification. Karl Deutsch, Ernst Haas, and Lucian Pye have all investigated the conditions for uniting different political units into a single political entity. Among th conditions that have been considered by these scholars as conducive to a peaceful political integration and unification are the sharing of a common memory and basic socio-cultural values, socio-economic interdependence, an accommodating attitude toward unification among the political elites of the various units, and mutual responsiveness based upon past experience. Judging by these criteria, the possibility of a peaceful unification of the PRC and the ROC into a single political entity in the foreseeable future is very slim.

In terms of the sharing of a common memory, recent survey research has shown that despite the more than 20 years of separation, the people of mainland China and Taiwan still share a rather similar socio-political culture. There are certain differences in the interaction patterns between the mainlanders and Taiwanese, but these differences did not create serious cleavages in their cultural and political outlook. Merely looking at these data, one may come to the conclusion that there would be little problem in uniting the people of mainland China and those of Taiwan. But possessing similar cultural-political traits is one thing, accepting different political ideology and the rule of a different political authority is quite another. Judging from the continuous flow of refugees from mainland China to the outside world, it is not feasible to expect that the people of Taiwan would be willing to accept the Communist ideology and join a political system from which many people are so eager to get out.

One of the basic factors that discourages the unification of Taiwan with the mainland is the much higher standard of living enjoyed by the Chinese people on Taiwan than that of their compatriots in mainland China. The standard of living of the people of Taiwan is far higher than that of mainland China. This is testified to by a higher adult literacy rate, more industrial and commercial population, higher per capita income, higher calorie per capita intake, and higher incidence of the possession of radios and telephones. Despite a recent claim made by Chou En-lai to the contrary, the people of the modernized Chinese society on Taiwan will probably have a lower standard of living if the island is incorporated in the state-controlled economy of Communist China.

In terms of the attitude of the ruling elites, there exist great mutual distrust and hostility between the Chinese Nationalists and Communists. This is an outgrowth of more than 40 years of life-and-death struggle between the two opposing political elites. There has been no lack of experience of negotiations and even collaboration between the Nationalists and the Communists. Yet each of thse experiences ended with bitter mutual accusation followed by more intensified conflicts. Since late 1971 the Chinese Communists have launched a peace offensive against the Nationalists. It took the form of inviting scholars of Chinese origin to visit mainland China, inducing pro-Communist nationalism among the overseas Chinese students over the Tiao-yü Tai incident, making proposals for peaceful resolution of the Taiwan question through a third, usually pro-Communist, party, and intensified broadcasts to the Nationalist-held offshore islands. Thus far, all the so-called "peace" overtures of the Chinese Communists have been met with stiff opposition and rejection by the Nationalists. The government of the ROC has recently reaffirmed its intention to stay in the democratic camp and to continue the national goal of the recovery of mainland China.

If a peaceful unification of mainland China and Taiwan is not currently feasible, how about unification through a military confrontation between the Nationalists and Chinese Communists? The probability of this happening is also very small. On the part of the Nationalists, they fully realize the military imbalance between themselves and the Communists, although they also believe that they have a better trained and equipped armed force. For this reason, the Nationalists have thus far refrained from any all-out military action

ˉagainst the Communists, but stress the principle of "seventy percent political struggle, and thirty percent military confrontation," to fulfill their goal of national unification. A Nationalist counterattack will be more likely if a large-scale military conflict occurs between the PRC and the USSR, or a serious and violent struggle over succession happens among various contenders after Mao's death, or the local military commanders in Fukien and Kwamgtung Provinces in Southern China rebel against the central authority in Peking and seek assistance from the Nationalists in Taiwan.

As for the Communists, their much larger military force of 2.8 million is scattered throughout the vast territories of mainland China. Prevention of a Russian attack in the Sinkiang province and Manchuria absorbed almost half of the military might of the Chinese Communists. Consequently, the amount of force the Chinese Communists could use for a military adventure in Taiwan is seriously limited. The likelihood of a Communist attack against Taiwan will increase if the conflicts' between the PRC and the USSR are significantly reduced, or if the United States severs diplomatic ties wth Taiwan and renounces the mutual defense treaty protecting the island, or if internal conflict or civic disturbance occur in Taiwan. At the present, none of the above conditions is likely to develop. Some of the China experts are even of the opinion that the Chinese Nationalists are able to defend themselves militarily without active U.S. participation. From the above analyses, we may conclude that the probability of a forced unification of mainland China and Taiwan through military action is quite small.

If neither peaceful unification nor military confrontation is feasible in the near future, how about the establishment of a Taiwanese nation on the island as a "permanent" solution to the problem? The answer to this question in that after UN admission and the recognition of Peking by many nations as the government of all China, it does not make much difference whether the people on the island of Taiwan officially declare their independence or not. It is not likely that the ROC can regain their seat in the UN General Assembly after such a declaration of independence, nor will it win diplomatic recognition with countries which have already recognized mainland China. For the Communist part, they may better tolerate a hostile but nevertheless Chinese political system on Taiwan than a legally independent Taiwanese nation separate from China.

For many years there has been a separatist movement supported by certain Taiwanese intellectuals who are dissatisfied with the Nationalist rule on Taiwan. Since the organizations and the activities of the so-called "Formosan (Taiwanese) Independence Movement" (FIM) are rather secretive, it is hard to assess the strength and the membership of the organization. It is known, however, that the major operational bases of the movement are found in Japan and in the United States.

Since the Nixon-Chou Shanghai Communique and since the recognition of the PRC by Japan, the FIM has been faced with serious problems of ideological confusion and internal factional divisions. The Chinese Communists have made some efforts to recruit the left wing of the FIM, yet without much success. With diminishing hope for support from either the United States or Japan, and with an increasing Communist threat against Taiwan, it is very likely that many of the members of FIM will seek reconciliation with the Chinese Nationalists to keep Taiwan a non –Communist society.

From the foregoing analysis, it is clear that the most likely course of development in the relations between mainland China and Taiwan is the continuation of a stalemate in the struggle for hegemony between the PRC and the ROC. Most likely, the struggle will take the form of intensified diplomatic, economic, and psychological warfare between the two political systems. As of this moment, the primary concern of the Chinese Communists seems to be the threat from the Soviet Union. As for the Chinese Nationalists, they are naturally more preoccupied with the threat coming from across the Taiwan Strait. Yet, with a booming economy, a combat-ready armed force, and an enlarged political base through a series of national, provincial, and local elections, held recently on the island, the government and the people of the ROC seem to be more determined than ever before to defend the fruits of their modernization efforts on Taiwan. They further hope that, through their determined efforts, their compatriots in mainland China may also share these fruits of success with them someday.

9. Official ROC Statements on U.S. Derecognition

[The following are excerpts from two official statements. The first is from President Chiang Ching-kuo of the ROC on December 29, 1978, after he received a 16-member mission led by U.S. Deputy Secretary of State Warren Christopher informing him of the impending severance of U.S. official relations with the ROC. President Chiang told the U.S. diplomats that future relations between the two countries must rest on five principles: "reality, continuity, security, legality and governmentality."

[The second statement was Premier Sun Yun-suan's oral report before the 65th session of the Legislative Yuan on February 22, 1980 on the future direction of the ROC's foreign relations.]

DECEMBER 29, 1978
The President explained the five principles as follows:

Continuity
The Republic of China and the United States have had a long-standing cooperative diplomatic relationship. During the Second World War, the two countries fought shoulder to shoulder. After the signing of the Sino-U.S. Mutual Defense Treaty in 1954, we strengthened our alliance further and made tremendous contributions to the security and peace of the Asian-Pacific region.

Unfortunately, the two countries have broken diplomatic ties, but the two peoples will always remain friendly and have common interests. Additionally, the two countries follow identical ideals of democracy and freedom. The two peoples should continue to strengthen their cooperation and promote their friendship.

Reality
Since its founding in 1911, the Republic of China has been an independent sovereign state and the sole genuine representative of Chinese culture and history. The Government of the Republic of China is a legitimately constituted government and its existence has always been an international reality. The international status and international personality of the Republic of China cannot be changed because of the recognition of the Chinese Communist regime by any country in the world. The United States should continue to recognize and respect the legal status and international personality of the Republic of China.

Security
Since the signing of the Sino-U.S. Mutual Defense Treaty twenty-four years ago, we have faithfully carried out all our obligations and responsibilities under the treaty. The United States has never failed to provide weapons to the Republic of China to enhance its defense capability. In substance, this treaty is a vital link in the chain of the collective defense system of free countries in the Western Pacific. The situation in this area remains unstable and insecure. The threat of invasion and subversion from the Communist forces, faced by the free countries, especially since the fall of Vietnam, is more serious than ever before. Consequently, we hope the United States can continue to provide effective guarantees of our security and remain committed to the sale of the defensive weapons we need to ensure the peace and security of the Western Pacific area, including the Republic of China.

Legality
Both the Republic of China and the United States are governed by law. From now on, the

Excerpts from ROC government releases, December 29, 1978 and February 22, 1980.

private interests of both Chinese and American citizens require the protection of definite legal provisions as well as government policy guidance. The United States has stated that after the termination of the mutual Defense Treaty, it will continue to be concerned about the peace, security and prosperity of this region, and that it will continue to supply the Republic of China with defensive weapons. The United States has also said that except for the Mutual Defense Treaty, all of the more than 50 other treaties and agreements will remain in full force and effect. These commitments and pledges and the establishment of proposed government-to-government representation and all other relations can be effectively carried out and preserved only by legislation.

Governmentality

The government of the United States has declared that it will continue to sell defensive weapons to the Republic of China and maintain cultural, economic, trade, scientific, technological and travel relations. Considering that activities of mutual benefit between the two countries are so numerous and of such a complex nature, it is impossible for any private organization or any individual to carry them out. To facilitate the continuation and enhancement of our relationship, it is essential that government-to-government representation be established in Taipei and Washington to administer all relations.

February 22, 1980

Premier Sun:

We are deeply aware that the more unfavorable the external situation, the greater the need to strengthen our external relations at the price of our blood, sweat and wisdom. In the last year, we have adhered to principle, taken an initial stand and worked earnestly to establish our diplomatic position.

Specifically, our endeavors have been directed to the strengthening of the policy-making and command center of our total diplomacy, the improvement of our diplomatic strategy and study of international issues, fortification of the coordination and cooperation of overseas organizations and personnel, and the cultivation of loyal and competent diplomats of principle. We have developed definite working plans as operative guidelines to strengthen overall foreign relations in the Americas, Europe, Africa, Southeast Asia and South Asia.

Strengthening of relations with the United States is our consistent policy. To do so will promote our mutual interests and safeguard the peace and security of Asia and even the world. Our relations with the United States have undergone some procedural changes but there also has been substantive progress. Especially during the last six months, the newly established representative organs of the two countries have carried out their work satisfactorily. Cultural, scientific, technological, financial, economic and trade relations have been continuously strengthened. Beginning this year, the United States has resumed the supplying of arms to the Republic of China, but still has not agreed to provide the equipment of which we are most in need.

Since the rupture of diplomatic relations with the United States, we have been striving to improve our relationships with the free nations of Europe in the expectation of opening up new international vistas. We have placed particular emphasis on augmenting economic, trade and cultural interflow with West Germany, France and Britain. After a year of hard work, some Western European nations have established representative offices in the Republic of China to promote mutually substantive relations. Additionally, we have liberalized trade restrictions applying to five Eastern European nations. This is a measure intended to diversify our trade and markets and is absolutely not to be considered as a token of any change in our basic anti-Communist position.

Most of the countries maintaining diplomatic relations with us are in Latin America. Although some countries in that area have had changes of government in the last six months, they have continued to maintain friendly ties with us in consequence of our timely measures to cope with the situation. From now on, we should certainly step up various forms of cooperation with friendly Latin America countries and cement our ties in that area. Unfortunately, drastic world changes—especially the coup in Iran and the Russian incursion into Afghanistan—have prompted more countries to embrace the illusion of "uniting with Communist China to restrain the Soviet Union." This led Colombia to establish diplomatic relations with Communist China. Even so, the countries of Latin America have traditionally maintained friendly relations with us and substantive relations with them are still to be considered good. We should further strengthen these ties.

Our relations with the Kingdom of Saudi Arabia have long been close. The joint efforts of the two governments have steadily enlarged the scope of cooperation in politics, economics, science, technology and hygiene in recent years. Beginning last January 1, Saudi Arabia increased its daily supply of crude oil to the Republic of China from 20,000 barrels to 50,000 barrels. The two governments recently signed an agreement calling for investment in a big fertilizer plant, thereby augmenting the relationship.

In developing our external relations, we obviously seek to expand our spheres of activities in order to frustrate the Chinese Communist conspiracy to isolate us, but we also are striving earnestly to fulfill our obligations to the world community. We have, for example, spared no efforts to rescue, receive and assist Indochinese refugees. We have repeatedly donated money and materials to serve this humane purpose. In addition to our original donations of US$500,000, NT$10 million and 10,000 tons of rice, we gave US$10 million worth of rice last November and committed ourselves to accept 1,000 more refugees. We also have done all we could to provide several friendly nations with agricultural, medical and technical assistance. We have dispatched 29 technical teams with personnel of 504 to 21 nations of Africa, the Asia-Pacific region, West Asia and Latin America. Besides this, we have held a ministerial economic conference with Costa Rica and have raised our economic cooperation conferences with Saudi Arabia and the Republic of South Africa from the vice ministerial to the ministerial level. Our country attaches great importance to these meetings. We believe that this approach of "doing our best" for friendship will gradually increase understanding of our country and contribute to the development of a world of friends.

International changes in recent years have made the position of the overseas Chinese more difficult. Patriotism triggered by the rupture of our U.S. diplomatic relations has shown that the more ominous the world situation, the greater the difficulties faced by the nation, the stronger the love and allegiance of the overseas Chinese for the motherland and its government. In the last year, we have seen the overseas Chinese bear the brunt of many crises and demonstrate their patriotism in actions as they attacked the enemy's united front with deeds. Their demonstration of fortitude, strength and righteousness have heightened the morale of the nation and provided strong assurance of our success in anti-Communism and national recovery.

10.   The Status of Taiwan

Victor Li

[In spite of the ROC's success during the past 30 years, a number of serious problems remain. One of these involves the international legal status of Taiwan after the U.S. switch of recognition to Peking. Here the problem is discussed by Victor Li, a prominent Chinese-American international law professor who is now elected President of the East-West Center in Hawaii.]

After January 1, 1979 we know what the United States does *not* regard Taiwan to be: it is not the *de jure* government of the state of China. Much less clear, however, is the question of what the United States considers Taiwan to be.

The Taiwan Relations Act does not directly address this issue. The report of the Senate Committee on Foreign Relations states:

> Considerable discussion has occured concerning the status of Taiwan under international law. The Committee concluded that it was unnecessary, in drafting this legislation, to address this issue since, for purposes of United States domestic law, the Executive Branch can be empowered, statutorily, to treat Taiwan as if it were a state. This is, in fact, precisely what the bill does . . .

Thus, the United States has not explicitly explained the legal rationale for preserving treaties and maintaining commercial, cultural, and other relations with an unrecognized entity.

The successor government theory provides one possible rationale. That is, the United States has treaty and other relations with the state of China. Prior to January 1 that state was represented by the ROC government. After the switch of recognition the United States regards the PRC as the successor government to the ROC. As such, the PRC assumes the rights and obligations of its predecessor. This theory is well known. For example, in 1971 the PRC was recognized by the United Nations as the only legitimate representative of China, and succeeded to the seat belonging to that state.

Some scholars argue that the successor government theory should be applied to the switch in recognition to the PRC. But such an approach would produce some highly unsatisfactory results. First, the PRC would succeed to the Mutual Defense Treaty and other agreements with the United States. These treaties would remain in force only as long as the PRC agrees, in an implied manner, that they should continue to serve as the bases of American relations with the Chinese territory of Taiwan. This means that China could withdraw its implied agreement at any time and terminate American treaty relations with Taiwan. Second, the United States would be in the absurd situation of having a mutual defense treaty with the PRC for the purpose of defending Taiwan from being attacked by the PRC.

In addition, since the PRC would be the sole legitimate government of all of China including Taiwan, the United States could have no direct relations with the authorities on Taiwan without the PRC's consent, even if that consent is only implied. Taiwan would have no capacity to conduct foreign affairs unless the PRC consented.

A second possible description of the legal status of Taiwan after withdrawal of recognition is that it is a "*de facto* entity with international personality." That is, while no longer regarded by the United States as a *de jure* government or state, nevertheless Taiwan continues to control a population and territory and to carry out the usual functions of government. Section 4 of the *Restatement, Second, Foreign Relations Law of the United States* provides:

Victor Li, (ed.) *The Future of Taiwan,* (New York: M. E. Sharpe, Inc., 1980), pp. 14-20. Copyright 1980 by M. E. Sharpe, Inc. Reprinted by permission of M. E. Sharpe, Inc. Armonk, New York 10504. Footnotes omitted.

Except as otherwise indicated, "state" as used in the Restatement of this Subject means an entity that has a defined territory and population under the control of a government and that engages in foreign relations.

In other words, whether Taiwan is regarded as a "state" or juridical person in international law depends on whether it carries out the usual functions of a state, and not whether it is recognized *de jure* by other states.

If Taiwan is a *de facto* entity with international personality, it may carry out the full range of foreign relations, including entering into international agreements and sending and receiving official missions.

The *de facto* entity concept is not a new idea. Prior to January 1, 1979, the United States dealt with the PRC on exactly such a basis. Although we did not extend *de jure* recognition to the PRC, official missions were exchanged, agreements were reached, American presidents visited the PRC, and a considerable amount of trade and travel was carried out between the two countries. No one seriously questioned the capacity of the PRC to engage in such relations.

I should note that this concept does not violate the principle of one-China. It addresses the present political realities without requiring or precluding eventual reunification or any other ultimate relationship between the PRC and Taiwan. Indeed, Vice-Premier Teng's indication that Taiwan may retain its own political and economic system as well as maintain separate armed forces acknowledges the same realities.

The United States Position

The PRC obviously views the switch of recognition as a successor government situation. In its unilateral statement of December 15, 1978 the Chinese government said:

> As is known to all, the Government of the People's Republic of China is the sole legal government of China and Taiwan is part of China . . . As for the way of bringing Taiwan back to the embrace of the motherland and reunifying the country, it is entirely China's internal affair.

The United States has not taken a definitive stand on the status of Taiwan. In the joint Communique of December 15, 1978, the United States "acknowledges the Chinese position that there is but one China and Taiwan is a part of China, [and] recognizes the People's Republic of China as the sole legal government of China. Within this context, the people of the United States will maintain cultural, commercial, and other unofficial relations with the people of Taiwan."

One possible interpretation of these statements is that the PRC is the successor government to the ROC: The state of China includes Taiwan, and the PRC is the sole legal government of this state. Moreover, since the United States can deal with Taiwan only "within this context," the United States acknowledges the PRC's ultimate legal authority over Taiwan, including the right to approve future U.S.-Taiwan relations.

An alternative interpretation is that "acknowledgement" of the Chinese position is not tantamount to accepting it. Consequently, the United States still retains the options of regarding the status of Taiwan as still "undetermined," dealing with it as a *de facto* entity with international personality, or at a later point explicitly accepting the PRC as the successor government to the ROC.

The word "acknowledge" presents a potentially serious linguistic discrepancy between the English and Chinese texts. The Shanghai Communique states: "The United States acknowledges that Chinese on both sides of the Strait agree that there is but one China and Taiwan is part of China. We do not challenge this position." The Chinese text uses a correct equivalent, *jen-shih,* for "acknowledges." In the December 15 communique "acknowledges" is rendered in Chinese as *ch'eng-jen,* a term carrying a clear connotation of acceptance or agreement. Reading the Chinese texts of the two communiques together, the United States has increased the degree of its acquiescence in the Chinese position from *jen-shih* (acknowledges or takes note) to *ch'eng-jen.* Administration officials have stated that, in interpreting this phrase, the United States will adhere only to the English version. Of course, China will adhere only to the Chinese version.

The United States may derive some short-term benefits from refusing to clarify its legal rationale for continued dealings with Taiwan. Explicitly calling Taiwan a *de facto* entity might annoy the PRC, while adopting the successor government theory would damage Taiwan. Nevertheless this policy of intentional ambiguity will be difficult to maintain for an indeterminate time.

Indeed, a great deal already has occurred which requires the United States to be increasingly specific about its view of the status of Taiwan. For example, Taiwan has deposited in American banks several billion dollars of its foreign exchange reserves. If the PRC were considered the successor government, it could assert that this money belongs to the "state of China" and should be handed over to the proper representative of that state, the PRC. The transfer of this vast sum would undercut any policy of ensuring that the people of Taiwan "face a peaceful and prosperous future."

The Taiwan Relations Act deals with this problem by providing in section 4(b)(3)(B) that the PRC does not succeed to the property of the ROC:

> [R]ecognition of the People's Republic of China shall not affect in any way the ownership of or other rights or interests in properties, tangible or intangible, and other things of value, owned or held on or prior to December 31, 1978, or thereafter acquired or earned by the governing authorities on Taiwan.

A related problem which is not completely resolved concerns the ownership of the former ROC embassy at Twin Oaks and other diplomatic and consular properties. The Senate version of the Act excluded diplomatic real property from the application of the section quoted above, and hence would have supported the taking over of Twin Oaks by the PRC. The Act, however, follows the House version, the legislative history of which indicates that this section applies to all property including diplomatic real property.

The PRC considers obtaining the state of China's diplomatic property to be an important symbolic act. The Executive for political reasons may want to allow this property to pass to the PRC. Ultimately, the courts may have to decide whether the PRC is the successor government to the ROC, and, if so, whether section 4(b)(3)(B) should be narrowly construed so that it is consistent with international law rules regarding the rights of successor governments.

The issue of whether the PRC is the successor government to the ROC will recur repeatedly in the future. For example, under what structure will athletes from the PRC and Taiwan participate in the Olympic Games? What are Taiwan's rights and obligations under bilateral and multilateral international agreements on civil aviation? If the PRC objects, can American commercial, cultural, and educational bodies legally have direct dealings with the Taiwan government? Each such question will require a specific response from the United States, which in turn will set a pattern of precedents for future dealings.

My guess is that in the coming months and years the United States will increasingly assert, although with some reluctance, that Taiwan is a *de facto* entity with international personality. This formulation is awkward both semantically and substantively. But since both the PRC and Taiwan agree on the principle of one-China, it is hardly appropriate for the United States, as an outsider, to propose any other position. Having to operate within this principle, the United States must use the *de facto* entity concept if it is to maintain economic, cultural, and other ties with Taiwan into the indefinite future.

Section 8

Security and Defense Capabilities

Edited by Michael Ying-mao Kau

Section 8
Security and Defense Capabilities

By Michael Y. M. Kau

Despite Peking's repeated claim that the Taiwan issue is "entirely China's own internal affair" in which no foreign powers are permitted to interfere, the realities surrounding the Taiwan issue over the last 30 years are far more complex. Taiwan has in fact emerged since 1950 as a major issue of international concern and controversy, which at times even brought the superpowers of the world to the brink of military confrontation. Ever since President Truman's statement of June 27, 1950 regarding Taiwan's future, Taiwan's security has become inseparable from the development and evolution of U.S. foreign policy and security strategy in Asia.[1]

A brief review of the key events which shaped the Republic of China's external security and military capabilities over the last three decades will help make the complexities of the case clearer. The year 1949 was probably the most disastrous year for the Chinese Nationalist Government. Internally, the Communists had just succeeded in occupying the entire mainland and seizing power by force. The defeated Nationalist forces were forced to withdraw in haste to Taiwan for safety and reorganization. Externally, the U.S., the staunchest ally of the Nationalists at that time, was prepared to follow a "hands-off" policy to allow the Chinese civil war to take its own natural course. The release of the "China White Paper" by the State Department on August 5, 1949 openly signaled Washington's intention to "write off" the Nationalist government in China.[2]

In contrast, the internal morale as well as outside support of the new revolutionary regime in Peking was at its highest. Riding on the tides of their successful military campaigns, the Communists began to prepare their final assault on the Nationalists across the Taiwan Strait to complete the task of national unification. The Soviets also agreed to throw in their support by signing a thirty-year treaty of military alliance with Peking on February 14, 1950. By acting expeditiously to deny the Nationalist forces a chance to recuperate and reorganize, the Communists hoped that they could just sail across the strait with junks and sampans to take over Taiwan.

War in Korea: The U.S. Changes Direction
The sudden outbreak of war in Korea on June 25, 1950, however, immediately changed the entire strategic outlook and military balance in the Taiwan Strait. U.S. strategic thinking and military deployments in the West-

Michael Y.M. Kau is Professor of Political Science, Brown University (Providence, R.I.).

ern Pacific were shifted quickly to a different gear. The U.S. responded to the North Korean attack on the South with the full power of U.S. air and naval forces. On June 27, President Truman ordered the U.S. 7th Fleet to move into the Taiwan Strait to protect Taiwan and Penghu (the Pescadores) from any Communist attack. Washington even went so far as to declare that "the determination of the future status of Formosa [Taiwan] must await the restoration of security in the Pacific, a peace settlement with Japan, or consideration by the U.S."[3] Meanwhile, the U.S. stepped up its military aid to all friendly countries throughout Southeast Asia.

The continued intensification of the Korean War and the subsequent intervention of Peking's "volunteers" in the fall of 1950 further stimulated the interest and resolve of the U.S. to build up Taiwan's military strength against the Communist threat of "liberation." Hence, U.S. economic and military aid began to pour into the island, and on May 2, 1951, a U.S. Military Assistance and Advisory Group was formally instituted on Taiwan to help train and equip the Nationalist Armed Forces. There is no question that the "neutralization" of the Taiwan Strait and the resumption of U.S. military aid following the Korean War gave the Nationalist government a desperately needed respite to recuperate from its defeat in the civil war on the China mainland.

The inauguration of the Eisenhower Administration in 1953 speeded up the process of U.S.-ROC military cooperation started earlier in 1950. Under the energetic stewardship of the anti-Communist Secretary of State, John Foster Dulles, the strategy of "containment" against Communism was extended to include the doctrine of "rollback." This was the heyday of the Cold War confrontation between East and West. Thus, Taiwan not only was integrated into the U.S.'s defense perimeter in the Western Pacific, which extended from Japan and South Korea in the north to the Philipines and Indochina in the south, but was even "unleashed" from the earlier Truman ban and given the leeway to recover the mainland.[4] The close military and political ties between the ROC and the U.S. were officially seated by a Mutual Defense Treaty, signed on December 2, 1954. In January of the following year, Congress was even persuaded to authorize the President "to employ the Armed Forces of the U.S. as he deems necessary for the specific purpose of securing and protecting Formosa [Taiwan] and the Pescadores [Penghu] against armed attack."[5]

While U.S. commitment to the security of Taiwan and Penghu against outside threat was always explicit and unequivocal, U.S. obligations to protect the offshore islands of Quemoy [Kinmen] and Matsu were deliberately kept ambiguous. As formulated in the Congressional authorization of January, 1955, the decision whether or not to use force to protect the offshore islands was left to the discretion of the President. He was authorized to use U.S. forces if, in his judgment, such action was "required" or "appropriate" in securing the defense of Taiwan. During the two Quemoy crises in 1954 and 1958, President Eisenhower judged the defense of the offshore islands to be truly essential to the security of Taiwan.[6] Despite heated debate, over the strategic values and the defensibility of Quemoy and Matsu during the the 1960 Presidential campaign between John F. Kennedy and Richard M. Nixon, it should be noted that President Kennedy later took exactly the same strong position as his predecessor had when a third offshore islands crisis developed in the summer of 1962. [7] For the next three Administrations, under Johnson, Nixon and Ford, the basic policy of unequivocally honoring U.S. commitments to Taiwan's security and taking a strong position on the defense of the offshore islands remained essentially unchanged.

The escalation of the war in Indochina in the 1960s greatly enhanced the strategic value of Taiwan to America's war efforts. Taiwan was used as a staging and logistic base for U.S. forces operating in Southeast Asia. During the peak of the Vietnam War, over 10,000 U.S. troops and advisors were stationed in Taiwan. Such extensive military cooperation between the two countries and a conspicuous U.S. military presence on the island, it goes without saying, further enhanced Taiwan's security position.

Aside from U.S. guarantees of its security, the 1960s also witnessed a dramatic transformation of Taiwan's armed forces into a modern military might, equipped with advanced weapon systems and a sophisticated command-communications structure. In the two decades since 1950, the U.S. poured over $2.5 billion in military aid into the island for the training and equipping of the ROC armed forces. [8]

In contrast, the People's Liberation Army (PLA) on the mainland suffered from recurrent political turmoil and factional struggle during the same period. The prolonged political chaos and economic setbacks during the Great Leap Forward of the 1950s deprived the PLA of much-needed time and resources to modernize. The worsening of the Sino-Soviet conflict after 1960 not only further denied China access to advanced military technology and modern weaponry, but also led the PLA to bloody confrontations with the Soviets.

Uncertainties of the 1970s

The 1970s, however, began with increasingly dark clouds of uncertainty over the issue of Taiwan's security. Major developments in the world arena, such as the winding down of the Vietnam War, the intensification of the dispute between Peking and Moscow, and the increasing challenge of growing Soviet might and expansionism, all brought pressure, on Washington to reexamine the validity of its Cold War strategy of the "containment" of China, which had been formulated to deal with the situations of the previous two decades. [9]

It was under this new mood of searching for a new strategy that President Nixon undertook his historic trip to Peking in February, 1972, and opened up a new era of accommodation and cooperation with the PRC. While both President Nixon and his successor, President Ford, were clearly interested in keeping the process and momentum of "normalization" going, it was equally evident that they were not prepared to push "normalization" at an expense unacceptable to the ROC. They were particularly unwilling to compromise on the existing U.S. security commitments to Taiwan by accepting Peking's demand for abrogating the 1954 Mutual Defense Treaty without getting in return Peking's explicit promise to renounce the use of force in settling the Taiwan issue. This stalemate throughout the Nixon and Ford Admnistrations following the initial breakthrough of 1972 clearly testified to the seriousness of the dilemma. Throughout the long negotiations, the U.S. remained firm and uncompromising on Taiwan's security.

It was not until December 15, 1978, when President Carter made his historic announcement of the completion of normalization, that a crisis of credibility began to surface with regard to Washington's resolve to protect Taiwan's security. After the announcement, it also became known that, in the first place, in accepting Peking's three demands including the termination of the Mutual Defense Treaty, no effort was made by the Carter Administration to negotiate for a PRC pledge not to use force against Taiwan. Secondly, under Peking's pressure, Carter even made further concessions by imposing a one-year moratorium on arms sales to Taiwan. Despite the Administration's repeated denials to the contrary, Carter advisors' strong desire to play the "China card" against what appeared to them to be growing Soviet expansionism must have been the single decisive factor hat influenced their willingness to derecognize the ROC and to take risks on the issue of Taiwan's security. [10]

The U.S. nation's reactions to Carter's important decision turned out to be rather predictable. While the public generally supported his initiatives in establishing diplomatic relations with the PRC, his weak and ambiguous approach to Taiwan was strongly criticized. The response of Congress was particularly critical. Even the most liberal-minded members of Congress openly attacked the Carter formula in regard to Taiwan's security as totally inadequate and highly risky. [11]

Efforts to provide remedies to the serious weaknesses of the Carter approach quickly gathered momentum in Congress, and by April, 1979, the Congress succeeded in producing an extraordinary piece of legislation, the Taiwan Relations Act (TRA). The Act in fact became a functional substitute of the 1954 Mutual Defense Treaty. The law declares explicitly:

It is the policy of the United States:

• to declare the peace and stability in the area are in the political, security, and economic interests of the United States, and are matters of international concern;

• to consider any effort to determine the future of Taiwan by other than peaceful means, including by boycotts or embargoes, a threat to the peace and security of the Western Pacific area and of grave concern to the United States;

• to provide Taiwan with arms of a defensive character; and

• to maintain the capacity of the United States to resist any resort to force or other forms of coercion that would jeopardize the security, or the social or economic system, of the people on Taiwan. [12]

The Act provides further that:

> The President is directed to inform the Congress promptly of any threat to the security or the social or economic system of the people on Taiwan and any danger to the interests of the United States arising therefrom. The President and the Congress shall determine, in accordance with constitutional processes, appropriate action by the United States in response to any such danger.

The dramatic victory of the Republican Party in the 1980 Presidential and Congressional elections signaled a strong shift in the nation's political moods. During his campaign Ronald Reagan, reflecting his long-held strong commitment to Taiwan, criticized Carter for paying "too high a price" in normalizing relations with Peking and for failing to implement the TRA faithfully and rigorously as required by the law.[13] The ascendence of Reagan to the Presidency has raised hopes for strengthening the established policy of honoring unequivocal U.S. commitments to the security of Taiwan, except that now it must be done within the framework of the new law, the TRA.

Reducing Security Dependence on the U.S.

Two crucial points emerge clearly from the record of U.S.-Taiwan relations over the past three decades: First, since 1950, Taiwan's security strategy in Asia. Second, the development and improvement of Taiwan's security position and defense capabilities has benefited almost exclusively from its close alliance with the U.S. In the 1950s and 1960s, the logic of Washington's strategic thinking and military planning dictated that the U.S. make Taiwan one of its closest allies in the Western Pacific. In the 1970s, although the strategic value of Taiwan to the U.S. was perceived to have declined as a result of the reduction of tensions in Southeast Asia, the moral obligations to the security and well-being of the 17 million people on Taiwan which the U.S. had assumed over the two preceeding decades, seems to have played a crucial role in persuading Washington to continue its long-standing security commitments.[14]

With hindsight and amidst anxieties and uncertainties in the three years since U.S. derecognition, the Taiwan Leadership began to realize with agony that the security of Taiwan under U.S. protection had been achieved only at a dangerously high price. Prior to the Nixon breakthrough and particularly before Carter's drastic move, the ROC had responded positively to U.S. strategic planning and relied heavily on the U.S.'s exclusive guarantees of security and arms supply. The guarantee under the Mutual Defense Treaty and the steady flow of U.S. weapons and military technology over the years had been the two legs on which Taiwan's security and survival rested. Consequently, Taiwan had become extremely dependent on, and vulnerable to, policy changes in Washington.

Carter's drastic shift of late 1978, therefore, amounted to amputation of one of Taiwan's "security legs" and serious injury to the other. Although

Congress came to the rescue by creating the TRA as a functional substitute for the previous treaty commitments, its intended effectiveness remains to be tested. After the Nixon "ambiguity" of 1972 and the Carter "shock" of 1978, one can be sure that Taiwan's confidence in, and trust of, Washington will no longer be the same.

U.S. Still an Indispensable Ally

Most of the leaders in Taiwan today continue to believe that despite all the defects and confusions in Washington's policy towards Taiwan, the U.S. is probably, on balance, still an indispensable ally for Taiwan. But at the same time a growing number of security strategists and planners are convinced that Taiwan should not allow its future security to be victimized for a second time through a total dependency on the U.S. To avoid the trap of exclusive reliance on one security partner in the future they reason, Taiwan must begin to explore seriously other options for security and survival.

Some of the options being explored are moderate in nature and can be and are being carried out in conjunction with its existing ties with the U.S. Since the derecognition shock of late 1978, Taiwan has actively pursued the additional strategy of (1) diversifying its sources of arms supplies, and (2) expanding substantive political, economic, and cultural ties with all nations, including the Communist countries of Eastern Europe. [15] Such a strategy is clearly designed to develop a broader and more secure base of arms supply and international trade, to hedge against the dangers of increasing political restrictions and uncertainties in dealing with the U.S. More recently, Taiwan entered into the final stage of negotiations with the Dutch government to purchase two submarines and related supportive equipment in a $500-million package. A contract was signed with South Africa in 1980 for long-term supplies of uranium, supposedly for use in Taiwan's expanding nuclear power projects. For a couple of years, Taiwan has been in touch with Israel to discuss possible purchase of military aircraft missiles and other advanced defense technology. [16] If these arms deals are consummated as planned, they will constitute a significant breakthrough in Taiwan's efforts to break away from a vulnerable dependency on the U.S.

Other options, such as developing nuclear weapons, establishing ties with the Soviet Union, and seeking a complete separation from China by declaring an independent Taiwan, would not only be drastic in nature but would run counter to the global and regional strategic interests of the U.S. [17] Admittedly, the risks involved in pursuing these options would be overwhelming, and their desired results are by no means assured. However, if and when Taiwan should perceive that its security is in peril and that U.S. commitments are not in the least credible, what Taiwan might do in the moment of desperation cannot be foretold. Should Taiwan be driven to any of these adventurous options, the impact on the existing delicate strategic balance in the Western Pacific would be most destabilizing and unpredictable. In this regard, the future of Taiwan's security cannot but remain, as Congress declares in the TRA, a matter of "grave concern" to the U.S.'s regional interests in Asia and to its global strategy for peace and stability.

NOTES

1. For comprehensive studies of the interactions among the U.S., the PRC and the ROC, see Hungdah Chiu, ed., *China and the Questions of Taiwan: Documents and Analysis* (New York: Praeger, 1973); *China: U.S. Policy Since 1945* (Washington, DC: Congressional Quarterly, 1980); and Harold C. Hinton, *China's Turbulent Quest* (London: Macmillan, 1970).

2. See, for example, John K. Fairbank, *The United States and China* (Cambridge, Ma. Harvard University Press, 1971), pp. 304-323.

3. See Selection A-1 of this Chapter. For the complications of the Korean War, see Allen S. Whiting, *China Crosses the Yalu* (London: Macmillan, 1960)

4. O. Edmund Clubb, "Formosa and the Off-shore Islands in American Policy," *Political Science Quarterly*, No. 74 (Dec. 1959), 517-531.

5. See Selection A-3.

6. See Selection A-4.

7. See Selection A-5.

8. See Niel H. Jacoby, *U.S. Aid to Taiwan* (New York: Praeger, 1966); and *Hearings on U.S. Security Agreements and Commitments Abroad Before the Committee on Foreign Relations, U.S. Senate, 91st Congress, Nov. 24-26, 1969 and May 8, 1970;* Part 4, Republic of China (Washington, D.C.: U.S. Government Printing Office, 1970).

9. A. Doak Barnett, *A New U.S. Policy Towards China* (Washington, D.C.: Brookings, 1971) and Ralph N. Clough, *East Asia and U.S. Security* (Washington, D.C.: Brookings, 1975).

10. James C. Hsiung, "The Conceptual Foundations of U.S. China Policy," *Occasional Papers / Reprints Series in Contemporary Asian Studies*, School of Law, University of Maryland, No. 2 (1980); Miles M. Costick and Brian Green, "The Arming of Red China," *Current Analysis*, XI: 9 (Nov. 15, 1980); and Edward N. Luttwak, "Against the China Card," *Commentary*, LXVI: 4 (Oct. 1978), 37-43.

11. See, for example, the Joint Resolution 31 on the peace and security of Taiwan sponsored by Senators Kennedy, Cranston and 29 other liberal Senators and their testimonies, in *Taiwan: Hearings Before the Committee on Foreign Relations, U.S. Senate, 96th Congress, Feb. 5-22, 1979* (Washington, D.C.: U.S. Government Printing Office, 1979), pp. 366-402.

12. See Selection A-8. For an excellent study of the Congress' effort, see Robert L. Downen, *The Taiwan Pawn in the China Game: Congress to the Rescue* (Washington, D.C.: Center for Strategic and International Studies, Georgetown University, 1979).

13. Ronald Reagan, "Decency for Taiwan," *The New York Times*, Jan. 28, 1979; Selection A-9 of this Chapter; and a report on Reagan's press conference, *The New York Times*, Aug. 26, 1980.

14. See, for example, Ray S. Cline's testimony, in *Taiwan: Hearings Before the Committee on Foreign Relations, U.S. Senate, 96th Congress, Feb. 5-22, 1979* (Washington, D.C.: U.S. Government Printing Office, 1979), pp. 576-582.

15. See Selection A-10.

16. A. James Gregor and Maria Hsia Chang, "Arms Control, Regional Stability and the Taiwan Relations Act," *The Journal of Strategic Studies*, III: 1 (May, 1980), 3-25. For a report on the Dutch-Taiwan deal, see *The New York Times*, Jan. 19, 1981. For trade with the Communist countries, including the Soviet Union, see *China Daily News* (New York), Mar. 6, 1980. For further discussions of Taiwan's nuclear option, see George H. Quester, "Taiwan and Nuclear Proliferation," *ORBIS*, XVIII: 1 (Spring, 1974); and Ernest Lefever, "U.S. Security Ties and the Nuclear Options: South Korea and Taiwan," *Asia & the World Forum*, No. 7 (Nov. 1977), 125-136.

17. See Selections D-2 and D-3. Also, *Beyond Normalization: Report of the UNA-USA National Policy Panel to Study US-China Relations* (New York: United Nations Association of the United States of America, 1979).

A. The Evolution of Security Strategy: From Alliance to Realignment

The development of Taiwan's security strategy since 1950 has been inseparable from U.S. strategic interests and foreign policy postures in Asia. The Nationalist Government on Taiwan has, throughout the years, responded cooperatively to the thrust of Washington's policy directions. Until President Carter's 1978 decision to terminate the 1954 Mutual Defense Treaty, Taiwan's security planning had been clearly marked by an exclusive and faithful reliance on its military and political alliance with the U.S. The dramatic Nixon visit to Peking in 1972, though, ushered in an era of increasing uncertainty and anxiety for the leadership of Taiwan. Although the U.S. resolve to protect Taiwan's security remains reasonably strong even after the U.S.-PRC normalization, the Taiwan authorities are convinced that for the sake of their long-term survival they must start exploring other security options as was noted above.

The documents selected in this subsection are designed to provide an overall picture of the evolution of Taiwan's security strategy from 1950 to the present, with special emphasis on Taiwan's security ties with the U.S. Consisting of ten watershed policy statements, these documents chronologically portray the evolution in the nature, scope and international contexts of U.S.—Taiwan security ties throughout the last three decades, (Selections 1-9). It is important to note that despite some variations in tone and style in which the U.S. commitment to Taiwan was expressed, the basic U.S. policy stance has been remarkably consistent, the only exception thus far being the period under the Carter Administration (see Selection 7). Carter's ambiguous and weak policy approach, however, was quickly augmented by the explicit and strong declaration adopted by Congress in the Taiwan Relations Act (Selection 8).

Candidate Reagan's "Five Guiding Principles for the Far East," presented in August, 1980, demonstrates unequivocally his full support of the traditional policy of a strong commitment to Taiwan's security (Selection 9). ROC Premier Sun Yun-suan's recent Administrative Report to the Legislative Yuan, for its part, reveals a sense of urgency within the ROC government that Taiwan must make still greater efforts to develop new ideas and strategies for its long-term survival and security (Selection 10).

1. EXCERPT FROM PRESIDENT TRUMAN'S STATEMENT ON THE MISSION OF THE U.S. SEVENTH FLEET IN THE FORMOSA AREA, June 27, 1950

The attack upon Korea makes it plain beyond all doubt that communism has passed beyond the use of subversion to conquer independent nations and will now use armed invasion and war. It has defied the orders of the Security Council of the United Nations issued to preserve international peace and security. In these circumstances, the occupation of Formosa by Communist forces would be a direct threat to the security of the Pacific area and to United States forces performing their lawful and necessary functions in that area.

Accordingly, I have ordered the Seventh Fleet to prevent any attack on Formosa. As a corollary of this action, I am calling upon the Chinese Government on Formosa to cease all air and sea operations against the mainland. The Seventh Fleet will see that this is done. The determination of the future status of Formosa must await the restoration of security in the Pacific, a peace settlement with Japan, or consideration by the United Nations.

American Foreign Policy, 1950-1955: Basic Documents (Washington, D.C.: U.S. Government Printing Office, 1957), II, p. 2467.

2. MUTUAL DEFENSE TREATY BETWEEN THE UNITED STATES AND THE REPUBLIC OF CHINA, December 2, 1954

The Parties to this Treaty,

Reaffirming their faith in the purposes and principles of the Charter of the United Nations and their desire to live in peace with all peoples and all Governments, and desiring to strengthen the fabric of peace in the West Pacific Area,

Recalling with mutual pride the relationship which brought their two peoples together in a common bond of sympathy and mutual ideas to fight side by side against imperialist aggression during the last war,

Desiring the declare publicly and formally their sense of unity and their common determination to defend themselves against external armed attack, so that no potential aggressor could be under the illusion that either of them stands alone in the West Pacific Area, and

Desiring further to strengthen their present efforts for collective defense for the preservation of peace and security pending the development of a more comprehensive system of regional security in the West Pacific Area,

Have agreed as follows:

Article I

The Parties undertake, as set forth in the Charter of the United Nations, to settle any international dispute in which they may be involved by peaceful means in such a manner that international peace, security and justice are not endangered and to refrain in their international relations from the threat or use of force in any manner inconsistent with the purposes of the United Nations.

United Nations Treaty Series, CCXLVIII (New York: The United Nations, 1958), pp. 214–216.

Article II

In order more effectively to achieve the objective of this Treaty, the Parties separately and jointly by self-help and mutual aid will maintain and develop their individual and collective capacity to resist armed attack and communist subversive activities directed from without against their territorial integrity and political stability.

Article III

The Parties undertake to strengthen their free institutions and to cooperate with each other in the development of economic progress and social well-being and to further their individual and collective efforts toward these ends.

Article IV

The Parties, through their Foreign Ministers or their deputies, will consult together from time to time regarding the implementation of this Treaty.

Article V

Each Party recognizes that an armed attack in the West Pacific Area directed against the territories of either of the Parties would be dangerous to its own peace and safety and declares that it would act to meet the common danger in accordance with its constitutional processes.

Any such armed attack and all measures taken as a result thereof shall be immediately reported to the Security Council of the United Nations. Such measures shall be terminated when the Security Council has taken the measures necessary to restore and maintain international peace and security.

Article VI

For the purposes of Articles II and V, the terms "territorial" and "territories" shall mean in respect of the Republic of China, Taiwan and the Pescadores; and in respect of the United States of America, the island territories in the West Pacific under its jurisdiction. The provisions of Articles II and V will be applicable to such other territories as may be determined by mutual agreement.

Article VII

The Government of the Republic of China grants, and the Government of the United States of America accepts, the right to dispose such United States land, air and sea forces in and about Taiwan and the Pescadores as may be required for their defense, as determined by mutual agreement.

Article VIII

This Treaty does not affect and shall not be interpreted as affecting in any way the rights and obligations of the Parties under the Charter of the United Nations or the responsibility of the United Nations for the maintenance of international peace and security.

Article IX

This Treaty shall be ratified by the Republic of China and the United States of America in accordance with their respective constitutional processes and will come into force when instruments of ratification thereof have been exchanged by them at Taipei.

Article X

This Treaty shall remain in force indefinitely. Either Party may terminate it one year after notice has been given to the other party.

3. U.S. CONGRESSIONAL AUTHORIZATION FOR THE PRESIDENT TO EMPLOY THE ARMED FORCES OF THE UNITED STATES TO PROTECT FORMOSA, THE PESCADORES, AND RELATED POSITIONS AND TERRITORIES OF THAT AREA, January 29, 1955

Whereas the primary purpose of the United States, in its relations with all other nations, is to develop and sustain a just and enduring peace for all; and

Whereas certain territories in the West Pacific under the jurisdiction of the Republic of China are now under armed attack, and threats and declarations have been and are being made by the Chinese Communists that such armed attack is in aid of and in preparation for armed attack on Formosa and the Pescadores; and;

Whereas such armed attack if continued would gravely endanger the peace and security of the West Pacific Area and particularly of Formosa and the Pescadores; and

Whereas the secure possession by friendly governments of the Western Pacific Island chain, of which Formosa is a part, is essential to the vital interests of the United States and all friendly nations in or bordering upon the Pacific Ocean; and

Whereas the President of the United States on January 6, 1955, submitted to the Senate for its advice and consent to ratification a Mutual Defense Treaty between the United States of America and the Republic of China, which recognizes that an armed attack in the West Pacific Area directed against territories, therein described, in the region of Formosa and the Pescadores, would be dangerous to the peace and safety of the parties to the treaty: Therefore be it

Resolved by the Senate and House of Representatives of the United States of America in Congress assembled, That the President of the United States be and he hereby is authorized to employ the Armed Forces of the United States as he deems necessary for the specific purpose of securing and protecting Formosa and the Pescadores against armed attack, this authority to include the securing and protection of such related positions and territories of that area now in friendly hands and the taking of such other measures as he judges to be required or appropriate in assuring the defense of Formosa and the Pescadores.

This resolution shall expire when the President shall determine that the peace and security of that area is reasonably assured by international conditions created by action of the United Nations or otherwise, and shall so report to the Congress.

United States Statutes at Large, LXLX (Washington, D.C.: U.S. Government Printing Office, 1955), p. 7.

4. U.S. SECRETARY OF STATE DULLES'
STATEMENT, September 4, 1958 (Excerpt)

I have reviewed in detail with the President the serious situation which has resulted from aggressive Chinese Communist military actions in the Taiwan (Formosa) Straits area. The President has authorized me to make the following statement.

1. Neither Taiwan (Formosa) nor the islands of Quemoy and Matsu have ever been under the authority of the Chinese Communists. Since the end of the Second World War, a period of over 13 years, they have continuously been under the authority of Free China, that is, the Republic of China.

2. The United States is bound by treaty to help to defend Taiwan (Formosa) from armed attack and the President is authorized by Joint Resolution of the Congress to employ the armed forces of the United States for the securing and protecting of related positions such as Quemoy and Matsu.

3. Any attempt on the part of the Chinese Communists now to seize these positions or any of them would be a crude violation of the principles upon which world order is based, namely, that no country should use armed force to seize new territory.

4. The Chinese Communists have, for about 2 weeks, been subjecting Quemoy to heavy artillery bombardment and, by artillery fire and use of small naval craft, they have been harassing the regular supply of the civilian and military population of the Quemoys, which totals some 125 thousand persons. The official Peiping radio repeatedly announces the purpose of these military operations to be to take by armed force Taiwan (Formosa), as well as Quemoy and Matsu. In virtually every Peiping broadcast Taiwan (Formosa) and the offshore islands are linked as the objective of what is called the "Chinese People's Liberation Army."

5. Despite, however, what the Chinese Communists say, and so far have done, it is not yet certain that their purpose is in fact to make an all-out effort to conquer by force Taiwan (Formosa) and the offshore islands. Neither is it apparent that such efforts as are being made, or may be made, cannot be contained by the courageous, and purely defensive, efforts of the forces of the Republic of China, with such substantial logistical support as the United States is providing.

7. The President and I earnestly hope that the Chinese Communist regime will not again, as in the case of Korea, defy the basic principle upon which world order depends, namely, that armed force should not be used to achieve territorial ambitions. And such naked use of force would pose an issue far transcending the offshore islands and even the security of Taiwan (Formosa). It would forecast a widespread use of force in the Far East which would endanger vital free world positions and the security of the United States. Acquiescence therein would threaten peace everywhere. We believe that the civilized world community will never condone overt military conquest as a legitimate instrument of policy.

8. The United States has not, however, abandoned hope that Peiping will stop short of defying the will of mankind for peace. This would not require it to abandon its claims, however ill-founded we may deem them to be. I recall that in the extended negotiations which the representatives of the United States and Chinese Communist regime conducted at Geneva between 1955 and 1958, a sustained effort was made by the United States to secure, with particular reference to the Taiwan area, a declaration of mutual and reciprocal renunciation of force, except in self-defense, which, however, would be without prejudice to the pursuit of policies by peaceful means. The Chinese Communists rejected any such declaration. We believe, however, that such a course of conduct constitutes the only civilized and acceptable procedure. The United States intends to follow that course, so far as it is concerned, unless and until the Chinese Communists, by their acts, leave us no choice but to react in defense of the principles to which all peace-loving governments are dedicated.

Department of State Bulletin, XXXIX: 1004 (Sept. 22, 1958), 445–446.

5. PRESIDENT KENNEDY'S STATEMENT ON
THE TAIWAN STRAIT, June 27, 1962

The Situation in the area of the Taiwan Strait is a matter of serious concern to this Government.

Very large movements of Chinese Communist forces into this area have taken place. The purpose of these moves is not clear. It seems important in these circumstances that the position of the United States Government be clearly understood.

Our basic position has always been that we are opposed to the use of force in this area. In earlier years, President Eisenhower made repeated efforts to secure the agreement of Communist China to the mutual renunciation of the use of force in the Taiwan area. And our support for this policy continues.

One possibility is that there might be aggressive action against the offshore islands of Matsu and Quemoy. In that event the policy of this country will be that established seven years ago under the Formosa resolution. The United States will take the action necessary to assure the defense of Formosa and the Pescadores.

In the last crisis in the Taiwan area in 1958, President Eisenhower made it clear that the United States would not remain inactive in the face of any aggressive action against the offshore islands which might threaten Formosa. In my own discussion of this issue, in the campaign of 1960, I made it quite clear that I was in agreement with President Eisenhower's position on this matter. I stated this position very plainly, for example, on October 16, 1960, and I quote:

"The position of the Administration has been that we would defend Quemoy and Matsu if there were an attack which was part of an attack on Formosa and the Pescadores. I don't want the Chinese Communists to be under any misapprehension.

"I support the Administration policy towards Quemoy and Matsu over the last five years."

Under this policy, sustained continuously by the United States Government since 1954, it is clear that any threat to the offshore islands must be judged in relation to its wider meaning for the safety of Formosa and the peace of the area.

Exactly what action would be necessary in the event of any such act of force would depend on the situation as it developed. But there must be no doubt that our policy, specifically including our readiness to take necessary action in the face of force, remains just what it has been on this matter since 1955.

It is important to have it understood that on this point the United States speaks with one voice. But I repeat that the purposes of the United States in this area are peaceful and defensive.

As Secretary Dulles said in 1955, and I quote: "The treaty arrangements which we have with the Republic of China make it quite clear that it is in our mutual contemplation that force shall not be used. The whole character of that treaty is defensive."

This continues to be the character of our whole policy in this area now.

Current History, No. 43 (Sept. 1962), 178.

6. PRESIDENT NIXON'S SECOND ANNUAL STATE OF THE WORLD REPORT, February 25, 1971 (Excerpt)

We are prepared to establish a dialogue with Peking. We cannot accept its ideological precepts, or the notion Communist China must exercize hegemony over Asia. But neither do we wish to impose on China an international position that denies its legitimate national interests.

The evolution of our dialogue with Peking cannot be at the expense of international order or our own commitments. Our attitude is public and clear. We will continue to honor our treaty commitments to the security of our Asian allies. An honorable relationship with Peking cannot be constructed at their expense.

Among these allies is the Republic of China. We have been associated with that government since its inception in 1911, and with particular intimacy when we were World War II allies. These were among the considerations behind the American decision to assist the Government of the Republic of China on Taiwan with its defense and economic needs.

Our present commitment to the security of the Republic of China on Taiwan stems from our 1954 treaty. The purpose of the treaty is exclusively defensive, and it controls the entire range of our military relationship with the Republic of China.

Our economic assistance to the Republic of China has had gratifying results. Beginning in 1951, the U.S. provided $1.5 billion in economic assistance. Its effective and imaginative use by the Government of the Republic of China and the people of Taiwan made it possible for us to terminate the program in 1965.

I am recalling the record of friendship, assistance, and alliance between the United States and the Government of the Republic of China in order to make clear both the vitality of this relationship and the nature of our defense relationship. I do not believe that this honorable and peaceful association need constitute an obstacle to the movement toward normal relations between the United States and the People's Republic of China. As I have tried to make clear since the beginning of my Administration, while I cannot foretell the ultimate resolution of the differences between Taipei and Peking, we believe these differences must be resolved by peaceful means.

In that connection, I wish to make it clear that the United States is prepared to see the People's Republic of China play a constructive role in the family of nations. The question of its place in the United Nations is not, however, merely a question of whether it should participate. It is also a question of whether Peking should be permitted to dictate to the world the terms of its participation. For a number of years attempts have been made to deprive the Republic of China of its place as a member of the United Nations and its Specialized Agencies. We have opposed these attempts. We will continue to oppose them.

China: U.S. Policy Since 1945 (Washington; D.C.: Congressional Quarterly, 1980), pp. 322–323.

7. REMARKS OF PRESIDENT CARTER ON ESTABLISHMENT OF DIPLOMATIC RELATIONS BETWEEN THE UNITED STATES OF AMERICA AND THE PEOPLE'S REPUBLIC OF CHINA, December 15, 1978

Good evening.

I would like to read a joint communique which is being simultaneously issued in Peking at this very moment by the leaders of the People's Republic of China:

Joint Communique on the Establishment of Diplomatic Relations Between the United States of America and the People's Republic of China, January 1, 1979.

The United States of America and the People's Republic of China have agreed to recognize each other and to establish diplomatic relations as of January 1st, 1979.

The United States recognizes the Government of the People's Republic of China as the sole legal government of China. Within this context, the people of the United States will maintain cultural, commercial and other unofficial relations with the people of Taiwan.

The United States of America and the People's Republic of China reaffirm the principles agreed on by the two sides in the Shanghai Communique of 1972 and emphasize once again that:

—Both sides wish to reduce the danger of international military conflict.

—Neither should seek hegemony—that is a dominance of one nation over the other—in the Asia-Pacific region or in any other region of the world and each is opposed to efforts by any other country or group of countries to establish such hegemony.

—Neither is prepared to negotiate on behalf of any other third party or to enter into agreements or understandings with the other directed at other states.

—The Government of the United States of America acknowledges the Chinese position that there is but one China and Taiwan is part of China.

—Both believe that normalization of Sino-American relations is not only in the interest of the Chinese and American peoples but also contributes to the cause of peace in Asia and in the world.

—The United States of America and the People's Republic of China will exchange Ambassadors and establish embassies on March 1, 1979.

Yesterday, our country and the People's Republic of China reached this final historic agreement.

On January 1, 1979, a little more than two weeks from now, our two governments will implement full normalization of diplomatic relations.

As a nation of gifted people who comprise about one-fourth of the total population of the earth, China plays, already, an important role in world affairs—a role that can only grow more important in the years ahead.

We do not undertake this important step for transient tactical or expedient reasons. In recognizing the People's Republic of China, that it is the single government of China, we are recognizing simple reality. But far more is involved in this decision that just recognition of a fact.

Before the estrangement of recent decades, the American and the Chinese people had a long history of friendship. We have already begun to rebuild some of those previous ties. Now, our rapidly expanding relationship requires the kind of structure that only full diplomatic relations will make possible.

The change than I am announcing tonight will be of great long-term benefit to the peoples of both our country and China—and, I believe, to all the peoples of the world.

Normalization—and the expanded commercial and cultural relations that it will bring—will contribute to the well-being of our own Nation, to our own national interest, and it will also enhance the stability of Asia.

White House Press Release, Dec. 15, 1978.

These more positive relations wih China can beneficially affect the world in which we live and the world in which our children will live.

We have already begun to inform our allies and other nations and the Members of the Congress of the details of our intended action. But I wish also tonight to convey a special message to the people of Taiwan—I have already communicated with the leaders in Taiwan—with whom the American people have had and will have extensive, close and friendly relations.

This is important between our two peoples.

As the United States asserted in the Shanghai Communique of 1972, issued on President Nixon's historic visit, we will continue to have an interest in the peaceful resolution of the Taiwan issue.

I have paid special attention to ensuring that normalization of relations between our country and the People's Republic will not jeopardize the well-being of the people of Taiwan.

The people of our country will mantain our current commercial, cultural, trade and other relations with Taiwan through nongovernmental means. Many other countries in the world are already successfully doing this.

These decisions and these actions open a new and important chapter in our country's history, and also in world affairs.

To strengthen and to expedite the benefits of this new relationship between China and the United States, I am pleased to announce that Vice Premier Teng has accepted my invitation and will visit Washington at the end of January. His visit will give our governments the opportunity to consult with each other on global issues and to begin working together to enhance the cause of world peace.

These events are the final result of long and serious negotiations begun by President Nixon in 1972, and continued under the leadership of President Ford. The results bear witness to the steady, determined and bipartisan effort of our country to build a world in which peace will be the goal and the responsibility of all nations.

The normalization of relations between the United States and China has no other purpose than this—the advancement of peace.

It is in this spirit, at this season of peace, that I take special pride in sharing this good news with you tonight.

8.   TAIWAN RELATIONS ACT
PUBLIC LAW 96–8—April 10, 1979 (Excerpts)

An Act

To help maintain peace, security, and stability in the Western Pacific and to promote the foreign policy of the United States by authorizing the continuation of commercial, cultural, and other relations between the people of the United States and the people on Taiwan, and for other purposes.

Be it enacted by the Senate and House of Representatives of the United States of America in Congress assembled,

---

U.S. Code, Title 22, §§ 3301–3316 (Supp. III, 1979) (Washington, D.C.: U.S. Government Printing Office, 1980), pp. 669–676.

SHORT TITLE

SECTION 1. This Act may be cited as the "Taiwan Relations Act."

FINDINGS AND DECLARATION OF POLICY

SEC. 2. (a) The President having terminated governmental relations between the United States and the governing authorities on Taiwan recognized by the United States as the Republic of China prior to January 1, 1979, the Congress finds that the enactment of this Act is necessary—

(1) to help maintain peace, security, and stability in the Western Pacific; and

(2) to promote the foreign policy of the United States by authorizing the continuation of commercial, cultural, and other relations between the people of the United States and the people of Taiwan.

(b) It is the policy of the United States—

(1) to preserve and promote extensive, close, and friendly commercial, cultural, and other relations between the people of the United States and the people on Taiwan, as well as the people on the China mainland and all other peoples of the Western Pacific area;

(2) to declare that peace and stability in the area are in the political, security, and economic interests of the United States, and are matters of international concern;

(3) to make clear that the United States decision to establish diplomatic relations with the People's Republic of China rests upon the expectation that the future of Taiwan will be determined by peaceful means;

(4) to consider any effort to determine the future of Taiwan by other than peaceful means, including by boycotts or embargoes, a threat to the peace and security of the Western Pacific area and of grave concern to the United States;

(5) to provide Taiwan with arms of a defensive character; and

(6) to maintain the capacity of the United States to resist any resort to force or other forms of coercion that would jeopardize the security, or the social or economic system, of the people on Taiwan.

(c) Nothing contained in this Act shall contravene the interest of the United States in human rights, especially with respect to the human rights of all the approximately eighteen million inhabitants of Taiwan. The preservation and enhancement of the human rights of all the people on Taiwan are hereby reaffirmed as objectives of the United States.

IMPLEMENTATION OF UNITED STATES POLICY WITH REGARD TO TAIWAN

SEC. 3 (a) In furtherance of the policy set forth in section 2 of this Act, the United States will make available to Taiwan such defense articles and defense services in such quantity as may be necessary to enable Taiwan to maintain a sufficient self-defense capacity.

(b) The President and the Congress shall determine the nature and quantity of such defense articles and services based solely upon their judgement of the needs of Taiwan, in accordance with procedures established by law. Such determination of Taiwan's defense needs shall include review by United States military authorities in connection with recommendations to the President and the Congress.

(c) The President is directed to inform the Congress promptly of any threat to the security or the social or economic system of the people on Taiwan and any danger to the interests of the United States arising therefrom. The President and the Congress shall determine in accordance with constitutional processes, appropriate action by the United States in response to any such danger.

REPORTING REQUIREMENT

SEC. 12 (a) The Secretary of State shall transmit to the Congress the text of any agreement to which the Institute is a party. However, any such agreement the immediate public disclosure of which would, in the opinion of the President, be prejudicial to the national security of the United States shall not be so transmitted to the Congress but shall be transmitted to the Committee on Foreign Affairs of the House of Representatives under an appropriate injunction of secrecy to be removed only upon due notice from the President.

(b) For purposes of subsection (a), the term "agreement" includes—

(1) any agreement entered into between the Institute and the governing authorities on Taiwan or the instrumentality established by Taiwan; and

(2) any agreement entered into between the Institute and an agency of the United States Government.

(c) Agreements and transactions made or to be made by or through the Institute shall be subject to the same congressional notification, review, and approval requirements and procedures as if such agreements and transactions were made by or through the agency of the United States Government on behalf of which the Institute is acting.

(d) During the two-year period beginning on the effective date of this Act, the Secretary of State shall transmit to the Speaker of the House of Representatives and the Committee on Foreign Relations of the Senate, every six months, a report describing and reviewing economic relations between the United States and Taiwan, noting any interference with normal commercial relations.

RULES AND REGULATIONS

SEC. 13. The President is authorized to prescribe such rules and regulations as he may deem appropriate to carry out the purposes of this Act. During the three-year period beginning on the effective date of this Act, such rules and regulations shall be terminated promptly to the Speaker of the House of Representatives and to the Committee on Foreign Relations of the Senate. Such action shall not, however, relieve the Institute of the responsibilities placed upon it by this Act.

CONGRESSIONAL OVERSIGHT

SEC. 14 (a) The Committee on Foreign Affairs of the House of Representatives, the Committee on Foreign Relations of the Senate, and other appropriate committees of the Congress shall monitor—

(1) the implementation of the provisions of this Act;

(2) the operation and procedures of the Institute;

(3) the legal and technical aspects of the continuing relationship between the United States and Taiwan; and

(4) the implementation of the policies of the United States concerning security and cooperation in East Asia.

(b) Such committees shall report, as appropriate to their respective Houses on the results of their monitoring.

9.   RONALD REAGAN'S STATEMENT ON TAIWAN
August 25, 1980

Ten days ago George Bush and I met with you here in Los Angeles on the occasion of his departure for Japan and China, a trip he undertook at my request. As we stressed at the time, the purpose of the trip was to provide for a candid exchange of views with leaders in both countries on a wide range of international topics of mutual interest. Ambassador Bush returned last evening, and has reported his findings in detail.

We are both very pleased with the results of his extensive discussions. In a series of meetings with distinguished leaders in Japan, including Prime Minister Suzuki, Former Prime Ministers Fukuda, Kishi and Miki, Foreign Minister Itoh and Minister of International Trade and Industry Tanaka, he had the opportunity to hear their views and recommendations concerning the future of U.S.–Japanese relations.

Our Republican Party Platform stresses that Japan will remain a pillar of our policy for Asia, and a Reagan-Bush Administration will work hard to insure that U.S.–Japanese relations are maintained in excellent condition, based on close consultation and mutual understanding.

Japan's role in the process of insuring peace in Asia is a crucial one, we must reinforce our ties with this close ally. Japan is our second most important trading partner, and we are her first. We have close ties in other fields, too. A most important example is the U.S.–Japan Mutual Security Treaty which recently marked its twentieth anniversary.

Understanding the Japanese perspective is important for the success of American policy. As Ambassador Bush will tell you in detail, he found Japanese leaders unanimous in their view that the United States must be a strong, reliable, leading partner.

I appreciate receiving their views, and I am grateful to them for the courtesies extended to Ambassador Bush. I would also like to express my appreciation to, and regard for, U.S. Ambassador Mike Mansfield, who also extended many courtesies.

Of equal importance was Ambassador Bush's trip to China, where he held a series of high-level meetings. As I said on August 16, "we have an obvious interest in developing our relationshp with China, an interest that goes beyond trade and cultural ties. It is an interest that is fundamental to a Reagan-Bush administration."

The meetings in Beijing provided for extensive exchanges of views. George has reported to me in great detail the points of similarity and agreement, as well as those of dissimilarity and disagreement. Since the objective of the trip was to have just such an exchange without necessarily reaching agreement, I believe that the objective was reached.

We now have received an updated, first-hand of China's views, and the Chinese leaders have heard our point of view.

While in Beijing, Ambassador Bush and Richard Allen met at length with Vice Premier Deng Xiaoping, Foreign Minister Huang Hua, as well as with other top foreign policy experts and military leaders. I appreciate the courtesies which the Chinese leaders extended to our party, and I also wish to thank U.S. Ambassador Leonard Woodcock for his kind assistance.

We now maintain full and friendly diplomatic relations with China. This relationship began only a few years ago, and it is one which we should develop and strengthen in the years ahead. It is a delicate relationship, and the Reagan-Bush Administration will handle it with care and respect, with due regard for our own vital interests in the world generally, and in the Pacific region specifically.

China and the United States have a common interest in maintaining peace so that our nations can grow and prosper. Our two-way trade has now reached approximately $3.5 billion annually, and China's program of modernization depends in a major way on Western and U.S. technology.

Along with many other nations, we and China share a deep concern about the pace and

Reagan Campaign Press Release, Aug. 25, 1980.

scale of the Soviet military buildup. Chinese leaders agree with Japanese leaders that the United States must be a strong and vigorous defender of peace, and they specifically favor us bolstering our defenses and our alliances.

It is quite clear that we do not see eye to eye on Taiwan. Thus, this is an appropriate time for me to state our position on this subject.

I'm sure that the Chinese leaders would place no value on our relations with them if they thought we would break commitments to them if a stronger power were to demand it. Based on my long-standing conviction that America can provide leadership and command respect only if it keeps its commitments to its friends, large and small, a Reagan-Bush Administration would observe these five principles in dealing with the China situation.

Guiding Principles for the Far East

First, U.S.–Chinese relations are important to American as well as Chinese interests. Our partnership should be global and strategic. In seeking improved relations with the People's Republic of China, I would extend the hand of friendship to all Chinese. In continuing our relations, which date from the historic opening created by President Nixon, I would continue the process of expanding trade, scientific, and cultural ties.

Second, I pledge to work for peace, stability and the economic growth of the Western Pacific area in cooperation with Japan, the People's Republic of China, the Republic of Korea and Taiwan.

Third, I will cooperate and consult with all countries of the area in a mutual effort to stand firm against aggression or search for hegemony which threaten the peace and stability of the area.

Fourth, I intend that United States relations with Taiwan will develop in accordance with the law of our land, the Taiwan Relations Act. This legislation is the product of our democratic process, and is designed to remedy the defects of the totally inadequate legislation proposed by Jimmy Carter.

By accepting China's three conditions for "normalization," Jimmy Carter made concessions that Presidents Nixon and Ford had steadfastly refused to make. I was and am critical of his decision because I believe he made concessions that were not necessary and not in our national interest. I felt that a condition of normalization—by itself a sound policy choice—should have been the retention of a liaison office on Taiwan of equivalent status to the one which we had earlier established in Beijing. With a persistent and principled negotiating position, I believe that normalization could ultimately have been achieved on this basis. But that is behind us now. My present concern is to safeguard the interests of the United States and to enforce the law of the land.

It was the timely action of the Congress, reflecting the strong support of the American people for Taiwan, that forced the changes in the inadequate bill which Mr. Carter proposed. Clearly, the Congress was unwilling to buy the Carter plan, which it believed would have jeopardized Taiwan's security.

This Act, designed by the Congress to provide adequate safeguards for Taiwan's security and well being, also provides the official basis for our relations with our long-time friend and ally. It declares our official policy to be one of maintaining peace and promoting extensive, close, and friendly relations between the United States and the 17 million people on Taiwan as well as the 1 billion people on the China mainland. It specifies that our official policy considers any effort to determine the future of Taiwan by other than peaceful means a threat to peace and of "grave concern" to the United States.

And, most important, it spells out our policy of providing defensive weapons to Taiwan and mandates the United States to maintain the means to "resist any resort to force or other forms of coercion" which threaten the security or the social or economic system of Taiwan.

This Act further spells out, in great detail, how the President of the United States, our highest elected official, shall conduct relations with Taiwan, leaving to his discretion the specific methods of achieving policy objectives. The Act further details how our official personnel (including diplomats) are to administer United States relations with Taiwan through the American Institute in Taiwan. It specifies that for that purpose they are to resign for the term of their duty in Taiwan and then be reinstated to their former agencies of the U.S. Government with no loss of status, seniority or pension rights.

The intent of the Congress is crystal clear. Our official relations with Taiwan will be funded by Congress with public monies, the expenditure of which will be audited by the Comptroller General of the United States; and Congressional oversight will be performed by two standing Committees of the Congress.

You might ask what I would do differently. I would not pretend, as Carter does, that the relationship we now have with Taiwan, enacted by our Congress, is not official.

I am satisfied that this Act provides an official and adequate basis for safeguarding our relationship with Taiwan, and I pledge to enforce it. But I will eliminate petty practices of the Carter Administration which are inappropriate and demeaning to our Chinese friends on Taiwan. For example, it is absurd and not required by the Act that our representatives are not permitted to meet with Taiwanese officials in their offices and ours. I will treat all Chinese officials with fairness and dignity.

I would not impose restrictions which are not required by the Taiwan Relations Act and which contravene its spirit and purpose. Here are other examples of how Carter has gone out of his way to humiliate our friends on Taiwan:

- Taiwanese officials are ignored at senior levels of the U.S. Government.
- The Taiwan Relations Act specifically requires that the Taiwanese be permitted to keep the same number of offices in this country as they had before. Previously, Taiwan had 14 such offices. Today there are but nine.
- Taiwanese military officers are no longer permitted to train in the United States or to attend service academies.
- Recently the Carter Administration attempted to ban all imports from Taiwan labeled "made in the Republic of China," but was forced to rescind the order after opposition began to mount in the Congress.
- The Carter Administration unilaterally imposed a one-year moratorium on arms supplies even though the Act specifies that Taiwan shall be provided with arms of a defense character.
- The Carter Administration abrogated the Civil Aviation Agreement with Taiwan, which had been in effect since 1947, in response to demands from the People's Republic of China.

I recognize that the People's Republic of China is not pleased with the Taiwan Relations Act which the United States Congress insisted on as the official basis for our relations with Taiwan. This was made abundantly clear to Mr. Bush, and, I'm told, is clear to the Carter Administration. But it *is* the law of our land.

Fifth, As President I will not accept the interference of any foreign power in the process of protecting American interests and carrying out the laws of our land. To do otherwise would be a dereliction of my duty as President.

It is my conclusion that the strict observance of these five principles will be in the best interests of the United States, the People's Republic of China and the people on Taiwan.

The specific implementation of these duties will have to await the results of the election in November, but in deciding what to do I will take into account the views of the People's Republic of China as well as Taiwan. It will be my firm intention to preserve the interests of the United States, and as President I will choose the methods by which this shall best be accomplished.

10. PREMIER SUN YUN-SUAN'S REPORT TO
THE LEGISLATIVE YUAN,
February 24, 1981 (Excerpts)

Opening Up a New Vista on the Diplomatic Front

External relations give us the opportunity to change the situation and create new opportunities for our country.

In our Republic's sixties, we lost some diplomatic friends because of international arrogance and shortsightedness, and faced difficulties with our membership in international organizations. As a result of our calm coping with the situation, people-to-people relations have been strengthened despite the termination of some government-to-government relationships; substantial relations have been furthered despite the conclusion of nominal relations. The increase in our economic and trade, scientific and technological, academic, cultural and athletic contacts with free countries have yielded mutual benefits, augmented friendly and cooperative relationships, and increased international understanding of our country's progress and prosperity.

In the last year, we have adhered to our basic spirit of national independence and to principles of equality and reciprocity as we followed a course of honesty and dignity in developing friendly relations with all democratic countries. We shall continue these efforts in the future. Strategically, we promote active diplomacy. Relying on our strength, we promote total diplomacy. Seeking openings on the diplomatic front, we promote diversified diplomacy.

In keeping with these guidelines, we have every confidence in our ability to expand our external activities. This is a breakdown of what we are doing:

—*Relations with the United States.* Since the establishment of formal relations between the United States and the Chinese Communist regime, we have adjusted our U.S. relations in accordance with requirements. Our government has made improvement of the U.S. relationship its consistent policy. In the last year, agreements have been signed involving air transportation, science and technology, textiles and immunities of representatives of the two sides. The United States has agreed to sell us some weapons, but we have to work harder to obtain more sophisticated weapons for strengthening our defense capability. With reorganization of the U.S. administration, it is to be hoped that our relationship will be further improved.

—*Relations with European countries.* We have made outstanding progress in promoting substantial relations with Europe during the last year: Such countries as Britain, France, West Germany, Spain, Holland, Greece, Austria and Belgium have established trade, financial and cultural organizations in the Republic of China. We have been able to set up corresponding establishments in many European countries. Following our purchase of Airbuses from France, the Western European countries have been paying more attention to the ROC trade potential. Relations with the Common Market have been improved. To diversify our markets and cope with international economic changes, the government approved direct trade with five Eastern European countries as of the end of 1979. The volume of this trade is being gradually developed.

—*Relations with African countries.* We are prepared to expand our technological cooperation programs from agriculture into industry, including development of small and medium enterprises, to move from bilateral to multilateral diplomacy and to include countries with which we have no diplomatic relations as well as those with which we do in order to help develop economies that will be resistant to Communist pressures. African nations that severed diplomatic relations with us have been watching our economic growth and our social stability and have come to miss the achievements made in the course of agricultural and other technological cooperation with us. They have indicated they would like to establish substantive economic, trade and technological relations with us either directly or indirectly. We are examining the situation and setting priorities.

Free China Weekly, XXII, 8 (March 1, 1981).

—*Relations with Latin American countries*. This is the area in which most of our diplomatic relationships are concentrated. Eleven countries still have formal diplomatic relations with us, and we have maintained representative offices in important countries with which we do not have formal relations. In this last year, we have augmented the number of official exchange visits with the countries in which we have embassies and enlarged the scope of cooperative activities. Where we have no diplomatic relations, we are continuing to seek or create favorable opportunities for elevating the status of our representation.

—*Relations with Middle Eastern countries*. Saudi Arabia has remained our firm friend with whom we have continued to enlarge and strengthen cooperation. At the end of last year, we held the ROC-Saudi Economic and Technical Cooperation Conference in Taipei and the ROC-Saudi Cultural Cooperation Conference in Riyadh. Relations were drawn closer when the first resident ambassador of Saudi Arabia assumed his post.

—*Exchange visits at higher levels*. Last March I accepted the invitations of the Republic of South Africa, Malawi, Swaziland and Lesotho and visited these countries. In May and June, Foreign Minister Chu Fu-sung visited six Central American and Caribbean countries. In September I visited the Central American states of Costa Rica, Panama and Dominica for a sincere exchange of views on the international situation and other matters of common interest with their chiefs of state and other high officials. In October, South African Prime Minister Pieter W. Botha and foreign ministers from some of the Latin American countries visited the Republic of China. These dignitaries were greatly interested in our progress in various fields during recent years and decided to enlarge and augment the scope of their countries' cooperation with us. We believe that closer and more amicable relationships will result from these activities.

Looking back over the past year, we can see that although we encountered difficulties on the diplomatic front, we also made some progress and established a new image internationally. International relationships are complex, however, and Chinese Communist conspiracies have no end. We must watch for changes and be ready to meet new challenges. As the sayings go, "People help those who help themselves" and "Righteous people can expect support." We are convinced that if we firmly adhere to our position and never cease to work hard, we shall be able to open up a new vista on the diplomatic front.

Looking Toward the Central Tasks in National Defense Development

In the current stage, national defense is stressing preparations for war and the development of national defense industry.

Our policy of building up the armed forces is intended to ensure the security of Taiwan, Penghu, Kinmen and Matsu and then to create opportunities for carrying out our task of mainland recovery. This means that our current defense and strategic policy must adhere to the principles of "integrating offense with defense" and "fighting independently." We shall stress both ideological warfare and offensive strategy. In the last year, these measures have been adopted in furtherance of our defense tasks:

—*Improvement of air defenses*. We have established an automated air defense system and prescribed joint combat areas where fighters, missiles and antiaircraft guns can be combined for effective integrated defense. Additionally, the government has decided to equip the Air Force with high performance jet fighters and antiaircraft guns. The number of missiles and combat planes is being increased and the training of air defense personnel stepped up. Air defense deployments over Taiwan, Kinmen, Matsu and Penghu are formidable and we control the air over the Taiwan Straits.

—*Strengthening superiority on the sea*. Our goals include the use of missiles as standard weapons, effective command control and vertical antisubmarine warfare. In this last year the government has carried out various measures to augment our supremacy on the sea, including the renovation of major weapons and equipment, improvement of air and sea spotting, improvement of antisubmarine warfare equipment and the development of new types of ships. The Self-Reliance Squadron of F5E jet fighters and Navy missile boats purchased with public donations have joined the combat forces, thereby contributing to public morale as well as to the strength of the armed forces.

—*Augmenting strength for ground warfare.* The Armed Forces seek increased firepo-wer and mobility for effective deployments in Taiwan, Penghu, Kinmen and Matsu. Besides drawing up long-range plans for the construction of military fortifications and adjusting the deployment of fighting units, the Armed Forces are accelarating the renewal of weapons and equipment, setting up stronger attack units and enhancing our ability to fight on the ground.

—*Establishing a flawless system of garrison security.* To guard against Chinese Communist infiltration and subversion, we have rallied the people to contribute their strength in opposing the united front. Infiltrators, surprise attacks and terrorism, thus ensuring the security and prosperity of our bastion of national revival.

I reported to the last two meetings of your esteemed Yuan that the government has established a special fund to accelerate development of national defense industry. The government has set up a special group to study and expedite this plan, relying on experts from at home and abroad. We hope that public and private cooperation will promote research on new weapons. As a result of joint efforts, we are engaged in 14 projects to develop armaments and have made progress. This suggests that we have the capability to build a national defense industry, are improving our technical skills, and are moving toward the manufacture of our own weapons.

The government has also moved to promote the cooperation between Armed Forces and people; improve the training of officers; augment military training in the schools; provide incentives for enlisted men and thereby strengthen grass roots leadership; and implement the "five-year plan for improving the life of officers and enlisted men" so as to elevate their morale. All of these programs have made good progress. The Vocational Assistance Commission for Retired Servicemen has recorded outstanding achievements in resettling retired servicemen, helping them find jobs, assuring them of medical care, sending them to school and providing employment overseas.

B.   Security Threats to Taiwan:
Armed Liberation or Peaceful Unification?

The periodic mass campaigns in the PRC to either "liberate" or "unify with" Taiwan remind one that Peking is the principal threat to the security of Taiwan. The first six documents all selected from official Chinese sources for this section demonstrate that the ultimate national goal of incorporating Taiwan into the motherland has been absolutely consistent throughout the last three decades.What has varied from time to time are tactics to be employed for achieving the ultimate goal of unification. Over the past 30 years Peking's tactics have alternated between periods of militant threat (Selections 11-14) and periods of peace overtures (Selections 15-16). When Secretary of State John Foster Dulles succeeded in persuading President Chiang Kai-shek in 1958 to agree to publicly renounce "the use of force" as the means of recovering the mainland, he was viciously attackes by the PRC as having been engaged in plotting to create "two Chinas" (Selection 12). Even amidst the most conciliatory mood of the Nixon visit of 1972, Peking reiterated its determination to liberate Taiwan (Selection 13).

Following the conclusion of normalization, Peking entered a phase of rigorous "peace" campaigns. It has urged Taipei repeatedly to open up postal services, tourist exchange and mutual trade between the two sides (Selections 15-16). At times, Peking even offered to allow Taiwan to retain its political and economic autonomy, and even its armed forces, as long as it was willing to surrender its sovereignty. Of course, this is not the first time that such "generous" offers were made by Peking. During the period of political moderation in the mid-1950's the offer made by Premier Chou was essentially the same in substance. It may be recalled that these peace overtures were reversed again and again during the radical campaigns of the Great Leap Forward and the Cultural Revolution. During the violent Quemoy Crisis of 1958, more than half a million artillery shells fell on the tiny offshore island. It is not hard to understand why the Nationalist leaders are extremely leery of any negotiations with Peking, because past experiences have shown that they invariably suffered whenever they negotiated with the Communists.

The bitter experience of Tibet's "peaceful liberation" is another chilling lesson that the people on Taiwan still remember. Peking's peace offer to Taiwan, in fact, bears a great similarity to the offer which the Tibetans accepted in 1951. However, it may be recalled, the PLA invaded Tibet in 1959, and ended the latter's legally guaranteed "autonomy" through a bloodbath of military suppression (Selection 17).

11.   FOREIGN MINISTER CHOU EN-LAI'S STATEMENT REFUTING TRUMAN'S STATEMENT ON TAIWAN, June 28, 1950 (Excerpt)

After instigating the puppet government of Syngman Rhee in South Korea to provoke civil war in Korea, President Truman of the United States of America made a statement on June 27, declaring that the United States Government had decided to prevent by armed force our liberation of Taiwan.

On Truman's order, the U.S. Seventh Fleet has moved to the coast of Taiwan.

On behalf of the Central People's Government of the People's Republic of China, I declare that Truman's statement of June 27 and the action of the U.S. navy constitute armed aggression against the territory of China and are a gross violation of the United Nations Charter. This violent, predatory action by the United States Government came as no surprise to the Chinese people but only increases their wrath, because the Chinese people have, over a long period, consistently exposed all the conspiratorial schemes of U.S. imperialism to commit aggression against China and seize Asia by force. In his statement, Truman merely discloses his premeditated plan and puts it into practice. In fact the attack by the puppet Korean troops of Syngman Rhee on the Korean Democratic People's Republic at the instigation of the United States Government was a premeditated move by the United States, designed to create a pretext for the United States to invade Taiwan, Korea, Vietnam and the Philippines. It is nothing but a further act of intervention by U.S. imperialism in the affairs of Asia.

On behalf of the Central People's Government of the People's Republic of China, I declare that, no matter what obstructive action U.S. imperialists may take, the fact that Taiwan is part of China will remain unchanged forever. This is not only a historical fact; it has also been confirmed by the Cairo and Potsdam Declarations and the situation since the surrender of Japan. All the people of our country will certainly fight as one man and to the end to liberate Taiwan from the grasp of the U.S. aggresssors. The Chinese people, who have defeated Japanese imperialism and Chiang Kai-shek, the hireling of U.S. imperialism, will surely succeed in driving out the U.S. aggressors and in recovering Taiwan and all other territories belonging to China.

Oppose U.S. Occupation of Taiwan and "Two Chinas" Plot (Peking: Foreign Languages Press, 1958), pp. 5–6.

12. DOCUMENT 63: "ON THE CHIANG KAI-SHEK—DULLES TALKS," *People's Daily,* October 30, 1958 (Excerpts)

Not long ago, U.S. Secretary of State Dulles went to Taiwan and held talks with Chiang Kai-shek. Now the United States is ballyhooing these talks as marking a change in U.S. policy toward China, as having strengthened the unity between the United States and Chiang Kai-shek and as a manifestation of U.S. peaceful intentions. There is indeed a change in U.S. policy toward China—its plot to create "two Chinas" is coming out into the open. This change, however, merely amounts to the implementation in another form of its policy of aggression and war against China. There are no peaceful intentions whatsoever about it. Dulles' aim in these talks was to force Chiang to accept the "two Chinas" scheme. He has actually made some gains in this respect. However, his dream is far from being realized. As to the lip service paid to greater unity, that is just so much eyewash. . . .

On the eve of publication of the communiqué on the Chiang-Dulles talks, U.S. Vice-President Richard Nixon declared publicly that there was a "need for an independent Chinese government to which both the twelve million people on Formosa and the millions more of overseas Chinese can owe allegiance." In the Chiang-Dulles joint communiqué of October 23, Dulles forced the Taiwan authorities to accept the so-called principle of no recourse to the use of force, and granted the Chiang Kai-shek clique the right to represent only "free China." This appeared to be an agreement between Chiang Kai-shek and Dulles. . . .

The creation of the "two Chinas," it must be pointed out, is merely a matter of expediency for the United States. The United States wants first to separate Taiwan from China and isolate it completely, so as to facilitate its control over the Chiang Kai-shek clique and strengthen its occupation of Taiwan. But this is only a first step. Once Taiwan should become a "*de facto* political unit" independent of China, the United States could then use some pretext or other to place it under trusteeship. In this way, the United States would take a double gain: on the one hand, it would legalize its seizure of Taiwan and turn that island into a U.S. colony; at the same time, by involving certain other countries, it would get them to share its responsibility for aggression. The Chiang Kai-shek clique clearly has no place in this sinister U.S. scheme. Nixon declared that the aim of the United States in the Far East was to make Taiwan an "island of freedom" rather than "to tie the United States policy to Chiang Kai-shek." Isn't the meaning of these words clear enough?

It is very absurd for the United States to abuse the principle of no recourse to the use of force in international relations, by trying to apply it to China's internal affairs. By so doing, the United States aims to tie the hands of the Taiwan authorities and make them completely subservient to the U.S. The Taiwan authorities are not unaware of this. That is why, after the release of the Chiang-Dulles joint communiqué, they made such a hullabaloo about there being reservations to their declaration on renunciation of the use of force. However, the United States featured this same declaration as its major victory. Both parties are clinging to their own interpretation and making a big fuss about it. It was in these circumstances that, at his press conference on October 28, Dulles, as if handing down a verdict, came out bluntly with the remark that, despite all their reservations, the Taiwan authorities "didn't have much chance of winning by force." Coming from Dulles, isn't this a deliberate attempt to make it difficult for the Taiwan authorities even to drag on their miserable existence?

We stated long ago that it is absolutely impossible for the U.S. to carry through its plot of creating "two Chinas" so as to occupy Taiwan indefinitly. The Chinese people who have stood up are confident that they can smash this U.S. plot. There is only one China in the world, not two. Every patriotic Chinese opposes the "two Chinas" scheme. The masses of overseas Chinese oppose it. Even the Taiwan authorities do not agree to it. On October 24, Chiang Kai-shek said that Taiwan and the mainland were part of the same entity, with a flesh and blood relationship, sharing the common weal and woe. We believe that the U.S. scheme to split China and create "two Chinas" will be utterly defeated if the whole Chinese people unite and face the foreign foe. . . .

Peking Review, No. 35 (Oct. 28, 1958), 9–11.

The United States realizes that a direct proposal of the "two Chinas" scheme just will not work. That is why it is employing a series of crafty devices such as demands for a cease-fire, renunciation of the use of force, reduction of Chiang Kai-shek's troops on the offshore islands, and so on and so forth. But no patriotic Chinese will permit the U.S. to use such devices to meddle in the internal affairs of China and realize its aim of creating "two Chinas."

The U.S. is purposely confusing public opinion in order to sell the world its scheme for the creation of "two Chinas". The U.S. says: just as there can be two Koreas, two Vietnams, two Germany's, why can't there be "two Chinas"? But this is absolutely ridiculous. The existence of two Germanys is an outcome of the Second World War. The division of Korea and Vietnam into northern and southern parts is a temporary state of affairs provided for by the relevant international agreements. They provide no basis for comparison with the forcible U.S. occupation of Taiwan and its obstruction of the unification of China. The U.S. has used every possible means and done its utmost to obstruct the unification of Germany, Korea and Viet-nam, and now it is trying to turn division of these three nations into a justification for creating "two Chinas" and perpetuating its occupation of Taiwan. Not only is this an utterly untenable position; it exposes the U.S. crimes of aggression all over the world . . .

Faced by the resolute opposition of the Chinese people, the U.S. is planning to implement its "two Chinas" plot by means of a so-called international settlement. It is trying to get the question of the situation in the Taiwan Straits area submitted to the United Nations. It is true that U.S. aggression against and interference in China have created tension in the Taiwan Straits area and the United Nations should have dealt with it, but since the People's Republic of China is deprived of its legitimate place in the United Nations, the United Nations has lost its competence to handle this question. As to the Chinese people's liberation of Taiwan, Penghu, Quemoy and Matsu to complete the unification of their motherland, this is an internal matter and the U.N. has no right to interfere in it at all. No Chinese with any sense of self-respect will ever agree to the submission of this question to the U.N. The U.S. is also trying to interfere in China's internal affairs and obstruct the Chinese people's liberation of Taiwan, Penghu, Quemoy and Matsu through some sort of international court, referendum, international mediation or other kind of so-called international settlement. The Chinese people will tolerate none of this. We are convinced that no fair-minded nation or people will fall into these U.S. traps.

13.   THE SHANGHAI COMMUNIQUE
February 28, 1972 (Excerpt)

The two sides reviewed the long-standing serious disputes between China and the United States. The Chinese side reaffirmed its position: That Taiwan question is the crucial question obstructing the normalization of relations between China and the United States; the Government of the People's Republic of China is the sole legal government of China; Taiwan is a province of China which has long been returned to the motherland; the liberation of Taiwan is China's internal affair in which no other country has the right to interfere; and all U.S. forces and military installations must be withdrawn from Taiwan. The Chinese Government firmly opposes any activities which aim at the creation of "one China, one Taiwan," "one China, two governments," "two Chinas," and "Independent Taiwan" or advocate that "the status of Taiwan remains to be determined."

The U.S. side declared: The United States acknowledges that all Chinese on either side of the Taiwan Strait maintain there is but one China and that Taiwan is a part of China. The United States Government does not challenge that position. It reaffirms its interest in a peaceful settlement of the Taiwan question by the Chinese themselves. With this prospect in mind, it affirms the ultimate objective of the withdrawal of all U.S. forces and military installations from Taiwan. In the meantime, it will progressively reduce its forces and military installations on Taiwan as the tension in the area diminishes.

U.S. Department of State Bulletin, Vol. 66, No. 1708 (Mar. 20, 1972), 435–438.

14. PREMIER HUA KUO-FENG'S REPORT ON
THE WORK OF THE GOVERNMENT
February 26, 1978 (Excerpt)

Taiwan is part of the sacred territory of China. The people in and from Taiwan are our kith and kin. The liberation of Taiwan and the unification of the motherland are the common aspirations of the whole Chinese people, our Taiwan compatriots included. We resolutely oppose anyone scheming to create what is called "two Chinas," "one China, one Taiwan," "one China, two governments" or an "independent Taiwan." We place our hopes on the people of Taiwan and resolutely support their patriotic struggle against imperialism and the Chiang clique. As for the military and administrative personnel of the Kuomintang in and from Taiwan, it has been our consistent policy that "all patriots belong to one big family," "whether they come over early or late." It is our hope that they will clearly see the general trend of events and take the road of patriotism and unification of the motherland. The Chinese People's Liberation Army must make all the preparations necessary for the liberation of Taiwan. We are determined to realize the behest of Chairman Mao and Premier Chou and, together with our Taiwan compatriots, accomplish the sacred task of liberating Taiwan and unifying the motherland . . .

The Sino–U.S. Shanghai Communiqué issued in 1972 has brought a new turn in the relations between the two countries. These relations will continue to improve provided the principles laid down in the Communiqué are seriously carried out. At present, the attitude of the U.S. government toward the question of Taiwan is the obstacle to the normalization of Sino-U.S. relations. The Chinese people are determined to liberate Taiwan. When and how is entirely China's internal affair, an internal affair which brooks no foreign interference whatsoever. If the relations between the two countries are to be normalized, the United States must sever its so-called diplomatic relations with the Chiang clique, withdraw all its armed forces and military installations from Taiwan and the Taiwan Straits area, and abrogate its so-called "mutual defense treaty" with the Chiang clique. This is the unswerving stand of the Chinese government.

Peking Review, No. 10 (March 10, 1978), 35 and 39.

15. PREMIER CHOU EN-LAI'S REPORT TO
THE NATIONAL PEOPLE'S CONGRESS
June 28, 1956 (Excerpts)

The Chinese people are determined to liberate Taiwan. This is the unshakable common will of the 600 million people of China.

The Chinese Government has repeatedly pointed out that there are two ways for the Chinese people to liberate Taiwan, that is, by war or by peaceful means, and that the Chinese people would seek to liberate Taiwan by peaceful means so far as it is possible. There is no doubt that if Taiwan can be liberated peacefully, it would be best for our country, for all the Chinese people and for Asian and world peace.

At present, the possibility of peacefully liberating Taiwan is increasing. This is first of all because the international situation is now definitely tending toward relaxation, and the United States armed occupation of Taiwan and interference in China's internal affairs are opposed by more and more peace-loving countries and peoples. As regards our in internal situation, our great motherland has grown even stronger and become even more consolidated. . . .

We have consistently stood for national solidarity and united resistance against external enemies. In the interest of our great motherland and our people, the Chinese Communists and the Kuomintang members have twice fought shoulder to shoulder against imperialism. After the conclusion of the War of Resistance to Japanese Aggression, we also made efforts to bring about internal peace. Even during the Chinese War of Liberation, when the Chinese people were forced to take up arms, and even after the mainland was liberated, we have never given up efforts for peaceful negotiations. Although in the past few years, owing to U.S. armed intervention, we and the Kuomintang military and political personnel on Taiwan have taken different paths, yet so long as we all hold supreme the interests of our nation and motherland, we can still link arms again and unite. We believe that our great nation, which experienced long years of suffering, will certainly be able through our own efforts to accomplish the complete unity of our motherland.

Now, on behalf of the Government, I formally state: We are willing to negotiate with the Taiwan authorities on specific steps and terms for the peaceful liberation of Taiwan, and we hope that the Taiwan authorities will send their representatives to Peking or other appropriate places, at a time which they consider appropriate, to begin these talks with us.

In order to unite all patriotic forces to realize at an early date the complete unification of our motherland, I wish here to declare once again that all patriotic people, regardless of whether they joined the patriotic ranks earlier or later, and regardless of how great the crimes they committed in the past may have been, will be treated in accordance with the principle that "patriots belong to one family" and the policy of no punishment for past misdeeds; they are all welcome to perform meritorious service for the peaceful liberation of Taiwan, and will be duly rewarded according to the degree of their merit and provided with appropriate jobs.

Our compatriots in Taiwan have always been an inseparable part of the Chinese people. We not only have constant concern for them and support them in various ways in their struggle against foreign rule, but also stand ready to welcome them at any time to participate in the socialist construction of the motherland and to share the glory of our nation.

We appreciate the situation in which all the Kuomintang military and political personnel on Taiwan whose homes are on the mainland find themselves, and we hope that they may soon realize their desire of reuniting with their families. They can communicate with their relatives and friends on the mainland; they can also return to the mainland for short visits to their relatives and friends. We are prepared to give them all kinds of convenience and assistance.

We hope the responsible Kuomintang military and political personages on Taiwan will

---

Oppose U.S. Occupation of Taiwan and "Two Chinas" Plot (Peking: Foreign Languages Press, 1958), pp. 41–51.

actively expedite the peaceful liberation of Taiwan. If they do so, they will surely earn the confidence and care of the motherland and the people. The treatment accorded to those commanders and soldiers who came over peacefully on the mainland is a precedent.

We also hope that all Kuomintang military and political personnel who are abroad will work for the peaceful liberation of Taiwan. Only thus can they escape the fate of leading the life of exiles in foreign lands, looked down upon by others.

We attach great importance to the positive role played by the broad mass of patriotic overseas Chinese in promoting the cause of the peaceful liberation of Taiwan. We hope that those few overseas Chinese who used to maintain or still maintain a hostile attitude toward the motherland will distinguish between right and wrong, see the direction in which events are moving, and, together with the broad mass of patriotic overseas Chinese, contribute toward the patriotic cause of the peaceful liberation of Taiwan.

The gate of the motherland is always wide open for all patriots. Every Chinese has both the right and the duty to make his contribution to the sacred cause of the unification of the motherland. With the unity of the entire nation and the efforts of all our people, the liberation of Taiwan will certainly be consummated.

16.   MESSAGE TO COMPATRIOTS IN TAIWAN FROM THE STANDING COMMITTEE OF THE FIFTH NATIONAL PEOPLE'S CONGRESS
December 26, 1978 (Excerpts)

Reunification of China today is consonant with popular sentiment and the general trend of development. The world in general recognizes only one China, with the Government of the People's Republic of China as its sole legal Government. The recent conclusion of the China-Japan Treaty of Peace and Friendship and the normalization of relations between China and the United States show still more clearly that no one can stop this trend. The present situation in the motherland, one of stability and unity, is better than ever. The people of all nationalities on the mainland are working hard with one will for the great goal of the four modernizations. It is our fervent hope that Taiwan returns to the embrace of the motherland at an early date so that we can work together for the great cause of national development. Our state leaders have firmly declared that they will take present realities into account in accomplishing the great cause of reunifying the motherland and respect the status quo on Taiwan and the opinions of people in all walks of life there and adopt reasonable policies and measures in settling the question of reunification so as not to cause the people of Taiwan any losses. On the other hand, people in all walks of life in Taiwan have expressed their yearning for their homeland and old friends, stated their desire "to identify themselves with and rejoin their kinsmen," and raised diverse proposals which are expressions of their earnest hope for an early return to the embrace of the motherland. As all conditions now are favourable for reunification and everything is set, no one should go against the will of the nation and against the trend of history.

We place hopes on the 17 million people on Taiwan and also the Taiwan authorities. The Taiwan authorities have always taken a firm stand of one China and have been opposed to an independent Taiwan. We have this stand in common and it is the basis for our co-operation. Our position has always been that all patriots belong to one family. The responsibility for reunifying the motherland rests with each of us. We hope the Taiwan authorities will treasure national interests and make valuable contributions to the reunification of the motherland.

Beijing Review, No. 1 (Jan. 5, 1979), 16–17.

The Chinese Government has ordered the People's Liberation Army to stop the bombardment of Jinman (Quemoy) and other islands as from today. A state of military confrontation between the two sides still exists along the Taiwan Straits. This can only breed manmade tension. We hold that first of all this military confrontation should be ended through discussion between the Government of the People's Republic of China and the Taiwan authorities so as to create the necessary prerequisites and a secure environment for the two sides to make contacts and exchanges in whatever area.

The prolonged separation has led to inadequate mutual understanding between the compatriots on the mainland and on Taiwan and various inconveniences for both sides. Since overseas Chinese residing in faraway foreign lands can return for visits and tours and hold reunions with their families, why can't compatriots living so near, on the mainland and on Taiwan, visit each other freely? We hold that there is no reason for such barriers to remain. We hope that at an early date transportation and postal services between both sides will be established to make it easier for compatriots of both sides to have direct contact, write to each other, visit relatives and friends, exchange tours and carry out academic, cultural, sports and technological interchanges.

Economically speaking, Taiwan and the mainland of the motherland were originally one entity. Unfortunately, economic ties have been suspended for many years. Construction is going ahead vigorously on the motherland and it is our wish that Taiwan also grows economically more prosperous. There is every reason for us to develop trade between us, each making up what the other lacks, and carry out economic exchanges. This is mutually required and will benefit both parties without doing any harm to either.

Dear compatriots in Taiwan,

The bright future of our great motherland belongs to us and to you. The reunification of the motherland is the sacred mission history has handed to our generation. Times are moving ahead and the situation is developing. The earlier we fulfill this mission, the sooner we can jointly write an unprecedented, brilliant page in the history for our country, catch up with advanced powers and work together with them for world peace, prosperity and progress. Let us join hands and work together for this glorious goal!

17. THE UNIFICATION OF TIBET
(Excerpts)

King C. Chen

A typical example of unification under the Peking government since 1949 is Tibet. It is relevant to the subject here because the Chinese leaders have repeatedly mentioned that Taiwan could have a high autonomous status like that of Tibet before 1959.

On May 23, 1951, the Peking government and the Tibetan government signed a 17-point accord entitled, "Agreement of the Central People's Government and the Local Government of Tibet on Measures for the Peaceful Liberation of Tibet." From the title of this agreement, one can simply judge that the Peking government, at the outset, made it clear that this was a unification issue that the Central government of China dealt with a local government in China. This accord, accordingly, was a document of domestic law, not of international law. Consequently, Peking's "peaceful liberation" of Tibet in 1959 was its own "domestic affair" in which no other nation could have the right to interfere.

After the Chinese occupying forces had entered Tibet, Chairman Mao Tse-tung on April 6, 1952 issued a "directive" for the takeover of Tibet. It can be summarized in five points: (1) Flexibility and gradualism in carrying out the agreement of 1951; (2) cooperation with pro-Peking Tibetans whereas isolating the resisters; (3) self-support in food production by the occupying military forces so as not to drain local economic resources; (4) the maintenance and development of Tibet's trade with India and China; and (5) insistence on the eventual reorganization of the Tibetan army and the ultimate military takeover. With this directive, Peking had waited for eight years (1952-59) before it "peacefully liberated" Tibet.

What had actually happened in Tibet in 1959, in a nutshell, was the Chinese military takeover with bloodshed. In doing so, Peking had violated Article 3 of the 1951 Agreement which provided that "the Tibetan people have the right of exercising national regional autonomy under the unified leadership of the Central People's Government." From March to October 1959, the Tibetan uprisings and the ensuing Chinese military repression cost about at least 10,000 Tibetan lives (about 1 percent of the population). 80,000 Tibetan refugees, including the Dalai Lama, fled to India and other countries.

On the basis of reports and studies by the International Commission of Jurists and individual scholars, several significant points can be drawn from the Tibetan experience of unification.

(1) Although the 1951 Chinese-Tibetan agreement was signed "under duress" and could accordingly be considered void, it was a domestic, not an international, agreement. Consequently, the Peking government's violation of this accord was not a breach of international law.

(2) The Tibetan government did not violate the 1951 agreement except for its reluctance to cooperate with the Chinese military authorities in taking over Tibet.

(3) While the Chinese government, according to the 1951 agreement, had the legal right to liberate and unify Tibet with China by peaceful means, the means that Peking employed to accomplish this goal in 1959 was military. In this context, the Tibetan case presents us with a serious question: Since Peking had failed to honor its written commitment to peaceful unification of Tibet, would she honor her verbal expectation of peaceful unification of Taiwan?

Human Rights Issue in Tibet

After the Chinese military occupied Tibet in 1959, human rights in that region were severely violated. According to various reports and studies by the International Commission of Jurists and individual journalists and scholars, the violation can be divided into the following categories:

Taiwan: Hearings Before the Committee on Foreign Relations, U.S. Senate, 96th Congress, February 5-22, 1979 (Washington, D.C.: U.S. Government Printing Office, 1979), pp. 822-824.

(1) Approximately 10,000 Tibetans out of 90,000 who revolted in 1959 were killed by the Chinese forces. 80,000 more fled Tibet. Later, defectors of the Chinese army reported about the reign of terror and repression in Tibet.

(2) Evidence proved the existence of enforced sterilization in Tibet by the Chinese authorities, although it was not in massive measure nor "Genocide." Forced labor was also imposed on the Tibetans.

(3) The Tibetans were deprived of their original religious freedom; it was transformed into Maoist worship.

(4) Serious food shortage occurred in Tibet after the Chinese military occupation and the Chinese authorities took almost no action to correct the situation.

Against the background, the General Assembly of the United Nations on October 21, 1959 adopted a resolution (introduced by Ireland and Malaya) calling for respect for the fundamental human rights of the Tibetan people and for their distinctive cultural and religious life. The vote was 45 to 9, with 26 abstentions. The United States approved it.

On December 20, 1961, the General Assembly once again adopted a four nation resolution (introduced by El Salvador, Malaya, Ireland and Thailand), solemnly renewing its 1950 call for the "cessation of practices which deprived the Tibetan people of their fundamental human rights and freedom, including their right to self-determination." The vote was 59 to 11, with 29 abstentions. The United States firmly supported.

The Carter Administration has once and again expressed its true concern over human rights. In late 1978 Amnesty International in its study, entitled "Political Imprisonment in the People's Republic of China," shows the record of the Chinese government's severe violation of human rights in that country. And yet, the human rights issue in Tibet has not been specifically voiced.

Appendix
Agreement between the Chinese Central People's Government and the Tibetan Government on the Administration of Tibet, May 23, 1951

1. The Tibetan people shall unite and drive out imperialist aggressive forces from Tibet so that the Tibetan people shall return to the big family of the motherland—the People's Republic of China.

2. The local government of Tibet shall actively assist the People's Liberation Army to enter Tibet and consolidate the national defenses.

3. In accordance with the policy toward nationalities laid down in the Common Program of the Chinese People's Political Consultative Conference, the Tibetan people have the right of exercising national regional autonomy under the unified leadership of the Central People's Government.

4. The central authorities will not alter the existing political system in Tibet. The central authorities also will not alter the established status, functions, and powers of the Dalai Lama. Officials of various ranks shall hold office as usual.

5. The established status, functions, and powers of the Panchen Ngoertehni shall be maintained.

6. By the established status, functions, and powers of the Dalai Lama and of the Panchen Ngoertehni are meant the status, functions, and powers of the Thirteenth Dalai Lama and of the Ninth Panchen Ngoerhtehni when they were in friendly and amicable relations with each other.

7. The policy of freedom of religious belief laid down in the Common Program of the Chinese People's Political Consultative Conference shall be carried out.

The religious beliefs, customs and habits of the Tibetan people shall be respected, and lama monasteries shall be protected. The central authorities will not effect a change in the income of the monasteries.

8. Tibetan troops shall be reorganized step by step into the People's Liberation Army and become a part of the national forces of the People's Republic of China.

9. The spoken and written language and school education etc. of the Tibetan nationality shall be developed step by step in accordance with the actual conditions in Tibet.

10. Tibetan agriculture, livestock raising, industry, and commerce shall be developed step by step, and the people's livelihood shall be improved step by step in accordance with the actual conditions in Tibet.

11. In matters related to various reforms in Tibet, there will be no compulsion on the part of the central authorities. The local government of Tibet should carry out reforms of its own accord, and, when the people raise demands for reform, they shall be settled by means of consultation with the leading personnel of Tibet.

12. Insofar as former pro-imperialist and pro-Kuomintang officials resolutely sever relations with imperialism and the Kuomintang and do not engage in sabotage or resistance, they may continue to hold office irrespective of their past.

13. The People's Liberation Army entering Tibet shall abide by all the above-mentioned policies and shall also be fair in all buying and selling and shall not arbitrarily take a needle or thread from the people.

14. The Central People's Government shall have the centralized handling of all external affairs of the area of Tibet, and there will be peaceful coexistence with neighboring countries and the establishment and development of fair commercial and trading relations with them on the basis of equality, mutual benefit, and mutual respect for territory and sovereignty.

15. In order to ensure the implementation of this agreement, the Central People's Government shall set up a military and administrative committee and a military area headquarters in Tibet, and, apart from the personnel sent there by the Central People's Government, shall absorb as many local Tibetan personnel as possible to take part in the work.

Local Tibetan personnel taking part in the military and administrative committee may include patriotic elements from the local government of Tibet, various districts and various principal monasteries; the name list shall be set forth after consultation between the representatives designated by the Central People's Government and various quarters concerned and shall be submitted to the Central People's Government for appointment.

16. Funds needed by the military and administrative committee, the military area headquarters, and the People's Liberation Army entering Tibet shall be provided by the Central People's Government. The local government of Tibet should assist the People's Liberation Army in the purchase and transport of food, fodder and other daily necessities.

17. This agreement shall come into force immediately after the signatures and seals are affixed to it.

Signed and sealed by delegates of the Central People's Government with full powers . . . [and] delegates with full powers of the local government of Tibet . . .

C.   Taiwan's Defense Capabilities and Arms Needs

The infusion of large quantities of U.S. military aid worth over $2.5 billion during the 1950's and 1960's enabled the Nationalist Armed Forces on Taiwan to transform themselves into an efficient fighting force with modern defense capabilities. Equipped with a wide array of advanced weapons and sophisticated command and communications systems supplied by the U.S., Taiwan's military forces are judged to be one of the best trained and equipped forces in Asia. Qualitatively, they are superior over their counterpart on the mainland in many aspects, especially in such important areas as jet fighters, missiles, and radars. This slight but crucial qualitative edge helped the Nationalists maintain their air and naval superiority over the Taiwan Strait. During the 1958 Quemoy confrontation, for instance, Taiwan's air force scored an impressive 1 : 15 kill-ratio in air combat against the Communist MiGs.

Quantitatively, however, as shown in the comparative data below, Taiwan is clearly no match to the mainland in practically every category. Due to its absolute quantitative strengths, it is generally held that China will be able to carry out a successful military assault on Taiwan if Peking chooses to do so. But the price they will have to pay would be so high—probably as high as one third of their entire air and naval forces—that they would be deterred from doing so in the near future.

It is abundantly clear, therefore, that the credibility of Taiwan's military deterrence rests ultimately on their qualitative superiority over their enemy, on the one hand, and on the availability of arms replenishment on a continuing basis from reliable sources, on the other. This may explain why the ROC leadership was so alarmed in 1979, when the Carter Administration decided to terminate the Mutual Defense Treaty and impose a moratorium on arms sales. Peking's emphasis on "military modernization" in recent years naturally gives Taiwan an even more heightened sense of urgency about the need to step up the pace of its own weapons upgrading and to develop an indigenous defense industry.

The two selections by Snyder, Gregor and Chang below provide detailed data on and excellent analyses of Taiwan's military capabilities in all key areas. They also identify and discuss the functions, priorities and quantities of the various types of arms urgently needed to make Taiwan's military deterrence credible vis-à-vis the military capabilities of Peking. It is worth noting that Admiral Edwin K. Snyder, having served as Commander of the U.S. Taiwan Defense Command between 1974 and 1977, is undoubtedly one of the few specialists who have both the professional expertise and personal experience to speak authoritatively on the subject of Taiwan's military capabilities.

18.   MILITARY STRENGTHS OF THE ROC & THE PRC

ROC (Taiwan) Armed Forces
Population: 17,500,000.
Military service: 2 years.
Total armed forces: 539,000.
Estimated GNP 1978: $23.4 bn.
Defence expenditure 1977-78: $1.7 bn.

PRC Armed Forces
Population: 958,000,000.
Military service: Army 2–4 years, Air
    Force 4 years, Navy 5 years.
Total regular forces: 4,360,000.
Estimated GNP 1978: $400 bn.
Defence expenditure 1978: $12 bn (Offi-
    cial); $40 bn (Western Estimate)

Strategic Forces:
ICBM: 2 CSS-3 (limited range).
IRBM: 50-70 CSS-2.
MRBM: 40-50 CSS-1.
Aircraft: about 90 Tu-16 med bbrs.

Army: 400,000
2 armd divs.
12 hy inf divs.
6 lt inf divs.
2 armd cav regts.
2 AB bdes.
4 special force gps.
1 SSM bn with *Honest John.*
3 SAM bns: 2 with 80 *Nike Hercules,* 1 with
    24 *HAWK.*
175 M-47/-48 med, 625 M-41 lt tks; 1,100
    M-113 APC; 550 105mm, 300 155mm
    guns/how; 350 75mm M-116 pack, 90
    203mm, 10 240mm how; 225 M-108
    105mm SP how, 81mm mor; *Kung Feng*
    126mm SP RL; *Honest John, Hsiung Feng*
    SSM; 150 M-18 76mm SP ATK guns, 500
    106mm RCL; 300 40mm AA guns (some
    SP); *Nike Hercules, HAWK,* 20 *Chapar-
    ral* SAM; 118 UH-1H, 2 KH-4, 7 CH-34
    hel.
(On order: 100 M-48 med tks; 100 M-109
    155mm, 25 M-110 203mm SP how; *TOW*
    ATGW, 24 *Improved HAWK* SAM.)

DEPLOYMENT: *Quemoy:* 60,000; *Matsu:*
    20,000.

RESERVES: 1,000,000.

Army: 3,600,000.
Main Forces:
    11 armd divs.
    115 inf divs.
    3 AB divs.
    40 arty divs (incl AA divs.)
    16 railway and construction engr divs.
    150 indep regts.

Local Forces:
    85 inf divs.
    130 indep regts.
11,000 Soviet IS-2 hy, T-34 and Chinese-
    produced Type-59/-63 med, Type-60
    (PT-76) amph and Type-62 lt tks; 1,500
    M-1967 APC; 16,000 122mm, 130mm,
    152mm guns/how, incl SU-76, SU-85,
    SU-100 and ISU-122 SP arty; 32,000
    82mm, 120mm, 160mm mor; 107mm,
    140mm RL; 75mm, 82mm RCL; 57mm,
    76mm, 85mm, 100mm ATK guns; 37mm,
    57mm, 85mm, 100mm AA guns.
(On order: *Milan, HOT* ATGW, *Crotale*
    SAM.)

DEPLOYMENT:
China is divided into 11 Military Regions
    (MR), in turn divided into Military Dis-
    tricts (MD), with usually two or three Dis-
    tricts to a Region. Divs are grouped into
    some 40 armies, generally of 3 inf divs, 3
    arty regts and, in some cases, 3 armd re-
    gts. Main Force (MF) divs are adminis-
    tered by Regions but are under central
    comd.

Data taken from The International Institute for Strategic Studies, *The Military Balance, 1979-1980* (Boulder, CO: WestView Press, 1980), pp. 60–65.

Navy: 35,000
2 ex-US *Guppy*-II submarines.
22 ex-US destroyers (10 *Gearing,* 2 with *Gabriel* SSM, 6 *with ASROC;* 8 *Summer,* 3 with *Gabriel* SSM; 4 *Fletcher* with *Chaparral* SAM).
11 ex-US frigates (10 APD37/87; 1 *Rudderow*).
3 ex-US *Auk* corvettes.
1 PSMM 5 FAC(M) with *Otomat* SSM.
6 FAC(T).
14 ex-US *Adjutant* coastal minesweepers.
51 landing vessels: 2 dock, 23 LST, 4 medium, 22 utility.
(On order: 2 PSMM 5 FAC(M) with *Otomat* SSM, *Harpoon, ASROC, Gabriel* SSM, *Sea Chaparral* SAM.)

RESERVES: 45,000.

Bases: Tsoying, Makung (Pescadores), Keelung.

Navy: 360,000, incl 38,000 Naval Air Force and 38,000 Marines; 25 major surface combat ships, 91 attack subs.
1 *Han* SSN.
1 G-class submarine (with SLBM tubes).
91 submarines (incl 68 Soviet R-, 21 W-class, 2 *Ming*).§
11 destroyers with *Styx* SSM: 7 *Luta* (more building), 4 ex-Sov *Gordy.*
14 frigates: 3 *Kiang Hu* and 4 ex-Sov *Riga* with *Styx* SSM, 2 *Kiang Tung* with SAM, 5 *Kiang Nan.*
9 patrol escorts.
160 FAC(M) with *Styx* SSM (80 *Osa/Hola,* 80 *Komar* and *Hoku*<).
20 *Kronstadt* large patrol craft.
23 *Hainan* FAC(P).
403 FAC(G) (25 *Shanghai* I, 340 *Shanghai* II, 6 *Haikou,* 30 *Swatow*<, 2 *Shantung* hydrofoils<).
220 FAC(T) (70 P6<, 120 *Hu Chwan*< hydrofoils, 30 P4<).
20 T43 ocean minesweepers.
15 ex-US 511-1152 LST, LSM, 16 inf landing ships, some 450 LCU.
1,000 coast and river defence craft (most <).

NAVAL AIR FORCE: 38,000; about 800 shore-based combat aircraft, organized into 4 bbr and 5 fighter divs, incl about 150 Il-28/B-5 torpedo-carrying, Tu-16 med and Tu-2 lt bbrs and some 575 fighters, incl MiG-17/F-4, MiG-19/F-6 and some F-9 *Fantan* A; a few Be-6 *Madge* MR ac; 50 Mi-4/H-5 hel and some lt tpt ac. Naval fighters are integrated into the AD system.

Marines: 39,000.
2 divs.
M-47 med tks; LVT-4 APC; 105mm, 155mm how; 106mm RCL.

RESERVES: 35,000.

Air Force: 65,000; 388 combat aircraft.
12 fighter sqns with 90 F-100A/F, 200 F-5A/E.
3 interceptor sqns with 63 F-104G.
1 recce sqn with 8 RF-104G.
1 MR sqn with 9 S-2A, 18-2E.
1 SAR sqn with 8 HU-16B ac, 10 UH-1H hel.
Tpts incl 30 C-46, 50 C-47, 1 C-118B, 40 C-119, 10 C-123, 1 Boeing 720B.
210 trainers, incl 55 PL-1B *Chien Shou,* 50 T-CH-1, 32 T-33, 30 T-38, F-5B/F, 3 TF-104G, 6 F-104D, F-100F.

Hel incl 95 UH-1H, 7 UH-19, 10 Bell 47G, 6 Hughes 500MD/ASW hel.
Sidewinder, Shafrir AAM, *Bullpup* ASM.
(On order: 48 F-5E/F fighters, 6 Hughes 500MD/ASW hel, *Maverick* ASM.)

RESERVES: 90,000.

Air Force: 400,000, incl strategic forces and 120,000 AD personnel; about 4,700 combat aircraft.
About 80–90 Tu-16/B-6 *Badger* and a few Tu-4 *Bull* med bbrs.
About 300 Il-28/B-5 *Beagle* and 100 Tu-2 *Bat* lt bbrs.
About 500 MiG-15/F-2 and F-9 *Fantan* A FB.
About 3,700 MiG-17/F-4/-5, MiG-19/F-6, 80 MiG-21/F-8 and some F-9 fighters organized into air divs and regts.
About 500 fixed-wing tpt ac, incl some 300 An-2/C-5, about 100 Li-2, 50 Il-14 and Il-18, some An-12/-24/-26, 18 *Trident.* 350 hel, incl Mi-4/H-5, Mi-8 and 13 *Super Frelon.* These could be supplemented by about 500 ac from the Civil Aviation Administration, of which about 150 are major tpts.
There is an AD system, capable of providing a limited defence of key urban and industrial areas, military installations and weapon complexes. Up to 4,000 naval and air force fighters are assigned to this role, also about 85 CSA-1 (SA-2) SAM and over 10,000 AA guns.

Para-Military Forces: 100,000 militia.

Para-Military Forces: Public security force and a civilian militia with various elements: the Armd Militia, up to 7 million, organized into about 75 divs and an unknown number of regts; the Urban Militia, of several million; the Civilian Production and Construction Corps, about 4 million; and the Ordinary and Basic Militia, 75–100 million, who receive some basic training but are generally unarmed.

19.   THE DEFENSE OF THE REPUBLIC OF CHINA
(Excerpts)
Edwin K. Snyder, A. James Gregor, and Maria Hsia Chang

Any discussion of the security of the Republic of China on Taiwan necessarily turns on the combat capabilities of the armed forces that would be involved in a military struggle for control of the island. Given the withdrawal of American forces from Taiwan, the immediate burden of defense against an attempted invasion by the People's Liberation Army (PLA) of the People's Republic of China becomes the responsibility of the Nationalist Chinese military.

Any appraisal of the force levels attainable by either party will inevitably involve the use of soft and highly perishable data. There are few things in the contemporary world more difficult to obtain than hard data on the military capabilities of either the ROC or the PRC. For every figure given, there is almost invariably another to be found—and the range of variation is often wide. Given the magnitude of the difference in overall capabilities, however, the elimination of these discrepancies would do little to alter the broad picture. The PRC enjoys almost a 10-to 1 superiority over the ROC in terms of personnel and in all categories of major military equipment. The PRC has the largest land army, the third largest air force, the third largest navy, and the third largest defense budget in the world.

Estimates of main force ground combat units commanded by the central Ministry of National Defense make the present manpower availability of the PRC approximately 3.4 to 3.6 million. Local militia, poorly trained and generally armed only with light weaponry, number about 7 million, organized into about 75 divisions.

The navy of the PRC lists approximately 300,000 men in active service, including 30,000 assigned to the naval air force and 38,000 to coastal defense detachments. Estimates of naval combatants identify 1 *Han*-class nuclear-powered submarine; 1 *G*-class submarine equipped with launching tubes for SLBMs (which as far as can be determined are unarmed); anywhere from 73 to 90 *R*-, *W*-, and *Ming*-class diesel-powered submarines; 7 *Luta*-class destroyers armed with Styx-type surface-to-surface missiles (SSMs); 4 Soviet-built *Gordy*-class destroyers also armed with Styx SSMs; 14 frigates at least 7 of which are armed with Styx SSMs; 14 patrol escort vessels; 39 subchasers; about 70 *Osa*- and 70 *Hoku*/*Komar*-type multipurpose missile patrol craft (PSMM); 140 P-4- and P-6-class motorized torpedo boats (MTB) that displace less than 100 tons; 105 *Hu Chwan* patrol hydrofoils that attain a top speed of 55 knots in calm seas and displace less than 100 tons; and 440 motorized gun boats (MGB) of the *Shanghai, Swatow*, and *Whampoa* classes; at least 30 minesweepers, about 18 of which are of the Soviet T-43 class, approximately 500 landing craft of assorted types; and over 300 coast and river defense regular navy vessels, almost all displacing less than 100 tons. The estimates of the total available units for the People's Liberation Army Navy (PLAN) range from about 1,680 to the Nationalist Chinese military intelligence estimate of 2,510.

The air force of the PRC counts about 400,000 men in its ranks, including in excess of 100,000 in the air defense (AD) organization and 15,000 pilots. The People's Liberation Army Air Force (PLAAF) deploys from 5,000 to 6,000 combat aircraft. The backbone of the air force is about 4,000 MiG-17 (F-4) and MiG-19 (F-6) interceptor-fighters, supplemented by about 100 Mig-21s and an indeterminate "small" number of F-9 (MiG-19 variants) fighter-bombers. The fighter-interceptor force is supplemented by a small tactical and strategic air force composed of about 80 Tu-16 (B6) medium bombers, 300-400 Il-28 (Beagle), and about 100 Tu-2 (Bat) light bombers. These are further supplemented by about 500 transport aircraft and about 350-400 helicopters.

Across the Taiwan Strait, the ROC maintains about half a million men under arms—

Edwin K. Snyder, A. James Gregor and Maria Hsia Chang, *The Taiwan Relations Act and the Defense of the Republic of China* (Berkeley, Ca: Institute of International Studies, University of California–Berkeley, 1980), pp. 24–45. Copyright 1980 by The Regents of the University of California. Reprinted by permission of the Regents. Footnotes omitted. The title is the Editor's.

330,000 in the main ground forces, 35,000 in the navy, 39,000 in the marines, and 70,000 in the air force. It deploys about 344 combatant units in its navy, including two former U.S. Navy submarines that underwent Greater Underwater Propulsion Program (GUPPY II) conversion during 1948-50; 21 or 22 destroyers of World War II vintage, almost all of which were modernized under the U.S. Navy's Fleet Rehabilitation and Modernization (FRAM) program. About half of these vessels have been or are being equipped with Gabriel-type SSMs. Ten or 11 armed frigates supplement the number of larger naval vessels, and there are about 37 torpedo, gun, and missile patrol boats, including 15 240-ton PSMMs (invarious stages of construction), each armed with one 76-mm. OTO Melara weapon and four SSM launchers. Among the patrol boats is a small (30-ton) vessel armed with a single 40-mm., radar-equipped cannon set amidships. (Ten more of these small patrol boats are expected to be commissioned shortly.)

The ROC Air Command (ROCAC) deploys about 316 combat aircraft. It is composed of 12 fighter squadrons equipped with 90 F-100A/F. (Sabre) and 165 F-5A/E (Tiger) aircraft and 3 interceptor squadrons deploying about 44 F-104G (Starfighter) aircraft. Eight F-104G aircraft have been modified to serve as reconnaissance platforms, and there are 9 S-2A/E (Tracker) craft serving rescue and anti-aubmarine warfare (ASW) functions. There are about 120 helicopters in the ROCAC inventory. The ROCAC has neither bomber nor specifically fighter-bomber units.

In sum, as previously noted, the PRC enjoys about 10-to-1 superiority over the ROC in terms of personnel and in all categories of major military equipment. Thus, apart from its local militia, the PRC has about 4.3 million men under arms; the ROC has about .5 million. The PRC navy deploys about 2,000 vessels—the ROC about 350. The PLAAF has about 4,500 fighter-interceptor aircraft—the ROC about 300. The PRC has about 10,000 tanks—the ROC less than 1,000. This asymmetry persists through all the conventional intermediate and minor weapons categories. Should nuclear weapons be included, the disparity in force levels becomes still more dramatic. The PRC has theater nuclear capability amounting to several hundred fission and fusion warheads with aircraft capable of tactical nuclear delivery. Land-based intermediate-range ballistic missile launchers, located on the mainland at at least 103 sites, are capable of targetting all of Taiwan. The ROC has no nuclear capability.

Given the massive disparity between these potential opponents, any suggestion that it is possible to bring the reactive and defense capabilities of the ROC up to levels that would be "self-sufficient" against attack by the PRC is transparent foolishness. Even without entertaining the possibility of nuclear assault, any determined attack by the PRC—now and for the forseeable future—would overwhelm the resistance of the ROC. The most competent estimates available indicate that the air force of the ROC would be neutralized by the overwhelming numbers of the PRC fighter force in two to three weeks. The PRC fleet of about 140 patrol boats, armed with SSMs, would find themselves opposed by—at best— 15 similarly armed ROC vessels. The 1,190 torpedo tubes of the PRC would face 132 tubes of the ROC. Given the neutralization of the ROCAC, the largest surface ships of the ROC—without tactical aircover and with most lacking significant air-defense capabilities—would themselves rapidly be neutralized, and the smaller patrol vessels would be scattered or destroyed. The military intelligence of the ROC estimates that the PRC now possesses about 500 regular naval craft capable of serving in a sealift capacity, while 700 other coastal vessels (the "seaborne militia") in the 500-ton-or-over category could be pressed into service in "boat-pack" waves for amphibious assault. Contrary to American estimates, ROC military intelligence claims that the PRC, mobilizing only 65 percent of its available sealift capablities, could transport about 18 infantry divisions to the Taiwan coast at one time. While the PRC has only limited airlift capabilities, there is every reason to believe that good use would be made of the 3 airborne paratroop divisions that at present are apparently up to operational strength. ROC coastal defenses could be degraded or supressed—given PRC Taiwan Strait tactical air superiority—by concentrated firepower delivered by patrol boats, destroyers, and armed frigates. PRC bombers, making a circuit from airfields about 150 miles away from the action front, could maintain unrelenting pressure on those defenses. Since most of the hardened defenses of the ROC are localized in the narrow northwestern plain of the island, there would be little defense in depth. Out-flanked by airlift forces and under steady bombardment from sea and air, the coastal defense of Taiwan could not long endure. In the process, the carnage and loss of military inventory on both sides would be oppressive. There would be widespread destruction of productive facilities and transportation infrastructure on Taiwan, of course, while the PRC would suffer substantial losses in aircraft and surface vessels as well as harrowing losses of ground troops.

In all probability, any determined amphibious assault on Taiwan by the armed forces of the PRC would have the general consequences described above, subject to certain qualifi-cations. For one thing, such a scenario would require the PLAAF's effective suppression of the air force of the ROC—no mean accomplishment. Although there is no question of the quantitative superiority of the PLAAF, it is clear that plane for plane and man for man the ROCAC is, at this time, qualitatively superior. By 1980 standards the MiG-17s and MiG-19s that constitute the bulk of the mainland air force are obsolescent. While the MiG-19 is a sturdy and dependable firing platform, it is at least marginally inferior to the F-5E—the present first-line fighter of the ROCAC. In addition, the Sidewinder air-to-air missiles (AAMs) with which the ROC aircraft are equipped seem to be significantly superior to the early Soviet-type Alkali and Atoll AAMs with which at least some of the PRC MiGs are armed. The avionics of PRC units, moreover, are relatively primitive. Most of the naviga-tional systems on PRC aircraft are visual, severely limiting their overwater and poor weather capabilities. PLAAF pilots rarely if ever make overwater flights; furthermore, their training in providing close support of ground troops is probably deficient at this time. Finally, the pilots of the PLAAF are considerably older than desireable to meet present-day demands for instant reaction times. Many younger pilots were purged during the "Great Proletarian Cultural Revolution," and the recruitment and training of new pilots seems to have been neglected for almost a decade. The costs of such qualitative inferiority are re-flected in the kill-ratios scored by American and ROC pilots in combat with the MiGs of the PRC. In major air battles between the PRC and the ROC in 1958, for example, the pilots in American-built F-86s of the ROCAC scored a kill-ratio of 15.5:1 against the MiG-17 pilots of the PLAAF. The air force of Mainland China would thus almost certainly have to sustain oppressive losses in any invasion attempt before the ROCAC had been neutralized.

In order to avoid such devastating losses, the PLAAF would have to cover and suppress the three or four military airbases now operational on Taiwan. But to accomplish that, the PLAAF would need to venture into unfamiliar airspace which has some of the most treach-erous air currents in the West Pacific region. Furthermore, it would have to operate in the detection and tracking envelope provided by the Taiwan air defense ground environment (ADGE) radar system that ties into a network of primary and secondary radars located along the defense perimeter and throughout the island. ADGE would allow multiple tracking of incoming aircraft targets covered by the entire network, separating military from nonmili-tary targets and generating vectors for the interception of attacking intruders; antiaircraft (AA) defense would be engaged semi-automatically.

The air defense system of the ROC includes at least four sophisticated AA battalions—two armed with Nike-Hercules and two with Hawk and newly acquired Chaparral surface-to-air missiles (SAMs). The Nike (MIH-14B), although in service for a quarter of a century, is an effective high-level antiaircraft deterrent; its slant range is about 30 miles, and it has destroyed targets at altitudes of 100,000 feet. The Hawk (MIM-23A) supplements the Nike as a superior low/medium-altitude missile, usually launched from a self-propelled vehicle; in service since 1959, it is credited with a high single-shot kill-probability. Conventional 40mm. AA batteries back up these more sophisticated systems, but their effectiveness is uncertain.

The ROC probably deploys no more than 120 sophisticated low/medium- and high-altitude missiles, and in massive air attacks their reactive capabilities would be rapidly degraded. As long as they are available, however, aggressor air units would be forced to hedge-hop to avoid detection and interdiction. Such maneuvers would put PLAAF aircraft at a considerable disadvantage-i.e., flying over unfamiliar terrain without ground-following radar. The available evidence suggests that the Chinese Communist air force is accustomed to a "defense mode," and is ill-suited to organized and aggressive ground support and low-level tactical attack. The medium and light bombers of the PLAAF coming in at medium and high altitudes would probably suffer serious attrition to SAM antiaircraft measures.

Even with tactical or absolute air superiority assured, landings by the PLA in any invasion of Taiwan would have to be made on coasts defended, to the depth possible, by onshore positions. In the northwest these positions are emplaced in hardened structures. Further south, mobile artillery, armored vehicle, machine gun, and automatic weapons fire would provide concentrated anti-personnel and anti-equipment defense. The slow gradient along the beachfronts from Tatu Chi to Tainan would make troop landings very hazardous, with infantry having to wade as much as 600 yards in the surf before reaching dry land. Given these considerations, attempts would probably be made to secure major port facilities at Taichung or Kaohsiung—sites that would be very heavily defended.

In any invasion effort the PRC would have an initial landing force of no more than 18 divisions—considerably less than the force proposed in a projected Allied landing on a Japanese-held Taiwan toward the close of World War II. In 1945 the Allies estimated that an invasion force of at least 300,000 troops would be needed to wrest the island away from less than 100,000 Japanese troops—35,000 of them in major ground combat units. In any contemporary attack the 18 divisions of a PRC amphibious landing force would number, at best, 250,000 troops, and they would be opposed by almost the same number. The "boat-packs" of the PRC, without sea-train capabilities, would have to secure port facilities early on, and make several transits of the 100-mile Taiwan Strait in order to deliver and support an attack force of sufficient number to ensure victory. Such a victory could be gained, but the defenders on Taiwan would make it very costly.

Most of the coastal defenses on Taiwan are arranged in self-contained compartments, serviced by stockpiles of military stores that would allow the ROC forces to independently sustain combat even if resupply was interdicted by PRC flank attacks and assault by tactical-attack and ground-support aircraft. Even after the ROC air defense had been suppressed, batteries of Honest John (MGR-1B) surface-to-surface missiles ensconced in hardened launch sites could inflict considerable damage on invading forces. An unguided ballistic vehicle with a range of 5-23 miles, the Honest John can destroy force elements of size. Any invasion force making it through this SSM shield would face the massed fire-power of conventional howitzer and cannon, ranging from 203mm. weapons to 40mm. AA guns. All these defenses would probably be supplemented by an indeterminate number of Taiwanese-built Gabriel-type SSMs redesigned for land-launch.

Because of restricted sea- and air-lift and logistic follow-on capabilities, the PLA would have to land substantially without armor on a cost defended by ground forces supported by two armored divisions and two armored cavalry regiments equipped with about 1,000 M-47/-48 medium and M-41/-24 light tanks, supplemented by about 300 M-113 armored personnel carriers. The PLA is now attempting to upgrade its antitank capabilities with the purchase of French man-portable, hand-held, antitank precision-guided weapons (to supplement the type 69 RFG-7 anti-tank launchers now in service), but the invading troops would have to pass through heavy suppression fire before these weapons could be effectively used. Little ground support could be expected from the PLAAF, so that landings would be very expensive for the PLA. The major engagements would be at landing points, and the ROC fire plan emphasizes heavy point-defense engagements on the beaches and immediately offshore. Given the configuration of PRC naval capabilities and the disabilities under which the PLAAF would be compelled to operate, the initial landings on the coast of Taiwan would almost certainly result in heavy losses of Communist personnel and equipment. Interdiction of support lines over the central mountaineous spine of Taiwan by PLAAF ground attack low-level fighter-bombers would complicate resupply problems for the ROC forces, and in time their stockpile of ordnance would be exhausted. Ultimately, given sufficient determination, beachheads and port facilities could be secured by the PLA and the island taken. Fighting would probably last a considerable time—its duration a function of the rapidity with which the ROCAC is supressed and ROC munitions supplies and morale exhausted. Combined casualities would run into the hundreds of thousands, the loss of air and naval units on both sides would be grievous, and much of the industrial and agricultural potential of the western side of Taiwan would be destroyed for years. . . .

Thus, even without major power guarantees for the security of Taiwan, it is not likely that the PRC, for the time being, will venture on an invasion of the island. But the initiative rests with Communist China. Should the PRC conceive the victory worth the exorbitant price it would have to pay, it could invade and occupy Taiwan. For that reason, the U.S. Joint Chiefs of Staff urged the Carter administration not to accede to normalization with the PRC until it had obtained a formal commitment from the Communist Chinese to abjure the use of force in resolving the Taiwan issue. The Carter administration failed to obtain such a guarantee, and as a consequence the Congress attempted to provide a *de facto* security arrangement that would be a functional surrogate for the lapsed mutual security treaty between the United States and the Republic of China.

Among the considerations reinforcing the Congressional disposition was the fact that the PRC was clearly prepared to practice "brinkmanship" when it felt that its vital national interests were involved. It had undertaken military adventures in the past that defied every rational calculation. In 1969, for example, the armed forces of the PRC engaged in regimental- and battalion-sized frontal conflict with Soviet forces along the Sino-Russian border—an adventure that might easily have expanded into tactical and strategic nuclear warfare. And in its "punitive" invasion of Vietnam in 1979, the PRC challenged the Soviet Union to come to the assistance of its Southeast Asian ally in what might well have been the opening of a major power conventional and/or nuclear confrontation. . . .

Communist China may well be prepared to absorb the costs involved in "liberating" Taiwan if those costs are restricted to losses in men and a modest loss in material. It might even be prepared to accept the loss of American and Japanese assistance. Only if an attack on Taiwan involved the serious risk of large-scale military intervention by one of the major powers could one conclude with any assurance that it would not be attempted. But the PRC cannot help but be cognizant that the likelihood of such intervention has become remote. Even though the Taiwan Relations Act has made any armed attack against Taiwan a matter of "grave concern" for the United States, no one seriously entertains the notion that American armed forces would be committed to its defense. After a decade of tortured withdrawal from military involvement in Asia by the United States, it is doubtful that even an invasion of Taiwan would lead to direct American military intervention. The "paper guarantee" of American concern for Taiwan is not likely to deter the PRC should it choose to exercise its military option against the ROC. The only provisions in the Taiwan Relations Act that offers substantial hope of enhanced security for the ROC are those that mandate the ongoing sale of arms to the military forces on Taiwan. Only if the military of the ROC can make invasion prohibitively costly to attackers can Taiwan enjoy some sense of security.

It is evident that the political and military leaders of the PRC are prepared to take considerable casualties and run grave risks in the pursuit of what they believe to be their national purpose. In the invasion of Vietnam the PLA may have suffered as many as 45,000 casualties, and the PRC faced possible Soviet retaliatory measures on its northern and western borders. Those costs and that risk were evidently acceptable, but the loss of expensive air force inventory apparently was not. Hundreds of PLAAF aircraft were massed along the China-Vietnam border, for example, but none made forays into the battle zone defended by fairly sophisticated Vietnamese antiaircraft defenses.

The PRC military has always been prepared to absorb massive manpower losses. The "human wave" tactics of the PLA in Korea and the recent manpower losses in Vietnam are evidence enough of that. Replacement infantry are not in short supply in Mainland China, but military hardware is another matter. The aircraft industry of the PRC, for instance, produces about 300 combat aircraft a year, while its shipyards produce one destroyer, 2 to 6 submarines, 7 *Osa/Hola*-class missile patrol boats, and 10 hydrofoils a year. Any significant loss in major military equipment would seriously reduce the force levels of the PLA, the PLAN, and the PLAAF, and impair their effectiveness as levers in international negotiation or as defenses against major power threats.

The abandonment of the "people's war" strategy by the PLA suggests an increasing concern about major military material. The PRC has always been frugal in its employment of military hardware, and the military of the PRC have been prepared to commit only limited quantities of major military items to combat. How much they might be prepared to commit (and risk losing) in an invasion of Taiwan is difficult to determine, but it is clear that the higher the probable costs, the less likely the prospect of an invasion.

After the lapse of the mutual defense treaty with the United States, Taiwan's security can be assured only to the extent that the ROC armed forces can inflict punishing damage on the invaders not only in terms of manpower (which the PRC can readily replace), but also in terms of major military hardware already in short supply if the Mainland Chinese should ever find themselves in serious confrontation with a major power.

America's determination to provide defensive arms to the ROC in sufficient quantity and quality to assure that very high costs will be paid by any invading force is the most direct way to discharge the popular and Congressional sense of obligation that found expression in the deliberations leading to the context, if the Congressional mandate to supply the ROC with "a sufficient self-defense capability" means anything at all, it means the provision of arms in sufficient quantity and quality to make the costs of invading Taiwan prohibitive.

After the lapse of the one-year moratorium on arms transfers to the ROC, the United States now has to decide on a policy governing military sales to Taipei. During the decade of negotiations between Peking and Washington, U.S. arms transfer policies were always clouded by prudent concern for the climate of international diplomacy. During those years ROC requests for an advanced all-weather fighter, for the Harpoon missile, and for torpedoes for their submarines were regularly rebuffed. In the course of Congressional deliberations prior to the marking-up of the Taiwan Relations Act, the issue of sales of the Harpoon to the ROC was raised, and there was a suggestion that both the State Department and the DOD wuld be reviewing the past deferment of sales of such weapons systems to the ROC. Harold Brown, the Secretary of Defense indicated that Harpoon had not been sold to the ROC prior to December, 1978 in order not to obstruct the normalization process, but that after the termination of the moratorium in December, 1979, the issue of such sales would be reconsidered.

Evidence of America's serious commitment to the security of Taiwan can only be conveyed by continued military sales of significant defensive weaponry to the ROC. Such sales would substantially increase the costs of misadventure by the PRC in the Taiwan Strait, reduce any disposition the PRC might entertain to resort to military force aganst the ROC, contribute to regional stability, and restore some credibility to the image of the United States as a responsible defense partner in the Pacific. There is a catalog of defense items whose sales would contribute to such ends. The ROC requires an SSM of longer range than the Gabriel, a larger number of smaller SSMs and SAMs already in limited supply in its inventory, as well as land mobile, one- or two-man portable SAMs, such as the Redeye (MIM-43A), to provide its ground forces effective defense against low-flying hostile aircraft. The Redeye, which is operational with U.S. ground forces, is an optically sighted infrared, heat-seeking missile that locks on to an opponent aircraft's engines. It has a range of about two miles and would provide mobile low-level defensive cover lacking in the present Nike-Hercules-Hawk-Chaparral SAM array.

Two recent wars—Vietnam and the Arab-Israeli Yom Kippur War—have shown that small antiaircraft missiles can significantly influence the course of combat. In South Vietnam the North Vietnamese forces deployed only a few hundred SA-7 (Grail) missiles, very similar to the American Redeye, and yet they mounted sufficient threat to force the U.S. and South Vietnamese air forces to restrict their customary modes of operation, making them less effective than they would have been otherwise. The PRC's indisposition to employ the 700 fighter and ground support aircraft it had on line in the immediate area of Communist China's "punitive" invasion of Vietnam suggests that the PLAAF fully appreciated the effectiveness of man-portable SAMs.

In the Yom Kippur War the Israeli air force was seriously hampered in its ground support efforts by a dense battlefield antiaircraft environment. Evasive action by aircraft under threat of heavy SAM fire often resulted in the jettisoning of ordnance that would otherwise be delivered on target. In substance, man-portable SAMs could not only increase the attrition rate of attacking aircraft, but also degrade their effectiveness as offensive weapons platforms. Such weapons are relatively inexpensive, require relatively little training for their employment, and need very little maintenance. Because they are small and do not require launch pads or vehicles, they are easily concealed, which enhances their battlefield effectiveness.

Since the ROC does not have the option of preemptive strikes against enemy airfields, the deployment of hand-held precision-guided SAMs would be a clear battlefield asset in protecting ground forces and critical targets from air attack. Such weapons cost between $5-10,000 each, while the cost of a single modern interceptor runs into millions of dollars. The cost-effectiveness of such defense is obvious, even if the kill-probability is only 5-10 percent.

The ROC already deploys a guided antitank (and anti-landing barge) weapon, the TOW (BGM-71), which like the Redeye is optically sighted. It has an effective range of about two miles and can be used against three surface targets within a 90-degree arc in less than 60 seconds. Under test conditions it was demonstrated that the TOW was also capable of hitting airborne helicopter targets. The TOW is an economical substitute for a 106mm. recoilless rifle, requires less training for its use, and is far more cost-effective. Precision-guided munitions (PGMs) like the Redeye and TOW are "equalizers"—high priority items for military forces facing a numerically dominant enemy that threatens to obtain tactical control over the battlefield environment. Since such weapons systems are manifestly defensive in the case of the ROC, their sale would be fully compatible with the mandate of the Taiwan Relations Act.

Such weapons could contribute to the stability of the region by increasing the cost to the aggressor in any attack. Moreover, should an attack be launched, such weapons might sustain the conflict long enough for the major powers to react, increasing the risk to the attacker. Only if the PRC could accomplish its purpose with singular dispatch could it hope to avoid the risk of some sort of involvement by the United States, Japan, or possibly even the Soviet Union. It would be much easier for the PRC to suppress the firepower of fixed emplacements and neutralize ROC airfields than it would be to search out and destroy hundreds of infantryman equipped with PGMs.

Given the circumstances of the ROC, its defense tactics are fairly restricted. The principal function of its armed services would be to inflict as much damage on the enemy as possible. Its first problem would be to obtain early warning of imminent attack. At the present time, the passive and active radar situated on the island extends at least 70 miles into the Taiwan Strait (given fixed mountain-top radar sites). This radar screen is supplemented by the reconaissance aircraft of the ROCAC. To date the PLAAF has not attempted to intercept ROC aircraft on reconnaisance missions so long as they do not penetrate Mainland Chinese airspace. The present warning system probably should be enhanced by an effective "look down radar" array—an airborne early warning (AEW) system capable of affording fully automatic detection and tracking over land and water. This would require an aircraft with a tactical data system which detects the presence, direction, and identity of surface and low-level targets in heavily trafficked environments. Discriminant radar (IFF) could distinguish friendly aircraft from those of any potential enemy. Moreover, such a system would provide early warning of any military buildup on the coast of mainland China that might signal preparations for a sea, air, or amphibious assault. The time required for the mobilization of sufficient force for such an assault would provide the defense systems of the ROC a long lead time, as well as allow the major powers to attempt to intercede before actual hostilities began.

The armed forces of the United States deploy at least two AEW aircraft the E-3A (AWACS) and the E-2C (Hawkeye)—that would be suitable for such purposes. The E-3A is a modified 707-32B airframe topped by a thirty-foot rotating radome. Under test conditions the E-3A demonstrated a sophisticated interoperability capacity by linking detection, tracking, and computing capabilities directly (in real time) to surface forces, such as SAMs, shipboard air defense systems, and ground control centers. The high resolution properties of its multimode radar enabled it to detect and track patrol boats and minesweepers at sea and targets as small as tanks and trucks on land.

The E-2C has much the same properties, but a far shorter range and loiter-time. It extends the radar horizon to a radius of about 200 miles and provides an air and surface surveillance of about 3 million cubic miles. It can simultaneously and automatically track over 250 surface-borne targets—and similarly process some 30 airborne intercepts. Since the F-5E Tiger, now in major service with the ROCAC, is a clear-weather fighter, the detection and directional radar assistance provided by the Hawkeye would permit greater safety and access to targets in even marginal atmospheric conditions characteristic of the Taiwan Strait. It could provide early warning of incoming, low-flying aircraft and surface vessels as small as patrol boats or motorized junks—targets not easily detected by land-based radar systems.

Not only would the F-5E enjoy significantly increased marginal weather safety and attack efficiency when guided by the E-2C, but also the over-the-horizon detection and threat assessment properties of the Hawkeye would make it possible to reduce the number of ROC interceptors kept aloft or maintained on alert status, thereby reducing personnel and unit maintenance costs for a small air force facing a quantitatively superior opponent.

For all that, the E-2C is an extremely expensive weapon system (although its unit costs are about one-quarter that of the E-3A), and it is so sophisticated it is doubtful the ROCAC now has the capability for its proper use and maintenance. But if these considerations do not preclude a request for its purchase by the ROC, the fact that it is clearly a defensive weapon already in service with the U.S. military (and which will soon be deployed by the Self-Defense Forces of Japan) renders its sale and transfer fully compatible with the legislative intent of the Taiwan Relations Act. The ROC is reported to have made inquiries in 1975 concerning the possible purchase of AEW craft for its air command. To date the U.S. government has not allowed the ROC to pursue these inquiries.

If the ROC possessed a sophisticated early warning system that could tie into the available ADGE radar network, its defense strategy could provide for the early and effective deployment of its limited fighter and attack aircraft resources. Air-launched Maverick (AGM-65A) "smart bombs," guided by a stabilized television camera in the nose which feeds video signals into automatic tracking circuits in the missile which in turn generate guidance signals, could be expected to exact a considerable toll among incoming large surface combatants or transports marginally equipped with antiaircraft defense.

The defense of Taiwan requires that the ROCAC deny the PLAAF air superiority for as long as possible in any full-scale invasion attempt. Without air superiority the naval forces of the PRC would be operating at very high risk. The Nationalists pilots attempting to maintain air control would enjoy considerable advantage. They would be operating defensively, close to their bases and would need to use less fuel to position themselves in the frontal attack area, which would allow them correspondingly more combat time. The pilots of the PLAAF, travelling longer distances to the battlefield area, would have less combat time; they would be operating in an unfamiliar overwater environment, and their aircraft would be at least marginally inferior to the best of their opponents.

Nonetheless, given the quantitative asymmetry between the two air forces, the ROCAC requires a high-speed, all-weather interceptor with heavier payload and a longer inflight combat time than the F-5E to afford it the opportunity of exploiting qualitative superiority. One available possibility for supplying such an advantage is the F-5G, a newly developed single-engined, high performance, all-weather version of the F-5, armed with Navy/Raytheon AIM-7 Sparrow AAMs. The Sparrow has a range of about 15 miles and can be used in both air-to-air and air-to-surface attack. A better choice, however, would be the F-16. The F-16 is a high-thrust, all-weather, lightweight fighter aircraft possessed of superior close-in, air-to-air combat characteristics. It is expected to outperform any known aircraft in its class for the foreseeable future, it incorporates the most modern avionics available, and it is relatively economical to procure, operate, and maintain. There are indications that facilities on Taiwan are capable of entering into co-production of the F-16 so that the ROC could manufacture the aircraft in its own plants.

The combat enhancement that would accrue with the availability of the F-5G, or preferably the F-16, would include the availability of an aerodynamically superior aircraft that could perform air-superiority, ground-support, and sea surface-attack missions. All-weather capabilities would permit the pilots of the ROCAC to exploit the weather conditions of the Taiwan Strait to advantage, allowing them to venture out when the MiGs of the PLAAF would be confined to their bases. The advanced avionics of the F-16 would allow the combat pilot a radar picture of either air or ship targets. The air or surface target can be locked on, and once lock-on has been achieved, the radar will initiate automatic target track in both range and azimuth, affording a high single-shot kill-probability.

On-line availability of such aircraft in the defense forces of the ROC would significantly affect the cost-accounting that would be required by the military leadership of the PRC in any plan of full-scale amphibious assault on Taiwan. Making such aircraft and their crews combat ready would require at least a two- to three-year lead time, of course. Concern for the security of Taiwan against determined invasion would counsel early sale and transfer of such military items.

Only if the air force of the ROC could maintain effective air-cover could its small navy operate with any probability of survival in the Taiwan Strait when opposed by the overwhelming numbers of combatants that could be mobilized by the PRC. In naval clashes with the PLAN in May, August, and November 1965, two ROC minesweepers were sunk and a third badly damaged. Beginning in 1969, when it became evident that the United States was beginning to consider rapprochement with the People's Republic of China, the ROC has attempted to enhance its naval forces. Its difficulties are monumental given its potential opponent, but its principal shortcomings are those which turn on inadequate AA and antimissile (AM) defenses. On any counterforce mission the ROC navy would be exposed to air attack. Most of its destroyers and frigates are armed with antiaircraft armament of World War II vintage—Bofors 40mm. cannon and 3-inch and 50-caliber rapid-fire guns—hardly deterrents to transsonic attack aircraft. Moreover, at present the major vessels of the ROC navy have no significant countermeasure capabilities against missile attack. Given the probability of such attacks from the swarm of PRC missile patrol boats, such a disability puts the navy of the ROC in acute risk in the event of determined conflict.

The destroyers used by the ROC in the Taiwan Strait were designed for openwater patrolling by the U.S. Navy, where they could operate under the cover of carrier-based aircraft outside the range of an opponent's land-based tactical air units. The ROC navy enjoys none of these circumstances. If any of its surface combatants are to survive any appreciable time in the event of a major conflict in the confined quarters of the Taiwan Strait, the ROCAC must maintain a significant measure of local air superiority to protect them, the AA weapons systems of such vessels must be significantly upgraded, and effective countermeasures must be developed against the SSMs now in use by the PLAN.

The first requirement for their survival could be met, at least partially, by the procurement of a number of high-performance, all-weather fighter aircraft to supplement the current inventory of the ROCAC. The second might be partially met, on an interim basis, by the employment of hand-held, man-portable, surface-to-air missiles that might force the aircraft of the PLAAF to be far more prudent in their attacks on surface ships than they would otherwise be. The third requirement could only be met by the deployment of electronic countermeasures (ECM) that would deflect any PLAN SSM assault.

Unlike the Israeli navy, somewhat similarly circumstanced, the ROC has neither the option nor the capabilities to attack the naval bases, installations, or equipment of the PLAN in its home ports. The first engagements would be at sea, and would probably expose the ships of the ROC to dense SSM fire. The 5-inch guns of many of the destroyers of the ROC do not have the range to counter missile patrol boat attacks. If ROC vessels are to survive, they require the same antimissile countermeasures that have become common in the Israeli navy.

In the naval engagements of the Yom Kippur War, when Israeli vessels engaged an enemy well-equipped with SSM capabilities, only their ECM allowed the devastating use of their Gabriel missiles against the opposing Styx. The Israelis sank 19 Arab vessels, including 10 missile patrol boats, without loss. In the Yom Kippur War, only Israeli air force aircover and effective ECM allowed the Israelis to prevail against a numerically superior enemy. In that conflict Israeli pilots brought down 265 Egyptian and 131 Syrian aircraft—mostly fighters more advanced in design and firepower than the MiGs in major operational use by the PLAAF. Although Israeli losses were high (102 aircraft), 40 percent of those losses were to enemy SAMs not yet available to the PRC. Egypt had 146 batteries of advanced antiaircraft SA-6 missiles, and Syria had 34 similar batteries. The Israeli air force had to contend with one of the most advanced and densely deployed SAM defense systems ever faced in combat (more hazardous than anything with which American pilots had to contend in North Vietnam). Only superior pilots, superior aircraft, and effective ECM allowed the Israeli air force and Israeli vessels to survive and prevail against quantitatively superior forces.

The array of weapons against which the ROC must defend itself in any major engagement with the PRC is far less sophisticated than those faced by the Israeli defense forces. The MiGs of the PLAAF are of the same family as those flown by Egyptians and Syrians, but of an earlier generation, and while the Styx SSMs of the PLAN are essentially the same as those in service in Egypt and Syria, they probably have not incorporated the modern innovations embodied in the Egyptian and Syrian versions. The defenses against the weaponry of the PRC, nonetheless, would be substantially the same as those employed by the Israeli combat forces. The ROC requires both high-performance, all-weather fighter aircraft (however few) and reasonably sophisticated ECM antimissile capabilities for its aircraft and surface vessels. Given such force enhancements, the ROC navy could employ its Gabriel-type SSMs to good effect.

In the immediate past the ROC military command has evinced an interest in supplementing its small fleet of missile patrol boats with Israeli SAAR II-class multipurpose guided missile craft (armed with Gabriel-type SSMs already on-line in the ROC navy). Smaller patrol boats are now being constructed in the shipyard facilities of Taiwan, and they will probably be armed with Gabriel-type, Sea Chapparal or alternative missile systems. These vessels would be supported by the short-range anti-aircraft SAM capabilities already operational on some older Fletcher-class ROC destroyers—capabilities that could be enhanced by low-cost man-portable SAMs.

It seems quite clear that the strategists and tacticians on Taiwan have settled on defense plans responsive to their short- and long-term needs. But to put together a really credible defense against invasion, the ROC must overcome a number of quite formidable problems. The first turns on access to the foreign military sales market in the United States. Over the years the ROC has attempted to purchase a number of major defense items in the United States, and either permission has been denied or relevant procurement decisions have been deferred. It is difficult to anticipate American policy with regard to future arms transfers to the ROC in the changing diplomatic environment that now prevails. In 1978 the Director of the Defense Security Assistance Agency of the DOD reported that sales of Maverick, Harpoon, and Chaparral missiles, precision-guided missiles like TOW and some SAMs, and aircraft such as F-16s and F-18s, as well as requests for less important pieces of military equipment, had been blocked by either the State, Defense, or Commerce departments of the federal government.

Yet the United States remains the supplier of choice for the ROC military command for a variety of reasons. Most of the ROC military have been trained with American equipment. American military equipment, furthermore, is among the best in the world. ROC representatives have long contact with American suppliers, and in a world in which the ROC no longer enjoys diplomatic recognition among the major suppliers, it is difficult for them to establish and secure access to alternative arms procurement markets.

The second problem to be dealt with in preparing the defense of Taiwan turns on the extremely high cost of major military equipment. In 1976 a single F-16 cost no less than $15 million. A SAAR IV missile patrol boat costs approximately $17-20 million. Any major acquisition of such items might severely strain the budget of the ROC, which is so intensively involved in the modernization and development of its economy. In 1977 the ROC purchased an estimated $235 million in arms from the United States and received credits estimated at $35 million. In 1978 agreements were entered into for $225 million in direct sales procurement and $25 million in funded foreign military sales (FMS) credits. Given such levels of procurement, the ROC could maintain a slow but steady enhancement of its defense posture. Its purchases would probably be a "high-low mix," with acquisition of some major military items (like E-2C units for AEW, and some air-superiority aircraft) and some relatively low-cost ECM equipment for antimissile defense, along with man-portable SAMs to neutralize low-flying enemy ground-support or naval-attack aircraft. Subsequent purchases, again in such a mix, would probably include items like multipurpose missile patrol boats and more precision-guided battlefield hardware. Ongoing purchases of SSMs, including the Harpoon (if it is allowed for purchase by the ROC), and follow-on supplies would exhaust Taiwan's annual military foreign purchase budget.

Given such procurement strategy, it would be at least a decade before the ROC could mount a defense that would make armed invasion an unacceptable option for the PRC. This assumes that the force levels of the PRC will not appreciably improve in the interim—an assumption that is difficult to defend.

All of this suggests that the ROC will probably attempt to significantly increase its military purchases in the United States. In 1978 the ROC had a military budget of over $2 billion, a substantial portion of which was designated for arms procurement in the West. Since the moratorium on FMS to the ROC did not allow them to purchase in the United States during 1979, the present funds available would permit the officials of Taiwan to make significant current offers for priority major military equipment they critically need.

In effect, an immediate improvement in the force posture of the ROC, and a corresponding decrement in any disposition on the part of the PRC to pursue military options, can be obtained without imposing an inordinate strain on the economy of Taiwan, given the temporary accumulation of funds not dispersed in 1979. The ROC regularly allocates the equivalent of between 7 to 9 percent of its gross domestic product (GNP) to military expenditures. At the moment, given the temporary surplus, the upgrading of the defenses of the ROC need not require a disabling increase—an increase that might impair its economic development and social welfare goals. In the future, the proportion of the GNP alocated to military enhancement will probably have to increase, but such increase can be monitored in order not to threaten other national goals as long as the United States allows the ROC to make arms purchases on a regular and predictable basis.

Under such conditions the ROC can gradually enhance its air-interception, early-warning, missile-delivery, and air, antimissile, and ground defense capabilities without threat to its economic stability. This would allow the maintenance of the existing relationship between the potential adversaries, and might allow some substantial improvements in ROC force levels. This would require that the provisions embodied in the Taiwan Relations Act be acted upon conscientiously, permitting the ROC access to the American procurement market, supplemented by some special consideration that would indicate acknowledgement of the special relationship that exists between the United States and Taiwan. That special consideration might well include the extension of FMS credits (now "phased out"), as well as special review of arms transfer requests made by the ROC. While most sales would continue to be cash sales, Taiwan's special circumstances and America's interest in the maintenance of regional stability in the Taiwan Strait would have to weigh in any executive policy decisions.

All of this can only be accomplished by a very careful consideration of all the complex variables that influence behaviors between the United States, the People's Republic of China, and the Republic of China on Taiwan. Arms transfers would have to be clearly defensive in character in order not to provoke the mainland Chinese. But firm resolve on the part of the United States to reduce the potential for violence in the Taiwan Strait by selected arms sale to Taiwan could only render the United States a more credible and responsible partner in any defensive alignments, whether those alignments involve the nations of the Asian littoral or the PRC itself. A weak or irresolute ally is unattractive to any defense partner, and any lack of concern on America's part for the future of its longtime ally could only be read as general unreliability by the political authorities in Peking. Finally, any lack of determination on the part of the United States might well be read by the PRC as a signal to undertake military adventure.

I have yet to mention the greatest threat to the Republic of China Navy and the maritime lifelines of the Republic of China. The People's Republic of China submarine force consists of almost double the number of attack submarines that we have in our whole Pacific fleet.

20. ADM. EDWIN K. SNYDER'S ASSESSMENT OF TAIWAN'S MILITARY CAPABILITIES
February 7, 1979

Admiral SNYDER. Mr. Chairman, distinguished Senators of the committee, it is an honor to be asked to testify before the Foreign Relations Committee on a subject that is very dear to my heart, the security and well-being of some very dear friends, not only of mine, but of all of us; that is, the people of the Republic of China.

As Commander of the United States Taiwan Defense Command from 1974 to August 1977, I was responsible to the Joint Chiefs of Staff for contingency planning for the defense of the Republic of China, including Taiwan and the Pescadores Islands.

My additionl responsibilities as Commander, United States Taiwan Defense Command, included supervising the submission of the Republic of China 5-year defense plan, which was prepared by the Chief Military Advisory Assistance Group to the Republic of China. As the ultimate consumer of any weapons systems purchased by the Republic of China, I was vitally interested that they be the weapons that would be the most effective.

A third major responsibility of my staff was the oversight concern for the readiness of the Chinese and American Forces that would be placed at our disposal should the need to defend ourselves ever arise. In this regard, we conducted frequent and regular joint training exercises with Republic of China Forces, including one large-scale war game on an annual basis.

So much for background. Mr. Chairman, I presume that the purpose of my presence today is to present an assessment of the capabilities of the armed forces of the Republic of China to defend itself.

First, let me say that in the event of a determined attempt by the People's Republic of China to conquer the Republic of China by military force without the aid of immediate and extensive U.S. aid, the Republic of China's Air Force would be neutralized within 2 to 3 weeks in my opinion by the overwhelming superiority of the Communist fighter inventory.

This is not to say that the Republic of China Air Force would not take a massive, and perhaps unacceptable, toll of the People's Republic of China aircraft. But a little over 200 modern fighters are no match for the 2,500 that are now in place facing Taiwan.

Second, let me say that the Republic of China Navy is no match for the increasing numbers of the People's Republic of China OSA patrol boats and modern destroyers, both armed with Styx type, surface-to-surface missiles. The 20-odd World War II destroyers in the Republic of China Navy, armed with 5-inch guns, are woefully inadequate to defend themselves against such firepower.

Taiwan: Hearings Before the Committee on Foreign Relations, U.S. Senate, 96th Congress, February 5-22, 1979 (Washington, D.C.: U.S. Government Printing Office, 1979), pp. 585-587, 653-655.

True, they are diesel submarines, but one must remember that our diesel submarines devastated the Japanese lines of communications against similar vintage antisubmarine capabilities in World War II.

It is my opinion that the People's Republic of China submarine force in concert with its surface and air forces could totally disrupt the lines of communications to Taiwan in short order should they ever get the order to do so.

I admit, Mr. Chairman, that I have given you a rather gloomy view of the Republic of China capabilities to "go it alone." I would point out, however, that until just several years ago, there was never any indication that they would be required to "go it alone."

In the past few years, the Republic of China Government has been exerting superhuman efforts and spending vast amounts of money to prepare itself. However, you don't just develop an effective ASW [antisubmarine warfare] capability overnight, nor an air defense, nor any other military capability. Today's weapons systems are too frightfully complex and expensive.

An additional problem is that, in my opinion, several vital weapons that Taiwan really needs have been withheld from them for political reasons.

On the brighter side, I would close with one final observation. The armed forces of the Republic of China are superbly led. They are fierce fighters and they are completely loyal to their government.

In spite of my foregoing comments, there is no doubt in my mind that any fight the People's Republic of China should pick with the Republic of China would be a very painful and costly undertaking.

[Admiral Snyder's answers to additional questions submitted by Senator Glenn.]

Question 1. Admiral Snyder, please give us your assessment of the military threat to Taiwan today and if you will, your view of how the situation will be ten years from now?

Answer. The major military threats to Taiwan today are (1) the PRC's overwhelming numbers of fighter aircraft that can be almost immediately brought to bear on the Taiwan front, (2) the burgeoning number of surface-to-surface, missile equipped, destroyers and patrol boats in the PRC Navy inventory, and (3) the large submarine inventory of the PRC. Since the PRC is embarked upon a modernization program, and since she has repeatedly stressed the importance of her military posture, I think the next 10 years will see a rapid modernization of the PRC military machine especially in view of their preoccupation with the Russian threat to the north and the unsettled conditions in S.E. Asia to the south. One of the major hindrances to a truly modern air force has been a weakness in aircraft engine technology. Their acquisition of Spey engines from Great Britain should lead to development of a much more effective Air Force. A number of other glaring military weaknesses such as poor command and control, computer technology and lines of communication (roads, merchant marine, commercial air, railroads) are almost certain to receive order of magnitude improvement once the door to U.S. technology is opened. I would say that the military threat to Taiwan will be greatly increased 10 years from now.

Question 2. Although I do not believe that PRC will use force against Taiwan any time in the forseeable future, I think it only prudent to consider the possibility of such a worse case occurring. With this in mind could you give us your assessment of the PRC's most likely courses of military action against Taiwan?

Answer. The most dangerous action that the PRC could participate right now is the declaration of an embargo on all commerce into Taiwan. She could state that Taiwan is a province of China, as finally recognized and acknowledged by all major powers, and that henceforth all deliveries to her "province" must clear customs through one of her seaports. She can back this declaration up by stating that a blockade exists, and any ship entering her sovereign waters (including those surrounding Taiwan) are subject to boarding and inspection. With her 70 plus submarines, 15 missiles equipped destroyer types and air cover from her 2,500 fighter aircraft, Taiwan would be hard pressed to prevent such an action; however, I am sure she would try! This would lead to a massive air war which, in my opinion, would see the ROC Air Force take a very high toll of PRC aircraft before their 200 modern fighters and air-to-air missile inventory was exhausted and destroyed. At this time the PRC would have total air supremacy and could work their will in bringing Taiwan to its knees economically. Somewhere along the line the U.S. government would have to make a very hard decision on the proper course of action under these circumstances.

In any event, if immediate and massive aid in the form of replacement aircraft, missiles, fuel, etc., is not provided, Taiwan is doomed.

I don't foresee any threat of invasion of Taiwan. Invasion is unnecessary if you can destroy your enemy by starving him economically.

Question 3. Who do you think would win an all out air war between the PRC and the ROC? What are the important variables that we must consider in assessing the air balance?

Answer. Unquestionably an all out air war would be won by the PRC on the strength of its overwhelming numbers. It wouldn't even have to be "all out" on the part of the PRC. She has over 5,000 fighters and 350 bombers. The ROC has only 200 fighters and no bombers. The 2,500 fighters opposite Taiwan could handle the ROC AF although the attrition would be immense. I anticipate the ROC AF could knock down up to 10 PRC fighters to everyone they lose—if they have enough air-to-air missiles. But plain arithmetic still reveals the ROC to be the loser.

The major variables in this equation are (1) How many aircraft and pilots are the PRC willing to sacrifice to take Taiwan. This is especially germaine since there are other trouble spots where this airpower may be urgently needed. (2) The effects of weather on air activity/capability. The weather around Taiwan is unpredictable and usually poor for air operations. This factor could be a life saver for the ROC Air Force and could lengthen their life line considerably; however, this factor is out of the control of both parties. (3) Command and control. The ROC AF command and control is far superior to that of the PRC and is an important factor in assessing the effectiveness of air power. This is especially true when you consider that the ROC AF would be in a totally defensive mode. (4) The ROC AF, by being constrained to short range defensive interceptors, has no means to attack and destroy the PRC airfields, radar sites, and lines of communications. This is a major shortcoming which allows the PRC to replace, restock, and rearm at will and without interference.

Question 4. When we in the U.S. are considering what weapon systems we will sell to Taiwan, do you believe we should stress the deterrence provided by a particular system or concentrate on deciding whether it is a defensive or offensive weapon?

—In a related question have you seen the list of major military sales that have been approved for Taiwan? (If no, provide him a copy)

—Do you think these sales are appropriate?

—Are there any weapon systems that you think should be added to the list? Why?

Answer. Weapons systems should be provided to the ROC that will make the risk associated with an attack on Taiwan unacceptable to the PRC. A good example is illustrated in the last question above. If a bombing attack on Taiwan meant an immediate response in kind on airfields and lines of communications on the mainland the PRC would certainly think long and hard about precipitating such an attack. The same reasoning applies to arming the ROC Navy with a credible deterrent to the Styx missile. If the PRC knew that their missile boats and destroyers were out gunned by ROC Navy surface-to-surface missiles, they wouldn't dare attempt a blockade of Taiwan ports.

I have the list of major military sales approved for Taiwan and I think they are excellent, as far as they go. You must remember, those sales were still predicated on the supposition that the ROC would have the assistance of the U.S. 7th Fleet, the 3rd and 5th U.S. Air Force, Army support from Hawaii and a steady supply of war materials from the U.S. in the event of hostilities. If the ROC has to go it alone, she needs much, much more.

In my opinion, the following weapons systems should be added to the list:

1. Advanced all weather fighter—F-16. This would insure continued ROC qualititative superiority for the forseeable future. In addition it would provide another crucial element to their defense, an all weather capability.

2. Reconnaissance aircraft—RF4E. These are urgently required to replace the aging and disappearing F-104.

3. Harpoon surface-to-surface missile—or suitable substitute. These are required to give the ROC Navy a fighting chance of survival against the PRC Navy.

4. Shipboard surface-to-air missile—for survival against PRC attack aircraft.

5. Mobile command and control radar sets. The ROC air defense radar sites are very vulnerable to enemy air attack. A mobile back-up system is vital to their air defense system. This item was always one of the first provided by the U.S. Army in major U.S./ROC exercises.

6. Anti-submarine torpedoes for the two ROC submarines. The most effective anti-sub weapon is another submarine. The ROC has two excellent ex-U.S. submarines but torpedoes for these subs have been withheld for political reasons. The time has come to give them defensive torpedoes.

7. To really see them bolster their anti-submarine defense posture I would recommend releasing about four more diesel submarines to the ROC. With a total of six defensive anti-submarine subs operating against a blockading force, the ROC would, in my opinion, be able to break the blockade.

8. The most urgent of all requirements of the ROC is the continued availability of U.S. spare parts and supplies for their U.S. originated arms. Without such responsive support, the ROC armed forces will rapidly degenerate into a third rate military force, easily mastered by PRC force of threat of force.

D.   Taiwan's Security Options and U.S. Policy

In normalizing relations with the PRC in 1978, President Carter decided to accept China's three basic demands with regard to Taiwan, that is, to sever diplomatic relations, to abrogate the security treaty, and to withdraw U.S. military presence. In return, Washington insisted that the U.S. would continue to have an "interest" in the peaceful resolution of the Taiwan issue and would continue to sell selective defensive arms to Taiwan. The concessions notwithstanding, the Carter Administration argued, Taiwan's security will be adequately protected. As principal reasons Carter officials suggested: First, the continued Sino-Soviet conflict in the north will not permit China to undertake military adventures in the south. Second, China does not have at the present time the amphibious capabilities required to carry out a well coordinated invasion across the Taiwan Strait. And, third, after having cultivated in recent years new economic and technological ties with the West to support its "four modernization" campaigns, the pragmatic Deng-Hua leadership cannot afford to antagonize the Western industrial powers by attacking Taiwan. The testimony by Defense Secretary Harold Brown before the Senate Foreign Relations Committee's Taiwan legislation hearings in February 1979 represents a comprehensive explanation of the Carter rationale (Selection 21).

The Carter Administration's rationale, however, was not widely accepted. As Michael Y. M. Kau pointed out in a paper presented at the Workshop on Taiwan sponsored by the Senate Foreign Relations Committee and the Congressional Research Service, the Administration's arguments involved assumptions and interpretations which were highly questionable or flawed (Selection 22). The fact that Congress was determined to force on the reluctant President a far stronger version of the Taiwan Omnibus Bill testified to the fact that the Congress, too, found the Administration's arguments unconvincing and dangerous. Senator Jesse Helms for one, was greatly troubled by the "motives" of Carter's new China policy (Selection 23).

The loss of confidence in Washington's resolve and sincerity to protect Taiwan, as John F. Copper argues, is bound to drive Taipei to explore other options for security (Selection 24). They might choose to develop nuclear bombs, seek alliance with the Russians, and/or declare de jure independence from China. The consequences of these adventurous options can be highly destabilizing to the balance of power in the Western Pacific and thus detrimental to the regional as well global security interests of the U.S. In this context, Senator Jesse Helms' advice that Washington should take a more careful look at the strategic and economic values of Taiwan deserves serious attention (Selection 23). As Taipei searches desperately for a best answer to its security, Washington should also ask, with all seriousness, what policy toward Taiwan will best serve U.S. strategic interests in Asia.

**21. DEFENSE SECRETARY HAROLD BROWN'S STATEMENT ON
NORMALIZATION AND TAIWAN'S SECURITY**
February 5, 1979

Mr. Chairman, I am pleased to participate in this Committee's hearings on the normalization of U.S. diplomatic relations with the People's Republic of China and the Taiwan
Omnibus legislation. In my opening statement, I will address two issues which I know are
of concern to many members of this committee.

—What are security implications for the U.S. of normalization?
—Have adequate provisions been made for the future security of Taiwan?

Security Implications

I would like to start by noting two important realities. First, China is an emerging power
which will exercise increasing influence on world events. This is a fact, not a consequence
of normalization. But the Administration's decision to complete the process begun in 1971
was designed to take this fact into account. Second, we now confront an Asia much less
menacing to the U.S. than it appeared—and was—in the 1950s when the Russians and
Chinese acted in concert.

As a result of the deepening Sino-Soviet rivalry, the USSR has had to deal with the
challenge to Soviet security from the PRC. Moscow has now deployed 20 to 25 percent of
its ground and tactical aviation forces along the Sino-Soviet border.

We did not precipitate the split between Moscow and Peking, and have no desire to see
the present level of Sino-Soviet differences intensify. The accompanying change in China's
orientation, however, does effect—and improve—our security by relieving us of the requirement we perceived in the past, of confronting two major adversaries on different
fronts. Military resources have been freed for other purposes, thereby importing greater
global flexibility to our military (particularly general purpose) forces. The Soviets, on the
other hand, now have to plan for what they view as a two-front security problem.

Moreover, Peking, in its desire for expanded ties with the U.S. has acquired additional
incentives for restraint on the Taiwan issue and for the pursuit of moderate policies elsewhere. For example, the People's Republic supports a strong NATO, endorses the preservation of the U.S.-Japanese defense relationship, applauds our presence in the Western
Pacific, actively encourages the growing cohesion of ASEAN, and shares our stake in
avoiding a renewal of war on the Korean peninsula. This is beneficial to the security of
many of our allies as well as to our own security.

To be sure, China's foreign policy goals and actions do not fully coincide with American
interests and policies. Nor can we expect the Chinese to neglect their own national interests
in pursuit of improved Sino-American relations any more than we are willing to subordinate
our interests to theirs. What is significant, however, is the substantial parallelism of U.S.-
PRC interests which permits us to maintain compatible approaches to many issues around
the globe that affect our national security in various dimensions.

Some of these benefits, of course, are not directly attributable to improvements in Sino-
American relations. The Sino-Soviet split would have persisted even without full normalization, as would some convergence of U.S. and Chinese security interests. However,
completion of the normalization process serves to reduce the future possibility that we
might slip back into a confrontation with the Chinese. It provides a framework for the
further reduction of tensions in the region. And it lays the groundwork for a major expansion in Sino-American cooperation. While the future contours of our relationship are yet to
be charted, I see no reason to expect that the interests which have led Chinese leaders to seek
normal relations with the U.S. will change in the forseeable future.

Finally, I would like to emphasize that establishment of U.S.-PRC diplomatic relations
and the removal of our military personnel from Taiwan will not significantly affect our
regional military posture. As the Committee well knows, our last combat forces were withdrawn from Taiwan four years ago.

Taiwan: Hearings Before the Committee on Foreign Relations, U.S. Senate, 96th Congress, February 5-22, 1979
(Washington, D.C.: U.S. Government Printing Office, 1979), pp. 35-38.

The Military Threat of Taiwan

Many individuals have asked why the U.S. did not insist on an explicit PRC renunciation of the use of force against Taiwan. The answer rests essentially on an assessment of what was diplomatically feasible and a judgement of the present and anticipated military threat to Taiwan's security. The State Department can best address the negotiating issue. For my part I want to emphasize my belief that for a variety of reasons PRC military action against Taiwan is extremely unlikely for the forseeable future.

Militarily, China is not now capable of mounting a successful combined air and sea invasion of Taiwan. Peking is now primarily concerned about the threat from the Soviet Union, which requires that it maintain large forces along its northern border. Nor can it ignore Soviet-supported Vietnam on its southern border. Any serious PRC effort to mount an attack on Taiwan would require seriously weakening China's border defenses. Though Peking could use its air and naval assets to degrade Taiwan's air force or attempt to blockade the island, such action could not be undertaken without great risk given the condition of China's air and naval forces, Taiwan's defense capabilities, and the likely international response to such actions. The PRC could thus have no confidence even in the outcome of these lesser attempts to harass Taiwan.

Let me turn in more detail to these military considerations. Although China has a large number of combat aircraft, many are obsolescent fighters based on Soviet technology of the early 1950s, which are limited in range and payload. Few are equipped with air-to-air missiles; and pilot proficiency is well below Taiwan's standards. Although China has a large diesel submarine fleet, its Navy is primarily a coastal defense force, and the PRC lacks the amphibious shipping necessary to mount a successful invasion of Taiwan. Nor can Peking expect to develop substantial amphibious forces before the mid-1980s even if they began a concentrated effort now.

For its part Taiwan possesses impressive deterrent capabilities of its own. The island's army numbers about 335,000 men; its air force 75,000; and its navy 70,000. Taiwan's air defense capability rests upon a mixture if surface-to-air missile battalions (Improved Hawk and Nike-Hercules), and an interceptor fleet of 300 aircraft (F-100s, F-104s and F-5Es). The latter are fitted with late model air-to-air missiles (AIM 9-J) which are more sophisticated than anything PRC can deploy. Taiwan has recently installed a semi-automated air defense radar system, augmented by mobile radars for extra insurance against surprise attack. Its command-and- control system is far more advanced than the PRC's as are its electronic counter-measures capabilities.

Beyond these military factors, there are a number of political constraints that will continue to make a PRC attack of Taiwan extremely unlikely. China has embarked on a massive effort to modernize its economy at a rapid pace. The efficacy of this undertaking depends heavily upon cooperative relations with the industrial democracies. Those relations would be jeopardized—indeed very probably ruptured—by an attack on Taiwan. Similarly, the Chinese are concerned with Moscow's growing influence in Vietnam and elsewhere in East Asia. That concern enhances Peking's stake in cultivating closer state-to-state relations with the ASEAN countries, which remain extremely sensitive to Taiwan's fate. Peking also must consider the possibility that any attack on Taiwan will evoke Japanese anxieties and precipitate a major reorientation of Japan's security policies with anti-Chinese overtones. Nor, I might add, can the Chinese discount the possibility of a U.S. military response.

The Administration has consistently affirmed a continuing U.S. interest in the future security and well-being of the people of Taiwan and its expectation—not hope, but expectation—that the Taiwan issue will be resolved peacefully. It is important to note that Peking has not challenged these statements. On the contrary, PRC spokesman no longer talk of "liberating" Taiwan. Vice-Premier Teng and others have repeatedly stated that reunification is not an immediate issue; and they have shown considerable flexibility in discussing the future status of Taiwan including an expressed willingness to see Taiwan retain some armed forces of its own as well as its economic and social system. To be sure, they have resisted any explicit commitment not to use force, which they regard ultimately as a matter of sovereignty. But Peking has decided to pursue the development of normal US—PRC relations despite the President's intention, publicly expressed, to assist the people of Taiwan in maintaining their defenses through sales of selected weapons of a defensive character.

The Normalization Agreement

Let me now review in more detail the basic elements of our normalization policy as they apply to our future security relations with Taiwan.

First, as I have just noted, the U.S. has and will retain an interest in what we expressly expect to be the peaceful resolution of the Taiwan issue by the parties directly concerned. This position is clearly known to Peking.

Second, in the recent normalization negotiations with the PRC, we insisted that termination of the Mutual Defense Treaty must be accomplished in accordance with its provisions, rather than abrogated as Peking proposed.

Third, despite the PRC's disagreement, we have expressed our intention to continue to extend to Taiwan access to selected items of defense equipment, including follow-on support for weapons systems previously supplied.

All arms we have agreed to sell to Taiwan, and which are now in the pipeline—and these amount to more than $50 million—will be delivered. No new commitments will be made during calendar year 1979, but thereafter we will resume sales of selected defensive arms taking into account the situation in the Taiwan Straits. The legal authority for future arms sales to Taiwan is provided for in the Omnibus Legislation currently before this committee.

Let me comment briefly on some of the reasons why we felt we could agree not to make any new commitments for arms sales to Taiwan during 1979. First, we did not wish to create an impression that we were loading Taiwan up with additional arms as an offset to normal relations with Peking. Such action would have implied an urgent need to shore up Taiwan's forces—a judgement at odds with our appraisal of Taiwan's current strength. Moreover, we had already approved an extensive arms sales program for FY 1979 which includes on-going deliveries that will not be completed until 1983. Hence, there was no pressing need for new sales to Taiwan during 1979.

Second, during CY 1979 we will be establishing a new legal basis for future arms sales to Taiwan through the passage of the Omnibus legislation, as well as establishing procedures for processing these sales in a manner compatible with the unofficial relations we shall conduct with the people of Taiwan.

The Future Security of Taiwan

In closing, let me emphasize that we will sustain our concern for the security and well-being of the people on Taiwan. And there are positive steps that we can and will take to express that concern in a tangible way. Of primary importance to Taiwan's security has been the island's ability to maintain modern military forces adequate for its self-defense. Over the years, the U.S. has given Taiwan access, through Foreign Military Sales (FMS) and commercial channels to selected defensive equipment, with particular emphasis on air and naval defenses. We will continue to do so.

We are also completing processing formalities, including the requisite notification of Congress, for the sale to Taiwan of those major items of military equipment approved late in 1978, including additional F-5E interceptor aircraft with improved weaponry such as precision-guided-munitions and Maverick missiles.

In sum, the U.S. is not "abandoning" Taiwan. Our interest in the future security of the people of the island and the peaceful resolution of the Taiwan issue by the Chinese themselves will continue.

22. THE SECURITY OF TAIWAN:
AN EVALUATION OF THE CARTER APPROACH

Michael Y. M. Kau

After decades of hard negotiations between Washington and Peking, President Carter made the historic announcement on December 15, 1978 that agreement had finally been reached between the United States and the People's Republic of China (PRC) on normalizing full diplomatic relations between the two countries. In reaching the agreement, the United States accepted the "three conditions" long insisted upon by Peking: that is, to break diplomatic relations with the Republic of China (ROC) on Taiwan, to terminate the Mutual Defense Treaty of 1954, and to withdraw American troops from the island. Moreover, the Carter Administration went beyond the commitment made by President Nixon in the Shanghai Communique of 1972 by "recognizing the Government of the People's Republic of China as the *sole* legal Government of China" and acknowledging the *Chinese position* that there is but one China and Taiwan is part of China [italic added]." The Joint Communique on normalization further stated that it was "within this context the people of the United States will maintain cultural, commerical and other unofficial relations with the people of Taiwan."

Concession to China's "three conditions" and the implicit acknowledgement of the PRC's sovereignty over Taiwan notwithstanding, the Carter Administration feels that the security of Taiwan and the well-being of its people would not be jeopardized. First, it is explained, the United States Government had made clear to the Chinese that "we have an *interest* in the peaceful resolution of the Taiwan issue and that we *expect* this issue to be settled peacefully by the Chinese themselves [italic added]." In the context of China's ambitious and energetic pursuit of "four modernizations" and its fundamental turn to the West and Japan for the supply of advanced technology and capital, it is extremely unlikely that China will use force on Taiwan at the risk of disrupting its newly cultivated ties with the United States and Japan, the two major powers which have shown great concern for the continued peace and prosperity of the island.

Second, the Administration points out that Taiwan has well-trained and well-equipped, modern armed forces. It air defense capability is highly advanced. Recently, for instance, a Hughes Radar System was installed on Taiwan to augment the mobile radars against surprise attacks. In contrast, despite its large land forces, the PRC's air force and navy are poorly equipped and technologically outmoded. China's armed forces also lack amphibious attack capability to carry out a large-scale operation across the Taiwan Strait. Besides, it is specially emphasized, the United States intends to continue to supply selected weapons to Taiwan for defensive purposes. More importantly, China is now under serious military pressure from the Soviets in the North and from the Vietnamese in the South. Under these circumstances, according to the Administration, it is virtually impossible that China might contemplate seriously to unify Taiwan by force. China simply cannot afford to ignore the 44 divisions of Soviet troops deployed along the 4,500-miles of its northern border.

Considerations such as these must have entered into the process of making the crucial decision by the Carter Administration not to raise or press for a formal pledge by Peking not to use force against Taiwan. Early in 1978, fears began to surface that the stalemate in negotiations might eventually stall the momentum of normalization so the Administration set a deadline to complete the arrangement for normalization by the end of the year. Despite the fact that Taiwan's security had been the most crucial issue throughout the negotiation since the first official contacts were established by President Nixon in 1972, the Carter Administration apparently concluded that Taiwan's security could be adequately protected by relying on the "expectation" and "interest" unilaterally expressed by the United States, on the one hand, and on both internal and external constraints limiting the range of China's policy choices and military options on the other. This low-key approach was also clearly

Taiwan: One Year After United States-China Normalization (A Workship Sponsored by the Committee on Foreign Relations, U.S. Senate and Congressional Research Service, Library of Congress), (Washington, D.C.: Government Printing Office, 1980), pp. 129-135.

reflected in the President's approach to the Taiwan Omnibus Bill proposed to Congress on January 26, 1979. In the Bill, the Administration deliberately and cautiously avoided including any clauses which addressed explicitly the issue of Taiwan's security. Nowhere in the Bill did the Administration mention Unitd States concern over a military attack or economic harassment of Taiwan by external forces or its determination to continue to provide arms sales to Taiwan to maintain the island's capabilities of self-defense.

The Congress, however, disagreed strongly with the Administration's informal and ambigious approach to the protection of Taiwan's security. Congressional leaders were quick to point out the inadequacies and dangers of such an approach. They contended that unless our resolve and commitment were stated formally and explicitly, United States credibility would be subject to needless doubts and speculations in the eyes of adversaries and friends as well. Worse still, the ambiguity and implicity of our stance might turn into a fertile ground for dangerous misinterpretations and miscalculations. Hence, in the Taiwan Relations Act, the Congress deemed it essential to strengthen the Administration's original proposal by writing into the legislation explicit United States concern and commitment to the safeguards for the security of Taiwan. The Act declares openly:

It is the policy of the United States —

(1) To preserve and promote extensive, close, and friendly commercial, cultural, and other relations between the people of the United States and the people on Taiwan . . .

(2) To declare that peace and stability in the area are in the political, security, and economic interests of the United States, and are matters of international concern;

(3) To make clear that the United States decision to establish diplomatic relations with the People's Republic of China rests upon the expectation that the future of Taiwan will be determined by peaceful means;

(4) To consider any effort to determine the future of Taiwan by other than peaceful means, including by boycotts or embargoes, a threat to the peace and security of the Western Pacific area and of grave concern to the United States;

(5) To provide Taiwan with arms of a defensive character; and

(6) To maintain the capacity of the United States to resist any resort to force or other form of coercion that would jeopardize the security, or the social or economic system, of the people on Taiwan.

Tests on the Carter Approach

Despite the Carter Administration's extraordinary efforts to be conciliatory and restraining on the sensitive issue of Taiwan's future security, Peking was not from the very beginning cooperative enough to reciprocate accordingly. While the Administration was simply expressing its "expectation" and "interest" that the future of Taiwan would be resolved peacefully, leaders in Peking were quick to contradict the Administration's position by declaring that to unify Taiwan was "entirely China's internal affair" with which no foreign powers were permitted to interfere. On several occasions, Deng Xiaoping put it bluntly: "We cannot commit ourselves to use no other than peaceful means . . . we cannot tie our hands in this matter.' On the issue of the United States' intention to continue to supply defensive arms to Taiwan following normalization, Hua Guofeng, in his press conference announcing normalization, flatly rejected the idea as "absolutely not acceptable."

It is worth noting that even though the Administration singled out its commitment to continue arms sales to Taiwan as the hard evidence of its continued concern for the island's future security, Peking's apparent ability to exert pressure on Washington became strikingly evident. Even before normalization took full effect, the Administration announced, belatedly, that it had put a one-year moratorium on new arms sales to Taiwan in 1979.

On the political front, the record of Peking's response in the past year appears to be more encouraging. Peking has toned down its verbal attacks on political leaders in Taiwan. The call for the "liberation of Taiwan" has now been replaced with a conciliatory appeal for the "unification of the motherland." In the meantime, Peking has offered to trade with Taiwan, open postal services, and permit travel across the Taiwan Strait. In his interview with Senator Sam Nunn in Peking, Deng Xiaoping even stated that if Taiwan would return to the motherland by acknowledging PRC sovereignty, it could preserve its own political and economic systems and maintain its own armed forces. Of course, the important catch in Deng's proposal is that Taiwan should abandon its sovereignty and independence first. Deng was also quick to add that if Taiwan refused to negotiate indefinitely or tried to seek a Soviet connection, the use of force might be necessary. While making concerted efforts of a peace offensive to put Taiwan in a defensive position, Peking stepped up over the year its "united front" campaign attempting to split the Nationalist leaders, the overseas Chinese and native Taiwanese, and to attract their sympathy and support for the cause of unification.

At the time of normalization, China specialists within the Administration argued that as China became more reliant on the West and Japan for the supply of technology and capital for its pursuit of "four modernizations," the ability of the West to influence China would increase accordingly. Developments in Indochina since last spring, however, raised serious doubt regarding such an argument. Strong objections by the United States and Japan notwithstanding, China went ahead and invaded Vietnam in February, 1979 to "teach the Vietnamese a lesson." Such behavior clearly demonstrates that China is prepared to use force if necessary to achieve what it considers as the nation's vital interest and legitimate claim. Admittedly, the implications of China's invasion of Vietnam on the issue of Taiwan's future security are by not means clear. Nevertheless, its possible implications are worth examining in light of the series of decisions and actions by China in committing force in Korea (1950–53), Quemoy (1958), Tibet (1959), India (1962) and the Soviet border (1969).

The Security Design and its Long-Term Problems

In the year following normalization, the Carter Administration's security design for Taiwan, though repeatedly challenged verbally by Chinese leaders in Peking, has not really been tested by action. In the near-term future, there is no compelling reason to believe that its major assumptions and rationale will not hold as long as no drastic realignment of the balance of power takes place domestically or internationally among the major powers. Hence, Taiwan's security in the foreseeable future under the safeguards of the Taiwan Relations Act causes no need for particular alarm. However, its long-term future is clearly far less certain. Uncertainties are bound to emerge from the inherent changeability and misconception of the assumptions upon which the Carter strategy is built.

To begin with, the "dependency-leverage" assumption, which stresses the rise of United States leverage over Peking as a result of increased dependence by China on Western technology and capital, clearly has its limits and flaws. Having learned a bitter lesson from the policy of "lean to the Soviet" in the 1950s and 1960s, China has in its current modernization campaign deliberately diversified the sources of its technological and capital intakes. As a matter of fact, even today China still carries on substantial trade with the Soviet Union and Eastern European Communist countries to avoid, in part, excessive economic dependency on the West. Moreover, growing economic involvement and cooperation between China and the West has to be viewed as a two-way interactions. The increasing participation by industrial countries in China's vast market naturally also creates a dependency in the opposite direction, where the West becomes dependent on China for its international trade, and thereby China will in time gain certain leverage over the West. It would not be surprising to see soon that China will be able to use its market and trade in a calculated manner to enhance its leverage over the West for noneconomic objectives.

Second, the Carter strategy for Taiwan's security is clearly based in part on the assumption that the Sino-Soviet disputes will not be reversed. Such an assumption of course has many problems. We know that in the past Mao's charismatic personality and ideological emphasis played a major role in the Sino-Soviet conflicts. Now that Mao is gone and all "China's Khrushchevs" are back in power, there are few differences in the ideological and policy orientations between the Soviet Union and China. The growing convergence of their respective ideological and policy perspectives may indeed serve as a basis for their reconciliation in the years ahead.

A third assumption on which the Carter strategy rests is the belief that Deng and his moderate and pragmatic colleagues will stay in power in the foreseeable future, and will continue to consolidate their leadership and pursue the policy of the Western connection. Hence, as long as China remains on the current track, it is believed, the security of Taiwan is assured. As has been pointed out frequently, Deng is now 76, and virtually all his senior colleagues are in their seventies. How much longer they can remain in charge certainly is an open question. There is little guarantee that his successors would pursue the same policy line as he has. A far more serious problem pertains to the pace and ultimate success of China's on-going modernation campaign. There is not doubt that the future of political stability and modernization in China has to rest ultimately on its economic progress. The "four modernizations" movement has surely unleashed the masses' energies and imaginations, but so have been their "rising expectations." Unless the pace of economic progress keeps up with the rapidly inflating expectations in the coming years, a resurgence of leftist, radical backlash will be inevitable. The behavior of the Chinese political system in the past three decades has shown a distinct and consistent pattern of periodic pendulum swings between the "leftist" and the rightist deviation every few years. Despite the massive campaign to purge the "Gang of Four" and their followers at the top, the socio-economic soils for the resurgence of radical politics remain fairly fertile. Should that happen, the current approach to the security of Taiwan as designed by the Carter Administration would naturally be rendered invalid.

Taiwan's Continuing Search for Viable Security Strategies

For the three decade prior to normalizations, Taiwan's security protection rested squarely on the explicit and formal commitment by the United States through the bilateral Mutual Defense Treaty signed in 1954 and the presence of American armed forces on the island and the Strait. Our resolve to protect Taiwan from external attacks was demonstrated to Peking unequivocally with action during the Quemoy Crisis of 1958. It is true that with heavy American military assistance Taiwan also built up its own sophisticated modern armed forces, especially its highly advanced Air Force. However, there is no doubt the primary deterrent to a Chinese attack remained the formal treaty commitment of the United States. The way President Carter handled the process as well as the substance of his normalization policy, therefore seriously eroded the Nationalists' confidence and trust in the Carter Administration. The violent riot which received the Christopher Mission in Taipei following the announcement of normalization reveals clearly the intensity and bitterness of their disappointment and frustration. Even though Congress had come to the rescue by writing into the Taiwan Relations Act explicit United States concern for and commitment to Taiwan's security, leaders in Taiwan remain painfully aware that the ultimate power of policy implementation rests in the hand of the United States President.

The shockwaves of normalization sent a loud and clear message to leaders in Taiwan that they had to make a drastic change in their security strategy: to shift from the total reliance on the United States to the new strategy of self-reliance and self-strengthening. Unfortunately, they discovered immediately that the task is not that easy. Over 95 percent of Taiwan's modern military arsenals and hardwares are entirely American-designed or American-made. It is virtually impossible to diversify at this stage the sources of military procurements. Taiwan has to return to the United States for support. The one-year moratorium on new arms sales for 1979 imposed by the Administration under pressure from Peking certainly makes the efforts even more difficult. Although the ban was just lifted at the end of last December, Taiwan will still have to cope with the administration's strict standard of selectivity and its extreme sensitivity to Peking's objections. The task is further compounded by the fact that, while China is expanding its military budget to speed up military modernization and to shop for advanced weapons and technologies in the world market, Taiwan has been placed under the most stringent constraints out of the post-normalization courtesy to Peking. As Taiwan runs into increasing obstacles in its attempt to expand and upgrade its defense capabilities, is military planners have become increasingly nervous that Taiwan's qualitative edge over China's quantitative strengths will diminish before long.

Confronted by tough dilemmas and uncertainties such as those just discussed, some leaders in Taiwan are beginning to find certain attractions in options such as "going nuclear," playing the "Russian card," and/or moving toward *de jure* separation from China. They are by no means not sophisticated enough to see the serious risks and high costs involved in such adventures. Some argue, however, that when there is no way out and when the ultimate survival of the nation is at stake, all the risks and costs are worth taking. Although there are not positive signs yet that the present leadership is actually pursuing any of those options, discussions of their desirability and feasibility have become more serious and widespread over the past year. It is clear that any active pursuit to those options by Taiwan at this time is bound to destabilize the peace and stability of the Western Pacific, complicate our security strategy, and damage our national interest in that region. It seems that such dangers can be effectively prevented, however, if the United States pays sufficient attention to the legitimate needs of Taiwan's defense capabilities and provides its leaders with a credible assurance for the island's security from outside attack.

Further Policy Considerations

China objects to United States arms sales to Taiwan, because such action by Washington will, in their view, encourage Taiwan not to negotiate with Peking for unification. Implicit in the argument are two assumptions: First, a militarily weak Taiwan is more likely to negotiate with Peking; and, second, the United States is obligated to weaken Taiwan's defense capabilities, so that the latter can be forced to negotiate. The validity of these assumptions is highly questionable. In the first place, contrary to Peking's argument, a secure and confident Taiwan may be more likely to go to the negotiation table. A strong case can be made that East and West Germany entered into serious negotiations in the past, and North and South Korea are in the process of negotiating, primarily because of the approximate parity in their respective military capabilities, and not because of their disparity in strength. As Taipei leaders have reiterated time and again, "nobody in his sane mind is willing to negotiate for his own surrender and demise." Hence, it is highly questionable that Taiwan would be prepared to enter into serious talks unless it has a strong sense of security and is reasonably confident of the credibility of its own defense capabilities.

Peking's second assumption implies that the United States has an obligation to weaken Taiwan militarily, so that the latter can be forced to enter into negotiations. It should be noted that neither the Shanghai Communique of 1972 nor the Joint Communique on Normalization of 1978 imposed such an obligation on the United States. In fact, our policy objective with regard to Taiwan as explicitly enunciated in the Taiwan Relations Act last March is to uphold the principle that the future of Taiwan should be resolved peacefully by the Chinese themselves and to make sure that Taiwan will not be coerced to negotiate under duress or by force. Continued sales of defenive arms to Taiwan, therefore, constitutes no more than a fulfillment of an avowed obligation of the United States to the people on Taiwan.

There is no doubt that the Carter Administration's China policy is not designed to "abandon" Taiwan. The Administration simply prefers to take a low-key and less formalized approach to the safeguards for Taiwan, which has the virtue of avoiding unnecessary embarrassments and confrontations with Peking. This approach, according to the Administration, is particularly important during the initial stage of contacts with China to advance cooperation on important international issues of common interests. Implicit in the approach is of course the tactics that when and if Peking violates our expressed "expectation" and "interest" with regard to the security of Taiwan, then the United States will escalate its response accordingly. In spite of the perceived virtue of this approach, one should bear in mind that as far as the future security of Taiwan is concerned, Peking's objective is indeed very different from ours. Their goal is to see further United States disengagement to facilitate the process of unification. There can be no doubt that they will use whatever opportunities available in the future to promote development in that direction. Here lies the inherent danger of the Carter approach. If the escalation of calculated response is what the Administration plans to take, they may have to take it sooner than expected. Worse still, once it gets started, the politics of escalation tends to develop a momentum of its own and eventually gets out of control. The high price we paid for the escalation of conflict in Vietnam is clearly a lesson the American people must not forget.

Perhaps having the lessons of the Korean and the Vietnam War in mind, Congress decided last spring to pursue a different approach with regard to the safeguarding of Taiwan's security: It chose to stress the strategy of explicit deterrence, instead of accepting the Administration's approach of calculated escalation. By making our stand and commitment to Taiwan's security crystal clear in advance, Congress hopes to achieve the effect of deterring potential adversaries from starting needless speculations or miscalculations which may escalate into further action and violence. This alternative approach did no doubt cause some embarrassment and controversy in Peking at the beginning, but the Congress believes that in the long run it will save the United States a great deal of needless troubles.

Although the "deterrence strategy" advocated by Congress eventually prevailed in the Taiwan Relations Act, various aspects of its implementation remain in the hands of the Administration and are yet to be seen. Unless the Administration carries out the intent and spirit of the legislation with rigor and clarity in the years ahead, the strategy may not work as effectively as designed to deter all temptations to tamper with the future security of Taiwan by outside powers.

The development of the Afghan crisis in recent months has greatly heightened the nation's interest in advancing further cooperation with China. Defense Secretary Harold Brown's trip to China in January sharpened the focus on the prospects of developing military ties with Peking. Brown was reported to have discussed with Chinese leaders a wide variety of military and security matters ranging from "parallel actions" to counter the Soviet invasion of Afghanistan to the transfer of advanced technologies to China. Deng Xiaoping told Brown that the United States should "do something in a down-to-earth way so as to defend peace against Soviet hegemonism." The sudden upsurge of euphoria over military cooperations between the two countries clearly reflects the irresistable attraction of the "China card," especially at a time of crisis vis-à-vis the Soviet Union. The Administration should, however, be reminded of both the promises as well as the pitfalls of playing such a card. Above all, we must be fully aware of the inherent fragility of the newly-developed relationship between the United States and China. It is clear that both countries came closer together in recent years based primarily on the compatability of well-calculated but transient strategic and economic interests, rather than on the basic political and economic cohesion of the two societies. It is true that both have considerable "parallel interests" at this time, but their respective political and economic systems are fundamentally different and unbridgeable. Progress made over the years cannot automatically preclude the possibility of abrupt disruption and deterioration in the future. One needs only to be reminded of how far apart both countries stand with regard to the issue of Taiwan's security.

Military and security specialists seems to differ on their assessments of strategic value of Taiwan to the security interest of the United States in Asia. However, they are virtually unanimous that it will be harmful to our national interest if Taiwan is allowed to fall under the control of an unfriendly or potentially unfriendly power. In this regard, the maintenance of the international status quo of Taiwan will probably best serve our national interest. While developing constructive ties with China based on the principle of mutual benefit, the United States should continue to strengthen and expand the broad friendly relationship developed with Taiwan over the last three decades. We should also bear in mind that the framework of security safeguards for the island as designed by the Taiwan Relations Act is yet to be tested. The precarious balance of power in Asia as demonstrated through the Iranian and Afghan crises in recent months clearly signal that our security interest in Taiwan should not be treated lightly. In the years ahead, more uncertainties are bound to emerge from the inherent dynamics of international rivalries and domestic political processes in the region. When the pressure of crisis is on, there will undoubtedly be temptations for the great powers to change the existing power equilibrium surrounding the island in their favor or similarly for the leadership in Taiwan to try out high-risk strategies for self-survival. To discourage and prevent such destabilizing attempts from taking place, the explicit and credible assurance for the island's security by the United States, in advance, will remain as the most effective and low-cost strategy.

23. SENATOR JESSE HELMS' VIEW ON THE CARTER POLICY AND THE STRATEGIC VALUE OF TAIWAN
(Excerpts)

The New China Policy places the United States in the moral position of an ambitious man who divorces his first wife to marry a socially prominent and attractive second wife, all the while promising wife No. 1 that they will continue to live together as though nothing had happened. Such an anomaly cannot lead to stability or fulfillment; in fact, it is bound to become a destabilizing element if the expectations of the new partner are not fulfilled.

The whole question of the future security of Taiwan is cast into a deep shade by the failure of the Administration to secure commitments and practical arrangements that would guarantee Taiwan's freedom of action. More deeply disturbing is not simply the failure to obtain such guarantees; the most damaging blow is the admission that Taiwan's future was conceded in advance to the will of Peking. The testimony of Ambassador Woodcock before this Committee was startling in its revelation of the abject capitulation of the United States before the rulers of Peking.

> It had been the American position that we were seeking a guarantee of the nonuse of force in the settlement of the Taiwan question. I personally came to the conclusion— and I am now speaking in personal terms—that to insist upon that would be to run into a roadblock because it was, in essence, the negotiation of sovereignty. It isn't a question of who we look upon in the situation. The Chinese in Peking and the Chinese in Taipei both insisted that there was one China. It was a question of trying to negotiate directly a guarantee of the nonuse of force by a sovereign government against what in the mind of that government is its own province.
>
> So central to our negotiations beginning in the period of July, 1978, was our insistance and our expectancy that it would be settled on a peaceful basis, but recognizing the roadblock of the sovereignty issue, which would have led the negotiations nowhere.
>
> I think in a very practical sense, I myself am convinced that we have the best possible assurance in that regard, and I think the statements particularly of Vice Premier Teng Hsiao-P'ing, beginning in late November of 1978, reiterated forcefully to the Nunn senatorial delegation of which Senator Glenn was a member, in early January 1979, that we are getting the most positive response from the Chinese government in this regard.
>
> The CHAIRMAN. At any time during the negotiations over the period that you were in Peking, was the matter of an express commitment by Peking against the use of force in settling the Taiwan question posed?
>
> Ambassador WOODCOCK. Not by me, sir. No.

Keeping in mind that the Ambassador was the sole channel for the negotiations which led to "normalization," we must conclude the following:

1. Peking considers that it has sovereign authority over Taiwan.

2. The use of force is the ultimate determinate of sovereignty.

3. Peking's ultimate sovereignty over Taiwan was a nonnegotiable item for Peking.

4. The United States view of Peking's sovereignty over Taiwan is irrelevant to Peking's intention to assert that sovereignty.

5. The United States, in refusing even to attempt to negotiate the question, conceded the ultimate disposition of Taiwan to Peking's authority.

6. The United States encourages the incorporation of Taiwan into the People's Republic of China by peaceful means.

7. The United States would be displeased if force were used to bring about unification, but we expect that "unification" by some means would be the "settlement" of the Taiwan question.

Taiwan Enabling Act: Report of the Committee on Foreign Relations, U.S. Senate, 96th Congress, March 1, 1979 (Washington, D.C.: U.S. Government Printing Office, 1979), pp. 46-60.

A "Decent Interval" for Taiwan

These conclusions, which flow indisputably from Ambassador Woodcock's testimony, can leave no particle of doubt that the New China Policy has already surrendered the legal and moral status of Taiwan to the Communist rulers of Peking. All that is retained is a pragmatic, under-the-table relationship, designed to provide a temporary umbrella, a "decent interval," as it were, to shield the people on Taiwan from an immediate blow, to give time to phase our American capital investment there if necessary, and to bamboozle the American people.

The impact of the new China policy is that both Peking and the United States agree that Taiwan has only one option: To come under Communist hegemony, to use the word that Peking always applies to the Soviet Union. The only question remaining for Taiwan is a question of timing. We are saying that Taiwan has no right to refuse indefinitely. And to help Taiwan to negotiate quickly, both the PRC and the United States hold the ultimate levers: the PRC retaining the right to use force, and the United States retaining the right to supply defensive weapons. Our right to supply weapons conceivably could be continued at such a level as to force the PRC into a better deal for Taiwan and for American investment there; but it could also be withheld if Taiwan were recalcitrant and refused to be absorbed into the Communist system. The execution of the New China Policy so far ought to be a warning to the people on Taiwan that the present leadership of the United States is willing to subordinate the human rights and dignity of the people on Taiwan to other considerations.

It is for this reason that I have found a widespread concern among my colleagues over the exact nature of the security guarantees to Taiwan. The question turns upon whether the policy of the United States is to support the indefinite autonomy of the people on Taiwan, or whether our security assistance is to support the interests of the New China Policy. The information, at first suppressed, that no new weapons would be supplied under the Mutual Defense Treaty during the last year of its existence is further evidence that the architects of the New China Policy are seeking to avoid any real test of our true intentions.

The notion that Taiwan's social, economic, and political autonomy could be preserved within the sovereignty of the PRC will hardly bear the least examination. The notorious example of Tibet, which concluded a written agreement with Peking guaranteeing its religious, social, and political systems, demonstrates the extent to which Peking will perpetuate cultural genocide. The example of Hong Kong, ostensibly under British rule, but in reality dominated by PRC finance, trade, kickbacks and corruption, survives because it fulfills a special need to which Taiwan would be superflous. Rather Taiwan could expect to become the victim of economic and political subversion—pressed from without by restriction and boycotts, and assaulted from within by seducing business leaders with special deals and economic dependencies. Once political control were established, key leaders and cultural figures would disappear for "reeducation."

Two Governments in One China

The New China Policy is predicated upon the expectation that Taiwan will eventually come under the domination of the Communist government in Peking. The Institute provides a restraining mechanism for slowing down that process; if strengthened, it could help thwart that process completely.

Hopefully, the Institute can provide a bridge to a more realistic China policy. The reality is that China has two governments which each effectively control different parts of Chinese territory. A realistic policy would recognize each government as competent in the territory it controls. There is no need to recognize the claim which each makes to the territory controlled by the other, nor is there any need to deny such claims. Above all, the United States should refrain from actions which would tend to coerce "unification."

The New China Policy is despicable not because it tries to deal with mainland China, but because its aim is to consign the people on Taiwan to a fate which they would not freely choose. It attempts to retain the substance of sovereignty for Taiwan while conceding the juridical basis for sovereignty to the Communist rulers of Peking. In-sofar as the the Institute retains the substance of a relationship with a sovereign power, the Institute should be encouraged and strengthened. For the decision of the President of the United States is not determinative *de jure* of the existence of a sovereign state. The Republic of China remains a sovereign state as long as it effectively controls its own territory. As long as a small nation retains the help of allies who will back up its sovereign powers with a defensive capability, it can retain its independence. The Institute, for the time being, can perform that function.

Congress must keep a close oversight on the Institute to ensure that it is used to preserve Taiwan's independent options, not to destroy them. Congress must avoid complicity in the New China Policy.

Three Major Issues

Three major issues were raised by the President's actions of December 15, 1978.

First, the President derecognized a long-time ally and friend, the Republic of China. This precipitate action not only was unnecessary, it came at the worst possible time. As the world looked to the United States for a demonstration of resolve and fidelity after a period of growing setbacks for American interests, the world saw instead vacillation, weakness and betrayal of friendship in the derecognition of the Republic of China.

It is not up to the Congress to change that action. The President may choose the nations he wishes to recognize, and which he does not. The issue of derecognition may well be a matter to be dealt with in the 1980 Presidential elections. That is a more proper forum for settlement of that issue.

The second issue raised by the President's actions of December 15, 1978, is the termination of a mutual defense treaty with an ally in time of peace.

Needless to say, this unprecedented action has not gone without notice by allies and opponents alike around the world. Despite Administration protestations to the contrary, many of our allies rightfully question the value of the United States' mutual security commitments. Newspaper reports that the Ambassador to the United States from one nation bordering the Indian Ocean littoral has sought to be moved to Moscow because "that is where the power is" cannot be brushed aside as reportage of a mere diplomatic aberration. How much the Presidential decision to abandon the people on Taiwan affected the Ambassador's decision one only can speculate; but it is difficult to believe that it had no effect.

The Congress may not be the proper forum to deal with the specific issue of termination of the treaty, *per se;* although Congress certainly must deal with the broader issue of the defense of the people on Taiwan. Already, a court suit has been undertaken to deal with the particulars of the treaty termination matter. Its outcome will say much about the scope of the President's power to terminate a treaty with an ally, unilaterally and without prior consultation with and approval by the Congress. At a time when the American public is wary of overextension of Executive power, a proper resolution of the issues raised in the suit will do much to define the limits of Executive power.

The final issue raised by the President's actions of December 15, 1978, is the protection of the interests of the people of the Unitd States in Taiwan, and the concurrent protection of the legitimate interests of our friends and allies, the people of the Republic of China on Taiwan. . . .

In spite of this legislation, there are many issues which need to be addressed by the Congress, so as not to jeopardize our valuable relations with the people on Taiwan. Foremost is the continuing interest of the people of the United States in the security and defense of the people on Taiwan. Nor should the value of Taiwan to legitimate U.S. and allied security interests in the Pacific be overlooked. Close scrutiny should be made of the People's Republic of China, not only in terms of what good can come of the new United States relations with that nation, but also what pitfalls exist for U.S. policymakers.

Taiwan, an Ally and Longstanding Friend

As America's eighth largest trading partner, the Republic of China remains an important economic asset of the United States. One expert has told me that withdrawal of Taiwan's funds from the banks in New York would precipitate a severe economic situation, forcing some banks to face possible bankruptcy as a result. Thus, many would not want to antagonize Taiwan too harshly.

Strategically, Taiwan serves as an important intelligence resource for the United States off the coast of mainland China. While some may contend that a larger U.S. presence in the PRC will facilitate intelligence gathering and obviate, somewhat, Taiwan's importance, many do not agree with that conclusion. One need only consider the restrictions on movement in the Soviet Union to see how the other major totalitarian state in the region deals with human intelligence gathering. The Taiwan post is so important for the United States, and will remain so. Nor should anyone be deluded into believing that such intelligence gathering is unnecessary, now that the United States has opened up full relations with Peking.

We must not forget that Peking views any relationship with the United States as only a matter of necessity—again, playing off the far barbarian against the near one. Peking's relationship with the United States still remains an adversary one over the long haul, as even top China hands in the Carter Administration are quick to admit.

With rumored new missile capability under development, with a missile possibly able to reach the United States said to be part of the Chinese strategic nuclear delivery program, the United States has every need to be wary of Peking's long-term intentions. Thus, the need continues for a Taiwan base, not only for intelligence gathering, but as an advance-base for U.S. forces in any emergency, either on the mainland, or in Japan or Korea.

Some may have forgotten that the Japanese attack on Pearl Harbor was launched from Taiwan, in part. Strategically, Taiwan sits in an important location, serving as a vital choke-point for shipping around the coast of China. This includes not only commercial shipping so vital to U.S. allies Japan and Korea; but also Soviet naval ships bound for action in the Southern Pacific or Indian Ocean.

Thus, the United States continues to have important economic and strategic interests in Taiwan.

nearby countries, and to the United States, because of fear of persecution under PRC rule. This could force these nations to face up to the realities of the problem, and to regard it as something other than simply a domestic Chinese issue. Conceivably, Taipei might also resort to terrorist tactics similar to those used by the Palestine Liberation Organization to win attention for its claim to self-determination, although it is certainly aware that few people would support such methods.

Indeed, an independence policy of some kind should be expected in reaction to President Carter's dramatic initiative. The implementation of such a policy probably does not involve undue risks from Taipei's point of view. This is not only because Taipei is already in a very difficult situation, and would weigh such a course against the risks already present; it also knows that the White House decision was taken against the sentiment of the Congress, the American people, and even world opinion. A declaration of independence would, on the other hand, put the United States in an awkward position. It would accentuate the differences between the White House and the Congress, as well as underscore the lack of public support for at least one aspect of American foreign policy. It would inevitably cause some strain in United States relations with Communist China, as Washington groped for the appropriate response to what would be an increasingly awkward new political reality.

Alignment with the Soviet Union

A second option for Taipei is to seek closer relations with the Soviet Union, leading to an agreement that would afford Taiwan some of the security it will lose when the U.S.-ROC defense treaty lapses at the end of 1979. Many observers have argued that such a development is not likely because of Taiwan's vital commercial relations with the West. It is also argued that Taipei could not trust the Kremlin. But there are also counterarguments. First, a secret agreement would not endanger Taiwan's commercial or other ties with the West and Japan. Second, it is uncertain in any event that Soviet ties with Taiwan would interfere with Taiwan's present foreign economic relationships. Soviet political and military ties with a number of other countries have not interfered with their capitalist-oriented economy or trade. Third, Taipei has undoubtedly come to distrust the United States, especially in view of the timing and modalities of Washington's recognition of Peking and abrogation of the defense treaty after numerous assurances to the contrary. For the moment, at least, Taipei could hardly perceive the Soviet Union as being much less reliable.

There is some evidence that there may already be a number of agreements or informal understandings in effect between Taipei and Moscow. Ever since 1960, when the Sino-Soviet break became formal, and especially after the onset of the Cultural Revolution in China in 1965, there has been accumulating evidence that the Soviet Union no longer perceived the incorporation of Taiwan by China to be in its interests. In 1965, pictures of the flag of the Republic of China were published in the Soviet Union, constituting—in Peking's view, at least—a recognition of the fact that the ROC is an independent nation. The following year, a Soviet magazine called Taiwan a "state"; and in 1967, this same use of words appeared in an official Tass release. In 1970, coinciding with Vice President Agnew's trip to Asia, the Soviet press called Taiwan a "country." In 1968 Victor Louis, a well-known unofficial representative of the Soviet government, visited Taiwan and conferred with Chiang Ching-kuo, who was then Defense Minister. In 1971, the Soviet Union's UN representative made reference to a Two Chinas solution to the Chinese representation question then before the world body.

Other facts suggest that the Soviet Union has a military interest in Taiwan, and that this view is reciprocated in Taipei. The ROC's armed forces tie down large numbers of Chinese troops across the Taiwan Strait in Fukien Province that might otherwise be shifted to the north to reinforce Chinese divisions on the Sino-Soviet border. In 1969, after the flareup on the border, and simultaneous with Moscow's demands that Peking negotiate forthwith, paramilitary forces from Taiwan raided a military installation in Fukien Province. China's defense plan announced the next year indicated that in the event of escalating hostilities with the Soviet Union, China would also have to prepare for an invasion from the east. Since the Soviet Union does not possess adequate capabilities for landing forces on the

Chinese coast, this had to refer to Taiwan. At almost the same time, Peking accused Taipei of holding talks with Soviet military representatives in Tokyo on problems of mutual interest. In 1973, just two days before Ambassador David Bruce went to Peking to head the United States "liaison office," two Soviet warships passed through the Taiwan Strait and circumnavigated the island. This was the first time that Soviet naval vessels passed through the Taiwan Strait since World War II. After President Carter's announcement on December 15, 1978, on recognition of Communist China, it was rumored that Soviet ships were again in the Taiwan Strait and had signaled to military installations on the coast of Taiwan.

Evidence on the Taiwan side also indicates a change in both attitude and policy toward the Soviet Union over a period of years. In the early 1960s, the government-controlled press in Taiwan stopped criticizing the Soviet Union as harshly as it had formerly; and, contrary to past practice, it began to discriminate between Soviet and Chinese communism. In 1969, the year after Victor Louis' trip to Taipei, the ROC Minister of Education travelled to the Soviet Union on a semi-official visit, accompanied by newspaper reporters. Chiang Ching-kuo's wife, who is Russian and whom he married in the Soviet Union, was subsequently seen in public more frequently, and the press was allowed to photograph her— again contrary to past practice. On a number of occasions, officials in Taipei have said that Taiwan plans to provide the Soviet Union with bases if the United States moves its embassy to Peking. In all cases, the reports were subsequently denied; but in view of the number of them, and the fact that the officials reportedly making them were not punished, it must be that they had official sanction, at least as trial balloons. The most recent reports of this character were made by a Greek newspaper editor who spent several weeks in Taiwan in 1975, and by South Korean sources in August, 1978. It is also note-worthy that a member of the National Assembly in Taipei made a similar statement at a meeting of that body after Carter's announcement on granting diplomatic recognition to Peking in December, 1978.

Peking's statements and reactions provide further evidence of the possibility of a Soviet connection. There is no question that Peking is concerned about the prospect of military and other ties between Moscow and Taipei. Communist leaders in Peking have frequently commented on the possibility of talks between Taipei and Moscow. In April, 1978, for example, Peking charged that secret conversations were going on between Moscow and Taipei in Vienna; and in July, Peking charged "collusion" between the Soviet Union and Taiwan.

Clearly Taipei and Moscow have parallel interests, and these have been underscored by the United States decision to recognize Peking. Moscow perceives that the United States is allying with Japan and China against the Soviet Union, and that its strategic interests in Northeast Asia may be threatened. Ties with Taiwan would also enhance Soviet efforts to establish an Asian "security system." While Taiwan's defenses are strong, ultimately the island would need outside help to repel an invasion. A Soviet promise to keep Sino-Soviet border tension high enough to prevent Chinese troops from massing in Fukien Province, or deliberately to heighten tensions if such a reinforcement began; or an agreement to interdict an invasion across the Strait by the use of Soviet naval forces; or the mere presence of Soviet military bases in Taiwan; would all serve to increase Taiwan's security.

Going Nuclear

A third option for Taiwan is to go nuclear. Again, many observers will argue that Taipei cannot and will not exercise this option for a number of reasons. There is, however, considerable evidence that Taiwan has already gone some distance in this direction. Like the other options, it is not an all-or-nothing decision at present. Taipei could go on to the last step prior to engineering an explosion, or could build weapons in secret without testing them; and in either case, it would retain a measure of ambiguity as to its nuclear status.

The argument that Taiwan has nuclear weapons capabilities is widely accepted. Scientists in Taiwan have been doing research on nuclear energy since the early 1950s; and since 1961, they have had a nuclear reactor with which to carry their research to more advanced levels. To date, more than a thousand scientists from Taiwan have received advanced nuclear training at institutions in the United States. Taipei has also purchased equipment abroad to build three nuclear power plants, with two nuclear generators in each. One generator is now in use and a second will go on stream in August this year. In the 1980s, nuclear power will—according to recent estimates—produce more than 40 percent of Taiwan's electricity. The byproducts of these power plants could provide the raw materials for a number of nuclear bombs if diverted to that purpose.

One of Taiwan's nuclear research reactors was purchased from Canada shortly before Ottawa granted diplomatic recognition to Peking. As a result, the reactor is no longer subject to inspection. The reactor was almost identical to the one that Canada sold to India, which was instrumental in India's engineering a nuclear explosion in 1974. Taiwan also has a facility for reprocessing spent fuel, which is probably the most important step in moving from the peaceful use of nuclear energy to the production of bombs. In 1976, it was reported that the Republic of China had secretly reprocessed some of the nuclear fuel it was using for experimental purposes. Westinghouse, the company that has contracted with Taiwan to build two of its nuclear power plants, and also the US Energy Research and Development Administration, the Joint Committee on Atomic Energy of the Congress, and the CIA have all judged Taiwan to be a potential nuclear power. In 1975, Premier Chiang Ching-kuo was reported to have stated that Taiwan has both the facilities and the capabilities to make nuclear weapons, and has considered building a nuclear arsenal. In other statements, Taipei has denied that it has any intention to build nuclear weapons; but presumably, the long-term validity of such assertions would depend on its perceptions of its security situation.

Together with the capability to build nuclear weapons, Taiwan also has a credible delivery system. Both the F-4 and the F-5 jet fighter planes which Taiwan currently uses can be fitted to carry nuclear weapons. Since these planes were used by US military forces in Taiwan and were so equipped at the time, presumably the ROC Air Force already has the know-how for this. Republic of China military forces may also be able to deliver an atomic warhead by missile. Its engineers have apparently acquired the sophisticated technology necessary to build the inertial navigational systems used in missiles. In the past year, Taiwan has in fact displayed locally built missiles. If it does not yet have a missile system capable of delivering nuclear weapons, it surely will have before long. In any event, in view of Taiwan's demonstrated capabilities to infiltrate men and material into China, it may not need such a sophisticated delivery system.

The question remains, Will Taipei see the need to go nuclear? The Republic of China signed the nuclear nonproliferation treaty, and in 1970 ratified it. Afterwards, however, it was expelled from the United Nations—under whose aegis it committed itself to the treaty. Thus, it could be argued that it has no responsibilities under the treaty. But Taipei's decision will probably rest on how it perceives the guarantees under the nonproliferation treaty. The United States and the Soviet Union have both guaranteed nonnuclear signatories protection from threat or attack by other nuclear countries. If Taipei sees this as effectively applying to Peking, then it will no doubt forego the decision to go nuclear. On the other hand, in view of President Carter's statement that Taiwan is a part of China, Taipei cannot reasonably assume that this will be the case—unless, of course, the guarantee comes from Moscow.

In the event that Peking is able to convince the United States and other important countries that the Taiwan question is purely an internal or domestic matter, Taipei may be compelled to exercise the nuclear option to prove that this is not the case. Certainly Taiwan could gain world attention by announcing the attainment of nuclear status or by testing a nuclear device; and this, in turn, would undoubtedly strengthen Taipei's claim to be recognized as a sovereign nation. Similarly, Taipei may see an advantage in going nuclear if Peking begins to threaten Taiwan in order to force it to negotiate incorporation, or if the PRC begins to prepare for military action against Taiwan. Finally, the burdensome costs of conventional weapons needed to guarantee its security may persuade Taipei to exercise the nuclear option.

It bears repeating at this point that Taipei can complete all of the initial steps in the process, or even build weapons, in secret and thereby avoid the unfavorable public repercussions of going nuclear. Indeed, it may already have nuclear weapons. Alternatively, Taipei can continue to keep the world guessing about its nuclear capabilities, while encouraging the belief that it may be close to, or already have, nuclear weapons. This would have almost the same effect as going nuclear without the accompanying problems.

Any of the three options just discussed might be taken; more probably, two or all of them would be exercised simultaneously. The decision to implement any or all of the options could be made immediately, or in the more distant future. The options may also be put into force gradually; while all of them entail both risks and undesirable repercussions, these may be minimized by moving slowly or secretly.

This situation creates potentially serious problems for the United States in Asia. What is the United States to do if Taiwan exercises one or more of its options? What will be the impact on United States-China relations? How will Japan react and how will this affect Sino-Japanese relations? More important, how will United States-Soviet relations be affected? These are questions that need to be given considerable thought. The implications of all of them are serious.

All of the options pose dangers to the stability of East Asia, and destabilization of the area would inevitably involve the United States. One should recall in this context that the United States fought its last three wars in Asia. Such action by Taiwan could lead to a deterioration of relations between China and the Soviet Union or between the United States and either or both of the two Communists superpowers. The triangular relationship is in many ways a fragile one. Likewise, Japan's role in Asia and its relations with China, Taiwan, and Southeast Asia, not to mention the Soviet Union, would also be seriously affected.

One alternative for the United States, mindful of the gravity of the possible results of a decision by Taiwan to exercise any or all of its options, is unilaterally—or in concert with the Soviet Union—and explicitly to promise Taipei nuclear protection under the 1968 non-proliferation treaty, including protection against an attack by Communist China. Similarly, the United States could go beyond what the Congress did in April to broaden the scope of US support for Taiwan's security or to make these "guarantees" more explicit and more formal. Another choice would be for the United States to redeploy the Seventh Fleet back to the Taiwan Strait, in order to forestall its use as an invasion route. Washington could rationalize this decision in terms of the rapid Soviet naval buildup in the region. Since Peking has suggested that the United States bolster its naval stength in the Pacific area, it could hardly oppose such a United States decision. Another choice for the United States would be to provide Taiwan with more sophisticated weapons. The decision to withhold weapons sales to Taiwan is of grave concern in Taipei, and does not bode well for the coming termination of the US-ROC defense pact.

Finally, the United States should deal with Taiwan as an independent nation-state, and help bolster its image in this respect. The people of Taiwan do not want to be incorporated or ruled by China, and it is not in the United States interest to allow or help this to happen. The credibility of the United States, upon which rests its strategic posture in Asia, would be still further undermined by abandoning a loyal ally to its fate. US support for a world legal order and a pluralist state system would similarly be questioned by the global community if Taiwan were taken over by the PRC. The same would be true of US human rights policy. It is one thing for the United States to acknowledge Peking's claim to Taiwan. It is quite another, however, to go beyond mere acknowledgment, and thereby leave Taiwan with no alternatives but to take options that are dangerous for itself, the United States, and the world.

Bibliography

SELECTED BIBLIOGRAPHY (By Topic)

I. Books

Cultural Values and Cultural Continuity

Aijmer, Göran. *The Religion of Taiwan Chinese in an Anthropological Perspective*. Gothenburg: University of Gothenburg, 1976.

Allen, Leonard B. "The Relevance of Sun Yat-sen Today," in Paul K. T. Sih (ed.) *Sun Yat-sen and China*. New York: St. John's University Press, 1974.

Chen, Chung-min. *Ancestor Worship and Clan Organization in a Rural Village of Taiwan*. Nankang, Taipei: Academia Sinica, Bulletin of the Institute of Ethnology, 23 (1967).

Chen, Chi-lu. *Material Culture of the Formosan Aborigines*. Taipei: The Taiwan Musuem, 1968.

Chiu, Ming-chung. *Two Types of Folk Piety: A Comparative Study of Two Folk Religions in Formosa*. Chicago: University of Chicago Press, 1970.

Cohen, Myron L. *House United, House Divided: The Chinese Family in Taiwan*. New York: Columbia University Press, 1976.

Cooke, David C. *Taiwan: Island China*. New York: Dodd, Mead & Company, 1975.

Deglopper, Donald R. "Doing Business in Lukang," in W. E. Willmott (ed.) *Economic Organization in Chinese Society*. Stanford, Ca.: Stanford University Press, 1972.

Diamond, Norma. *K'un Shen: A Taiwan Village*. New York: Holt, Rinehard and Winston, 1969.

Eberhard, Wolfram. *Moral and Social Values of the Chinese: Collected Essays*. San Francisco and Taipei: Chinese Materials and Research Aids Service Center, 1971.

_____. *Studies in Taiwanese Folktales*. Taipei: The Orient Cultural Service, 1974.

Feuchtwang, Stephen. "City Temples in Taipei under Three Regimes," in Mark Elvin, and G. William Skinner (eds.) *The Chinese City between Two Worlds*. Stanford, California: Stanford University Press, 1974.

Freedman, Ronald, and John Y. Takeshita. *Family Planning in Taiwan*. Princeton: Princeton University Press, 1969.

Fried, Morton H. "Some Political Aspects of Clanship in a Modern Chinese City," in Marc J. Swartz, Victor W. Turner, and Arthur Tuden (eds.) *Political Anthropology*. Chicago: Aldine Publishing Company, 1966.

Gallin, Bernard. *Hsin Hsing, Taiwan: A Chinese Village in Change*. Berkeley, California: University of California Press, 1966.

_____. "Rural to Urban Migration in Taiwan: Its Impact on Chinese Family and Kinship," in David C. Buxbaum (ed.) *Chinese Family Law and Social Change in Historical and Comparative Perspective*. Seattle, Washington: University of Washington Press, 1978.

Gallin, Bernard, and Rita Gallin. "The Integration of Village Migrants in Taipei," in Mark Elvin and G. William Skinner (eds.) *The Chinese City between Two Worlds*. Stanford, Ca.: Stanford University Press, 1974.

_____. "Sociopolitical Power and Sworn Brother Groups in Chinese Society: A Taiwanese Case," in R. N. Adams and R. D. Fogelson (eds.) *The Anthropology of Power*. New York: Academic Press, 1977.

Goddard, W. G. *Formosa: A Study in Chinese History*. East Lansing, Michigan: Michigan State University Press, 1966.

Gordon, Leonard H. D. (ed.) *Taiwan: Studies in Chinese Local History.* New York: Columbia University Press, 1970.

Hanson, Eric O. *Catholic Politics in China and Korea.* Maryknoll, New York: Orbis Books, 1980.

Hsia, C. T. "The Continuing Obsession with China: Three Contemporary Writers," in Paul K. T. Sih (ed.) *China's Literary Image.* New York: St. John's University Press, 1975.

————. *A History of Modern Chinese Fiction.* Second ed. New Haven: Yale University Press, 1971.

Hsia, Tsi-an. "Taiwan," in C. T. Hsia. *A History of Modern Chinese Fiction.* First ed. New Haven: Yale University Press, 1961.

Jordan, David K. *Gods, Ghosts, and Ancestors: The Folk Religion of a Taiwanese Village.* Berkeley, California: University of California Press, 1972.

Lau, Joseph S. M. (ed.) *Chinese Stories from Taiwan 1960-1970.* New York: Columbia University Press, 1976.

Liao, David C. E. *The Unresponsive: Resistent of Neglected? The Hakka Chinese in Taiwan Illustrate a Common Mission Problem.* Chicago: Moody Press, 1972.

Long, Howard R. *The People of Mushan: Life in a Taiwanese Village.* Missouri: University of Missouri Press, 1961.

Lin, Huai-min. "Homecoming," in Pang-yuan Chi, John J. Deeney, Ho Hsin, Wu Hsi-chen, and Yü Kuang-chung (eds. and comps.) *An Anthology of Contemporary Chinese Literature Taiwan: 1949-1974.* Taipei, Taiwan: National Institute for Compilation and Translation, 1975.

Meskill, Johanna Menzel. "The Lins of Wufeng: The Rise of a Taiwanese Gentry Family," in Leonard H. D. Gordon (ed.) *Taiwan Studies in Chinese Local History.* New York: Columbia University Press, 1970.

Olsen, Nancy J. "Changing Family Attitudes of Taiwanese Youth," in Richard W. Wilson, Amy A. Wilson, and Sidney L. Greenblatt (eds.) *Value Change in Chinese Society.* New York: Praeger, 1979.

Ou-yang, Tzu. "Vase," in Pang-yuan Chi, John J. Deeney, Ho Hsin, Wu Hsi-chen, and Yü Kuang-chung (eds. and comps.) *An Anthology of Contemporary Chinese Literature Taiwan: 1949-1974.* Taipei, Taiwan: National Institute for Compilation and Translation, 1975.

Pai, Hsien-yung. "One Winter Evening," in Pang-yuan Chi, John J. Deeney, Ho Hsin, Wu Hsi-chen, and Yu Kuang-chung (eds. and comps.) *An Anthology of Contemporary Chinese Literature Taiwan: 1949-1974.* Taipei, Taiwan: National Institute for Compilation and Translation, 1975.

Pasternak, Burton. "The Sociology of Irrigation: Two Taiwanese Villages," in W. E. Willmott (ed.) *Economic Organization in Chinese Society.* Stanford, Ca: Stanford University Press, 1972.

Rohsenow, Hill Gates. *Prosperity Settlement: The Politics of Paipai in Taipei, Taiwan.* Unpublished Ph.D dissertation, University of Michigan, 1973.

Sih, Paul K. T. (ed.) *China's Literary Image.* New York: St. John's University Press, 1975.

Ssu-ma, Chung-yuan. "The Mountain," in Pang-yuan Chi, John J. Deeney, Ho Hsin, Wu Hsi-chen, and Yü Kuang-chung (eds. and comps.) *An Anthology of Contemporary Chinese Literature Taiwan: 1949-1974.* Taipei, Taiwan: National Institute for Compilation and Translation, 1975.

Thompson, Laurence G. *Chinese Religion: An Introduction.* Second ed. Encino, California: Dickenson Publishing Company, Inc., 1975.

Tong, Hollington K. *Christianity in Taiwan: A History.* Taipei, Taiwan: Hollington Tong, 1961.

Uhalley, Stephen, Jr. "The Taiwanese in Taiwan" in Joseph M. Kitagawa (ed.), *Understanding Modern China.* Chicago: Quadrangle Books, 1969.

Walters, Jo Neher. *Taiwan—Beautiful Island.* New York: Exposition Press, 1972.

Wang, Sung-hsing. Taiwanese Architecture and the Supernatural," in Arthur P. Wolf (ed.) *Religion and Ritual in Chinese Society.* Stanford, California: Stanford University Press, 1974.

Wolf, Margery. *The House of Lim—A Study of a Chinese Farm Family.* New York: Appleton-Century Crofts, 1968.

Wu, Juu-huey. *The Continuity of China's Moral Heritage.* Taipei: Bureau of Cultural Affairs, Ministry of Education, Republic of China, 1972.

Yen, Yuan-shu. "New Trends in the Study of Classical Chinese Literature in the Republic of China," in Paul K. T. Sih (ed.) *China's Literary Image.* New York: St. John's University Press, 1975.

———. "Social Realism in Recent Chinese Fiction in Taiwan," in *Thirty Years of Turmoil in Asian Literature.* Taipei: The Taipei Chinese Center, International P.E.N., 1976.

Yip, Wai-lim (ed.) *Modern Chinese Poetry: Twenty Poets from the Republic of China, 1955-1965.* Iowa City: University of Iowa Press, 1970.

Education

Barendsen, Robert Dale. *Higher Educational Institutions in Taiwan.* Washington, D.C.: Government Printing Office, U.S. Office of Education, Bulletin No. 18, 1966.

Kao, Charles H. C. *Brain Drain: A Case Study of China.* Taipei, Taiwan: Mei Ya Publications, Inc., 1971.

Kaser, Davis. *Book Pirating in Taiwan.* Philadelphia: University of Pennsylvania Press, 1969.

Thelin, Mark C. (ed.) *Two Taiwanese Villages.* New York: United Board for Christian Higher Education in Asia, 1976.

Tsurumi, E. Patricia. *Japanese Colonial Education in Taiwan, 1895-1945.* Cambridge, Massachusetts: Harvard University Press, 1977.

Wilson, Richard W. *Learning to be Chinese: The Political Socialization of Children in Taiwan.* Cambridge, Massachusetts: The M.I.T. Press, 1970.

Economic Development

Behmron, Jack N. and Harvey W. Wallender. *Transfers of Manufacturing Technology within Multinational Enterprises.* Cambridge, Massachusetts: Ballinger Company, 1976.

Chen, Edward K. Y. *Hyper-growth in Asian Economics: A Comparative Study of Hong Kong, Japan, Korea, Singapore, and Taiwan.* New York: Holmes and Meier Publishers, Inc., 1979.

Chang, Yen-t'ien. "Taiwan: Economic Development and Population Policy," in Dun J. Li (ed.) *Modern China.* New York: Charles Scribner's Sons, 1978.

Cheng, Chen. *Land Reform in Taiwan.* Taipei, Taiwan: China Publishing Co., 1961.

Fei, John C. H., Gustav Ranis, and Shirley W. Y. Kuo. *Growth with Equity: The Taiwan Case.* New York: Oxford University Press, 1979.

Galenson, Walter (ed.) *Economic Growth and Structural Change in Taiwan: The Post-war Experience of the Republic of China.* Ithaca, New York: Cornell University Press, 1979.

Ho, Samuel P. S. *Economic Development of Taiwan 1860-1970.* New Haven, Connecticut: Yale University Press, 1978.

Ho, Yhi-min. *Agricultural Development of Taiwan 1903-1970.* Tennessee: Vanderbilt University Press, 1966.

Hou, Chi-ming and Tzong-shian Yu (eds.) *Modern Chinese Economic History.* Nankang, Taipei: The Institute of Economics, Academia Sinica, 1979.

Hsieh, S. C. and T. H. Lee. *Agricultural Development and its Contributions to Economic Growths in Taiwan—Input-Output and Productivity Analysis of Taiwan Agricultural Development.* Taipei: Joint Commission on Rural Construction, 1966.

Hsing, Mo-huan. *Taiwan: Industrialization and Trade Policies.* London: Oxford University Press, 1971.

Jacoby, Neil H. *U.S. Aid to Taiwan: A Study of Foreign Aid, Self-help and Development.* New York: Praeger, 1966.

Kahn, Herman. *World Economic Development, 1979 and Beyond.* Boulder, Colorado: Westview Press, 1979.

Keefer, James F. *Taiwan's Agricultural Growth during the 1970's.* Washington, D.C.: Economic Research Service, U.S. Department of Agriculture, 1971.

Koo, Anthony Y. C. *The Role of Land Reform in Economic Development, A Case Study of Taiwan.* New York: Praeger, 1968.

Kuo, Wan Yong. "Technical Change, Foreign Investment and Growth in the Manufacturing Industries, 1952-1970," in Shinichi Ichimura (ed.) *The Economic Development of East and Southeast Asia.* Honolulu: University Press of Hawaii, 1967.

Lee, Teng-hui. *Intersectoral Capital Flows in the Economic Development of Taiwan 1895-1960.* Ithaca, New York: Cornell University Press, 1971.

Lin, Ching-yuan. *Industrialization in Taiwan, 1946-1972: Trade and Import Substitution Policies for Developing Countries.* New York: Praeger, 1973.

Lionberger, Herbert F. and H. C. Chang. *Farm Information for Modernizing Agriculture: The Taiwan System.* New York: Praeger, 1970.

Myers, Ramon H. "The Economic Development of Taiwan," in Hungdah Chiu (ed.) *China and the Question of Taiwan.* New York: Praeger, 1973.

Negandhi, Anant R. *Management and Economic Development: The Case of Taiwan.* The Hague: Martinus Nijhoff, 1973.

Olson, Gary L. *U.S. Foreign Policy and the Third World Peasant: Land Reform in Asia and Latin America.* New York: Praeger, 1974

People's Daily. "The Weakness of Taiwan's Economy," in Dun J. Li (ed.) *Modern China.* New York: Charles Scribner's Sons, 1978.

Population Papers. Nankang, Taipei: The Institute of Economics, Academia Sinica, 1973.

Rostow, W. W. *The World Economy: History and Prospects.* Austin, Texas: University of Texas Press, 1978.

Shen, T. H. *The Sino-American Joint Commission on Rural Reconstruction.* Ithaca, New York: Cornell University Press, 1970.

Tai, Hung-chao. "The Koumintang and Modernization in Taiwan," in Samuel P. Huntington and Clement H. Moore (eds.) *Authoritarian Politics in Modern Society.* New York: Basic Books, 1970.

_____. *Land Reforms and Politics: A Comparative Analysis.* Berkeley, California: University of California Press, 1974.

Willmott, W. E. (ed.) *Economic Organization in Chinese Society.* Stanford, California: Stanford University Press, 1972.

Wu, Kuang-hua and Chiao Wei-cheng (eds.) *JCRR and Agricultural Development in Taiwan.* Taipei, Taiwan: The Joint Commission on Rural Construction, 1978.

Yang, Martin M. C. *Socio-economic Results of Land Reform in Taiwan.* Honolulu: East-West Center Press, 1970.

Yum, Kwang Sup. *Successful Economic Development of the Republic of China in Taiwan.* New York: Vantage Press, 1968.

Social Conditions and Social Change

Appleton, Sheldon. "Sex, Values, and Change on Taiwan," in Richard W. Wilson, Amy A. Wilson, and Sidney L. Greenblatt (eds.) *Value Change in Chinese Society.* New York: Praeger, 1979.

Bessac, Frank B. *An Example of Social Change in Taiwan Related to Land Reform.* Missoula, Montana: Department of Anthropology, University of Montana, 1967.

Grichting, Wolfgang. *The Value System on Taiwan, 1970.* Taipei, Taiwan: Privately printed, 1971.

Liao, Cheng-hung, and Martin C. Yang. *Socio-economic Change in Rural Taiwan, 1950–1978*. Taipei: Department of Agricultural Extension, National Taiwan University, 1979.

Wu, Tsong-shien. *The Value of Children: A Cross-national Study*. Honolulu: East-West Population Institute, 1977.

Law and Justice

Buxbaum, David C. (ed.) *Chinese Family Law and Social Change*. Seattle: University of Washington Press, 1978.

Chao, Shou-po. *Comparative Aspects of Conflict of Laws in Domestic Relations*. Unpublished Ph.D dissertation, University of Illinois, Urbana, 1973.

Gallin, Bernard. "Conflict Resolution in Changing Chinese Society: A Taiwanese Study," in M. J. Swartz, A. Tuden, and V. W. Turner (eds.) *Political Anthropology*. Chicago: Aldine Publishing Company, 1966.

———. "Mediation in Changing Chinese Society in Rural Taiwan," in D. Buxbaum (ed.) *Traditional and Modern Legal Institutions in Asia and Africa*. Leiden: Brill, 1967.

Ma, Herbert H. P. "American Influence on the Formation of the Constitution and Constitutional Law of the Republic of China: Past History and Future Prospects," in Lawrence W. Beer (ed.) *Constitutionalism in Asia: Views of the American Influence*, Berkeley, California: University of California Press, 1979.

Seymour, James D. "Republic of China," in Albert P. Blaustein and Gisbert H. Flanz (eds.) *Constitutions of the Countries of the World*. Dobbs Ferry, New York: Oceana Publications, Inc., 1974.

Domestic Politics

Clough, Ralph N. *Island China*. Cambridge, Massachusetts: Harvard University Press, 1978.

Edmonds, L. G. *Taiwan—The Other China*. New York: Bobbs-Merrill Co., 1971.

Fitch, Geraldine. *Formosa Beachhead*. Chicago: Henry Regnery Company, 1953.

Han, Lih-wu. *Taiwan Today*. Taipei, Taiwan: Institute of International Relations, 1974.

Huang, Mab. *Intellectual Ferment for Political Reforms in Taiwan, 1971-1973*. Ann Arbor, Michigan: Center for Chinese Studies, University of Michigan, 1976.

Jacobs, J. Bruce. *Local Politics in Rural Taiwan: A Field Study of Kuan-hsi, Face, and Faction in Matsu Township*. Unpublished Ph.D dissertation, Columbia University, 1975.

Jo, Yung-hwan (ed.) *Taiwan's Future*. Tempe, Arizona: Arizona State University, 1974.

Kerr, George H. *Formosa Betrayed*. Boston: Houghton Mifflin Company, 1965.

Lerman, Arthur J. *Taiwan's Politics: The Provincial Assemblyman's World*. Washington, D.C.: University Press of America, 1978.

Linebarger, Paul M. A. Djang Chu, and Ardath W. Burks. *Far Eastern Government and Politics*. Second ed. Princeton, New Jersey: Van Nostrand, 1956.

Lumley, F. A. *The Republic of China under Chiang Kai-shek*. London: Barrie and Jenkins, 1976.

Mancall, Mark (ed.) *Formosa Today*. New York: Praeger, 1964.

Mason, Bruce B. *Local Government in Taiwan: Some Observations*. Tempe, Arizona: Bureau of Government Research, Arizona State University, No.10, 1964.

Mendel, Douglass, Jr. *The Politics of Formosan Nationalism*. Berkeley, California: University of California Press, 1970.

Moody, Peter R. *Opposition and Dissent in Contemporary China*. Stanford, California: Hoover Institute Press, Stanford University, 1977.

Peng, Ming-min. *A Taste of Freedom; Memoirs of a Formosan Independence Leader*. New York: Holt, Rinehart and Winston, 1972.

Pillsbury, Michael P. *The Political Environment on Taiwan*. P-5375, Santa Monica, Calif.: Rand Corporation, April, 1975.

Pinkerman, John. *An American View of Taiwan Miracle*. Taipei: China Publishing Company, 1970.

Rankin, Karl L. *China Assignment*. Seattle: University of Washington Press, 1967.

Riggs, Fred W. *Formosa under Chinese Nationalist Rule*. New York: Macmillan Co., 1952.

Shieh, Milton J. T. *The Kuomintang: Selected Historical Documents, 1894-1969*. New York: Center of Asian Studies, St. John's University, 1970.

Sih, Paul K. T. (ed.) *Taiwan in Modern Times*. New York: St. John's University, 1973.

The Truth About the February 28, 1947 Incident in Taiwan. Taichung: Historical Research Commission of Taiwan Province, 1967.

Tung, William L. *The Political Institutions of Modern China*. The Hague: Martinus Nijhoff, 1968.

Walker, Richard L. "Taiwan's Movement into Political Modernity, 1945-1972," in Paul K. T. Sih (ed.) *Taiwan in Modern Times*. New York: St. John's University, 1973.

Wei, Yung. "Political Development in the Republic of China on Taiwan," in Hungdah Chiu (ed.) *China and the Question of Taiwan*. New York: Praeger, 1973.

———. "Taiwan: A Modernizing Chinese Society," in Paul K. T. Sih (ed.) *Taiwan in Modern Times*. New York: St. John's University, 1973.

Williams, Jack F. (ed.) *The Taiwan Issue: Proceedings of the Symposium, November 6, 1975*. East Lansing: Asian Studies Center, Michigan State University, 1976.

Foreign Relations

Bachrack, Stanley D. *The Committee of One Million*. New York: Columbia University Press, 1976.

Barnett, Robert W. "A Future for Taiwan," in Gene T. Hsiao (ed.) *Sino-American Detente*. New York: Praeger, 1974.

Bueler, William M. *U.S. China Policy and the Problem of Taiwan*. Boulder: Colorado Associated University Press, 1971.

Chaffee, Frederick H. *et. al. Area Handbook for the Republic of China*. Washington, D.C.: U.S. Government Printing Office, 1968.

China and the United Nations. New York: Carnegie Endowment for International Peace, 1959.

China and U.S. Far East Policy, 1945-1967. Washington, D.C.: Congressional Quarterly Service, 1967.

Chinese People's Institute of Foreign Affairs. *Oppose U.S. Occupation of Taiwan and "Two China" Plot*. Peking: Foreign Languages Press, 1958.

Chiu, Hungdah. "China, the United States, and the Question of Taiwan," in Hungdah Chiu (ed.) *China and the Question of Taiwan*. New York: Praeger, 1973.

———. *China and the Taiwan Issue*. New York: Praeger, 1979.

Cohen, Jerome Alan, *et. al. Taiwan and American Policy, The Dilemma in U.S.–China Relations*. New York: Praeger, 1971.

Dowen, Robert L. *The Taiwan Pawn in the China Game: Congress to the Rescue*. Washington, D.C.: The Center for Strategic and International Studies, Georgetown University, 1979.

Goldwater, Barry M. *China and the Abrogation of Treaties*. Washington, D.C.: Heritage Foundation, 1978.

Kintner, William R. and John F. Copper. *A Matter of Two Chinas*. Philadelphia: Foreign Policy Research Institute, 1979.

Lasswell, Harold D. and Chen Lung-chu. *Formosa, China, and the United Nations*. New York: St. Martin's Press, 1967.

Li, Victor. *Derecognizing Taiwan: The Legal Problems*. Washington, D.C.: Carnegie Endowment for International Peace, 1977.

_____. *The Future of Taiwan*. New York: M. E. Sharpe, 1980.

Moorsteen, Richard, and Morton Abramowitz. *Remaking China Policy: U.S.–China Relations and Government Decision-making*. Cambridge, Massachusetts: Harvard University Press, 1971.

Morello, Frank P. *The International Legal Status of Formosa*. The Hague: Martinus Nijhoff, 1966.

Morgenthau, Hans J. "The Formosa Resolution of 1955," in Hans J. Morganthau. *The Impasse of American Foreign Policy*. Chicago: University of Chicago Press, 1962.

Myers, Ramon H. (ed.) *Two Chinese States: U.S. Foreign Policy and Interests*. Stanford, California: Hoover Institution Press, Stanford University, 1978.

Norma, Schroder. "Economic Costs and Benefits," in Ramon H. Myers (ed.) *Two Chinese States: U.S. Foreign Policy and Interests*. Stanford, California: Hoover Institution Press, Stanford University, 1978.

Pillsbury, Michael. *Taiwan's Fate: Two Chinas but Not Forever*. Santa Monica, Calif.: Rand Corporation, 1975.

Rowe, David N. *The Carter China Policy: Results and Prospects*. Branford, Connecticut: David N. Rowe, 1980.

_____. *U.S. China Policy Today*. Washington, D.C.: University Professors for Academic Order, 1979.

Shen, James C. H. *The View from Twin Oaks: A Collection of Selected Speeches, 1971-1978*. Vol. I and II. Washington, D.C.: n.p., 1978.

Thayer, Nathanniel B. "China, The Formosa Question," in Gregory Henderson, Richard N. Lebow, and John G. Stoessinger (eds.) *Divided Nations in a Divided World*. New York: David McKay Company, Inc., 1974.

Tierney, John, Jr. (ed.) *About Face: The China Decision and Its Consequences*. New Rochelle, New York: Arlington House Publishers, 1979.

Tsou, Tang. *Embroilment over Quemoy: Mao, Chiang, and Dulles*. Salt Lake City: University of Utah Press, 1959.

Wall, R. F. "Formosa and the Chinese Off-shore Islands," in G. Barraclough (ed.) *Survey of International Affairs 1956-1958*. London: Oxford University Press, 1962.

Washington Lobby, The. Third ed. Washington, D.C.: Congressional Quarterly Service, 1979.

Wei, Yung. "Unification or Confrontation," in Ray E. Johnston, *The Politics of Division, Partition, and Unification*. New York: Praeger, 1976.

Security and Defense Capabilities

Chiang, Wei-kuo. *The Strategic Significance of Taiwan in the Global Strategic Picture*. Taipei, Taiwan: Li Min Cultural Publication, Inc., 1977.

Clechman, Barry M., and Robert P. Berman. (eds.) *Guide to Far Eastern Navies*. Annapolis: Naval Institute, 1978.

Clough, Ralph N. *East Asia and U.S. Security*. Washington, D.C.: The Brookings Institution, 1975.

_____. *Island China*. Cambridge, Massachusetts: Harvard University Press, 1978.

Dupuy, Trevor N., Grace P. Hayes, and John A. C. Andrews. *The Almanac of World Military Power*. Third ed. New York: R. R. Bowker Company, 1974.

East, W. Gordon, O. H. K. Spate, and Charles A. Fisher (eds.), new ed., *The Changing Map of Asia: A Political Geography*. Great Britain: Methuen & Co., 1971.

Gregor, James and Maria Hsia Chang, "The Military Defense of the Republic of China," in *Struggles for Change in Mainland China*. Taipei: Institute of International Relations, 1980.

Hsieh, Chiao-min. *Taiwan—Ilha Formosa: A Geography in Perspective*. Washington, D.C.: Butterworths, 1964.

Kallgren, Joyce K. "Nationalist Chinese Military Strength: Its Use in South-east Asia," in
     K. K. Sinha (ed.) *Problems of Defence of South and East Asia*. Bombay, India:
     Manaktalas, 1969.
U.S. Office of Naval Operations. *Taiwan (Formosa)*. Washington, D.C.: Naval Depart-
     ment, 1944.
Overholt, William H. (ed.) *Asia's Nuclear Future*. Boulder, Colorado: Westview Press,
     1977.
Snyder, Edwin K. *et. al. The Taiwan Relations Act and the Defense of the Republic of
     China*. Berkeley, Ca.: Institute of International Studies, University of California,
     1980.
Whitson, William W. "Political and Military Dimensions," in Ramon H. Myers (ed.) *Two
     Chinese States: U.S. Foreign Policy and Interests*. Stanford, California: Hoover Insti-
     tution Press, Stanford University, 1978.
Wu, Chen-tsai. "Role of the Republic of China in Collective Defense," in K. K. Sinha
     (ed.) *Problems of Defence of South and East Asia*. Bombay, India: Manaktalas, 1969.

II. Articles in Learned Journals

Abbreviations for the Journals

ACAD SINICA PA SOC SCI	*Academia Sinica Papers in Social Sciences* (Nankang, Taipei)
AM J INT LAW	*American Journal of International Law* (Washington, D.C.)
AM POL SCI R	*American Political Science Review* (Washington, D.C.)
AN AM ACAD POL SOC SCI	*Annals of the American Academy of Political and Social Science* (Philadelphia, Pa.)
AS AFF	*Asian Affairs* (New York)
AS CULT Q	*Asian Culture Quarterly* (Taipei)
AS FORUM	*Asiam Forum* (Tempe, Arizona)
AS OUTLOOK	*Asian Outlook* (Taipei)
AS PROFILE	*Asian Profile* (Hong Kong)
AS STUD	*Asian Studies* (Quezon City)
AS SUV	*Asian Survey* (Berkeley, Ca.)
ASIA Q	*Asian Quarterly* (Brussels)
AUST Q	*Australian Quarterly* (Sidney)
CHIN CULT	*Chinese Culture* (Taipei)
CHIN J ADMIN	*Chinese Journal of Administration* (Taipei)
CHIN PEN	*Chinese Pen, The* (Taipei)
CHINA FORUM	*China Forum* (Taipei)
CHINA Q	*China Quarterly* (London)
CUR HIST	*Current History* (Philadelphia, Pa.)
DISSENT	*Dissent* (New York)
EAST AS CULT STUD	*East Asian Culture Studies* (Taipei)
ECON DEV CULT CHANGE	*Economic Development and Cultural Change* (Chicago, Ill.)
FOR AFF	*Foreign Affairs* (Baltimore, Md.)
FOR POL	*Foreign Policy* (New York)
FOR POL BUL	*Foreign Policy Bulletin*
FRANCE-ASIE	*France-Asie* (Paris)
FREE CHINA R	*Free China Review* (Taipei)
GEOG MAG	*Geographical Magazine* (London)
HUMAN ORG	*Human Organization* (New York)
IND J INT LAW	*Indian Journal of International Law* (New Delhi)
IND J PUB ADMIN	*Indian Journal of Public Administration* (New Delhi)
IND Q	*India Quarterly* (New Delhi)
INTERECON	*Intereconomics* (Munich, Germany)

INT POL	*International Politics*
INT SECURITY	*International Security* (Cambridge, Mass.)
INT TRADE LAW J	*International Trade Law Journal* (Baltimore, Md.)
ISS STUD	*Issues and Studies* (Taipei)
J AS STUD	*Journal of Asian Studies* (Ann Arbor, Mich.)
J SOC SCI	*Journal of Social Science* (Taipei)
KOREA WORLD AFF	*Korea and World Affairs* (Soeul)
LIT EAST WEST	*Literature East and West* (College Park, Md.)
MOD CHINA	*Modern China* (Beverly Hills, Ca.)
MONDA LING-PROB	*La Monda Lingro-Problemo* (The Hague)
OCCAS PA/RE SERIES CONT AS STUDY	*Occasional Papers/Reprints Series in Contemporary Asian Studies* (College Park, MD.)
ORBIS	*Orbis* (Philadelphia, Pa.)
PAC AFF	*Pacific Affairs* (Vancouver, B.C.)
PAC COM	*Pacific Community* (Tokyo)
PAC VIEWPT	*Pacific Viewpoint* (New Zealand)
PETRO ECON	*Petroleum Economist* (England)
POL SCI Q	*Political Science Quarterly* (New York)
POLITICS	*Politics* (Australia)
RURAL SOCIOLOGY	*Rural Sociology* (University Park, Pa.)
SINO–AM RELS	*Sino–American Relations* (Hwa Kang, Taipei)
SOCIAL PSYCHOLGY	*Social Psychology* (Washington, D.C.)
STUD ASIA	*Studies on Asia*
UKRANIAN Q	*Ukranian Quarterly* (New York)
UNITED ASIA	*United Asia* (Taipei)
VANDERBILT J TRANS LAW	*Vanderbilt Journal of Transnational Law* (Nashville, Tennessee)
WASHINGTON LAW R	*Washington Law Review* (Seattle, Washington)
WEST POL Q	*Western Political Quarterly* (Salt Lake City, Utah)
WORLD T	*World Today* (London)
YALE LAW J	*Yale Law Journal* (New Haven, Conn.)

Cultural Values and Cultural Continuity

Chen, Yu-Ching. "President Chiang Kai-shek and Chinese Cultural Renaissance," *AS CULT Q*, 3 (Spring, 1975), 27-42.

———. "Chinese Culture vs. Anti-Chinese Culture—Declaration of the Kuomintang on its 80th Founding Anniversary," *CHIN CULT*, 16 (March, 1975), 115-116.

Chu, Pao-tang. "Buddhist Organization in Taiwan," *CHIN CULT*, 10 (June, 1969), 98-132.

———. "Dragon Boat Festival, May 8," *AS OUTLOOK*, 5 (June, 1970), 23 and 29.

———. "Festivals in the Republic of China," *AS OUTLOOK*, 5 (February, 1970), 37-40 and 42.

Hung, Joe. "Religious Activities on Taiwan," *AS CULT Q*, 4 (Spring, 1976), 72-75.

Jacobs, J. Bruce. "A Preliminary Model of Particularistic Ties in Chinese Political Alliances: *Kan-ch'ing* and *Kuan-hsi* in a Rural Taiwanese Township," *CHINA Q*, No. 78 (June, 1979), 237-273.

Johnson, Irmgard. "Whatever Happened to Peking Opera?" *AS AFF*, II (July-August, 1975), 379-390.

Jordan, David K. "Language Choice and Interethnic Relations in Taiwan," *MONDA LING-PROB*, 5 (1973), 35-44.

Kallgren, Joyce K. "Nationalist China: The Continuing Dilemma of the 'Mainland' Philosophy," AS SURV, III (January, 1963), 11-16.

Kitagawa, Joseph M. "Buddhism in Taiwan Today," *FRANCE-ASIE*, 18 (1962), 439-444.

Lee, Wen-jer. "Taiwan and Dr. Sun's Revolution," *FREE CHINA R*, 15 (November, 1965), 9-14.

Metzger, Thomas A. "On Chinese Political Culture," *J AS STUD*, XXXII (November, 1972), 101-105.

O'Hara, Albert R. "A Factual Survey of Taipei's Temples and Their Functions," *J SOC SCI*, 17 (July, 1967), 323-337.

Palandri, Angela Jung. "Current Trends in Taiwan Poetry: Creativeness versus Conformity," *LIT EAST WEST*, XV (1971), 447-459.

Plummer, Mark. "Taiwan: Toward a Second Generation of Mainland Life," *AS SURV*, X (January, 1970), 18-24.

Saso, Michael. "The Taoist Tradition in Taiwan," *CHINA Q*, No. 41 (January-March, 1971), 83-102.

Starr, Kenneth. "Cultural Problems on Nationalist Taiwan," *FRANCE-ASIE*, 18 (1962), 539-560.

Tozer, Warren. "Taiwan's Cultural Renaissance: A Preliminary View," *CHINA Q*, No. 43 (July-September, 1970), 81-99.

Uhalley, Stephen, Jr. "Taiwan's Response to the Cultural Revolution," *AS SURV*, VII (November, 1967), 824-929.

Wang, Sung-hsing. "Family Structure and Economic Development in Taiwan," *Bulletin of the Institute of Ethnology, Academia Sinica*, No. 44, Autumn, 1977.

Wei, Yung. "A Methodological Critique of Current Studies on Chinese Political Culture," unpublished paper delivered at XXVI Annual Meeting of the Association for Asian Studies, Boston, April 1-3.

Yen, C. K. "Rotarianism and Confucianism," *CHIN CULT*, 16 (June, 1975), 3-8.

Yip, Wai-lim (ed.) "Chinese Arts and Literature: A Survey of Recent Trends," *OCCAS PA/ RE SERIES CONT AS STUD*, No.9, 1977, 126 pp.

Education

Appleton, S. "The Political Socialization of Taiwan's College Students," *AS SURV*, X (October, 1970), 910-923.

———. "Regime Support among Taiwan High School Students," *AS STUD*, 13 (August, 1973), 750-760.

————. "Silent Students and the Future of Taiwan," *PAC AFF*, 43 (Summer, 1970), 227-239.

————. "The Social and Political Impact of Education in Taiwan," *AS SURV*, XVI (August, 1976), 703-720.

————. "Taiwanese and Mainlanders on Taiwan: A Survey off Student Attitudes," *CHINA Q*, No. 44 (October-December, 1970), 38-65.

Hong, L. K. "Taiwanese Students in the U.S.," *SOCIAL PSYCHOLOGY*, (December, 1978), 342-346.

Lew, William J. F. "Education in Taiwan," *AS AFF*, Vol. 3, No.5 (May-June, 1978) 317-322.

Martin, Roberta. "The Socialization of Children in China and Taiwan: An Analysis of Elementary School Textbooks," *CHINA Q*. 62 (June, 1975), 242-262.

Wilson, Richard. "A Comparison of Political Attitudes of Taiwanese Children and Mainlander Children on Taiwan," *AS SURV*, VIII (December, 1968), 988-1000.

Economic Development

Barnett, R. W. "China and Taiwan: The Economic Issues," *FOR AFF*, L (April, 1972), 444-458.

Brandt, K. "Economic Development: Lessons of Statecraft in Taiwan," *ORBIS*, XI (Winter, 1968), 1067-1080.

Caldwell, J. Alexander. "The Financial System in Taiwan: Structure, Functions, and Issues for the Future," *AS SURV*, XVI (August, 1976), 729-751.

Chang, David W. "U.S. Aid and Economic Growth in Taiwan," *AS SURV*, V (March, 1965), 152–161.

Cheng, Peter P. "Taiwan: Protective Adjustment Economy," *AS SURV*, XV (January, 1975), 20-24.

Freeberne, Michael. "Lonely Taiwan Sows for the Future," GEOG MAG, No.4, (January, 1972), 268-274.

Gallin, Bernard. "Social Effects of Land Reform In Taiwan," *HUMAN ORG*, 22 (Summer, 1963), 109-112.

Glass, Sheppard. "Some Effects of Formosa's Economic Growth," *CHINA Q*, No. 15 (July-September, 1963), 12-34.

Ho, Samuel P. S. "The Economic Development of Colonial Taiwan: Evidence and Interpretation," *J AS STUD*, 34 (February, 1975), 417-439.

Klatt, Werner. "An Asian Success Story: Peaceful Agricultural Revolution in Taiwan," *ISS STUD*, VIII (April, 1972), 50-53.

Myers, Ramon H. and Norman Schroder. "American's Economic Stake in Taiwan," *AS AFF*, III (November-December, 1975), 99-106.

Pan, Lien-fan. "The Urban Land Reform in Republic of China," *CHIN CULT*, 16 (March, 1975), 105-114.

Pannell, Clifton W. "Urban Land Consolidation and City Growth in Taiwan," *PAC VIEWPT*, 15 (September, 1974), 111-122.

Prybyla, Jan S. "The Economy of Taiwan: A Study in Development," AS AFF, III (July-August, 1976), 347-363,

————. "The Societal Objective of Wealth, Growth, Stability and Equity in Taiwan," *OCCAS PA/RE SERIES CONT AS STUD*, No.4, 1978 (16), 31pp.

————. "Some Reflexions on Derecognition and the Economy of Taiwan," in *Taiwan: One Year after United States-China Normalization*, a workshop sponsored by the Committee on Foreign Relations, United States Senate and Congressional Research Service, Library of Congress, June, 1980. Washington, D.C.: U.S. Government Printing Office, 1980.

Simon, Dennis Fred. "Technology Transfer and Technology Policies in Taiwan," unpublished paper delivered at the Annual Meeting of the Association for Asian Studies, Charlottesville, Virginia, November 15, 1980.

Speare, Alden, Jr., "Urbanization and Migration in Taiwan," *ECO DEV CULT CHANGE,* Vol. 22, No. 2 (January, 1974).

Sun, Chen, "Prospects of the Taiwan Economy," *FREE CHINA R* (Taipei), Vol. LII, No. 5 (November, 1979).

Tsiang, Y. S. "The Role of Engineering Technological Education in the Economic Development of Taiwan," *St. John's Papers in Asian Studies,* No. 20. Jamaica, New York: St. John's University, 1972, 1-7.

von Gessel, Marinus. "American Businessmen's Views on the Investment Climate in Taiwan, ROC," Industry of Free China (Taipei), Vol. LIII, No.4 (April, 1980).

Webb, L. "Taiwan: The Economic Prospects," *AUST Q,* 28 (December, 1956), 7-18.

Wu, Yuan-li and Yeh Kung-chia (eds.) "Growth, Distribution, and Societal Change: Essays on the Economy of the Republic of China," *OCCAS PA / RE SERIES CONT AS STUD,* No. 3, 1978, 227pp.

_____. "Income Distribution in the Process of Economic Growth of the Republic of China," *OCCAS PA / RE SERIES CONT AS STUD,* No. 2, 1977, 45pp.

_____. "The Survival of Development of Taiwan," *AS AFF,* I (September-October, 1973), 42-48.

Young, Frank J. "Problems of Manpower Development in Taiwan," *AS SURV,* XVI (August, 1976), 721-728.

Yu, T. L. "Retrospect and Prospect of Industrial Development in Taiwan in 1980s," *Economic Review* (Taipei), The International Commercial Bank of China, Taipei, July-August, 1980.

Social Conditions and Social Change

Chen, Shao-hsing. "Trend Report of Studies in Social Stratification and Social Mobility in Taiwan," *EAST AS CULT STUD,* 4 (March, 1965), 38-51.

Chu, Godwin C. "Impact of Mass Media on a Gemeinschaft-like Social Structure," *RURAL SOCIOLOGY,* 33 (June, 1968), 189-199.

Diamond, Norma. "Women under the Kuomintang Rule—Variations on the Feminine Mystique," *MOD CHINA,* 1 (January, 1975), 3-45.

Eberhard, Wolfram. "Labor Mobility in Taiwan," *AS SURV,* II (May, 1962), 38-56.

Ho, Samuel P. S. "Decentralized Industrialization and Rural Development: Evidence from Taiwan," *ECON DEV CULT CHANGE,* 28 (October, 1979), 77-96.

_____. "Industrialization in Taiwan: Recent Trends and Problems," *PAC AFF,* 48 (Spring, 1975), 27-41.

Marsh, Robert M. "The Taiwanese of Taipei: Some Major Aspects of Their Social Structure and Attitudes," *J AS STUD,* 27 (May, 1968), 571-584.

Olsen, Nancy J. "Social Class and Rural-Urban Patterning of Socialization in Taiwan," *J AS STUD,* 34 (May, 1975), 659-674.

Sih, Paul K. T. "Taiwan: A Modernizing Chinese Society," *CHIN CULT,* 13 (December, 1972), 27-37.

Wang, Charlotte Shiang-yun. "Social Mobility in Taiwan," *Papers in Social Sciences,* No. 80-3. Taipei: Academia Sinica, 1980.

Wei, Yung. "Modernizing Process in Taiwan: An Allocative Analysis," *AS SURV,* XVI (March, 1976), 249-269.

Wilson, Richard W. "Some Rural-Urban Comparisons of Political Socialization in Taiwan," *AS STUD,* 10 (April, 1972), 108-130.

Yuan. D. Y. and Edward G. Stockwell. "The Rural-Urban Continuum: A Case Study of Taiwan," *RURAL SOCIOLOGY,* 29 (September, 1964), 247-260.

Law and Justice

Chang, Ya-yun. "A Comparative Study between the Five-power Constitution and Other Constitutions," *CHINA FORUM,* 2 (January, 1975), 97-138.

Cheng, Sheldon S. D. "A Study of the Temporary Provisions of the Constitution of the Republic of China," *CHIN CULT,* 13 (December, 1972), 38-57.

Fa, Jyh-pin. "A Comparative Study of Judicial Review under Nationalist Chinese and American Constitutional Law," *OCCAS PA/RE SERIES CONT AS STUD,* No.3, 1980 (32)

Heuser, Robert. "Legal Aspects of Trade with and Investment in the Republic of China: The German Experience." *INT TRADE LAW J* 3, No. 1 (Fall, 1977), 177-188.

Hsu, Cheng-hsi. "The American and Chinese Legislative Systems," *SINO-AM RELA,* 1 (Winter, 1975), 76-86.

Peng, Ming-min. "Political Offences in Taiwan: Laws and Problems," *CHINA Q,* No. 47 (June-September, 1971), 471-493.

Pound, Roscoe, "Progress of the Law in China," *WASHINGTON LAW R,* Vol. 23 (1948), pp. 346-356.

Domestic Politics

Appleton, S. C. "Taiwan: Portents of Change," *AS SURV,* XI (January, 1971), 68-73.

———. "Taiwan: The Year it Finally Happened," *AS STUD,* 12 (January, 1972), 32-37.

Chen, Lucy H. "Literary Formosa," *CHINA Q,* No.15 (July-September, 1963), 75-85.

Chen, Theodore H. E. "Taiwan After Chiang Kai-shek," *CUR HIST,* 69 (September, 1975), 90-93 and 99.

———. "Taiwan's Future," *CUR HIST,* 77 (September, 1979), 71-73 and 83-84.

Cheng, Peter P. "Taiwan 1975: A Year of Transition," *AS SURV,* XVI (January, 1976), 645-654.

Cole, A. B. "Political Roles of Taiwanese Enterprise," *AS SURV,* VII (September, 1967), 61-65.

Copper, J. F. "Taiwan in 1980: Entering a New Decade," *AS SURV,* XXI, No. 1 (January, 1981), 51–62.

Crissman. Lawrence W. "Each for His Own: Taiwanese Political Response to KMT Local Administration," unpublished paper delivered at the London-Cornell Project for East and Southeast Asian Studies, Ste. Adele-en-Quebec, Canada, August 24-29, 1969.

Durdin, Tillman. "Chiang Ching-kuo and Taiwan: A Profile," *ORBIS,* XVIII (Winter, 1975), 1023-1042.

Dutt, V. P. "Formosa, Background Notes," *IND Q,* 7 (January-March, 1951), 60-70.

Feng, Yukon. "Changes in the Chinese Political System," *CHIN J ADMIN,* 3 (July, 1964), 36-38.

Gordon, Leonard H. D. and Sidney Chang. "Fairbank and his Critics in the Republic of China," *J AS STUD,* 30 (November, 1970), 137-149.

Gurtov, Melvin. "Recent Developments on Formosa," *CHINA Q,* No. 31. (July-September, 1967), 59-95.

———. "Taiwan in 1966: Political Regidity, Economic Growth," *AS SURV,* VII (January, 1967), 40-45.

Hsieh, Erh-yi. "The System of Punishment of Public Officials," *CHIN J ADMIN,* No. 4 (January, 1965), 22-29.

Israel, John. "Politics on Formosa," *CHINA Q.* No. 15 (July-September, 1963), 3-11.

Jacobs, J. Bruce. "The Cultural Bases of Factional Alignment and Division in a Rural Taiwanese Township," *J AS STUD,* XXXVI (November, 1976), 79-97.

———. "Paradoxes in the Politics of Taiwan: Lessons for Comparative Politics," *POL,* 13 (November, 1978), 239-247.

———. "Recent Leadership and Political Trends in Taiwan," *CHINA Q,* No.45 (January-March, 1971), 129-154.

_____. "Taiwan 1972: Political Season," *AS SURV,* XIII (January, 1973), 102-112.

_____. "Taiwan 1973: Consolidation of the Succession," *AS STUD,* 14 (January, 1974), 22-29.

_____. "Taiwan 1979: 'Normalcy' after 'Normalization,' " *AS SURV,* XX (January, 1980), 84-93.

_____. "Taiwan's Press Political Communication Link and Research Resource," *CHINA Q,* No. 68 (December, 1976), 778-788.

Kagan, Richard C. "Taiwan: Another Greece," *Dissent,* XVI (January-February, 1969), 64-68.

Kallgren, Joyce K. "Nationalist China: Political Inflexibility and Economic Accomodation," *AS SURV,* IV (January, 1964), 638-645.

_____. "Nationalist China: Problems of a Modernizing Taiwan," *AS SURV,* V (January, 1965), 12-17.

_____. "Vietnam and Politics in Taiwan," *AS SURV,* VI (January, 1966), 28-33.

Lee, Kuo-wei. "A Study of Social Background and Recruitment Process of Local Political Decision-makers in Taiwan," *IND J PUB ADMIN,* 18 (April-June, 1972), 227-244.

Lerman, Arthur J. "National Elite and Local Politician in Taiwan," *AM POL SCI R,* LXXI (December, 1977), 1406-1422.

Linebarger, Paul M. A. "Guam and Taiwan: Some Political Contrasts," *WORLD AFF,* 128 (April 6, 1965), 14-20.

_____. "The Republic of China on Taiwan: A Descriptive Appraisal," *WORLD AFF,* 126 (Spring, 1963), 5-16.

Mancall, M. "Succession and Myth in Taiwan," *J INT AFF,* 18 (1964), 12-20.

McBeath, Geeald. "Taiwan in 1976: Chiang in the Saddle," *AS SURV,* XVII (January, 1977), 18-26.

Mei, Wen-li. "The Intellectuals on Formosa," *CHINA Q,* No. 15 (July-September, 1963), 65-74.

Meisner, Maurice. "The Development of Formosan Nationalism," *CHINA Q,* No. 15 (July-September, 1963), 91-106.

Mirsky, Jonathan. "Some Impressions of Formosa," *CHINA Q,* No. 15 (July-September, 1963), 86-90.

Nickum, James E. and David C. Schak. "Living Standards and Economic Development in Shanghai and Taiwan," *CHINA Q,* No.77 (March, 1979), 25-49.

Ong, Joktik. "A Formosan's View of the Formosan Independence Movement," *CHINA Q,* No.15 (July-September, 1963), 107-114.

Plummer, Mark. "Taiwan: The 'New Look' in Government," *AS SURV,* IX (January, 1969), 18-22.

_____. "Taiwan: The Other China," *CUR HIST,* 51 (September, 1966), 165-171 and 178.

_____. "Taiwan's Chinese Nationalist Government," *CUR HIST,* 61 (September, 1971), 171-176.

Ravenholt, A. "Formosa Today," *FOR AFF,* XXX (July, 1952), 612-624.

Srinivasen, K. "Taiwan is Confident of the Future," *ISS STUD,* VIII (April, 1972), 40-43.

Tien, Hung-mao. "Taiwan in Transition: Prospects for Sociopolitical Change," *CHINA Q,* No. 64 (December, 1975), 615-644.

Wang, Gung-hsing. "Nationalist Government Policies, 1949-1951," *AN AM ACAD POL SOC SCI,* 277 (September, 1951), 213-223.

Wurfel, David. "Taiwanese Nationalism: Problems for United States Policy," *STUD ASIA,* 4 (1963), 101-119.

Foreign Relations

Bellows, Thomas J. "Taiwan's Foreign Policy in the 1970s: A Case Study of Adaptation and Viability," *AS SURV,* XVI (July, 1976), 593-610.

Bowles, C. "China Problem Reconsidered," *FOR AFF,* XXXVIII (April, 1960), 476-486.

Bueler, W. M. "Taiwan: A Problem of International Law or Politics?" *WORLD T,* 27 (June, 1971), 256-266.

Chang, Pao-min. "Choices for Taiwan," *WORLD T,* 34 (September, 1978), 364-374.

Chen Lung-chu and W. M. Reisman. "Who owns Taiwan? A Search for International Title," *YALE LAW J,* LXXXI (March, 1972), 599–671.

Chen, Yu-ching. "World Situation and National Destiny," *CHIN CULT,* 14 (March, 1973), 25-33.

Cheng, P. P. "Taiwan and the Two Chinas," *CUR HIST,* 57 (September, 1969), 168-174 and 177.

———. "The Taiwan Tangle Today: A Taiwanese View," *AS PROFILE,* 3 (December, 1975), 557-562.

Ching, Frank. "Most Envied Province," *FOR POL,* 36 (Fall, 1979), 122-146.

Chiu, Hungdah. "Normalizing Relations with China: Some Practical and Legal Problems," *AS AFF,* IV (November-December, 1977), 67-87.

———. "The Outlook for Taiwan," *AS AFF,* VII (January/February, 1980), 137-147.

Chiu, Hungdah and David Simon (eds.) "Legal Aspects of U.S.-Republic of China Trade and Investment—Proceedings of a Regional Conference of the American Society of International Law," *OCCAS PA/RE SERIES CONT AS STUD,* No.10, 1977, 217pp.

Clubb, O. E. "Sino-American Relations and the Future of Formosa," *POL SCI Q,* 80 (March, 1965), 1-21.

Copper, John F. "The Future of Taiwan: An Analysis of its Legal and Political Status," *ASIA Q,* 3 (1973), 195-220.

———. "Prospects for the Unification of Taiwan with China," *PAC COM,* 7 (January, 1976), 271-282.

———. "Taiwan's Options," *AS AFF,* VI (May-June, 1979), 282-294.

———. "Taiwan's Strategy and America's China Policy," *ORBIS,* XXI (Summer, 1977), 261-676.

Dean, Acheson. "United States Foreign Policy and Formosa," *FOR AFF,* XXXIII (April, 1955), 360-375.

Editorial. "The Cases of Taiwan and Ukraine: An Unacceptable Analogy," *UKRANIAN Q,* XXVII, No. 4 (Autumn, 1971) 341-347.

Gable, Carl I. "Taiwan Relations Act: Legislative Recognition," *VANDERBILT J. TRANS LAW* 12 (Summer, 1979), 511-32.

Gilbert, Lewis. "Peking and Taipei," *CHINA Q,* No. 15 (July-September, 1963), 56-64.

Halbach, Axel J. "Taiwan and the People's Republic of China, Foes or Partners?" *INTERECON,* (May-June, 1979), 145-154.

Harkavy, Robert E. "The Pariah State Syndrome," *ORBIS,* XXI (Fall, 1977), 623-649.

Hinton, Harold C. "Who Needs Peking? The Case Against Normalization," *KOREA WORLD AFF,* 2 (Winter, 1978), 519-525.

Hsiao, Frank S. T. and Laurence R. Sullivan. "The Politics of Reunification: Beijing's Initiative on Taiwan," *AS SURV,* XX (August, 1980), 789-802.

Hsiung, James C. "The Conceptual Foundations of U.S. China Policy: A Critical Review," *OCCAS PA/RE SERIES CONT AS STUD,* No.2, 1980 (31), 17pp.

———. "U.S. Relations with China in the Post-Kissingerian Era: A Sensible Policy for the 1980's," *AS SURV,* XVII (August, 1977), 691-710.

Hsu, King-yi. "America's National Interests and its Continued Support of the Republic of China," *ISS STUD,* X (March, 1974), 69-77.

———. "Taiwan's Response to Peking's United Front Tactics," *AS AFF,* Vol. 8, No. 2, (November/December, 1980), 89-112.

Iriye, Akira. "Dilemmas of American Policy Towards Formosa," *CHINA Q,* No. 15 (July-September, 1963), 51-55.

Jensen, B. "Eisenhower's Full Powers for Formosa and their Constitutional Basis," *INT POL,* (1955), 45-48.

Kau, Michael Y. M. *et. al.* "Public Opinion and Our China Policy," *AS AFF,* V (January-February, 1978), 133-147.

Keeton, G. W. "The Problem of Formosa," *WORLD AFF,* 5 (January, 1951), 4-12.

Kindermann, Gottfried-Karl. "Washington between Beijing and Taipei: The Restructured Triangle, 1978-1980), *AS SURV,* XX (May, 1980), 457-476.

Klatt, W. "Taiwan and the Foreign Investor," *PAC AFF,* 50 (Winter, 1977-1978), 644-659.

Klein, Donald. "Formosa's Diplomatic World," *CHINA Q.* No. 15 (July-September, 1963), 45-50.

Levi, W. "Formosa's Diplomatic World," *CHINA Q,* No. 15 (July-September, 1963), 45-50.

———. "Formosa and the China Issue," *CUR HIST,* 41 (December, 1961), 321-328.

Li, K. T. "Republic of China's Aid to Developing Nations," *PAC COM,* 1 (July, 1970), 664-671.

Li, Thian-hok. "The China Impasse: A Formosan View," *FOR AFF,* XXXVI (April, 1958), 437-448.

Li, Victor and John W. Lewis. "Resolving the China Dilemma: Advancing Normalization, Preserving Security," *INT SECURITY,* 2 (SUMMER, 1977), 11-23.

Mendel, D. H., Jr. "Japan's Taiwan Tangle," *AS SURV,* IV (October, 1964), 1073-1084.

———. "Japanese Policy and Views toward Formosa," *J AS STUD,* 28 (May, 1969), 513-534.

———. "Japanese Public Views on Taiwan's Future," *AS SURV,* XV (March, 1975), 215-220.

———. "Taiwan and Trade in Japan's Mainland Chinese Policy," *AS FORUM,* IV (October-December, 1972), 9-16.

O'Connell, D. P. "The Status of Formosa and the Chinese Recognition Problem," *AM J INT LAW,* L (April, 1956), 405–416.

Overholt, W. H. "Would Chiang Find Mao an Unacceptable Strange Bedfellow?" *AS SURV,* XIV (August, 1974), 679-699.

Thompson, Thomas N. "Taiwan's Ambiguous Destiny," *AS SURV,* XVI (July, 1976), 611-619.

Trager, Frank N. "A 'Willy Brandt' Solution for China?" *AS AFF,* III (September-October, 1975), 1-6.

Phillips, C. S., Jr. "International Legal Status of Formosa," *WEST POL Q,* 10 (June, 1957), 276-289.

Ravenal, E. C. "Approaching China, Defending Taiwan," *FOR AFF,* L (October, 1971), 44-58.

Rowe, David. "Republic of China: Post-United Nations," *ISS STUD,* VIII (May, 1972), 20-26.

Saxena, J. N. "The Legal Status of Taiwan," *IND J INT LAW,* 12 (January, 1972), 100-108.

Scalapino, Robert A. "What Should the U.S. Do about Taiwan?" *FOR POL BUL,* 40 (November 15, 1960), 36-38.

Simmons, Robert T. "Taiwan and China: The Delicate Courtship," *CUR HIST,* 65 (September, 1973), 111-114 and 134.

Slawecki, L. M. S. "The Two Chinas in Africa," *FOR AFF,* XLI (January, 1963), 398-409.

Solomon, Richard H. "Thinking through the China Problem," *FOR AFF,* LVI (January, 1978), 324-356.

Stockwin, Harvey. "A Hong-Kong–Macau–Taiwan Triangle?" *The Round Table,* No. 273 (January 1979), pp. 20-30.

U.S. Senate, Committee on Foreign Relations, "Implementation of the Taiwan Relations Act: The First Year." (A Staff Report), 96th Congress, 2d session. (Washington, D.C.: U.S. Government Printing Office, 1980).

U.S. Senate, Committee on Foreign Relations, and Library of Congress Congressional Research Service, "Taiwan: One Year After U.S.-China Normalization," (A Workshop). (Washington, D.C.: U.S. Government Printing Office, 1980).

Unger, L. "Derecognition Worked," *FOR POL,* 36 (Fall, 1979), 105-121.

Weiss, Thomas, "Taiwan and U.S. Policy," *ORBIS,* XII (Winter, 1969), 1165-1187.

Woodman, D. "Korea, Formosa, and World Peace," *POL Q,* 21 (October-December, 1950), 364-373.

Wright, Quincy. "The Chinese Recognition Problem," *AM J INT LAW,* 49 (July, 1955), 320-338.

Wu, Chun-tsai. "Change in the World Situation and the Republic of China," *PAC COM,* 2 (October, 1970), 144-155.

Zagoria, Donald S. "Normalizing Relations with China without 'Abandoning' Taiwan," *PAC COM,* 9 (November, 1977), 73-83.

Security and Defense Capabilities

Chen, King C. "Peking's Attitude Toward Taiwan," *AS SURV.* XVII (October, 1977), 903-918.

Clubb, O. E. "Formosa and the Offshore Islands in American Policy, 1950-1955," *POL SCI Q.* 74 (December, 1959), 517-531.

Fifield, R. H. "Strategic Formosa," *CUR HIST,* 16 (April, 1949), 217-220.

Fleming, D. F. "Our Brink of War Diplomacy in the Formosa Strait," *WEST POL Q,* (September, 1956), 535-552.

Fraser, A. M. "Military Posture and Strategic Policy in the Republic of China," *AS AFF,* I (May-June, 1974), 306-318.

Hsu, King-yi. "Sino-American Relations and the Security of Taiwan," *AS AFF,* VI (September-October, 1978), 48-66.

Kallgren, Joyce. "Nationalist China's Armed Forces," *CHINA Q,* No. 15 (July-September, 1963), 35-44.

"President Kennedy's Statement on the Taiwan Strait," *CUR HIST,* 43 (September, 1962), 178.

Quester, George H. "Taiwan and Nuclear Proliferation," *ORBIS,* XVIII (Spring, 1974), 140-150.

Roucek, Joseph S. "The Geopolitics of Formosa," *UNITED ASIA,* 15 (April, 1963), 305-308.

_____. "Taiwan in Geopolitics," *UKRANIAN Q.* 35 (Autumn, 1979), 267-278.

Segal, Jeffrey. "Taiwan: Reality Intrudes into Oil Plans," *PETRO ECON,* (May, 1979), 185-187.

Tsou, Tang. "The Quemoy Imbroglio: Chiang Kai-shek and the United States, *West POL Q,* 12 (December, 1959), 1075-1091.

Wu, Yuan-li. "Economic Development and International Security in Northeast Asia: Some Issues of Political and Economic Interaction," *KOREA WORLD AFF,* 2 (Fall, 1978), 369-379.

Biographical Sketches of
the Advisers and Editors

• WINBERG CHAI, who received his Ph.D. from New York University, is the author of more than 15 books and numerous articles on China. Formerly Vice President for Academic Affairs at the University of South Dakota, he is Distinguished Professor of International Studies and Humanities.

• THEODORE HSI-EN CHEN, Emeritus Professor of Education and Asian Studies, University of Southern California, is the author of nine books and more than 100 articles, mostly in the field of Chinese education in the 20th century. Formerly Dean and President of Fukien Christian University in Foochow, China, he helped organize and inaugurate Tunghai University as a representative of the United Board for Christian Higher Education in Asia.

• HUNGDAH CHIU (S.J.D., Harvard Law School) is Professor of Law at the University of Maryland School of Law. He is the author of *The Capacity of International Organizations to Conclude Treaties* and *The People's Republic of China and the Law of Treaties;* and co-author of *People's China and International Law: A Documentary Study* (1974), which was awarded a certificate of merit by the American Society of International Law in 1976. He has edited *China and the Question of Taiwan* (1973), *China and the Taiwan Issue* (1979), and *Agreements of the People's Republic of China, 1966-1980: A Calendar* (1981); and coedited *Agreements of the People's Republic of China, 1949-1967: A Calendar* (1968), *Law in Chinese Foreign Policy* (1972), *Legal Aspects of U.S.-Republic of China Trade and Investment* (1977), and *The Chinese Connection and Normalization* (1980). He has also contributed more than 40 articles to various learned journals.

• JOHN F. COPPER is Associate Professor of International Studies at Southwestern University, Memphis, Tennessee. He is the author of *China's Foreign Aid: An Instrument of Peking's Foreign Policy* (1976), (with William R. Kintner) *A Matter of Two Chinas: The China-Taiwan Issue in U.S. Foreign Policy* (1979), *China's Global Role: An Analysis of Peking's National Power Capabilities in the Context of an Evolving International System* (1980), in addition to numerous articles on Asian and international affairs in learned journals. He has spent more than ten years in Asia.

- JYH-PIN FA, (S.J.D., Virginia) is Associate Professor of Law at National Chengchi University and is the author of *A Comparative Study of Judicial Review under Nationalist Chinese and American Constitutional Law* (1980)

- JAMES C. HSIUNG, who received his Ph.D. in political science from Columbia University, is Professor of Politics at New York University. Among his many publications are: *Ideology and Practice: The Evolution of Chinese Communism* (1970); *Law and Policy in China's Foreign Relations* (1972); *The Logic of Maoism* (1974); and *China in the Global Community* (1980). His forthcoming volume is *Asia and U.S. Foreign Policy* (Praeger, November, 1981).

- CHO-YUN HSU was educated at National Taiwan University (B.A. and M.A.) and University of Chicago (Ph.D.). Before joining the faculty of history, University of Pittsburgh in 1970 he had taught at National Taiwan University. He is the author of *Ancient China in Transition* (1965) and the *Han Agriculture* (1980) as well as several articles on Chinese history and society, in both Chinese and English. He has been elected to life membership of Academia Sinica, Taiwan.

- CHALMERS JOHNSON is Professor and former Chairman of the Department of Political Science, at the University of California, Berkeley. He has written extensively on politics of modern China and Japan. His most recent works are *MITI and the Japanese Miracle* (Stanford University Press) and *Japan's Public Policy Companies* (American Enterprise Institute).

- MICHAEL Y. M. KAU is Professor of Political Science at Brown University, and Editor of the journal *Chinese Law and Government*. He is the author of *The People's Liberation Army and China's Nation-Building; The Lin Piao Affair: Power Politics and Military Coup,* and numerous articles on East Asian politics and international relations. Dr. Kau received his M.A. and Ph.D. from Cornell University, and conducted extensive field research and lectures in Japan, Taiwan, China, England, and the Soviet Union.

- THOMAS A. METZGER, who received his Ph.D. from Harvard University in 1967, is currently Professor of Chinese History at the University of California, San Diego. He has written two books: *The Internal Organization of Ch'ing Bureaucracy* (Harvard University Press, 1967) and *Escape from Predicament: Neo-Confucianism and China's Evolving Political Culture* (Columbia University Press, 1977).

- RAMON H. MYERS received his Ph.D. in economics from the University of Washington (Seattle) in 1960. His research and teaching has focused on Chinese economic history, especially agrarian problems of Taiwan and mainland China. He is Curator-Scholar of the East Asian Collection and Senior Fellow in the Hoover Institution on War, Revolution and Peace, at Stanford University. His current research involves editing a volume of papers on American foreign policy toward Asia in the 1980's and beyond.

- JAN S. PRYBYLA is Professor of Economics at Pennsylvania State University and Visiting Professor of Economics and Oriental Studies (1981), University of Arizona at Tucson. He is the author of *The Political Economy of Communist China* (1970); *Issues in Socialist Economic Modernization* (Praeger, 1980); and *The Chinese Economy: Problems and Policies* (University of South Carolina Press 1978; 2nd rev. ed., 1981). He has also written extensively on the economy of the Republic of China on Taiwan.

- ROBERT A. SCALAPINO is Robson Research Professor of Government and Director of the Institute of East Asian Studies, University of California, at Berkeley. He is also editor of *Asian Survey,* a scholarly monthly publication. His recent books include *Elites in the People's Republic of China, Asia and the Road Ahead,* and *The Foreign Policy of Modern Japan.*

- YU-MING SHAW, who received his doctorate from the University of Chicago, is Associate Professor of History, University of Notre Dame. He is the author of *Studies on Sino-American Relations*, editor of *Problems in Twentieth-Century Chinese Christianity,* and co-editor of *China and Christianity: Historical and Future Encounters.* He has also published articles dealing with Sino-American relations, modern Chinese history, and contemporary Chinese affairs. His book-length study — "John Leighton Stuart and Twentieth-Century Sino-American Relations" — is forthcoming.

- RICHARD L. WALKER is on leave from the University of South Carolina, where he is the James F. Byrnes Professor of International Relations and the Director of the Institute of International Studies. He is the author of fifteen books and a contributor to more than fifty others. His books include *China under Communism* (1955); *Ancient China* (1969); *Prospects in the Pacific* (1972); *Asia in Perspective* (1974); and *Ancient Japan* (1975). He has also written numerous articles and reviews in scholarly and popular journals. He is currently U.S. Ambassador to the Republic of Korea. His association with this book project predated his ambassadorial appointment.

• C. MARTIN WILBUR is George Sansom Professor Emeritus of Chinese History and a Senior Research Associate of the East Asian Institute, Columbia University, where he taught for 29 years. Author of *Sun Yat-sen: Frustrated Patriot*, and numerous articles and books concerning Chinese history, he has visited the Republic of China many times.

• YUAN-LI WU received his B.Sc. (Economics) and Ph.D. degrees at the University of London. He is a Professor of Economics at the University of San Francisco and a Consultant at the Hoover Institution, Stanford University. Dr. Wu was U.S. Assistant Secretary of Defense during 1969-1970. He is recipient of the Meritorious Civilian Service Award of the Department of Defense. Among his recent publications on Asia and International economic and strategic topics are: *Raw Material Supply in a Multipolar World; Economic Development in Southeast Asia: The Chinese Dimension,* which he co-authored with C. H. Wu; "U.S. Foreign Economic Policy: Politico-Economic Linkages" in *The United States in the 1980's;* and *The Economic Condition of Chinese Americans,* which he edited.